ELEMENTS

OF

PLANE AND SPHERICAL

TRIGONOMETRY,

WITH THEIR APPLICATIONS TO

MENSURATION, SURVEYING, AND NAVIGATION.

BY ELIAS LOOMIS, LL.D.,

PROFESSOR OF MATHEMATICS AND NATURAL PHILOSOPHY IN THE UNIVERSITY OF THE CITY OF NEW YORK, AUTHOR OF A "COURSE OF MATHEMATICS," ETC.

FOURTEENTH EDITION.

NEW YORK:
HARPER & BROTHERS, PUBLISHERS,
FRANKLIN SQUARE.
1859.

PREFACE.

THE following treatise constitutes the third volume of a course of Mathematics designed for colleges and high schools, and is prepared upon substantially the same model as the works on Algebra and Geometry. It does not profess to embody every thing which is known on the subject of Trigonometry, but it contains those principles which are most important on account of their applications, or their connection with other parts of a course of mathematical study. The aim has been to render every principle intelligible, not by the repetition of superfluous words, but by the use of precise and appropriate language. Whenever it could conveniently be done, the most important principles have been reduced to the form of theorems or rules, which are distinguished by the use of italic letters, and are designed to be committed to memory. The most important instruments used in Surveying are fully described, and are illustrated by drawings.

The computations are all made by the aid of natural numbers, or with logarithms to six places; and by means of the accompanying tables, such computations can be performed with great facility and precision This volume, having been used by several successive classes, has been subjected to the severest scrutiny, and the present edition embodies all the alterations which have been suggested by experience in the recitation room.

CONTENTS.

BOOK I.

THE NATURE AND PROPERTIES OF LOGARITHMS.

BOOK II.

PLANE TRIGONOMETRY.

BOOK III.

MENSURATION OF SURFACES AND SOLIDS.

BOOK IV.

SURVEYING.

BOOK V.

NAVIGATION.

BOOK VI.

SPHERICAL TRIGONOMETRY.

TRIGONOMETRY.

BOOK I.

THE NATURE AND PROPERTIES OF LOGARITHMS.

ARTICLE 1. Logarithms are numbers designed to diminish the labor of Multiplication and Division, by substituting in their stead Addition and Subtraction. All numbers are regarded as powers of some one number, which is called the *base* of the system; and the exponent of that power of the base which is equal to a given number, is called the logarithm of that number.

The base of the common system of logarithms (called, from their inventor, Briggs' logarithms) is the number 10. Hence all numbers are to be regarded as powers of 10. Thus, since

$10^0=1$,	0	is the	logarithm of	1	in Briggs'	system;
$10^1=10$,	1	"	"	10	"	"
$10^2=100$,	2	"	"	100	"	"
$10^3=1000$,	3	"	"	1000	"	"
$10^4=10000$,	4	"	"	10,000	"	"
&c.,			&c.,		&c.;	

whence it appears that, in Briggs' system, the logarithm of every number between 1 and 10 is some number between 0 and 1, *i. e.*, is a proper fraction. The logarithm of every number between 10 and 100 is some number between 1 and 2, *i. e.*, is 1 plus a fraction. The logarithm of every number between 100 and 1000 is some number between 2 and 3, *i. e.*, is 2 plus a fraction, and so on.

(2.) The preceding principles may be extended to fractions by means of negative exponents. Thus, since

$10^{-1}=0.1$,	-1	is the	logarithm of	0.1	in Briggs'	system;
$10^{-2}=0.01$,	-2	"	"	0.01	"	"
$10^{-3}=0.001$,	-3	"	"	0.001	"	"
$10^{-4}=0.0001$	-4	"	"	0.0001	"	"
&c.,			&c.,		&c.	

Hence it appears that the logarithm of every number between 1 and 0.1 is some number between 0 and −1, or may be represented by −1 plus a fraction; the logarithm of every number between 0.1 and .01 is some number between −1 and −2, or may be represented by −2 plus a fraction; the logarithm of every number between .01 and .001 is some number between −2 and −3, or is equal to −3 plus a fraction, and so on.

The logarithms of most numbers, therefore, consist of an integer and a fraction. The integral part is called the *characteristic*, and may be known from the following

RULE.

The characteristic of the logarithm of any number greater than unity, is one less than the number of integral figures in the given number.

Thus the logarithm of 297 is 2 plus a fraction; that is, the characteristic of the logarithm of 297 is 2, which is one less than the number of integral figures. The characteristic of the logarithm of 5673.29 is 3; that of 73254.1 is 4, &c.

The characteristic of the logarithm of a decimal fraction is a negative number, and is equal to the number of places by which its first significant figure is removed from the place of units.

Thus the logarithm of .0046 is −3 plus a fraction; that is, the characteristic of the logarithm is −3, the first significant figure, 4, being removed three places from units.

(3.) Since powers of the same quantity are multiplied by adding their exponents (*Alg.*, Art. 50),

The logarithm of the product of two or more factors is equal to the sum of the logarithms of those factors.

Hence we see that if it is required to multiply two or more numbers by each other, we have only to add their logarithms: the sum will be the logarithm of their product. We then look in the table for the number answering to that logarithm, in order to obtain the required product.

Also, since powers of the same quantity are divided by subtracting their exponents (*Alg.*, Art. 66),

The logarithm of the quotient of one number divided by an-

other, is equal to the difference of the logarithms of those numbers.

Hence we see that if we wish to divide one number by another, we have only to subtract the logarithm of the divisor from that of the dividend; the difference will be the logarithm of their quotient.

(4.) Since, in Briggs' system, the logarithm of 10 is 1, if any number be multiplied or divided by 10, its logarithm will be increased or diminished by 1; and as this is an integer, it will only change the characteristic of the logarithm, without affecting the decimal part. Hence

The decimal part of the logarithm of any number is the same as that of the number multiplied or divided by 10, 100, 1000, &c.

Thus, the logarithm of		65430	is 4.815777;
"	"	6543	is 3.815777;
"	"	654.3	is 2.815777;
"	"	65.43	is 1.815777;
"	"	6.543	is 0.815777;
"	"	.6543	is $\bar{1}$.815777;
"	"	.06543	is $\bar{2}$.815777;
"	"	.006543	is $\bar{3}$.815777.

The minus sign is here placed *over* the characteristic, to show that *that* alone is negative, while the decimal part of the logarithm is positive.

TABLE OF LOGARITHMS.

(5.) A table of logarithms usually contains the logarithms of the entire series of natural numbers from 1 up to 10,000, and the larger tables extend to 100,000 or more. In the smaller tables the logarithms are usually given to five or six decimal places; the larger tables extend to seven, and sometimes eight or more places.

In the accompanying table, the logarithms of the first 100 numbers are given with their characteristics; but, for all other numbers, the decimal part only of the logarithm is given, while the characteristic is left to be supplied, according to the rule in Art. 2.

(6.) *To find the Logarithm of any Number between* 1 *and* 100.

Look on the first page of the accompanying table, along the column of numbers under N., for the given number, and against it, in the next column, will be found the logarithm with its characteristic. Thus,

opposite 13 is 1.113943, which is the logarithm of 13;
" 65 is 1.812913, " " 65.

To find the Logarithm of any Number consisting of three Figures.

Look on one of the pages of the table from 2 to 20, along the left-hand column, marked N., for the given number, and against it, in the column headed 0, will be found the decimal part of its logarithm. To this the characteristic must be prefixed, according to the rule in Art. 2. Thus

the logarithm of 347 will be found, from page 8, 2.540329;
" " 871 " " 18, 2.940018.

As the first two figures of the decimal are the same for several successive numbers in the table, they are not repeated for each logarithm separately, but are left to be supplied. Thus the decimal part of the logarithm of 339 is .530200. The first two figures of the decimal remain the same up to 347; they are therefore omitted in the table, and are to be supplied.

To find the Logarithm of any Number consisting of four Figures.

Find the three left-hand figures in the column marked N., as before, and the fourth figure at the head of one of the other columns. Opposite to the first three figures, and in the column under the fourth figure, will be found four figures of the logarithm, to which two figures from the column headed 0 are to be prefixed, as in the former case. The characteristic must be supplied according to Art. 2. Thus

the logarithm of 3456 is 3.538574;
" " 8765 is 3.942752.

In several of the columns headed 1, 2, 3, &c., small dots are found in the place of figures. This is to show that the two figures which are to be prefixed from the first column have changed, and they are to be taken from the horizontal line directly *below*. The place of the dots is to be supplied with ciphers. Thus

the logarithm of 2045 is 3.310693;
" " 9777 is 3.990206.

The two leading figures from the column 0 must also be taken from the horizontal line below, if any dots have been passed over on the same horizontal line. Thus

the logarithm of 1628 is 3.211654.

To find the Logarithm of any Number containing more than four Figures.

(7.) By inspecting the table, we shall find that, within certain limits, the differences of the logarithms are nearly proportional to the differences of their corresponding numbers. Thus

the logarithm of 7250 is 3.860338;
" " 7251 is 3.860398;
" " 7252 is 3.860458;
" " 7253 is 3.860518.

Here the difference between the successive logarithms, called *the tabular difference*, is constantly 60, corresponding to a difference of unity in the natural numbers. If, then, we suppose the logarithms to be proportional to their corresponding numbers (as they are nearly), a difference of 0.1 in the numbers should correspond to a difference of 6 in the logarithms; a difference of 0.2 in the numbers should correspond to a difference of 12 in the logarithms, &c. Hence

the logarithm of 7250.1 must be 3.860344;
" " 7250.2 " 3.860350;
" " 7250.3 " 3.860356.

In order to facilitate the computation, the tabular difference is inserted on page 16 in the column headed D., and the proportional part for the fifth figure of the natural number is given at the bottom of the page. Thus, when the tabular difference is 60, the corrections for .1, .2, .3, &c., are seen to be 6, 12, 18, &c.

If the given number was 72501, the characteristic of its logarithm would be 4, but the decimal part would be the same as for 7250.1.

If it were required to find the correction for a sixth figure in the natural number, it is readily obtained from the Proportional Parts in the table. The correction for a figure in the sixth place must be one tenth of the correction for the same figure if it stood in the fifth place. Thus, if the correction for .5 is 30, the correction for .05 is obviously 3.

As the differences change rapidly in the first part of the table, it was found inconvenient to give the proportional parts for each tabular difference; accordingly, for the first seven pages, they are only given for the *even* differences, but the proportional parts for the odd differences will be readily found by inspection.

Required the logarithm of 452789.

The logarithm of 452700 is 5.655810.

The tabular difference is 96.

Accordingly, the correction for the fifth figure, 8, is 77, and for the sixth figure, 9, is 8.6, or 9 nearly. Adding these corrections to the number before found, we obtain 5.655896.

The preceding logarithms do not pretend to be perfectly exact, but only the nearest numbers limited to six decimal places. Accordingly, when the fraction which is omitted exceeds half a unit in the sixth decimal place, the last figure must be increased by unity.

Required the logarithm of 8765432.

The logarithm of 8765000 is	6.942752
Correction for the fifth figure, 4,	20
" " sixth figure, 3,	1.5
" " seventh figure, 2,	0.1
Therefore the logarithm of 8765432 is	6.942774.

Required the logarithm of 234567.

The logarithm of 234500 is	5.370143
Correction for the fifth figure, 6,	111
" " sixth figure, 7,	13
Therefore the logarithm of 234567 is	5.370267.

To find the Logarithm of a Decimal Fraction

(8.) According to Art. 4, the decimal part of the logarithm of any number is the same as that of the number multiplied or divided by 10, 100, 1000, &c. Hence, for a decimal fraction, we find the logarithm as if the figures were integers, and prefix the characteristic according to the rule of Art. 2.

EXAMPLES.

The logarithm	of 345.6	is	2.538574;
"	" 87.65	is	1.942752;
"	" 2.345	is	0.370143;
"	" .1234	is	$\bar{1}.091315$;
"	" .005678	is	$\bar{3}.754195$.

To find the Logarithm of a Vulgar Fraction.

(9.) We may reduce the vulgar fraction to a decimal, and find its logarithm by the preceding article; or, since the value of a fraction is equal to the quotient of the numerator divided by the denominator, we may, according to Art. 3, *subtract the logarithm of the denominator from that of the numerator;* the difference will be the logarithm of the fraction.

Ex. 1. Find the logarithm of $\frac{3}{16}$, or 0.1875.

From the logarithm of 3,	0.477121,
Take the logarithm of 16,	1.204120.
Leaves the logarithm of $\frac{3}{16}$, or .1875,	$\bar{1}.273001$.

Ex. 2. The logarithm of $\frac{4}{55}$ is $\bar{2}.861697$.

Ex. 3. The logarithm of $\frac{123}{876}$ is $\bar{1}.147401$.

To find the Natural Number corresponding to any Logarithm.

(10.) Look in the table, in the column headed 0, for the first two figures of the logarithm, neglecting the characteristic; the other four figures are to be looked for in the same column, or in one of the nine following columns; and if they are exactly found, the first three figures of the corresponding number will be found opposite to them in the column headed N., and the fourth figure will be found at the top of the page. This number must be made to correspond with the characteristic of the given logarithm by pointing off decimals or annexing ciphers. Thus the natural number belonging to the log. 4.370143 is 23450;
" " " " 1.538574 is 34.56.

If the decimal part of the logarithm can not be exactly found in the table, look for the nearest less logarithm, and take out the four figures of the corresponding natural number as before; the additional figures may be obtained by means of the Proportional Parts at the bottom of the page.

Required the number belonging to the logarithm 4.368399.
On page 6, we find the next less logarithm .368287.

The four corresponding figures of the natural number are 2335. Their logarithm is less than the one proposed by 112. The tabular difference is 186; and, by referring to the bottom of page 6, we find that, with a difference of 186, the figure corresponding to the proportional part 112 is 6. Hence the five figures of the natural number are 23356; and, since the characteristic of the proposed logarithm is 4, these five figures are all integral.

Required the number belonging to logarithm 5.345678.
The next less logarithm in the table is 345570.
Their difference is 108.
The first four figures of the natural number are 2216.

With the tabular difference 196, the fifth figure, corresponding to 108, is seen to be 5, with a remainder of 10. To find the sixth figure corresponding to this remainder 10, we may multiply it by 10, making 100, and search for 100 in the same line of proportional parts. We see that a difference of 100 would give us 5 in the fifth place of the natural number. Therefore, a difference of 10 must give us 5 in the sixth place of the natural number. Hence the required number is 221655.

In the same manner we find
the number corresponding to log. 3.538672 is 3456.78;
" " " 1.994605 is 98.7654;
" " " $\bar{1}.647817$ is .444444.

Multiplication by Logarithms.

(11.) According to Art. 3, the logarithm of the product of two or more factors is equal to the sum of the logarithms of those factors. Hence, for multiplication by logarithms, we have the following

Rule.

Add the logarithms of the factors; the sum will be the logarithm of their product.

Ex. 1. Required the product of 57.98 by 18.

The logarithm of 57.98 is 1.763278
" " 18 is 1.255273

The logarithm of the product 1043.64 is 3.018551

Ex. 2. Required the product of 397.65 by 43.78.

Ans., 17409.117.

Ex. 3. Required the continued product of 54.32, 6.543, and 12.345.

The word *sum*, in the preceding rule, is to be understood in its algebraic sense; therefore, if any of the characteristics of the logarithms are *negative*, we must take the difference between their sum and that of the positive characteristics, and prefix the sign of the greater. It should be remembered that the decimal part of the logarithm is invariably positive; hence that which is carried from the decimal part to the characteristic must be considered positive.

Ex. 4. Multiply 0.00563 by 17.

The logarithm of 0.00563 is $\bar{3}.750508$
" " 17 is 1.230449

Product, 0.09571, whose logarithm is $\bar{2}.980957$.

Ex. 5. Multiply 0.3854 by 0.0576. *Ans.*, 0.022199.

Ex. 6. Multiply 0.007853 by 0.00476.

Ans., 0.00003738.

Ex. 7. Find the continued product of 11.35, 0.072, and 0.017.

(12.) *Negative* quantities may be multiplied by means of logarithms in the same manner as positive, the proper sign being prefixed to the result according to the rules of Algebra. To distinguish the negative sign of a natural number from the negative characteristic of a logarithm, we append the letter n to the logarithm of a negative factor. Thus

the logarithm of -56 we write 1.748188 n.

Ex. 8. Multiply 53.46 by -29.47.

The logarithm of 53.46 is 1.728029
" " -29.47 is 1.469380 n.

Product, -1575.47, log. 3.197409 n.

Ex. 9. Find the continued product of 372.1, $-.0054$, and -175.6.

Ex. 10. Find the continued product of -0.137, -7.689, and $-.0376$.

DIVISION BY LOGARITHMS.

(13.) According to Art. 3, the logarithm of the quotient of one number divided by another is equal to the difference of the logarithms of those numbers. Hence, for division by logarithms, we have the following

RULE.

From the logarithm of the dividend, subtract the logarithm of the divisor; the difference will be the logarithm of the quotient.

Ex. 1. Required the quotient of 888.7 divided by 42.24.

The logarithm of	888.7 is	2.948755
" "	42.24 is	1.625724
The quotient is 21.039, whose log. is		1.323031.

Ex. 2. Required the quotient of 3807.6 divided by 13.7.
Ans., 277.927.

The word *difference*, in the preceding rule, is to be understood in its algebraic sense; therefore, if the characteristic of one of the logarithms is negative, or the lower one is greater than the upper, we must change the sign of the subtrahend, and proceed as in addition. If unity is carried from the decimal part, this must be considered as positive, and must be united with the characteristic before its sign is changed.

Ex. 3. Required the quotient of 56.4 divided by 0.00015.

The logarithm of	56.4 is	1.751279
" "	0.00015 is	$\bar{4}$.176091
The quotient is 376000, whose log. is		5.575188.

This result may be verified in the same way as subtraction in common arithmetic. The remainder, added to the subtrahend, should be equal to the minuend. This precaution should always be observed when there is any doubt with regard to the sign of the result.

Ex. 4. Required the quotient of .8692 divided by 42.258.
Ans.

Ex. 5. Required the quotient of .74274 divided by .00928.

Ex. 6. Required the quotient of 24.934 divided by .078541.

Negative quantities may be divided by means of logarithms

in the same manner as positive, the proper sign being prefixed to the result according to the rules of Algebra.

Ex. 7. Required the quotient of −79.54 divided by 0.08321

Ex. 8. Required the quotient of −0.4753 divided by −36.74.

INVOLUTION BY LOGARITHMS.

(14.) It is proved in Algebra, Art. 340, that the logarithm of any power of a number is equal to the logarithm of that number multiplied by the exponent of the power. Hence, to involve a number by logarithms, we have the following

RULE.

Multiply the logarithm of the number by the exponent of the power required.

Ex. 1. Required the square of 428.

$$\begin{array}{rr} \text{The logarithm of 428 is} & 2.631444 \\ & 2 \\ \hline \text{Square, 183184, log.} & 5.262888. \end{array}$$

Ex. 2. Required the 20th power of 1.06.

$$\begin{array}{rr} \text{The logarithm of 1.06 is} & 0.025306 \\ & 20 \\ \hline \text{20th power, 3.2071, log.} & 0.506120. \end{array}$$

Ex. 3. Required the 5th power of 2.846.

It should be remembered, that what is carried from the decimal part of the logarithm is positive, whether the characteristic is positive or negative.

Ex. 4. Required the cube of .07654.

$$\begin{array}{rr} \text{The logarithm of .07654 is} & \bar{2}.883888 \\ & 3 \\ \hline \text{Cube, .0004484, log.} & \bar{4}.651664. \end{array}$$

Ex. 5. Required the fourth power of 0.09874.

Ex. 6. Required the seventh power of 0.8952.

EVOLUTION BY LOGARITHMS.

(15.) It is proved in Algebra, Art. 341, that the logarithm of any root of a number is equal to the logarithm of that number divided by the index of the root. Hence, to extract the root of a number by logarithms, we have the following

RULE.

Divide the logarithm of the number by the index of the root required.

Ex. 1. Required the cube root of 482.38.

The logarithm of 482.38 is 2.683389.

Dividing by 3, we have 0.894463, which corresponds to 7.842, which is therefore the root required.

Ex. 2. Required the 100th root of 365.

Ans., 1.0608.

When the characteristic of the logarithm is negative, and is not divisible by the given divisor, we may increase the characteristic by any number which will make it exactly divisible, provided we prefix an equal positive number to the decimal part of the logarithm.

Ex. 3. Required the seventh root of 0.005846.

The logarithm of 0.005846 is $\bar{3}.766859$, which may be written $\bar{7}+4.766859$.

Dividing by 7, we have $\bar{1}.680980$, which is the logarithm of .4797, which is, therefore, the root required.

This result may be verified by multiplying $\bar{1}.680980$ by 7, the result will be found to be $\bar{3}.766860$.

Ex. 4. Required the fifth root of 0.08452.

Ex. 5. Required the tenth root of 0.007815.

PROPORTION BY LOGARITHMS.

(16.) The fourth term of a proportion is found by multiplying together the second and third terms, and dividing by the first. Hence, to find the fourth term of a proportion by logarithms,

Add the logarithms of the second and third terms, and from their sum subtract the logarithm of the first term.

Ex. 1. Find a fourth proportional to 72.34, 2.519, and 357.48

Ans., 12.448.

(17.) When one logarithm is to be subtracted from another, it may be more convenient to convert the subtraction into an addition, which may be done by first subtracting the given logarithm from 10, adding the difference to the other logarithm, and afterward rejecting the 10.

The difference between a given logarithm and 10 is called its *complement;* and this is easily taken from the table by beginning at the left hand, subtracting each figure from 9, except the last significant figure on the right, which must be subtracted from 10.

To subtract one logarithm from another is the same as to add its complement, and then reject 10 from the result. For $a-b$ is equivalent to $10-b+a-10$.

To work a proportion, then, by logarithms, we must

Add the complement of the logarithm of the first term to the logarithms of the second and third terms.

The characteristic must afterward be diminished by 10.

Ex. 2. Find a fourth proportional to 6853, 489, and 38750.

The complement of the logarithm of	6853	is 6.164119
The logarithm of	489	is 2.689309
" "	38750	is 4.588272
The fourth term is 2765, whose logarithm is		3.441700.

One advantage of using the complement of the first term in working a proportion by logarithms is, that it enables us to exhibit the operation in a more compact form.

Ex. 3. Find a fourth proportional to 73.84, 658.3, and 4872.,

Ans.

Ex. 4. Find a fourth proportional to 5.745, 781.2, and 54.27.

BOOK II.

PLANE TRIGONOMETRY.

(18.) TRIGONOMETRY *is the science which teaches how to determine the several parts of a triangle from having certain parts given.*

Plane Trigonometry treats of plane triangles; Spherical Trigonometry treats of spherical triangles.

(19.) The circumference of every circle is supposed to be divided into 360 equal parts, called *degrees ;* each degree into 60 *minutes*, and each minute into 60 *seconds.* Degrees, minutes, and seconds are designated by the characters °, ′, ″. Thus 23° 14′ 35″ is read 23 degrees, 14 minutes, and 35 seconds.

Since an angle at the center of a circle is measured by the arc intercepted by its sides, a right angle is measured by 90°, two right angles by 180°, and four right angles are measured by 360°.

(20.) The *complement* of an arc is what remains after subtracting the arc from 90°. Thus the arc DF is the complement of AF. The complement of 25° 15′ is 64° 45′.

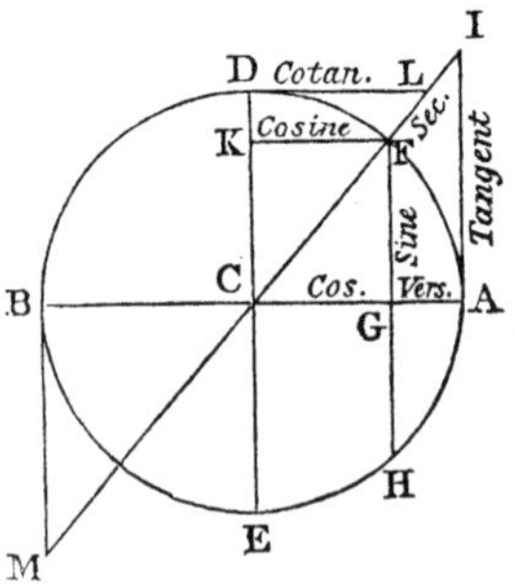

In general, if we represent any arc by A, its complement is 90°−A. Hence, if an arc is greater than 90°, its complement must be negative. Thus, the complement of 100° 15′ is −10° 15′. Since the two acute angles of a right-angled triangle are together equal to a right angle, each of them must be the complement of the other.

(21.) The *supplement* of an arc is what remains after subtracting the arc from 180°. Thus the arc BDF is the supplement of the arc AF. The supplement of 25° 15′ is 154° 45′.

In general, if we represent any arc by A, its supplement is

180°−A. Hence, if an arc is greater than 180°, its supplement must be negative. Thus the supplement of 200° is −20°. Since in every triangle the sum of the three angles is 180°, either angle is the supplement of the sum of the other two.

(22.) *The sine of an arc is the perpendicular let fall from one extremity of the arc on the radius passing through the other extremity.* Thus FG is the sine of the arc AF, or of the angle ACF.

Every sine is half the chord of double the arc. Thus the sine FG is the half of FH, which is the chord of the arc FAH, double of FA. The chord which subtends the sixth part of the circumference, or the chord of 60°, is equal to the radius (*Geom.*, Prop. IV., B. VI.); hence the sine of 30° is equal to half of the radius.

(23.) The *versed sine* of an arc is that part of the diameter intercepted between the sine and the arc. Thus GA is the versed sine of the arc AF.

(24). *The tangent of an arc is the line which touches it at one extremity, and is terminated by a line drawn from the center through the other extremity.* Thus AI is the tangent of the arc AF, or of the angle ACF.

(25.) *The secant of an arc is the line drawn from the center of the circle through one extremity of the arc, and is limited by the tangent drawn through the other extremity.*

Thus CI is the secant of the arc AF, or of the angle ACF.

(26.) The *cosine* of an arc is the sine of the complement of that arc. Thus the arc DF, being the complement of AF, FK is the sine of the arc DF, or the cosine of the arc AF.

The *cotangent* of an arc is the tangent of the complement of that arc. Thus DL is the tangent of the arc DF, or the cotangent of the arc AF.

The *cosecant* of an arc is the secant of the complement of that arc. Thus CL is the secant of the arc DF, or the cosecant of the arc AF.

In general, if we represent any angle by A,

$$\text{cos. } A = \text{sine } (90° - A).$$
$$\text{cot. } A = \text{tang. } (90° - A).$$
$$\text{cosec. } A = \text{sec. } (90° - A).$$

Since, in a right-angled triangle, either of the acute angles is the complement of the other, the sine, tangert, and secant of one of these angles is the cosine, cotangent, and cosecan of the other.

(27.) The sine, tangent, and secant of an arc are equal to the sine, tangent, and secant of its supplement. Thus FG is the sine of the arc AF, or of its supplement, BDF. Also, AI, the tangent of the arc AF, is equal to BM, the tangent of the arc BDF. And CI, the secant of the arc AF, is equal to CM, the secant of the arc BDF.

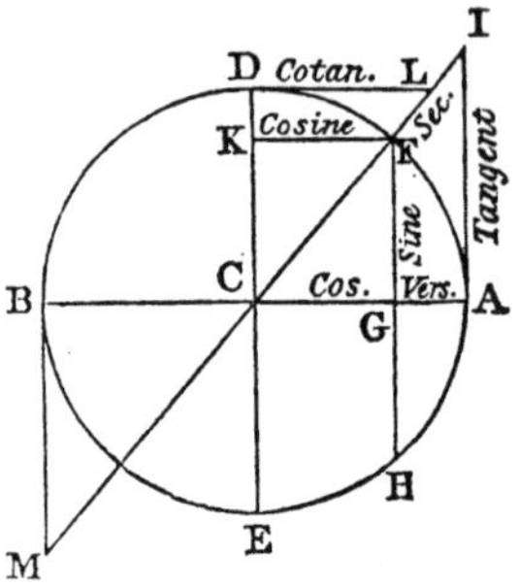

The versed sine of an acute angle, ACF, is equal to the radius *minus* the cosine CG. The versed sine of an obtuse angle, BCF, is equal to radius *plus* the cosine CG; that is, to BG.

(28.) The relations of the sine, cosine, &c., to each other, may be derived from the proportions of the sides of similar triangles. Thus the triangles CGF, CAI, CDL, being similar, we have,

1. CG : GF : : CA : AI; that is, representing the arc by A, and the radius of the circle by R, cos. A : sin. A : : R : tang. A.

$$\text{Whence tang. A}=\frac{\text{R sin. A}}{\text{cos. A}}.$$

2. CG : : CF : CA : CI; that is, cos. A : R : : R : sec. A.

$$\text{Whence sec. A}=\frac{\text{R}^2}{\text{cos. A}}.$$

3 GF : CG : : CD : DL; that is, sin. A : cos. A : : R : cot. A.

$$\text{Whence cot. A}=\frac{\text{R cos. A}}{\text{sin. A}}.$$

4 GF : CF : : CD : CL; that is, sin. A : R : : R : cosec. A.

$$\text{Whence cosec. A}=\frac{\text{R}^2}{\text{sin. A}}.$$

5. AI : AC : : CD : DL; that is, tang. A : R : : R : cot. A.

$$\text{Whence tang. A.}=\frac{\text{R}^2}{\text{cot. A}}.$$

The preceding values of tangent and cotangent, secant and cosecant will be frequently referred to hereafter, and should be carefully committed to memory.

Also, in the right-angled triangle CGF, we find $CG^2+GF^2=CF^2$; that is, $\sin.^2A+\cos.^2A=R^2$; or,

The square of the sine of an arc, together with the square of its cosine, is equal to the square of the radius.

$$\text{Hence } \sin. A=\pm\sqrt{R^2-\cos.^2A}.$$

$$\text{And } \cos. A=\pm\sqrt{R^2-\sin.^2A}.$$

(29.) A table of *natural sines, tangents,* &c., is a table giving the lengths of those lines for different angles in a circle whose radius is unity.

Thus, if we describe a circle with a radius of one inch, and divide the circumference into equal parts of ten degrees, we shall find

the	sine of	10°	equals	0.174	inch;
"	"	20°	"	0.342	"
"	"	30°	"	0.500	"
"	"	40°	"	0.643	"
"	"	50°	"	0.766	"
"	"	60°	"	0.866	"
"	"	70°	"	0.940	"
"	"	80°	"	0.985	"
"	"	90°	"	1.000	"

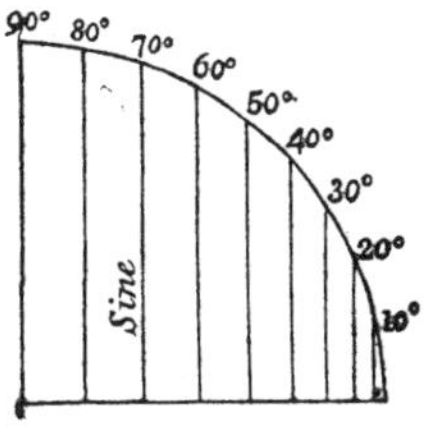

If we draw the tangents of the same arcs, we shall find

the	tangent of	10°	equals	0.176	inch;.
"	"	20°	"	0.364	"
"	"	30°	"	0.577	"
"	"	40°	"	0.839	"
"	"	45°	"	1.000	"
"	"	50°	"	1.192	"
"	"	60°	"	1.732	"
"	"	70°	"	2.747	"
"	"	80°	"	5.671	"
"	"	90°	"	infinite.	

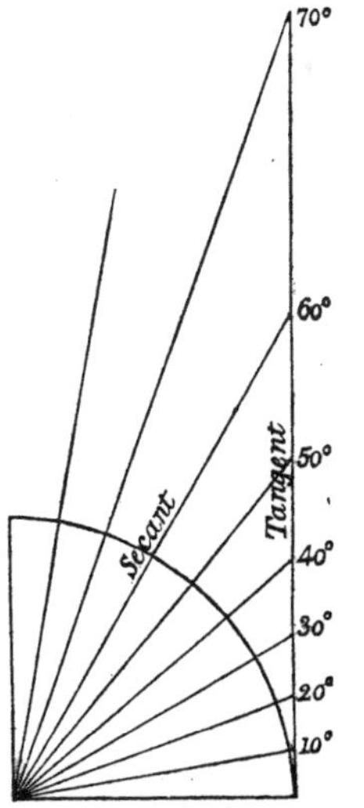

Also, if we draw the secants of the same arcs, we shall find that

the	secant of	10°	equals	1.015	inch;
"	"	20°	"	1.064	"
"	"	30°	"	1.155	"
"	"	40°	"	1.305	"

the secant of 50° equals 1.556 inch;
" " 60° " 2.000 "
" " 70° " 2.924 "
" " 80° " 5.759 "
" " 90° " infinite.

In the accompanying table, pages 116–133, the sines, cosines, tangents, and cotangents are given for every minute of the quadrant to six places of figures.

(30.) *To find from the table the natural sine, cosine, &c., of an arc or angle.*

If a sine is required, look for the degrees at the *top* of the page, and for the minutes on the *left;* then, directly under the given number of degrees at the top of the page, and opposite to the minutes on the left, will be found the sine required. Since the radius of the circle is supposed to be unity, the sine of every arc below 90° is less than unity. The sines are expressed in decimal parts of radius; and, although the decimal point is not written in the table, it must always be prefixed. As the first two figures remain the same for a great many numbers in the table, they are only inserted for every ten minutes, and the vacant places must be supplied from the two leading figures next preceding. Thus, on

page 120, the sine of 25° 11′ is 0.425516;
page 126, " " 51° 34′ is 0.783332, &c.

The tangents are found in a similar manner. Thus

the tangent of 31° 44′ is 0.618417;
" " 65° 27′ is 2.18923.

The same number in the table is both the sine of an arc and the cosine of its complement. The degrees for the cosines must be sought at the bottom of the page, and the minutes on the right. Thus,

on page 130, the cosine of 16° 42′ is 0.957822;
on page 118, " " 73° 17′ is 0.287639, &c.

The cotangents are found in the same manner. Thus

the cotangent of 19° 16′ is 2.86089;
" " 54° 53′ is 0.703246.

It is not necessary to extend the tables beyond a quadrant, because the sine of an angle is equal to that of its supplement (Art. 27). Thus

the sine of 143° 24′ is 0.596225;
" cosine of 151° 23′ is 0.877844;
" tangent of 132° 36′ is 1.08749;
" cotangent of 116° 7′ is 0.490256, &c.

(31.) If a sine is required for an arc consisting of degrees, minutes, and *seconds*, we must make an allowance for the seconds in the same manner as was directed in the case of logarithms, Art. 7; for, within certain limits, the differences of the sines are proportional to the differences of the corresponding arcs. Thus

the sine of 34° 25′ is .565207;
" " 34° 26′ is .565447.

The difference of the sines corresponding to one minute of arc, or 60 seconds, is .000240. The proportional part for 1″ is found by dividing the tabular difference by 60, and the quotient, .000004, is placed at the bottom of page 122, in the column headed 34°. The correction for any number of seconds will be found by multiplying the proportional part for 1″ by the number of seconds.

Required the natural sine of 34° 25′ 37″.

The proportional part for 1″, being multiplied by 37, becomes 148, which is the correction for 37″. Adding this to the sine of 34° 25′, we find

the sine of 34° 25′ 37″ is .565355.

Since the proportional part for 1″ is given to *hundredths* of a unit in the sixth place of figures, after we have multiplied by the given number of seconds, we must reject the last two figures of the product.

In the same manner we find

the cosine of 56° 34′ 28″ is .550853.

It will be observed, that since the cosines decrease while the arcs increase, the correction for the 28″ is to be subtracted from the cosine of 56° 34′.

In the same manner we find

the natural sine of 27° 17′ 12″ is 0.458443;
" " cosine of 45° 23′ 23″ is 0.702281;
" " tangent of 63° 32′ 34″ is 2.00945;
" " cotangent of 81° 48′ 56″ is 0.143825

(32.) *To find the number of degrees, minutes, and seconds belonging to a given sine or tangent.*

If the given sine or tangent is found exactly in the table, the corresponding degrees will be found at the top of the page, and the minutes on the left hand. But when the given number is not found exactly in the table, look for the sine or tangent which is next less than the proposed one, and take out the corresponding degrees and minutes. Find, also, the difference between this tabular number and the number proposed, and divide it by the proportional part for 1″ found at the bottom of the page; the quotient will be the required number of seconds.

Required the arc whose sine is .750000.

The next less sine in the table is .749919, the arc corresponding to which is 48° 35′. The difference between this sine and that proposed is 81, which, divided by 3.21, gives 25. Hence the required arc is 48° 35′ 25″.

In the same manner we find

the arc whose tangent is 2.00000 is 63° 26′ 6″.

If a cosine or cotangent is required, we must look for the number in the table which is next greater than the one proposed, and then proceed as for a sine or tangent. Thus

the arc whose cosine is .40000 is 66° 25′ 18″;
" " " cotangent is 1.99468 is 26° 37′ 34″.

(33.) On pages 134–5 will be found a table of natural secants for every ten minutes of the quadrant, carried to seven places of figures. The degrees are arranged in order in the first vertical column on the left, and the minutes at the top of the page. Thus

the secant of 21° 20′ is 1.073561;
" " 81° 50′ is 7.039622.

If a secant is required for a number of minutes not given in the table, the correction for the odd minutes may be found by means of the last vertical column on the right, which shows the proportional part for one minute.

Let it be required to find the secant of 30° 33′

The secant of 30° 30′ is 1.160592.

The correction for 1′ is 198.9, which, multiplied by 3, becomes 597. Adding this to the number before found, we obtain 1.161189.

For a cosecant, the degrees must be sought in the right-hand vertical column, and the minutes at the bottom of the page. Thus

the cosecant of 47° 40′ is 1.352742;
" " 38° 33′ is 1.604626.

(34.) When the natural sines, tangents, &c., are used in proportions, it is necessary to perform the tedious operations of multiplication and division. It is, therefore, generally preferable to employ the *logarithms* of the sines; and, for convenience, these numbers are arranged in a separate table, called *logarithmic sines*, &c. Thus

the natural sine of 14° 30′ is 0.250380.
Its logarithm, found from page 6, is $\bar{1}.398600$.

The characteristic of the logarithm is *negative*, as must be the case with all the sines, since they are less than unity. To avoid the introduction of negative numbers in the table, we increase the characteristic by 10, making 9.398600, and this is the number found on page 38 for the logarithmic sine of 14° 30′. The radius of the table of logarithmic sines is therefore, properly, 10,000,000,000, whose logarithm is 10.

(35.) The accompanying table contains the logarithmic sines and tangents for every ten seconds of the quadrant. The degrees and seconds are placed at the top of the page, and the minutes in the left vertical column. After the first two degrees, the three leading figures in the table of sines are only given in the column headed 0″, and are to be prefixed to the numbers in the other columns, as in the table of logarithms of numbers. Also, where the leading figures change, this change is indicated by dots, as in the former table. The correction for any number of seconds less than 10 is given at the bottom of the page.

(36.) *To find the logarithmic sine or tangent of a given arc.*

Look for the degrees at the top of the page, the minutes on the left hand, and the next less number of seconds at the top; then, under the seconds, and opposite to the minutes, will be found four figures, to which the three leading figures are to be prefixed from the column headed 0″; to this add the proportional part for the odd seconds at the bottom of the page.

Required the logarithmic sine of 24° 27′ 34″.

The logarithmic sine of 24° 27′ 30″ is	9.617033
Proportional part for 4″ is	18
Logarithmic sine of 24° 27′ 34″ is	9.617051.

Required the logarithmic tangent of 73° 35′ 43″.

The logarithmic tangent 73° 35′ 40″ is	10.531031
Proportional part for 3″ is	23
Logarithmic tangent of 73° 35′ 43″ is	10.531054.

When a cosine is required, the degrees and seconds must be sought at the bottom of the page, and the minutes on the right, and the correction for the odd seconds must be subtracted from the number in the table.

Required the logarithmic cosine of 59° 33′ 47″.

The logarithmic cosine of 59° 33′ 40″ is	9.704682
Proportional part for 7″ is	25
Logarithmic cosine of 59° 33′ 47″ is	9.704657.

So, also, the logarithmic cotangent of 37° 27′ 14″ is found to be 10.115744.

It will be observed that for the cosines and cotangents, the seconds are numbered from 10″ to 60″, so that if it is required to find the cosine of 25° 25′ 0″ we must look for 25° 24′ 60″; and so, also, for the cotangents.

(37.) The proportional parts given at the bottom of each page correspond to the degrees at the top of the page, increased by 30′, and are not strictly applicable to any other number of minutes; nevertheless, the differences of the sines change so slowly, except near the commencement of the quadrant, that the error resulting from using these numbers for every part of the page will seldom exceed a unit in the sixth decimal place. For the first two degrees, the differences change so rapidly that the proportional part for 1″ is given for each minute in the right-hand column of the page. The correction for any number of seconds less than ten will be found by multiplying the proportional part for 1″ by the given number of seconds.

Required the logarithmic sine of 1° 17′ 33″.

The logarithmic sine of 1° 17′ 30″ is 8.352991.

The correction for 3″ is found by multiplying 93.4 by 3, which gives 280. Adding this to the above tabular number, we obtain for

the sine of 1° 17′ 33″, 8.353271.

A similar method may be employed for several of the first degrees of the quadrant, if the proportional parts at the bottom of the page are not thought sufficiently precise. This correction may, however, be obtained pretty nearly by inspection, from comparing the proportional parts for two successive degrees. Thus, on page 26, the correction for 1″, corresponding to the sine of 2° 30′, is 48; the correction for 1″, corresponding to the sine of 3° 30′, is 34. Hence the correction for 1″, corresponding to the sine of 3° 0′, must be about 41; and, in the same manner, we may proceed for any other part of the table.

(38.) Near the close of the quadrant, the tangents vary so rapidly that the same arrangement of the table is adopted as for the commencement of the quadrant. For the last, as well as the first two degrees of the quadrant, the proportional part to 1″ is given for each minute separately. These proportional parts are computed for the minutes placed opposite to them, increased by 30″, and are not strictly applicable to any other number of seconds; nevertheless, the differences for the most part change so slowly, that the error resulting from using these numbers for every part of the same horizontal line is quite small. When great accuracy is required, the table on page 114 may be employed for arcs near the limits of the quadrant. This table furnishes the differences between the logarithmic sines and the logarithms of the arcs expressed in seconds. Thus

the logarithmic sine of 0° 5′, from page 22, is	7.162696
the logarithm of 300″ (=5′) is	2.477121
the difference is	4.685575.

This is the number found on page 114, under the heading *log. sine A−log. A″*, opposite to 5 min.; and, in a similar manner, the other numbers in the same column are obtained. These numbers vary quite slowly for two degrees; and hence, to find the logarithmic sine of an arc less than two degrees, we have but to add the logarithm of the arc expressed in seconds to the appropriate number found in this table.

Required the logarithmic sine of 0° 7′ 22″.

Tabular number from page 114,	4.685575
The logarithm of 442″ is	2.645422
Logarithmic sine of 0° 7′ 22″ is	7.330997.

The logarithmic tangent of an arc less than two degrees is found in a similar manner.

Required the logarithmic tangent of 0° 27′ 36″.

Tabular number from page 114,	4.685584
The logarithm of 1656″ is	3.219060
Logarithmic tangent of 0° 27′ 36″ is	7.904644.

The column headed *log. cot. A+log. A″*, is found by adding the logarithmic cotangent to the logarithm of the arc expressed in seconds. Hence, to find the logarithmic cotangent of an arc less than two degrees, we must subtract from the tabular number the logarithm of the arc in seconds.

Required the logarithmic cotangent of 0° 27′ 36″.

Tabular number from page 114,	15.314416
The logarithm of 1656″ is	3.219060
Logarithmic cotangent of 0° 27′ 36″ is	12.095356.

The same method will, of course, furnish cosines and cotangents of arcs near 90°.

(39.) The secants and cosecants are omitted in this table, since they are easily derived from the cosines and sines. We have found, Art. 28, secant $=\frac{R^2}{\text{cosine}}$; or, taking the logarithms,

log. secant $=2.\ \text{log. R}-\text{log. cosine}$
$=20-\text{log. cosine}.$

Also, cosecant $=\frac{R^2}{\text{sine}}$,

or log. cosecant $=20-\text{log. sine}$. That is,

The logarithmic secant is found by subtracting the logarithmic cosine from 20; *and the logarithmic cosecant is found by subtracting the logarithmic sine from* 20.

Thus we have found the logarithmic sine of 24° 27′ 34″ to be 9.617051.

Hence the logarithmic cosecant of 24° 27′ 34″ is 10.382949

The logarithmic cosine of 54° 12′ 40″ is 9.767008.
Hence the logarithmic secant of 54° 12′ 40″ is 10.232992.

(40.) *To find the arc corresponding to a given logarithmic sine or tangent.*

If the given number is found exactly in the table, the corresponding degrees and seconds will be found at the top of the page, and the minutes on the left. But when the given number is not found exactly in the table, look for the sine or tangent which is next less than the proposed one, and take out the corresponding degrees, minutes, and seconds. Find, also, the difference between this tabular number and the number proposed, and corresponding to this difference, at the bottom of the page, will be found a certain number of seconds which is to be added to the arc before found.

Required the arc corresponding to the logarithmic sine 9.750000.

The next less sine in the table is 9.749987.

The arc corresponding to which is 34° 13′ 0″.

The difference between its sine and the one proposed is 13, corresponding to which, at the bottom of the page, we find 4″ nearly. Hence the required arc is 34° 13′ 4″.

In the same manner, we find the arc corresponding to logarithmic tangent 10.250000 to be 60° 38′ 57″.

When the arc falls within the first two degrees of the quadrant, the odd seconds may be found by dividing the difference between the tabular number and the one proposed, by the proportional part for 1″. We thus find the arc corresponding to logarithmic sine 8.400000 to be 1° 26′ 22″ nearly.

We may employ the same method for the last two degrees of the quadrant when a tangent is given; but near the limits of the quadrant it is better to employ the auxiliary table on page 114. The tabular number on page 114 is equal to log. sin. A—log. A″. Hence log. sin. A— tabular number =log. A″; that is, if we subtract the corresponding tabular number on page 114, from the given logarithmic sine, the remainder will be the logarithm of the arc expressed in seconds.

Required the arc corresponding to logarithmic sine 7.000000.

We see, from page 22, that the arc must be nearly 3′; the corresponding tabular number on page 114 is 4.685575

The difference is 2.314425,
which is the logarithm of 206.″265.

Hence the required arc is 3′ 26.″265.

Required the arc corresponding to log. sine 8.000000.

We see from page 22, that the arc is about 34′. The corresponding tabular number from page 114 is 4.685568, which, subtracted from 8.000000, leaves 3.314432, which is the logarithm of 2062.″68. Hence the required arc is

34′ 22.″68.

In the same manner, we find the arc corresponding to logarithmic tangent 8.184608 to be 0° 52′ 35″.

SOLUTIONS OF RIGHT-ANGLED TRIANGLES.

THEOREM I.

(41.) *In any right-angled triangle, radius is to the hypothenuse as the sine of either acute angle is to the opposite side, or the cosine of either acute angle to the adjacent side.*

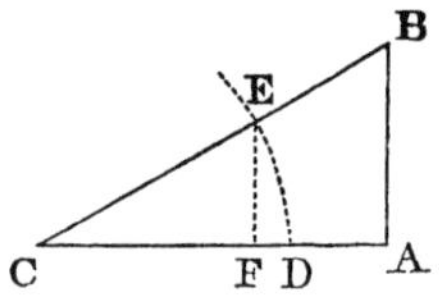

Let the triangle CAB be right angled at A, then will

R : CB : : sin. C : BA : : cos. C : CA.

From the point C as a center, with a radius equal to the radius of the tables, describe the arc DE, and on AC let fall the perpendicular EF. Then EF will be the sine, and CF the cosine of the angle C. Because the triangles CAB, CFE are similar, we have

CE : CB : : EF : BA,

or R : CB : : sin. C : BA.

Also, CE : CB : : CF : CA,

or R : CB : : cos. C : CA.

THEOREM II.

(42.) *In any right-angled triangle, radius is to either side as the tangent of the adjacent acute angle is to the opposite side, or the secant of the same angle to the hypothenuse.*

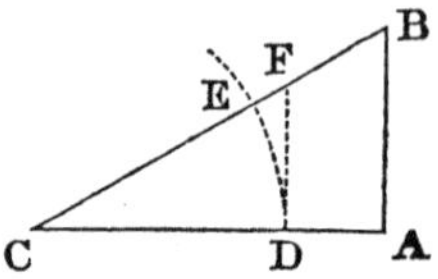

Let the triangle CAB be right angled at A, then will

R : CA : : tang. C : AB : : sec. C : CB.

From the point C as a center, with a radius equal to the radius of the tables, describe the arc DE, and from the point D draw DF perpendicular to CA. Then DF will be the tangent, and CF the secant of the angle C. Because the triangles CAB, CDF are similar, we have CD : CA : : DF : AB,

or R : CA : : tang. C : AB.

Also, CD : CA : : CF : CB,

or R : CA : : sec. C : CB.

(43.) In every plane triangle there are *six* parts : three sides and three angles. Of these, any three being given, provided one of them is a side, the others may be determined. In a right-angled triangle, one of the six parts, viz., the right angle, is always given; and if one of the acute angles is given, the other is, of course, known. Hence the number of parts to be considered in a right-angled triangle is reduced to *four*, any two of which being given, the others may be found.

It is desirable to have appropriate names by which to designate each of the parts of a triangle. One of the sides adjacent to the right angle being called the base, the other side adjacent to the right angle may be called the perpendicular. The three sides will then be called the hypothenuse, base, and perpendicular. The base and perpendicular are sometimes called the legs of the triangle. Of the two acute angles, that which is adjacent to the base may be called the angle at the base, and the other the angle at the perpendicular.

We may, therefore, have four cases, according as there are given,

1. The hypothenuse and the angles;
2. The hypothenuse and a leg;
3. One leg and the angles; or,
4. The two legs.

All of these cases may be solved by the two preceding theorems.

CASE I.

(44.) *Given the hypothenuse and the angles, to find the base and perpendicular.*

This case is solved by Theorem I.

Radius : *hypothenuse* : : *sine of the angle at the base* : *perpendicular* ;

: : *cosine of the angle at the base* : *base*

Ex. 1. Given the hypothenuse 275, and the angle at the base 57° 23′, to find the base and perpendicular.

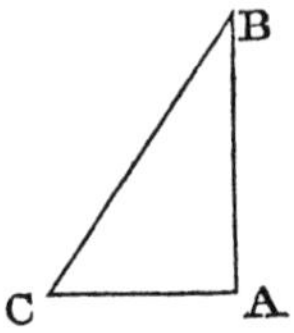

The natural sine of 57° 23′ is .842296;
" cosine " .539016.

Hence 1 : 275 : : .842296 : 231.631=AB.
1 : 275 : : .539016 : 148.229=AC.

The computation is here made by natural numbers. If we work the proportion by logarithms, we shall have

Radius,	10.000000
Is to the hypothenuse 275	2.439333
As the sine of C 57° 23′	9.925465
To the perpendicular 231.63	2.364798.

Also, Radius,	10.000000
Is to the hypothenuse 275	2.439333
As the cosine of C 57° 23′	9.731602
To the base 148.23	2.170935.

Ex. 2. Given the hypothenuse 67.43, and the angle at the perpendicular 38° 43′, to find the base and perpendicular.

Ans. The base is 42.175, and perpendicular 52.612.

The student should work this and the following examples both by natural numbers and by logarithms, until he has made himself perfectly familiar with both methods. He may then employ either method, as may appear to him most expeditious.

CASE II.

(45.) *Given the hypothenuse and one leg, to find the angles and the other leg.*

This case is solved by Theorem I.

Hypothenuse : *radius* : : *base* : *cosine of the angle at the base.*

Radius : *hypothenuse* : : *sine of the angle at the base* : *perpendicular.*

When the perpendicular is given, perpendicular must be substituted for base in this proportion.

Ex. 1. Given the hypothenuse 54.32, and the base 32.11, to find the angles and the perpendicular.

By natural numbers, we have

54.32 : 1 : : 32.11 : .591127, which is the cosine of 53° 45′ 47″, the angl › at the base.

Also, 1 : 54.32 : : .806580 : 43.813=the perpendicular.

The computation may be performed more expeditiously by logarithms, as in the former case.

Ex. 2. Given the hypothenuse 332.49, and the perpendicular 98.399, to find the angles and the base.

Ans. The angles are 17° 12′ 51″ and 72° 47′ 9″; the base, 317.6.

CASE III.

(46.) *Given one leg and the angles, to find the other leg and hypothenuse.*

This case is solved by Theorem II.

Radius : base : : tangent of the angle at the base : the perpendicular.

: : secant of the angle at the base : hypothenuse.

When the perpendicular is given, perpendicular must be substituted for base in this proportion.

Ex. 1. Given the base 222, and the angle at the base 25° 15′, to find the perpendicular and hypothenuse.

By natural numbers, we have

1 : 222 : : .471631 : 104.70, perpendicular;

: : 1.105638 : 245.45, hypothenuse.

The computation should also be performed by logarithms, as in Case I.

Ex. 2. Given the perpendicular 125, and the angle at the perpendicular 51° 19′, to find the hypothenuse and base.

Ans. Hypothenuse, 199.99; base, 156.12.

CASE IV.

(47.) *Given the two legs, to find the angles and hypothenuse.*

This case is solved by Theorem II.

Base : radius : : perpendicular : tangent of the angle at the base.

Radius : base : : secant of the angle at the base : hypothenuse.

Ex. 1. Given the base 123, and perpendicular 765, to find the angles and hypothenuse.

By natural numbers, we have

123 : 1 : : 765 : 6.219512, which is the tangent of 80° 51′ 57″, the angle at the base.

1 : 123 : : 6.300479 : 774.96, hypothenuse.

The computation may also be made by logarithms, as in Case I.

Ex. 2. Given the base 53, and perpendicular 67, to find the angles and hypothenuse.

Ans. The angles are 51° 39′ 16″ and 38° 20′ 44″; hypothenuse, 85.428.

Examples for Practice.

1. Given the base 777, and perpendicular 345, to find the hypothenuse and angles.

This example, it will be seen, falls under Case IV.

2. Given the hypothenuse 324, and the angle at the base 48° 17′, to find the base and perpendicular.

3. Given the perpendicular 543, and the angle at the base 72° 45′, to find the hypothenuse and base.

4. Given the hypothenuse 666, and base 432, to find the angles and perpendicular.

5. Given the base 634, and the angle at the base 53° 27′, to find the hypothenuse and perpendicular.

6. Given the hypothenuse 1234, and perpendicular 555, to find the base and angles.

(48.) When two sides of a right-angled triangle are given, the third may be found by means of the property that the square of the hypothenuse is equal to the sum of the squares of the other two sides.

Hence, representing the hypothenuse, base, and perpendicular by the initial letters of these words, we have

$$h=\sqrt{b^2+p^2}\,;\quad b=\sqrt{h^2-p^2}\,;\quad p=\sqrt{h^2-b^2}.$$

Ex. 1. If the base is 2720, and the perpendicular 3104, what is the hypothenuse? *Ans.*, 4127.1.

Ex. 2. If the hypothenuse is 514, and the perpendicular 432, what is the base?

SOLUTIONS OF OBLIQUE-ANGLED TRIANGLES.

THEOREM I.

(49.) *In any plane triangle, the sines of the angles are proportional to the opposite sides.*

Let ABC be any triangle, and from one of its angles, as C, let CD be drawn perpendicular to AB. Then, because the triangle ACD is right angled at D, we have

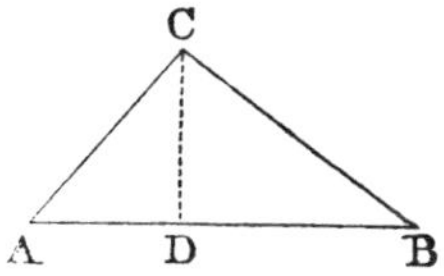

R : sin. A : : AC : CD; whence R×CD=sin. A×AC.

For the same reason,

R : sin. B : : BC : CD; whence R×CD=sin. B×BC.

Therefore, sin. A×AC=sin. B×BC,

or sin. A : sin. B : : BC : AC.

THEOREM II.

(50.) *In any plane triangle, the sum of any two sides is to their difference, as the tangent of half the sum of the opposite angles is to the tangent of half their difference.*

Let ABC be any triangle; then will

$$CB+CA : CB-CA :: \text{tang.}\frac{A+B}{2} : \text{tang.}\frac{A-B}{2}.$$

Produce AC to D, making CD equal to CB, and join DB. Take CE equal to CA, draw AE, and produce it to F. Then AD is the *sum* of CB and CA, and BE is their *difference.*

The sum of the two angles CAE, CEA, is equal to the sum of CAB, CBA, each being the supplement of ACB (*Geom.*, Prop. 27, B. I.). But, since CA is equal to CE, the angle CAE is equal to the angle CEA; therefore, CAE is the *half sum* of the angles CAB, CBA. Also, if from the greater of the two angles CAB, CBA, there be taken their half sum, the remainder, FAB, will be their *half difference* (*Algebra*, p. 68).

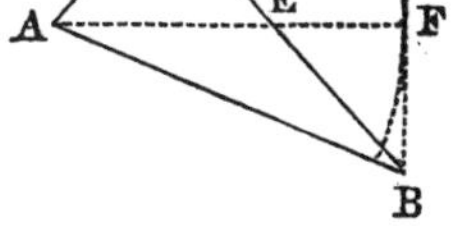

Since CD is equal to CB, the angle ADF is equal to the angle EBF; also, the angle CAE is equal to AEC, which is equal to the vertical angle BEF. Therefore, the two triangles DAF, BEF, are mutually equiangular; hence the two angles at F are equal, and AF is perpendicular to DB. If, then, AF be made radius, DF will be the tangent of DAF, and BF will be the tangent of BAF. But, by similar triangles, we have

$$AD : BE :: DF : BF; \text{ that is,}$$

$$CB+CA : CB-CA :: \text{tang.} \frac{A+B}{2} : \text{tang.} \frac{A-B}{2}.$$

THEOREM III.

(51.) *If from any angle of a triangle a perpendicular be drawn to the opposite side or base, the whole base will be to the sum of the other two sides, as the difference of those two sides is to the difference of the segments of the base.*

For demonstration, see Geometry, Prop. 31, Cor., B. IV.

(52). In every plane triangle, three parts must be given to enable us to determine the others; and of the given parts, one, at least, must be a side. For if the angles only are given, these might belong to an infinite number of different triangles In solving oblique-angled triangles, four different cases may therefore be presented. There may be given,

1. Two angles and a side;
2. Two sides and an angle opposite one of them;
3. Two sides and the included angle; or,
4. The three sides.

We shall represent the three angles of the proposed triangle by A, B, C, and the sides opposite them, respectively, by a, b, c.

CASE I.

(53.) *Given two angles and a side, to find the third angle and the other two sides.*

To find the third angle, add the given angles together, and subtract their sum from 180°.

The required sides may be found by Theorem I. The proportion will be,

The sine of the angle opposite the given side : the given side :: the sine of the angle opposite the required side : the required side.

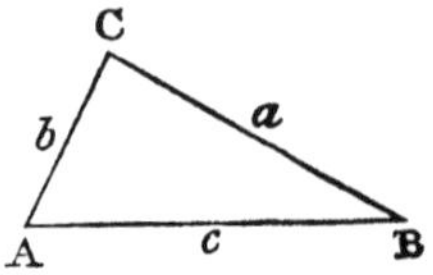

Ex. 1. In the triangle ABC, there are given the angle A, 57° 15′, the angle B, 35° 30′, and the side c, 364, to find the other parts.

The sum of the given angles, subtracted

from 180°, leaves 87° 15′ for the angle C. Then, to find the side a, we say, sin. C : c : : sin. A : a.

By natural numbers,

$$.998848 : 364 :: .841039 : 306.49 = a.$$

This proportion is most easily worked by logarithms, thus:

As the sine of the angle C, 87° 15′, comp.,	0.000500
Is to the side c, 364,	2.561101
So is the sine of the angle A, 57° 15′,	9.924816
To the side a, 306.49,	2.486417.

To find the side b:

sin. C : c : : sin. B : b.

By natural numbers,

$$.998848 : 364 :: .580703 : 211.62 = b.$$

The work by logarithms is as follows:

sin. C, 87° 15′, comp.,	0.000500
: c, 364,	2.561101
: : sin. B, 35° 30′,	9.763954
: b, 211.62,	2.325555.

Ex. 2. In the triangle ABC, there are given the angle A, 49° 25′, the angle C, 63° 48′, and the side c, 275, to find the other parts. *Ans.*, B=66° 47′; a=232.766; b=281.67.

CASE II.

(54.) *Given two sides and an angle opposite one of them, to find the third side and the remaining angles.*

One of the required angles is found by Theorem I. The proportion is,

The side opposite the given angle : *the sine of that angle* : : *the other given side* : *the sine of the opposite angle.*

The third angle is found by subtracting the sum of the other two from 180°; and the third side is found as in Case I.

If the side BC, opposite the given angle A, is shorter than the other given side AC, the solution will be *ambiguous;* that is, two different triangles, ABC, AB′C, may be formed, each of which will satisfy the conditions of the problem.

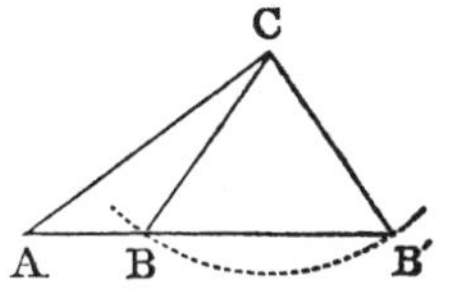

The numerical result is also ambiguous, for the fourth term

of the first proportion is a sine of an angle. But this may be the sine either of the *acute* angle AB′C, or of its supplement, the obtuse angle ABC (Art. 27). In practice, however, there will generally be some circumstance to determine whether the required angle is acute or obtuse. If the given angle is obtuse, there can be no ambiguity in the solution, for then the remaining angles must of course be acute.

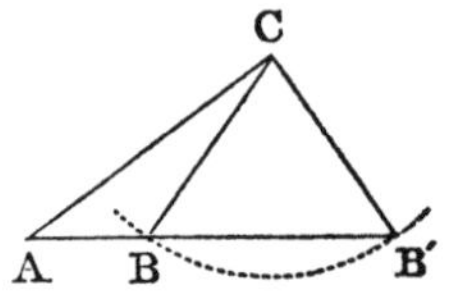

Ex. 1. In a triangle, ABC, there are given AC, 458, BC, 307, and the angle A, 28° 45′, to find the other parts.

To find the angle B:

BC : sin. A : : AC : sin. B.

By natural numbers,

307 : .480989 : : 458 : .717566, sin. B, the arc corresponding to which is 45° 51′ 14″, or 134° 8′ 46″.

This proportion is most easily worked by logarithms, thus·

BC, 307, comp.,	7.512862
: sin. A, 28° 45′,	9.682135
: : AC, 458,	2.660865
: sin. B, 45° 51′ 14″, or 134° 8′ 46″,	9.855862.

The angle ABC is 134° 8′ 46″, and the angle AB′C, 45° 51′ 14″. Hence the angle ACB is 17° 6′ 14″, and the angle ACB′, 105° 23′ 46″.

To find the side AB:

sin. A : CB : : sin. ACB : AB.

By logarithms,

sin. A, 28° 45′, comp.,	0.317865
: CB, 307,	2.487138
: : sin. ACB, 17° 6′ 14″,	9.468502
: AB, 187.72,	2.273505.

To find the side AB′:

sin. A : CB′ : : sin. ACB′ : AB′.

By logarithms,

sin. A, 28° 45′, comp.,	0.317865
: CB′, 307,	2.487138
: : sin. ACB′, 105° 23′ 46″,	9.984128
: AB′, 615.36,	2.789131.

Ex. 2. In a triangle, ABC, there are given AB, 532, BC, 358, and the angle C, 107° 40′, to find the other parts.

Ans. A=39° 52′ 52″; B=32° 27′ 8″; AC=299.6.

In this example there is no ambiguity, because the given angle is obtuse.

CASE III.

(55.) *Given two sides and the included angle, to find the third side and the remaining angles.*

The *sum* of the required angles is found by subtracting the given angle from 180°. The *difference* of the required angles is then found by Theorem II. Half the difference added to half the sum gives the greater angle, and, subtracted, gives the less angle. The third side is then found by Theorem I.

Ex. 1. In the triangle ABC, the angle A is given 53° 8′; the side c, 420, and the side b, 535, to find the remaining parts.

The sum of the angles B+C=180°−53° 8′=126° 52′.

Half their sum is 63° 26′.

Then, by Theorem II.,

535+420 : 535−420 : : tang. 63° 26′ : tang. 13° 32 25″,

which is half the difference of the two required angles.

Hence the angle B is 76° 58′ 25″, and the angle C, 49° 53′ 35″.

To find the side a:

sin. C : c : : sin. A : a=439.32.

Ex. 2. Given the side c, 176, a, 133, and the included angle B, 73°, to find the remaining parts.

Ans., b=187.022, the angle C, 64° 9′ 3″, and A, 42° 50′ 57″.

CASE IV.

(56.) *Given the three sides, to find the angles.*

Let fall a perpendicular upon the longest side from the opposite angle, dividing the given triangle into two right-angled triangles. The two segments of the base may be found by Theorem III. There will then be given the hypothenuse and one side of a right-angled triangle to find the angles.

Ex. 1. In the triangle ABC, the side a is 261, the side b, 345, and c, 395. What are the angles?

Let fall the perpendicular CD upon AB.

Then, by Theorem III.,

$$AB : AC+CB :: AC-CB : AD-DB;$$

or $$395 : 606 :: 84 : 128.87.$$

Half the difference of the segments added to half their sum gives the greater segment, and subtracted gives the less segment.

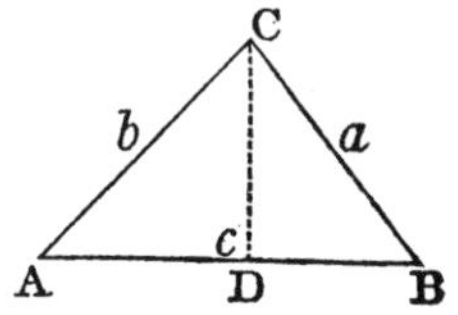

Therefore, AD is 261.935, and BD, 133.065.

Then, in each of the right-angled triangles, ACD, BCD, we have given the hypothenuse and base, to find the angles by Case II. of right-angled triangles. Hence

$$AC : R :: AD : \cos. A=40° 36' 13'';$$

$$BC : R :: BD : \cos. B=59° 20' 52''.$$

Therefore the angle C=80° 2′ 55″.

Ex. 2. If the three sides of a triangle are 150, 140, and 130, what are the angles?

Ans., 67° 22′ 48″, 59° 29′ 23″, and 53° 7′ 49″

Examples for Practice.

1. Given two sides of a triangle, 478 and 567, and the included angle, 47° 30′, to find the remaining parts.

2. Given the angle A, 56° 34′, the opposite side, *a*, 735, and the side *b*, 576, to find the remaining parts.

3. Given the angle A, 65° 40′, the angle B, 74° 20′, and the side *a*, 275, to find the remaining parts.

4. Given the three sides, 742, 657, and 379, to find the angles.

5. Given the angle A, 116° 32′, the opposite side, *a*, 492, and the side *c*, 295, to find the remaining parts.

6. Given the angle C, 56° 18′, the opposite side, *c*, 184, and the side *b*, 219, to find the remaining parts.

This problem admits of two answers.

INSTRUMENTS USED IN DRAWING.

(57.) The following are some of the most important instruments used in drawing.

I. The *dividers* consist of two legs, revolving upon a pivot at one extremity. The joints should be composed of two different metals, of unequal hardness: one part, for example, of steel, and the other of brass or silver, in order that they may move upon each other with greater

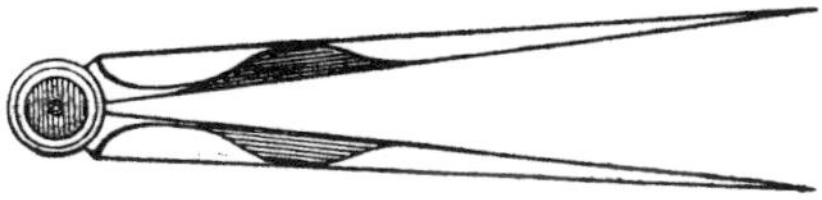

freedom. The points should be of tempered steel, and when the dividers are closed, they should meet with great exactness. The dividers are often furnished with various appendages, which are exceedingly convenient in drawing. Sometimes one of the legs is furnished with an adjusting screw, by which a slow motion may be given to one of the points, in which case they are called *hair compasses.* It is also useful to have a movable leg, which may be removed at pleasure, and other parts fitted to its place; as, for example, a long beam for drawing large circles, a pencil point for drawing circles with a pencil, an ink point for drawing black circles, &c.

(58.) II. The *parallel rule* consists of two flat rules, made of wood or ivory, and connected together by two cross-bars of

equal length, and parallel to each other. This instrument is useful for drawing a line parallel to a given line, through a given point. For this purpose, place the edge of one of the flat rules against the given line, and move the other rule until its edge coincides with the given point. A line drawn along its edge will be parallel to the given line.

(59.) III. The *protractor* is used to lay down or to measure angles. It consists of a semicircle, usually of brass, and is divided into degrees, and sometimes smaller portions, the center of the circle being indicated by a small notch.

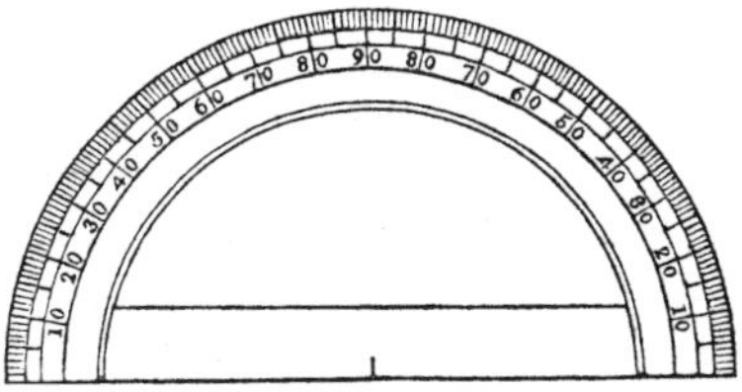

To lay down an angle with the protractor, draw a base line, and apply to it the edge of the protractor, so that its center shall fall at the angular point. Count the degrees contained in the proposed angle on the limb of the circle, and mark the extremity of the arc with a fine dot. Remove the instrument, and through the dot draw a line from the angular point; it will give the angle required. In a similar manner, the inclination of any two lines may be measured with the protractor.

(60.) IV. The *plane scale* is a ruler, frequently two feet in length, containing a line of *equal parts*, *chords*, *sines*, *tangents*, &c. For a scale of equal parts, a line is divided into inches and tenths of an inch, or half inches and twentieths. When smaller fractions are required, they are obtained by means of the *diagonal scale*, which is constructed in the following manner. Describe a square inch, ABCD, and divide

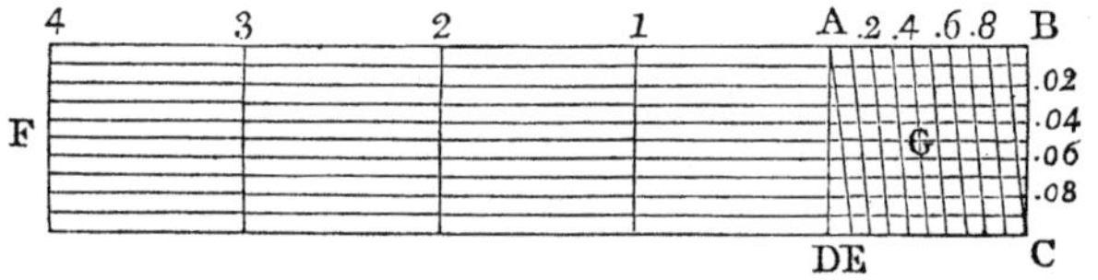

each of its sides into ten equal parts. Draw diagonal lines from the first point of division on the upper line, to the second on the lower; from the second on the upper line, to the third on the lower, and so on. Draw, also, other lines parallel to AB, through the points of division of BC. Then, in the triangle ADE, the base, DE, is one tenth of an inch; and, since the line AD is divided into ten equal parts, and through the points of division lines are drawn parallel to the base, forming nine smaller triangles, the base of the least is one tenth of DE, that is, .01 of an inch; the base of the second is .02 of an inch; the third, .03, and so on. Thus the diagonal scale furnishes us *hundredths* of an inch. To take off from the scale a line of given length, as, for example, 4.45 inches, place one foot of the dividers at F, on the sixth horizontal line, and extend the other foot to G, the fifth diagonal line.

A half inch or less is frequently subdivided in the same manner.

(61.) A *line of chords*, commonly marked CHO., is found on most plane scales, and is useful in setting off angles. To form this line, describe a circle with any convenient radius, and divide the circumference into degrees. Let the length of the chords for every degree of the quadrant be determined and laid off on a scale: this is called a line of chords.

Since the chord of 60° is equal to radius, in order to lay

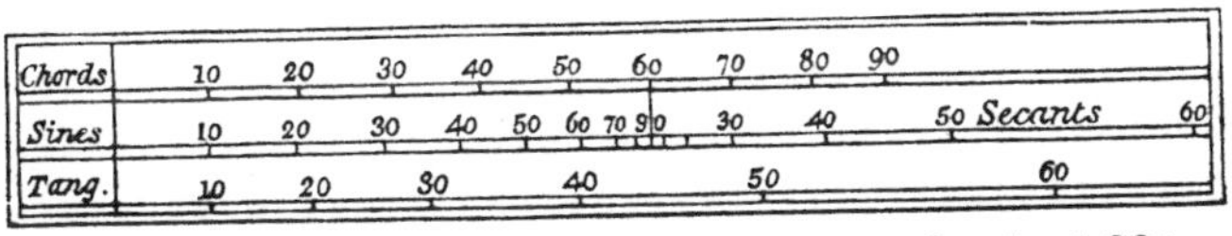

down an angle, we take from the scale the chord of 60°, and with this radius describe an arc of a circle. Then take from the scale the chord of the given angle, and set it off upon the former arc. Through these two points of division draw lines to the center of the circle, and they will contain the required angle.

The line of sines, commonly marked SIN., exhibits the lengths of the sines to every degree of the quadrant, to the same radius as the line of chords. The line of tangents and the line of secants are constructed in the same manner. Since the sine of 90° is equal to radius, and the secant of 0° is the same, the graduation on the line of secants begins where the line of sines ends.

On the back side of the plane scale are often found lines representing the logarithms of numbers, sines, tangents, &c. This is called Gunter's Scale.

(62.) V. The *Sector* is a very convenient instrument in drawing. It consists of two equal arms, movable about a pivot as a center, having several scales drawn on the faces, some single, others double. The single scales are like those upon a common Gunter's scale. The double scales are those which proceed from the center, each being laid twice on the same face of the instrument, viz., once on each leg. The double scales are a scale of lines, marked Lin. or L.; the scale of chords, sines, &c. On each arm of the sector there is a diagonal line, which diverges from the central point like the radius of a circle, and these diagonal lines are divided into equal parts.

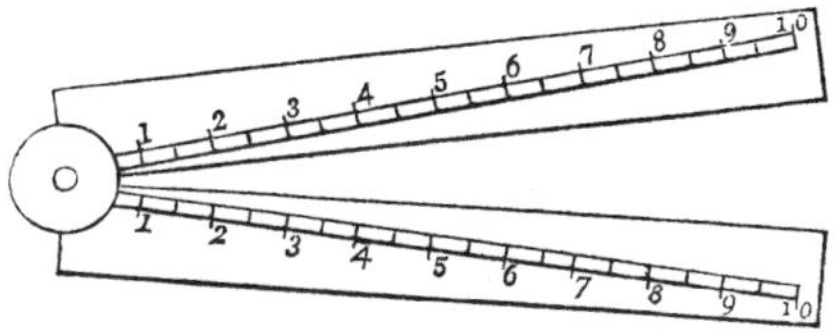

The advantage of the sector is to enable us to draw a line

upon paper to any scale; as, for example, a scale of 6 feet to the inch. For this purpose, take an inch with the dividers from the scale of inches; then, placing one foot of the dividers at 6 on one arm of the sector, open the sector until the other foot reaches to the same number on the other arm. Now, regarding the lines on the sector as the sides of a triangle, of which the line measured from 6 on one arm to 6 on the other arm is the base, it is plain that if any other line be measured across the angle of the sector, the bases of the triangles thus formed will be proportional to their sides. Therefore, a line of 7 feet will be represented by the distance from 7 to 7, and so on for other lines.

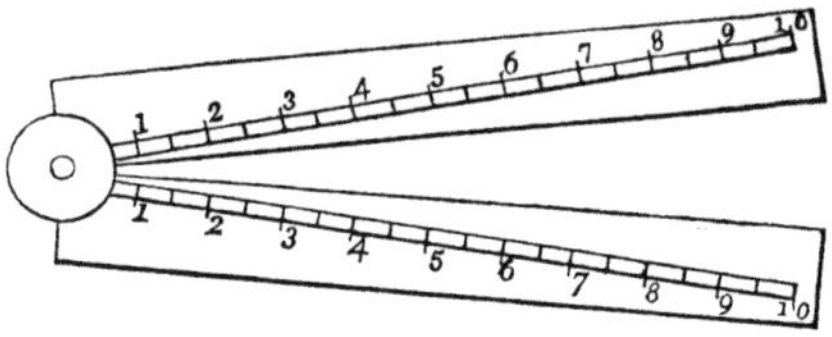

The sector also contains a line of chords, arranged like the line of equal parts already mentioned. Two lines of chords are drawn, one on each arm of the sector, diverging from the central point. This double line of chords is more convenient than the single one upon the plane scale, because it furnishes chords to *any radius*. If it be required to lay down any angle, as, for example, an angle of 25°, describe a circle with any convenient radius. Open the sector so that the distance from 60 to 60, on the line of chords, shall be equal to this radius. Then, preserving the same opening of the sector, place one foot of the dividers upon the division 25 on one scale, and extend the other foot to the same number upon the other scale: this distance will be the chord of 25 degrees, which must be set off upon the circle first described.

The lines of sines, tangents, &c., are arranged in the same manner.

(63.) By means of the instruments now enumerated, all the cases in Plane Trigonometry may be solved mechanically. The sides and angles which are *given* are laid down according to the preceding directions, and the *required* parts are then measured from the same scale. The student will do well to exercise himself upon the following problems:

I. *Given the angles and one side of a triangle*, to find, by construction, the other two sides.

Draw an indefinite straight line, and from the scale of equal parts lay off a portion, AB, equal to the given side. From each extremity lay off an angle equal to one of the adjacent angles, by means of a protractor or a scale of chords. Extend the two lines till they intersect, and measure their lengths upon the same scale of equal parts which was used in laying off the base.

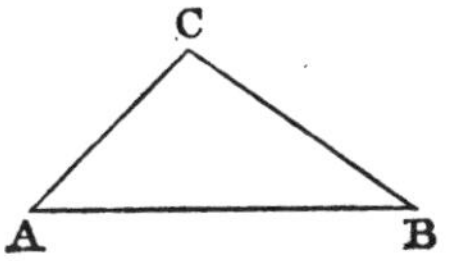

Ex. 1. Given the angle A, 45° 30′, the angle B, 35° 20′, and the side AB, 432 rods, to construct the triangle, and find the lengths of the sides AC and BC.

The triangle ABC may be constructed of any dimensions whatever; all which is essential is that its angles be made equal to the given angles. We may construct the triangle upon a scale of 100 rods to an inch, in which case the side AB will be represented by 4.32 inches; or we may construct it upon a scale of 200 rods to an inch; that is, 100 rods to a half inch, which is very conveniently done from a scale on which a half inch is divided like that described in Art. 60; or we may use any other scale at pleasure. It should, however, be remembered, that the required sides must be measured upon the *same* scale as the given sides.

Ex. 2. Given the angle A, 48°, the angle C, 113°, and the side AC, 795, to construct the triangle.

II. *Given two sides and an angle opposite one of them*, to find the other parts.

Draw the side which is adjacent to the given angle. From one end of it lay off the given angle, and extend a line indefinitely for the required side. From the other extremity of the first side, with the remaining given side for radius, describe an arc cutting the indefinite line. The point of intersection will determine the third angle of the triangle.

Ex. 1. Given the angle A, 74° 45′, the side AC, 432, and the side BC, 475, to construct the triangle, and find the other parts.

Ex. 2. Given the angle A, 105°, the side BC, 498, and the side AC, 375, to construct the triangle.

III. *Given two sides and the included angle*, to find the other parts.

Draw one of the given sides. From one end of it lay off the given angle, and draw the other given side, making the required angle with the first side. Then connect the extremities of the two sides, and there will be formed the triangle required.

Ex. 1. Given the angle A, 37° 25′, the side AC, 675, and the side AB, 417, to construct the triangle, and find the other parts.

Ex. 2. Given the angle A, 75°, the side AC, 543, and the side AB, 721, to construct the triangle.

IV. *Given the three sides*, to find the angles.

Draw one of the sides as a base; and from one extremity of the base, with a radius equal to the second side, describe an arc of a circle. From the other end of the base, with a radius equal to the third side, describe a second arc intersecting the former; the point of intersection will be the third angle of the triangle.

Ex. 1. Given AB, 678, AC, 598, and BC, 435, to find the angles.

Ex. 2. Given the three sides 476, 287, and 354, to find the angles.

Values of the Sines, Cosines, &c., of certain Angles

(64.) We propose now to examine the changes which the sines, cosines, &c., undergo in the different quadrants of a circle. Draw two diameters, AB, DE, perpendicular to each other, and suppose one of them to occupy a horizontal position, the other a vertical. The angle ACD is called the *first* quadrant, the angle DCB the *second* quadrant, the angle BCE the *third* quadrant, and the angle ECA the *fourth* quadrant; that is, the first quadrant is above the horizontal diameter, and on the right of the vertical diameter; the second quadrant is above the horizontal diameter, and on the left of the vertical, and so on.

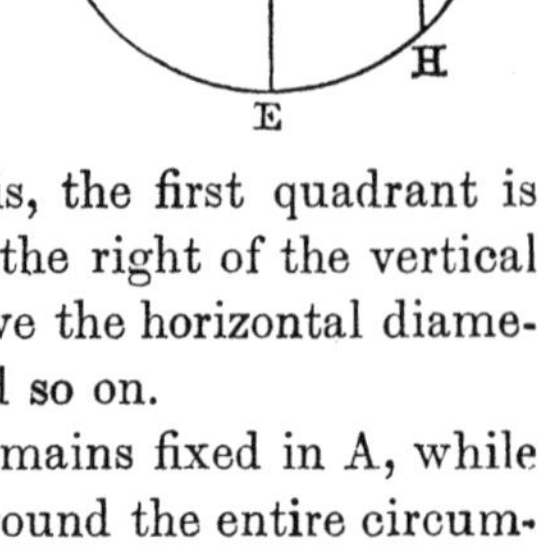

Suppose one extremity of the arc remains fixed in A, while the other extremity, marked F, runs round the entire circumference in the direction ADBE.

When the point F is at A, or when the arc AF is zero, the sine is zero. As the point F advances toward D, the sine increases; and when the arc AF becomes 45°, the triangle CFG being isosceles, we have FG : CF : : 1 : $\sqrt{2}$ (*Geom.*, Prop. 11, Cor. 3, B. IV.); or sin. 45° : R : : 1 : $\sqrt{2}$.

Hence, $$\sin. 45° = \frac{R}{\sqrt{2}} = \tfrac{1}{2}R\sqrt{2}.$$

The sine of 30° is equal to half radius (Art. 22). Also, since sin. A $= \sqrt{R^2 - \cos.^2 A}$, the sine of 60°, which is equal to the cosine of 30°, $= \sqrt{R^2 - \frac{1}{4}R^2} = \sqrt{\frac{3}{4}R^2} = \frac{1}{2}R\sqrt{3}$.

The arc AF continuing to increase, the sine also increases till F arrives at D, at which point the sine is equal to the radius; that is, the sine of 90°=R.

As the point F advances from D toward B, the sines diminish, and become zero at B; that is, the sine of 180°=0.

In the third quadrant, the sine increases again, becomes equal to radius at E, and is reduced to zero at A.

(65.) When the point F is at A, the cosine is equal to radius. As the point F advances toward D, the cosine decreases, and the cosine of 45°=sine 45°$=\frac{1}{2}R\sqrt{2}$. The arc continuing to increase, the cosine diminishes till F arrives at D, at which point the cosine becomes equal to zero. The cosine in the second quadrant increases, and becomes equal to radius at B; in the third quadrant it decreases, and becomes zero at E; in the fourth quadrant it increases again, and becomes equal to radius at A.

(66.) The tangent begins with zero at A, increases with the arc, and at 45° becomes equal to radius. As the point F approaches D, the tangent increases very rapidly; and when the difference between the arc and 90° is less than any assignable quantity, the tangent is greater than any assignable quantity. Hence the tangent of 90° is said to be infinite.

In the second quadrant the tangent is at first infinitely great, and rapidly diminishes till at B it is reduced to zero. In the third quadrant it increases again, becomes infinite at E, and is reduced to zero at A.

The cotangent is equal to zero at D and E, and is infinite at A and B.

(67.) The secant begins with radius at A, increases through

the first quadrant, and becomes infinite at D; diminishes in the second quadrant, till at B it is equal to the radius; increases again in the third quadrant, and becomes infinite at E; decreases in the fourth quadrant, and becomes equal to the radius at A.

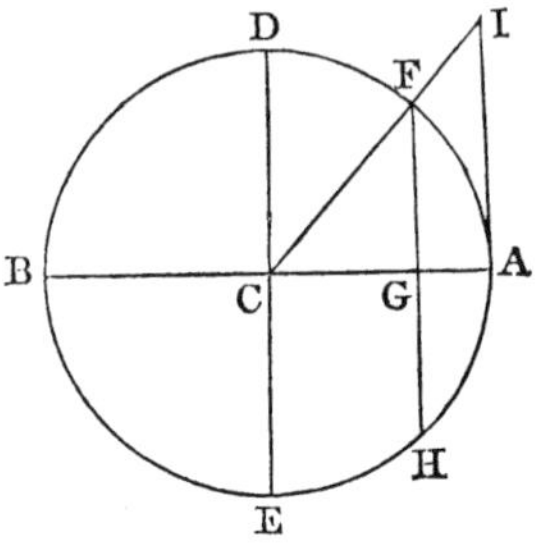

The cosecant is equal to radius at D and E, and is infinite at A and B.

(68.) Let us now consider the algebraic signs by which these lines are to be distinguished. In the first and second quadrants, the sines fall *above* the diameter AB, while in the third and fourth quadrants they fall *below*. This opposition of directions ought to be distinguished by the algebraic signs; and if one of these directions is regarded as positive, the other ought to be considered as negative. It is generally agreed to consider those sines which fall *above* the horizontal diameter as positive; consequently, those which fall *below* must be regarded as negative. That is, the sines are positive in the first and second quadrants, and negative in the third and fourth.

In the first quadrant the cosine falls on the *right* of DE, but in the second quadrant it falls on the *left*. These two lines should obviously have opposite signs, and it is generally agreed to consider those which fall to the right of the vertical diameter as positive; consequently, those which fall to the left must be considered negative. That is, the cosines are positive in the first and fourth quadrants, and negative in the second and third.

(69.) The signs of the tangents are derived from those of the sines and cosines. For tang. $=\frac{\text{R. sin.}}{\text{cos.}}$ (Art. 28). Hence, when the sine and cosine have like algebraic signs, the tangent will be positive; when unlike, negative. That is, the tangent is positive in the first and third quadrants, and negative in the second and fourth.

Also, cotangent $=\frac{\text{R}^2}{\text{tang.}}$ (Art. 28); hence the tangent and cotangent have always the same sign.

We have seen that sec. $=\frac{R^2}{\cos.}$; hence the secant must have the same sign as the cosine.

Also, cosec. $=\frac{R^2}{\sin.}$; hence the cosecant must have the same sign as the sine.

(70.) The preceding results are exhibited in the following tables, which should be made perfectly familiar:

	First quad.	*Second* quad.	*Third* quad.	*Fourth* quad.
Sine and cosecant,	+	+	−	−
Cosine and secant,	+	−	−	+
Tangent and cotangent,	+	−	+	−

	0°	90°	180°	270°	360°
Sine,	0	+R	0	−R	0
Cosine,	+R	0	−R	0	+R
Tangent,	0	∞	0	∞	0
Cotangent,	∞	0	∞	0	∞
Secant,	+R	∞	−R	∞	+R
Cosecant,	∞	+R	∞	−R	∞

(71.) In Astronomy we frequently have occasion to consider arcs greater than 360°. But if an entire circumference, or any number of circumferences, be added to any arc, it will terminate in the same point as before. Hence, if C represent an entire circumference, or 360°, and A any arc whatever, we shall have

$$\sin. A=\sin. (C+A)=\sin. (2C+A)=\sin. (3C+A)=, \&c.$$

The same is true of the cosine, tangent, &c.

We generally consider those arcs as positive which are estimated from A in the direction ADBE. If, then, an arc were estimated in the direction AEBD, it should be considered as negative; that is, if the arc AF be considered positive, AH must be considered negative. But the latter belongs to the fourth quadrant; hence its sine is negative. Therefore, sin. $(-A)=-\sin. A$.

The cosine CG is the same for both the arcs AF and AH.

Hence, $\cos. (-A)=\cos. A.$

Also, $\text{tang.} (-A)=-\text{tang.} A.$

And $\cot. (-A)=-\cot. A.$

TRIGONOMETRICAL FORMULÆ.

(72.) *Expressions for the sine and cosine of the sum and difference of two arcs.*

Let AB and BD represent any two given arcs; take BE equal to BD: it is required to find an expression for the sine of AD, the sum, and of AE, the difference of these arcs.

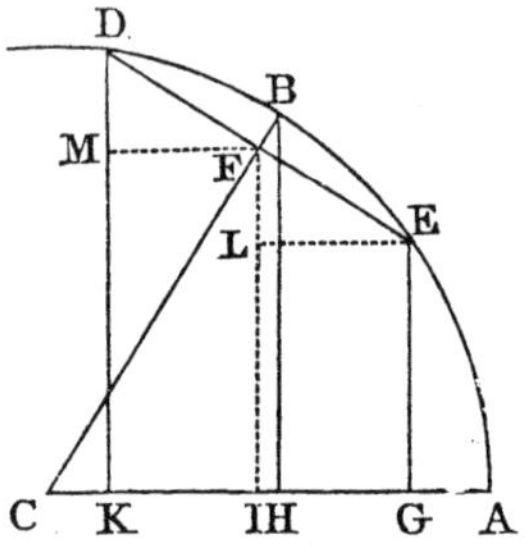

Put AB$=a$, and BD$=b$; then AD$=a+b$, and AE$=a-b$. Draw the chord DE, and the radius CB, which may be represented by R. Since DB is by construction equal to BE, DF is equal to FE, and therefore DE is perpendicular to CB. Let fall the perpendiculars EG, BH, FI, and DK upon AC, and draw EL, FM parallel to AC.

Because the triangles BCH, FCI are similar, we have

$$\text{CB : CF :: BH : FI; or R : cos. } b \text{ :: sin. } a \text{ : FI.}$$

Therefore, $$\text{FI}=\frac{\text{sin. } a \text{ cos. } b}{\text{R}}.$$

Also, $\text{CB : CF :: CH : CI; or R : cos. } b \text{ :: cos. } a \text{ : CI.}$

Therefore, $$\text{CI}=\frac{\text{cos. } a \text{ cos. } b}{\text{R}}.$$

The triangles DFM, CBH, having their sides perpendicular each to each, are similar, and give the proportions

$$\text{CB : DF :: CH : DM; or R : sin. } b \text{ :: cos. } a \text{ : DM.}$$

Hence $$\text{DM}=\frac{\text{cos. } a \text{ sin. } b}{\text{R}}.$$

Also, $\text{CB : DF :: BH : FM; or R : sin. } b \text{ :: sin. } a \text{ : FM.}$

Hence $$\text{FM}=\frac{\text{sin. } a \text{ sin. } b}{\text{R}}.$$

But $\text{FI}+\text{DM}=\text{DK}=\text{sin. }(a+b)$;

and $\text{CI}-\text{FM}=\text{CK}=\text{cos. }(a+b)$.

Also, $\text{FI}-\text{FL}=\text{EG}=\text{sin. }(a-b)$;

and $\text{CI}+\text{EL}=\text{CG}=\text{cos. }(a-b)$.

Hence, $$\text{sin. }(a+b)=\frac{\text{sin. } a \text{ cos. } b+\text{cos. } a \text{ sin. } b}{\text{R}} \quad (1)$$

$$\text{cos. }(a+b)=\frac{\text{cos. } a \text{ cos. } b-\text{sin. } a \text{ sin. } b}{\text{R}} \quad (2)$$

$$\sin.(a-b)=\frac{\sin. a \cos. b-\cos. a \sin. b}{R} \quad (3)$$

$$\cos.(a-b)=\frac{\cos. a \cos. b+\sin. a \sin. b}{R} \quad (4)$$

(73.) *Expressions for the sine and cosine of a double arc.*

If, in the formulas of the preceding article, we make $b=a$ the first and second will become

$$\sin. 2a=\frac{2 \sin. a \cos. a}{R},$$

$$\cos. 2a=\frac{\cos.^2 a-\sin.^2 a}{R}.$$

Making radius equal to unity, and substituting the values of sin. a, cos. a. &c., from Art. 28, we obtain

$$\sin. 2a=\frac{2 \text{ tang. } a}{1+\text{tang.}^2 a},$$

$$\cos. 2a=\frac{1-\text{tang.}^2 a}{1+\text{tang.}^2 a}.$$

(74.) *Expressions for the sine and cosine of half a given arc.*

If we put $\frac{1}{2}a$ for a in the preceding equations, we obtain

$$\sin. a=\frac{2 \sin. \frac{1}{2}a \cos. \frac{1}{2}a}{R},$$

$$\cos. a=\frac{\cos.^2 \frac{1}{2}a-\sin.^2 \frac{1}{2}a}{R}.$$

We may also find the sine and cosine of $\frac{1}{2}a$ in terms of a.

Since the sum of the squares of the sine and cosine is equal to the square of radius, we have

$$\cos.^2 \tfrac{1}{2}a+\sin.^2 \tfrac{1}{2}a=R^2.$$

And, from the preceding equation,

$$\cos.^2 \tfrac{1}{2}a-\sin.^2 \tfrac{1}{2}a=R \cos. a.$$

If we subtract one of these from the other, we have

$$2 \sin.^2 \tfrac{1}{2}a=R^2-R \cos. a.$$

And, adding the same equations,

$$2 \cos.^2 \tfrac{1}{2}a=R^2+R \cos. a.$$

Hence, $\sin. \frac{1}{2}a=\sqrt{\frac{1}{2}R^2-\frac{1}{2}R \cos. a}$;

$$\cos. \tfrac{1}{2}a=\sqrt{\tfrac{1}{2}R^2+\tfrac{1}{2}R \cos. a}.$$

(75.) *Expressions for the products of sines and cosines.*

By adding and subtracting the formulas of Art. 72, we obtain

$$\sin.(a+b)+\sin.(a-b)=\frac{2}{R}\sin. a\cos. b.$$

$$\sin.(a+b)-\sin.(a-b)=\frac{2}{R}\cos. a\sin. b;$$

$$\cos.(a+b)+\cos.(a-b)=\frac{2}{R}\cos. a\cos. b;$$

$$\cos.(a-b)-\cos.(a+b)=\frac{2}{R}\sin. a\sin. b.$$

If, in these formulas, we make $a+b=A$, and $a-b=B$; that is, $a=\frac{1}{2}(A+B)$, and $b=\frac{1}{2}(A-B)$, we shall have

$$\sin. A+\sin. B=\frac{2}{R}\sin.\tfrac{1}{2}(A+B)\cos.\tfrac{1}{2}(A-B) \quad (1)$$

$$\sin. A-\sin. B=\frac{2}{R}\sin.\tfrac{1}{2}(A-B)\cos.\tfrac{1}{2}(A+B) \quad (2)$$

$$\cos. A+\cos. B=\frac{2}{R}\cos.\tfrac{1}{2}(A+B)\cos.\tfrac{1}{2}(A-B) \quad (3)$$

$$\cos. B-\cos. A=\frac{2}{R}\sin.\tfrac{1}{2}(A+B)\sin.\tfrac{1}{2}(A-B) \quad (4)$$

(76.) Dividing formula (1) by (2), and considering that $\frac{\sin. a}{\cos. a}=\frac{\text{tang. } a}{R}$ (Art. 28), we have

$$\frac{\sin. A+\sin. B}{\sin. A-\sin. B}=\frac{\sin.\frac{1}{2}(A+B)\cos.\frac{1}{2}(A-B)}{\sin.\frac{1}{2}(A-B)\cos.\frac{1}{2}(A+B)}=\frac{\text{tang.}\frac{1}{2}(A+B)}{\text{tang.}\frac{1}{2}(A-B)};$$

that is,

The sum of the sines of two arcs is to their difference, as the tangent of half the sum of those arcs is to the tangent of half their difference.

Dividing formula (3) by (4), and considering that $\frac{\cos.}{\sin.}=\frac{\cot.}{R}$ $=\frac{R}{\text{tang.}}$ (Art. 28), we have

$$\frac{\cos. A+\cos. B}{\cos. B-\cos. A}=\frac{\cos.\frac{1}{2}(A+B)\cos.\frac{1}{2}(A-B)}{\sin.\frac{1}{2}(A+B)\sin.\frac{1}{2}(A-B)}=\frac{\cot.\frac{1}{2}(A+B)}{\text{tang.}\frac{1}{2}(A-B)};$$

that is,

The sum of the cosines of two arcs is to their difference, as the cotangent of half the sum of those arcs is to the tangent of half their difference.

From the first formula of Art. 74, by substituting A+B for *a*, we have

$$\sin. (A+B)=\frac{2 \sin. \frac{1}{2}(A+B)\times\cos. \frac{1}{2}(A+B)}{R}.$$

Dividing formula (1), Art. 75, by this, we obtain

$$\frac{\sin. A+\sin. B}{\sin. (A+B)}=\frac{\sin. \frac{1}{2}(A+B) \cos. \frac{1}{2}(A-B)}{\sin. \frac{1}{2}(A+B) \cos. \frac{1}{2}(A+B)}=\frac{\cos. \frac{1}{2}(A-B)}{\cos. \frac{1}{2}(A+B)};$$

that is,

The sum of the sines of two arcs is to the sine of their sum, as the cosine of half the difference of those arcs is to the cosine of half their sum.

If we divide equation (1), Art. 72, by equation (3), we shall have

$$\frac{\sin. (a+b)}{\sin. (a-b)}=\frac{\sin. a \cos. b+\cos. a \sin. b}{\sin. a \cos. b-\cos. a \sin. b}.$$

By dividing both numerator and denominator of the second member by cos. a cos. b, and substituting $\frac{\text{tang.}}{R}$ for $\frac{\sin.}{\cos.}$, we obtain

$$\frac{\sin. (a+b)}{\sin. (a-b)}=\frac{\text{tang. } a+\text{tang. } b}{\text{tang. } a-\text{tang. } b};$$ that is,

The sine of the sum of two arcs is to the sine of their difference, as the sum of the tangents of those arcs is to the difference of the tangents.

From equation (3), Art. 72, by dividing each member by cos a cos. b, we obtain

$$\frac{\sin. (a-b)}{\cos. a \cos. b}=\frac{\sin. a \cos. b-\cos. a \sin. b}{R \cos. a \cos. b}=\frac{\text{tang. } a-\text{tang. } b}{R^2};$$

that is,

The sine of the difference of two arcs is to the product of their cosines, as the difference of their tangents is to the square of radius.

(77.) *Expressions for the tangents of arcs.*

If we take the expression $\text{tang. }(a+b)=\frac{R \sin. (a+b)}{\cos. (a+b)}$ (Art. 28), and substitute for sin. $(a+b)$ and cos. $(a+b)$ their values given in Art. 72, we shall find

$$\text{tang. } (a+b)=\frac{R (\sin. a \cos. b+\cos. a \sin. b)}{\cos. a \cos. b-\sin. a \sin. b}.$$

But sin $a=\frac{\cos. a \text{ tang. } a}{R}$, and sin. $b=\frac{\cos. b \text{ tang. } b}{R}$ (Art. 28).

If we substitute these values in the preceding equation, and divide all the terms by cos. a cos. b, we shall have

$$\text{tang. }(a+b)=\frac{R^2(\text{tang. } a+\text{tang. } b)}{R^2-\text{tang. } a \text{ tang. } b}.$$

In like manner we shall find

$$\text{tang. }(a-b)=\frac{R^2(\text{tang. } a-\text{tang. } b)}{R^2+\text{tang. } a \text{ tang. } b}.$$

Suppose $b=a$, then

$$\text{tang. } 2a=\frac{2R^2 \text{ tang. } a}{R^2-\text{tang.}^2 a}.$$

Suppose $b=2a$, then

$$\text{tang. } 3a=\frac{R^2(\text{tang. } a+\text{tang. } 2a)}{R^2-\text{tang. } a \text{ tang. } 2a}.$$

In the same manner we find

$$\text{cot. }(a+b)=\frac{\text{cot. } a \text{ cot. } b-R^2}{\text{cot. } b+\text{cot. } a},$$

$$\text{cot. }(a-b)=\frac{\text{cot. } a \text{ cot. } b+R^2}{\text{cot. } b-\text{cot. } a}.$$

(78.) When the three sides of a triangle are given, the angles may be found by the formula

$$\sin. \tfrac{1}{2}A=R\sqrt{\frac{(S-b)(S-c)}{bc}},$$

where S represents half the sum of the sides a, b, and c.

Demonstration.

Let ABC be any triangle; then (*Geom.*, Prop. 12, B. IV.),

$$BC^2=AB^2+AC^2-2AB\times AD.$$

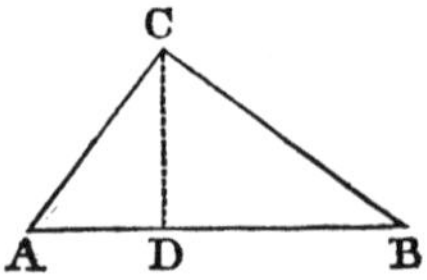

Hence, $AD=\frac{AB^2+AC^2-BC^2}{2AB}$.

But in the right-angled triangle ACD, we have

$$R : AC :: \cos. A : AD.$$

Hence, $$\cos. A=\frac{R\times AD}{AC};$$

or, by substituting the value of AD,

$$\cos. A=R\times\frac{AB^2+AC^2-BC^2}{2AB\times AC}.$$

Let a, b, c represent the sides opposite the angles A, B, C;

then,
$$\cos. A=R\times\frac{b^2+c^2-a^2}{2bc}.$$

By Art. 74, we have $2\sin.^2\tfrac{1}{2}A=R^2-R\cos. A$.

Substituting for cos. A its value given above, we obtain

$$2\sin.^2\tfrac{1}{2}A=R^2-R^2\times\frac{b^2+c^2-a^2}{2bc}=R^2\times\frac{2bc+a^2-b^2-c^2}{2bc}$$
$$=\frac{R^2\times(a+b-c)(a+c-b)}{2bc}.$$

Put $S=\tfrac{1}{2}(a+b+c)$, and we obtain, after reduction,

$$\sin.\tfrac{1}{2}A=R\sqrt{\frac{(S-b)(S-c)}{bc}}.$$

In the same manner we find

$$\sin.\tfrac{1}{2}B=R\sqrt{\frac{(S-a)(S-c)}{ac}}.$$

$$\sin.\tfrac{1}{2}C=R\sqrt{\frac{(S-a)(S-b)}{ab}}.$$

Ex. 1. What are the angles of a plane triangle whose sides are 432, 543, and 654?

Here $S=814.5$; $S-b=382.5$; $S-c=271.5$.

log. 382.5		2.582631
log. 271.5		2.433770
log. b, 432	comp.	7.364516
log. c, 543	comp.	7.265200
		2) 19.646117
sin. $\tfrac{1}{2}$A, 41° 42′ 36½″.		9.823058.
Angle A=83° 25′ 13″.		

In a similar manner we find the angle B=41° 0′ 39″, and the angle C=55° 34′ 8″.

Ex. 2. What are the angles of a plane triangle whose sides are 245, 219, and 91?

(79.) *On the computation of a table of sines, cosines, &c.*

In computing a table of sines and cosines, we begin with finding the sine and cosine of *one minute*, and thence deduce the sines and cosines of larger arcs. The sine of so small an angle as one minute is nearly equal to the corresponding arc. The radius being taken as unity, the semicircumference is known to be 3.14159. This being divided successively by 180 and 60, gives .0002908882 for the arc of one minute, which may be regarded as the sine of one minute.

$$\text{The cosine of } 1' = \sqrt{1-\sin.^2} = 0.9999999577.$$

The sines of very small angles are nearly proportional to the angles themselves. We might then obtain several other sines by direct proportion. This method will give the sines correct to five decimal places, as far as two degrees. By the following method they may be obtained with greater accuracy for the entire quadrant.

By Art. 75, we have, by transposition,

$$\sin.(a+b)=2\sin.a\cos.b-\sin.(a-b),$$
$$\cos.(a+b)=2\cos.a\cos.b-\cos.(a-b).$$

If we make $a=b$, $2b$, $3b$, &c., successively, we shall have

$$\sin.2b=2\sin.b\cos.b;$$
$$\sin.3b=2\sin.2b\cos.b-\sin.b,$$
$$\sin.4b=2\sin.3b\cos.b-\sin.2b,$$
&c., &c.

$$\cos.2b=2\cos.b\cos.b-1;$$
$$\cos.3b=2\cos.2b\cos.b-\cos.b;$$
$$\cos.4b=2\cos.3b\cos.b-\cos.2b,$$
&c., &c.

Whence, making $b=1'$, we have

$$\sin.2'=2\sin.1'\cos.1' =.000582;$$
$$\sin.3'=2\sin.2'\cos.1'-\sin.1'=.000873;$$
$$\sin.4'=2\sin.3'\cos.1'-\sin.2'=.001164,$$
&c., &c.

$$\cos.2'=2\cos.1'\cos.1'-1=0.999999;$$
$$\cos.3'=2\cos.2'\cos.1'-\cos.1'=0.999999;$$
$$\cos.4'=2\cos.3'\cos.1'-\cos.2'=0.999999,$$
&c., &c.

The tangents, cotangents, secants, and cosecants are easily derived from the sines and cosines. Thus,

$$\text{tang.}1'=\frac{\sin.1'}{\cos.1'};\qquad \cot.1'=\frac{\cos.1'}{\sin.1'};$$

$$\sec.1'=\frac{1}{\cos.1'};\qquad \text{cosec.}1'=\frac{1}{\sin.1'};$$

&c., &c.

BOOK III.

MENSURATION OF SURFACES.

(80.) THE *area* of a figure is the space contained within the line or lines by which it is bounded. This area is determined by finding how many times the figure contains some other surface, which is assumed as the *unit of measure.* This unit is commonly a *square;* such as a square inch, a square foot, a square rod, &c.

The *superficial* unit has generally the same name as the *linear* unit, which forms the side of the square. Thus,

the side of a square inch is a linear inch;
" " of a square foot is a linear foot;
" " of a square yard is a linear yard, &c.

There are some superficial units which have no corresponding linear units of the same name, as, for example, an acre.

The following table contains the square measures in common use:

Table of Square Measures.

Sq. Inches.	*Sq. Feet.*	*Sq. Yards.*	*Sq. Rods.*	*S. Ch's.*	*Acres.*	*M.*
144=	1					
1296=	9 =	1				
39204=	272¼=	30¼=	1			
627264=	4356 =	484 =	16=	1		
6272640=	43560 =	4840 =	160=	10=	1	
4014489600=	27878400 =	3097600 =	102400=	6400=	640=	1

PROBLEM I.

(81.) *To find the area of a parallelogram.*

RULE I.

Multiply the base by the altitude.

For the demonstration of this rule, see Geometry, Prop. 5, B. IV.

Ex. 1. What is the area of a parallelogram whose base is 17.5 rods, and the altitude 13 rods?

Ans., 227.5 square rods.

Ex. 2. What is the area of a square whose side is 315.7 feet? *Ans.*, 99666.49 square feet.

Ex. 3. What is the area of a rectangular board whose length is 15.25 feet, and breadth 15 inches?

Ans., 19.0625 square feet.

Ex. 4. How many square yards are there in the four sides of a room which is 18 feet long, 15 feet broad, and 9 feet high?

Ans., 66 square yards.

(82.) If the sides and angles of a parallelogram are given, the perpendicular height may be found by Trigonometry. For DE is one side of a right-angled triangle, of which AD is the hypothenuse. Hence,

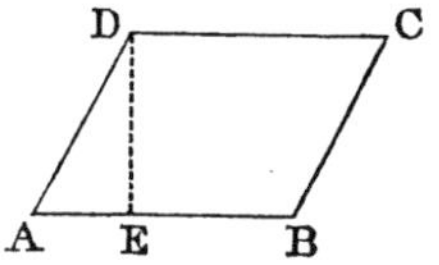

$$R : AD :: \sin. A : DE;$$

from which $$DE=\frac{AD\times \sin. A}{R}.$$

Therefore, *the area*$=AB\times DE=\dfrac{AB\times AD\times \sin. A}{R}.$

Hence we derive

RULE II.

Multiply together two adjacent sides, and the sine of the included angle.

Ex. 1. What is the area of a parallelogram having an angle of 58°, and the including sides 36 and 25.5 feet?

Ans. The area$=36\times 25.5\times .84805$ (natural sine of 58°)$=$ 778.508 square feet.

The computation will generally be most conveniently performed by logarithms.

Ex. 2. What is the area of a rhombus, each of whose sides is 21 feet 3 inches, and each of the acute angles 53° 20′?

Ans., 362.209 feet.

Ex. 3. How many acres are contained in a parallelogram one of whose angles is 30°, and the including sides are 25.35 and 10.4 chains? *Ans.*, 13 acres, 29.12 rods

PROBLEM II.

(83.) *To find the area of a triangle.*

RULE I.

Multiply the base by half the altitude.

For demonstration, see Geometry, Prop. 6, B. IV.

Ex. 1. How many square yards are contained in a triangle whose base is 49 feet, and altitude $25\frac{1}{4}$ feet?

Ans., 68.736.

Ex. 2. What is the area of a triangle whose base is 45 feet, and altitude 27.5 feet? *Ans.*, 618.75 square feet.

(84.) When two sides and the included angle are given, we may use

RULE II.

Multiply half the product of two sides by the sine of the included angle.

The reason of this rule is obvious, from Art. 82, since a triangle is half of a parallelogram, having the same base and altitude.

Ex. 1. What is the area of a triangle of which two sides are 45 and 32 feet, and the included angle 46° 30′?

Ans. The area$=45\times16\times.725374$ (natural sine of 46° 30′)$=$ 522.269 feet.

Ex. 2. What is the area of a triangle of which two sides are 127 and 96 feet, and the included angle 67° 15′?

Ans.

(85.) When the three sides are known, we may use

RULE III.

From half the sum of the three sides subtract each side severally; multiply together the half sum and the three remainders, and extract the square root of the product.

Demonstration.

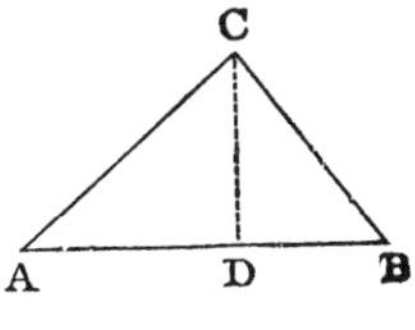

Let a, b, c denote the sides of the triangle ABC; then, by Geometry, Prop. 12, B. IV., we have $BC^2=AB^2+AC^2-2AB\times AD$, or $a^2=b^2+c^2-2c\times AD$; whence,

$$AD=\frac{b^2+c^2-a^2}{2c}.$$

But $$CD^2=AC^2-AD^2;$$

hence $$CD^2=b^2-\frac{(b^2+c^2-a^2)^2}{4c^2}=\frac{4b^2c^2-(b^2+c^2-a^2)^2}{4c^2},$$

or $$CD=\frac{\sqrt{4b^2c^2-(b^2+c^2-a^2)^2}}{2c}.$$

But *the area* $=\frac{AB\times CD}{2}=\frac{1}{4}\sqrt{4b^2c^2-(b^2+c^2-a^2)^2}$.

The quantity under the radical sign being the difference of two squares, may be resolved into the factors $2bc+(b^2+c^2-a^2)$ and $2bc-(b^2+c^2-a^2)$; and these, in the same manner, may be resolved into $(b+c+a)\times(b+c-a)$,
and $(a+b-c)\times(a-b+c)$.

Hence, if we put S equal to $\frac{a+b+c}{2}$, we shall have

$$\text{the } area=\sqrt{S(S-a)(S-b)(S-c)}.$$

Ex. 1. What is the area of a triangle whose sides are 125, 173, and 216 feet?

Here $S=257$, $S-b=84$,
$S-a=132$, $S-c=41$.

Hence the *area* $=\sqrt{257\times132\times84\times41}=10809$ square feet.

Ex. 2. How many acres are contained in a triangle whose sides are 49, 50.25, and 25.69 chains?

Ans., 61 acres, 1 rood, 39.68 perches.

Ex. 3. What is the area of a triangle whose sides are 234, 289, and 345 feet?

Ans.

(86.) In an equilateral triangle, one of whose sides is a, the expression for the area becomes

$$\sqrt{\tfrac{3}{2}a\times\tfrac{1}{2}a\times\tfrac{1}{2}a\times\tfrac{1}{2}a}$$
$$=\frac{a^2\sqrt{3}}{4};$$

that is, the area of an equilateral triangle is equal to on fourth the square of one of its sides multiplied by the square root of 3.

Ex. What is the area of a triangle whose sides are each 37 feet? *Ans.*, 592.79 feet.

PROBLEM III.

(87.) *To find the area of a trapezoid.*

RULE.

Multiply half the sum of the parallel sides into their perpendicular distance.

For demonstration, see Geometry, Prop. 7, B. IV.

Ex. 1. What is the area of a trapezoid whose parallel sides are 156 and 124, and the perpendicular distance between them 57 feet?

Ans., 7980 feet.

Ex. 2. How many square yards in a trapezoid whose parallel sides are 678 and 987 feet, and altitude 524 feet?

Ans.

PROBLEM IV.

(88.) *To find the area of an irregular polygon.*

RULE.

Draw diagonals dividing the polygon into triangles, and find the sum of the areas of these triangles.

Ex. 1. What is the area of a quadrilateral, one of whose diagonals is 126 feet, and the two perpendiculars let fall upon it from the opposite angles are 74 and 28 feet?

Ans., 6426 feet.

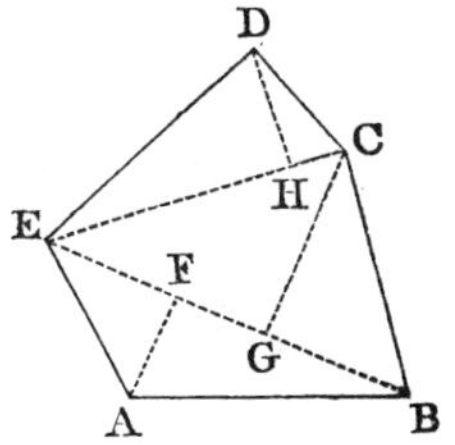

Ex. 2. In the polygon ABCDE, there are given EC=205, EB=242, AF=65, CG=114, and DH=110, to find the area.

Ans.

(89.) If the diagonals of a quadrilateral are given, the area may be found by the following

RULE.

Multiply half the product of the diagonals by the sine of the angle at their intersection.

Demonstration.

The sines of the four angles at E are all equal to each other since the adjacent angles AED, DEC are the supplements of each other (Art. 27). But, according to the Rule, Art. 84, the area of

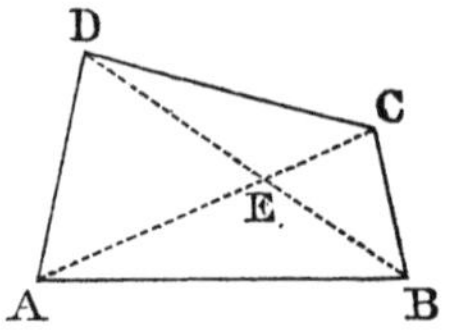

the triangle ABE$=\frac{1}{2}$AE$\times$BE$\times$sine E ;
" " AED$=\frac{1}{2}$AE$\times$DE$\times$sine E ;
" " BEC$=\frac{1}{2}$BE$\times$EC$\times$sine E ;
" " DEC$=\frac{1}{2}$DE$\times$EC$\times$sine E.

Therefore,

the area of ABCD$=\frac{1}{2}$(AE+EC)$\times$(BE+ED)$\times$sine E
$=\frac{1}{2}$AC$\times$BD$\times$sine E.

Ex. 1. If the diagonals of a quadrilateral are 34 and 56 rods, and if they intersect at an angle of 67°, what is the area?

Ans., 876.32.

Ex. 2. If the diagonals of a quadrilateral are 75 and 49, and the angle of intersection is 42°, what is the area?

Ans.

PROBLEM V.

(90.) *To find the area of a regular polygon.*

RULE I.

Multiply half the perimeter by the perpendicular let fall from the center on one of the sides.

For demonstration, see Geometry, Prop. 7, B. VI.

Ex. 1. What is the area of a regular pentagon whose side is 25, and the perpendicular from the center 17.205 feet?

Ans., 1075.31 feet.

Ex. 2. What is the area of a regular octagon whose side is 53, and the perpendicular 63.977?

Ans.

(91.) When the perpendicular is not given, it may be computed from the perimeter and number of sides. If we divide 360 degrees by the number of sides of the polygon, the quotient will be the angle ACB at the center, subtended by one of the sides. The perpendicular CD bisects the side AB, and the angle ACB. Then, in the triangle ACD, we have (Art. 42),

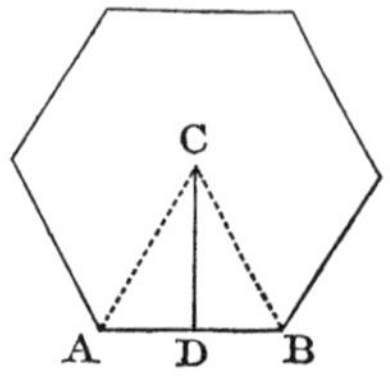

R : AD : cot. ACD : CD ; that is,

Radius is to half of one of the sides of the polygon, as the cotangent of the opposite angle is to the perpendicular from the center.

Ex. 3. Find the area of a regular hexagon whose side is 32 inches.

The angle ACD is $\frac{1}{12}$ of $360°=30°$. Then

$$R : 16 :: \cot. 30° : 27.7128 = CD, \text{ the perpendicular;}$$
$$\text{and the area} = 27.7128 \times 16 \times 6 = 2660.4288.$$

Ex. 4. Find the area of a regular decagon whose side is 46 feet. *Ans.*, 16280.946.

(92.) In this manner was computed the following table of the areas of regular polygons, in which the side of each polygon is supposed to be a unit.

TABLE OF REGULAR POLYGONS.

Names.	*Sides.*	*Areas.*
Triangle,	3	0.4330127.
Square,	4	1.0000000.
Pentagon,	5	1.7204774.
Hexagon,	6	2.5980762.
Heptagon,	7	3.6339124.
Octagon,	8	4.8284271.
Nonagon,	9	6.1818242.
Decagon,	10	7.6942088.
Undecagon,	11	9.3656399.
Dodecagon,	12	11.1961524.

By the aid of this table may be computed the area of any other regular polygon having not more than twelve sides. For, since the areas of similar polygons are as the *squares* of their homologous sides, we derive

RULE II.

Multiply the square of one of the sides of the polygon by the area of a similar polygon whose side is unity.

Ex. 5. What is the area of a regular nonagon whose side is 63? *Ans.*, 24535.66.

Ex. 6. What is the area of a regular dodecagon whose side is 54 feet? *Ans.*, 32647.98 feet.

PROBLEM VI.

(93.) *To find the circumference of a circle from its diameter.*

RULE.

Multiply the diameter by 3.14159.

For the demonstration of this rule, see Geometry, Prop. 13, Cor. 2, B. VI.

When the diameter of the circle is small, and no great accuracy is required, it may be sufficient to employ the value of π to only 4 or 5 decimal places. But if the diameter is large, and accuracy is required, it will be necessary to employ a corresponding number of decimal places of π. The value of π to ten decimal places is 3.14159,26536,

and *its logarithm is* 0.497150.

Ex. 1. What is the circumference of a circle whose diameter is 125 feet?

Ans., 392.7 feet.

Ex. 2. If the diameter of the earth is 7912 miles, what is its circumference?

Ans., 24856.28 miles.

Ex. 3. If the diameter of the earth's orbit is 189,761,000 miles, what is its circumference?

Ans., 596,151,764 miles.

To obtain this answer, the value of π must be taken to at least eight decimal places.

PROBLEM VII.

(94.) *To find the diameter of a circle from its circumference.*

RULE I.

Divide the circumference by 3.14159.

This rule is an obvious consequence from the preceding. To divide by a number is the same as to multiply by its *reciprocal;* and, since multiplication is more easily performed than division, it is generally most convenient to multiply by the reciprocal of π, which is 0.3183099. Hence we have

RULE II.

Multiply the circumference by 0.31831.

Ex. 1. What is the diameter of a circle whose circumference is 875 feet?

Ans., 278.52 feet.

Ex. 2. If the circumference of the moon is 6786 miles, what is its diameter?

Ans., 2160 miles.

Ex. 3. If the circumference of the moon's orbit is 1,492,987 miles, what is its diameter?

Ans., 475,233 miles.

PROBLEM VIII.

(95.) *To find the length of an arc of a circle.*

RULE I.

As 360 *is to the number of degrees in the arc, so is the circumference of the circle to the length of the arc.*

This rule follows from Prop. 14, B. III., in Geometry, where it is proved that angles at the center of a circle have the same ratio with the intercepted arcs.

Ex. 1. What is the length of an arc of 22°, in a circle whose diameter is 125 feet?

The circumference of the circle is found to be 392.7 feet.

Then 360 : 22 : : 392.7 : 23.998 feet.

Ex. 2. If the circumference of the earth is 24,856.28 miles, what is the length of one degree?

Ans., 69.045 miles.

RULE II.

(96.) *Multiply the diameter of the circle by the number of degrees in the arc, and this product by* 0.0087266.

Since the circumference of a circle whose diameter is unity is 3.14159, if we divide this number by 360, we shall obtain the length of an arc of *one* degree, viz., 0.0087266. If we multiply this decimal by the number of degrees in any arc, we shall obtain the length of that arc in a circle whose diameter is unity; and this product, multiplied by the diameter of any other circle, will give the length of an arc of the given number of degrees in that circle.

Ex. 3. What is the length of an arc of 25°, in a circle whose radius is 44 rods?

Ans., 19.198 rods.

Ex. 4. What is the length of an arc of 11° 15′, in a circle whose diameter is 1234 feet?

Ans., 121.147 feet.

(97.) If the number of degrees in an arc is not given, it may be computed from the radius of the circle, and either the chord or height of the arc. Thus, let AB be the chord, and DE the height of the arc ADB, and C the center of the circle. Then, in the right-angled triangle ACE,

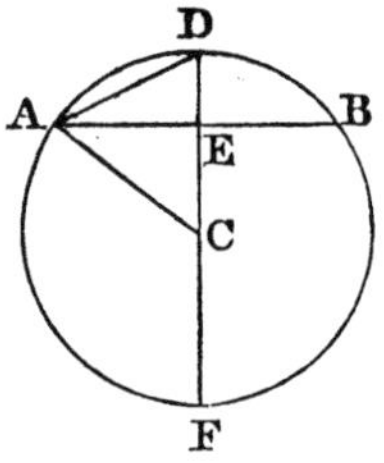

$$AC : R :: \begin{cases} AE : \text{sin. } ACE, \\ CE : \text{cos. } ACE, \end{cases}$$

either of which proportions will give the number of degrees in half the arc.

If only the chord and height of the arc are given, the diameter of the circle may be found. For, by Geometry, Prop. 22, Cor., B. IV.,

$$DE : AE :: AE : EF.$$

Ex. 5. What is the length of an arc whose chord is 6 feet, in a circle whose radius is 9 feet?

Ans., 6.117 feet.

PROBLEM IX.

(98.) *To find the area of a circle.*

RULE I.

Multiply the circumference by half the radius.

For demonstration, see Geometry, Prop. 12, B. VI.

RULE II.

Multiply the square of the radius by 3.14159.

See Geometry, Prop 13, Cor. 3, B. VI.

Ex. 1. What is the area of a circle whose diameter is 18 feet?

Ans., 254.469 feet.

Ex. 2. What is the area of a circle whose circumference is 74 feet?

Ans., 435.766 feet.

Ex. 3. What is the area of a circle whose radius is 125 yards?

Ans., 49087.38 yards.

PROBLEM X.

(99.) *To find the area of a sector of a circle.*

RULE I.

Multiply the arc of the sector by half its radius.

See Geometry, Prop. 12, Cor., B. VI.

RULE II.

As 360 *is to the number of degrees in the arc, so is the area of the circle to the area of the sector.*

This follows from Geometry, Prop. 14, Cor. 2, B. III.

Ex. 1. What is the area of a sector whose arc is 22°, in a circle whose diameter is 125 feet?

The length of the arc is found to be 23.998.

Hence the area of the sector is 749.937.

Ex. 2. What is the area of a sector whose arc is 25°, in a circle whose radius is 44 rods?

Ans., 422.367 rods.

Ex. 3. What is the area of a sector less than a semicircle. whose chord is 6 feet, in a circle whose radius is 9 feet?

Ans., 27.522 feet.

PROBLEM XI.

(100.) *To find the area of a segment of a circle.*

RULE.

Find the area of the sector which has the same arc, and also the area of the triangle formed by the chord of the segment and the radii of the sector.

Then take the sum of these areas if the segment is greater than a semicircle, but take their difference if it is less.

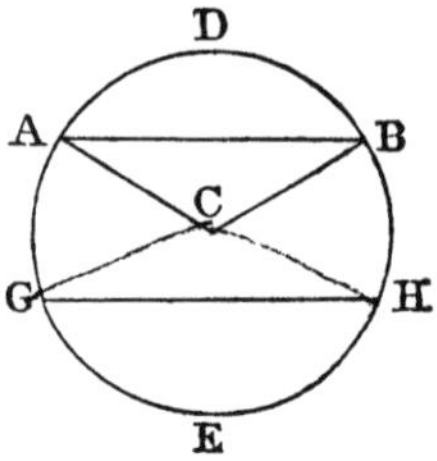

It is obvious that the segment AEB is equal to the sum of the sector ACBE and the triangle ACB, and that the segment ADB is equal to the difference between the sector ACBD and the triangle ACB.

Ex. 1. What is the area of a segment whose arc contains 280°, in a circle whose diameter is 50?

The whole circle	=	1963.495
The sector	=	1527.163
The triangle	=	307.752
The segment	=	1834.915, *Ans.*

Ex. 2. What is the area of a segment whose chord is 20 feet, and height 2 feet?

Ans., 26.8788 feet.

Ex. 3. What is the area of a segment whose arc is 25°, in a circle whose radius is 44 rods?

Ans.

(101.) The area of the zone ABHG, included between two parallel chords, is equal to the difference between the segments GDH and ADB.

Ex. 4. What is the area of a zone, one side of which is 96, and the other side 60, and the distance between them 26?

Ans., 2136.7527.

The radius of the circle in this example will be found to be 50.

PROBLEM XII.

(102.) *To find the area of a ring included between the circumferences of two concentric circles.*

RULE.

Take the difference between the areas of the two circles; or, *Subtract the square of the less radius from the square of the greater, and multiply their difference by* 3.14159.

For, according to Geometry, Prop. 13, Cor. 3, B. VI.,

the area of the greater circle is equal to πR^2,

and the area of the smaller, πr^2.

Their difference, or the area of the ring, is $\pi (R^2 - r^2)$.

Ex. 1. The diameters of two concentric circles are 60 and 50. What is the area of the ring included between their circumferences?

Ans., 863.938.

Ex. 2. The diameters of two concentric circles are 320 and 280 What is the area of the ring included between their circumferences?

Ans., 18849.55

PROBLEM XIII.

(103.) *To find the area of an ellipse.*

RULE.

Multiply the product of the semi-axes by 3.14159.

For demonstration, see Geometry, Ellipse, Prop. 21.

Ex. 1. What is the area of an ellipse whose major axis is 70 feet, and minor axis 60 feet?

Ans., 3298.67 feet.

Ex. 2. What is the area of an ellipse whose axes are 340 and 310?

Ans., 82780.896

PROBLEM XIV.

(104.) *To find the area of a parabola.*

RULE.

Multiply the base by two thirds of the height.

For demonstration, see Geometry, Parabola, Prop. 12.

Ex. 1. What is the area of a parabola whose base is 18 feet, and height 5 feet?

Ans., 60 feet.

Ex. 2. What is the area of a parabola whose base is 525 feet, and height 350 feet?

Ans., 122500 feet

MENSURATION OF SOLIDS.

(105.) The common measuring unit of solids is a *cube*, whose faces are squares of the same name; as, a cubic inch, a cubic foot, &c. This measuring unit is not, however, of necessity a cube whose faces are squares of the same name. Thus a bushel may have the form of a cube, but its faces can only be expressed by means of some unit of a different denomination. The following is

The Table of Solid Measure.

1728	cubic inches	=	1 cubic foot.
27	cubic feet	=	1 cubic yard.
$4492\frac{1}{8}$	cubic feet	=	1 cubic rod.
231	cubic inches	=	1 gallon (liquid measure).
268.8	cubic inches	=	1 gallon (dry measure).
2150.4	cubic inches	=	1 bushel.

PROBLEM I.

(106.) *To find the surface of a right prism.*

RULE.

Multiply the perimeter of the base by the altitude for the convex surface. To this add the areas of the two ends when the entire surface is required.

See Geometry, Prop. 1, B. VIII.

Ex. 1. What is the entire surface of a parallelopiped whose altitude is 20 feet, breadth 4 feet, and depth 2 feet?

Ans., 256 square feet.

Ex. 2. What is the entire surface of a pentagonal prism whose altitude is 25 feet 6 inches, and each side of its base 3 feet 9 inches?

Ans., 526.513 square feet.

Ex. 3. What is the entire surface of an octagonal prism whose altitude is 12 feet 9 inches, and each side of its base 2 feet 5 inches?

Ans., 302.898 square feet.

PROBLEM II.

(107.) *To find the solidity of a prism.*

RULE.

Multiply the area of the base by the altitude.

See Geometry, Prop. 11, B. VIII.

Ex. 1. What is the solidity of a parallelopiped whose altitude is 30 feet, breadth 6 feet, and depth 4 feet?

Ans., 720 cubic feet.

Ex. 2. What is the solidity of a square prism whose altitude is 8 feet 10 inches, and each side of its base 2 feet 3 inches?

Ans., $44\frac{23}{32}$ cubic feet.

Ex. 3 What is the solidity of a pentagonal prism whose altitude is 20 feet 6 inches, and its side 2 feet 7 inches?

Ans., 235.376 cubic feet.

PROBLEM III.

(108.) *To find the surface of a regular pyramid.*

RULE.

Multiply the perimeter of the base by half the slant height for the convex surface. To this add the area of the base when the entire surface is required.

See Geometry, Prop. 14, B. VIII.

Ex. 1. What is the entire surface of a triangular pyramid whose slant height is 25 feet, and each side of its base 5 feet?

Ans., 198.325 square feet.

Ex. 2. What is the entire surface of a square pyramid whose slant height is 30 feet, and each side of the base 4 feet?

Ans., 256 square feet.

Ex. 3. What is the entire surface of a pentagonal pyramid whose slant height is 20 feet, and each side of the base 3 feet?

Ans., 165.484 square feet.

PROBLEM IV.

(109.) *To find the solidity of a pyramid.*

RULE.

Multiply the area of the base by one third of the altitude.

See Geometry, Prop. 17, B. VIII.

Ex. 1. What is the solidity of a triangular pyramid whose altitude is 25 feet, and each side of its base 6 feet?

Ans., 129.904 cubic feet.

Ex. 2. What is the solidity of a square pyramid whose slant height is 22 feet, and each side of its base 10 feet?

Ans., 714.143 cubic feet.

Ex. 3. What is the solidity of a pentagonal pyramid whose altitude is 20 feet, and each side of its base 3 feet?

Ans., 103.228 cubic feet.

PROBLEM V.

(110.) *To find the surface of a frustum of a regular pyramid.*

RULE.

Multiply half the slant height by the sum of the perimeters of the two bases for the convex surface. To this add the areas of the two bases when the entire surface is required.

See Geometry, Prop. 14, Cor. 1, B. VIII.

Ex. 1. What is the entire surface of a frustum of a square pyramid whose slant height is 15 feet, each side of the greater base being 4 feet 6 inches, and each side of the less base 2 feet 10 inches?

Ans., 248.278 square feet.

Ex. 2. What is the entire surface of a frustum of an octagonal pyramid whose slant height is 14 feet, and the sides of the ends 3 feet 9 inches, and 2 feet 3 inches?

Ans., 428.344 square feet.

PROBLEM VI.

(111.) *To find the solidity of a frustum of a pyramid.*

RULE.

Add together the areas of the two bases, and a mean proportional between them, and multiply the sum by one third of the altitude.

See Geometry, Prop. 18, B. VIII.

When the pyramid is regular, it is generally most convenient to find the area of its base by Rule II., Art. 92. If we put a to represent one side of the lower base, and b one side of the upper base, and the tabular number from Art. 92 by

T, the area of the lower base will be a^2T; that of the upper base will be b^2T; and the mean proportional will be abT. Hence, if we represent the height of the frustum by h, its solidity will be

$$(a^2+b^2+ab)\frac{hT}{3}.$$

Ex. 1. What is the solidity of a frustum of an hexagonal pyramid whose altitude is 15 feet, each side of the greater end being 3 feet, and that of the less end 2 feet?

Ans., 246.817 cubic feet.

Ex. 2. What is the solidity of a frustum of an octagonal pyramid whose altitude is 9 feet, each side of the greater end being 30 inches, and that of the less end 20 inches?

Ans., 191.125 cubic feet.

Definition.

(112.) A *wedge* is a solid bounded by five planes, viz., a rectangular base, ABCD, two trapezoids, ABFE, DCFE, meeting in an edge, and two triangular ends, ADE, BCF. The *altitude* of the wedge is the perpendicular drawn from any point in the edge to the plane of the base, as EH.

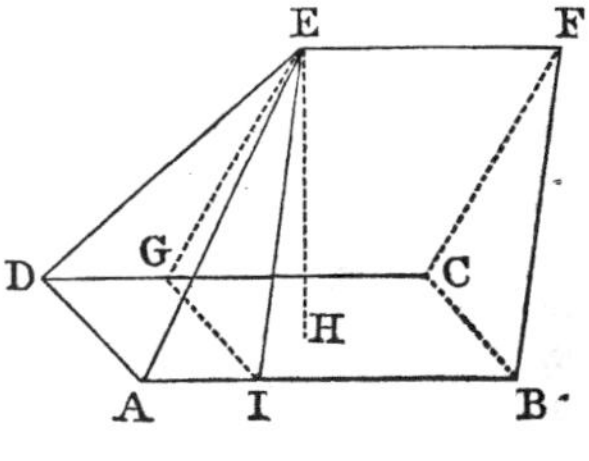

PROBLEM VII.

(113.) *To find the solidity of a wedge.*

RULE.

Add the length of the edge to twice the length of the base, and multiply the sum by one sixth of the product of the height of the wedge and the breadth of the base.

Demonstration.

Put L=AB, the length of the base;
" l=EF, the length of the edge;
" b=BC, the breadth of the base;
" h=EH, the altitude of the wedge.

Now, if the length of the base is equal to that of the edge, it is evident that the wedge is half of a prism of the same base and height. If the length of the base is greater than that of the edge, let a plane, EGI, be drawn parallel to BCF. The wedge will be divided into two parts, viz., the pyramid E—AIGD, and the triangular prism BCF—G.

The solidity of the former is equal to $\frac{1}{3}bh(\text{L}-l)$, and that of the latter is $\frac{1}{2}bhl$. Their sum is

$$\tfrac{1}{2}bhl+\tfrac{1}{3}bh(\text{L}-l)=\tfrac{1}{6}bh3l+\tfrac{1}{6}bh2\text{L}-\tfrac{1}{6}bh2l=\tfrac{1}{6}bh(2\text{L}+l).$$

If the length of the base is less than that of the edge, the wedge will be equal to the difference between the prism and pyramid, and we shall have

$$\tfrac{1}{2}bhl-\tfrac{1}{3}bh(l-\text{L}),$$

which is equal to

$$\tfrac{1}{2}bhl+\tfrac{1}{3}bh(\text{L}-l),$$

the same result as before.

Ex. 1. What is the solidity of a wedge whose base is 30 inches long and 5 inches broad, its altitude 12 inches, and the length of the edge 2 feet?

Ans., 840 cubic inches.

Ex. 2. What is the solidity of a wedge whose base is 40 inches long and 7 inches broad, its altitude 18 inches, and the length of the edge 30 inches?

Ans., 2310 cubic inches.

Definition.

(114.) A *rectangular prismoid* is a solid bounded by six planes, of which the two bases are rectangles having their corresponding sides parallel, and the four upright sides of the solid are trapezoids.

PROBLEM VIII.

To find the solidity of a rectangular prismoid.

RULE.

Add together the areas of the two bases, and four times the area of a parallel section equally distant from the bases, and multiply the sum by one sixth of the altitude.

Demonstration.

Put L and B=length and breadth of one base;

Put l and b =length and breadth of the other base;
" M " m=length and breadth of middle sec.;
" h =the altitude of the prismoid.

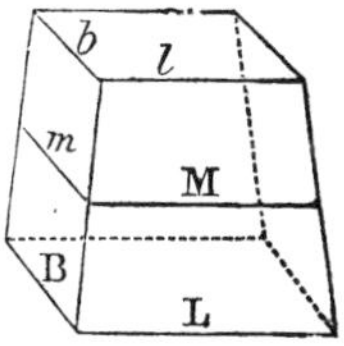

It is evident that if a plane be made to pass through the opposite edges of the upper and lower bases, the prismoid will be divided into two wedges, whose bases are the bases of the prismoid, and whose edges are L and l. The solidity of these wedges, and, consequently, that of the prismoid, is

$$\tfrac{1}{6}Bh(2L+l)+\tfrac{1}{6}bh(2l+L)=\tfrac{1}{6}h(2BL+Bl+2bl+bL).$$

But, since M is equally distant from L and l, we have

$$2M=L+l, \text{ and } 2m=B+b;$$

hence $\quad 4Mm=(L+l)(B+b)=BL+Bl+bL+bl.$

Substituting $4Mm$ for its value in the preceding expression, we obtain for the solidity of the prismoid

$$\tfrac{1}{6}h(BL+bl+4Mm).$$

Ex. 1. What are the contents of a log of wood, in the form of a rectangular prismoid, the length and breadth of one end being 16 inches and 12 inches, and of the other 7 inches and 4 inches, the length of the log being 24 feet?

Ans., $16\frac{1}{3}$ cubic feet.

Ex. 2. What is the solidity of a log of hewn timber, whose ends are 18 inches by 15, and 14 inches by $11\frac{1}{2}$, its length being 18 feet? *Ans.*, $26\frac{31}{48}$ cubic feet.

PROBLEM IX.

To compute the excavation or embankment for a rail-way.

(115.) By the preceding rule may be computed the amount of excavation or embankment required in constructing a railroad or canal. If we divide the line of the road into portions so small that each may be regarded as a straight line, and suppose an equal number of transverse sections to be made, the excavation or embankment between two sections may be regarded as a prismoid, and its contents found by the preceding rule.

Let ABCD represent the lower surface of the supposed excavation, which we will assume to be parallel to the horizon; and let EFGH represent the upper surface of the excavation projected on a horizontal plane. Also, let E′A′B′F′, G′C′D′H represent the vertical sections at the extremities. If we suppose vertical planes to pass through the lines AC, BD, the middle part of the excavation, or that contained between these vertical planes, will be a rectangular prismoid, of which A′B′KI will be one base, and C′D′ML the other base. Its solidity will therefore be given by Art. 114. The parts upon each side of the middle prismoid are also halves of rectangular prismoids; or, if the two parts are equal, they may be regarded as constituting a second prismoid, one of whose bases is the sum of the triangles A′E′I, B′F′K; and the other base is the sum of the triangles C′G′L, D′H′M. Therefore the volume of the entire solid is equal to the product of one sixth of its length, by the sum of the areas of the sections at the two extremities, and four times the area of a parallel and equidistant section.

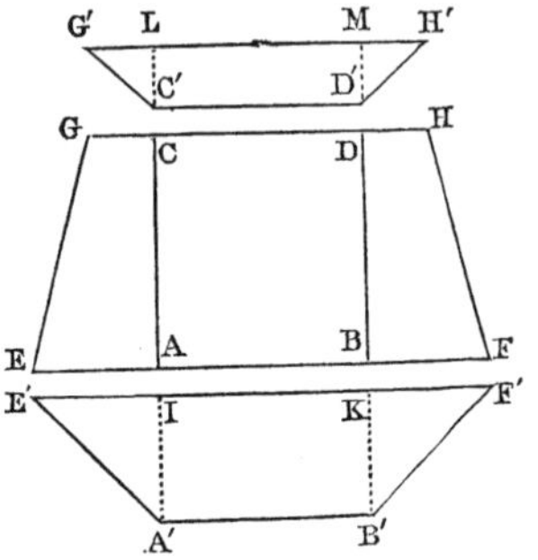

Ex. 1. Let ABCDEFG represent the profile of a tract of

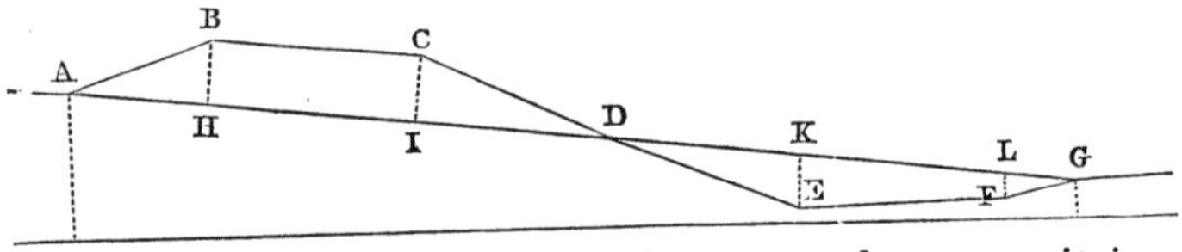

land selected for the line of a rail-way; and suppose it is required, by cutting and embankment, to reduce it from its present hilly surface to one uniform slope from the point A to the point G.

The distance AH is 561 feet; the distance DK is 820 feet;
" " HI is 858 feet; " " KL is 825 feet;
" " ID is 825 feet; " " LG is 330 feet.
The perpendicular BH is 18 feet; the perpendicular KE is 19 feet;
" " CI is 20 feet; " " LF is 8 feet.

The annexed figure represents a cross section, showing the form of the excavation.

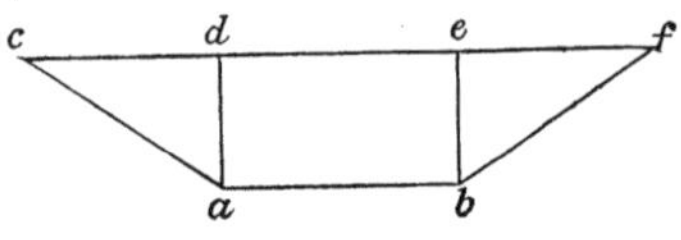

The base of the cutting is to

be 50 feet wide, the slope $1\frac{1}{2}$ horizontal to 1 perpendicular; that is, where the depth *ad* is 10 feet, the width of the slope *cd* at the surface will be 15 feet.

Calculation of the portion ABH.

Since BH is 18 feet, the length of *cd* in the cross section will be 27 feet, and *cf*, the breadth at the top of the section, will be 104 feet. We accordingly find, by Art. 87, the area of the trapezoid forming the cross section at BH equal to

$$\frac{104+50}{2}\times 18=1386 \text{ feet.}$$

For the middle section, the height is 9 feet, *cd* is 13.5 feet, and *cf* is 77 feet. The area of the cross section is therefore equal to

$$\frac{77+50}{2}\times 9=571.5.$$

The solid ABH will therefore be equal to

$$(1386+4\times 571.5)\,\frac{561}{6}=343332 \text{ cubic feet, or}$$

12716 cubic yards.

Calculation of the portion BCIH.

Since CI is 20 feet, the length of *cd* is 30 feet, and *cf* is 110 feet. The area of the section at CI is therefore equal to

$$\frac{110+50}{2}\times 20=1600.$$

For the middle section, the height is 19 feet, *cd* is 28.5 feet, and *cf* is 107 feet. The area of the cross section is therefore equal to

$$\frac{107+50}{2}\times 19=1491.5.$$

The solid BCIH will therefore be equal to

$$(1386+1600+4\times 1491.5)\,\frac{858}{6}=1280136 \text{ cubic feet, or}$$

47412.4 cubic yards.

Calculation of the portion CID.

The height of the middle section is 10 feet; therefore *cf* is 80 feet, and the area of the cross section is

$$\frac{80+50}{2}\times 10=650.$$

The solid CID will therefore be equal to

$$(1600+4\times 650)\,\frac{825}{6}=577500 \text{ cubic feet, or}$$

21388.9 cubic yards.

The entire amount of excavation therefore is,

ABH=	12716.0	cubic yards.
BCIH=	47412.4	"
CDI=	21388.9	"
Total excavation,	81517.3	"

The following is a cross section, showing the form of the embankment.

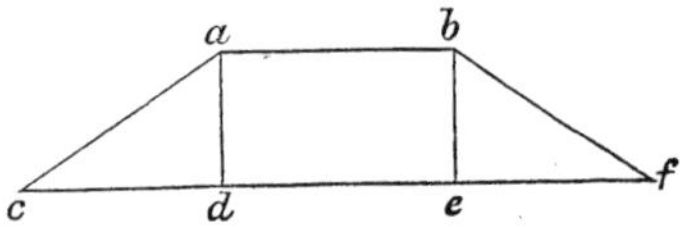

The top of the embankment is to be 50 feet wide, the slope 2 to 1; that is, where the height *ad* is 10 feet, the base *cd* is to be 20 feet.

Calculation of the portion DKE.

Since EK is 19 feet, the length of *cd* is 38 feet, and *cf* is 126 feet. The area of the cross section at EK is therefore equal to

$$\frac{126+50}{2}\times 19=1672.$$

For the middle section, the height is 9.5 feet; *cd* is therefore 19 feet, and *cf* is 88 feet. The area of the cross section is therefore

$$\frac{88+50}{2}\times 9.5=655.5$$

The solid DKE is therefore equal to

$$(1672+4\times 655.5)\frac{820}{6}=586846.7 \text{ cubic feet, or}$$

21735.1 cubic yards.

Calculation of the portion KEFL.

Since LF is 8 feet, *cd* is 16 feet, and *cf* is 82 feet. The area of the section at LF is therefore equal to

$$\frac{82+50}{2}\times 8=528.$$

The height of the middle section is 13.5 feet; therefore *cd* is 27 feet, and *cf* is 104 feet. The area of the cross section is therefore equal to

$$\frac{104+50}{2}\times 13.5=1039.5.$$

The solid KEFL will therefore be equal to

$$(1672+528+4\times 1039.5)\frac{825}{6}=874225 \text{ cubic feet, or}$$

32378.7 cubic yards.

Calculation of the portion LFG.

The height of the middle section is 4 feet; therefore *cf* is 66 feet, and the area of the cross section is equal to

$$\frac{66+50}{2}\times 4=232.$$

The solid LFG will therefore be equal to

$$(528+4\times 232)\frac{330}{6}=80080 \text{ cubic feet, or}$$

2965.9 cubic yards.

The entire amount of embankment therefore is

DKE=	21735.1	cubic yards.
KEFL=	32378.7	"
LFG=	2965.9	"
Total embankment,	57079.7	"

Ex. 2. Compute the amount of excavation of the hill ABCD from the following data:

The distance AH is 325 feet; the perpendicular BH is 12 feet;
" " HI is 672 feet; " " CI is 13 feet.
" " ID is 534 feet.

The base of the cutting to be 50 feet wide, and the slope $1\frac{1}{2}$ horizontal to 1 perpendicular. *Ans.*, 33969 cubic yards.

PROBLEM X.

(116.) *To find the surface of a regular polyedron.*

RULE.

Multiply the area of one of the faces by the number of

faces; or, *Multiply the square of one of the edges by the surface of a similar solid whose edge is unity.*

Since all the faces of a regular polyedron are equal, it is evident that the area of one of them, multiplied by their number, will give the entire surface. Also, regular solids of the same name are similar, and similar polygons are as the squares of their homologous sides (*Geom.*, Prop. 26, B. IV.). The following table shows the surface and solidity of regular polyedrons whose edge is unity. The surface is obtained by multiplying the area of one of the faces, as given in Art. 92, by the number of faces. Thus the area of an equilateral triangle, whose side is 1, is 0.4330127. Hence the surface of a regular tetraedron

$$=.4330127\times4=1.7320508,$$

and so on for the other solids.

A Table of the regular Polyedrons whose Edges are unity

Names.	*No. of Faces.*	*Surface.*	*Solidity.*
Tetraedron,	4	1.7320508	0.1178513.
Hexaedron,	6	6.0000000	1.0000000.
Octaedron,	8	3.4641016	0.4714045.
Dodecaedron,	12	20.6457288	7.6631189.
Icosaedron,	20	8.6602540	2.1816950.

Ex. 1. What is the surface of a regular octaedron whose edges are each 8 feet?

Ans., 221.7025 feet.

Ex. 2. What is the surface of a regular dodecaedron whose edge is 12 feet?

Ans., 2972.985 feet.

PROBLEM XI.

(117.) *To find the solidity of a regular polyedron.*

RULE.

Multiply the surface by one third of the perpendicular let fall from the center on one of the faces; or, *Multiply the cube of one of the edges by the solidity of a similar polyedron, whose edge is unity.*

Since the faces of a regular polyedron are similar and equal, and the solid angles are all equal to each other, it is evident that the faces are all equally distant from a point in the solid called the center. If planes be made to pass through the center and the several edges of the solid, they will divide it into as many equal pyramids as it has faces. The base of each pyramid will be one of the faces of the polyedron; and since their altitude is the perpendicular from the center upon one of the faces, the solidity of the polyedron must be equal to the areas of all the faces, multiplied by one third of this perpendicular.

Also, similar pyramids are to each other as the cubes of their homologous edges (*Geom.*, Prop. 17, Cor. 3, B. VIII.). And since two regular polyedrons of the same name may be divided into the same number of similar pyramids, they must be to each other as the cubes of their edges.

(118.) The solidity of a tetraedron whose edge is unity, may be computed in the following manner:

Let C—ABD be a tetraedron. From one angle, C, let fall a perpendicular, CE, on the opposite face; draw EF perpendicular to AD; and join CF, AE. Then AEF is a right-angled triangle, in which EF, being the sine of 30°, is one half of AE or BE; and therefore FE is one third of BF or CF. Hence the cosine of the angle CFE is equal to $\frac{1}{3}$; that is, the angle of inclination of the faces of the polyedron is 70° 31′ 44″. Also, in the triangle CAF, CF is the sine of 60°, which is 0.866025. Hence, in the right-angled triangle CEF, knowing one side and the angles, we can compute CE, which is found to be 0.8164966. Whence, knowing the base ABD (Art. 92), we obtain the solidity of the tetraedron =0.1178513.

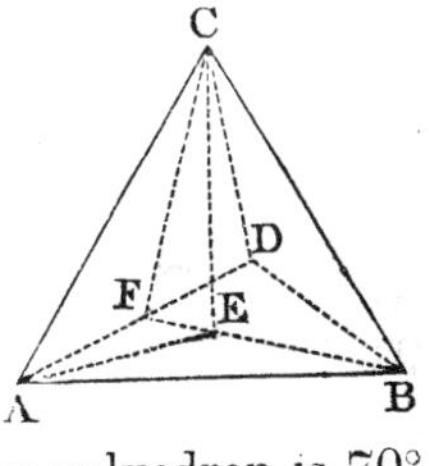

In a somewhat similar manner may the solidities of the other regular polyedrons, given in Art. 116, be obtained.

Ex. 1. What is the solidity of a regular tetraedron whose edges are each 24 inches?

Ans., 0.9428 feet.

Ex. 2. What is the solidity of a regular icosaedron whose edges are each 20 feet?

Ans., 17453.56 feet.

THE THREE ROUND BODIES.

PROBLEM I.

(119.) *To find the surface of a cylinder.*

RULE.

Multiply the circumference of the base by the altitude for the convex surface. To this add the areas of the two ends when the entire surface is required.

See Geometry, Prop. 1, B. X.

Ex. 1. What is the convex surface of a cylinder whose altitude is 23 feet, and the diameter of its base 3 feet?

Ans., 216.77 square feet.

Ex. 2. What is the entire surface of a cylinder whose altitude is 18 feet, and the diameter of its base 5 feet?

Ans.

PROBLEM II.

(120.) *To find the solidity of a cylinder.*

RULE.

Multiply the area of the base by the altitude.

See Geometry, Prop. 2, B. X.

Ex. 1. What is the solidity of a cylinder whose altitude is 18 feet 4 inches, and the diameter of its base 2 feet 10 inches?

Ans., 115.5917 cubic feet.

Ex. 2. What is the solidity of a cylinder whose altitude is 12 feet 11 inches, and the circumference of its base 5 feet 3 inches?

Ans., 28.3308 cubic feet.

PROBLEM III.

(121.) *To find the surface of a cone.*

RULE.

Multiply the circumference of the base by half the side for the convex surface; to which add the area of the base when the entire surface is required.

See Geometry, Prop. 3, B. X.

Ex. 1. What is the entire surface of a cone whose side is 10 feet, and the diameter of its base 2 feet 3 inches?

Ans., 39.319 square feet.

Ex. 2. What is the entire surface of a cone whose side is 15 feet, and the circumference of its base 8 feet?

Ans., 65.093 square feet.

PROBLEM IV.

(122.) *To find the solidity of a cone.*

RULE.

Multiply the area of the base by one third of the altitude.

See Geometry, Prop. 5, B. X.

Ex. 1. What is the solidity of a cone whose altitude is 12 feet, and the diameter of its base $2\frac{1}{2}$ feet?

Ans., 19.635 cubic feet.

Ex. 2. What is the solidity of a cone whose altitude is 25 feet, and the circumference of its base 6 feet 9 inches?

Ans.

PROBLEM V.

(123.) *To find the surface of a frustum of a cone.*

RULE.

Multiply half the side by the sum of the circumferences of the two bases for the convex surface; to this add the areas of the two bases when the entire surface is required.

See Geometry, Prop. 4, B. X.

Ex. 1. What is the entire surface of a frustum of a cone, the diameters of whose bases are 9 feet and 5 feet, and whose side is 16 feet 9 inches?

Ans., 451.6036 square feet.

Ex. 2. What is the convex surface of a frustum of a cone whose side is 10 feet, and the circumferences of its bases 6 feet and 4 feet?

Ans., 50 square feet.

PROBLEM VI.

(124.) *To find the solidity of a frustum of a cone.*

RULE

Add together the areas of the two bases, and a mean proportional between them, and multiply the sum by one third of the altitude.

See Geometry, Prop. 6, B. X.

If we put R and r for the radii of the two bases, then πR^2 will represent the area of one base, πr^2 the area of the other, and πRr the mean proportional between them. Hence, if we represent the height of the frustum by h, its solidity will be

$$\frac{\pi h}{3}(R^2+r^2+Rr).$$

Ex. 1. What is the solidity of a frustum of a cone whose altitude is 20 feet, the diameter of the greater end 5 feet, and that of the less end 2 feet 6 inches?

Ans., 229.074 cubic feet

Ex. 2. The length of a mast is 60 feet, its diameter at the greater end is 20 inches, and at the less end 12 inches: what is its solidity? *Ans.*, 85.521 cubic feet

PROBLEM VII.

(125.) *To find the surface of a sphere.*

RULE.

Multiply the diameter by the circumference of a great circle; or, Multiply the square of the diameter by 3.14159.

See Geometry, Prop. 7, B. X.

Ex. 1. Required the surface of the earth, its diameter being 7912 miles. *Ans.*, 196,662,896 square miles.

Ex. 2. Required the surface of the moon, its circumference being 6786 miles. *Ans.*

PROBLEM VIII.

(126.) *To find the solidity of a sphere.*

RULE.

Multiply the surface by one third of the radius; or, Multiply the cube of the diameter by $\frac{1}{6}\pi$; *that is, by* 0.5236.

See Geometry, Prop. 8, B. X.

Where great accuracy is required, the value of $\frac{1}{6}\pi$ must be taken to more than four decimal places. Its value, correct to ten decimal places, is .52359,87756.

Ex. 1. What is the solidity of the earth, if it be a sphere 7912 miles in diameter?

Ans., 259,332,805,350 cubic miles.

Ex. 2. If the diameter of the moon be 2160 miles, what is its solidity? *Ans.*

PROBLEM IX.

(127.) *To find the surface of a spherical zone.*

RULE.

Multiply the altitude of the zone by the circumference of a great circle of the sphere.

See Geometry, Prop. 7, Cor. 1, B. X.

Ex. 1. If the diameter of the earth be 7912 miles, what is the surface of the torrid zone, extending 23° 27′ 36″ on each side of the equator?

Ans., 78,293,218 square miles.

Let PEP′Q represent a meridian of the earth; EQ the equator; P, P′ the poles; AB one of the tropics, and GH one of the polar circles. Then PK will represent the height of one of the frigid zones, KD the height of one of the temperate zones, and CD half the height of the torrid zone.

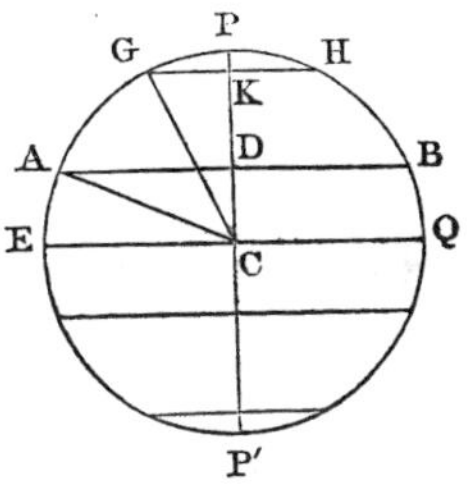

Each of the angles ACE, CAD, and GCK is equal to 23° 27′ 36″.

In the right-angled triangle ACD,

R : AC : : sin. CAD : CD.

Also, in the ight-angled triangle CGK,

R : CG : : cos. GCK : CK,

Then · PK=PC−KC.

Where great accuracy is required, the sine and cosine of 23° 27′ 36″ must be taken to more than six decimal places. The following values are correct to ten decimal places:

Natural sine of 23° 27′ 36″=.39810,87431.

" cosine of 23° 27′ 36″=.91733,82302.

Ex. 2. If the polar circle extends 23° 27′ 36″ from the pole find the convex surface of either frigid zone.

Ans., 8,128,252 square miles.

Ex. 3. On the same suppositions, find the surface of each of the temperate zones.

Ans., 51,056,587 square miles.

PROBLEM X.

(128.) *To find the solidity of a spherical segment with one base.*

RULE.

Multiply half the height of the segment by the area of the base, and the cube of the height by .5236, *and add the two products.*

See Geometry, Prop. 9, B. X.

Ex. 1. What is the solidity of either frigid zone, supposing the earth to be 7912 miles in diameter, the polar circles extending 23° 27′ 36″ from the poles?

Ans., 1,292,390,176 cubic miles.

(129.) The solidity of a spherical segment of two bases is the difference between two spherical segments, each having a single base.

Ex. 2. On the same supposition as in Ex. 1, find the solidity of either temperate zone.

Ans., 55,032,766,543 cubic miles

Ex. 3. Find the solidity of the torrid zone.

Ans., 146,682,491,911 cubic miles

PROBLEM XI.

(130.) *To find the area of a spherical triangle.*

RULE.

Compute the surface of the quadrantal triangle, or one eighth of the surface of the sphere. From the sum of the three angles subtract two right angles; divide the remainder by 90, *and multiply the quotient by the quadrantal triangle*

See Geometry, Prop. 20, B. IX.

Ex. 1. What is the area of a triangle on a sphere whose diameter is 10 feet, if the angles are 55°, 60°, and 85°?

Ans., 8.7266 square feet.

Ex. 2. If the angles of a spherical triangle measured on the surface of the earth are 78° 4′ 10″, 59° 50′ 54″, and 42° 5′ 37″, what is the area of the triangle, supposing the earth a sphere, of which the diameter is 7912 miles?

Ans., 3110.794 square miles.

If the excess of the angles above two right angles is expressed in seconds, we must divide it by 90 degrees also expressed in seconds; that is, by 324,000.

PROBLEM XII.

(131.) *To find the area of a spherical polygon.*

RULE.

Compute the surface of the quadrantal triangle. From the sum of all the angles subtract the product of two right angles by the number of sides less two; divide the remainder by 90, *and multiply the quotient by the quadrantal triangle.*

See Geometry, Prop. 21, B. IX.

Ex. 1. What is the area of a spherical polygon of 5 sides on a sphere whose diameter is 10 feet, supposing the sum of the angles to be 640 degrees?

Ans., 43.633 square feet.

Ex. 2. The angles of a spherical polygon, measured on the surface of the earth, are
62° 33′ 13″;
135° 8′ 26″;
149° 16′ 9″;
111° 45′ 8″;
105° 59′ 7″;
155° 19′ 12″.

Required the area of the polygon.

Ans., 5690.477 square miles.

BOOK IV.

SURVEYING.

(132.) The term *Surveying* includes the measurement of heights and distances, the determination of the area of portions of the earth's surface, and their delineation upon paper.

Since the earth is spherical, its surface is not a plane surface, and if large portions of the earth are to be measured, the curvature must be taken into account; but in ordinary surveying, the portions of the earth are supposed to be so small that the curvature may be neglected. The parts surveyed are therefore regarded as plane figures.

(133.) If a plummet be freely suspended by a line, and allowed to come to a state of rest, this line is called a *vertical line.*

Every plane passing through a vertical line is a *vertical plane.*

A line perpendicular to a vertical line is a *horizontal line.*

A plane perpendicular to a vertical line is a *horizontal plane.*

A *vertical angle* is one the plane of whose sides is vertical.

A *horizontal angle* is one the plane of whose sides is horizontal.

An *angle of elevation* is a vertical angle having one side horizontal and the other an ascending line, as the angle BAD.

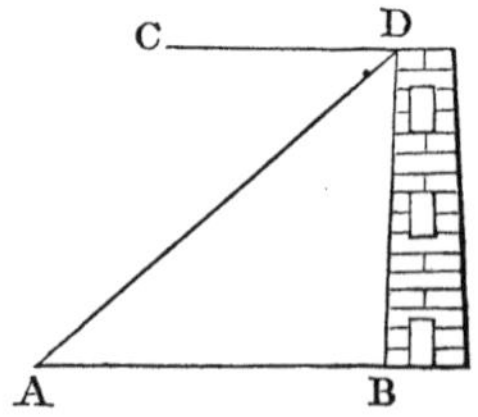

An *angle of depression* is a vertical angle having one side horizontal and the other a descending line, as the angle CDA.

(134.) When distances are to be found by trigonometrical computation, it is necessary to measure at least one line upon the ground, and also as many angles as may be necessary to render three parts of every triangle known.

In the measurement of lines, the unit commonly employed by surveyors is a chain four rods or sixty-six feet in length, called *Gunter's Chain*, from the name of the inventor. This chain is divided into 100 links. Sometimes a half chain is used, containing 50 links.

Hence, 1 chain = 100 links = 66 feet;
1 rod = 25 links = $16\frac{1}{2}$ feet;
1 link = 7.92 inches = $\frac{2}{3}$ of a foot nearly.

(135.) *To measure a horizontal line.*

To mark the termination of the chain in measuring, ten iron pins should be provided, about a foot in length.

Let the person who is to go foremost in carrying the chain, and who is called the leader, take one end of the chain and the ten pins; and let another person take the other end of the chain, and hold it at the beginning of the line to be measured. When the leader has advanced until the chain is stretched tight, he must set down one pin at the end of the chain, the other person taking care that the chain is in the direction of the line to be measured. Then measure a second chain in the same manner, and so on until all the marking pins are exhausted. A record should then be made that ten chains have been measured, after which the marking pins should be returned to the leader, and the measurement continued as before until the whole line has been passed over.

It is generally agreed to refer all surfaces to a horizontal plane. Hence, when an inclined surface, like the side of a hill, is to be measured, the chain should be maintained in a horizontal position. For this purpose, in ascending a hill, the hind end of the chain should be raised from the ground until it is on a level with the fore end, and should be held vertically over the termination of the preceding chain. In descending a hill, the fore end of the chain should be raised in the same manner.

INSTRUMENTS FOR MEASURING ANGLES.

In measuring angles, some instrument is used which contains a portion of a graduated circle divided into degrees and minutes. These instruments may be adapted to measuring either horizontal or vertical angles. The instrument most frequently employed for measuring horizontal angles is called

THE SURVEYOR'S COMPASS.

(136.) The principal parts of this instrument are a compass-box, a magnetic needle, two sights, and a stand for its support. The compass-box, ABC, is circular, generally about six inches in diameter, and at its center is a small pin on which the magnetic needle is balanced. The circumference of the box is divided into degrees, and sometimes to half degrees; and the degrees are numbered from the extremities of a diameter both ways to 90°. The sights, DE, FG, are placed at right angles

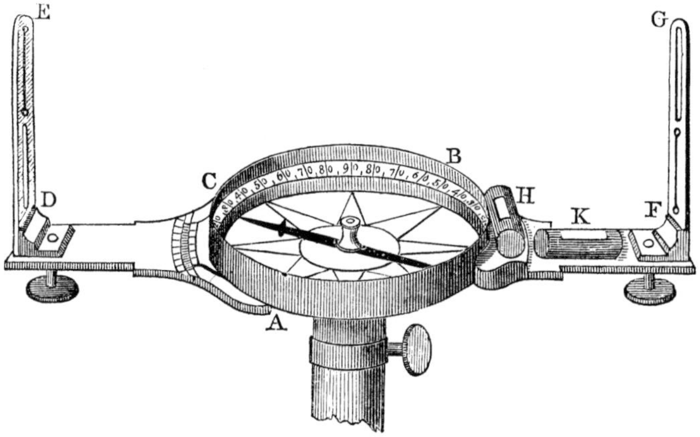

to the plane of the graduated circle, and in each of these there is a large and small aperture for convenience of observation The instrument, when used, is mounted on a tripod, or a single staff pointed with iron at the bottom, so that it may be firmly placed in the ground.

Sometimes two spirit levels, H and K, are attached, to indicate when the plane of the graduated circle is brought into a horizontal position.

(137.) When the magnetic needle is supported so as to turn freely, and is allowed to come to a state of rest, the direction it assumes is called the *magnetic meridian*, one end of the needle indicating the north point and the other the south.

A horizontal line perpendicular to a meridian is an east and west line

All the meridians passing through a survey of moderate extent, are considered as straight lines parallel to each other.

The *bearing* or *course* of a line is the angle which it makes with a meridian passing through one end; and it is reckoned from the north or south point of the horizon, toward the east or west.

Thus, if NS represent a meridian, and the angle NAB is 40°, then the bearing of AB from the point A is 40° to the west of north, and is written N. 40° W., and read north forty degrees west.

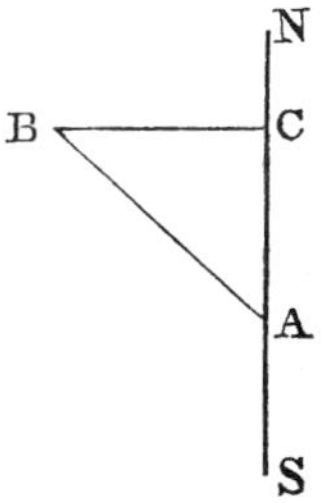

The *reverse bearing* of a line is the bearing taken from the other end of the line.

The forward bearing and reverse bearing of a line are equal angles, but lie between directly opposite points. Thus, if the bearing of AB from A is N. 40° W., the bearing of the same line from B is S. 40° E.

(138.) For measuring vertical angles, the instrument commonly used is

A QUADRANT.

It consists of a quarter of a circle, usually made of brass, and its limb, AB, is divided into degrees and minutes, numbered from A up to 90°. It is furnished either with a pair of plain sights or with a telescope, CD, which is to be directed toward the object observed. A plumb line, CE, is suspended from the center of the quadrant, and indicates when the radius CB is brought into a vertical position.

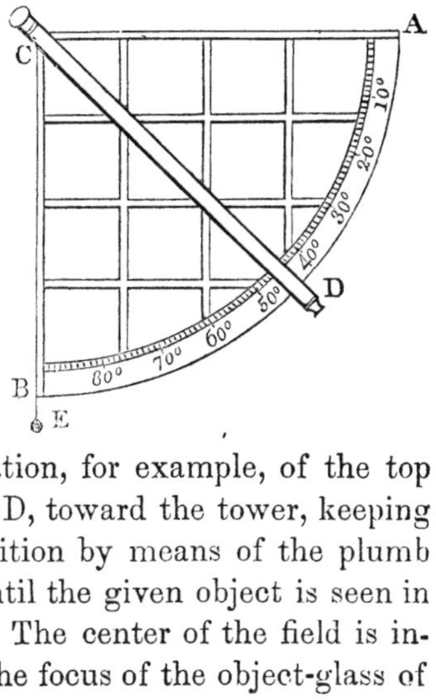

To measure the angle of elevation, for example, of the top of a tower, point the telescope, CD, toward the tower, keeping the radius, CB, in a vertical position by means of the plumb line, CE. Move the telescope until the given object is seen in the middle of the field of view. The center of the field is indicated by two wires placed in the focus of the object-glass of the telescope, one wire being vertical and the other horizontal. When the horizontal wire is made to coincide with the summit of the tower, the angle of elevation is shown upon the arc AB by means of an index which moves with the telescope.

As the arc is not commonly divided into parts smaller than half degrees, when great accuracy is required, some contrivance is needed for obtaining smaller fractions of a degree. This is usually effected by a vernier.

(139.) A *Vernier* is a scale of small extent, graduated in such a manner that, being moved by the side of a fixed scale, we are enabled to measure minute portions of this scale. The length of this movable scale is equal to a certain number of parts of that to be subdivided, but it is divided into parts one more or one less than those of the primary scale taken for the length of the vernier. Thus, if we wish to measure hundredths of an inch, as in the case of a barometer, we first divide an inch into ten equal parts. We then construct a vernier equal in length to 11 of these divisions, but divide it into 10 equal parts, by which means each division on the vernier is $\frac{1}{10}$th longer than a division of the primary scale.

Thus, let AB be the upper end of a barometer tube, the mercury standing at the point C; the scale is divided into inches and tenths of an inch, and the middle piece, numbered from 1 to 9, is the vernier that slides up and down, having 10 of its divisions equal to 11 divisions of the scale, that is, to $\frac{11}{10}$ths of an inch. Therefore, each division of the vernier is $\frac{11}{100}$ths of an inch; or one division of the vernier exceeds one division of the scale by $\frac{1}{100}$th of an inch. Now, as the sixth division of the vernier (in the figure) coincides with a division of the scale, the fifth division of the vernier will stand $\frac{1}{100}$th of an inch above the nearest division of the scale; the fourth division $\frac{2}{100}$ths of an inch, and the top of the vernier will be $\frac{6}{100}$ths of an inch above the next lower division of the scale; *i. e.*, the top of the vernier coincides with 29.66 inches upon the scale. In practice, therefore, we ob-

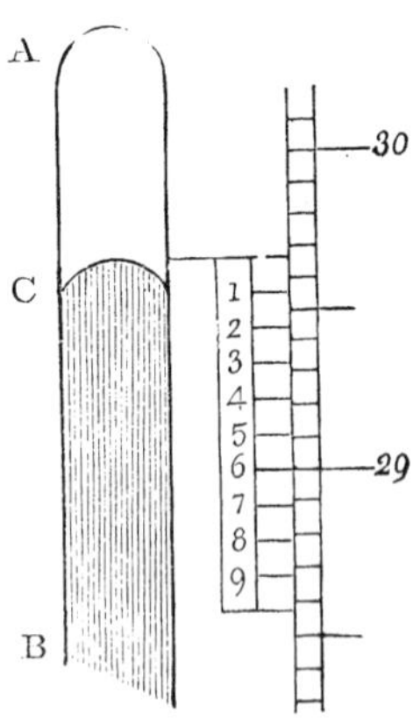

serve what division of the vernier coincides with a division of the scale; this will show the hundredths of an inch to be added to the tenths next below the vernier at the top.

A similar contrivance is applied to graduated circles, to obtain the value of an arc with greater accuracy. If a circle is graduated to half degrees, or 30′, and we wish to measure single minutes by the vernier, we take an arc equal to 31 divisions upon the limb, and divide it into 30 equal parts. Then each division of the vernier will be equal to $\frac{31}{60}$ths of a degree, while each division of the scale is $\frac{30}{60}$ths of a degree. That is, each space on the vernier exceeds one on the limb by 1′.

In order, therefore, to read an angle for any position of the vernier, we pass along the vernier until a line is found coinciding with a line of the limb. The number of this line from the zero point indicates the minutes which are to be added to the degrees and half degrees taken from the graduated circle. Sometimes a vernier is attached to the common surveyor's compass.

(140.) An instrument in common use for measuring both horizontal and vertical angles is

THE THEODOLITE.

The theodolite has two circular brass plates, C and D (see fig. next page), the former of which is called the *vernier plate*, and the latter the *graduated limb*. Both have a horizontal motion about the vertical axis, E. This axis consists of two parts, one external, and the other internal; the former secured to the graduated limb, D, and the latter to the vernier plate, C, so that the vernier plate turns freely upon the lower. The edge of the lower plate is divided into degrees and half degrees, and this is subdivided by a vernier attached to the upper plate into single minutes. The degrees are numbered from 0 to 360.

The parallel plates, A and B, are held together by a ball which rests in a socket. Four screws, three of which, *a*, *a*, *a*, are shown in the figure, turn in sockets fixed to the lower plate, while their heads press against the under side of the upper plate, by which means the instrument is leveled for observation. The whole rests upon a tripod, which is firmly attached to the body of the instrument.

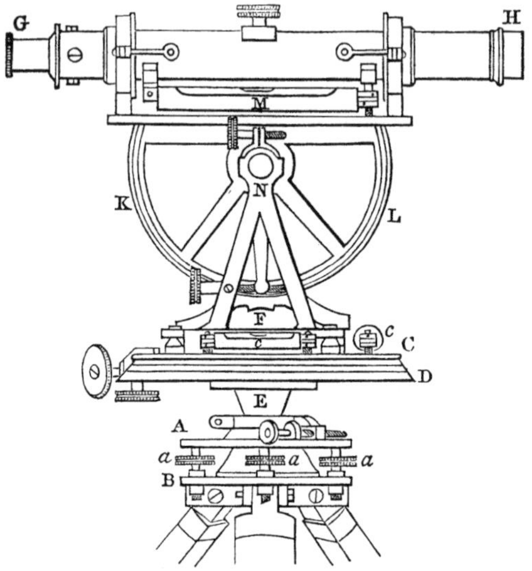

To the vernier plate, two spirit-levels, *c*, *c*, are attached at right angles to each other, to determine when the graduated limb is horizontal. A compass, also, is placed at F. Two frames, one of which is seen at N, support the pivots of the horizontal axis of the vertical semicircle KL, on which the telescope, GH, is placed. One side of the vertical arc is divided into degrees and half degrees, and it is divided into single minutes by the aid of its vernier. The graduation commences at the middle of the arc, and reads both ways to 90°. Under and parallel to the telescope is a spirit-level, M, to show when the telescope is brought to a horizontal position. To enable us to direct the telescope upon an object with precision, two lines called wires are fixed at right angles to each other in the focus of the telescope.

To measure a Horizontal Angle with the Theodolite.

(141.) Place the instrument exactly over the station from which the angle is to be measured; then level the instrument by means of the screws, *a*, *a*, bringing the telescope over each pair alternately until the two spirit-levels on the vernier plate retain their position, while the instrument is turned entirely round upon its axis. Direct the telescope to one of the objects to be observed, moving it until the cross-wires and object coincide. Now read off the degrees upon the graduated limb, and the minutes indicated by the vernier. Next, release the upper plate (leaving the graduated limb undisturbed), and move it round until the telescope is directed to the second object, and make the cross-wires bisect this object, as was done by the first. Again, read off the vernier; the difference between this and the former reading will be the angle required.

The magnetic bearing of an object is determined by simply reading the angle pointed out by the compass-needle when the object is bisected.

To measure an Angle of Elevation with the Theodolite.

(142.) Direct the telescope toward the given object so that it may be bisected by the horizontal wire, and then read off the arc upon the vertical semicircle. After observing the object with the telescope in its natural position, it is well to revolve the telescope in its supports until the level comes uppermost, and repeat the observation. The mean of the two measures may be taken as the angle of elevation.

By the aid of the instruments now described, we may determine the distance of an inaccessible object, and its height above the surface of the earth.

HEIGHTS AND DISTANCES.

PROBLEM I.

(143.) *To determine the height of a vertical object situated on a horizontal plane.*

Measure from the object to any convenient distance in a straight line, and then take the angle of elevation subtended by the object.

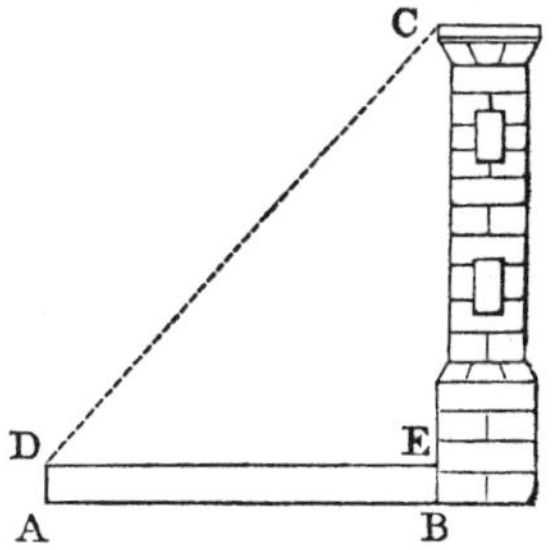

If we measure the distance DE, and the angle of elevation CDE, there will be given, in the right-angled triangle CDE, the base and the angles, to find the perpendicular CE (Art. 46). To this we must add the height of the instrument, to obtain the entire height of the object above the plane AB.

Ex. 1. Having measured AB equal to 100 feet from the bottom of a tower on a horizontal plane, I found the angle of elevation, CDE, of the top to be 47° 30′, the center of the quadrant being five feet above the ground. What is the height of the tower?

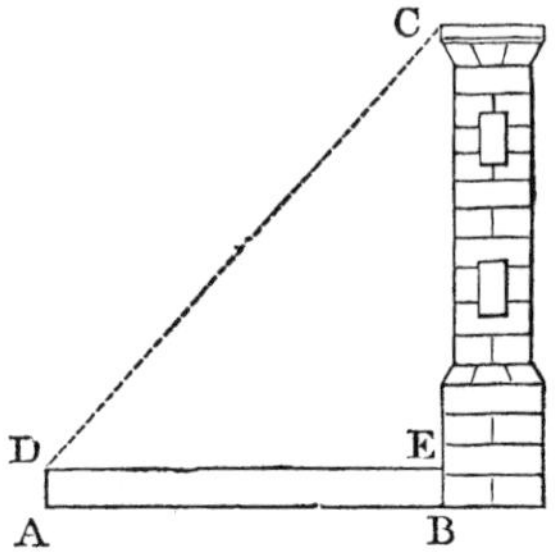

R : tang. CDE : : DE : CE=109.13. To which add five feet, and we obtain the height of the tower, 114.13 feet.

Ex. 2. From the edge of a ditch 18 feet wide, surrounding a fort, the angle of elevation of the wall was found to be 62° 40′. Required the height of the wall, and the length of a ladder necessary to reach from my station to the top of it.

Ans. The height is 34.82 feet. Length of ladder, 39.20 feet.

PROBLEM II.

(144.) *To find the distance of a vertical object whose height is known.*

Measure the angle of elevation, and we shall have given the angles and perpendicular of a right-angled triangle to find the base (Art. 46).

Ex. 1. The angle of elevation of the top of a tower whose height was known to be 143 feet, was found to be 35°. What was its distance?

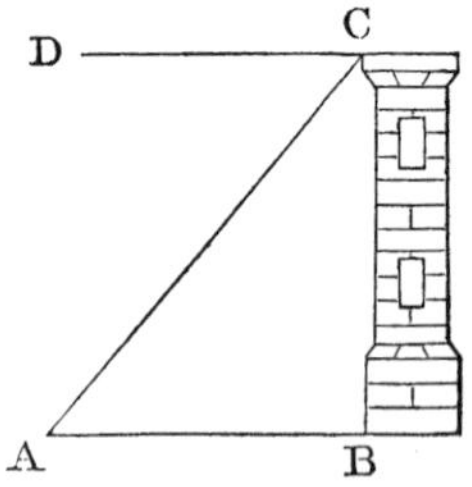

Here we have given the angles of the triangle ABC, and the side CB, to find AB.

Ans., 204.22 feet.

If the observer were stationed at the top of the tower BC, he might find the length of the base AB by measuring the angle of depression DCA, which is equal to BAC.

Ex. 2. From the top of a ship's mast, which was 80 feet above the water, the angle of depression of another ship's hull was found to be 20°. What was its distance?

Ans., 219.80 feet.

PROBLEM III.

(145.) *To find the height of a vertical object standing on an inclined plane.*

Measure the distance from the object to any convenient station, and observe the angles which the base-line makes with lines drawn from its two ends to the top of the object.

If we measure the base-line AB, and the two angles ABC, BAC, then, in the triangle ABC, we shall have given one side and the angles to find BC.

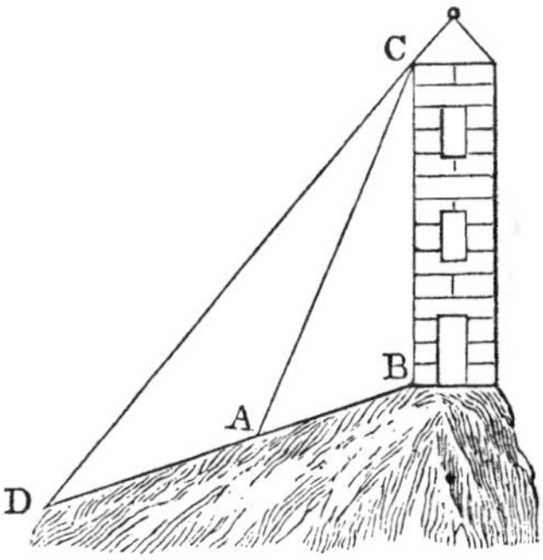

Ex. 1. Wanting to know the height of a tower standing on an inclined plane, BD, I measured from the bottom of the tower a distance, AB, equal to 165 feet; also the angle ABC, equal to 107° 18′, and the angle BAC, equal to 33° 35′. Required the height of the object.

$$\text{sin. ACB : AB : : sin. BAC : BC}=144.66 \text{ feet.}$$

The height, BC, may also be found by measuring the distances BA, AD, and taking the angles BAC, BDC. The difference between the angles BAC and BDC will be the angle ACD. There will then be given, in the triangle DAC, one side and all the angles to find AC; after which we shall have, in the triangle ABC, two sides and the included angle to find BC.

Ex. 2. A tower standing on the top of a declivity, I measured 75 feet from its base, and then took the angle BAC, 47° 50′; going on in the same direction 40 feet further, I took the angle BDC, 38° 30′. What was the height of the tower?

Ans., 117.21 feet.

PROBLEM IV.

(146.) *To find the distance of an inaccessible object.*

Measure a horizontal base-line, and also the angles between this line and lines drawn from each station to the object. Let C be the object inaccessible from A and B. Then, if the distance between the stations A and B be measured, as also the angles at A and B, there will be given, in the triangle ABC, the side AB and the angles, to find AC and BC, the distances of the object from the two stations.

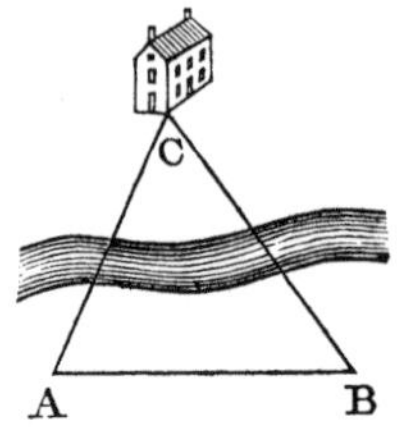

Ex. 1. Being on the side of a river, and wanting to know the distance to a house which stood on the other side, I measured 400 yards in a right line by the side of the river, and found that the two angles at the ends of this line, formed by the other end and the house, were 73° 15′ and 68° 2′. What was the distance between each station and the house?

The angle C is found to be 38° 43′. Then

$$\text{sin. C} : \text{AB} :: \begin{cases} \text{sin. A} : \text{BC}=612.38; \\ \text{sin. B} : \text{AC}=593.09. \end{cases}$$

Ex. 2. Two ships of war, wishing to ascertain their distance from a fort, sail from each other a distance of half a mile, when they find that the angles formed between a line from one to the other, and from each to the fort, are 85° 15′ and 83° 45′. What are the respective distances from the fort?

Ans., 4584.52 and 4596.10 yards.

PROBLEM V.

(147.) *To find the distance between two objects separated by an impassable barrier.*

Measure the distance from any convenient station to each of the objects, and the angle included between those lines.

If we wish to know the distance between the places C and B, both of which are accessible, but separated from each other by water, we may measure the lines AC and AB, and also the angle A. We shall then have given two sides of a triangle and the included angle to find the third side.

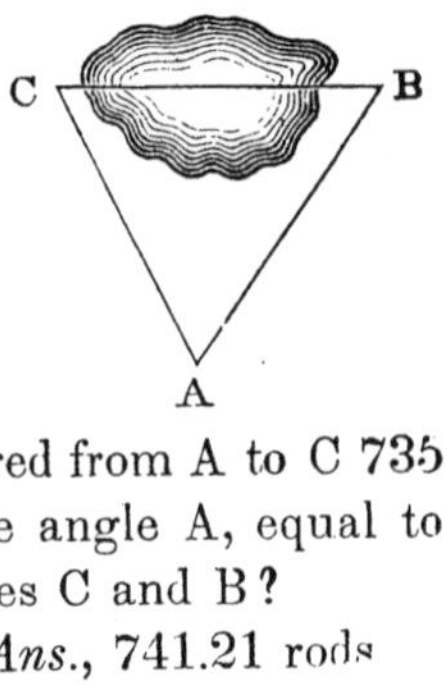

Ex. 1. The passage between the two objects C and B being obstructed, I measured from A to C 735 rods, and from A to B 840 rods; also, the angle A, equal to 55° 40′. What is the distance of the places C and B?

Ans., 741.21 rods

Ex. 2. In order to find the distance between two objects, C and B, which could not be directly measured, I measured from C to A 652 yards, and from B to A 756 yards; also, the angle A equal to 142° 25′. What is the distance between the objects C and B?

Ans.

PROBLEM VI.

(148.) *To find the height of an inaccessible object above a horizontal plane.*

First Method.—Take two stations in a vertical plane passing through the top of the object; measure the distance between the stations and the angle of elevation at each.

If we measure the base AB, and the angles DAC, DBC, then, since CBA is the supplement of DBC, we shall have, in the triangle ABC, one side and all the angles to find BC. Then, in the right-angled triangle DBC, we shall have the hypothenuse and the angles to find DC.

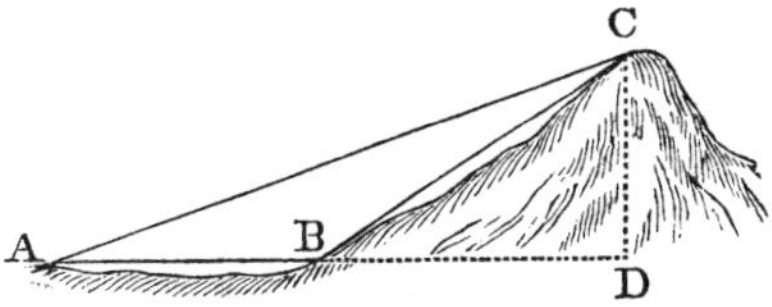

Ex. 1. What is the perpendicular height of a hill whose angle of elevation, taken at the bottom of it, was 46°; and 100 yards farther off, on a level with the bottom of it, the angle was 31°?

Ans., 143.14 yards.

Ex. 2. The angle of elevation of a spire I found to be 58°, and going 100 yards directly from it, found the angle to be only 32°. What is the height of the spire, supposing the instrument to have been five feet above the ground at each observation?

Ans., 104.18 yards.

(149.) *Second Method.*—Measure any convenient base-line, also the angles between this base and lines drawn from each of its extremities to the foot of the object, and the angle of elevation at one of the stations.

Let DC be the given object. If we measure the horizontal base-line AB, and the angles CAB, CBA, we can compute the distance BC. Also, if we observe the angle of elevation CBD, we shall have given, in the right-angled triangle BCD, the base and angles to find the perpendicular.

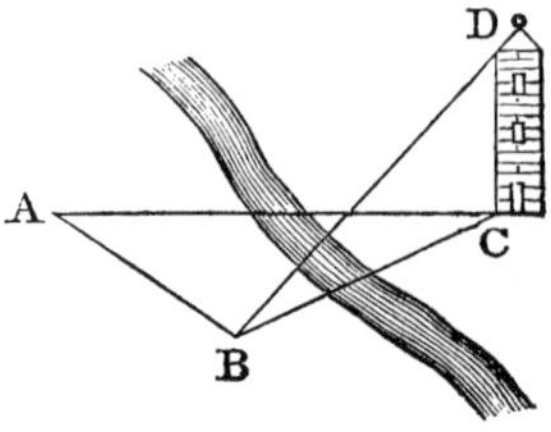

Ex. 1. Being on one side of a river, and wanting to know the height of a spire on the other side, I measured 500 yards, AB, along the side of the river, and found the angle ABC=74° 14′, and BAC=49° 23′; also, the angle of elevation CBD=11° 15′. Required the height of the spire. *Ans.*, 271.97 feet.

Ex. 2. To find the height of an inaccessible castle, I measured a line of 73 yards, and at each end of it took the angle of position of the object and the other end, and found the one to be 90°, and the other 61° 45′; also, the elevation of the castle from the latter station, 10° 35′. Required the height of the castle. *Ans.*, 86.45 feet.

PROBLEM VII.

(150.) *To find the distance between two inaccessible objects.*

Measure any convenient base-line, and the angles between this base and lines drawn from each of its extremities to each of the objects.

Let C and D be the two inaccessible objects. If we measure a base-line, AB, and the angles DAB, DBA, CAB, CBA, then, in the triangle DAB, we shall have given the side AB and all the angles to find BD; also, in the triangle ABC, we shall have one side and all the angles to find BC; and then, in the triangle BCD, we shall have two sides, BD, BC, with the included angle, to find DC.

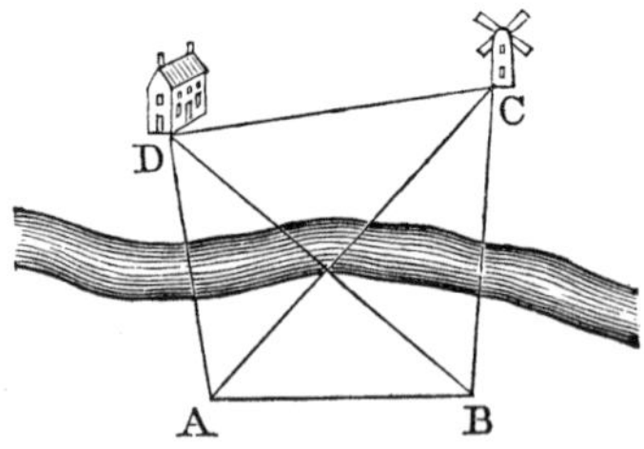

Ex. 1. Wanting to know the distance between a house and a mill, which were separated from me by a river, I measured a base-line, AB, 300 yards, and found the angle CAB=58° 20′, CAD=37°, ABD=53° 30′, DBC=45° 15′. What is the distance of the house from the mill? *Ans.*, 479.80 yards.

Ex. 2. Wanting to know the distance between two inaccessible objects, C and D, I measured a base-line, AB, 28.76 rods, and found the angle CAB=33°, CAD=66°, DBA=59° 45′, and DBC=76°. What is the distance from C to D?

Ans., 97.696 rods.

THE DETERMINATION OF AREAS.

(151.) The *area* or *content* of a tract of land is the *horizontal* surface included within its boundaries.

When the surface of the ground is broken and uneven, it is very difficult to ascertain exactly its actual surface. Hence it has been agreed to refer every surface to a horizontal plane; and for this reason, in measuring the boundary lines, it is necessary to reduce them all to horizontal lines.

The measuring unit of surfaces chiefly employed by surveyors is the *acre*, or ten square chains.

One quarter of an acre is called a rood.

Since a chain is four rods in length, a square chain contains sixteen square rods; and an acre, or ten square chains, contains 160 square rods. Square rods are called *perches*. The area of a field is usually expressed in acres, roods, and perches, designated by the letters A., R., P.

When the lengths of the bounding lines of a field are given in chains and links, the area is obtained in square chains and square links. Now, since a link is $\frac{1}{100}$ of a chain, a square link will be $\frac{1}{100}\times\frac{1}{100}$ of a square chain; that is, $\frac{1}{10000}$ of a chain. Hence we have the following

TABLE.

1 square chain=10,000 square links.
1 acre=10 square chains=100,000 square links.
1 acre=4 roods=160 perches.

If, then, the linear dimensions are links, the area will be expressed in square links, and may be reduced to square chains by cutting off *four* places of decimals; if *five* places be cut off, the remaining figures will be *acres*. If the decimal part of an acre be multiplied by 4, it will give the roods, and the resulting decimal, multiplied by 40, will give the perches.

(152.) The *difference of latitude*, or the *northing* or *southing* of a line, is the distance that one end is further north or south than the other end.

Thus, if NS be a meridian passing through the end A of the line AB, and BC be perpendicular to NS, then is AC the difference of latitude, or northing of AB.

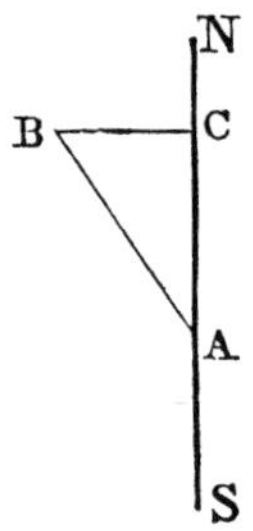

The *departure*, or the *easting* or *westing* of a line, is the distance that one end is further east or west than the other end.

Thus BC is the departure or westing of the line AB.

It is evident that the distance, difference of latitude, and departure form a right-angled triangle, of which the distance is the hypothenuse.

The meridian distance of a point is the perpendicular let fall from the given point on some assumed meridian, and is east or west according as this point lies on the east or west side of the meridian.

The meridian distance of a line is the distance of the middle point of that line from some assumed meridian.

(153.) When a piece of ground is to be surveyed, we begin at one corner of the field, and go entirely around the field, measuring the length of each of the sides with a chain, and their bearings with a compass.

Plotting a Survey.

When a field has been surveyed, it is easy to draw a plan of it on paper. For this purpose, draw a line to represent the meridian passing through the first station; then lay off an angle equal to the angle which the first side of the field makes with the meridian, and take the length of the side from a scale of equal parts. Through the extremity of this side draw a second meridian parallel to the first, and proceed in the same manner with the remaining sides. This method will be easily understood from an example.

EXAMPLE 1.

Draw a plan of a field from the following courses and distances, as given in the field-book.

Stations.	Bearings.	Distances.
1	N. 45° E.	9.30 chains.
2	S. 60° E.	11.85 "
3	S. 20° W.	5.30 "
4	S. 70° W.	10.90 "
5	N. 31° W.	9.40 "

Draw NS to represent a meridian line; in NS take any convenient point, as A, for the first station, and lay off an angle, NAB, equal to 45°, the bearing from A to B, which will give the direction from A to B. Then, from the scale of equal parts, make AB equal to 9.30, the length of the first side; this will give the station B. Through B draw a second meridian parallel to NS; lay off an angle of 60°, and make the line BC equal to 11.85. Proceed in the same manner with the other sides. If the survey is correct, and the plotting accurately performed, the end of the last side, EA, will fall on A, the place of beginning. This plot is made on a scale of 10 chains to an inch.

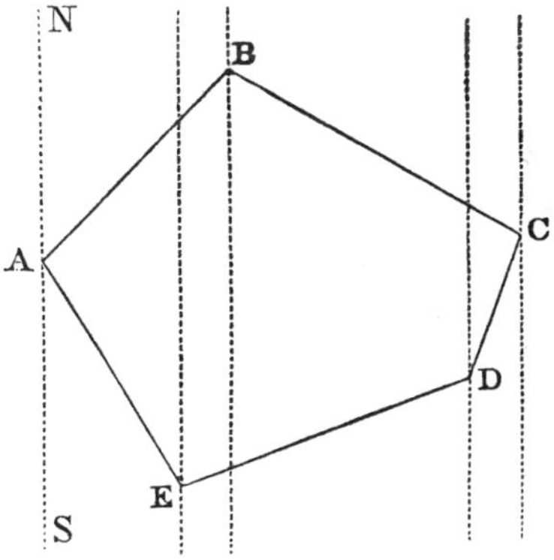

(154.) To avoid the inconvenience of drawing a meridian through each angle of the field, the sides may be laid down from the angles which they make with each other, instead of the angles which they make with the meridian. Reverse one of the bearings, if necessary, so that both bearings may run from the same angular point; then the angle which any two contiguous sides make with each other may be determined from the following

RULES.

1. If both courses are north or south, and both east or west, *subtract the less from the greater.*

2. If both are north or south, but one east and the other west, *add them together.*

3. If one is north and the other south, but both east or west, *subtract their sum from* 180°.

4. If one is north and the other south, one east and the other west, *subtract their difference from* 180°.

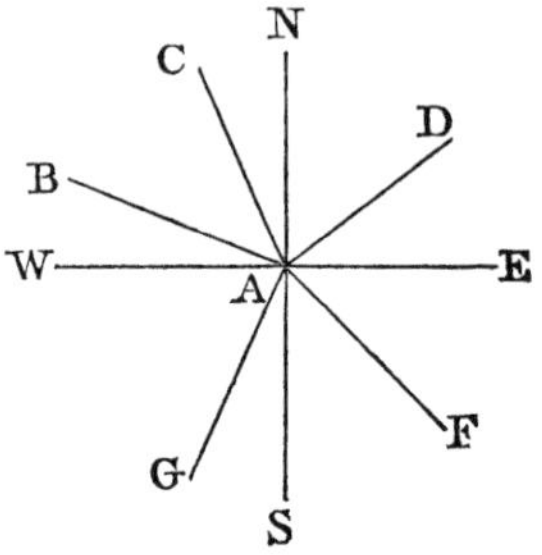

Thus the angle CAB is equal to NAB−NAC.

The angle CAD is equal to NAC +NAD.

The angle DAF is equal to 180° −(NAD+SAF).

The angle CAF is equal to 180° −(SAF−NAC).

In the preceding example we accordingly find the angle

ABC=105°. DEA=101°.
BCD=100°. EAB=104°.
CDE=130°.

With these angles the field may be plotted without drawing parallels.

EXAMPLE 2.

The following field notes are given to protract the survey:

Stations.	Bearings.	Distances.
1	N. 50° 30′ E.	16.50 chains.
2	S. 68° 15′ E.	14.20 "
3	S. 9° 45′ E.	8.45 "
4	S. 21° 0′ W.	6.84 "
5	S. 73° 30′ W.	12.31 "
6	N. 78° 15′ W.	9.76 "
7	N. 15° 30′ W.	11.55 "

THE TRAVERSE TABLE.

(155.) The accompanying traverse table shows the difference of latitude and the departure to four decimal places, for distances from 1 to 10, and for bearings from 0° to 90°, at intervals of 15′. If the bearing is less than 45°, the angle will be found on the left margin of one of the pages of the table, and the distance at the top or bottom of the page; the difference of latitude will be found in the column headed *Lat.* at the top of the page, and the departure in the column headed *Dep.* If the bearing is more than 45°, the angle will be found on the right margin, and the difference of latitude will be found in the column marked *Lat.* at the bottom of the page, and the departure in the other column. The latitudes and departures for different distances with the same bearing are proportional to the distances. Therefore the distances may be reckoned as tens, hundreds, or thousands, if the place of the decimal point in each departure and difference of latitude be changed accordingly.

Ex. 1. To find the latitude and departure for the course 45° and the distance 93.

Under distance 9 on page 141, and opposite 45°, will be found latitude 6.3640 and departure 6.3640. Hence, for distance 90, the latitude is 63.640, and adding the latitude for the distance 3, viz., 2.121, we find the latitude for distance 93 to be 65.761.

Ex. 2. To find the latitude and departure for the course 60° and the distance 11.85.

The latitude for	10	is	5.0000.	Departure	for	10	is	8.6603.
" " "	1	is	.5000.	"	"	1	is	.8660.
" " "	.8	is	.4000.	"	"	.8	is	.6928.
" " "	.05	is	.0250.	"	"	.05	is	.0433.
Latitude for	11.85	is	5.9250.	Depart.	for	11.85	is	10.2624.

Ex. 3. To find the latitude and departure for the course 20° and the distance 5.30.

Ans. Latitude 4.98, and departure 1.81.

The traverse table may be used not only for obtaining departure and difference of latitude, but for finding by inspection the sides and angles of any right-angled triangle; for the latitude and departure form the two legs of a right-angled triangle, of which the distance is the hypothenuse, and the course is one of the acute angles.

In this manner we find the latitude and departure for each side of the field given in Example 1, page 105, to be as in the following table:

	Courses.	Distances.	Latitude.		Departure.		Cor. Lat.	Cor. Dep.	Balanced.			
			N.	S.	E.	W.			N.	S.	E.	W.
1	N. 45° E.	9 30	6.58		6.58			+.01	6.58		6.59	
2	S. 60° E.	11.85		5.92	10.26		+.01	+.01		5.93	10.27	
3	S. 20° W.	5.30		4.98		1.81		−.01		4.98		1.80
4	S. 70° W.	10.90		3.73		10.24		−.01		3.73		10.23
5	N. 31° W.	9 40	8.06			4.84		−.01	8.06			4.83
	Perimeter	46.75	14 64	14.63	16.84	16.89			14.64	14.64	16 86	16.86

(156.) When a field has been correctly surveyed, and the latitudes and departures accurately calculated, the sum of the northings should be equal to the sum of the southings, and the sum of the eastings equal to the sum of the westings. If the northings do not agree with the southings, and the eastings with the westings, there must be an error either in the survey or in the calculation. In the preceding example, the northings exceed the southings by one link, and the westings exceed the eastings by five links. Small errors of this kind are unavoidable; but when the error does not exceed one link to a distance of three or four chains, it is customary to distribute the error among the sides by the following proportion:

As the perimeter of the field,
Is to the length of one of the sides,
So is the error in latitude or departure,
To the correction corresponding to that side.

This correction, when applied to a column in which the sum of the numbers is too small, is to be *added;* but if the sum of the numbers is too great, it is to be *subtracted.*

We thus obtain the corrections in columns 8 and 9 of the preceding table; and applying these corrections, we obtain the *balanced* latitudes and departures, in which the sums of the northings and southings are equal, and also those of the eastings and westings.

As the computations are generally carried to but two decimal places, the corrections of the latitudes and departures are only required to the nearest link, and these corrections may often be found by mere inspection without stating a formal proportion. Thus, in the preceding example, since the departures require a correction of five links, and the field has five sides which are not very unequal, it is obvious that we must make a correction of one link on each side.

It is the opinion of some surveyors that when the error in latitude or departure exceeds one link for every five chains of the perimeter, the field should be resurveyed; but most surveyors do not attain to this degree of accuracy. The error, however, should never exceed one link to a distance of two or three chains.

(157.) *To find the area of the field.*

Let ABCDE be the field to be measured. Through A, the most western station, draw the meridian NS, and upon it let fall the perpendiculars BF, CG, DH, EI.

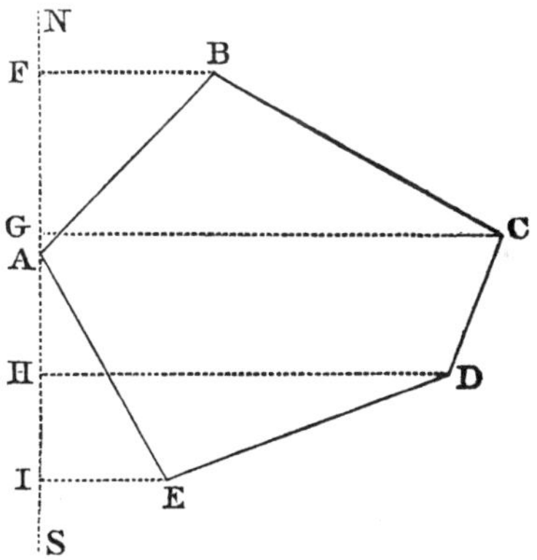

Then the area of the required field is equal to FBCDEI−(ABF+AEI).

But FBCDEI is equal to the sum of the three trapezoids FBCG, GCDH, HDEI.

Also, if the sum of the parallel sides FB, GC be multiplied by FG, it will give twice the area of FBCG (Art. 87). The sum of the sides GC, DH, multiplied by GH, gives twice the area of GCDH; and the sum of HD, IE, multiplied by HI, gives twice the area of HDEI.

Now BF is the departure of the first side, GC is the sum of the departures of the first and second sides, HD is the algebraic sum of the three preceding departures, IE is the algebraic sum of the four preceding departures. Then the sum of the parallel sides of the trapezoids is obtained by adding together the preceding meridian distances two by two; and if these sums are multiplied by FG, GH, &c., which are the corresponding latitudes, it will give the double areas of the trapezoids.

(158.) It is most convenient to reduce all these operations to a tabular form, according to the following

RULE.

Having arranged the balanced latitudes and departures in

their appropriate columns, draw a meridian through the most eastern or western station of the survey, and, calling this the first station, form a column of double meridian distances.

The double meridian distance of the first side is equal to its departure; and the double meridian distance of any side is equal to the double meridian distance of the preceding side, plus its departure, plus the departure of the side itself.

Multiply each double meridian distance by its corresponding northing or southing, and place the product in the column of north or south areas. The difference between the sum of the north areas and the sum of the south areas will be double the area of the field.

It must be borne in mind that by the term *plus* in this rule is to be understood the algebraic sum. Hence, when the double meridian distance and the departure are both east or both west, they must be added together; but if one be east and the other west, the one must be subtracted from the other.

The double meridian distance of the last side should always be equal to the departure for that side. This coincidence affords a check against any mistake in forming the column of double meridian distances.

The preceding example will then be completed as follows:

	N.	S.	E.	W.	D.M.D.	N. Areas.	S. Areas.
1	6.58		6.59		6.59	43.3622	
2		5.93	10.27		23.45		139.0585
3		4.98		1.80	31.92		158.9616
4		3.73		10.23	19.89		74.1897
5	8.06			4.83	4.83	38.9298	
						82.2920	372.2098

Twice the figure FBCDEI is 372.2098 square chains.
Twice the figure FBAEI is 82.2920 "
The difference is . . . . 289.9178 "

Therefore the area of the field is 144.9589 square chains, or 14.49589 acres, which is equal to 14 acres, 1 rood, 39 perches.

Ex. 2. It is required to find the contents of a tract of land of which the following are the field notes:

Stations.	Bearings.	Distances.
1	N. 50° 30′ E.	16.50 chains.
2	S. 68° 15′ E.	14.20 "
3	S. 9° 45′ E.	8.45 "
4	S. 21° 0′ W.	6.84 "
5	S. 73° 30′ W.	12.31 "
6	N. 78° 15′ W.	9.76 "
7	N. 17° 0′ W.	11.64 "

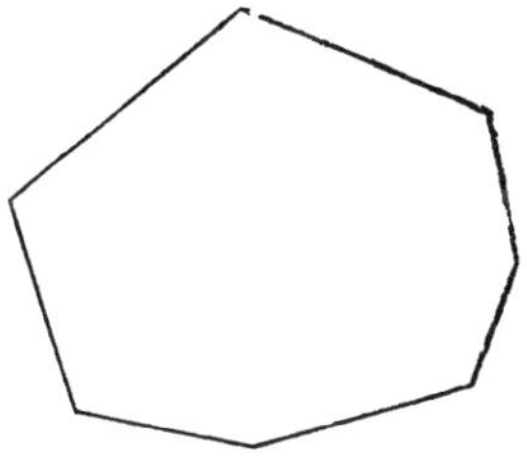

Calculation.

	Courses.	Dist.	Dif. Lat.		Departure.		Cor.	Balanced.				D.M.D.	N. Areas.	S. Areas.
			N.	S.	E.	W.		N.	S.	E.	W.			
1	N. 50° 30′ E.	16.50	10.50		12.73		.03	10.47		12.70		12.70	132.9690	
2	S. 68° 15′ E.	14.20		5.26	13.19		.03		5.29	13.16		38.56		203.9824
3	S. 9° 45′ E.	8.45		8.33	1.43		.01		8.34	1.42		53.14		443.1876
4	S. 21° 0′ W.	6.84		6.39		2.45	.01		6.40		2.46	52.10		333.4400
5	S. 73° 30′ W.	12.31		3.50		11.80	.02		3.52		11.82	37.82		133.1264
6	N. 78° 15′ W.	9.76	1.99			9.56	.02	1.97			9.58	16.42	32.3474	
7	N. 17° 0′ W.	11.64	11.13			3.40	.02	11.11			3.42	3.42	37.9962	
		79.70	23.62	23.48	27.35	27.21		23.55	23.55	27.28	27.28		203.3126	1113.7364
			Error .14		Error .14									203.3126

2)910.4238

Ans., 45 A., 2 R., 3 P. . . 455.2119.

Ex. 3. Required the area of a tract of land of which the following are the field notes:

Stations.	Bearings.	Distances.
1	N. 58° 45′ E.	19.84 chains.
2	N. 39° 30′ E.	10.45 "
3	S. 45° 15′ E.	37.26 "
4	S. 52° 30′ W.	21.53 "
5	S. 34° 0′ E.	9.12 "
6	S. 66° 15′ W.	27.69 "
7	N. 12° 45′ E.	24.31 "
8	N. 48° 15′ W.	24.60 "

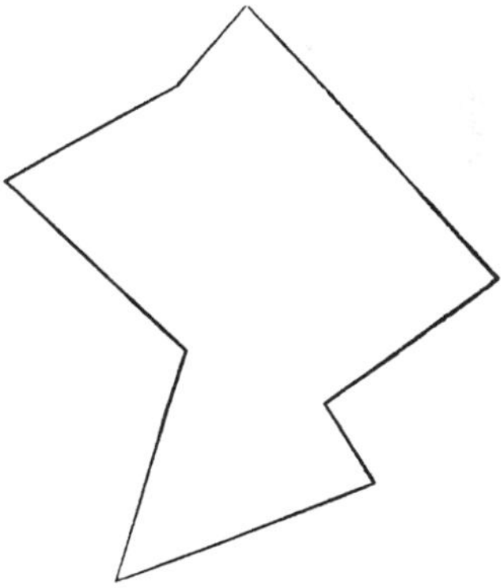

Ans., 130 A., 2 R., 23 P.

Ex. 4. Required the area of a piece of land from the following field notes:

Stations.	Bearings.	Distances.
1	N. 5° 15′ E.	15.17 chains.
2	N. 45° 45′ E.	16.83 "
3	N. 32° 0′ W.	14.26 "
4	N. 88° 30′ E.	19.54 "
5	S. 28° 15′ E.	17.92 "
6	S. 40° 45′ W.	9.71 "
7	S. 31° 30′ E.	22.65 "
8	S. 14° 0′ W.	18.39 "
9	S. 82° 45′ W.	24.80 "
10	N. 23° 15′ W.	26.31 "

Ans., 173 A., 0 R., 23 P.

Ex. 5. Required the area of a field from the following notes:

Stations.	Bearings.	Distances.
1	N. 32° 15′ E.	28.74 chains.
2	N. 17° 45′ E.	21.59 "
3	S. 81° 30′ E.	13.38 "
4	S. 9° 45′ W.	11.92 "
5	S. 43° 0′ E.	19.65 "
6	N. 25° 30′ E.	17.26 "
7	S. 78° 15′ E.	18.87 "
8	S. 5° 45′ W.	31.41 "
9	S. 37° 30′ W.	26.13 "
10	N. 69° 0′ W.	23.86 "
11	S. 74° 15′ W.	20.91 "
12	N. 27° 30′ W.	23.20 "

Ans., 304 A., 2 R., 9 P.

Ex. 6. Required the area of a field from the following notes:

Stations.	Bearings.	Distances.
1	N. 36° 15′ E.	24.73 chains.
2	N. 7° 45′ E.	11.58 "
3	N. 79° 30′ E.	15.39 "
4	S. 86° 45′ E.	20.56 "
5	S. 12° 15′ W.	18.14 "
6	S. 25° 0′ E.	21.92 "
7	S. 58° 30′ W.	29.27 "
8	N. 34° 0′ W.	19.81 "
9	N. 81° 15′ W.	21.24 "

Ans., 179 A., 1 R., 6 P.

(159) The field notes from which the area is to be computed may be imperfect. There may be obstacles which prevent the measuring of one side, or the notes may be defaced so as to render some of the numbers illegible. If the bearings and lengths of all the sides of a field *except one* are given, the remaining side may easily be found by calculation. For the difference between the sum of the northings and the sum of the southings of the given sides will be the northing or southing of the remaining side; and the difference between the sum of the eastings and the sum of the westings of the given sides will be the easting or westing of the remaining side. Having, then, the difference of latitude and departure of the required side, its length and direction are easily found by Trigonometry (Art. 47).

Ex. Given the bearings and lengths of the sides of a tract of land as follows:

Stations.	Bearings.	Distances.
1	N. 18° 15′ E.	8.93 chains.
2	N. 79° 45′ E.	15.64 "
3	S. 25° 0′ E.	14.27 "
4	*Unknown.*	*Unknown.*
5	N. 87° 30′ W.	18.52 chains.
6	N. 41° 15′ W.	12.18 "

Required the bearing and distance of the fourth side.

Ans., S. 15° 33′ E., distance 8.62 chains.

(160.) There is another method of finding the area of a field which may be practiced when great accuracy is not required It consists in first drawing a plan of the field, as in Art. 153 then dividing the field into triangles by diagonal lines, and measuring the bases and perpendiculars of the triangles upon the same scale of equal parts by which the plot was drawn. Thus, if we take Ex. 1, and draw the diagonals AC, AD, the field will be divided into three triangles, whose area is easily found when we know

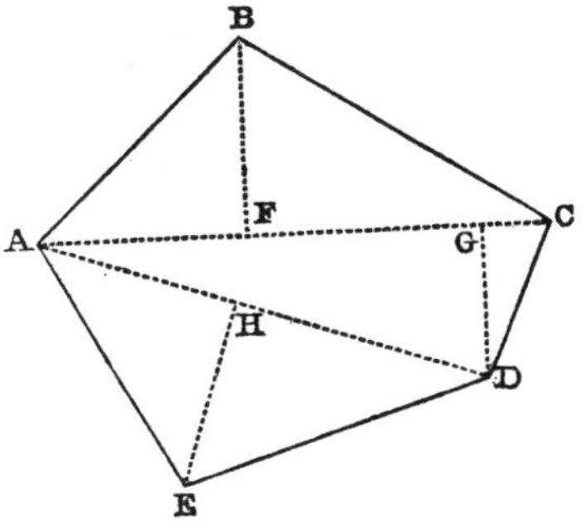

the diagonals AC, AD, and the perpendiculars BF, DG, EH. The diagonal AC is found by measurement upon the scale of equal parts to be 16.87; the diagonal AD is 15.67; the perpendicular BF is 6.30; DG is 4.92; and EH is 6.42. Hence

the triangle	ABC=16.87×3.15=	53.14
" "	ADC=16.87×2.46=	41.50
" "	ADE=15.67×3.21=	50.30
the figure ABCDE	=	144.94 sq. chains.

This method of finding the area of a field is very expeditious, and when the plot is carefully drawn, may afford results sufficiently precise for many purposes.

(161.) *To survey an irregular boundary by means of offsets.*

When the boundaries of a field are very irregular, like a river or lake shore, it is generally best to run a straight line, coming as near as is convenient to the true boundary, and measure the perpendicular distances of the prominent points of the boundary from this line.

Let ABCD be a piece of land to be surveyed; the land being bounded on the east by a lake, and on the west by a creek We select stations A, B, C, D, so as to form a polygon which shall embrace most of the proposed field, and find its area. We then measure perpendiculars *aa'*, *bb'*, *cc'*, &c., as also the distances A*a*, *ab*, *bc*, &c. Then, considering the spaces A*aa'*, *abb'a'*, &c., as triangles or trapezoids, their area may be computed; and, adding these areas to the figure ABCD, we shall obtain the area of the proposed field nearly.

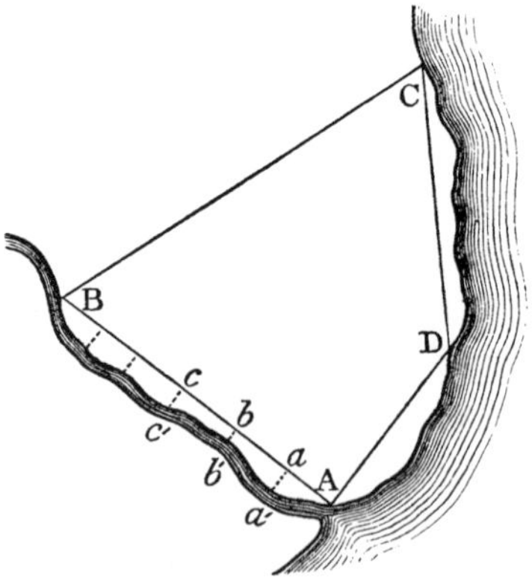

(162.) *To determine the bearing and distance from one point to another by means of a series of triangles.*

When it is required to find the distance between two points remote from each other, we form a series of triangles such that the first and second triangles may have one side in common; the second and third, also, one side in common; the third and fourth, &c. We then measure one side of the first triangle for a *base line*, and all the angles in each of the triangles. These data are sufficient to determine the length of the sides of each triangle; for in the first triangle we have one side and the angles to find the other sides. When these are found, we shall have one side and all the angles of a second triangle to find the other sides. In the same manner we may calculate the dimensions of the third triangle, the fourth, and so on. We shall illustrate this method by an example taken from the Coast Survey of the United States.

The object here is to make a survey of Chesapeake Bay and its vicinity; to determine with the utmost precision the position of the most prominent points of the country, to which subordinate points may be referred, and thus a perfect map of the country be obtained. Accordingly, a level spot of ground was selected on the eastern side of the bay, on Kent Island, where a base line, AB, of more than five miles in length, was measured with every precaution. A station, C, was also selected upon the other side of the bay, near Annapolis, so situated that it was visible from A and B. The three angles of the triangle ABC were then measured with a large theodolite, after which the length of BC may be computed. A fourth station, D, is now taken on the western shore of the bay, visible from C and B, and all the angles of the triangle BCD are measured, when the line BD can be computed. A fifth station, E, is now taken on an island near the eastern shore, visible both from B and D, and all the angles of the triangle BDE are measured, when DE can be computed. Also, all the angles of the triangle DEF are measured, and EF is computed. Then all the angles of the triangle EFG are meas-

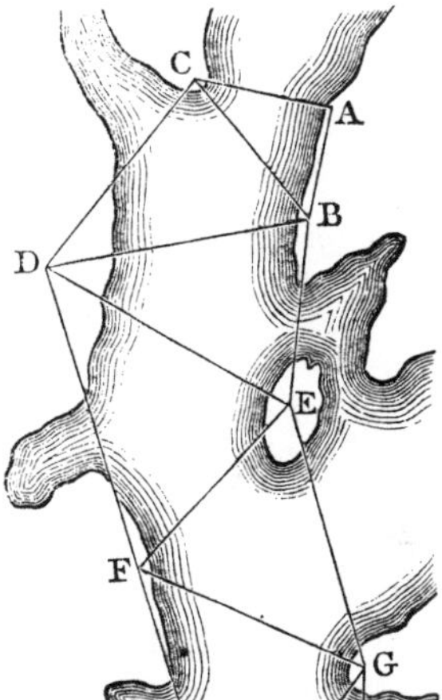

ured, and FG is computed. So, also, all the angles of the triangle FGH are measured, and GH is computed; and thus a chain of triangles may be extended along the entire coast of the United States. To test the accuracy of the work, it is common to measure a side in one of the triangles remote from the first base, and compare its measured length with that deduced by computation from the entire series of triangles. This line is called a *base of verification.* Such a base has been measured on Long Island; and, indeed, several bases have been measured on different points of the coast. These are all connected by a triangulation, and thus the length of a side in any triangle may be deduced from more than one base line, and the agreement of these results is a test of the accuracy of the entire work. Thus the length of one of the sides of a triangle which was twelve miles, as deduced from the Kent Island base, differed only twenty inches from that derived from the Long Island base, distant two hundred miles.

The superiority of this method of surveying arises from the circumstance that it is necessary to measure but a small number of base lines along a coast of a thousand or more miles in extent; and for these the most favorable ground may be selected any where in the vicinity of the system of triangles. All the other quantities measured are angles; and the precision of these measurements is not at all impaired by the inequalities of the surface of the ground. Indeed, mountainous countries afford peculiar facilities for a trigonometrical survey, since they present heights of ground visible to a great distance, and thus permit the formation of triangles of very large dimensions.

(163.) *To divide an irregular piece of land into any two given parts.*

We first run a line, by estimation, as near as may be to the required division line, and compute the area thus cut off. If this is found too large or too small, we add or subtract a triangle, or some other figure, as the case may require. Suppose it is required to divide the field ABCDEFGHI into two equal parts, by a line IL, running from the corner I to the opposite side CD. We first draw a line from I to D, and compute the area of the part DEFGHI; and, knowing the area of the entire field, we learn the area which must be contained in the triangle DIL, in order that IL may divide the field into two equal parts. Having the bearings and distances of the sides DE, EF, &c., we can compute the bearing and distance of DI. Thus the angle IDK is known; and, having the hypothenuse ID, we can compute the length of the perpendicular IK let fall on CD. Now the base of a triangle must be equal to its area divided by half the altitude. Hence, if we divide the area of the triangle DIL by half of IK, it will give DL.

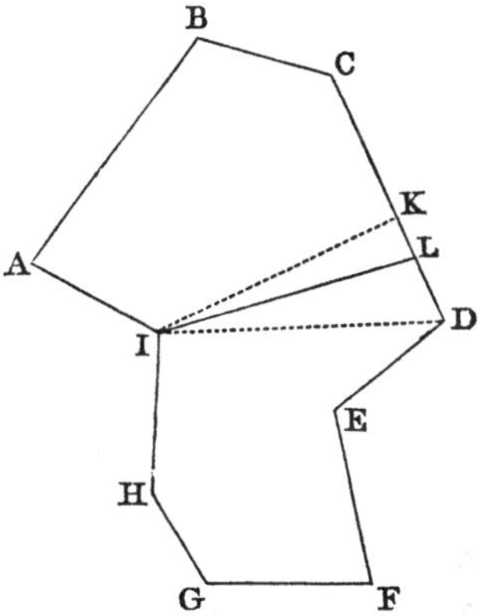

In a similar manner we might proceed if it was required to divide a tract of land into any two given parts.

Variation of the Needle.

(164.) The line indicated by a magnetic needle, when freely supported and allowed to come to a state of rest, is called the *magnetic meridian.* This does not generally coincide with the *astronomical meridian*, which is a true north and south line.

The angle which the magnetic meridian makes with the true meridian is called the *variation of the needle*, and is said to be east or west, according as the north end of the needle points east or west of the north pole of the earth.

The variation of the needle is different in different parts of the earth. In some parts of the United States it is 10° west, and in others 10° east, while at other places the variation has every intermediate value. Even at the same place, the variation does not remain constant for any length of time. Hence it is necessary frequently to determine the amount of the variation, which is easily done when we know the position of the true meridian. The latter can only be determined by astronomical observations. The best method is by observations of the pole star. If this star were exactly at the pole, it would always be on the meridian; but, being at a distance of about a degree and a half from the pole, it revolves about the pole in a small circle in a little less than 24 hours. In about six hours from its passing the meridian above the pole, it attains its greatest distance west of the meridian; in about six hours more it is on the meridian beneath the pole; and in about six hours more it attains its greatest distance east of the meridian. If the star can be observed at the instant when it is on the meridian, either above or below the pole, a true north and south line may be obtained.

(165.) The following table shows the time of the pole star's passing the meridian above the pole for every fifth day of the year:

	1st Day.	6th Day.	11th Day.	16th Day.	21st Day.	26th Day.
	h. m.	h. m.	h. m.	h. m.	h. m.	h. m.
January . . .	6 20 P.M.	6 0 P.M.	5 41 P.M.	5 21 P.M.	5 1 P.M.	4 42 P.M.
February. . .	4 18 "	3 58 "	3 39 "	3 19 "	3 0 "	2 40 "
March	2 28 "	2 8 "	1 49 "	1 29 "	1 9 "	0 50 "
April	0 26 "	0 7 "	11 47 A.M.	11 27 A.M.	11 8 A.M.	10 48 A.M.
May	10 28 A.M.	10 9 A.M.	9 49 "	9 29 "	9 9 "	8 50 "
June	8 26 "	8 7 "	7 47 "	7 27 "	7 8 "	6 48 "
July	6 28 "	6 9 "	5 49 "	5 29 "	5 10 "	4 50 "
August	4 27 "	4 7 "	3 47 "	3 27 "	3 8 "	2 48 "
September . .	2 25 "	2 5 "	1 45 "	1 26 "	1 6 "	0 46 "
October . . .	0 26 "	0 7 "	11 43 P.M.	11 24 P.M.	11 4 P.M.	10 44 P.M.
November . .	10 21 P.M.	10 1 P.M.	9 41 "	9 22 "	9 2 "	8 42 "
December . .	8 23 "	8 3 "	7 43 "	7 24 "	7 4 "	6 44 "

If the pole star passes the meridian in the daytime, it can not be observed without a good telescope; but $11^{h.}\ 58^{m.}$ after the dates in the above table, the star will be on the meridian *below* the pole, and during the whole year, except in summer, the pole star may be seen with the naked eye on the meridian either above or below the pole. These observations are best made with a theodolite, but they may be made with a common compass. At $5^{h.}\ 59^{m.}$ after the dates in the above table, the star will have attained its greatest distance west of the meridian; and $5^{h.}\ 59^{m.}$ before these dates, it will be at its greatest distance east of the meridian. In summer, therefore, we may observe the greatest eastern elongation of the pole star, at which time the star is 1° 55′ east of the true meridian for all places in the neighborhood of New York. Making this allowance, a true meridian is easily obtained; after which, the variation of the needle is determined by placing a compass upon this line, turning the sights in the same direction, and noting the angle shown by the needle.

The following table shows the angle which the plane of the

meridian makes with a vertical plane passing through the pole star, when at its greatest eastern or western elongation, for any latitude from 30° to 44°.

Lat. 30°	Lat. 32°	Lat. 34°	Lat. 36°	Lat. 38°	Lat. 40°	Lat. 42°	Lat. 44°
1° 41′	1° 43′	1° 45′	1° 48′	1° 51′	1° 54′	1° 58′	2° 2′

(166.) The variation of the needle, in 1840, for several parts of the United States, was as follows:

Burlington, Vt. . .	9° 27′ W.	Buffalo, N. Y. . .	1° 37′ W.
Boston, Mass. . .	9° 12′ W.	Cleveland, Ohio .	0° 19′ E.
Albany, N. Y. . .	6° 58′ W.	Detroit, Mich. . .	1° 56′ E.
New Haven, Ct. .	6° 13′ W.	Charleston, S. C. .	2° 44′ E.
New York City .	5° 34′ W.	Cincinnati, Ohio .	4° 46′ E.
Philadelphia . . .	4° 8′ W.	Mobile, Ala. . . .	7° 5′ E.
Washington City .	1° 20′ W.	St. Louis, Mo. . .	8° 37′ E.

Since 1840, the variation in New England has increased about five minutes annually; in New York and Pennsylvania it has increased from three to four minutes annually. In the Western States it decreases at about the same rate, and in the Southern States it decreases about two minutes annually.

LEVELING.

(167.) *Leveling* is the art of determining the difference of level between two or more places.

The surface of an expanse of tranquil water, or any surface parallel to it, is called a *level surface.* Points situated in a level surface are said to be on the *same level*, and a line traced on such a surface is called *a line of true level.*

On account of the globular figure of the earth, a level surface is not a plane surface. It is nearly spherical; and in the common operations of leveling it is regarded as perfectly so. Hence every point of a level surface is regarded as at the same distance from the center of the earth; and the *difference of level* of two places is the difference between their distances from the center.

A line of *apparent level* is a straight line tangent to the surface of the earth.

Thus, if AB represent the surface of the ocean, the two places A and B are said to be on the same level; but if AD be drawn tangent to the arc AB at A, then AD is a line of apparent level.

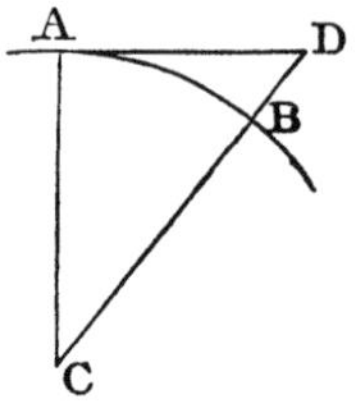

This is the line which is indicated by a leveling instrument placed at A. The theodolite may be employed for tracing horizontal lines; but if nothing further were required, there would be no occasion for graduated circles, and several parts of the theodolite might be dispensed with. A leveling instrument, therefore, usually consists of a large spirit level attached to a telescope, mounted upon a stand in a manner similar to the theodolite.

(168.) The surveyor should also be provided with a pair of *leveling staves*. A leveling staff consists of a rectangular bar of wood six feet in length, divided to inches and sometimes tenths of an inch, and having a groove running its entire length. A smaller staff of the same length, called a *slide*, also divided into inches, is inserted in this groove, and moves freely along it.

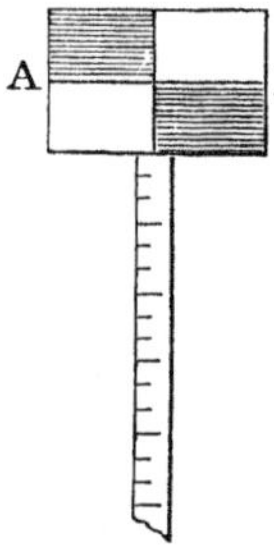

At the upper end of the slide is a rectangular board called a *vane*, AB, about six inches wide. The vane is divided into four equal parts by two lines, one horizontal and the other vertical. Two opposite parts of the vane are painted white, and the other two black, in order that they may be distinguished at a great distance.

To find the difference of level between any two points.

(169.) Set up the leveling staves perpendicular to the horizon, and at equal distances from the leveling instrument. Having adjusted the level by means of the proper screws, turn the telescope to one of the staves, and direct an assistant to slide up the vane until the line AB coincides with the center of the telescope, and note the height of this line from the ground. Turn the telescope to the other staff, and repeat the same operation. Level in the same manner from the second station to the third, from the third to the fourth, &c. Then the difference between the sum of the heights at the back stations and at the forward stations will be equal to the difference of level between the first station and the last.

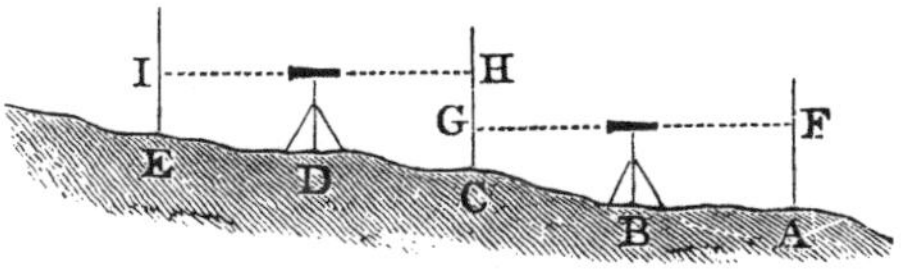

If we wish to level from A to E, we set up the staves at a convenient distance, AC, and midway between them place the level B. Observe where the line of level, FG, cuts the rods, and note the heights AF, CG. Their difference is the difference of level between the first and second stations. Take up the level and place it at D, midway between the rods C and E, and observe where the line of level, HI, cuts the rods, and note the heights CH, EI.

Then FA−CG=the ascent from A to C,

and CH−EI =the ascent from C to E.

Therefore (FA+CH)−(CG+EI)=the entire ascent from A to E; and in the same manner we may find the difference of level for any distance; that is, *the difference between the sum of the heights at the back stations and at the forward stations is equal to the difference of level between the first station and the last.*

(170.) The following is a copy of the field notes for running a level from A to E:

	Back sights.		*Fore sights.*	
	Feet.	Inches.	Feet.	Inches.
	0	4	3	2
	5	10	5	7
	4	2	4	3
	5	6	1	2
	4	11	3	2
	4	7	1	3
	6	1	2	0
Sum	31	5	Sum 20	7

The back sights being greater in amount than the forward sights, it is evident that E is higher than A by 10 feet 10 inches.

The heights indicated by the leveling staves are sometimes read off by the assistant, but it is better for the observer to read off the quantities himself through the telescope of his leveling instrument. This may easily be done provided the graduation of the staff is perfectly distinct; and in that case it is only necessary to rely upon the assistant to hold the staff perpendicularly. To enable him to do this, a small plummet is suspended in a groove cut in the side of the staff.

(171.) It must be observed that the lines GF, HI are lines of *apparent* level, and not of *true* level; nevertheless, we shall obtain the true difference of level between A and E by this method if the leveling instrument is placed midway between the leveling staves, because the points G and F will in that case be at equal distances from the earth's center. If the level is not placed midway between the staves, then we must apply a correction for the difference between the true and apparent level.

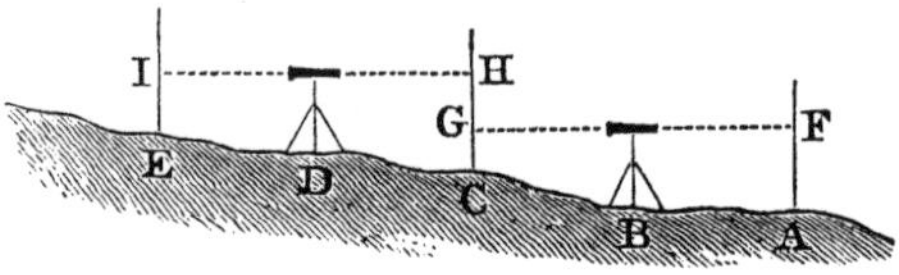

(172.) *To find the difference between the true and apparent level.*

Let C be the center of the earth, AB a portion of its surface, and AD a tangent to the earth's surface at A; then BD is the difference between the true and apparent level for the distance AD.

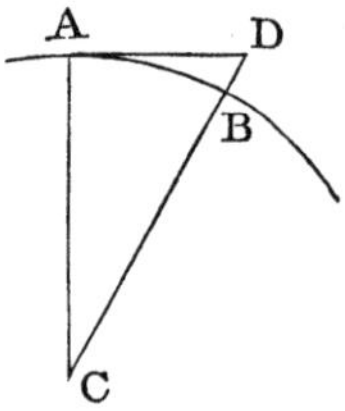

Now, by Geom., Prop. 11, B. IV.,

$$CD^2 = AC^2 + AD^2.$$

Hence $$CD = \sqrt{AC^2 + AD^2},$$

and $$BD = \sqrt{AC^2 + AD^2} - BC.$$

If we put $R = BC$, the radius of the earth,

$d = AD$,

and $h = BD$, the difference between the true and apparent level, we shall have

$$h = \sqrt{R^2 + d^2} - R;$$

that is, to find the difference between the true and apparent level for any distance, *add the square of the distance to the square of the earth's radius, extract the square root of the sum, and subtract the radius of the earth.*

If BD represent a mountain, or other elevated object, then AD will represent the distance at which it can be seen in consequence of the curvature of the earth.

Ex. 1. If the diameter of the earth be 7912 miles, and if Mount Ætna can be seen at sea 126 miles, what is its height?

Ans., 2 miles.

Ex. 2. If a straight line from the summit of Chimborazo touch the surface of the ocean at the distance of 179 miles, what is the height of the mountain? *Ans.*, 4.05 miles.

From the preceding formula we obtain

$$R^2+d^2=(R+h)^2$$
$$=R^2+2Rh+h^2,$$

that is, $$d^2=2Rh+h^2.$$

But in the common operations of leveling, h is very small in comparison with the radius of the earth, and h^2 is very small in comparison with $2Rh$. If we neglect the term h^2, we have

$$d^2=2Rh;$$

whence $$h=\frac{d^2}{2R};$$

that is, *the difference between the true and apparent level is nearly equal to the square of the distance divided by the diameter of the earth.*

Ex. 1. What is the difference between the true and apparent level for one mile, supposing the diameter of the earth to be 7912 miles? *Ans.*, 8.008 inches, or 8 inches nearly.

Ex. 2. What is the difference between the true and apparent level for half a mile? *Ans.*, 2 inches.

In the equation $h=\frac{d^2}{2R}$, since 2R is a constant quantity, h varies as d^2; that is, *the difference between the true and apparent level varies as the square of the distance.*

Hence, the difference for 1 mile being 8 inches,

						Ft.	In.
the difference for	2 miles is	$8\times2^2=$	32	inches	=	2	8.
"	" 3	"	$8\times3^2=$	72 "	=	6	0.
"	" 4	"	$8\times4^2=$	128 "	=	10	8.
"	" 5	"	$8\times5^2=$	200 "	=	16	8.
"	" 6	"	$8\times6^2=$	288 "	=	24	0, &c.

Topographical Maps.

(173.) It is sometimes required to determine and represent upon a map the undulations and inequalities in the surface of a tract of land. Such a map should give a complete view of the ground, so as to afford the means for an appropriate location of buildings or extensive works. For this purpose, we suppose the surface of the ground to be intersected by a number of horizontal planes, at equal distances from each other. The lines in which these planes meet the surface of the ground, being transferred to paper, will indicate the variations in the inclination of the ground; for it is obvious that the curves will be nearer together or further apart, according as the ascent is steep or gentle.

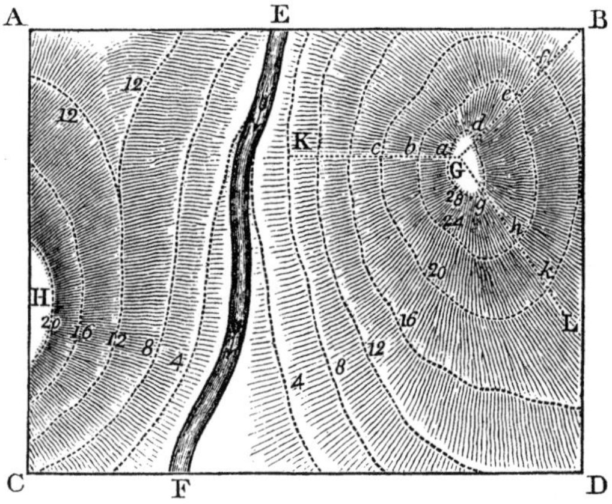

Thus, let ABCD be a tract of broken ground, divided by a stream, EF, the ascent being rapid on each bank, the ground swelling to a hill at G, and also at H. It is required to represent these inequalities upon paper, so as to give an exact idea of the face of the ground. The lowest point of the ground is at F. Suppose the tract to be intersected by a horizontal plane four feet above F, and let this plane intersect the surface of the ground in the undulating lines marked 4, one on each side of the stream. Suppose a second horizontal plane to be drawn eight feet above F, and let it intersect the surface of the ground in the lines marked 8. Let other horizontal planes be drawn at a distance of 12, 16, 20, 24, &c., feet above the point F. The projection of these lines of level upon paper shows at a glance the outline of the tract. We perceive that on the right bank of the stream the ground rises more rapidly on the upper than on the lower portion of the map, as is shown by the lines of level being nearer to one another. On the right bank of the stream the ascent is uninterrupted until we reach G, which is the summit of the hill. Beyond G the ground descends again toward B. On the left bank of the stream the ground rises to H; but toward A the level line of 12 feet divides into two branches, and between them the ground is nearly level.

(174.) The surveys requisite for the construction of such a map may be made with a theodolite or common level.

The object is to trace a series of level lines upon the surface of the ground. For this purpose we may select any point on the surface of a hill, place the level there, and run a level line around the hill, measuring the distances, and also the angles, at every change of direction. We may then select a second point at any convenient distance above or below the former, and trace a second level line around the hill, and so on for as many curves as may be thought necessary. Such a method, however, would not always be most convenient in practice.

(175.) The following method may sometimes be preferable: Set up the level on the summit of the hill at G, and fix the vane on the leveling staff at an elevation of four feet in addition to the height of the telescope above the ground. Then direct an assistant to carry the leveling staff, holding it in a vertical position, toward K, till he arrives at a point, as *a*, where the vane appears to coincide with the cross wires of the telescope. This will determine one point of the curve line four feet below G. The assistant may then proceed to the line GB, and afterward to GL, moving backward or forward in each of those directions till he finds points, as *d* and *g*, at which the vane coincides with the cross wires of the telescope. The horizontal distance between G and *a*, G and *d*, G and *g*, must then be measured.

If the leveling staff is sufficiently long, the vane may be fixed on it at the height of eight feet, in addition to the height of the telescope at G; and the assistant, placing himself in the directions GK, GB, GL, must move till the vane appears to coincide with the cross wires as before. The horizontal distances *ab*, *de*, *gh*, must then be measured, and stakes driven into the ground at *b*, *e*, and *h*.

The level must now be removed to *b;* and the vane being fixed on the staff at a height equal to four feet, together with the height of the instrument from the ground at *b*, the assistant must proceed in the direction *b*K, and stop at *c* when the vane coincides with the cross wires; then the horizontal distance of *c* from *b* must be measured. In a like manner, the operations may be continued from *b* or *c* as far as necessary toward K; then, commencing at *e*, and afterward at *h*, they may be continued in the same way toward B and L respectively.

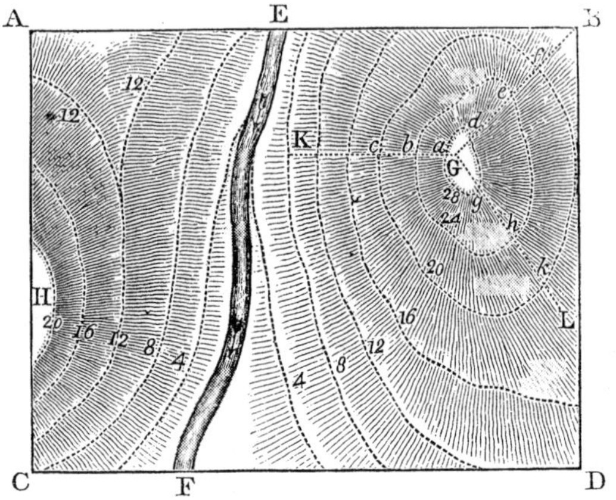

The angles which the directions GK, GB, GL make with the magnetic meridian being found with the compass, these directions may be represented on paper. Then the measured distances G*a*, *ab*, &c.; G*d*, *de*, &c.; G*g*, *gh*, &c., being set off on those lines of direction, curves drawn through *a*, *d*, *g*; *b*, *e*, *h*; *c*, *f*, *k*, &c., will show the contour of the hill.

The map is shaded so as to indicate the hills and slopes by drawing fine lines, as in the figure, perpendicular to the horizontal curves.

(176.) Another method, which may often be more convenient than either of the preceding, is as follows: From the summit of the hill measure any line, as GK, and at convenient points of this line let stakes be driven, and their distances from G be carefully measured. Then determine the difference of level of all these points; and if the assumed points do not fall upon the horizontal curves which are required to be delineated, we may, by supposing the slope to be uniform from one stake to another, compute by a proportion the points where the horizontal curves for intervals of four feet intersect the line GK. The same may be done for the lines GB and GL, and for other lines, if they should be thought necessary.

(177.) If the surface of the ground is gently undulating, it may be more convenient to run across the tract a number of lines parallel to one another. Drive stakes at each extremity ot these lines, and also at all the points along them where there is any material change in the inclination of the ground, and find the difference of level between all these stakes, and their distances from each other. Then, if we wish to draw upon a map the level lines at intervals of 4, 6, or 10 feet, we may compute in the manner already explained the points where the horizontal curves intersect each of the parallel lines. The curve lines are then to be drawn through these points, according to the judgment of the surveyor.

(178.) If it is required to draw a *profile* of the ground, for example, from G to K, draw a straight line, G′K, to represent a horizontal line to which the heights are referred, and set off G′a′, G′b′, G′c′, &c., equal to the distances of the stations from the beginning of the line. At the points G′, a′, b′, &c., erect perpendiculars, G′G, a′a, &c., and make them equal to the heights of the respective stations. Through the tops of these perpendiculars draw the curved line GK, and it will be the profile of the hill in the direction of the line GK.

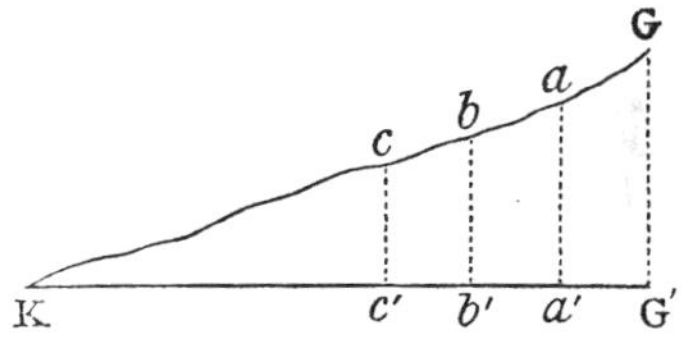

On setting out Rail-way Curves.

(179.) It is of course desirable that the line of a rail-way should be perfectly straight and horizontal. This, however, is seldom possible for any great distance; and when it becomes necessary to change the direction of the line, it should be done gradually by a curve. The curve almost universally employed for this purpose is the arc of a circle, and such an arc may be traced upon the ground by either of the following methods.

First Method.—When the center of the circle can be seen from every part of the curve.

Let AB, CD be two straight portions of a road which it is desired to connect by an arc of a circle. Set up a theodolite at B and another at C, and from each point range a line at right angles to the lines AB and CD respectively; and at the intersection of these lines, E, which will be the center of the circle, erect a signal which can be seen from any point between B and C. Produce the lines AB and CD until they meet in F, and on these lines drive stakes at equal distances, a_1, a_2, a_3, commencing from the points B and C. If r represents the radius of the circle, and d the distance between the points a_1, a_2, a_3, &c., then (Art. 172),

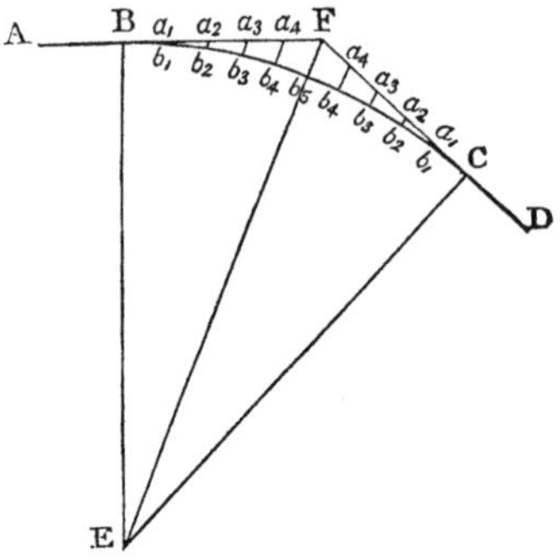

$$\sqrt{r^2+d^2}-r$$

will be the distance which must be set off from the first point a_1, in the direction a_1E, to obtain a point of the circular arc. In like manner,

$$\sqrt{r^2+(2d)^2}-r$$

will be the distance to be set off from the point a_2, in the direction a_2E; and, generally,

$$\sqrt{r^2+(nd)^2}-r$$

will be the distance to be set off at the nth points from B and C. For example, let r be one mile, or 5280 feet, and d equal to 100 feet; then,

$$\sqrt{5280^2+100^2}-5280=.94 \text{ feet},$$

will be the distance a_1b_1. In a similar manner, we find at

a_2, or 200 feet from B,	the offset	will be	3.79	feet.
a_3, or 300	"	"	"	8.52	"
a_4, or 400	"	"	"	15.13	"
a_5, or 500	"	"	"	23.62	"

(180.) *Second Method.*—When the center of the circle can not be seen from every part of the curve, the offsets may be set off perpendicularly to the tangent BF, in which case they must be computed from the formula

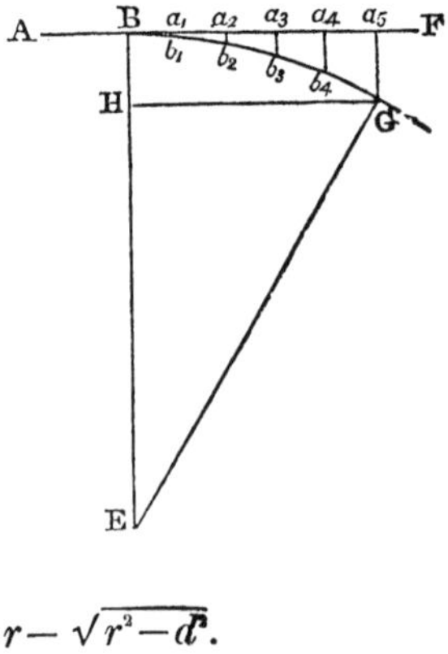

$$r-\sqrt{r^2-d^2}.$$

For, in the annexed figure,

$$\text{EH}=\sqrt{\text{GE}^2-\text{GH}^2},$$

that is, $\text{EH}=\sqrt{r^2-d^2}$.

And $$a_5\text{G}=\text{BH}=\text{BE}-\text{HE}=r-\sqrt{r^2-d^2}.$$

If $r=5280$ feet, we shall find the offsets at intervals of 100 feet to be

$$a_1b_1 = .95 \text{ feet.}$$
$$a_2b_2 = 3.79 \text{ "}$$
$$a_3b_3 = 8.53 \text{ "}$$
$$a_4b_4 = 15.17 \text{ "}$$
$$a_5b_5 = 23.73 \text{ "}$$

For small distances, the offsets will be given with sufficient accuracy by the formula

$$\frac{d^2}{2r},$$

see Art. 172.

It is very common for surveyors, after they have found the first point, b_1, of the curve, to join the points B, b_1, and produce the line Bb_1 to the distance d, and from the end of this line set off an offset to determine the point b_2; then, producing the line b_1b_2, set off a third offset to determine the point b_3, and so on. The objection to this method is, that any error committed in setting out one of the points of the curve will occasion an error in every succeeding one. Whenever this method, therefore, is employed, it should be checked by determining the position of every fourth or fifth point by independent computation and measurement.

(181.) *Third Method.*—Where the radius of the curve is small, place a theodolite at B, and point its telescope toward

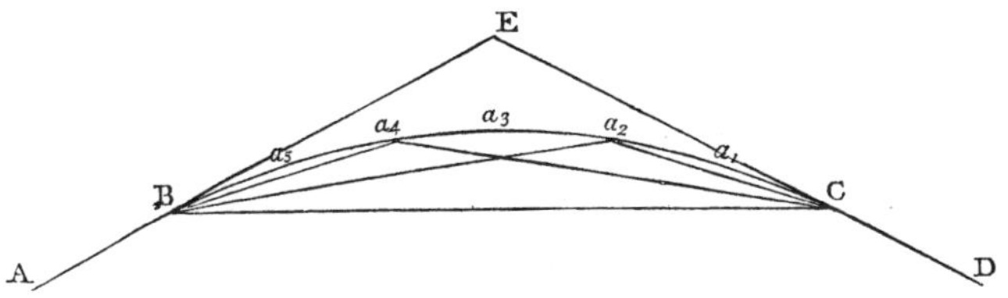

C. Place another theodolite at C, and point its telescope toward E, the point of intersection of the lines AB, CD produced. Then, if the former be moved through any number of degrees toward a_1, and the latter the same number of degrees toward a_1, the point a_1 will be a point of the curve, for the angle Ba_1C will be equal to BCD (*Geom.*, Prop. 16, B. III.). In the same manner, a_2, a_3, &c., any number of points of the curve, may be determined. It will be most convenient to move the theodolites each time through an even number of degrees, for example, an arc of two degrees, and a stake must be driven at each of the points of intersection a_1, a_2, a_3, &c. The accuracy of this method is independent of any undulations in the surface of the ground, so that in a hilly country this method may be preferable to any other.

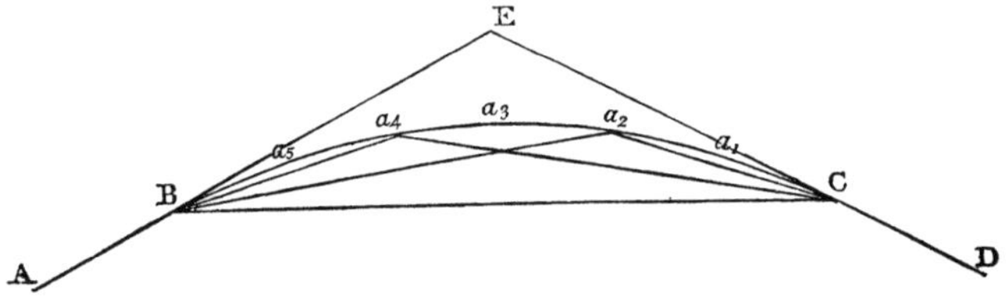

When the position of one end of the curve is not absolutely determined, the engineer may proceed more rapidly. Suppose it is required to trace an arc of a circle having a curvature of two degrees for a hundred feet.

Place a theodolite at C, the point where the curve commences, and lay off from the line CE, toward B, an angle of two degrees, and in the direction of the axis of the instrument set off a distance of 100 feet, which will give the first point a_1 of the curve. Next lay off from CE an angle of four degrees, and from a_1 set off a distance of 100 feet, and the point where this line cuts the axis of the instrument produced will be the second point a_2. In the same manner, lay off from CE an angle of six degrees, and from a_2 set off a distance of 100 feet, and the point where it cuts the axis of the instrument produced will be the third point a_3. All the points a_1, a_2, a_3, etc., thus determined lie in the circumference of a circle (*Geom.*, Prop. 15, B. III.). Circles thus drawn are generally made with a curvature of one or two degrees, or some convenient fraction of a degree, for every hundred feet. This method is very extensively practiced in the United States.

Surveying Harbors.

(182.) In surveying a harbor, it is necessary to determine the position of the most conspicuous objects, to trace the outline of the shore, and discover the depth of water in the neighborhood of the channel. A smooth, level piece of ground is chosen, on which a base line of considerable length is measured, and station staves are fixed at its extremities. We also erect station staves on all the prominent points to be surveyed, forming a series of triangles covering the entire surface of the harbor. The angles of these triangles are now measured with a theodolite, and their sides computed. After the principal points have been determined, subordinate points may be ascertained by the compass or plane table.

Let the following figure be a map of a harbor to be survey-

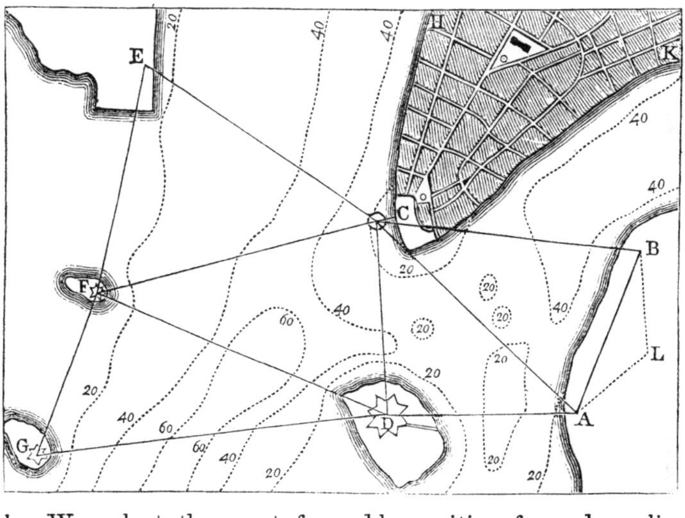

ed. We select the most favorable position for a base line, which is found to be on the right of the harbor, from A to B. We also erect station flags at the points C, D, E, F, and G. Having carefully measured the base line AB, we measure the three angles of the triangle ABC, which enables us to compute the remaining sides. We then measure the three angles of the triangle ACD, and by means of the side AC, just computed, we are enabled to compute AD and CD. We then measure the three angles of the triangle CDF, and by means of the side CD, just found, we are enabled to compute CF and DF. Proceeding in the same manner with the triangles CEF, DFG, we are enabled, after measuring the angles, to compute the sides.

(183.) Having determined the main points of the harbor, we may proceed to a more detailed survey by means of the chain and compass. If it is required to trace the shore, HCK, we commence at H, and observe the bearings with the compass, and measure the distances with the chain. Where the shore is undulating, it is most convenient to run a straight line for a considerable distance, and at frequent intervals measure off-sets to the shore.

When a great many objects are to be represented upon a map, the most convenient instrument is

The Plane Table.

(184.) The plane table is a board about sixteen inches square, designed to receive a sheet of drawing paper, and has two plates of brass upon opposite sides, confined by screws, for stretching and retaining the paper upon the board. The margin of the board is divided to 360 degrees from a center C, in the middle of the board, and these are subdivided as minutely as the size of the table will admit. On one side of the board there is usually a diagonal scale of equal parts. A compass box is sometimes attached, which renders the plane table capable of answering the purpose of a surveyor's compass.

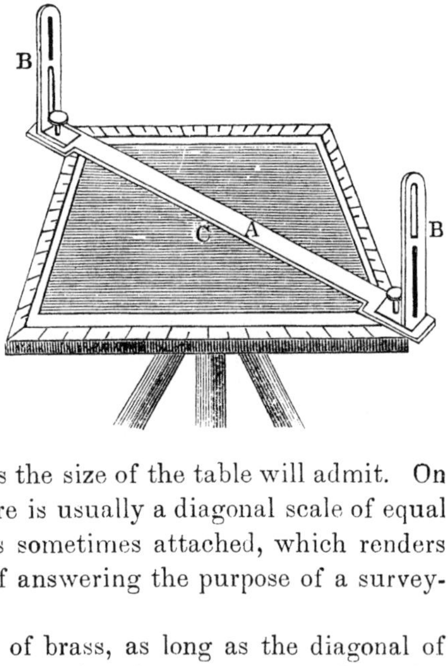

The ruler, A, is made of brass, as long as the diagonal of the table, and about two inches broad. A perpendicular sight-vane, B, B, is fixed to each extremity of the ruler, and the eye looking through one of them, the vertical thread in the other is made to bisect any required distant object.

To the under side of the table, a center is attached with a ball and socket, or parallel plate screws, like those of the theodolite, by which it can be placed upon a staff-head; and the table may be made horizontal by means of a detached spirit level

(185.) To prepare the table for use, it must be covered with drawing paper. Then set up the instrument at one of the stations, for example, B (see fig. on p. 131), and fix a needle in the table at the point on the paper representing that station, and place the edge of the ruler against the needle. Then direct the sights to the station A, and by the side of the ruler draw a line upon the paper to represent the direction of AB. Then, with a pair of dividers, take from the scale a certain number of equal parts to represent the base, and lay off this distance on the base line. Having drawn the base line, move the ruler around the needle, direct the sights to any object, as L, and keeping it there, draw a line along the edge of the ruler. Then direct the sights in the same manner to any other objects which are required to be sketched, drawing lines in their respective directions, taking care that the table remains steady during the operation.

Now remove the instrument to the other extremity of the base A, and place the point of the paper corresponding to that extremity directly over it. Place the edge of the ruler on the base line, and turn the table about till the sights are directed to the station B. Then placing the edge of the ruler against the needle, direct the sights in succession to all the objects observed from the other station, drawing lines from the point A in their several directions. The intersections of these lines with those drawn from the point B will determine the positions of the several objects on the map.

In this manner the plane table may be employed for filling in the details of a map; setting it up at the most remarkable spots, and sketching by the eye what is not necessary should be more particularly determined, the paper will gradually become a representation of the country to be surveyed.

To determine the Depth of Water.

(186.) Let signals be established on the principal shoals and along the edges of the channel, by erecting poles or anchoring buoys, and let their bearings be observed from two stations of the survey. Then in each triangle there will be known one side and the angles, from which the other sides may be computed, and their positions thus become known. Then ascertain the precise depth of water at each of the buoys, and proceed in this manner to determine as many points as may be thought necessary.

If an observer is stationed with a theodolite at each extremity of the base line, we may dispense with the erection of permanent marks upon the water. One observer in a boat may make a sounding for the depth of water, giving a signal at the same instant to two observers at the extremities of the base line. The direction of the boat being observed at that instant from two stations, the precise place of the boat can be computed. In this way soundings may be made with great expedition.

There is also another method, still more expeditious, which may afford results sufficiently precise in some cases. Let a boat be rowed uniformly across the harbor from one station to another, for example, from D to G (see fig. on p. 131), and let a series of soundings be made as rapidly as possible, and the instant of each sounding be recorded. Then, knowing the entire length of the line DG, and the time of rowing over it, we may find by proportion the approximate position of the boat at each sounding.

If the soundings are made in tide waters, the times of high water should be observed, and the time of each sounding be recorded, so that the depth of water at high or low tide may be computed. In the maps of the United States Coast Survey, the soundings are all reduced to low-water mark, and the number of feet which the tide rises or falls is noted upon the map

(187.) The results of the soundings may be delineated upon a map in the same manner as the observations of level on page 124. We draw lines joining all those points where the depth of water is the same, for example, 20 feet. Such a line is seen to be an undulating line running in the direction from E to G. We draw another line connecting all those points where the depth of water is 40 feet. This line runs somewhat to the east of the former line, but nearly parallel with it. We draw other lines for depths of 60 feet, &c. The lines being thus drawn, a mere glance at the map will show nearly the depth of water at any point of the harbor.

BOOK V.

NAVIGATION.

(188.) NAVIGATION is the art of conducting a ship at sea from one port to another.

There are two methods of determining the situation of a vessel at sea. The one consists in finding by astronomical observations her latitude and longitude; the other consists in measuring the ship's course, and her progress every day from the time of her leaving port, from which her place may be computed by trigonometry. The latter method is the one to be now considered.

(189.) The figure of the earth is nearly that of a sphere, and in navigation it is considered perfectly spherical. The *earth's axis* is the diameter around which it revolves once a day. The extremities of this axis are the terrestrial *poles;* one is called the north pole, and the other the south pole.

The *equator* is a great circle perpendicular to the earth's axis.

Meridians are great circles passing through the poles of the earth. Every place on the earth's surface has its own meridian.

(190.) The *longitude* of any place is the arc of the equator intercepted between the meridian of that place and some assumed meridian to which all others are referred. In most countries of Europe, that has been taken as the standard meridian which passes through their principal observatory. The English reckon longitude from the Observatory of Greenwich; and in the United States, we have usually adhered to the English custom, though we believe the time has come when longitude should be reckoned from the Observatory of Washington.

Longitude is usually reckoned east and west of the first meridian, from 0° to 180°.

The difference of longitude of two places is the arc of the equator included between their meridians. It is equal to the difference of their longitudes if they are on the same side of the first meridian, and to the sum of their longitudes if on opposite sides.

(191.) The *latitude* of a place is the arc of the meridian passing through the place, which is comprehended between that place and the equator.

Latitude is reckoned north and south of the equator, from 0° to 90°.

Parallels of latitude are the circumferences of small circles parallel to the equator.

The *difference of latitude* of two places is the arc of a meridian included between the parallels of latitude passing through those places. It is equal to the difference of their latitudes if they are on the same side of the equator, and to the sum of their latitudes if on opposite sides.

The *distance* is the length of the line which a vessel describes in a given time.

The *departure* of two places is the distance of either place from the meridian of the other. If the two places are on the same parallel, the departure is the distance between the places. Otherwise, we divide the distance AB into portions A*b*, *bc*, *cd*, &c., so small that the curvature of the earth may be neglected. Through these points we draw the meridians P*b*, P*c*, &c., and the parallels *be*, *cf*, &c. Then the departure for A*b* is *eb*, for *bc* it is *fc*; and the whole departure from A to B is $eb+fc+gd+h\text{B}$; that is, the sum of the departures corresponding to the small portions into which the distance is divided.

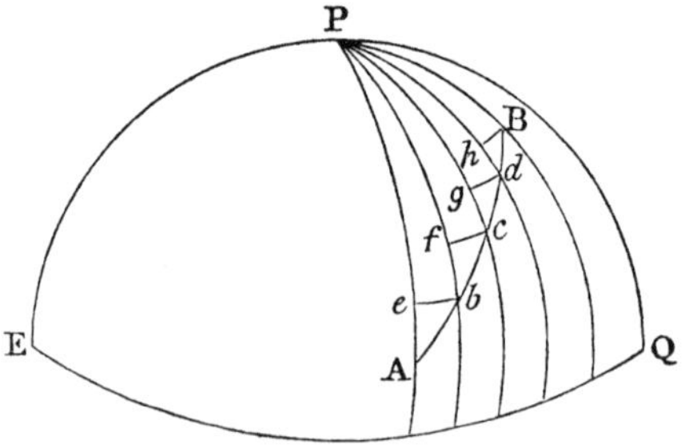

Distance, departure, and difference of latitude are measured in nautical miles, one of which is the 60th part of a degree at the equator. A nautical mile is nearly one sixth greater than an English statute mile.

The *course* of a ship is the angle which the ship's path makes with the meridian. A ship is said to continue on the same course when she cuts every meridian which she crosses at the same angle. The path thus described is not a straight line, but a curve called a *rhumb-line.*

The course of a ship is given by the mariner's compass.

(192.) The *mariner's compass* consists of a circular piece of paper, called a card, attached to a magnetic needle, which is balanced on a pin so as to move freely in any direction. Directly over the needle, a line is drawn on the card, one end of which is marked N, and the other S. The circumference is divided into thirty-two equal parts called rhumbs or *points*, each point being subdivided into four equal parts called *quarter points.*

The points of the compass are designated as follows, beginning at north and going east: north, north by east, north-north-east, northeast by north, northeast, and so on, as shown in the annexed figure.

The interval between two adjacent points is 11° 15′, which is the eighth part of a quadrant. On the inside of the compass-box a black line is drawn perpendicular to the horizon, and the compass should be so placed that a line drawn from this mark through the center of the card may be parallel to the keel of the ship. The part of the card which coincides with this mark will then show the point of the compass to which the keel is directed. The compass is suspended in its box in such a manner as to maintain a horizontal position, notwithstanding the motion of the ship.

The following table shows the number of degrees and minutes corresponding to each point of the compass:

North.		Pts.		Pts.	South.	
N. by E.	N. by W.	1	11° 15′	1	S. by E.	S. by W.
N.N.E.	N.N.W.	2	22° 30′	2	S.S.E.	S.S.W.
N.E. by N.	N.W. by N.	3	33° 45′	3	S.E. by S.	S.W. by S.
N.E.	N.W.	4	45° 0′	4	S.E.	S.W.
N.E. by E.	N.W. by W.	5	56° 15′	5	S.E. by E.	S.W. by W.
E.N.E.	W.N.W.	6	67° 30′	6	E.S.E.	W.S.W.
E. by N.	W. by N.	7	78° 45′	7	E. by S.	W. by S.
East.	West.	8	90° 0′	8	East.	West.

(193.) The ship's rate of sailing is measured by a *log-line.* The log-line is a cord about 300 yards long, which is wound

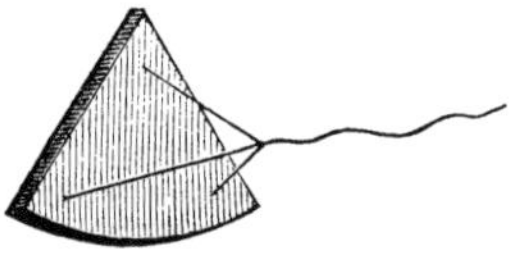

round a reel, one end being attached to a piece of thin board called a log. This board is in the form of a sector of a circle, the arc of which is loaded with lead sufficient to give the board a vertical position when thrown upon the water. This is designed to prevent the log from being drawn along after the vessel while the line is running off the reel.

The time is measured by a sand-glass, through which the sand passes in *half a minute*, or the 120th part of an hour.

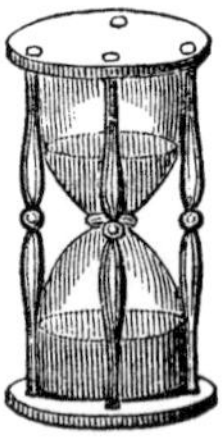

The log-line is divided into equal parts called *knots*, each of which is 50 feet, or the 120th part of a nautical mile. Now, since a knot has the same ratio to a nautical mile that half a minute has to an hour, it follows, that if the motion of a ship is uniform, she sails as many miles in an hour as she does knots in half a minute. If, then, seven knots are observed to run off in half a minute, the ship is sailing at the rate of seven miles an hour.

PLANE SAILING.

(194.) *Plane sailing* is the method of calculating a ship's place at sea by means of the properties of a plane triangle. The particulars which are given or required are four, viz., the distance, course, difference of latitude, and departure. Of these, any two being given, the others may be found.

Let the figure EPQ represent a portion of the earth's surface, P the pole, and EQ the equator. Let AB be a rhumb-line, or the track described by a ship in sailing from A to B on a uniform course. Let the whole distance be divided into portions Ab, bc, &c., so small that the curvature of the earth may be neglected. Through the points of division draw the meridians Pb, Pc, &c., and the parallels eb, fc, &c. Then, since the course is every where the same, each of the angles eAb, fbc, &c., is equal to the course. The distances Ae, bf, &c., are the differences of latitude of A and b, b and c, &c. Also, eb, fc, &c., are the departures for the same distances. Hence the difference of latitude from A to B is equal to

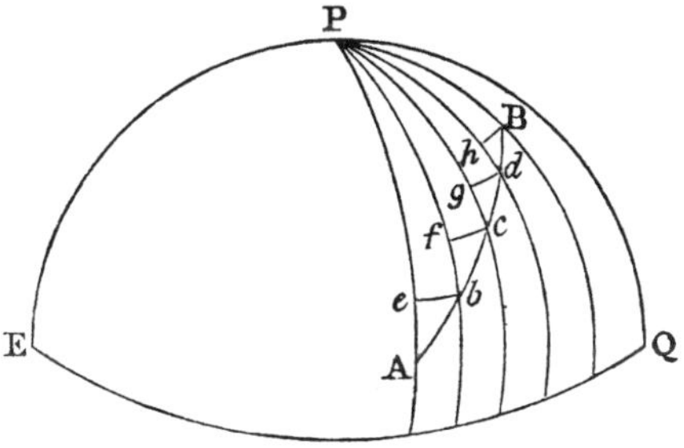

$$Ae+bf+cg+dh,$$

and the departure is equal to

$$eb+fc+gd+hB.$$

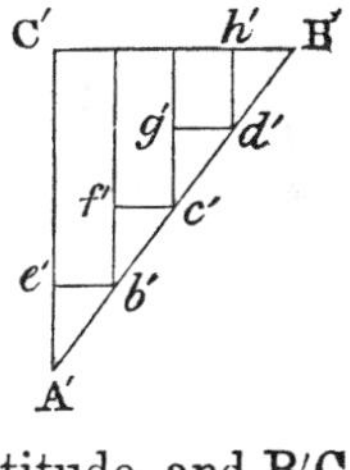

Construct the triangle A′B′C′ so that A′$b'e'$ shall be equal to Abe, $b'c'f'$ shall be equal to bcf, $c'd'g'$ equal to cdg, and d'B′h' equal to dBh. Then A′B′ represents the distance sailed, B′A′C′ the course, A′C′ the difference of latitude, and B′C the departure; that is, the distance, difference of latitude, and departure are correctly represented by the hypothenuse and sides of a right-angled triangle, of which the angle opposite to the departure is the course. Of these four quantities, any two being given, the others may be found.

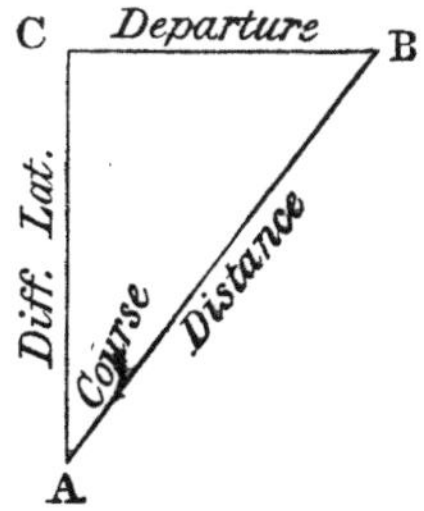

Plane sailing does not assume the earth's surface to be a plane, and does not involve any error even in great distances.

EXAMPLES.

1. A ship sails from Vera Cruz N.E. by N. 74 miles. Required her departure and difference of latitude.

According to the principles of right-angled triangles, Art. 44.

Radius : *distance* : : *sin. course* : *departure.*

: : *cos. course* : *diff. latitude.*

The course is three points, or 33° 45′; hence we obtain

Departure =41.11 miles.

Diff. latitude=61.53 miles.

2. A ship sails from Sandy Hook, latitude 40° 28′ N., upon a course E.S.E., till she makes a departure of 500 miles. What distance has she sailed, and at what latitude has she arrived?

By Trigonometry, Art. 44,

Sin. course : *departure* : : *radius* : *distance,*

: : *cos. course* : *diff. latitude*

Ans. Distance =541.20 miles.

Diff. latitude=207.11 miles, or 3° 27′.

Hence the latitude at which she has arrived is 37° 1′ N.

3. The bearing of Sandy Hook from Bermuda is N. 42° 56′ W., and the difference of latitude 486 miles. Required the distance and departure.

By Trigonometry, Art. 46,

Radius : *diff. latitude* : : *tang. course* : *departure,*

: : *sec. course* : *distance.*

Ans. Distance =663.8 miles.

Departure=452.1 miles.

4. A ship sails from Bermuda, latitude 32° 22′ N., a distance of 666 miles, upon a course between north and east, until she finds her departure 444 miles. What course has she sailed, and what is her latitude?

By Trigonometry, Art. 44,

Distance : *radius* : : *departure* : *sin. course,*

Radius : *distance* : : *cos. course* : *diff. latitude.*

Ans. Latitude= 40° 38′ N.

Course =N. 41° 49′ E.

5. The distance from Vera Cruz, latitude 19° 12′ N., to Pensacola, latitude 30° 19′ N., is 820 miles. Required the bearing and departure.

By Trigonometry, Art. 45,

Distance : *radius* : : *diff. latitude* : *cos. course*,
Radius : *distance* : : *sin. course* : *departure*.

Ans. Bearing $=$N. 35° 34′ E.
Departure$=$476.95 miles.

6. A ship sails from Sandy Hook upon a course between south and east to the parallel of 35°, when her departure was 300 miles. Required her course and distance.

By Trigonometry, Art. 47,

Diff. latitude : *radius* : : *departure* : *tang. course*,
Radius : *diff. latitude* : : *sec. course* : *distance*.

Ans. Course S. 42° 27′ E.
Distance 444.5 miles.

TRAVERSE SAILING.

(195.) A *traverse* is the irregular path of a ship when sailing on different courses.

The object of *traverse sailing* is to reduce a traverse to a single course, when the distances sailed are so small that the curvature of the earth may be neglected. When a ship sails on different courses, the difference of latitude is equal to the difference between the sum of the northings and the sum of the southings; and, neglecting the earth's curvature, the departure is equal to the difference between the sum of the eastings and the sum of the westings. If, then, the difference of latitude and the departure for each course be taken from the traverse table, and arranged in appropriate columns, the difference of latitude for the whole time may be obtained exactly, and the departure nearly, by addition and subtraction; and the corresponding distance and course may be determined as in plane sailing.

EXAMPLES.

1. A ship sails on the following successive tracks:

1.	N.E.	23	miles.
2.	E.S.E.	45	"
3.	E. by N.	34	"
4.	North	29	"
5.	N. by W.	31	"
6.	N.N.E.	17	"

Find the course and distance for the whole traverse.

We form a table as below, entering the courses from the table of rhumbs, page 138, and then enter the latitudes and departures taken from the traverse table.

Traverse Table.

No.	Course.	Distance.	N.	S.	E.	W.
1	N. 45° E.	23	16.26		16.26	
2	S. 67° 30′ E.	45		17.22	41.57	
3	N. 78° 45′ E.	34	6.63		33.35	
4	North.	29	29.00			
5	N. 11° 15′ W.	31	30.40			6.05
6	N. 22° 30′ E.	17	15.71		6.51	
Sum of columns . . .			98.00	17.22	97.69	6.05
			17.22		6.05	
Diff. latitude			=80.78 N.	Dep.	=91.64 E.	

Hence the course is found by plane sailing N. 48° 36′ E., and the distance =122.2 miles.

The proportions are

Diff. latitude : radius : : departure : tang. course,

Radius : diff. latitude : : sec. course : distance.

2. A ship leaving Sandy Hook makes the following courses and distances:

1. S.E. 25 miles.
2. E.S.E. 32 "
3. East 17 "
4. E. by S. 51 "
5. South 45 "
6. S. by E. 63 "

Required her latitude, the distance made, and the direct course.

Ans. Latitude=38° 1′ N.
Distance=193.7 miles.
Course =S. 40° 47′ E.

3. A ship from Pensacola, latitude 30° 19′, sails on the following successive courses:

1. South 48 miles.
2. S.S.W. 23 "
3. S.W. 32 "

4. S.W. by S. 76 miles.
5. West 17 "
6. W.S.W. 54 "

Required her latitude, direct course, and distance.

Ans. Latitude= 27° 23′ N.
Course =S. 38° 39′ W.
Distance =225.0 miles.

4. A ship from Bermuda, latitude 32° 22′, sails on the following successive courses:

1. N.E. 66 miles.
2. N.N.E. 14 "
3. N.E. by E. 45 "
4. East 21 "
5. E. by N. 32 "

Required her latitude, direct course, and distance.

Ans. Latitude= 33° 53′ N.
Course =N. 57° 22′ E.
Distance=168.4 miles.

(196.) When the water through which a ship is moving has a progressive motion, the ship's progress is affected in the same manner as if she had sailed in still water, with an additional course and distance equal to the direction and motion of the current.

Ex. 5. If a ship sail 125 miles N.N.E. in a current which sets W. by N. 32 miles in the same time, required her true course and distance.

Form a traverse table containing the course sailed by the ship and the progress of the current, and find the difference of latitude and departure. The resulting course and distance is found as in the preceding examples.

Traverse Table.

Courses.	Distance.	N.	E.	W.
N. 22° 30′ E	125	115.49	47.84	
N. 78° 45′ W.	32	6.24		31.39

Diff. latitude . . . =121.73 47.84 31.39
31.39

Departure . . . . =16.45 E.

Hence the course is found by plane sailing N. 7° 42′ E., and the distance=122.8 miles.

Ex. 6. A ship sails S. by E. for two hours at the rate of 9 miles an hour; then S. by W. for five hours at the rate of 8 miles an hour; and during the whole time a current sets W. by N. at the rate of two and a half miles an hour. Required the direct course and distance.

Ans. The course is S. 21° 51′ W.
Distance 57.6 miles.

PARALLEL SAILING.

(197.) *Parallel sailing* is when a ship sails exactly east or west, and therefore remains constantly on the same parallel of latitude. In this case the departure is equal to the distance sailed, and the difference of longitude may be found by the following

THEOREM.

The cosine of the latitude of the parallel is to radius, as the distance run is to the difference of longitude.

Let P be the pole of the earth, C the center, AB a portion of the equator, and DE any parallel of latitude; then will CA be the radius of the equator, and FD the radius of the parallel. Let DE be the distance sailed by the ship on the parallel of latitude, then the difference of longitude will be measured by AB, the arc intercepted on the equator by the meridians passing through D and E.

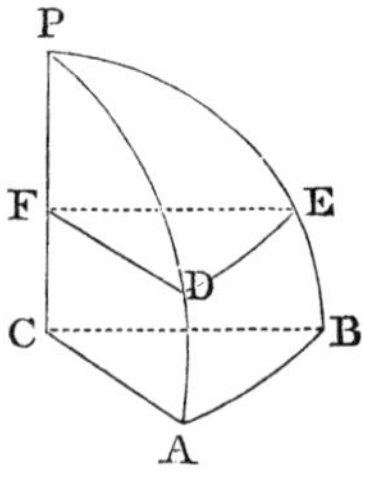

Since AB and DE correspond to the equal angles ACB, DFE, they are similar arcs, and are to each other as their radii. Hence

FD : CA : : *arc* DE : *arc* AB.

But FD is the sine of PD, or the cosine of AD, that is, the cosine of the latitude, and CA is the radius of the sphere; hence

Cosine of latitude : R : : *distance* : *diff. longitude.*

Cor. Like portions of different parallels of latitude are to each other as the cosines of the latitudes.

The length of a degree of longitude in different parallels may be computed by this theorem. A degree of longitude at the equator being 60 nautical miles, a degree in latitude 40° may be found by the proportion

R : cosine 40° : : 60 : 45.96, the required length.

The following table is computed in the same manner.

(198.) *Table showing the length of a degree of longitude for each degree of latitude.*

Lat.	Miles.	Lat.	Miles.	Lat.	Miles.	Lat.	Miles.	Lat.	Miles.	Lat.	Miles.
1	59.99	16	57.68	31	51.43	46	41.68	61	29.09	76	14.52
2	59.96	17	57.38	32	50.88	47	40.92	62	28.17	77	13.50
3	59.92	18	57.06	33	50.32	48	40.15	63	27.24	78	12.47
4	59.85	19	56.73	34	49.74	49	39.36	64	26.30	79	11.45
5	59.77	20	56.38	35	49.15	50	38.57	65	25.36	80	10.42
6	59.67	21	56.01	36	48.54	51	37.76	66	24.40	81	9.39
7	59.55	22	55.63	37	47.92	52	36.94	67	23.44	82	8.35
8	59.42	23	55.23	38	47.28	53	36.11	68	22.48	83	7.31
9	59.26	24	54.81	39	46.63	54	35.27	69	21.50	84	6.27
10	59.09	25	54.38	40	45.96	55	34.41	70	20.52	85	5.23
11	58.90	26	53.93	41	45.28	56	33.55	71	19.53	86	4.19
12	58.69	27	53.46	42	44.59	57	32.68	72	18.54	87	3.14
13	58.46	28	52.98	43	43.88	58	31.80	73	17.54	88	2.09
14	58.22	29	52.48	44	43.16	59	30.90	74	16.54	89	1.05
15	57.96	30	51.96	45	42.43	60	30.00	75	15.53	90	0.00

Let ABC represent a right-angled triangle; then, by Trigonometry, Art. 41,

cos. B : R : : AB : BC.

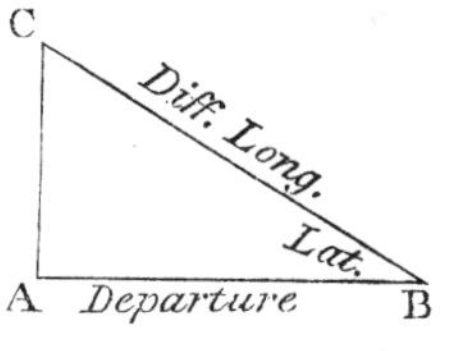

But, by the preceding Theorem, we have

cos. lat. : R : : *depart.* : *diff. long.*,

from which we see that if one leg of a right-angled triangle represent the distance run on any parallel, and the adjacent acute angle be made equal to the degrees of latitude of that parallel, then the hypothenuse will represent the difference of longitude.

EXAMPLES.

1. A ship sails from Sandy Hook, latitude 40° 28′ N., longitude 74° 1′ W., 618 miles due east. Required her present longitude.

Cos. 40° 28′ : R : : 618 : 812′.3=13° 32′, the difference of longitude.

This, subtracted from 74° 1′, leaves 60° 29′ W., the longitude required.

2. A ship in latitude 40° sails due east through nine degrees of longitude. Required the distance run.

Ans. 413.66 miles.

3. A ship having sailed on a parallel of latitude 261 miles, finds her difference of longitude 6° 15′. What is her latitude?

Ans. Latitude 45° 54′.

4. Two ships in latitude 52° N., distant from each other 95 miles, sail directly south until their distance is 150 miles What latitude do they arrive at?

Ans. Latitude 13° 34′.

MIDDLE LATITUDE SAILING.

(199.) By the method just explained may be found the longitude which a ship makes while sailing on a parallel of latitude. When the course is oblique, the departure may be found by plane sailing, but a difficulty is found in converting this departure into difference of longitude.

If a ship sail from A to B, the departure is equal to $eb+fc+gd+h$B, which is less than AC, but greater than DB. Navigators have assumed that the departure was equal to the distance between the meridians PA, PB, measured on a parallel EF, equidistant from A and B, called the *middle latitude*.

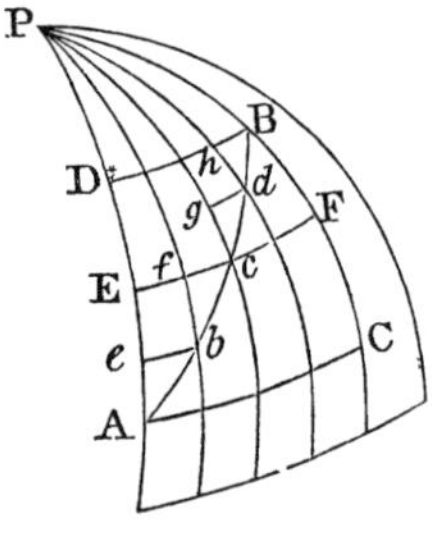

The middle latitude is equal to *half the sum* of the two extreme latitudes, if both are north or both south; but to *half their difference*, if one is north and the other south.

The principle assumed in middle latitude sailing is not perfectly correct. For long distances the error is considerable, but the method is rendered perfectly accurate by applying to the middle latitude a correction which is given in the accompanying tables, page 149.

(200.) It has been shown that when a ship sails upon an oblique course, the distance, departure, and difference of latitude may be represented by the sides of a right-angled triangle. The difference of longitude is derived from the departure, in the same manner as in parallel sailing, the ship being supposed to sail on the middle latitude parallel. Hence, if we combine the triangle ABC for plane sailing with the triangle BCD for parallel sailing, we shall obtain a triangle ABD, by which all the cases of middle latitude sailing may be solved.

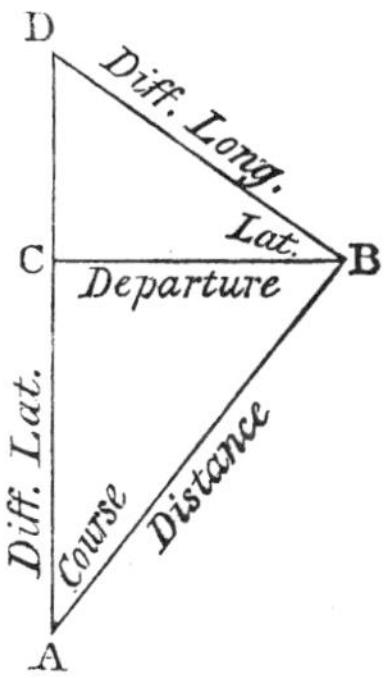

In the triangle BCD,

Cos. CBD : BC : : R : BD;

that is, *cosine of middle latitude is to the departure, as radius is to the difference of longitude.*

In the triangle ABD, since the angle D is the complement of CBD, which represents the middle latitude, we have

Sin. D : AB : : sin. A : BD;

that is, *cosine of middle latitude is to the distance, as the sine of the course is to the difference of longitude.*

In the triangle ABC, we have the proportion

AC : BC : : R : tang. A.

But we have before had the proportion

Cos. CBD : BC : : R : BD.

The means being the same in these two proportions, we have

Cos. CBD : AC : : tang. A : BD;

that is, *cosine of middle latitude is to the difference of latitude, as the tangent of the course is to the difference of longitude.*

The middle latitude should always be corrected according to the table on page 149. The given middle latitude is to be looked for either in the first or last vertical column, opposite to which, and under the given difference of latitude, is inserted the proper correction in minutes, which must be *added* to the middle latitude to obtain the latitude in which the meridian distance is exactly equal to the departure. Thus, if the middle latitude is 41°, and the difference of latitude 14°, the correction will be found to be 25′, which, added to the middle latitude, gives the corrected middle latitude 41° 25′.

EXAMPLES.

1. Find the bearing and distance of Liverpool, latitude 53° 22′ N., longitude 2° 52′ W., from New York, latitude 40° 42′ N., longitude 74° 1′ W.

Here are given two latitudes and longitudes to find the course and distance.

The difference of latitude is	12° 40′= 760′.
The difference of longitude is	71° 9′=4269′.
The middle latitude is	47° 2′.
To which add the correction from p. 149	22′.
The corrected middle latitude is . . .	47° 24′.

Then, according to the third of the preceding theorems,

Diff. lat. : *cos. mid. lat.* : : *diff. long.* : *tang. course*=N. 75° 16′ E

To find the distance by plane sailing,

Cos. course : *diff. latitude* : : R : *distance*=2988.4 miles.

2. A ship sailed from Bermuda, latitude 32° 22′ N., longitude 64° 38′ W., a distance of 500 miles, upon a course W.N W. Required her latitude and longitude at that time.

By plane sailing,

R : *distance* : : *cos. course* : *diff. latitude*= 191.3.

Therefore the required latitude is	35° 33′;
the middle latitude	33° 58′;
and the corrected middle latitude	33° 59′

Then we have

Cos. mid. lat. : *distance* : : *sin. course* : *diff. long.*=557′.1.

Therefore the longitude required is 73° 55′.

3. A ship sails southeasterly from Sandy Hook, latitude 40° 28′ N., longitude 74° 1′ W., a distance of 395 miles, when her latitude is 34° 40′ N. Required her course and longitude.

Ans. Course S. 28° 14′ E.
Longitude 70° 5′ W.

4. A ship sails from Brest, latitude 48° 23′ N., longitude 4° 29′ W., upon a course W.S.W., till her departure is 556 miles. Required the distance sailed and the place of the ship.

Ans. Distance 601.8 miles.
Latitude 44° 33′ N.
Longitude 17° 57′ W.

MERCATOR'S SAILING.

(201.) Mercator's sailing is a method of computing difference of longitude on the principles of Mercator's chart. On this chart, the meridians, instead of converging toward the poles as they do on the globe, are drawn *parallel* to each other, by which means the distance of the meridians is every where

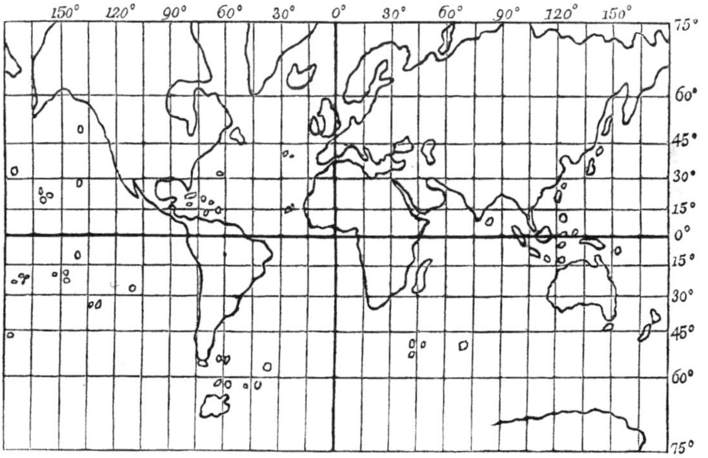

made too great except at the equator. To compensate for this, in order that the outline of countries may not be too much distorted, the degrees of latitude are proportionally enlarged, so that the distance between the parallels of latitude increases from the equator to the poles. In latitude 60° the distance of the meridians is twice as great, compared with a degree at the equator, as it is upon a globe, and a degree of latitude is here represented twice as great as near the equator. The diameter of an island in latitude 60° is represented twice as great as if it was on the equator, and its area four times too great. In latitude 70° 32′ the distance of the meridians is three times too great, in latitude 75° 31′ four times too great, and so on, by which means the relative dimensions of countries in high latitudes is exceedingly distorted. On this account it is not common to extend the chart beyond latitude 75°.

(202.) The distance of any parallel upon Mercator's chart from the equator has been computed, and is exhibited in the accompanying tables, pages 142–8, which is called a Table of *Meridional Parts.* This table may be computed in the following manner:

According to Art. 197, cosine of latitude is to radius, as the departure is to the difference of longitude; that is, as a part of a parallel of latitude is to a like part of the equator, or any meridian.

But by Art. 28, cosine : R : : R : secant; hence

$1'$ *of a parallel* : $1'$ *of a meridian* : : R : *sec. latitude.*

But on Mercator's chart the distance between the meridians is the same in all latitudes; that is, a minute on a parallel of latitude is equal to a minute at the equator, or a geographical mile. Hence *the length of one minute, on any part of a meridian, is equal to the secant of the latitude.* Thus,

The *first* minute of the meridian = the secant of $1'$;
second " " = " $2'$,
third " " = " $3'$,
&c., &c.

The table of meridional parts is formed by adding together the minutes thus found. Thus,

Mer. parts of $1'$=sec. $1'$;
Mer. parts of $2'$=sec. $1'$+sec. $2'$;
Mer. parts of $3'$=sec. $1'$+sec. $2'$+sec. $3'$;
Mer. parts of $4'$=sec. $1'$+sec. $2'$+sec. $3'$+sec. $4'$,
&c., &c., &c.

Since the secants of small arcs are nearly equal to radius or unity, if the meridional parts are only given to one tenth of a mile, we shall have

The meridional parts of $1'$=1.0 mile;
" " " $2'$=2.0 "
" " " $3'$=3.0 "
" " " $4'$=4.0 " &c.,

as shown in the table on page 142.

At 2° 33′ the sum of the small fractions omitted becomes greater than half of one tenth, and the meridional parts of 2° 33′ is 153.1; that is, the meridional parts exceed by one tenth of a mile the minutes of latitude. At 3° 40′ the excess is two tenths of a mile; at 4° 21′ the excess is three tenths;

and as the latitude increases, the meridional parts increase more rapidly, as is seen from the table.

An arc of Mercator's meridian contained between two parallels of latitude is called *meridional difference of latitude* It is found by subtracting the meridional parts of the less latitude from the meridional parts of the greater, if both are north or south, or by adding them together if one is north and the other south. Thus,

The lat. of New York is	40° 42′;	meridional parts=	2677.8,
" New Orleans	29° 57′:	" "	1884.9.
The true diff. of lat. is	10° 45′;	mer. diff. lat. is	792.9.

If one latitude and the meridional difference of latitude be given, the true difference of latitude may be found by reversing this process. Thus,

The meridional parts for New Orleans . . .	=1884.9.
Meridional difference of latitude between New York and New Orleans	= 792.9.
Therefore the meridional parts for New York	=2677.8,

and the corresponding latitude from the table is 40° 42′.

(203.) If we take the figure ABC for plane sailing, as on page 139, and produce AC to E, making AE equal to the meridional difference of latitude, then will DE represent the difference of longitude corresponding to the departure BC. For we have seen (Art. 202) that the departure is to the difference of longitude as radius is to the secant of latitude, which is also the ratio of the true difference of latitude to the meridional difference of latitude.

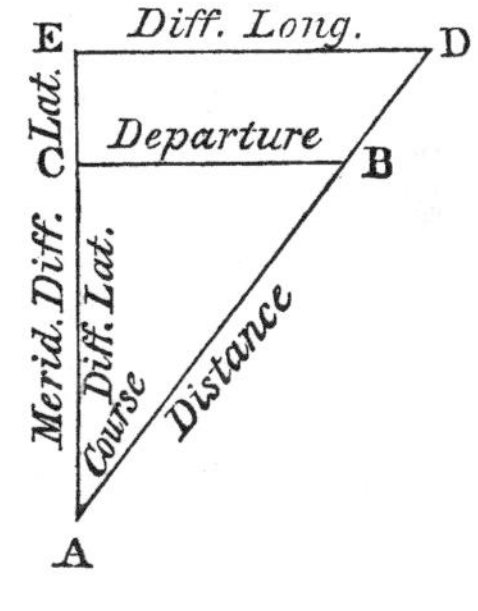

Now, from the similarity of the triangles ABC, ADE, we have

$$AC : AE :: BC : DE ;$$

that is, *the true difference of latitude is to the meridional difference of latitude, as the departure is to the difference of longitude.*

Also, in the triangle ADE, we have

$$R : \tan. A :: AE : DE ;$$

that is, *radius is to the tangent of the course, as the meridional difference of latitude is to the difference of longitude.*

EXAMPLES.

1. Find the bearing and distance from Sandy Hook, latitude 40° 28′ N., longitude 74° 1′ W., to Havre, latitude 49° 29′ N., longitude 0° 6′ E.

The true difference of latitude is 9° 1′= 541′;
meridional difference of latitude =767.1;
difference of longitude is 74° 7′=4447.

Hence, to find the course by the preceding proportion,

Mer. diff. lat. : *diff. long.* : : R : *tan. course*=N. 80° 13′ E.

To find the distance by plane sailing,

Cos. course : *true diff. lat.* : : R : *distance*=3183.8 miles.

2. Find the bearing and distance from Nantucket Shoals, in latitude 41° 4′ N., longitude 69° 55′ W., to Cape Clear, in latitude 51° 26′ N., longitude 9° 29′ W.

Ans. Course N. 76° E.
Distance 2572.9 miles.

3. A ship sails from Sandy Hook a distance of 600 miles upon a course S. by E. Required the place of the ship.

The difference of latitude may be found by plane sailing, the difference of longitude by Mercator's sailing.

Ans. Latitude 30° 39′.5 N.
Longitude 71° 36′.7 W.

4. A ship sails from St. Augustine, latitude 29° 52′ N., longitude 81° 25′ W., upon a course N.E. by E., until her latitude is found to be 34° 40′ N. What is then her longitude, and what distance has she run?

Ans. Longitude=72° 55′ W.
Distance =518.4 miles.

5. A ship sails from Bermuda upon a course N.W. by W. until her longitude is found to be 69° 30′ W. What is then her latitude, and what distance has she run?

Ans. Latitude 35° 4′ N.
Distance 291.6 miles.

6. A ship sailing from Madeira, latitude 32° 38′ N, longitude 16° 55′ W., steers westerly until her latitude is 40° 2′ N.,

and her departure 2425 miles. Required her course, distance and longitude.

Ans. Course N. 79° 37′ W.
Distance 2465.3 miles.
Longitude 67° 9′.3 W.

7. Find the bearing and distance from Sandy Hook, latitude 40° 28′ N., longitude 74° 1′ W., to the Cape of Good Hope, latitude 34° 22′ S., longitude 18° 30′ E.

Ans. Course
Distance

CHARTS.

(204.) The charts commonly used in navigation are *plane charts*, or *Mercator's chart*. In the construction of the former, the portion of the earth's surface which is represented is supposed to be a *plane*. The meridians are drawn parallel to each other, and the lines of latitude at equal distances. The distance between the parallels should be to the distance between the meridians, as radius to the cosine of the middle latitude of the chart. A chart of moderate extent constructed in this manner will be tolerably correct. The distance of the meridians in the *middle* of the chart will be exact, but on each side it will be either too great or too small.

When large portions of the earth's surface are to be represented, the error of the plane chart becomes excessive. To obviate this inconvenience Mercator's chart has been constructed. Upon this chart the meridians are represented by parallel lines, and the distance between the parallels of latitude is proportioned to the meridional difference of latitude, as represented on page 149.

We have seen that the meridional difference of latitude is to the difference of longitude as radius is to the tangent of the course. Hence, while the course remains unchanged, the ratio of the meridional difference of latitude to the difference of longitude is *constant;* and, therefore, every rhumb line will be represented on Mercator's chart by a *straight* line. This property renders Mercator's chart peculiarly convenient to navigators

The preceding sketch affords a very incomplete view of the present state of the science of navigation. The most accurate method of ascertaining the situation of a vessel at sea is by means of astronomical observations. For these, however, the student must be referred to some treatise on Astronomy.

BOOK VI.

SPHERICAL TRIGONOMETRY.

(205.) SPHERICAL trigonometry teaches how to determine the several parts of a spherical triangle from having certain parts given.

A spherical triangle is a portion of the surface of a sphere, bounded by three arcs of great circles, each of which is less than a semicircumference.

RIGHT-ANGLED SPHERICAL TRIANGLES.

THEOREM I.

(206.) *In any right-angled spherical triangle, the sine of the hypothenuse is to radius, as the sine of either side is to the sine of the opposite angle.*

Let ABC be a spherical triangle, right-angled at A; then will the sine of the hypothenuse BC be to radius, as the sine of the side AC is to the sine of the angle ABC.

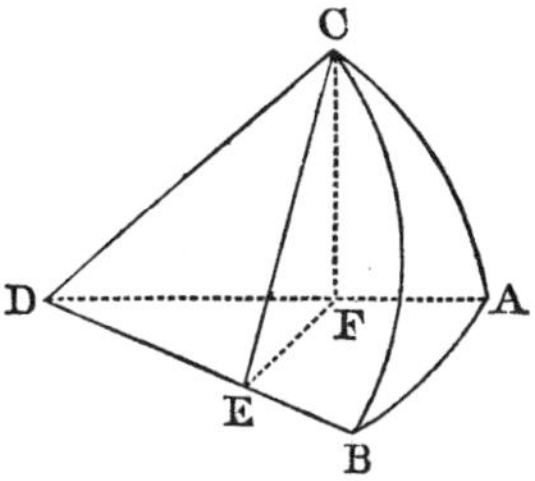

Let D be the center of the sphere; join AD, BD, CD, and draw CE perpendicular to DB, which will, therefore, be the sine of the hypothenuse BC. From the point E draw the straight line EF, in the plane ABD, perpendicular to BD, and join CF. Then, because DB is perpendicular to the two lines CE, EF, it is perpendicular to the plane CEF; and, consequently, the plane CEF is perpendicular to the plane ABD (*Geom.*, Prop. 6, B. VII.). But the plane CAD is also perpendicular to the plane ABD; therefore their line of common section, CF, is perpendicular to the plane ABD; hence CFD, CFE are right angles, and CF is the sine of the arc AC.

Now, in the right-angled plane triangle CFE,

CE : radius : : CF : sine CEF.

But since CE and FE are both at right angles to DB, the angle CEF is equal to the inclination of the planes CBD, ABD; that is, to the spherical angle ABC. Therefore,

sine BC : R : : sine AC : sine ABC.

(207.) *Cor.* 1. In any right-angled spherical triangle, *the sines of the sides are as the sines of the opposite angles.*

For, by the preceding theorem,

sine BC : R : : sine AC : sine ABC,

and sine BC : R : : sine AB : sine ACB;

therefore, sine AC : sine AB : : sine ABC : sine ACB.

Cor. 2. In any right-angled spherical triangle, *the cosine of either of the sides is to radius, as the cosine of the hypothenuse is to the cosine of the other side.*

Let ABC be a spherical triangle, right-angled at A. Describe the circle DE, of which B is the pole, and let it meet the three sides of the triangle ABC produced in D, E, and F. Then, because BD and BE are quadrants, the arc DF is perpendicular to BD. And since BAC is a right angle, the arc AF is perpendicular to BD. Hence the point F, where the arcs FD, FA intersect each other, is the pole of the arc BD (*Geom.*, Prop. 5, Cor. 2, B. IX.), and the arcs FA, FD are quadrants.

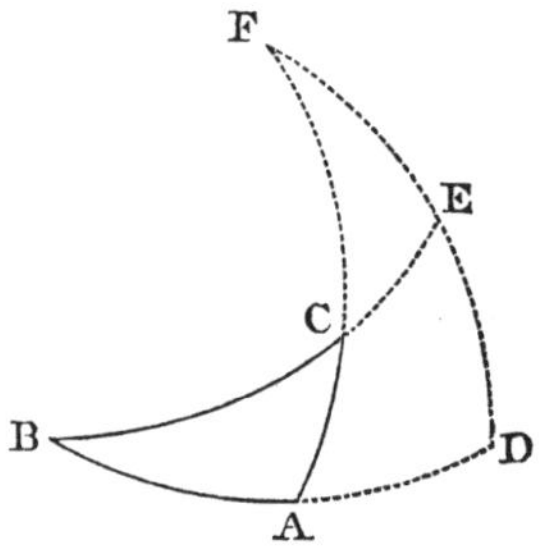

Now, in the triangle CEF, right-angled at the point E, according to the preceding theorem, we have

sine CF : R : : sine CE : sine CFE.

But CF is the complement of AC, CE is the complement of BC, and the angle CFE is measured by the arc AD, which is the complement of AB. Therefore, in the triangle ABC, we have

cos. AC : R : : cos. BC : cos. AB.

Cor. 3. In any right-angled spherical triangle, *the cosine of either of the sides is to radius, as the cosine of the angle opposite to that side is to the sine of the other angle.*

For, in the triangle CEF, we have

sine CF : R : : sine EF : sine ECF.

But sine CF is equal to cos. CA. EF is the complement of

ED, which measures the angle ABC, that is, sine EF is equal to cos. ABC, and sine ECF is the same as sine ACB; therefore,

cos. AC : R : : cos. ABC : sine ACB

THEOREM II.

(208.) *In any right-angled spherical triangle, the sine of either of the sides about the right angle is to the cotangent of the adjacent angle, as the tangent of the remaining side is to radius.*

Let ABC be a spherical triangle, right-angled at A; then will the sine of the side AB be to the cotangent of the angle ABC, as the tangent of the side AC is to radius.

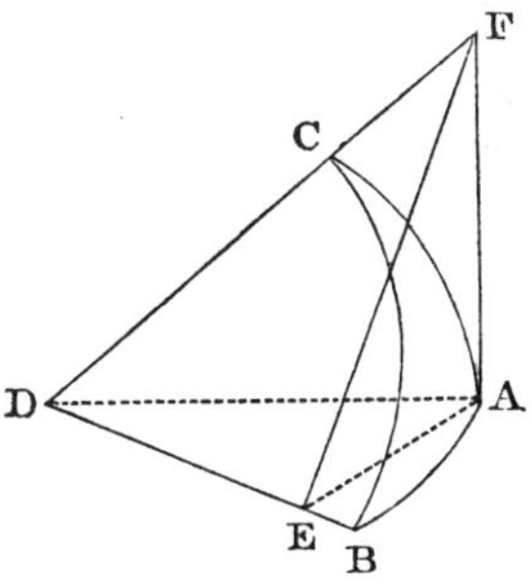

Let D be the center of the sphere; join AD, BD, CD; draw AE perpendicular to BD, which will, therefore, be the sine of the arc AB. Also, from the point E in the plane BDC, draw the straight line EF perpendicular to BD, meeting DC produced in F, and join AF. Then will AF be perpendicular to the plane ABD, because, as was shown in the preceding theorem, it is the common section of the two planes ADF, AEF, each perpendicular to the plane ADB. Therefore FAD, FAE are right angles, and AF is the tangent of the arc AC.

Now, in the triangle AEF, right-angled at A, we have

AE : radius : : AF : tang. AEF.

But AE is the sine of the arc AB, AF is the tangent of the arc AC, and the angle AEF is equal to the inclination of the planes CBD, ABD, or to the spherical angle ABC; hence

sine AB : R : : tang. AC : tang. ABC.

And because, Art. 28,

R : cot. ABC : : tang. ABC : R;

therefore, sine AB : cot. ABC : : tang. AC : R.

(209.) *Cor.* 1. In any right-angled spherical triangle, *the cosine of the hypothenuse is to the cotangent of either of the oblique angles, as the cotangent of the other oblique angle is to radius.*

Let ABC be a spherical triangle, right-angled at A. Describe the circle DEF, of which B is the pole, and construct the complemental triangle CEF, as in Cor. 2, Theorem I.

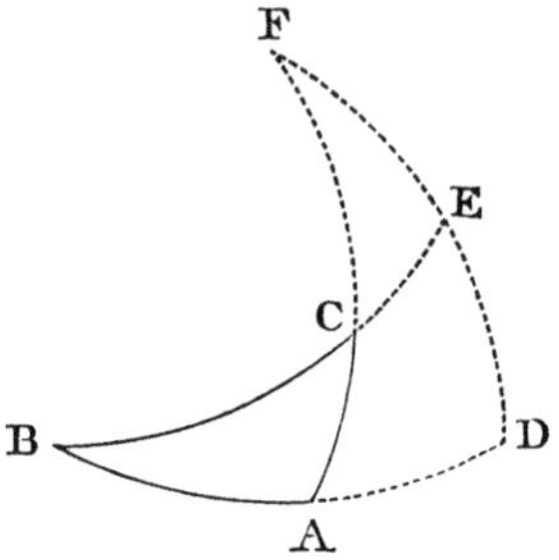

Then, in the triangle CEF, according to the preceding theorem, we have

sine CE : cot. ECF : : tan. EF : R.

But CE is the complement of BC, EF is the complement of ED, the measure of the angle ABC; and the angle ECF is equal to ACB, being its vertical angle; hence

cos. BC : cot. ACB : : cot. ABC : R.

Cor. 2. In any right-angled spherical triangle, *the cosine of either of the oblique angles is to the tangent of the adjacent side, as the cotangent of the hypothenuse is to radius.*

For, in the complemental triangle CEF, according to the preceding theorem, we have

sine EF : cot. CFE : : tan. CE : R;

hence, in the triangle ABC,

cos. ABC : tan. AB : : cot. BC : R.

Napier's Rule of the Circular Parts.

(210.) The two preceding theorems, with their corollaries, are sufficient for the solution of all cases of right-angled spherical triangles, and a rule was invented by Napier by means of which these principles are easily retained in mind.

If, in a right-angled spherical triangle, we set aside the right angle, and consider only the five remaining parts of the triangle, viz., the three sides and the two oblique angles, then the two sides which contain the right angle, and the complements of the other three, viz., of the two angles and the hypothenuse, are called the *circular parts.*

Thus, in the triangle ABC, right-angled at A, the circular parts are AB, AC, with the complements of B, BC, and C.

When, of the five circular parts, any one is taken for the *middle part,* then, of the remaining four, the two which are immediately adjacent to it on the right and left are called the *adjacent parts ;* and the other two, each of which is separated from the middle by an adjacent part, are called *opposite parts.*

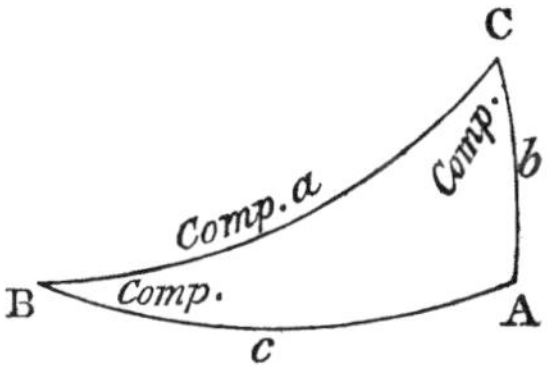

In every question proposed for solution, three of the circular parts are concerned, two of which are given, and one required ; and of these three, the middle part must be such that the other two may be equidistant from it; that is, may be either *both adjacent* or *both opposite parts.* The value of the part required may then be found by the following

RULE OF NAPIER.

(211.) *The product of the radius and the sine of the middle part, is equal to the product of the tangents of the adjacent parts, or to the product of the cosines of the opposite parts.*

It will assist the learner in remembering this rule to remark, that the first syllable of each of the words *tangent* and *adjacent* contains the same vowel *a*, and the first syllable of the words *cosine* and *opposite* contains the same vowel *o*.

It is obvious that the cosine of the complement of an angle is the sine of that angle, and the tangent of a complement is a cotangent, and vice versa.

In the triangle ABC, if we take the side b as the middle part, then the side c and the complement of the angle C are the adjacent parts, and the complements of the angle B and of the hypothenuse a are the opposite parts. Then, according to Napier's rule, $\text{R sin. } b = \text{tan. } c \text{ cot. C},$

which corresponds with Theorem II.

Also, by Napier's rule,

$$\text{R sin. } b = \text{sin. } a \text{ sin. B},$$

which corresponds with Theorem I.

Making each of the circular parts in succession the middle part, we obtain the ten following equations :

$$\text{R sin. } b = \text{sin. } a \text{ sin. B} = \text{tan. } c \text{ cot. C}.$$
$$\text{R sin. } c = \text{sin. } a \text{ sin. C} = \text{tan. } b \text{ cot. B}.$$
$$\text{R cos. B} = \text{cos. } b \text{ sin. C} = \text{cot. } a \text{ tan. } c.$$
$$\text{R cos. } a = \text{cos. } b \text{ cos. } c = \text{cot. B cot. C}.$$
$$\text{R cos. C} = \text{cos. } c \text{ sin. B} = \text{cot. } a \text{ tan. } b.$$

(212.) In order to determine whether the quantity sought is less or greater than 90°, the algebraic sign of each term should be preserved whenever one of them is negative. If the quantity sought is determined by means of its cosine, tangent, or cotangent, the algebraic sign of the result will show whether this quantity is less or greater than 90°; for the cosines, tangents, and cotangents are positive in the first quadrant, and negative in the second. But since the sines are positive in both the first and second quadrants, when a quantity is determined by means of its sine, this rule will leave it ambiguous whether the quantity is less or greater than 90°. The ambiguity may, however, generally be removed by the following rule.

In every right-angled spherical triangle, an oblique angle and its opposite side are always of the same species; that is, both are greater, or both less than 90°.

This follows from the equation

$$\text{R sin. } b = \text{tan. } c \text{ cot. C};$$

where, since sin. b is always positive, tan. c must always have the same sign as cot. C; that is, the side c and the opposite angle C both belong to the same quadrant.

(213.) When the given parts are a side and its opposite angle, the problem admits of two solutions; for two right-angled spherical triangles may always be found, having a side and its opposite angle the same in both, but of which the remaining sides and the remaining angle of the one are the supplements of the remaining sides and the remaining angle of the other. Thus, let BCD, BAD be the halves of two great circles, and let the arc CA be drawn perpendicular to BD; then ABC, ADC are two right-angled triangles, having the side AC common, and the opposite angle B equal to the angle D; but the side DC is the supplement of BC, AD is the supplement of AB, and the angle ACD is the supplement of ACB.

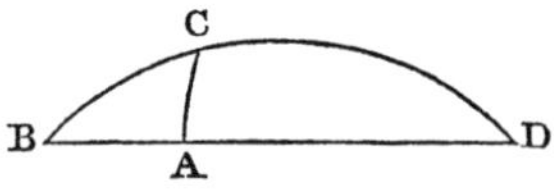

EXAMPLES.

1. In the right-angled spherical triangle ABC, there are given $a=63°\ 56'$ and $b=40°$. Required the other side c, and the angles B and C.

To find the side c.

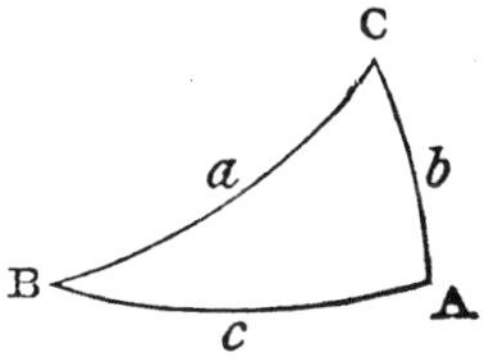

Here the circular parts concerned are the two legs and the complement of the hypothenuse; and it is evident that if the complement of a be made the *middle part*, b and c will be *opposite parts;* hence, by Napier's rule,

$$\text{R} \cos. a = \cos. b \cos. c;$$

or, reducing this equation to a proportion,

$$\cos. b : \text{R} :: \cos. a : \cos. c = 54° 59' 49''.$$

To find the angle B.

Here b is the *middle part*, and the complements of B and a are *opposite parts;* hence

$$\text{R} \sin. b = \cos. (\text{comp. } a) \times \cos. (\text{comp. B}) = \sin. a \sin. \text{B},$$

or $\quad \sin. a : \text{R} :: \sin. b : \sin. \text{B} = 45° 41' 25''.$

B is known to be an acute angle, because its opposite side is less than 90°.

To find the angle C.

Here the complement of C is the *middle part;* also b and the complement of a are *adjacent parts;* hence

$$\text{R} \cos. \text{C} = \cot. a \tan. b,$$

or $\quad \text{R} : \tan. b :: \cot. a : \cos. \text{C} = 65° 45' 57''.$

Ex. 2. In a right-angled triangle ABC, there are given the hypothenuse $a = 91° 42'$, and the angle $\text{B} = 95° 6'$. Required the remaining parts.

To find the angle C.

Make the complement of the hypothenuse the middle part; then $\quad \text{R} \cos. a = \cot. \text{B} \cot. \text{C}.$

Whence $\quad \text{C} = 71° 36' 47''.$

To find the side c.

Make the complement of the angle B the middle part; and we have $\quad \text{R} \cos. \text{B} = \cot. a \tan. c.$

Whence $\quad c = 71° 32' 14''.$

To find the side b.

Make the side b the middle part; then

$$R \sin. b = \sin. a \sin. B.$$

Whence $b = 95° 22' 30''$.

b is known to be greater than a quadrant, because its opposite angle is obtuse.

Ex. 3. In the right-angled triangle ABC, the side *b* is 26° 4′, and its opposite angle B 36°. Required the remaining parts.

Ans. $\begin{cases} a = 48° 22' 52'', \text{ or } 131° 37' 8'' \\ c = 42° 19' 17'', \text{ or } 137° 40' 43''. \\ C = 64° 14' 26'', \text{ or } 115° 45' 34''. \end{cases}$

This example, it will be seen, admits of two solutions, conformably to Art. 213.

Ex. 4. In the right-angled spherical triangle ABC, there are given the side *c*, 54° 30′, and its adjacent angle B, 44° 50′. Required the remaining parts.

Ans. $\begin{cases} C = 65° 49' 53''. \\ a = 63° 10' 4''. \\ b = 38° 59' 11'' \end{cases}$

Why is not the result ambiguous in this case?

Ex. 5. In the right-angled spherical triangle ABC, the side *b* is 55° 28′, and the side *c* 63° 15′. Required the remaining parts.

Ans. $\begin{cases} a = 75° 13' 2''. \\ B = 58° 25' 47''. \\ C = 67° 27' 1''. \end{cases}$

Ex. 6. In the right-angled spherical triangle ABC, there are given the angle B=69° 20′, and the angle C=58° 16′. Required the remaining parts.

Ans. $\begin{cases} a = 76° 30' 37''. \\ b = 65° 28' 58''. \\ c = 55° 47' 46''. \end{cases}$

(214.) A triangle, in which one of the sides is equal to a quadrant, may be solved upon the same principles as right-angled triangles, for its polar triangle will contain a right angle. See *Geom.*, Prop. 9, B. IX.

Ex. 7. In the spherical triangle ABC, the side BC=90°, the angle C=42° 10′, and the angle A=115° 20′. Required the remaining parts.

Taking the supplements of the given parts, we shall have

in the polar triangle the hypothenuse $a'=180°-115° 20'=64°$ $40'$, and one of the sides, $c'=180°-42° 10'=137° 50'$, from which, by Napier's rule, we find

$$B'=115° 23' 20''.$$
$$C'=132° \; 2' 13''.$$
$$b'=125° 15' 36''.$$

Hence, taking the supplements of these arcs, we find the parts of the required triangle are

$$AC=64° 36' 40''.$$
$$AB=47° 57' 47''.$$
$$B=54° 44' 24''.$$

Ex. 8. In the spherical triangle ABC, the side AC=90°, the angle C=69° 13′ 46″, and the angle A=72° 12′ 4″. Required the remaining parts.

$$Ans. \begin{cases} AB=70° \; 8' 39''. \\ BC=73° 17' 29''. \\ B=96° 13' 23 \end{cases}$$

OBLIQUE-ANGLED SPHERICAL TRIANGLES.

THEOREM III.

(215.) *In any spherical triangle, the sines of the sides are proportional to the sines of the opposite angles.*

In the case of right-angled spherical triangles, this proposition has already been demonstrated. Let, then, ABC be an oblique-angled triangle; we are to prove that

sin. BC : sin. AC : : sin. A : sin. B.

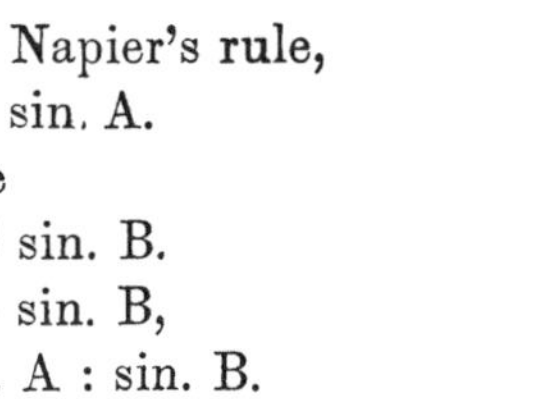

Through the point C draw an arc of a great circle CD perpendicular to AB. Then, in the spherical triangle ACD, right-angled at D, we have, by Napier's rule,

$$R \sin. CD=\sin. AC \sin. A.$$

Also, in the triangle BCD, we have

$$R \sin. CD=\sin. BC \sin. B.$$

Hence sin. AC sin. A=sin. BC sin. B,

or sin. BC : sin. AC : : sin. A : sin. B.

(216.) *Cor.* 1. In any spherical triangle, *the cosines of the sides are proportional to the cosines of the segments of the base, made by a perpendicular from the opposite angle.*

For, by Theorem I., Cor. 2,

cos. CD : R : : cos. AC : cos. AD.

Also, cos. CD : R : : cos. BC : cos. BD.

Hence cos. AC : cos. BC : : cos. AD : cos. BD.

Cor. 2. *The cosines of the angles at the base are proportional to the sines of the segments of the vertical angle.*

For, by Theorem I., Cor. 3,

cos. CD : R : : cos. A : sin. ACD.

Also, cos. CD : R : : cos. B : sin. BCD.

Hence cos. A : cos. B : : sin. ACD : sin. BCD.

Cor. 3. *The sines of the segments of the base are reciprocally proportional to the tangents of the angles at the base.*

For, by Theorem II.,

sin. AD : R : : tan. CD : tan. A.

Also, sin. BD : R : : tan. CD : tan. B.

Hence sin. AD : sin. BD : : tan. B : tan. A.

Cor. 4. *The cotangents of the two sides are proportional to the cosines of the segments of the vertical angle.*

For, by Theorem II., Cor. 2,

cos. ACD : cot. AC : : tan. CD : R.

Also, cos. BCD : cot. BC : : tan. CD : R.

Hence cos. ACD : cos. BCD : : cot. AC : cot. BC.

THEOREM IV.

(217.) *If from an angle of a spherical triangle a perpendicular be drawn to the base, then the tangent of half the sum of the segments of the base is to the tangent of half the sum of the sides, as the tangent of half the difference of the sides is to the tangent of half the difference of the segments of the base.*

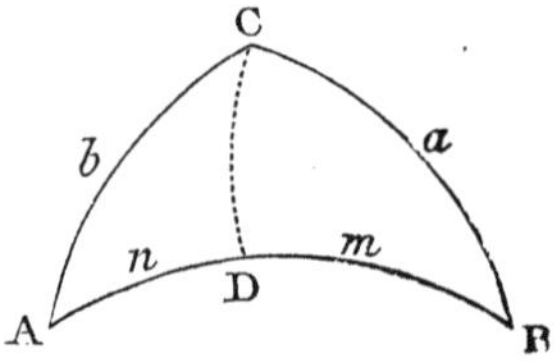

Let ABC be any spherical triangle, and let CD be drawn from C perpendicular to the base AB; then tan. $\frac{1}{2}$(BD+AD) : tan. $\frac{1}{2}$(BC+AC) : : tan. $\frac{1}{2}$(BC−AC) : tan. $\frac{1}{2}$(BD−AD).

Let BC=a, AC=b, BD=m, and AD=n. Then, by Theorem III., Cor. 1,

cos. a : cos. b : : cos. m : cos. n.

Whence, Geom., Prop. 7, Cor., B. II.,

$\cos. b+\cos. a : \cos. b-\cos. a :: \cos. n+\cos. m : \cos. n-\cos. m$

But by Trig., Art. 76,

$\cos. b+\cos. a : \cos. b-\cos. a :: \cot. \frac{1}{2}(a+b) : \tan. \frac{1}{2}(a-b).$

Also, by the same Art.,

$\cos. n+\cos. m : \cos. n-\cos. m :: \cot. \frac{1}{2}(m+n) : \tan. \frac{1}{2}(m-n).$

Therefore

$\cot. \frac{1}{2}(a+b) : \cot. \frac{1}{2}(m+n) :: \tan. \frac{1}{2}(a-b) : \tan. \frac{1}{2}(m-n).$

But, since tangents are reciprocally as their cotangents, Art. 28, we have

$\cot. \frac{1}{2}(a+b) : \cot. \frac{1}{2}(m+n) :: \tan. \frac{1}{2}(m+n) : \tan. \frac{1}{2}(a+b)$

Hence

$\tan. \frac{1}{2}(m+n) : \tan. \frac{1}{2}(a+b) :: \tan. \frac{1}{2}(a-b) : \tan. \frac{1}{2}(m-n).$

(218.) In the solution of oblique-angled spherical triangles, six cases may occur, viz.:

1. Given two sides and an angle opposite one of them.
2. Given two angles and a side opposite one of them.
3. Given two sides and the included angle.
4. Given two angles and the included side.
5. Given the three sides.
6. Given the three angles.

CASE I.

(219.) *Given two sides and an angle opposite one of them, to find the remaining parts.*

In the triangle ABC, let there be given the two sides AC and BC, and the angle A opposite one of them. The angle B may be found by Theorem III.

sin. BC : sin. AC : : sin. A : sin. B.

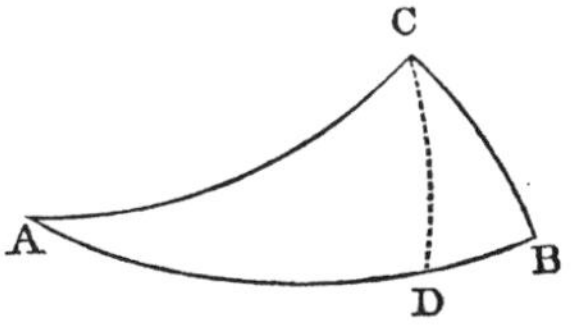

From the angle C let fall the perpendicular CD upon the side AB. The triangle ABC is divided into two right-angled triangles, in each of which there is given the hypothenuse and the angle at the base. The remaining parts may then be found by Napier's rule.

Ex. 1. In the oblique-angled spherical triangle ABC, the

side AC=70° 10′ 30″, BC=80° 5′ 4″, and the angle A=33° 15′ 7″. Required the other parts.

sin BC : sin. AC : : sin. A : sin. B=31° 34′ 38″.

Then, in the triangle ACD,

R cos. AC=cot. A cot. ACD.

Whence ACD=77° 27′ 47″.

Also, in the triangle BCD,

R cos. BC=cot. B cot. BCD.

Whence BCD= 83° 57′ 29″.

Therefore ACB=161° 25′ 16″.

To find the side AB.

sin. A : sin. ACB : : sin. BC : sin. AB=145° 5′ 0″.

When we have given two sides and an opposite angle, there are, in general, two solutions, each of which will satisfy the conditions of the problem. If the side AC, the angle A, and the side opposite this angle are given, then, with the latter for radius, describe an arc cutting the arc AB in the points B and B′. The arcs CB, CB′ will be equal, and each of the triangles ACB, ACB′ will satisfy the conditions of the problem. There is the same ambiguity in the numerical computation. The angle B is found by means of its *sine*. But this may be the sine either of ABC, or of its *supplement* AB′C (Art. 27). In the preceding example, the first proportion leaves it ambiguous whether the angle B is 31° 34′ 38′, or its supplement 148° 25′ 22″. In order to avoid false solutions, we should remember that *the greater side of a spherical triangle must lie opposite the greater angle, and conversely* (*Geom.*, Prop. 17, B. IX.). Thus, since in the preceding example the side AC is less than BC, the angle B must be less than A, and, therefore, can not be obtuse.

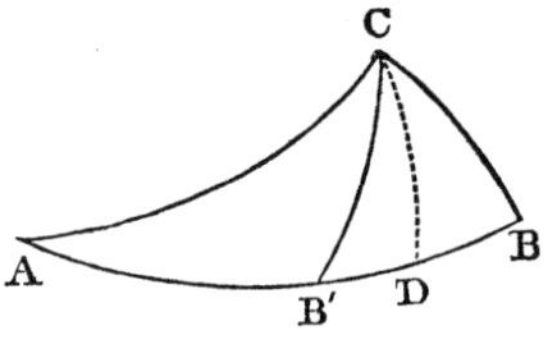

If the quantity sought is determined by means of its cosine, tangent, or cotangent, the algebraic sign of the result will show whether this quantity is less or greater than 90°; for the cosines, tangents, and cotangents are positive in the first quadrant, and negative in the second. Hence the algebraic sign of each term of a proportion should be preserved whenever one of them is negative.

Ex. 2. In the spherical triangle ABC, the side $a=124° 53'$, $b=31° 19'$, and the angle $A=16° 26'$. Required the remaining parts.

$$Ans. \begin{cases} B=\ 10° 19' 34'' \\ C=171° 48' 22'' \\ c=155° 35' 22''. \end{cases}$$

CASE II.

(220.) *Given two angles and a side opposite one of them, to find the remaining parts.*

In the triangle ABC let there be given two angles, as A and B, and the side AC opposite to one of them. The side BC may be found by Theorem III.

sin. B : sin. A : : sin. AC : sin. BC.

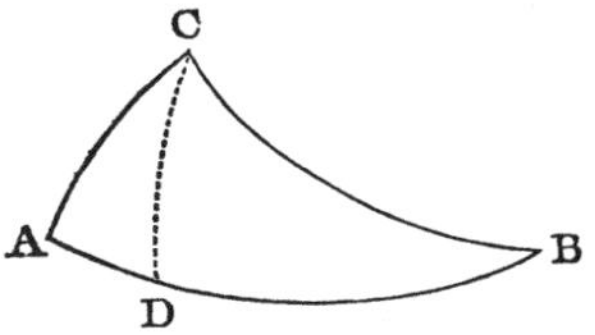

From the unknown angle C draw CD perpendicular to AB; then will the triangle ABC be divided into two right-angled triangles, in each of which there is given the hypothenuse and the angle at the base. Whence we may proceed by Napier's rule, as in Case I.

Ex. 1. In the oblique-angled spherical triangle ABC, there are given the angle $A=52° 20'$, $B=63° 40'$, and the side $b=83° 25'$. Required the remaining parts.

sin. B : sin. A : : sin. AC : sin. BC$=61° 19' 53''$.

Then, in the triangle ACD,

cot. AC : R : : cos. A : tan. AD$=79° 18' 17''$.

Also, in the triangle BCD,

cot. BC : R : : cos. B : tan. BD$=39° 3' 8''$.

Hence AB$=118° 21' 25''$.

To find the angle ACB.

sin. BC : sin. AB : : sin. A : sin. ACB$=127° 26' 47''$.

When we have given two angles and an opposite side, there are, in general, two solutions, each of which will satisfy the conditions of the problem. If the angle A, the side AC, and the angle opposite this side are given, then through the point C there may generally be drawn two arcs of great circles CB, CB′, making the same angle with AB, and each of the triangles ABC, AB′C will satisfy the conditions of the problem. There is the same ambiguity in the numerical computation, since the side BC is found by means of its *sine* (Art. 27). In the preceding example, however, there is no ambiguity, because the angle A is less than B, and, therefore, the side a must be less than b, that is, less than a quadrant.

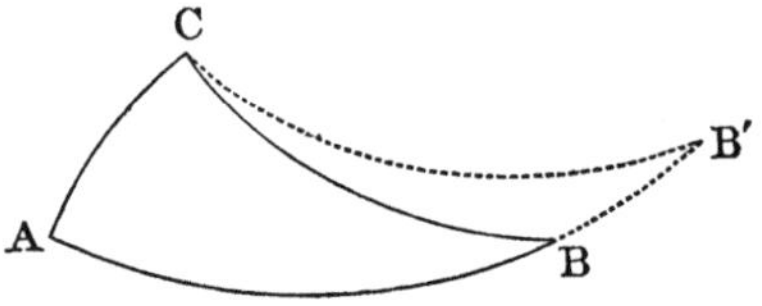

Ex. 2. In the oblique-angled spherical triangle ABC, the angle A is 128° 45′, the angle C=30° 35′, and BC=68° 50′. Required the remaining parts.

It will be observed that in this case the perpendicular BD, drawn from the angle B, falls without the triangle ABC, and therefore the side AC is the difference between the segments CD and AD.

Ans. { AB=37° 28′ 20″, AC=40° 9′ 4″, B =32° 37′ 58″.

CASE III.

(221.) *Given two sides and the included angle, to find the remaining parts.*

In the triangle ABC let there be given two sides, as AB, AC, and the included angle A. Let fall the perpendicular CD on the side AB; then, by Napier's rule,

R cos. A=tan. AD cot. AC.

Having found the segment AD, the segment BD becomes known; then, by Theorem III., Cor. 3,

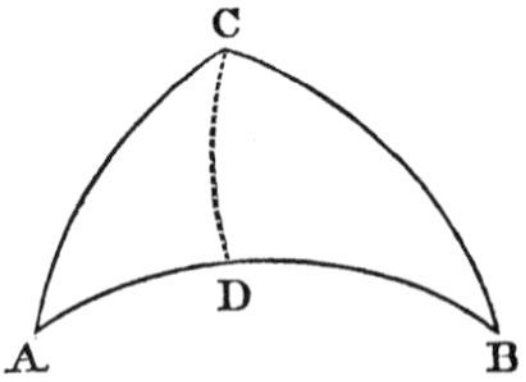

sin. BD : sin. AD : : tan. A : tan. B.

The remaining parts may now be found by Theorem III.

Ex. 1. In the spherical triangle ABC, the side AB=73° 20′, AC=41° 45′, and the angle A=30° 30′. Required the remaining parts.

cot. AC : cos. A : : R : tan. AD=37° 33′ 41″.

Hence BD=35° 46′ 19″.

sin. BD : sin. AD : : tan. A. : tan. B=31° 33′ 43″.

Also, by Theorem III., Cor. 1,

cos. AD : cos. BD : : cos. AC : cos. BC=40° 13′ 0″.

Then, by Theorem III.,

sin. BC : sin. AB : : sin. A : sin. ACB=131° 8′ 47″.

Ex. 2. In the spherical triangle ABC, the side AB=78° 15′, AC=56° 20′, and the angle A=120°. Required the other parts.

Ans. B = 48° 57′ 29″. C = 62° 31′ 40″. BC=107° 7′ 45″

CASE IV.

(222.) *Given two angles and the included side, to find the remaining parts.*

In the triangle ABC let there be given two angles, as A and ACB, and the side AC included between them. From C let fall the perpendicular CD on the side AB. Then, by Napier's rule,

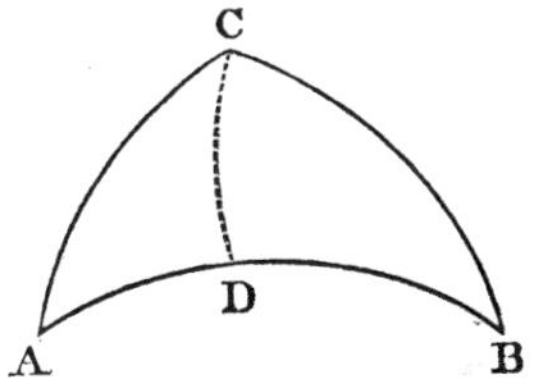

R cos. AC=cot. A cot. ACD.

Having found the angle ACD, the angle BCD becomes known; then, by Theorem III., Cor. 4,

cos. ACD : cos. BCD : : cot. AC : cot. BC.

The remaining parts may now be found by Theorem III.

Ex. 1. In the spherical triangle ABC, the angle A=32° 10′, the angle ACB=133° 20′, and the side AC=39° 15′. Required the other parts.

cot. A : cos. AC : : R : cot. ACD=64° 1′ 57″.

Hence BCD=69° 18′ 3″.

Then

cos. ACD : cos. BCD : : cot. AC : cot. BC=45° 20′ 43″.

Also, by Theorem III., Cor. 2,

sin. ACD : sin. BCD : : cos. A : cos. B=28° 15′ 47″.

Then, by Theorem III.,

sin. B : sin. ACB : : sin. AC : sin. AB=76° 23′ 5″.

Ex. 2. In the spherical triangle ABC, the angle A=125° 20′, the angle C=48° 30′, and the side AC=83° 13′. Reauired the remaining parts.

Ans. $\begin{cases} AB = 56° 39' 9''. \\ BC = 114° 30' 24''. \\ B = 62° 54' 38''. \end{cases}$

CASE V.

(223.) *Given the three sides of a spherical triangle, to find the angles.*

In the triangle ABC let there be given the three sides. From one of the angles, as C, draw CD perpendicular to AB. Then, by Theorem IV., tan. $\frac{1}{2}$AB : tan. $\frac{1}{2}$(AC+BC) : tan. $\frac{1}{2}$(AC−BC) : tan. $\frac{1}{2}$(AD−BD).

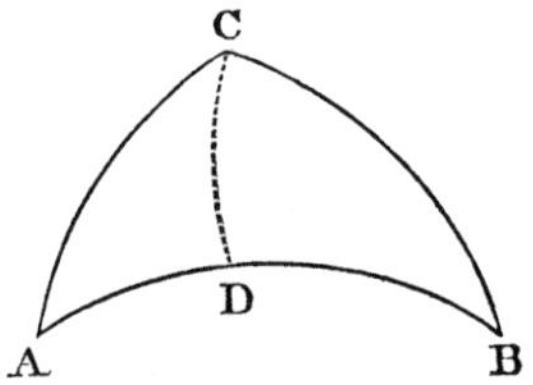

Hence AD and BD become known; then, by Napier's rule,

R cos. A=tan. AD cot. AC.

The other angles may now be easily found.

It is generally most convenient to let fall the perpendicular upon the longest side of the triangle.

Ex. 1. In the spherical triangle ABC, the side AB=112° 25′, AC=60° 20′, and BC=81° 10′. Required the angles.

tan. 56° 12$\frac{1}{2}$′ : tan. 70° 45′ : : tan. 10° 25′ : tan. 19° 24′ 26″.

Hence AD=36° 48′ 4″, and BD=75° 36′ 56″.

Then R : tan. AD : : cot. AC : cos. A=64° 46′ 36″.

Also, R : tan. BD : : cot. BC : cos. B=52° 42′ 12″.

Then sin. AC : sin. AB : : sin. B : sin. ACB=122° 11′ 6″.

Ex. 2. In the spherical triangle ABC, the side AB=40° 35′, AC=39° 10′, and BC=71° 15. Required the angles.

Ans. $\begin{cases} A = 130° 35' 55''. \\ B = 30° 25' 34''. \\ C = 31° 26' 32''. \end{cases}$

CASE VI.

(224.) *Given the three angles of a spherical triangle, to find the sides.*

If A, B, C are the angles of the given triangle, and *a*, *b*, *c* its sides, then 180°−A, 180°−B, and 180°−C are the sides of its polar triangle, whose angles may be found by Case V. Then the supplements of those angles will be the sides a, b, c of the proposed triangle.

Ex. 1. In the spherical triangle ABC, the angle A=125° 34′, B=98° 44′, and C=61° 53′. Required the sides.

The sides of the polar triangle are

54° 26′, 81° 16′, and 118° 7′.

From which, by Case V., the angles are found to be

134° 6′ 21″, 41° 28′ 17″, and 53° 34′ 47″.

Hence the sides of the proposed triangle are

AB=45° 53′ 39″, BC=138° 31′ 43″, and AC=126° 25′ 13″.

Ex. 2. In the spherical triangle ABC, the angle A=109° 55′, B=116° 38′, and C=120° 43′. Required the sides.

Ans. $\begin{cases} a = 98° \, 21' \, 20''. \\ b = 109° \, 50' \, 10''. \\ c = 115° \, 13' \, 7'' \end{cases}$

TRIGONOMETRICAL FORMULÆ.

(225.) Let ABC be any spherical triangle, and from the angle B draw the arc BD perpendicular to the base AC. Represent the sides of the triangle by a, b, c, and the segment AD by x; then will CD be equal to $b-x$.

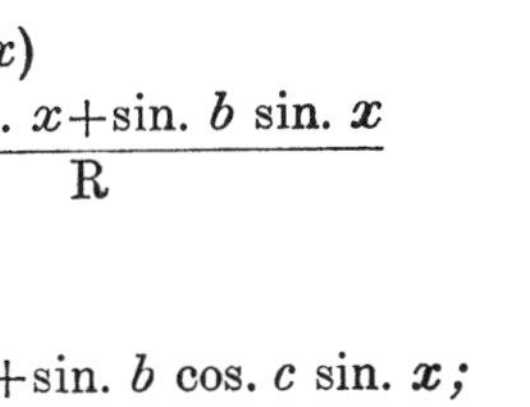

By Theorem III., Cor., 1,

$$\cos. c : \cos. a :: \cos. x : \cos. (b-x)$$

$$:: \cos. x : \frac{\cos. b \cos. x + \sin. b \sin. x}{R}$$

(Trig., Art. 72), formula (4).

Whence

$$R \cos. a \cos. x = \cos. b \cos. c \cos. x + \sin. b \cos. c \sin. x;$$

or, dividing each term by cos. x, and substituting the value of $\frac{\sin. x}{\cos. x}$ (Art. 28), we obtain

$$R^2 \cos. a = R \cos. b \cos. c + \sin. b \cos. c \tan. x.$$

But by Theorem II., Cor. 2, we have

$$\tan. x = \frac{R \cos. A}{\cot. c} = \frac{\cos. A \sin. c}{\cos. c} \text{ (Art. 28).}$$

Hence $R^2 \cos. a = R \cos. b . \cos. c + \sin. b \sin. c \cos. A$, (1) from which all the formulæ necessary for the solution of spherical triangles may be deduced.

In a similar manner we obtain

$$R^2 \cos. b = R \cos. a \cos. c + \sin. a \sin. c \cos. B, \quad (2)$$

$$R^2 \cos. c = R \cos. a \cos. b + \sin. a \sin. b \cos. C. \quad (3)$$

These equations express the following Theorem:

The square of radius multiplied by the cosine of either side of a spherical triangle, is equal to radius into the product of the cosines of the two other sides, plus the product of the sines of those sides into the cosine of their included angle.

(226.) From equation (1) we obtain, by transposition,

$$\cos. A = \frac{R^2 \cos. a - R \cos. b \cos. c}{\sin. b \sin. c},$$

a formula which furnishes an angle of a triangle when the three sides are known.

If we add R to each member of this equation, we shall have

$$R + \cos. A = \frac{R^2 \cos. a + R \sin. b \sin. c - R \cos. b \cos. c}{\sin. b \sin. c}.$$

But, by Art. 74, $R + \cos. A = \frac{2 \cos.^2 \frac{1}{2}A}{R}$.

And, by Art. 72, formula (2), by transposition,

$$R \sin. b \sin. c - R \cos. b \cos. c = -R^2 \cos. (b+c).$$

Hence, by substitution, we obtain

$$\frac{2 \cos.^2 \frac{1}{2}A}{R} = \frac{R^2(\cos. a - \cos. (b+c))}{\sin. b \sin. c}$$

$$= \frac{2R \sin. \frac{1}{2}(a+b+c) \sin. \frac{1}{2}(b+c-a)}{\sin. b \sin. c},$$

by Art. 75, formula (4).

If, then, we put $s = \frac{1}{2}(a+b+c)$, that is, half the sum of the sides, we shall find

$$\cos. \tfrac{1}{2}A = R\sqrt{\frac{\sin. s \sin. (s-a)}{\sin. b \sin. c}}. \quad (4)$$

By subtracting cos. A from R instead of adding, we shall obtain, in a similar manner,

$$\sin. \tfrac{1}{2}A = R\sqrt{\frac{\sin. (s-b) \sin. (s-c)}{\sin. b \sin. c}}. \quad (5)$$

Either formula (4) or (5) may be employed to compute the angles of a spherical triangle when the three sides are known, and this method may be preferred to that of Art. 223.

Ex. 1. In a spherical triangle there are given $a=63° 50'$, $b=80° 19'$, and $c=120° 47'$. Required the three angles.

Here half the sum of the sides is $132° 28'=s$.

Also, $s-a=68° 38'$.

Using formula (4), we have

log. sine s,	132° 28′ . .	9.867862
log. sine $(s-a)$,	68° 38′ . .	9.969075
$-$log. sine b,	80° 19′ comp.	0.006232
$-$log. sine c,	120° 47′ comp.	0.065952
	Sum	19.909121
log. cos. $\frac{1}{2}$A,	25° 45′ 19″	9.954560.

Hence the angle $A=51° 30' 38''$.

The remaining angles may be found by Theorem III., or by formulas similar to formula (4).

$$\cos. \tfrac{1}{2}B=R\sqrt{\frac{\sin. s \sin. (s-b)}{\sin. a \sin. c}}.$$

$$\cos. \tfrac{1}{2}C=R\sqrt{\frac{\sin. s \sin. (s-c)}{\sin. a \sin. b}}.$$

We thus find the angle $B= 59° 16' 46''$,

and $C=131° 28' 36''$.

Ex. 2. In a spherical triangle there are given $a=115° 20'$, $b=57° 30'$, and $c=82° 28'$. Required the three angles.

Ans. $\begin{cases} A=126° 35' \ 2''. \\ B= 48° 31' 42''. \\ C= 61° 43' 58''. \end{cases}$

(227.) By means of the polar triangle, we may convert the preceding formulæ for angles into formulæ for the sides of a triangle, since the angles of every triangle are the supplements of the sides of its polar triangle. Let, then, a', b', c', A', B', C' represent the sides and angles of the polar triangle, and we shall have

$$A=180°-a', \quad B=180°-b', \quad C=180°-c',$$
$$a=180°-A', \quad b=180°-B', \quad c=180°-C'$$

Therefore
$$\sin. \tfrac{1}{2}A=\sin. (90°-\tfrac{1}{2}a')=\cos. \tfrac{1}{2}a',$$
$$\cos. \tfrac{1}{2}A=\cos. (90°-\tfrac{1}{2}a')=\sin. \tfrac{1}{2}a',$$

$$\sin. b = \sin. (180° - B') = \sin. B',$$
$$\sin. c = \sin. (180° - C') = \sin. C'.$$

Also, if we put S'=half the sum of the angles of the polar triangle, we shall have

$$a+b+c=540° - (A'+B'+C'),$$

or
$$s = 270° - S',$$

whence
$$\sin. s = -\cos. S',$$

$$\sin. (s-a) = \sin. [90° - (S'-A')] = \cos. (S'-A'),$$
$$\sin. (s-b) = \cos. (S'-B'),$$
$$\sin. (s-c) = \cos. (S'-C').$$

By substituting these values in formula (5), Art. 226, and omitting all the accents, since the equations are applicable to any triangle, we obtain

$$\cos. \tfrac{1}{2}a = R\sqrt{\frac{\cos. (S-B) \cos. (S-C)}{\sin. B \sin. C}}; \qquad (6)$$

and formula (4) becomes

$$\sin. \tfrac{1}{2}a = R\sqrt{\frac{-\cos. S \cos. (S-A)}{\sin. B \sin. C}}, \qquad (7)$$

which formulæ enable us to compute the sides of a triangle when the three angles are known; and this method may be preferred to that of Art. 224.

In a similar manner, by means of the polar triangle, we derive from formula (1), Art. 225, the equation

$$R^2 \cos. A = \cos. a \sin. B \sin. C - R \cos. B \cos. C; \qquad (8)$$

that is, *the square of radius multiplied by the cosine of either angle of a spherical triangle, is equal to the product of the sines of the two other angles into the cosine of their included side, minus radius into the product of their cosines.*

Ex. 1. In a spherical triangle ABC, there are given $A = 130° \ 30'$, $B = 30° \ 50'$, and $C = 32° \ 5'$. Required the three sides.

Here half the sum of the angles is $96° \ 42' \ 30'' = S$.

Also,
$$S-A = -33° \ 47' \ 30'',$$
$$S-B = 65° \ 52' \ 30'',$$
$$S-C = 64° \ 37' \ 30''$$

Using formula (6), we have

log. cos. (S−B),	65° 52′ 30″	.	9.611435
log. cos. (S−C),	64° 37′ 30″	.	9.631992
−log. sin. B,	30° 50′ comp.		0.290270
−log. sin. C,	32° 5′ comp.		0.274781
		Sum	19.808478.
log. cos. $\frac{1}{2}a$,	36° 40′ 1″		9.904239.

Hence the side a=73° 20′ 2″.

The remaining sides may be found by Theorem III., or by formulas similar to formula (6).

$$\cos.\ \tfrac{1}{2}b = \mathrm{R}\sqrt{\frac{\cos.\ (\mathrm{S}-\mathrm{A})\cos.\ (\mathrm{S}-\mathrm{C})}{\sin.\ \mathrm{A}\sin.\ \mathrm{C}}},$$

$$\cos.\ \tfrac{1}{2}c = \mathrm{R}\sqrt{\frac{\cos.\ (\mathrm{S}-\mathrm{A})\cos.\ (\mathrm{S}-\mathrm{B})}{\sin.\ \mathrm{A}\sin.\ \mathrm{B}}}.$$

We thus find the side b=40° 13° 12″,

and c=42° 0′ 12″.

Ex. 2. In the spherical triangle ABC, the angle A=129° 30′, B=54° 35′, and C=63° 5′. Required the three sides.

Ans. a=120° 57′ 5″.
b= 64° 55′ 37″
c= 82° 19′ 0″.

(228.) Formula (1), Art. 225, will also furnish a new test for removing the ambiguity of the solution in Case I. of oblique angled triangles. For we have

$$\cos.\ \mathrm{A} = \frac{\mathrm{R}^2 \cos.\ a - \mathrm{R}\cos.\ b\cos.\ c}{\sin.\ b\sin.\ c}.$$

Now if cos. a is greater than cos. b, we shall have

$$\mathrm{R}^2 \cos.\ a > \mathrm{R}\cos.\ b\cos.\ c,$$

or the sign of the second member of the equation will be the same as that of cos. a, since the denominator is necessarily positive, and cos. c is less than radius. Hence cos. A and cos. a will have the same sign; or A and a will be of the same species when cos a>cos. b, or sin. a<sin. b; that is,

If the sine of the side opposite to the required angle is less than the sine of the other given side, there will be but one triangle.

But if cos. a is less than cos. b, then such a value may be given to c as to render

$$R^2 \cos. a < R \cos. b \cos. c,$$

or the sign of the second member of the equation will depend upon the value of cos. c; that is, c may be taken so as to render cos. A either positive or negative. Hence

If the sine of the side opposite to the required angle is greater than the sine of the other given side, there will be two triangles which fulfill the given conditions.

(229.) Formula (8), Art. 227, will furnish a test for removing the ambiguity in Case II. of oblique-angled triangles. For we have

$$\cos. a = \frac{R^2 \cos. A + R \cos. B \cos. C}{\sin. B \sin. C};$$

from which it follows, as in the preceding article, that if cos. A is greater than cos. B, A and a will be of the same species. But if cos. A is less than cos. B, then such values may be given to C as to render cos. a either positive or negative. Hence

If the sine of the angle opposite to the required side is less than the sine of the other given angle, there will be but one triangle;

But, *if the sine of the angle opposite to the required side is greater than the sine of the other given angle, there will be two triangles which fulfill the given conditions.*

SAILING ON AN ARC OF A GREAT CIRCLE.

(230.) It is demonstrated in *Geom.*, Prop. 3, B. IX., that the shortest path from one point to another on the surface of a sphere is the arc of a great circle which joins the two given points. Hence, if it is desired to sail from one port to another by the shortest route, it is necessary to follow an arc of a great circle, and this arc generally does not coincide with a rhumb-line.

The bearing and distance from one place to another on the arc of a great circle may be computed from the latitudes and longitudes of the places by means of Spherical Trigonometry

Thus, let P be the pole of the earth, EQ a part of the equator, and A and B the two given places comprehended between the meridians PE and PQ. Then PA is the complement of the latitude of A, PB is the complement of the latitude of B, and the angle P is measured by the arc EQ, which is the difference of longitude between the two places. Hence, in the triangle ABP, we have given two sides AP, BP, and the included angle P, from which we may compute the side AB, and the angles A and B, according to Case III. of oblique-angled triangles.

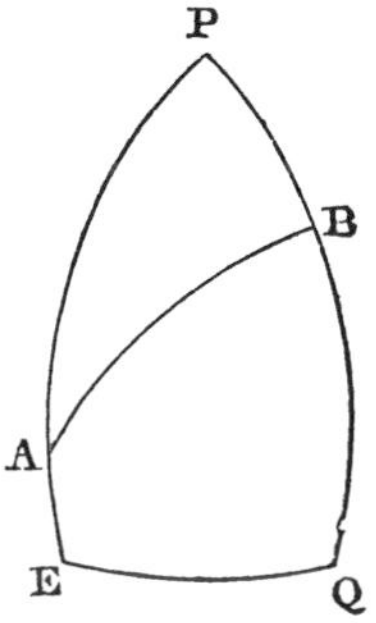

Ex. 1. Required the course and distance from Nantucket Shoals, in latitude 41° 4′ N., longitude 69° 55′ W., to Cape Clear, in latitude 51° 26′ N., longitude 9° 29′ W., on the arc of a great circle.

Here we have given

the angle P=69° 55′− 9° 29′=60° 26′;
the side PA=90° −41° 4′=48° 56′;
the side PB=90° −51° 26′=38° 34′.

Then cot. PB : cos. P : : R : tan. PD=21° 28′ 35″.
Whence AD=27° 27′ 25″.
Also sin. AD : sin. PD : : tan. P : tan. A =54° 27′ 21 ,
and sin. A : sin. PB : : sin. P : sin. AB=41° 47′ 28′.

41° 47′ 28″ is equal to 2507.47 nautical miles.

Hence the course from Nantucket Shoals to Cape Clear is N. 54° 27′ E., and the distance is 2507.47 miles.

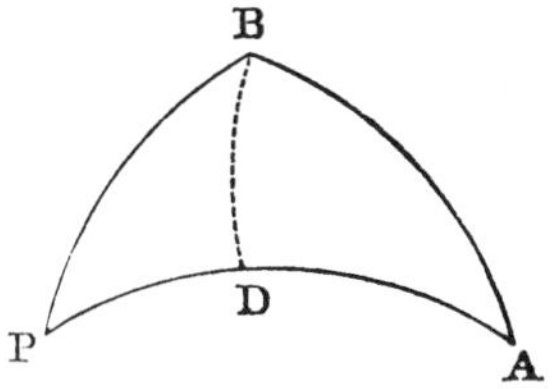

According to Mercator's sailing, the course on a rhumb-line, found on page 152, is N. 76° E., and the distance 2572.9 miles. Hence the distance on an arc of a great circle is 65.4 miles less than on a rhumb-line, and the former course is 21½ degrees more northerly than the latter.

While sailing on a rhumb-line the course of a ship remains always the same, but while sailing on an arc of a great circle the course is continually changing. The preceding course is that with which the ship starts from Nantucket, and a new computation of the course should be made every day or two; or it might be more convenient to compute beforehand the position of the points in which the great circle intersects the meridians for every five degrees of longitude, and the ship might be steered upon a direct course for these points successively.

Ex. 2. Required the course and distance from Nantucket Shoals to Gibraltar, in latitude 36° 6′ N., longitude 5° 21′ W., on the shortest route.

Ans. The course is N. 73° 29′ E
Distance 2974.1 miles.

Ex. 3. Required the course and distance from Sandy Hook, in latitude 40° 28′ N., longitude 74° 1′ W., to Madeira, in latitude 32° 38′ N., longitude 16° 55′ W., on the shortest route.

Ans. The course is N. 80° 53′ E.
Distance 2744.1 miles.

Ex. 4. Required the course and distance from Sandy Hook to St. Jago, in latitude 14° 54′ N., longitude 23° 30′ W., on the shortest route.

Ans. The course is S. 74° 46′ E.
Distance 3037.6 miles.

Ex. 5. Required the course and distance from Sandy Hook to the Cape of Good Hope, in latitude 34° 22′ S., longitude 18° 30′ E., on the shortest route.

Ans. The course is S. 63° 48′ E
Distance 6792 miles.

EXAMPLES FOR PRACTICE.

PLANE TRIGONOMETRY.

Prob. 1. Given the three sides of a triangle, 627, 718.9, and 1140, to find the angles.

Ans. 29° 44′ 2″, 34° 39′ 26″, and 115° 36′ 32″.

Prob. 2. In the triangle ABC, the angle A is given 89° 45′ 43″, the side AB 654, and the side AC 460, to find the remaining parts.

Ans. BC=798; the angle B=35° 12′ 1″, and the angle C=55° 2′ 16″.

Prob. 3. In the triangle ABC, the angle A is given 56° 12′ 45″, the side BC 2597.84, and the side AC 3084.33, to find the remaining parts.

Ans. B=80° 39′ 40″, C=43° 7′ 35″, c=2136.8;
or, B=99 20 20, C=24 26 55, c=1293.8.

Prob. 4. In the triangle ABC, the angle A is given 44° 13′ 24″, the angle B 55° 59′ 58″, and the side AC 368, to find the remaining parts.

Ans. C=79° 46′ 38″, AB=436.844, and BC=309.595.

Prob. 5. In a right-angled triangle, if the sum of the hypothenuse and base be 3409 feet, and the angle at the base 53° 12′ 14″, what is the perpendicular?

Ans. 1707.2 feet.

Prob. 6. In a right-angled triangle, if the difference of the hypothenuse and base be 169.9 yards, and the angle at the base 42° 36′ 12″, what is the length of the perpendicular?

Ans. 435.732 yards.

Prob. 7. In a right-angled triangle, if the sum of the base and perpendicular be 123.7 feet, and the angle at the base 58° 19′ 32″, what is the length of the hypothenuse?

Ans. 89.889 feet.

Prob. 8. In a right-angled triangle, if the difference of the base and perpendicular be 12 yards, and the angle at the base 38° 1′ 8″, what is the length of the hypothenuse?

Ans. 69.81 yards.

Prob. 9. A May-pole, 50 feet 11 inches high, at a certain time will cast a shadow 98 feet 6 inches long; what, then, is the breadth of a river which runs within 20 feet 6 inches of the foot of a steeple 300 feet 8 inches high, if the steeple at the same time throws its shadow 30 feet 9 inches beyond the stream?

Ans. 530 feet 5 inches.

Prob. 10. A ladder 40 feet long may be so placed that it shall reach a window 33 feet from the ground on one side of the street, and by turning it over, without moving the foot out of its place, it will do the same by a window 21 feet high on the other side. Required the breadth of the street.

Ans. 56.649 feet.

Prob. 11. A May-pole, whose top was broken off by a blast of wind, struck the ground at the distance of 15 feet from the foot of the pole; what was the height of the whole May-pole, supposing the length of the broken piece to be 39 feet?

Ans. 75 feet.

Prob. 12. How must three trees, A, B, C, be planted, so that the angle at A may be double the angle at B, the angle at B double the angle at C, and a line of 400 yards may just go round them?

Ans. AB=79.225, AC=142.758, and BC=178.017 yards.

Prob. 13. The town B is half way between the towns A and C, and the towns B, C, and D are equidistant from each other. What is the ratio of the distance AB to AD?

Ans. As unity to $\sqrt{3}$.

Prob. 14. There are two columns left standing upright in the ruins of Persepolis; the one is 66 feet above the plain, and the other 48. In a straight line between them stands an ancient statue, the head of which is 100 feet from the summit of the higher, and 84 feet from the top of the lower column, the base of which measures just 74 feet to the centre of the figure's base. Required the distance between the tops of the two columns.

Ans. 156.68 feet.

Prob. 15. Prove that $\text{tang.}\,(45^\circ - b) = \dfrac{1 - \text{tang.}\,b}{1 + \text{tang.}\,b}$.

Prob. 16. One angle of a triangle is 45°, and the perpendicular from this angle upon the opposite base divides the base into two parts, which are in the ratio of 2 to 3. What are the parts into which the vertical angle is divided by this perpendicular?

Ans. 18° 26′ 6″ and 26° 33′ 54″.

Prob. 17. Prove that $\sin. 3b = 3 \sin. b - 4 \sin.^3 b$.

Prob. 18. One side of a triangle is 25, another is 22, and the angle contained by these two sides is half that of the angle opposite the side 25. What is the value of the included angle?

Ans. 39° 58′ 51″.

Prob. 19. One side of a triangle is 25, another is 22, and the angle contained by these two sides is half that of the angle opposite the side 22. What is the value of the included angle?

Ans. 30° 46′ 38″.

Prob. 20. Two sides of a triangle are in the ratio of 11 to 9, and the opposite angles have the ratio of 3 to 1. What are those angles?

Ans. The sine of the smaller of the two angles is $\frac{2}{3}$, and of the greater $\frac{22}{27}$; the angles are 41° 48′ 37″ and 125° 25′ 51″.

Prob. 21. One side of a triangle is 15, and the difference of the two other sides is 6; also, the angle included between the first side and the greater of the two others is 60°. What is the length of the side opposite to this angle?

Ans. 57.

Prob. 22. One side of a triangle is 15, and the difference of the two other sides is 6; also, the angle opposite to the greater of the two latter sides is 60°. What is the length of said side?

Ans. 13.

Prob. 23. One side of a triangle is 15, and the opposite angle is 60°; also, the difference of the two other sides is 6. What are the lengths of those sides?

Ans. 11.0712 and 17.0712.

Prob. 24. The perimeter of a triangle is 100; the perpendicular let fall from one of the angles upon the opposite base is 30, and the angle at one end of this base is 50°. What is the length of the base?

Ans. 30.388.

MENSURATION OF SURFACES AND SOLIDS.

Prob. 1. The base of a triangle is 20 feet, and its altitude 18 feet. It is required to draw a line parallel to the base so as to cut off a trapezoid containing 80 square feet. What is the length of the line of section, and its distance from the base of the triangle?

Ans. Length 14.907 feet; distance from base 4.584 feet.

Prob. 2. The base of a triangle is 20 feet, one angle at the base is 63° 26′, and the other angle at the base is 56° 19′. It is required to draw a line parallel to the base, so as to cut off a trapezoid containing 109 square feet. What is the length of the line of section, and its distance from the base of the triangle?

Ans. Length 12.070 feet; distance from base 6.797 feet.

Prob. 3. In a perpendicular section of a ditch, the breadth at the top is 26 feet, the slopes of the sides are each 45°, and the area 140 square feet. Required the breadth at bottom and the depth of the ditch.

Ans. Breadth 10.77 feet; depth 7.615 feet.

Prob. 4. The altitude of a trapezoid is 23 feet; the two parallel sides are 76 and 36 feet; it is required to draw a line parallel to the parallel sides, so as to cut off from the smaller end of the trapezoid a part containing 560 square feet. What is the length of the line of section, and its distance from the shorter of the two parallel sides?

Ans. Length 56.954 feet; distance 12.048 feet.

Prob. 5. From the greater end of a trapezoidal field whose parallel ends and breadth measure 12, 8, and $10\frac{1}{2}$ chains respectively, it is required to cut off an area of six acres by a fence parallel to the parallel sides of the field. What is the length of the fence, and its distance from the greater side.

Ans. Length of fence 9.914 chains; distance from greater side 5.476 chains.

Prob. 6. There are three circles whose radii are 20, 28, and 29 inches respectively. Required the radius of a fourth circle, whose area is equal to the sum of the areas of the other three.

Ans. 45 inches.

Prob. 7. In constructing a rail-road, the pathway of which is 24 feet broad, it is necessary to make a cutting 40 feet in depth; what must be the breadth of the cutting at top, supposing the slopes of the sides to be 65°?

Ans. 61.305 feet.

Prob. 8. The sides of a quadrilateral field are 690 yards, 467 yards, 359 yards, and 428 yards; also, the angle contained between the first and second sides is 57° 30′, and the angle between the third and fourth sides 122° 30′. Required the area of the field.

Ans. 200677.2 square yards.

Prob. 9. There are two regular pentagons, one inscribed in a circle, and the other described about it; and the difference of the areas of the pentagons is 10 square inches. Required the radius of the circle.

Ans. 8.926 inches.

Prob. 10. What is the length of a chord cutting off one third part of a circle, whose diameter is 289 feet.

Ans. 278.67 feet.

Prob. 11. The area of a triangle is 1012; the length of the side a is to that of b as 4 to 3, and c is to b as 3 to 2. Required the length of the sides.

Ans. $a=52.470$, $b=39.353$, $c=59.029$.

Prob. 12. The area of a triangle is 144, the base is 24, and one of the angles at the base is 30°. Required the other sides of the triangle.

Ans. 24 and 12.4233.

Prob. 13. Seven men bought a grinding-stone of 60 inches diameter, each paying one seventh part of the expense. What part of the diameter must each grind down for his share?

Ans. The 1st, 4.4508 inches; 2d, 4.8400 inches; 3d, 5.3535 inches; 4th, 6.0765 inches; 5th, 7.2079 inches; 6th, 9.3935 inches; 7th, 22.6778 inches.

Prob. 14. The area of an equilateral triangle is 17 square feet and 83 square inches. What is the length of each side?

Ans. 76.45 inches.

Prob. 15. The parallel sides of a trapezoid are 20 and 12 feet, and the other sides are 15 and 17 feet. Required the area of the trapezoid.

Ans. 240 square feet.

Prob. 16. How many square yards of canvas are required to make a conical tent which is 20 feet in diameter and 12 feet high?

Ans. 54.526 square yards.

Prob. 17. The circumference of an hexagonal pillar is 7 feet, and the height 11 feet 2 inches. Required the solid contents of the pillar.

Ans. 39.488 cubic feet.

Prob. 18. The base of the great pyramid of Egypt is a square whose side measures 746 feet, and the altitude of the pyramid is 450 feet. Required the volume of the pyramid.

Ans. 83,477,400 cubic feet.

Prob. 19. A side of the base of a frustum of a square pyramid is 25 inches, a side of the top is 9 inches, and the height is 20 feet. Required the volume of the frustum.

Ans. 43.102 cubic feet.

Prob. 20. Three persons, having bought a sugar-loaf, would divide it equally among them by sections parallel to the base. It is required to find the altitude of each person's share, supposing the loaf to be a cone whose height is 20 inches.

Ans. 13.8672, 3.6044, and 2.5284 inches.

Prob. 21. If a cubical foot of brass were to be drawn into wire of one thirtieth of an inch in diameter, it is required to determine the length of the said wire, allowing no loss in the metal.

Ans. 55003.94 yards; or 31 miles 443.94 yards.

Prob. 22. How high above the surface of the earth must a person be raised to see one third of its surface?

Ans. The height of its diameter.

Prob. 23. If a heavy sphere, whose diameter is 4 inches, be let fall into a conical glass full of water, whose diameter is 5, and altitude 6 inches, it is required to determine how much water will run over.

Ans. 26.272 cubic inches.

Prob. 24. The capacity of a cylinder is a cubic feet, and its convex surface is b square feet. Required the dimensions of the cylinder.

Ans. Radius of base$=\frac{2a}{b}$, and altitude$=\frac{b^2}{4a\pi}$.

Prob. 25. A triangular pyramid, the sides of whose base are

13, 14, and 15 inches respectively, and whose altitude is 16 inches, is cut, at the distance of 2 inches from the vertex, by a plane parallel to the base. Required the volume of the frustum of the pyramid.

Ans. 447.125 cubic inches.

Prob. 26. The altitude of a cone is 10 inches, and the radius of its base is 5 inches. At what distance from the base must a plane pass parallel to the base, so as to cut off a frustum whose capacity is 20 cubic inches?

Ans. 0.2614 inches.

SURVEYING.

Prob. 1. The angle of elevation of a spire I found to be 39° 27′, and going directly from it 225 feet on a horizontal plane, I found the angle to be only 24° 38′. What is the height of the spire, and the distance from its base to the second station?

Ans. Height 238.02 feet, distance 508.18 feet.

Prob. 2. Wishing to know the distance of an inaccessible object, I measured a horizontal base-line 1328 feet, and found the angles at the ends of this line were 84° 23′ and 43° 19′. What was the distance of the object from each end of the base-line?

Ans. 1151.44 feet, and 1670.35 feet.

Prob. 3. Wishing to know the distance between two inaccessible objects, C and D, I measured a base-line, AB, 3784 feet, and found the angle BAD=47° 32′, the angle DAC=39° 53′, the angle ABC=46° 34′, and the angle CBD=38° 1′. What is the distance from C to D?

Ans. 3257.36 feet.

Prob. 4. Suppose a light-house built on the top of a rock; the distance between the place of observation and that part of the rock which is level with the eye, and directly under the building, is 1860 feet; the distance from the top of the rock to the place of observation is 2538 feet, and from the top of the building 2550 feet. Required the height of the light-house.

Ans. 17 feet 7 inches.

Prob. 5. At 85 feet distance from the bottom of a tower, standing on a horizontal plane, the angle of its elevation was found to be 52° 30′. Required the altitude of the tower.

Ans. 110½ feet.

Prob. 6. At a certain station, the angle of elevation of an inaccessible tower was 26° 30′; but, measuring 225 feet in a direct line toward it, the angle was then found to be 51° 30′. Required the height of the tower, and its distance from the last station. *Ans.* Height 186 feet, distance 147 feet.

Prob. 7. To find the distance of an inaccessible castle gate, I measured a line of 73 yards, and at each end of it took the angle of position of the object and the other end, and found the one to be 90°, and the other 61° 45′. Required the distance of the castle from each station.

Ans. 135.8 yards, and 154.2 yards.

Prob. 8. From the top of a tower 143 feet high, by the seaside, I observed that the angle of depression of a boat was 35°. What was its distance from the bottom of the tower?

Ans. 204.22 feet.

Prob. 9. I wanted to know the distance between two places, A and B, but could not meet with any station from whence I could see both objects. I measured a line CD=200 yards; from C the object A was visible, and from D the object B was visible, at each of which places I set up a pole. I also measured FC=200 yards, and DE=200 yards, and at F and E set up poles. I then measured the angle AFC=83°, ACF=54° 31′, ACD=53° 30′, BDC=156° 25′, BDE=54° 30′, and BED=88° 30′. Required the distance from A to B.

Ans. 345.5 yards.

Prob. 10. From the top of a light-house, the angle of depression of a ship at anchor was 3° 38′, and at the bottom of the light-house the angle of depression was 2° 43′. Required the horizontal distance of the vessel, and the height of the promontory above the level of the sea, the light-house being 85 feet high. *Ans.* Distance 5296.4 feet, height 251.3 feet.

Prob. 11. An observer, seeing a cloud in the west, measured its angle of elevation, and found it to be 64°. A second observer, situated half a mile due east from the first station, and on the same horizontal plane, found its angle of elevation at the same moment of time to be only 35°. Required the perpendicular height of the cloud, and its distance from each observer.

Ans. Perpendicular height 935.75 yards, distances 1041.1 and 1631.4 yards.

Prob. 12. An observer, seeing a balloon in the north, measured its angle of elevation, and found it to be 36° 52′. A second observer, situated one mile due south from the first station, and on the same horizontal plane, found its angle of elevation at the same instant to be only 30° 58′. Required the perpendicular height of the balloon, and its distance from each observer.

Ans. Perpendicular height 3.003 miles, distances 5.006 and 5.837 miles.

Prob. 13. From a window near the bottom of a house which seemed to be on a level with the bottom of a steeple, I found the angle of elevation of the top of the steeple to be 40° ; then from another window, 21 feet directly above the former, the like angle was 37° 30′. What was the height and distance of the steeple? *Ans.* Height 245.51 feet, distance 292.59 feet.

Prob. 14. Wanting to know my distance from an inaccessible object, P, on the other side of a river, and having no instrument for taking angles, but a chain for measuring distances, from each of two stations, A and B, which were taken at 300 yards asunder, I measured in a direct line from the object P 60 yards, viz., AC and BD each equal to 60 yards; also, the diagonal AD measured 330 yards, and the diagonal BC 336 yards. What was the distance of the object P from each station A and B? *Ans.* AP=321.76 yards, BP=300.09 yards.

Prob. 15. Having at a certain (unknown) distance taken the angle of elevation of a steeple, I advanced 60 yards nearer on level ground, and then observed the angle of elevation to be the complement of the former. Advancing 20 yards still nearer, the angle of elevation now appeared to be just double of the first. Required the altitude of the steeple.

Ans. 74.162 yards.

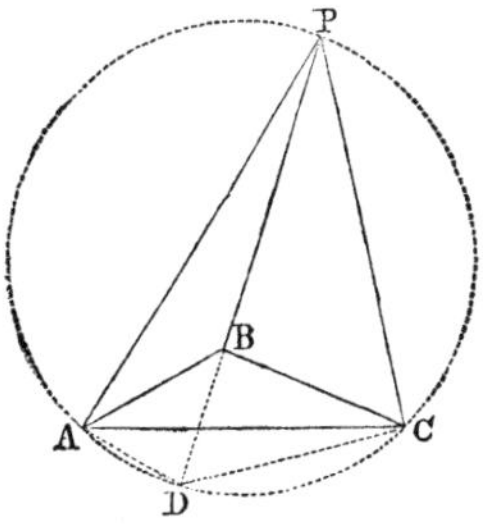

Prob. 16. In a garrison there are three remarkable objects, A, B, C, whose distances from each other are known to be, AB 213, AC 424, and BC 262 yards. I am desirous of knowing my position and distance at a station, P, from which I observed the angle APB, 13° 30′, and the angle CPB, 29° 50′.

Ans. AP=605.7122, BP=429.6814, CP=524.2365.

Prob. 17. Supposing the object B to be on the opposite side of the line AC (see figure to Prob. 16), and that the distances of the objects were, AB=8 miles, AC=12 miles, and BC=$7\frac{1}{5}$ miles; also, the angle APB=19°, and the angle CPB=25°. It is required to find the distances AP, BP, and CP.

Ans. AP=9.4711 miles, BP=16.3369 miles, CP=16.8485 miles.

Prob. 18. In a pentangular field, beginning with the south side, and measuring round toward the east, the first or south side was 27.35 chains, the second 31.15 chains, the third 23.70 chains, the fourth 29.25 chains, and the fifth 22.20 chains; also, the diagonal from the first angle to the third was 38.00 chains, and that from the third to the fifth was 40.10 chains. Required the area of the field.

Ans. 117 *A.* 2 *R.* 39 *P.*

Prob. 19. The following are the dimensions of a five-sided field, ABCDE: the side AB=19.40 chains, and the angle B 110° 30′; the side BC=15.55 chains, and the angle C 117° 45′; the side CD=21.25 chains, and the angle D 91° 20′; and the side DE=27.41 chains. Required the area of the field.

Ans. 66 *A.* 2 *R.* 24 *P.*

Prob. 20. From a station, H, near the middle of a field, ABCDEF, from which I could see all the angles, I measured the distances to the several corners, and measured the angles formed at H by those distances, as follows:

Distances.		*Angles.*	
AH, 43.15	chains;	AHB, 60°	30′.
BH, 29.82	"	BHC, 47	40
CH, 35.61	"	CHD, 49	50
DH, 50.10	"	DHE, 57	10
EH, 46.18	"	EHF, 64	15
FH, 36.06	"	FHA, 80	35

Required the area of the field.

Ans. 412 *A.* 1 *R.* 17 *P.*

NAVIGATION.

Prob. 1. From a ship at sea I observed a point of land to bear east by south, and, after sailing northeast 12 miles, I observed again, and found its bearing to be southeast by east. How far was the last observation made from the point of land?

Ans. 26.07 miles.

Prob. 2. If a ship in latitude 50° N., sails 52 miles in the direction southwest by south, what latitude has she arrived in, and how much farther to the west?

Ans. Latitude 49° 16.′8 N.; west, 28.9 miles.

Prob. 3. Two ships sail from the same port; the one sails east-northeast 85 miles, the other sails east by south till the first ship bears northwest by west. What is the distance of the second ship from the port, and also from the first ship?

Ans. From the port, 184.7 miles; from the first ship, 123.4 miles.

Prob. 4. Two ports lie east and west of each other; a ship sails from each, namely, the ship from the west port sails northeast 89 leagues, and the other sails 80 leagues, when she meets the former. Required the latter ship's course, and the distance between the two ports.

Ans. Course, N. 51° 52′ W.; distance, 112.3 leagues.

Prob. 5. Two ships sail from a certain port; the one sails south by east 45 leagues, and the other south-southwest 64 leagues. What is the bearing and distance of the first ship from the second?

Ans. Bearing, N. 65° 44′ E.; distance, 36.5 leagues.

Prob. 6. A ship sailing northwest, two islands appear in sight, of which the one bears north, and the other west-northwest; but, after sailing 20 leagues, the former bears northeast, and the latter west by south. What is the distance asunder of the two islands? *Ans.* 32.38 leagues.

Prob. 7. To a vessel sailing on a certain course, a headland was observed to bear due west; four hours after which it was seen at west-southwest; and six hours after this, the vessel continuing to run at the same rate, its bearing was found to be south-southwest. What was the vessel's course at the time?

Ans. N. 42° 35′ W.

Prob. 8. Two ships of war, intending to cannonade a fort, are, by the shallowness of the water, kept so far from it that they suspect their guns can not reach it with effect. In order, therefore, to measure the distance, they separate from each other 500 rods; then each ship observes the angle which the other ship and the fort subtend, which angles are 38° 16′ and 37° 9′. What, then, is the distance between each ship and the fort?

Ans. 312 rods and 320 rods.

Prob. 9. A ship from the latitude 42° 18′ N., sails southwest by south until her latitude is 40° 18′ N. What direct distance has she sailed, and how many miles has she sailed to the westward?

Ans. Distance run 144.3 miles, and has sailed to westward 80.2 miles.

Prob. 10. A ship having run due east for three days, at the rate of eight knots an hour, finds she has altered her longitude 15 degrees. What parallel of latitude did she sail on?

Ans. Latitude 50° 12′.

Prob. 11. A ship in latitude 43° 30′ N., and longitude 44° W., sails southeasterly 532 miles, until her departure from the meridian is 420 miles. Required the course steered, and the latitude and longitude of the ship.

Ans. Course S. 52° 8′ E., latitude 38° 3.′5 N., longitude 34° 45′ W.

Prob. 12. A ship from latitude 43° 20′ N., and longitude 52° W., sails E.S.E. until her departure is 745 miles. Required the distance sailed, and the latitude and longitude of the ship.

Ans. Distance 806.4 miles, latitude 38° 11.′5 N., longitude 35° 36′ W.

Prob. 13. If the height of the mountain called the Peak of Teneriffe be 4 miles, and the angle taken at the top of it, as formed between a plumb-line and a line conceived to touch the earth in the horizon, or farthest visible point, be 87° 25′ 55″, it is required from hence to determine the magnitude of the whole earth, and the utmost distance that can be seen on its surface from the top of the mountain, supposing the earth to be a perfect sphere.

Ans. Distance 178.458 miles, diameter 7957.793 miles.

Prob. 14. Required the course and distance from St. Jago, one of the Cape Verd islands, in latitude 14° 56′ N., to the island of St. Helena, in latitude 15° 45′ S., their difference of longitude being 30° 12′.

Ans. Course S. 44° 12′ E., distance 2567.8 miles.

Prob. 15. A ship from the latitude of 49° 57′ N., and longitnde of 30° W., sails S. 39° W., till she arrives in the latitude of 45° 31′ N. Required the distance run, and the longitude of the ship.

Ans. Distance 342.3 miles, longitude of ship 35° 21′ W.

Prob. 16. Find the bearing and distance from San Francisco, latitude 37° 48′ N., longitude 122° 28′ W., to Jeddo, latitude 35° 40′ N., longitude 139° 40′ E., by Mercator's sailing.

Ans. Course S. 88° 26′ W., distance 4705 miles.

Prob. 17. Find the bearing and distance from San Francisco to Batavia in Java, latitude 6° 9′ S., longitude 106° 53′ E., by Mercator's sailing.

Ans. Course S. 70° 12′ W., distance 7783 miles.

Prob. 18. Find the bearing and distance from San Francisco to Port Jackson, latitude 33° 51′ S., longitude 151° 14′ E., by Mercator's sailing.

Ans. Course S. 48° 18′ W., distance 6462 miles.

Prob. 19. Find the bearing and distance from San Francisco to Otaheite, latitude 17° 29′ S., longitude 149° 29′ W., by Mercator's sailing.

Ans. Course S. 24° 44′ W., distance 3652 miles.

Prob. 20. Find the bearing and distance from San Francisco to Valparaiso, latitude 33° 2′ S., longitude 71° 41′ W., by Mercator's sailing.

Ans. Course S. 33° 47′ E., distance 5354 miles.

SPHERICAL TRIGONOMETRY.

Prob. 1. In the right-angled spherical triangle ABC, there are given the angle C 23° 27′ 42″, and the side *b* 10° 39′ 40″. Required the angle B, and the sides *a* and *c*.

$$Ans. \begin{cases} a = 11^\circ\ 35'\ 49''. \\ c = 4^\circ\ 35'\ 26''. \\ B = 66^\circ\ 58'\ 1''. \end{cases}$$

Prob. 2. In the spherical triangle ABC, the side BC = 90°, the side AB = 32° 57′ 6″, and the side AC = 66° 32′. Required the angles.

$$Ans. \begin{cases} A = 132^\circ\ 2'\ 44''. \\ B = 42^\circ\ 56'\ 12''. \\ C = 23^\circ\ 49'\ 26''. \end{cases}$$

Prob. 3. In the right-angled spherical triangle ABC, there are given the angle B=47° 54′ 20″, and the angle C=61° 50′ 29″. Required the sides.

Ans. $\begin{cases} a=61° \ 4' \ 56''. \\ b=40° \ 30' \ 20''. \\ c=50° \ 30' \ 30''. \end{cases}$

Prob. 4. In the spherical triangle ABC, the side AC=90°, the side AB=115° 9′, and the angle B=101° 40′. Required the remaining parts.

Ans. $\begin{cases} BC=113° \ 18' \ 7''. \\ A=115° \ 54' \ 46''. \\ C=117° \ 33' \ 49''. \end{cases}$

Prob. 5. In the spherical triangle ABC, the angle A=130° 5′ 22″, the angle C=36° 45′ 28″, and the side AC=44° 13′ 45″. Required the remaining parts.

Ans. $\begin{cases} AB=51° \ 6' \ 12''. \\ BC=84° \ 14' \ 29''. \\ B=32° \ 26' \ 6''. \end{cases}$

Prob. 6. In the spherical triangle ABC, the angle A=33° 15′ 7″, B=31° 34′ 38″, and C=161° 25′ 17″. Required the sides.

Ans. $\begin{cases} a=80° \ 5' \ 4''. \\ b=70° \ 10' \ 30''. \\ c=145° \ 5' \ 2''. \end{cases}$

Prob. 7. In the spherical triangle ABC, the side AB=112° 22′ 58″, AC=52° 39′ 4″, and BC=89° 16′ 53″. Required the angles.

Ans. $\begin{cases} A=70° \ 39' \ 0''. \\ B=48° \ 36' \ 0''. \\ C=119° \ 15' \ 0''. \end{cases}$

Prob. 8. In the spherical triangle ABC, the side AB=76° 35′ 36″, AC=50° 10′ 30″, and the angle A=34° 15′ 3″. Required the remaining parts.

Ans. $\begin{cases} B=42° \ 15' \ 13''. \\ C=121° \ 36' \ 20''. \\ BC=40° \ 0' \ 10''. \end{cases}$

Prob. 9. The latitudes of the observatories of Paris and Pekin are 48° 50′ 14″ N. and 39° 54′ 13″ N., and their difference of longitude is 114° 7′ 30″. What is their distance?

Ans. 73° 56′ 40″.

Prob. 10. Required the course and distance from New York, latitude 40° 43′ N., longitude 74° 0′ W., to San Francisco, latitude 37° 48′ N., longitude 122° 28′ W., on the shortest route.

Ans. The course is S. 78° 16′ W.
Distance, 2229.8 nautical miles.

Prob. 11. Required the course and distance from San Francisco, latitude 37° 48′ N., longitude 122° 28′ W., to Jeddo, in latitude 35° 40′ N., longitude 139° 40′ E., on the shortest route.

Ans. The course is N. 56° 41′ W.
Distance, 4461.9 nautical miles.

Prob. 12. Required the course and distance from San Francisco to Batavia in Java, latitude 6° 9′ S., longitude 106° 53′ E., on the shortest route.

Ans. The course is N. 67° 30′ W.
Distance, 7516 nautical miles.

Prob. 13. Required the course and distance from San Francisco to Port Jackson, latitude 33° 51′ S., longitude 151° 14′ E., on the shortest route.

Ans. The course is S. 59° 50′ W.
Distance, 6444 nautical miles.

Prob. 14. Required the course and distance from San Francisco to Otaheite, latitude 17° 29′ S., longitude 149° 29′ W., on the shortest route.

Ans. The course is S. 30° 31′ W.
Distance, 3514.8 nautical miles.

Prob. 15. Required the course and distance from San Francisco to Valparaiso, latitude 33° 2′ S., longitude 71° 41 W., on the shortest route.

Ans. The course is S. 55° 9′ E.
Distance, 5108.5 nautical miles.

Prob. 16. Suppose two ports, one in north latitude 30°, and the other in north latitude 40°, the difference of longitude between them being 50°. Required the bearing and distance of each of those ports from an island that lies in south latitude 18°. and which is equally distant from both of the said ports.

Ans. Bearing from first port, S. 40° 52′ 9″ E.
Bearing from second port, S. 15 9 47 W.
The distance, 59° 23′ 19″ = 3563.3 nautical miles.

THE END.

N

TABLES

OF

LOGARITHMS OF NUMBERS

AND OF

SINES AND TANGENTS

FOR EVERY

TEN SECONDS OF THE QUADRANT,

WITH OTHER USEFUL TABLES.

BY ELIAS LOOMIS, LL.D.,

PROFESSOR OF MATHEMATICS AND NATURAL PHILOSOPHY IN THE UNIVERSITY OF THE CITY OF NEW YORK, AND AUTHOR OF "A COURSE OF MATHEMATICS."

SEVENTH EDITION.

NEW-YORK:

HARPER & BROTHERS, PUBLISHERS,

329 & 331 PEARL STREET,

FRANKLIN SQUARE.

1859.

CONTENTS.

PREFACE.

THE accompanying tables were designed to afford the means of performing trigonometrical computations with facility and precision. The tables chiefly used in this country for purposes of education extend to six decimal places, like those in the present collection; but the precision which they are designed to furnish is only attained by a serious expenditure of labor. In the Table of Logarithms of Numbers they do not furnish the correction for a fifth figure in the natural number, and the labor of computing this correction is such that I always prefer the use of Hutton's Tables, extending to seven places, even in computations to which six-place logarithms are abundantly competent. In the present collection, the correction for a fifth figure of the natural number is introduced at the bottom of each page, and the table is thus rendered nearly as useful as one of the common kind extending to 100,000. The whole has been carefully compared with standard authors, and nearly a dozen errors have thus been detected in the common tables.

The principal table in this collection is that of Logarithmic Sines and Tangents. The common tables in this country extend only to minutes, with differences to 100″. If, in a trigonometrical computation, angles are only required to the nearest minute, tables to five places are quite sufficient; but if the computation is to be carried to seconds, these can only be obtained from the common tables by a great expenditure of time and labor. In the present collection, the sines and tangents are furnished to every ten seconds of the quadrant, and at the bottom of each page is given the correction for any number of seconds less than ten, so that the precision of seconds can be obtained with almost the same facility as that of minutes with the tables in common use. Moreover, near the limits of the quadrant, by means of an auxiliary table, sines and tangents are readily obtained, even for a fraction of a second. The method of arrangement of the sines and tangents was suggested by a table in Mackay's Longitude; but the errors of that table, amounting to several thousand, have been corrected by a careful comparison with the work of Ursinus. By comparison with the same standard, more than two hundred errors (chiefly in the final figures) have been detected in the tables in common use.

The Table of Natural Sines and Tangents is of less use than the logarithmic; nevertheless, it is often important for reference, particularly in analytical geometry and the calculus; and it is useful as a stepping-stone to assist the beginner in comprehending the nature of logarithmic sines and tangents. The Traverse Table commonly used in this country furnishes the latitude and departure to every quarter degree of the quadrant, for distances from 1 to 100, and occupies ninety pages. The accompanying table occupies but six pages, and yields ten times greater precision.

The Table of Meridional Parts extends to tenths of a mile, and great care has been taken to insure its accuracy. For this purpose, I have compared all the similar tables within my reach, and among them have found two which appeared to have been computed independently. Between them there were detected 674 discrepancies in the final figures. These cases were all recomputed, and 78 errors were detected in the best copy compared. It is probable that the numbers in this table are not in every instance true to the *nearest* tenth of a mile; but it is believed that the remaining errors are few in number, as well as minute. This table is confidently pronounced more accurate than any similar one with which I have been able to compare it.

The Table of Corrections to Middle Latitude was computed entirely anew. The corresponding table in common use, which was originally computed by Workman, contains more than four hundred errors, several of them amounting to two minutes.

On the whole, it is believed that the accompanying tables will be found more convenient to the computer than any tables of six decimal places hitherto published in this country; and that they will be pronounced sufficiently extensive for all purposes of academic and collegiate instruction, as well as for practical mechanics and surveyors.

EXPLANATION OF THE TABLES.

TABLE OF LOGARITHMS OF NUMBERS, pp. 1–20.

LOGARITHMS are numbers contrived to diminish the labor of Multiplication and Division by substituting in their stead Addition and Subtraction. All numbers are regarded as powers of some one number, which is called the *base* of the system; and the exponent of that power of the base which is equal to a given number, is called the logarithm of that number.

The base of the common system of logarithms (called, from their inventor, Briggs' logarithms) is the number 10. Hence all numbers are to be regarded as powers of 10. Thus, since

$10^0=1$,	0 is the logarithm of	1	in Briggs' system;	
$10^1=10$,	1 " "	10	"	"
$10^2=100$,	2 " "	100	"	"
$10^3=1000$,	3 " "	1000	"	"
$10^4=10{,}000$,	4 " "	10,000	"	"
&c.,	&c.,		&c.;	

whence it appears that, in Briggs' system, the logarithm of every number between 1 and 10 is some number between 0 and 1, *i. e.*, is a proper fraction. The logarithm of every number between 10 and 100 is some number between 1 and 2, *i. e.*, is 1 plus a fraction. The logarithm of every number between 100 and 1000 is some number between 2 and 3, *i. e.*, is 2 plus a fraction, and so on.

The preceding principles may be extended to fractions by means of negative exponents. Thus, since

$10^{-1}=0.1$,	—1 is the logarithm of	0.1	in Briggs' system;	
$10^{-2}=0.01$,	—2 " "	0.01	"	"
$0^{-3}=0.001$,	—3 " "	0.001	"	"
$10^{-4}=0.0001$,	—4 " "	0.0001	"	"
&c.,	&c.,		&c.	

Hence it appears that the logarithm of every number between 1 and 0.1 is some number between 0 and —1, or may be represented by —1 plus a fraction; the logarithm of every number between 0.1 and .01 is some number between —1 and —2, or may be represented by —2 plus a fraction; the logarithm of every number between .01 and .001 is some number between —2 and —3, or is equal to —3 plus a fraction, and so on.

The logarithms of most numbers, therefore, consist of an integer and a fraction. The integral part is called the *characteristic*, and may be known from the following

RULE.

The characteristic of the logarithm of a number greater than unity, is one less than the number of integral figures in the given number.

Thus the logarithm of 297 is 2 plus a fraction; that is, the characteristic of the logarithm of 297 is 2, which is one less than the number of integral figures. The characteristic of the logarithm of 5673.29 is 3; that of 73254.1 is 4, &c.

The characteristic of the logarithm of a decimal fraction is a negative number, and is equal to the number of places by which its first significant figure is removed from the place of units.

Thus the logarithm of .0046 is —3 plus a fraction; that is, the characteristic of the logarithm is —3, the first significant figure 4 being removed three places from units.

The accompanying table contains the logarithms of all numbers from 1 to 10,000 carried to 6 decimal places.

To find the Logarithm of any Number between 1 *and* 100.

Look on the first page of the table, along the column of numbers under N, for the given number, and against it, in the next column, will be found the logarithm, with its characteristic. Thus,

opposite 13 is 1.113943, which is the logarithm of 13;
" 65 is 1.812913, " " 65.

To find the Logarithm of any Number consisting of three Figures.

Look on one of the pages from 2 to 20, along the left-hand column marked N, for the given number, and against it, in the column headed 0, will be found the decimal part of its logarithm. To this the characteristic must be prefixed, according to the rule already given. Thus

the logarithm of 347 will be found, from page 8, to be 2.540329;
" " 871 " " " 18, " 2.940018.

As the first two figures of the decimal are the same for several successive numbers in the table, they are not repeated for each logarithm separately, but are left to be supplied. Thus the decimal part of the logarithm of 339 is .530200. The first two figures of the decimal remain the same up to 347; they are therefore omitted in the table, and are to be supplied.

To find the Logarithm of any Number consisting of four Figures.

Find the three left-hand figures in the column marked N as before, and the fourth figure at the head of one of the other columns. Opposite to the first three figures, and in the column under the fourth figure, will be found four figures of the logarithm, to which two figures from the column headed 0 are to be prefixed, as in the former case. The characteristic must be supplied by the usual rule. Thus

the logarithm of 3456 is 3.538574;
" " 8765 is 3.942752.

In several of the columns headed 1, 2, 3, &c., small dots are found in the place of figures. This is to show that the two figures which are to be prefixed from the first column have changed, and they are to be taken from the horizontal line directly *below*. The place of the dots is to be supplied with ciphers. Thus

the logarithm of 2045 is 3.310693;
" " 9777 is 3.990206.

The two leading figures from the column 0 must also be taken from the horizontal line below, if any dots have been passed over on the same horizontal line. Thus

the logarithm of 1628 is 3.211654.

To find the Logarithm of any Number containing more than four Figures.

By inspecting the table, we shall find that within certain limits the logarithms are nearly proportional to their corresponding numbers. Thus

the logarithm of 7250 is 3.860338;
" " 7251 is 3.860398;
" " 7252 is 3.860458;
" " 7253 is 3.860518.

Here the difference between the successive logarithms, called the *tabular difference*, is constantly 60, corresponding to a difference of unity in the natural numbers. If, then, we suppose the logarithms to be proportional to their corresponding numbers (as they are nearly), a difference of 0.1 in the numbers should correspond to a difference of 6 in the logarithms; a difference of 0.2 in the numbers should correspond to a difference of 12 in the logarithms, &c. Hence

the logarithm of 7250.1 must be 3.860344;
" " 7250.2 " 3.860350;
" " 7250.3 " 3.860356;
&c., &c.

In order to facilitate the computation, the tabular difference is inserted on page 16 in the column headed D, and the proportional part for the fifth figure of the natural number is given at the bottom of the page. Thus, when the tabular difference is 60, the corrections for .1, .2, .3, &c., are seen to be 6, 12, 18, &c.

If the given number was 72501, the characteristic of its logarithm would be 4, but the decimal part would be the same as for 7250.1

If it were required to find the correction for a sixth figure in the natural number, it is readily obtained from the Proportional Parts in the table. Thus, if the correction for .5 is 30, the correction for .05 is obviously 3.

As the differences change rapidly in the first part of the table, it was found inconvenient to give the proportional parts for each tabular difference; accordingly, for the first seven pages they are only given for the *even* differences, but the proportional parts for the odd differences will be readily found by inspection.

Required the logarithm of 452789.

The logarithm of 452700 is 5.655810

The tabular difference is 96.

Accordingly, the correction for the fifth figure, 8, is 77, and for the sixth figure, 9, is 8.6, or 9 nearly. Adding these corrections to the number before found, we obtain 5.655896.

The preceding logarithms do not pretend to be perfectly exact, but only the nearest numbers having but six decimal places. Accordingly when the fraction which is omitted exceeds half a unit in the sixth decimal place, the last figure must be increased by unity.

Required the logarithm of 8765432.

The logarithm of 8765000 is	6.942752
Correction for the fifth figure 4,	20
" " sixth figure 3,	1.5
" " seventh figure 2,	0.1
Therefore the logarithm of 8765432 is	6.942774.

Required the logarithm of 234567.

The logarithm of 234500 is	5.370143
Correction for the fifth figure 6,	111
" " sixth figure 7,	13
Therefore the logarithm of 234567 is	5.370267.

To find the Logarithm of a Decimal Fraction.

The decimal part of the logarithm of any number is the same as that of the number multiplied or divided by 10, 100, 1000, &c. Hence, for a decimal fraction, we find the logarithm as if the figures were integers and prefix the characteristic according to the usual rule.

EXAMPLES.

The logarithm of 345.6	is 2.538574;
" " 87.65	is 1.942752;
" " 2.345	is 0.370143;
" " .1234	is $\bar{1}$.091315;
" " .005678	is $\bar{3}$.754195.

The minus sign is placed *over* the characteristic to show that this alone is negative, while the decimal part of the logarithm is positive.

To find the Logarithm of a Vulgar Fraction.

We may reduce the vulgar fraction to a decimal, and find its logarithm by the preceding rule; or, since the value of a fraction is equal to the quotient of the numerator divided by the denominator, we may subtract the logarithm of the denominator from that of the numerator; the difference will be the logarithm of the quotient.

Required the logarithm of $\frac{3}{16}$, or 0.1875.

From the logarithm of 3,	0.477121,
Subtract the logarithm of 16,	1.204120.
Leaves logarithm of $\frac{3}{16}$, or .1875,	$\bar{1}$.273001.

In the same manner we find

the logarithm of $\frac{4}{55}$ is $\bar{2}$.861697;
" " $\frac{123}{876}$ is $\bar{1}$.147401.

To find the natural Number corresponding to any Logarithm.

Look in the table in the column headed 0 for the first two figures of the logarithm, neglecting the characteristic; the other four figures are to be looked for in the same column, or in one of the nine following columns; and if they are exactly found, the first three figures of the corresponding number will be found opposite to them in the column headed N, and the fourth figure will be found at the top of the page. This number must be made to correspond with the characteristic of the given logarithm by pointing off decimals or annexing ciphers. Thus

the natural number belonging to the logarithm 4.370143 is 23450;
" " " " 1.538574 is 34.56.

If the decimal part of the logarithm can not be exactly found in the table, look for the nearest less logarithm, and take out the four figures of the corresponding natural number as before; the additional figures may be obtained by means of the Proportional Parts at the bottom of the page.

Required the number belonging to the logarithm 4.368399.
On page 6, we find the next less logarithm .368287.

The four corresponding figures of the natural number are 2335. Their logarithm is less than the one proposed by 112. The tabular difference is 186; and, by referring to the bottom of page 6, we find that, with a difference of 186, the figure corresponding to the Proportional Part 112 is 6. Hence the five figures of the natural number are 23356; and, since the characteristic of the proposed logarithm is 4, these five figures are all integral.

Required the number belonging to logarithm 5.345678.
The next less logarithm in the table is .345570
Their difference is 108.

The first four figures of the natural number are 2216.

With the tabular difference 196, the fifth figure corresponding to 108 is seen to be 5, with a remainder of 10, which furnishes a sixth figure 5 nearly. Hence the required number is 221655.

In the same manner we find

the number corresponding to logarithm 3.538672 is 3456.78;
" " " 1.994605 is 98.7654;
" " " $\bar{1}$.647817 is .444444.

TABLE OF NATURAL SINES AND TANGENTS, pp. 116–133.

This is a table of natural sines and tangents for every degree and minute of the quadrant, carried to six places of figures. Since the radius of the circle is supposed to be unity, the sine of every arc below 90° is less than unity. These sines are expressed in decimal parts of the radius; and, although the decimal point is not written in the table, it must always be prefixed. The degrees are arranged in order at the top of the page, and the minutes in the left hand vertical column. Directly under the given number of degrees at the top of the page, and opposite to the minutes on the left, will be found the sine required. The two leading figures are repeated at intervals of ten minutes. Thus

the sine of 6° 27′ is .112336;
" " 28° 53′ is .483028.

The same number in the table is both the sine of an arc and the cosine of its complement. The degrees for the cosines must be sought at the bottom of the page, and the minutes on the right. Thus

the cosine of 62° 25′ is .463038;
" " 84° 23′ is .097872.

If a sine is required for an arc consisting of degrees, minutes, and *seconds*, it may be found by means of the line at the bottom of each page, which gives the proportional part corresponding to one second of arc

Required the sine of 8° 9′ 10″.

The sine of 8° 9′ is .141765.

By referring to the bottom of page 116, in the column under 8°, we find the correction for 1″ is 4.80; hence the correction for 10″ must be 48, which, added to the number above found, gives for the sine of 8° 9′ 10″, .141813.

In the same manner we find

the cosine of 56° 34′ 28″ is .550853.

It will be observed, that since the cosines decrease while the arcs increase, the correction for the 28″ is to be subtracted from the cosine of 56° 34′.

The arrangement of the table of natural tangents is similar to that of the table of sines. The tangents for arcs less than 45° are all less than radius, and consist wholly of decimals. For arcs above 45°, the tangents are all greater than radius, and contain both integral and decimal figures. The proportional parts at the bottom of each page enable us readily to find the correction for seconds. Thus

the natural tangent of 32° 29′ 18″ is .636784;
" " 74° 35′ 55″ is 3.63014.

To find the Number of Degrees, Minutes, and Seconds belonging to a given Sine or Tangent.

If the given sine or tangent is found exactly in the table, the corresponding degrees will be found at the top of the page, and the minutes on the left hand. But when the given number is not found exactly in the table, look for the sine or tangent which is next less than the proposed one, and take out the corresponding degrees and minutes. Find, also, the difference between this tabular number and the number proposed, and divide it by the proportional part for 1″ found at the bottom of the page; the quotient will be the required number of seconds.

Required the arc whose sine is .750000.

The next less sine in the table is .749919, the arc corresponding to which is 48° 35′. The difference between this sine and that proposed is 81, which, divided by 3.21, gives 25. Hence the required arc is 48° 35′ 25″.

In the same manner we find

the arc whose tangent is 2.000000, to be 63° 26′ 6″.

TABLE OF NATURAL SECANTS, pp. 134–5.

This is a table of natural secants for every ten minutes of the quadrant carried to seven places of figures. The degrees are arranged in order in the first vertical column on the left, and the minutes at the top of the page. Thus

the secant of 21° 20′ is 1.073561;
" " 81° 50′ is 7.039622.

If a secant is required for a number of minutes not given in the table, the correction for the odd minutes may be found by means of the last vertical column on the right, which shows the proportional part for one minute.

Let it be required to find the secant of 30° 33′.

The secant of 30° 30′ is 1.160592.

The correction for 1′ is 198.9, which, multiplied by 3, gives 597 Adding this to the number before found, we obtain 1.161189.

For a cosecant, the degrees must be sought in the right-hand vertical column, and the minutes at the bottom of the page. Thus

the cosecant of 47° 40′ is 1.352742.

TABLE OF LOGARITHMIC SINES AND TANGENTS, pp. 21–115.

This is a table of the logarithms of the sines and tangents for every ten seconds of the quadrant, carried to six places of decimals The degrees and seconds are placed at the top of the page, and the minutes in the left vertical column. After the first two degrees, the three leading figures in the table of sines are only given in the column headed 0″, and are to be prefixed to the numbers in the other columns, as in the table of logarithms of numbers. Also, where the leading figures change, this change is indicated by dots, as in the former table. The correction for any number of seconds less than 10 is given at the bottom of the page.

To find the Logarithmic Sine or Tangent of a given Arc.

Look for the degrees at the top of the page, the minutes on the left hand, and the next less tenth second at the top; then, under the seconds, and opposite to the minutes, will be found four figures, to which the three leading figures are to be prefixed from the column headed 0″; to this add the proportional part for the odd seconds from the bottom of the page.

Required the logarithmic sine of 24° 27′ 34″.

The logarithmic sine of 24° 27′ 30″ is	9.617033.
Proportional part for 4″ is	18.
Logarithmic sine of 24° 27′ 34″ is	9.617051.

This is the logarithm of .414049 found in the table of natural sines on page 120. The natural sine being less than unity, the characteristic of its logarithm is negative. To obviate this inconvenience, the characteristics in the table have all been increased by 10; or the logarithmic sines may be regarded as the logarithms of natural sines computed for a radius of 10,000,000,000.

Required the logarithmic tangent of 73° 35′ 43″.

The logarithmic tangent of 73° 35′ 40″ is	10.531031.
Proportional part for 3″ is	23.
Logarithmic tangent of 73° 35′ 43″	10.531054.

When a cosine is required, the degrees and seconds must be sought at the bottom of the page, and the minutes on the right, and the correction for the odd seconds must be subtracted from the number in the table.

Required the logarithmic cosine of 59° 33′ 47″.

The logarithmic cosine of 59° 33′ 40″ is	9.704682.
Proportional part for 7″ is	25.
Logarithmic cosine of 59° 33′ 47″ is	9.704657.

So, also, the logarithmic cotangent of 37° 27′ 14″ is found to be 10.115744.

The proportional parts given at the bottom of each page correspond to the degrees at the top of the page increased by 30′, and are not strictly applicable to any other number of minutes; nevertheless, the differences of the sines change so slowly, except near the commencement of the quadrant, that the error resulting from using these numbers for every part of the page will seldom exceed a unit in the sixth decimal place. For the first two degrees, the differences change so rapidly that the proportional part for 1″ is given for each minute in the right-hand column of the page. The correction for any number of seconds less than ten will be found by multiplying the proportional part for 1″ by the given number of seconds.

Required the logarithmic sine of 1° 17′ 33″.

The logarithmic sine of 1° 17′ 30″ is 8.352991

The correction for 3″ is found by multiplying 93.4 by 3, which gives 280. Adding this to the above tabular number, we obtain

the sine of 1° 17′ 33″, 8.353271.

A similar method may be employed for several of the first degrees of the quadrant, if the proportional parts at the bottom of the page are not thought sufficiently precise. This correction may, however, be obtained pretty nearly by inspection from comparing the proportional parts for two successive degrees. Thus, on page 26, the correction for 1″, corresponding to the sine of 2° 30′, is 48; the correction for 1″, corresponding to the sine of 3° 30′, is 34. Hence the correction for 1″, corresponding to the sine of 3° 0′, must be about 41; and in the same manner we may proceed for any other part of the table.

Near the close of the quadrant, the tangents vary so rapidly, that the same arrangement of the table is adopted as for the commencement of the quadrant. For the last as well as the first two degrees of the quadrant, the proportional part to 1″ is given for each minute separately. These proportional parts are computed for the minutes placed opposite to them. increased by 30″, and are not strictly applicable to any other number of seconds; nevertheless, the differences for the most part change so slowly, that the error resulting from using these numbers for every part of the same horizontal line is quite small. When great accuracy is required, the table on page 114 may be employed for arcs near the limits of the quadrant. This table furnishes the differences between the logarithmic sines and the logarithms of the arcs expressed in seconds. Thus

the logarithmic sine of 0° 5′ is	7.162696;
the logarithm of 300″ (=5′) is	2.477121;
the difference is	4.685575.

This is the number found on page 114, under the heading *log. sine A—log. A″*, opposite 5 min.; and in a similar manner the other numbers in the same column are obtained. These numbers vary quite slowly for two degrees; and hence, to find the logarithmic sine of an arc less than two degrees, we have but to add the logarithm of the arc expressed in seconds to the appropriate number found in this table.

Required the logarithmic sine of 0° 7′ 22″.

Tabular number from page 114,	4.685575.
The logarithm of 442″ is	2.645422.
Logarithmic sine of 0° 7′ 22″ is	7.330997

The logarithmic tangent of an arc less than two degrees is found in a similar manner.

Required the logarithmic tangent of 0° 27′ 36″.

Tabular number from page 114,	4.685584.
The logarithm of 1656″ is	3.219060.
Logarithmic tangent of 0° 27′ 36″ is	7.904644.

The column headed *log. cot. A+log. A″* is found by adding the logarithmic cotangent to the logarithm of the arc expressed in seconds. Hence, to find the logarithmic cotangent of an arc less than two degrees, we must subtract from the tabular number the logarithm of the arc in seconds.

Required the logarithmic cotangent of 0° 27′ 36″.

Tabular number from page 114,	15.314416.
The logarithm of 1656″ is	3.219060.
Logarithmic cotangent of 0° 27′ 36″ is	12.095356.

The same method will, of course, furnish cosines and cotangents of arcs near 90°.

The secants and cosecants are omitted in this table, since they are easily derived from the cosines and sines.

The logarithmic secant is found by subtracting the logarithmic cosine from 20; *and the logarithmic cosecant is found by subtracting the logarithmic sine from* 20.

Thus we have found the logarithmic sine of 24° 27′ 34″ to be 9.617051. Hence the logarithmic cosecant of 24° 27′ 34″ is 10.382949.

The logarithmic cosine of 54° 12′ 40″ is 9.767008.
Hence the logarithmic secant of 54° 12′ 40″ is 10.232992.

To find the Arc corresponding to a given Logarithmic Sine or Tangent

If the given number is found exactly in the table, the corresponding degrees and seconds will be found at the top of the page, and the minutes on the left. But when the given number is not found exactly in the table, look for the sine or tangent which is next less than the proposed one, and take out the corresponding degrees, minutes, and seconds. Find, also, the difference between this tabular number and the number proposed, and, corresponding to this difference, at the bottom of the page will be found a certain number of seconds, which is to be added to the arc before found.

Required the arc corresponding to the logarithmic sine 9.750000.
The next less sine in the table is 9.749987.
The arc corresponding to which is 34° 13′ 0″.

The difference between its sine and the one proposed is 13, corresponding to which, at the bottom of the page, we find 4″ nearly. Hence the required arc is 34° 13′ 4″.

In the same manner we find the arc corresponding to logarithmic tan gent 10.250000, to be 60° 38′ 57″.

When the arc falls within the first two degrees of the quadrant, the odd seconds may be found by dividing the difference between the tabular number and the one proposed, by the proportional part for 1″. We thus find the arc corresponding to logarithmic sine 8.400000, to be 1° 26′ 22″ nearly.

We may employ the same method for the last two degrees of the quadrant when a tangent is given; but near the limits of the quadrant it is better to employ the auxiliary table on page 114. If we subtract the corresponding tabular number on page 114 from the given logarithmic sine, the remainder will be the logarithm of the arc expressed in seconds.

Required the arc corresponding to logarithmic sine 7.000000.

We see, from page 22, that the arc must be nearly 3′; the correspond ing tabular number on page 114 is 4.685575.

The difference is 2.314425;

which is the logarithm of 206.″265.

Hence the required arc is 3′ 26.″265.

In the same manner we find the arc corresponding to logarithmic tangent 8.184608, to be 0° 52′ 35″.

TABLE FOR THE LENGTHS OF CIRCULAR ARCS, p. 135.

This table contains the lengths of every single degree up to 60, and at intervals of ten degrees up to 180; also for every minute and second up to 20. The lengths are all expressed in decimal parts of radius.

Required the length of an arc of 57° 17′ 44.″8.

Take out from their respective columns the lengths answering to each of these numbers singly, and add them all together thus:

57°	0.9948377
17′	.0049451
40″	.0001939
4″	.0000194
0.″8	.0000039
The sum is	1.0000000.

That is, the length of an arc of 57° 17′ 44.″8 is equal to the radius of the circle.

TRAVERSE TABLE, pp. 136–141.

This table shows the difference of latitude and the departure to four decimal places for distances from 1 to 10, and for bearings from 0° to 90°, at intervals of 15′. If the bearing is less than 45°, the angle will be found on the left margin of one of the pages of the table, and the distance at the top or bottom of the page; the difference of latitude wil be found in the column headed *lat.* at the top of the page, and the departure in the column headed *dep.* If the bearing is more than 45°, the angle will be found on the right margin, and the difference of latitude will be found in the column marked *lat.* at the bottom of the page, and the departure in the other column. The latitudes and departures for different distances with the same bearing, are proportional to the distances. Therefore the distances may be reckoned as tens, hundreds, or thousands, if the place of the decimal point in each departure and difference of latitude be changed accordingly.

Required the latitude and departure for the distance 32.25, and the bearing 10° 30′.

On page 136, opposite to 10° 30′, we find the following latitudes and departures, proper attention being paid to the position of the decimal points.

Distance.	*Diff. Lat.*	*Dep.*
30	29.498	5.467
2	1.966	.364
.2	.197	.036
.05	.049	.009
32.25	31.710	5.876.

TABLE OF MERIDIONAL PARTS, pp. 142–148.

This table gives the length of the enlarged meridian on Mercator's Chart to every minute of latitude expressed in geographical miles and tenths of a mile. The degrees of latitude are arranged in order at the top of the page, and the minutes on both the right and left margins. Under the degrees and opposite to the minutes are placed the meridional parts corresponding to any latitude less than 80°. Thus

the meridional parts for latitude 12° 23′ are 748.9;
" " " 57° 42′ are 4260.5.

TABLE OF CORRECTIONS TO MIDDLE LATITUDE, p. 149.

This table is used in Navigation for correcting the middle latitude The given middle latitude is to be found either in the first or last vertical column, opposite to which, and under the given difference of latitude is inserted the proper correction in minutes, to be added to the middle latitude to obtain the latitude in which the meridian distance is accurately equal to the departure. Thus, if the middle latitude is 41°, and the difference of latitude 14°, the correction will be found to be 25′ which, added to the middle latitude, gives the corrected middle latitude 41° 25′.

A TABLE

OF

LOGARITHMS OF NUMBERS

FROM 1 TO 10,000.

N.	Log.	N.	Log.	N.	Log.	N.	Log.
1	0.000000	26	1.414973	51	1.707570	76	1.880814
2	0.301030	27	1.431364	52	1.716003	77	1.886491
3	0.477121	28	1.447158	53	1.724276	78	1.892095
4	0.602060	29	1.462398	54	1.732394	79	1.897627
5	0.698970	30	1.477121	55	1.740363	80	1.903090
6	0.778151	31	1.491362	56	1.748188	81	1.908485
7	0.845098	32	1.505150	57	1.755875	82	1.913814
8	0.903090	33	1.518514	58	1.763428	83	1.919078
9	0.954243	34	1.531479	59	1.770852	84	1.924279
10	1.000000	35	1.544068	60	1.778151	85	1.929419
11	1.041393	36	1.556303	61	1.785330	86	1.934498
12	1.079181	37	1.568202	62	1.792392	87	1.939519
13	1.113943	38	1.579784	63	1.799341	88	1.944483
14	1.146128	39	1.591065	64	1.806180	89	1.949390
15	1.176091	40	1.602060	65	1.812913	90	1.954243
16	1.204120	41	1.612784	66	1.819544	91	1.959041
17	1.230449	42	1.623249	67	1.826075	92	1.963788
18	1.255273	43	1.633468	68	1.832509	93	1.968483
19	1.278754	44	1.643453	69	1.838849	94	1.973128
20	1.301030	45	1.653213	70	1.845098	95	1.977724
21	1.322219	46	1.662758	71	1.851258	96	1.982271
22	1.342423	47	1.672098	72	1.857332	97	1.986772
23	1.361728	48	1.681241	73	1.863323	98	1.991226
24	1.380211	49	1.690196	74	1.869232	99	1.995635
25	1.397940	50	1.698970	75	1.875061	100	2.000000

N.B. In the following table, the two leading figures in the first column of logarithms are to be prefixed to all the numbers of the same horizontal line in the next nine columns; but when a point (.) occurs, its place is to be supplied by a cipher, and the two leading figures are to be taken from the next lower line.

N	0	1	2	3	4	5	6	7	8	9	D.
100	000000	0434	0868	1301	1734	2166	2598	3029	3461	3891	432
101	4321	4751	5181	5609	6038	6466	6894	7321	7748	8174	428
102	8600	9026	9451	9876	.300	.724	1147	1570	1993	2415	424
103	012837	3259	3680	4100	4521	4940	5360	5779	6197	6616	419
104	7033	7451	7868	8284	8700	9116	9532	9947	.361	.775	416
105	021189	1603	2016	2428	2841	3252	3664	4075	4486	4896	412
106	5306	5715	6125	6533	6942	7350	7757	8164	8571	8978	408
107	9384	9789	.195	.600	1004	1408	1812	2216	2619	3021	404
108	033424	3826	4227	4628	5029	5430	5830	6230	6629	7028	400
109	7426	7825	8223	8620	9017	9414	9811	.207	.602	.998	396
110	041393	1787	2182	2576	2969	3362	3755	4148	4540	4932	393
111	5323	5714	6105	6495	6885	7275	7664	8053	8442	8830	389
112	9218	9606	9993	.380	.766	1153	1538	1924	2309	2694	386
113	053078	3463	3846	4230	4613	4996	5378	5760	6142	6524	382
114	6905	7286	7666	8046	8426	8805	9185	9563	9942	.320	379
115	060698	1075	1452	1829	2206	2582	2958	3333	3709	4083	376
116	4458	4832	5206	5580	5953	6326	6699	7071	7443	7815	373
117	8186	8557	8928	9298	9668	..38	.407	.776	1145	1514	369
118	071882	2250	2617	2985	3352	3718	4085	4451	4816	5182	366
119	5547	5912	6276	6640	7004	7368	7731	8094	8457	8819	363
120	9181	9543	9904	.266	.626	.987	1347	1707	2067	2426	360
121	082785	3144	3503	3861	4219	4576	4934	5291	5647	6004	357

Differences. Proportional Parts.

N.	0	1	2	3	4	5	6	7	8	9	D.
	434	43	87	130	174	217	260	304	347	391	
	432	43	86	130	173	216	259	302	346	389	
	430	43	86	129	172	215	258	301	344	387	
	428	43	86	128	171	214	257	300	342	385	
	426	43	85	128	170	213	256	298	341	383	
	424	42	85	127	170	212	254	297	339	382	
	422	42	84	127	169	211	253	295	338	380	
	420	42	84	126	168	210	252	294	336	378	
	418	42	84	125	167	209	251	293	334	376	
	416	42	83	125	166	208	250	291	333	374	
	414	41	83	124	166	207	248	290	331	373	
	412	41	82	124	165	206	247	288	330	371	
	410	41	82	123	164	205	246	287	328	369	
	408	41	82	122	163	204	245	286	326	367	
	406	41	81	122	162	203	244	284	325	365	
	404	40	81	121	162	202	242	283	323	364	
	402	40	80	121	161	201	241	281	322	362	
	400	40	80	120	160	200	240	280	320	360	
	398	40	80	119	159	199	239	279	318	358	
	396	40	79	119	158	198	238	277	317	356	
	394	39	79	118	158	197	236	276	315	355	
	392	39	78	118	157	196	235	274	314	353	
	390	39	78	117	156	195	234	273	312	351	
	388	39	78	116	155	194	233	272	310	349	
	386	39	77	116	154	193	232	270	309	347	
	384	38	77	115	154	192	230	269	307	346	
	382	38	76	115	153	191	229	267	306	344	
	380	38	76	114	152	190	228	266	304	342	
	378	38	76	113	151	189	227	265	302	340	
	376	38	75	113	150	188	226	263	301	338	
	374	37	75	112	150	187	224	262	299	337	
	372	37	74	112	149	186	223	260	298	335	
	370	37	74	111	148	185	222	259	296	333	
	368	37	74	110	147	184	221	258	294	331	
	366	37	73	110	146	183	220	256	293	329	
	364	36	73	109	146	182	218	255	291	328	
	362	36	72	109	145	181	217	253	290	326	
	360	36	72	108	144	180	216	252	288	324	

N.	0	1	2	3	4	5	6	7	8	9	D.
122	086360	6716	7071	7426	7781	8136	8490	8845	9198	9552	355
123	9905	.258	.611	.963	1315	1667	2018	2370	2721	3071	351
124	093422	3772	4122	4471	4820	5169	5518	5866	6215	6562	349
125	6910	7257	7604	7951	8298	8644	8990	9335	9681	..26	346
126	100371	0715	1059	1403	1747	2091	2434	2777	3119	3462	343
127	3804	4146	4487	4828	5169	5510	5851	6191	6531	6871	341
128	7210	7549	7888	8227	8565	8903	9241	9579	9916	.253	338
129	110590	0926	1263	1599	1934	2270	2605	2940	3275	3609	335
130	3943	4277	4611	4944	5278	5611	5943	6276	6608	6940	333
131	7271	7603	7934	8265	8595	8926	9256	9586	9915	.245	330
132	120574	0903	1231	1560	1888	2216	2544	2871	3198	3525	328
133	3852	4178	4504	4830	5156	5481	5806	6131	6456	6781	325
134	7105	7429	7753	8076	8399	8722	9045	9368	9690	..12	323
135	130334	0655	0977	1298	1619	1939	2260	2580	2900	3219	321
136	3539	3858	4177	4496	4814	5133	5451	5769	6086	6403	318
137	6721	7037	7354	7671	7987	8303	8618	8934	9249	9564	315
138	9879	.194	.508	.822	1136	1450	1763	2076	2389	2702	314
139	143015	3327	3639	3951	4263	4574	4885	5196	5507	5818	311
140	6128	6438	6748	7058	7367	7676	7985	8294	8603	8911	309
141	9219	9527	9835	.142	.449	.756	1063	1370	1676	1982	307
142	152288	2594	2900	3205	3510	3815	4120	4424	4728	5032	305
143	5336	5640	5943	6246	6549	6852	7154	7457	7759	8061	303
144	8362	8664	8965	9266	9567	9868	.168	.469	.769	1068	301
145	161368	1667	1967	2266	2564	2863	3161	3460	3758	4055	299
146	4353	4650	4947	5244	5541	5838	6134	6430	6726	7022	297
147	7317	7613	7908	8203	8497	8792	9086	9380	9674	9968	295
148	170262	0555	0848	1141	1434	1726	2019	2311	2603	2895	293

Differences.	Proportional Parts. 1	2	3	4	5	6	7	8	9
358	36	72	107	143	179	215	251	286	322
356	36	71	107	142	178	214	249	285	320
354	35	71	106	142	177	212	248	283	319
352	35	70	106	141	176	211	246	282	317
350	35	70	105	140	175	210	245	280	315
348	35	70	104	139	174	209	244	278	313
346	35	69	104	138	173	208	242	277	311
344	34	69	103	138	172	206	241	275	310
342	34	68	103	137	171	205	239	274	308
340	34	68	102	136	170	204	238	272	306
338	34	68	101	135	169	203	237	270	304
336	34	67	101	134	168	202	235	269	302
334	33	67	100	134	167	200	234	267	301
332	33	66	100	133	166	199	232	266	299
330	33	66	99	132	165	198	231	264	297
328	33	66	98	131	164	197	230	262	295
326	33	65	98	130	163	196	228	261	293
324	32	65	97	130	162	194	227	259	292
322	32	64	97	129	161	193	225	258	290
320	32	64	96	128	160	192	224	256	288
318	32	64	95	127	159	191	223	254	286
316	32	63	95	126	158	190	221	253	284
314	31	63	94	126	157	188	220	251	283
312	31	62	94	125	156	187	218	250	281
310	31	62	93	124	155	186	217	248	279
308	31	62	92	123	154	185	216	246	277
306	31	61	92	122	153	184	214	245	275
304	30	61	91	122	152	182	213	243	274
302	30	60	91	121	151	181	211	242	272
300	30	60	90	120	150	180	210	240	270
298	30	60	89	119	149	179	209	238	268
296	30	59	89	118	148	178	207	237	266
294	29	59	88	118	147	176	206	235	265

N.	0	1	2	3	4	5	6	7	8	9	D.
149	173186	3478	3769	4060	4351	4641	4932	5222	5512	5802	291
150	6091	6381	6670	6959	7248	7536	7825	8113	8401	8689	289
151	8977	9264	9552	9839	.126	.413	.699	.986	1272	1558	287
152	181844	2129	2415	2700	2985	3270	3555	3839	4123	4407	285
153	4691	4975	5259	5542	5825	6108	6391	6674	6956	7239	283
154	7521	7803	8084	8366	8647	8928	9209	9490	9771	..51	281
155	190332	0612	0892	1171	1451	1730	2010	2289	2567	2846	279
156	3125	3403	3681	3959	4237	4514	4792	5069	5346	5623	278
157	5900	6176	6453	6729	7005	7281	7556	7832	8107	8382	276
158	8657	8932	9206	9481	9755	..29	.303	.577	.850	1124	274
159	201397	1670	1943	2216	2488	2761	3033	3305	3577	3848	272
160	4120	4391	4663	4934	5204	5475	5746	6016	6286	6556	271
161	6826	7096	7365	7634	7904	8173	8441	8710	8979	9247	269
162	9515	9783	..51	.319	.586	.853	1121	1388	1654	1921	267
163	212188	2454	2720	2986	3252	3518	3783	4049	4314	4579	266
164	4844	5109	5373	5638	5902	6166	6430	6694	6957	7221	264
165	7484	7747	8010	8273	8536	8798	9060	9323	9585	9846	262
166	220108	0370	0631	0892	1153	1414	1675	1936	2196	2456	261
167	2716	2976	3236	3496	3755	4015	4274	4533	4792	5051	259
168	5309	5568	5826	6084	6342	6600	6858	7115	7372	7630	258
169	7887	8144	8400	8657	8913	9170	9426	9682	9938	.193	256
170	230449	0704	0960	1215	1470	1724	1979	2234	2488	2742	254
171	2996	3250	3504	3757	4011	4264	4517	4770	5023	5276	253
172	5528	5781	6033	6285	6537	6789	7041	7292	7544	7795	252
173	8046	8297	8548	8799	9049	9299	9550	9800	..50	.300	250
174	240549	0799	1048	1297	1546	1795	2044	2293	2541	2790	249
175	3038	3286	3534	3782	4030	4277	4525	4772	5019	5266	248
176	5513	5759	6006	6252	6499	6745	6991	7237	7482	7728	246
177	7973	8219	8464	8709	8954	9198	9443	9687	9932	.176	245
178	250420	0664	0908	1151	1395	1638	1881	2125	2368	2610	243
179	2853	3096	3338	3580	3822	4064	4306	4548	4790	5031	242
180	5273	5514	5755	5996	6237	6477	6718	6958	7198	7439	241
181	7679	7918	8158	8398	8637	8877	9116	9355	9594	9833	239

N.	0 (Differences.)	1 (Proportional Parts.)	2	3	4	5	6	7	8	9	D.
	292	29	58	88	117	146	175	204	234	263	
	290	29	58	87	116	145	174	203	232	261	
	288	29	58	86	115	144	173	202	230	259	
	286	29	57	86	114	143	172	200	229	257	
	284	28	57	85	114	142	170	199	227	256	
	282	28	56	85	113	141	169	197	226	254	
	280	28	56	84	112	140	168	196	224	252	
	278	28	56	83	111	139	167	195	222	250	
	276	28	55	83	110	138	166	193	221	248	
	274	27	55	82	110	137	164	192	219	247	
	272	27	54	82	109	136	163	190	218	245	
	270	27	54	81	108	135	162	189	216	243	
	268	27	54	80	107	134	161	188	214	241	
	266	27	53	80	106	133	160	186	213	239	
	264	26	53	79	106	132	158	185	211	238	
	262	26	52	79	105	131	157	183	210	236	
	260	26	52	78	104	130	156	182	208	234	
	258	26	52	77	103	129	155	181	206	232	
	256	26	51	77	102	128	154	179	205	230	
	254	25	51	76	102	127	152	178	203	229	
	252	25	50	76	101	126	151	176	202	227	
	250	25	50	75	100	125	150	175	200	225	
	248	25	50	74	99	124	149	174	198	223	
	246	25	49	74	98	123	148	172	197	221	
	244	24	49	73	98	122	146	171	195	220	
	242	24	48	73	97	121	145	169	194	218	
	240	24	48	72	96	120	144	168	192	216	

N.	0	1	2	3	4	5	6	7	8	9	D.
182	260071	0310	0548	0787	1025	1263	1501	1739	1976	2214	238
183	2451	2688	2925	3162	3399	3636	3873	4109	4346	4582	237
184	4818	5054	5290	5525	5761	5996	6232	6467	6702	6937	235
185	7172	7406	7641	7875	8110	8344	8578	8812	9046	9279	234
186	9513	9746	9980	.213	.446	.679	.912	1144	1377	1609	233
187	271842	2074	2306	2538	2770	3001	3233	3464	3696	3927	232
188	4158	4389	4620	4850	5081	5311	5542	5772	6002	6232	230
189	6462	6692	6921	7151	7380	7609	7838	8067	8296	8525	229
190	8754	8982	9211	9439	9667	9895	.123	.351	.578	.806	228
191	281033	1261	1488	1715	1942	2169	2396	2622	2849	3075	227
192	3301	3527	3753	3979	4205	4431	4656	4882	5107	5332	226
193	5557	5782	6007	6232	6456	6681	6905	7130	7354	7578	225
194	7802	8026	8249	8473	8696	8920	9143	9366	9589	9812	223
195	290035	0257	0480	0702	0925	1147	1369	1591	1813	2034	222
196	2256	2478	2699	2920	3141	3363	3584	3804	4025	4246	221
197	4466	4687	4907	5127	5347	5567	5787	6007	6226	6446	220
198	6665	6884	7104	7323	7542	7761	7979	8198	8416	8635	219
199	8853	9071	9289	9507	9725	9943	.161	.378	.595	.813	218
200	301030	1247	1464	1681	1898	2114	2331	2547	2764	2980	217
201	3196	3412	3628	3844	4059	4275	4491	4706	4921	5136	216
202	5351	5566	5781	5996	6211	6425	6639	6854	7068	7282	214
203	7496	7710	7924	8137	8351	8564	8778	8991	9204	9417	213
204	9630	9843	..56	.268	.481	.693	.906	1118	1330	1542	212
205	311754	1966	2177	2389	2600	2812	3023	3234	3445	3656	211
206	3867	4078	4289	4499	4710	4920	5130	5340	5551	5760	210
207	5970	6180	6390	6599	6809	7018	7227	7436	7646	7854	209
208	8063	8272	8481	8689	8898	9106	9314	9522	9730	9938	208
209	320146	0354	0562	0769	0977	1184	1391	1598	1805	2012	207
210	2219	2426	2633	2839	3046	3252	3458	3665	3871	4077	206
211	4282	4488	4694	4899	5105	5310	5516	5721	5926	6131	205
212	6336	6541	6745	6950	7155	7359	7563	7767	7972	8176	204
213	8380	8583	8787	8991	9194	9398	9601	9805	...8	.211	203
214	330414	0617	0819	1022	1225	1427	1630	1832	2034	2236	202
215	2438	2640	2842	3044	3246	3447	3649	3850	4051	4253	202
216	4454	4655	4856	5057	5257	5458	5658	5859	6059	6260	201
217	6460	6660	6860	7060	7260	7459	7659	7858	8058	8257	200
218	8456	8656	8855	9054	9253	9451	9650	9849	..47	.246	199
219	340444	0642	0841	1039	1237	1435	1632	1830	2028	2225	198
220	2423	2620	2817	3014	3212	3409	3606	3802	3999	4196	197
N.	0	1	2	3	4	5	6	7	8	9	D.

Differences.	Proportional Parts.								
238	24	48	71	95	119	143	167	190	214
236	24	47	71	94	118	142	165	189	212
234	23	47	70	94	117	140	164	187	211
232	23	46	70	93	116	139	162	186	209
230	23	46	69	92	115	138	161	184	207
228	23	46	68	91	114	137	160	182	205
226	23	45	68	90	113	136	158	181	203
224	22	45	67	90	112	134	157	179	202
222	22	44	67	89	111	133	155	178	200
220	22	44	66	88	110	132	154	176	198
218	22	44	65	87	109	131	153	174	196
216	22	43	65	86	108	130	151	173	194
214	21	43	64	86	107	128	150	171	193
212	21	42	64	85	106	127	148	170	191
210	21	42	63	84	105	126	147	168	189
208	21	42	62	83	104	125	146	166	187
206	21	41	62	82	103	124	144	165	185
204	20	41	61	82	102	122	143	163	184
202	20	40	61	81	101	121	141	162	182
200	20	40	60	80	100	120	140	160	180
198	20	40	59	79	99	119	139	158	178

N.	0	1	2	3	4	5	6	7	8	9	D.
221	344392	4589	4785	4981	5178	5374	5570	5766	5962	6157	196
222	6353	6549	6744	6939	7135	7330	7525	7720	7915	8110	195
223	8305	8500	8694	8889	9083	9278	9472	9666	9860	..54	194
224	350248	0442	0636	0829	1023	1216	1410	1603	1796	1989	193
225	2183	2375	2568	2761	2954	3147	3339	3532	3724	3916	
226	4108	4301	4493	4685	4876	5068	5260	5452	5643	5834	192
227	6026	6217	6408	6599	6790	6981	7172	7363	7554	7744	191
228	7935	8125	8316	8506	8696	8886	9076	9266	9456	9646	190
229	9835	..25	.215	.404	.593	.783	.972	1161	1350	1539	189
230	361728	1917	2105	2294	2482	2671	2859	3048	3236	3424	188
231	3612	3800	3988	4176	4363	4551	4739	4926	5113	5301	
232	5488	5675	5862	6049	6236	6423	6610	6796	6983	7169	187
233	7356	7542	7729	7915	8101	8287	8473	8659	8845	9030	186
234	9216	9401	9587	9772	9958	.143	.328	.513	.698	.883	185
235	371068	1253	1437	1622	1806	1991	2175	2360	2544	2728	184
236	2912	3096	3280	3464	3647	3831	4015	4198	4382	4565	
237	4748	4932	5115	5298	5481	5664	5846	6029	6212	6394	183
238	6577	6759	6942	7124	7306	7488	7670	7852	8034	8216	182
239	8398	8580	8761	8943	9124	9306	9487	9668	9849	..30	181
240	380211	0392	0573	0754	0934	1115	1296	1476	1656	1837	
241	2017	2197	2377	2557	2737	2917	3097	3277	3456	3636	180
242	3815	3995	4174	4353	4533	4712	4891	5070	5249	5428	179
243	5606	5785	5964	6142	6321	6499	6677	6856	7034	7212	178
244	7390	7568	7746	7923	8101	8279	8456	8634	8811	8989	
245	9166	9343	9520	9698	9875	..51	.228	.405	.582	.759	177
246	390935	1112	1288	1464	1641	1817	1993	2169	2345	2521	176
247	2697	2873	3048	3224	3400	3575	3751	3926	4101	4277	
248	4452	4627	4802	4977	5152	5326	5501	5676	5850	6025	175
249	6199	6374	6548	6722	6896	7071	7245	7419	7592	7766	174
250	7940	8114	8287	8461	8634	8808	8981	9154	9328	9501	173
251	9674	9847	..20	.192	.365	.538	.711	.883	1056	1228	
252	401401	1573	1745	1917	2089	2261	2433	2605	2777	2949	172
253	3121	3292	3464	3635	3807	3978	4149	4320	4492	4663	171
254	4834	5005	5176	5346	5517	5688	5858	6029	6199	6370	
255	6540	6710	6881	7051	7221	7391	7561	7731	7901	8070	170
256	8240	8410	8579	8749	8918	9087	9257	9426	9595	9764	169
257	9933	.102	.271	.440	.609	.777	.946	1114	1283	1451	
258	411620	1788	1956	2124	2293	2461	2629	2796	2964	3132	168
259	3300	3467	3635	3803	3970	4137	4305	4472	4639	4806	167
260	4973	5140	5307	5474	5641	5808	5974	6141	6308	6474	
261	6641	6807	6973	7139	7306	7472	7638	7804	7970	8135	166
262	8301	8467	8633	8798	8964	9129	9295	9460	9625	9791	165
263	9956	.121	.286	.451	.616	.781	.945	1110	1275	1439	

N.	0 (Differences)	1	2	3	4	5	6	7	8	9	D.
Differences. / Proportional Parts.	196	20	39	59	78	98	118	137	157	176	
	194	19	39	58	78	97	116	136	155	175	
	192	19	38	58	77	96	115	134	154	173	
	190	19	38	57	76	95	114	133	152	171	
	188	19	38	56	75	94	113	132	150	169	
	186	19	37	56	74	93	112	130	149	167	
	184	18	37	55	74	92	110	129	147	166	
	182	18	36	55	73	91	109	127	146	164	
	180	18	36	54	72	90	108	126	144	162	
	178	18	36	53	71	89	107	125	142	160	
	176	18	35	53	70	88	106	123	141	158	
	174	17	35	52	70	87	104	122	139	157	
	172	17	34	52	69	86	103	120	138	155	
	170	17	34	51	68	85	102	119	136	153	
	168	17	34	50	67	84	101	118	134	151	
	166	17	33	50	66	83	100	116	133	149	
	164	16	33	49	66	82	98	115	131	148	

N.	0	1	2	3	4	5	6	7	8	9	D.
264	421604	1768	1933	2097	2261	2426	2590	2754	2918	3082	164
265	3246	3410	3574	3737	3901	4065	4228	4392	4555	4718	
266	4882	5045	5208	5371	5534	5697	5860	6023	6186	6349	163
267	6511	6674	6836	6999	7161	7324	7486	7648	7811	7973	162
268	8135	8297	8459	8621	8783	8944	9106	9268	9429	9591	
269	9752	9914	..75	.236	.398	.559	.720	.881	1042	1203	161
270	431364	1525	1685	1846	2007	2167	2328	2488	2649	2809	
271	2969	3130	3290	3450	3610	3770	3930	4090	4249	4409	160
272	4569	4729	4888	5048	5207	5367	5526	5685	5844	6004	159
273	6163	6322	6481	6640	6799	6957	7116	7275	7433	7592	
274	7751	7909	8067	8226	8384	8542	8701	8859	9017	9175	158
275	9333	9491	9648	9806	9964	.122	.279	.437	.594	.752	
276	440909	1066	1224	1381	1538	1695	1852	2009	2166	2323	157
277	2480	2637	2793	2950	3106	3263	3419	3576	3732	3889	
278	4045	4201	4357	4513	4669	4825	4981	5137	5293	5449	156
279	5604	5760	5915	6071	6226	6382	6537	6692	6848	7003	155
280	7158	7313	7468	7623	7778	7933	8088	8242	8397	8552	
281	8706	8861	9015	9170	9324	9478	9633	9787	9941	..95	154
282	450249	0403	0557	0711	0865	1018	1172	1326	1479	1633	
283	1786	1940	2093	2247	2400	2553	2706	2859	3012	3165	153
284	3318	3471	3624	3777	3930	4082	4235	4387	4540	4692	
285	4845	4997	5150	5302	5454	5606	5758	5910	6062	6214	152
286	6366	6518	6670	6821	6973	7125	7276	7428	7579	7731	
287	7882	8033	8184	8336	8487	8638	8789	8940	9091	9242	151
288	9392	9543	9694	9845	9995	.146	.296	.447	.597	.748	
289	460898	1048	1198	1348	1499	1649	1799	1948	2098	2248	150
290	2398	2548	2697	2847	2997	3146	3296	3445	3594	3744	
291	3893	4042	4191	4340	4490	4639	4788	4936	5085	5234	149
292	5383	5532	5680	5829	5977	6126	6274	6423	6571	6719	
293	6868	7016	7164	7312	7460	7608	7756	7904	8052	8200	148
294	8347	8495	8643	8790	8938	9085	9233	9380	9527	9675	
295	9822	9969	.116	.263	.410	.557	.704	.851	.998	1145	147
296	471292	1438	1585	1732	1878	2025	2171	2318	2464	2610	
297	2756	2903	3049	3195	3341	3487	3633	3779	3925	4071	146
298	4216	4362	4508	4653	4799	4944	5090	5235	5381	5526	
299	5671	5816	5962	6107	6252	6397	6542	6687	6832	6976	145
300	7121	7266	7411	7555	7700	7844	7989	8133	8278	8422	
301	8566	8711	8855	8999	9143	9287	9431	9575	9719	9863	144
302	480007	0151	0294	0438	0582	0725	0869	1012	1156	1299	
303	1443	1586	1729	1872	2016	2159	2302	2445	2588	2731	143
304	2874	3016	3159	3302	3445	3587	3730	3872	4015	4157	
305	4300	4442	4585	4727	4869	5011	5153	5295	5437	5579	142
306	5721	5863	6005	6147	6289	6430	6572	6714	6855	6997	
307	7138	7280	7421	7563	7704	7845	7986	8127	8269	8410	141
308	8551	8692	8833	8974	9114	9255	9396	9537	9677	9818	
309	9958	..99	.239	.380	.520	.661	.801	.941	1081	1222	140
310	491362	1502	1642	1782	1922	2062	2201	2341	2481	2621	
311	2760	2900	3040	3179	3319	3458	3597	3737	3876	4015	139
N.	**0**	**1**	**2**	**3**	**4**	**5**	**6**	**7**	**8**	**9**	**D.**

Differences.		Proportional Parts.									
	162	16	32	49	65	81	97	113	130	146	
	160	16	32	48	64	80	96	112	128	144	
	158	16	32	47	63	79	95	111	126	142	
	156	16	31	47	62	78	94	109	125	140	
	154	15	31	46	62	77	92	108	123	139	
	152	15	30	46	61	76	91	106	122	137	
	150	15	30	45	60	75	90	105	120	135	
	148	15	30	44	59	74	89	104	118	133	
	146	15	29	44	58	73	88	102	117	131	
	144	14	29	43	58	72	86	101	115	130	
	142	14	28	43	57	71	85	99	114	128	
	140	14	28	42	56	70	84	98	112	126	

N.	0	1	2	3	4	5	6	7	8	9	D.
312	494155	4294	4433	4572	4711	4850	4989	5128	5267	5406	139
313	5544	5683	5822	5960	6099	6238	6376	6515	6653	6791	
314	6930	7068	7206	7344	7483	7621	7759	7897	8035	8173	138
315	8311	8448	8586	8724	8862	8999	9137	9275	9412	9550	
316	9687	9824	9962	..99	.236	.374	.511	.648	.785	.922	137
317	501059	1196	1333	1470	1607	1744	1880	2017	2154	2291	
318	2427	2564	2700	2837	2973	3109	3246	3382	3518	3655	136
319	3791	3927	4063	4199	4335	4471	4607	4743	4878	5014	
320	5150	5286	5421	5557	5693	5828	5964	6099	6234	6370	
321	6505	6640	6776	6911	7046	7181	7316	7451	7586	7721	135
322	7856	7991	8126	8260	8395	8530	8664	8799	8934	9068	
323	9203	9337	9471	9606	9740	9874	...9	.143	.277	.411	134
324	510545	0679	0813	0947	1081	1215	1349	1482	1616	1750	
325	1883	2017	2151	2284	2418	2551	2684	2818	2951	3084	133
326	3218	3351	3484	3617	3750	3883	4016	4149	4282	4415	
327	4548	4681	4813	4946	5079	5211	5344	5476	5609	5741	
328	5874	6006	6139	6271	6403	6535	6668	6800	6932	7064	132
329	7196	7328	7460	7592	7724	7855	7987	8119	8251	8382	
330	8514	8646	8777	8909	9040	9171	9303	9434	9566	9697	131
331	9828	9959	..90	.221	.353	.484	.615	.745	.876	1007	
332	521138	1269	1400	1530	1661	1792	1922	2053	2183	2314	
333	2444	2575	2705	2835	2966	3096	3226	3356	3486	3616	130
334	3746	3876	4006	4136	4266	4396	4526	4656	4785	4915	
335	5045	5174	5304	5434	5563	5693	5822	5951	6081	6210	129
336	6339	6469	6598	6727	6856	6985	7114	7243	7372	7501	
337	7630	7759	7888	8016	8145	8274	8402	8531	8660	8788	
338	8917	9045	9174	9302	9430	9559	9687	9815	9943	..72	128
339	530200	0328	0456	0584	0712	0840	0968	1096	1223	1351	
340	1479	1607	1734	1862	1990	2117	2245	2372	2500	2627	
341	2754	2882	3009	3136	3264	3391	3518	3645	3772	3899	127
342	4026	4153	4280	4407	4534	4661	4787	4914	5041	5167	
343	5294	5421	5547	5674	5800	5927	6053	6180	6306	6432	126
344	6558	6685	6811	6937	7063	7189	7315	7441	7567	7693	
345	7819	7945	8071	8197	8322	8448	8574	8699	8825	8951	
346	9076	9202	9327	9452	9578	9703	9829	9954	..79	.204	125
347	540329	0455	0580	0705	0830	0955	1080	1205	1330	1454	
348	1579	1704	1829	1953	2078	2203	2327	2452	2576	2701	
349	2825	2950	3074	3199	3323	3447	3571	3696	3820	3944	124
350	4068	4192	4316	4440	4564	4688	4812	4936	5060	5183	
351	5307	5431	5555	5678	5802	5925	6049	6172	6296	6419	
352	6543	6666	6789	6913	7036	7159	7282	7405	7529	7652	123
353	7775	7898	8021	8144	8267	8389	8512	8635	8758	8881	
354	9003	9126	9249	9371	9494	9616	9739	9861	9984	.106	
355	550228	0351	0473	0595	0717	0840	0962	1084	1206	1328	122
356	1450	1572	1694	1816	1938	2060	2181	2303	2425	2547	
357	2668	2790	2911	3033	3155	3276	3398	3519	3640	3762	121
358	3883	4004	4126	4247	4368	4489	4610	4731	4852	4973	
359	5094	5215	5336	5457	5578	5699	5820	5940	6061	6182	
360	6303	6423	6544	6664	6785	6905	7026	7146	7267	7387	120
361	7507	7627	7748	7868	7988	8108	8228	8349	8469	8589	

N.	0	1	2	3	4	5	6	7	8	9	D.
Differences.	138	Proportional Parts. 14	28	41	55	69	83	97	110	124	
	136	14	27	41	54	68	82	95	109	122	
	134	13	27	40	54	67	80	94	107	121	
	132	13	26	40	53	66	79	92	106	119	
	130	13	26	39	52	65	78	91	104	117	
	128	13	26	38	51	64	77	90	102	115	
	126	13	25	38	50	63	76	88	101	113	
	124	12	25	37	50	62	74	87	99	112	
	122	12	24	37	49	61	73	85	98	110	
	120	12	24	36	48	60	72	84	96	108	

N.	0	1	2	3	4	5	6	7	8	9	D.
362	558709	8829	8948	9068	9188	9308	9428	9548	9667	9787	120
363	9907	..26	.146	.265	.385	.504	.624	.743	.863	.982	
364	561101	1221	1340	1459	1578	1698	1817	1936	2055	2174	119
365	2293	2412	2531	2650	2769	2887	3006	3125	3244	3362	
366	3481	3600	3718	3837	3955	4074	4192	4311	4429	4548	
367	4666	4784	4903	5021	5139	5257	5376	5494	5612	5730	118
368	5848	5966	6084	6202	6320	6437	6555	6673	6791	6909	
369	7026	7144	7262	7379	7497	7614	7732	7849	7967	8084	
370	8202	8319	8436	8554	8671	8788	8905	9023	9140	9257	117
371	9374	9491	9608	9725	9842	9959	..76	.193	.309	.426	
372	570543	0660	0776	0893	1010	1126	1243	1359	1476	1592	
373	1709	1825	1942	2058	2174	2291	2407	2523	2639	2755	116
374	2872	2988	3104	3220	3336	3452	3568	3684	3800	3915	
375	4031	4147	4263	4379	4494	4610	4726	4841	4957	5072	
376	5188	5303	5419	5534	5650	5765	5880	5996	6111	6226	115
377	6341	6457	6572	6687	6802	6917	7032	7147	7262	7377	
378	7492	7607	7722	7836	7951	8066	8181	8295	8410	8525	
379	8639	8754	8868	8983	9097	9212	9326	9441	9555	9669	114
380	9784	9898	..12	.126	.241	.355	.469	.583	.697	.811	
381	580925	1039	1153	1267	1381	1495	1608	1722	1836	1950	
382	2063	2177	2291	2404	2518	2631	2745	2858	2972	3085	
383	3199	3312	3426	3539	3652	3765	3879	3992	4105	4218	113
384	4331	4444	4557	4670	4783	4896	5009	5122	5235	5348	
385	5461	5574	5686	5799	5912	6024	6137	6250	6362	6475	
386	6587	6700	6812	6925	7037	7149	7262	7374	7486	7599	112
387	7711	7823	7935	8047	8160	8272	8384	8496	8608	8720	
388	8832	8944	9056	9167	9279	9391	9503	9615	9726	9838	
389	9950	..61	.173	.284	.396	.507	.619	.730	.842	.953	
390	591065	1176	1287	1399	1510	1621	1732	1843	1955	2066	111
391	2177	2288	2399	2510	2621	2732	2843	2954	3064	3175	
392	3286	3397	3508	3618	3729	3840	3950	4061	4171	4282	
393	4393	4503	4614	4724	4834	4945	5055	5165	5276	5386	110
394	5496	5606	5717	5827	5937	6047	6157	6267	6377	6487	
395	6597	6707	6817	6927	7037	7146	7256	7366	7476	7586	
396	7695	7805	7914	8024	8134	8243	8353	8462	8572	8681	
397	8791	8900	9009	9119	9228	9337	9446	9556	9665	9774	109
398	9883	9992	.101	.210	.319	.428	.537	.646	.755	.864	
399	600973	1082	1191	1299	1408	1517	1625	1734	1843	1951	
400	2060	2169	2277	2386	2494	2603	2711	2819	2928	3036	108
401	3144	3253	3361	3469	3577	3686	3794	3902	4010	4118	
402	4226	4334	4442	4550	4658	4766	4874	4982	5089	5197	
403	5305	5413	5521	5628	5736	5844	5951	6059	6166	6274	
404	6381	6489	6596	6704	6811	6919	7026	7133	7241	7348	107
405	7455	7562	7669	7777	7884	7991	8098	8205	8312	8419	
406	8526	8633	8740	8847	8954	9061	9167	9274	9381	9488	
407	9594	9701	9808	9914	..21	.128	.234	.341	.447	.554	
408	610660	0767	0873	0979	1086	1192	1298	1405	1511	1617	106

N.	0	1	2	3	4	5	6	7	8	9	D.
Differences.	119	Proportional Parts. 12	24	36	48	60	71	83	95	107	
	118	12	24	35	47	59	71	83	94	106	
	117	12	23	35	47	59	70	82	94	105	
	116	12	23	35	46	58	70	81	93	104	
	115	12	23	35	46	58	69	81	92	104	
	114	11	23	34	46	57	68	80	91	103	
	113	11	23	34	45	57	68	79	90	102	
	112	11	22	34	45	56	67	78	90	101	
	111	11	22	33	44	56	67	78	89	100	
	110	11	22	33	44	55	66	77	88	99	
	109	11	22	33	44	55	65	76	87	98	
	108	11	22	32	43	54	65	76	86	97	
	107	11	21	32	43	54	64	75	86	96	

N.	0	1	2	3	4	5	6	7	8	9	D.
409	611723	1829	1936	2042	2148	2254	2360	2466	2572	2678	106
410	2784	2890	2996	3102	3207	3313	3419	3525	3630	3736	
411	3842	3947	4053	4159	4264	4370	4475	4581	4686	4792	
412	4897	5003	5108	5213	5319	5424	5529	5634	5740	5845	105
413	5950	6055	6160	6265	6370	6476	6581	6686	6790	6895	
414	7000	7105	7210	7315	7420	7525	7629	7734	7839	7943	
415	8048	8153	8257	8362	8466	8571	8676	8780	8884	8989	
416	9093	9198	9302	9406	9511	9615	9719	9824	9928	..32	104
417	620136	0240	0344	0448	0552	0656	0760	0864	0968	1072	
418	1176	1280	1384	1488	1592	1695	1799	1903	2007	2110	
419	2214	2318	2421	2525	2628	2732	2835	2939	3042	3146	
420	3249	3353	3456	3559	3663	3766	3869	3973	4076	4179	103
421	4282	4385	4488	4591	4695	4798	4901	5004	5107	5210	
422	5312	5415	5518	5621	5724	5827	5929	6032	6135	6238	
423	6340	6443	6546	6648	6751	6853	6956	7058	7161	7263	
424	7366	7468	7571	7673	7775	7878	7980	8082	8185	8287	102
425	8389	8491	8593	8695	8797	8900	9002	9104	9206	9308	
426	9410	9512	9613	9715	9817	9919	..21	.123	.224	.326	
427	630428	0530	0631	0733	0835	0936	1038	1139	1241	1342	
428	1444	1545	1647	1748	1849	1951	2052	2153	2255	2356	101
429	2457	2559	2660	2761	2862	2963	3064	3165	3266	3367	
430	3468	3569	3670	3771	3872	3973	4074	4175	4276	4376	
431	4477	4578	4679	4779	4880	4981	5081	5182	5283	5383	100
432	5484	5584	5685	5785	5886	5986	6087	6187	6287	6388	
433	6488	6588	6688	6789	6889	6989	7089	7189	7290	7390	
434	7490	7590	7690	7790	7890	7990	8090	8190	8290	8389	
435	8489	8589	8689	8789	8888	8988	9088	9188	9287	9387	99
436	9486	9586	9686	9785	9885	9984	..84	.183	.283	.382	
437	640481	0581	0680	0779	0879	0978	1077	1177	1276	1375	
438	1474	1573	1672	1771	1871	1970	2069	2168	2267	2366	
439	2465	2563	2662	2761	2860	2959	3058	3156	3255	3354	
440	3453	3551	3650	3749	3847	3946	4044	4143	4242	4340	98
441	4439	4537	4636	4734	4832	4931	5029	5127	5226	5324	
442	5422	5521	5619	5717	5815	5913	6011	6110	6208	6306	
443	6404	6502	6600	6698	6796	6894	6992	7089	7187	7285	
444	7383	7481	7579	7676	7774	7872	7969	8067	8165	8262	
445	8360	8458	8555	8653	8750	8848	8945	9043	9140	9237	97
446	9335	9432	9530	9627	9724	9821	9919	..16	.113	.210	
447	650308	0405	0502	0599	0696	0793	0890	0987	1084	1181	
448	1278	1375	1472	1569	1666	1762	1859	1956	2053	2150	
449	2246	2343	2440	2536	2633	2730	2826	2923	3019	3116	
450	3213	3309	3405	3502	3598	3695	3791	3888	3984	4080	96
451	4177	4273	4369	4465	4562	4658	4754	4850	4946	5042	
452	5138	5235	5331	5427	5523	5619	5715	5810	5906	6002	
453	6098	6194	6290	6386	6482	6577	6673	6769	6864	6960	
454	7056	7152	7247	7343	7438	7534	7629	7725	7820	7916	
455	8011	8107	8202	8298	8393	8488	8584	8679	8774	8870	95
456	8965	9060	9155	9250	9346	9441	9536	9631	9726	9821	
457	9916	..11	.106	.201	.296	.391	.486	.581	.676	.771	

N.	0	1	2	3	4	5	6	7	8	9	D.
Differences.	106 Proportional Parts.	11	21	32	42	53	64	74	85	95	
	105	11	21	32	42	53	63	74	84	95	
	104	10	21	31	42	52	62	73	83	94	
	103	10	21	31	41	52	62	72	82	93	
	102	10	20	31	41	51	61	71	82	92	
	101	10	20	30	40	51	61	71	81	91	
	100	10	20	30	40	50	60	70	80	90	
	99	10	20	30	40	50	59	69	79	89	
	98	10	20	29	39	49	59	69	78	88	
	97	10	19	29	39	49	58	68	78	87	
	96	10	19	29	38	48	58	67	77	86	

N.	0	1	2	3	4	5	6	7	8	9	D.
458	660865	0960	1055	1150	1245	1339	1434	1529	1623	1718	95
459	1813	1907	2002	2096	2191	2286	2380	2475	2569	2663	
460	2758	2852	2947	3041	3135	3230	3324	3418	3512	3607	94
461	3701	3795	3889	3983	4078	4172	4266	4360	4454	4548	
462	4642	4736	4830	4924	5018	5112	5206	5299	5393	5487	
463	5581	5675	5769	5862	5956	6050	6143	6237	6331	6424	
464	6518	6612	6705	6799	6892	6986	7079	7173	7266	7360	
465	7453	7546	7640	7733	7826	7920	8013	8106	8199	8293	93
466	8386	8479	8572	8665	8759	8852	8945	9038	9131	9224	
467	9317	9410	9503	9596	9689	9782	9875	9967	..60	.153	
468	670246	0339	0431	0524	0617	0710	0802	0895	0988	1080	
469	1173	1265	1358	1451	1543	1636	1728	1821	1913	2005	
470	2098	2190	2283	2375	2467	2560	2652	2744	2836	2929	92
471	3021	3113	3205	3297	3390	3482	3574	3666	3758	3850	
472	3942	4034	4126	4218	4310	4402	4494	4586	4677	4769	
473	4861	4953	5045	5137	5228	5320	5412	5503	5595	5687	
474	5778	5870	5962	6053	6145	6236	6328	6419	6511	6602	
475	6694	6785	6876	6968	7059	7151	7242	7333	7424	7516	91
476	7607	7698	7789	7881	7972	8063	8154	8245	8336	8427	
477	8518	8609	8700	8791	8882	8973	9064	9155	9246	9337	
478	9428	9519	9610	9700	9791	9882	9973	..63	.154	.245	
479	680336	0426	0517	0607	0698	0789	0879	0970	1060	1151	
480	1241	1332	1422	1513	1603	1693	1784	1874	1964	2055	90
481	2145	2235	2326	2416	2506	2596	2686	2777	2867	2957	
482	3047	3137	3227	3317	3407	3497	3587	3677	3767	3857	
483	3947	4037	4127	4217	4307	4396	4486	4576	4666	4756	
484	4845	4935	5025	5114	5204	5294	5383	5473	5563	5652	
485	5742	5831	5921	6010	6100	6189	6279	6368	6458	6547	89
486	6636	6726	6815	6904	6994	7083	7172	7261	7351	7440	
487	7529	7618	7707	7796	7886	7975	8064	8153	8242	8331	
488	8420	8509	8598	8687	8776	8865	8953	9042	9131	9220	
489	9309	9398	9486	9575	9664	9753	9841	9930	..19	.107	
490	690196	0285	0373	0462	0550	0639	0728	0816	0905	0993	
491	1081	1170	1258	1347	1435	1524	1612	1700	1789	1877	88
492	1965	2053	2142	2230	2318	2406	2494	2583	2671	2759	
493	2847	2935	3023	3111	3199	3287	3375	3463	3551	3639	
494	3727	3815	3903	3991	4078	4166	4254	4342	4430	4517	
495	4605	4693	4781	4868	4956	5044	5131	5219	5307	5394	
496	5482	5569	5657	5744	5832	5919	6007	6094	6182	6269	87
497	6356	6444	6531	6618	6706	6793	6880	6968	7055	7142	
498	7229	7317	7404	7491	7578	7665	7752	7839	7926	8014	
499	8101	8188	8275	8362	8449	8535	8622	8709	8796	8883	
500	8970	9057	9144	9231	9317	9404	9491	9578	9664	9751	
501	9838	9924	..11	..98	.184	.271	.358	.444	.531	.617	
502	700704	0790	0877	0963	1050	1136	1222	1309	1395	1482	86
503	1568	1654	1741	1827	1913	1999	2086	2172	2258	2344	
504	2431	2517	2603	2689	2775	2861	2947	3033	3119	3205	
505	3291	3377	3463	3549	3635	3721	3807	3893	3979	4065	
506	4151	4236	4322	4408	4494	4579	4665	4751	4837	4922	
507	5008	5094	5179	5265	5350	5436	5522	5607	5693	5778	

N.	0	1	2	3	4	5	6	7	8	9	D.
Differences.	95	10	19	29	38	48	57	67	76	86	
	94	9	19	28	38	47	56	66	75	85	
	93	9	19	28	37	47	56	65	74	84	
	92	9	18	28	37	46	55	64	74	83	
	91	9	18	27	36	46	55	64	73	82	
	90	9	18	27	36	45	54	63	72	81	
	89	9	18	27	36	45	53	62	71	80	
	88	9	18	26	35	44	53	62	70	79	
	87	9	17	26	35	44	52	61	70	78	
	86	9	17	26	34	43	52	60	69	77	

Proportional Parts.

N.	0	1	2	3	4	5	6	7	8	9	D.
508	705864	5949	6035	6120	6206	6291	6376	6462	6547	6632	85
509	6718	6803	6888	6974	7059	7144	7229	7315	7400	7485	
510	7570	7655	7740	7826	7911	7996	8081	8166	8251	8336	
511	8421	8506	8591	8676	8761	8846	8931	9015	9100	9185	
512	9270	9355	9440	9524	9609	9694	9779	9863	9948	..33	
513	710117	0202	0287	0371	0456	0540	0625	0710	0794	0879	
514	0963	1048	1132	1217	1301	1385	1470	1554	1639	1723	84
515	1807	1892	1976	2060	2144	2229	2313	2397	2481	2566	
516	2650	2734	2818	2902	2986	3070	3154	3238	3323	3407	
517	3491	3575	3659	3742	3826	3910	3994	4078	4162	4246	
518	4330	4414	4497	4581	4665	4749	4833	4916	5000	5084	
519	5167	5251	5335	5418	5502	5586	5669	5753	5836	5920	
520	6003	6087	6170	6254	6337	6421	6504	6588	6671	6754	83
521	6838	6921	7004	7088	7171	7254	7338	7421	7504	7587	
522	7671	7754	7837	7920	8003	8086	8169	8253	8336	8419	
523	8502	8585	8668	8751	8834	8917	9000	9083	9165	9248	
524	9331	9414	9497	9580	9663	9745	9828	9911	9994	..77	
525	720159	0242	0325	0407	0490	0573	0655	0738	0821	0903	
526	0986	1068	1151	1233	1316	1398	1481	1563	1646	1728	82
527	1811	1893	1975	2058	2140	2222	2305	2387	2469	2552	
528	2634	2716	2798	2881	2963	3045	3127	3209	3291	3374	
529	3456	3538	3620	3702	3784	3866	3948	4030	4112	4194	
530	4276	4358	4440	4522	4604	4685	4767	4849	4931	5013	
531	5095	5176	5258	5340	5422	5503	5585	5667	5748	5830	
532	5912	5993	6075	6156	6238	6320	6401	6483	6564	6646	
533	6727	6809	6890	6972	7053	7134	7216	7297	7379	7460	81
534	7541	7623	7704	7785	7866	7948	8029	8110	8191	8273	
535	8354	8435	8516	8597	8678	8759	8841	8922	9003	9084	
536	9165	9246	9327	9408	9489	9570	9651	9732	9813	9893	
537	9974	..55	.136	.217	.298	.378	.459	.540	.621	.702	
538	730782	0863	0944	1024	1105	1186	1266	1347	1428	1508	
539	1589	1669	1750	1830	1911	1991	2072	2152	2233	2313	
540	2394	2474	2555	2635	2715	2796	2876	2956	3037	3117	80
541	3197	3278	3358	3438	3518	3598	3679	3759	3839	3919	
542	3999	4079	4160	4240	4320	4400	4480	4560	4640	4720	
543	4800	4880	4960	5040	5120	5200	5279	5359	5439	5519	
544	5599	5679	5759	5838	5918	5998	6078	6157	6237	6317	
545	6397	6476	6556	6635	6715	6795	6874	6954	7034	7113	
546	7193	7272	7352	7431	7511	7590	7670	7749	7829	7908	79
547	7987	8067	8146	8225	8305	8384	8463	8543	8622	8701	
548	8781	8860	8939	9018	9097	9177	9256	9335	9414	9493	
549	9572	9651	9731	9810	9889	9968	..47	.126	.205	.284	
550	740363	0442	0521	0600	0678	0757	0836	0915	0994	1073	
551	1152	1230	1309	1388	1467	1546	1624	1703	1782	1860	
552	1939	2018	2096	2175	2254	2332	2411	2489	2568	2647	
553	2725	2804	2882	2961	3039	3118	3196	3275	3353	3431	78
554	3510	3588	3667	3745	3823	3902	3980	4058	4136	4215	
555	4293	4371	4449	4528	4606	4684	4762	4840	4919	4997	
556	5075	5153	5231	5309	5387	5465	5543	5621	5699	5777	
557	5855	5933	6011	6089	6167	6245	6323	6401	6479	6556	
558	6634	6712	6790	6868	6945	7023	7101	7179	7256	7334	
N.	0	1	2	3	4	5	6	7	8	9	D.

Differences.	Proportional Parts.									
	86	9	17	26	34	43	52	60	69	77
	85	9	17	26	34	43	51	60	68	77
	84	8	17	25	34	42	50	59	67	76
	83	8	17	25	33	42	50	58	66	75
	82	8	16	25	33	41	49	57	66	74
	81	8	16	24	32	41	49	57	65	73
	80	8	16	24	32	40	48	56	64	72
	79	8	16	24	32	40	47	55	63	71
	78	8	16	23	31	39	47	55	62	70

N.	0	1	2	3	4	5	6	7	8	9	D.
559	747412	7489	7567	7645	7722	7800	7878	7955	8033	8110	78
560	8188	8266	8343	8421	8498	8576	8653	8731	8808	8885	77
561	8963	9040	9118	9195	9272	9350	9427	9504	9582	9659	
562	9736	9814	9891	9968	..45	.123	.200	.277	.354	.431	
563	750508	0586	0663	0740	0817	0894	0971	1048	1125	1202	
564	1279	1356	1433	1510	1587	1664	1741	1818	1895	1972	
565	2048	2125	2202	2279	2356	2433	2509	2586	2663	2740	
566	2816	2893	2970	3047	3123	3200	3277	3353	3430	3506	
567	3583	3660	3736	3813	3889	3966	4042	4119	4195	4272	
568	4348	4425	4501	4578	4654	4730	4807	4883	4960	5036	76
569	5112	5189	5265	5341	5417	5494	5570	5646	5722	5799	
570	5875	5951	6027	6103	6180	6256	6332	6408	6484	6560	
571	6636	6712	6788	6864	6940	7016	7092	7168	7244	7320	
572	7396	7472	7548	7624	7700	7775	7851	7927	8003	8079	
573	8155	8230	8306	8382	8458	8533	8609	8685	8761	8836	
574	8912	8988	9063	9139	9214	9290	9366	9441	9517	9592	
575	9668	9743	9819	9894	9970	..45	.121	.196	.272	.347	75
576	760422	0498	0573	0649	0724	0799	0875	0950	1025	1101	
577	1176	1251	1326	1402	1477	1552	1627	1702	1778	1853	
578	1928	2003	2078	2153	2228	2303	2378	2453	2529	2604	
579	2679	2754	2829	2904	2978	3053	3128	3203	3278	3353	
580	3428	3503	3578	3653	3727	3802	3877	3952	4027	4101	
581	4176	4251	4326	4400	4475	4550	4624	4699	4774	4848	
582	4923	4998	5072	5147	5221	5296	5370	5445	5520	5594	
583	5669	5743	5818	5892	5966	6041	6115	6190	6264	6338	74
584	6413	6487	6562	6636	6710	6785	6859	6933	7007	7082	
585	7156	7230	7304	7379	7453	7527	7601	7675	7749	7823	
586	7898	7972	8046	8120	8194	8268	8342	8416	8490	8564	
587	8638	8712	8786	8860	8934	9008	9082	9156	9230	9303	
588	9377	9451	9525	9599	9673	9746	9820	9894	9968	..42	
589	770115	0189	0263	0336	0410	0484	0557	0631	0705	0778	
590	0852	0926	0999	1073	1146	1220	1293	1367	1440	1514	
591	1587	1661	1734	1808	1881	1955	2028	2102	2175	2248	73
592	2322	2395	2468	2542	2615	2688	2762	2835	2908	2081	
593	3055	3128	3201	3274	3348	3421	3494	3567	3640	3713	
594	3786	3860	3933	4006	4079	4152	4225	4298	4371	4444	
595	4517	4590	4663	4736	4809	4882	4955	5028	5100	5173	
596	5246	5319	5392	5465	5538	5610	5683	5756	5829	5902	
597	5974	6047	6120	6193	6265	6338	6411	6483	6556	6629	
598	6701	6774	6846	6919	6992	7064	7137	7209	7282	7354	
599	7427	7499	7572	7644	7717	7789	7862	7934	8006	8079	72
600	8151	8224	8296	8368	8441	8513	8585	8658	8730	8802	
601	8874	8947	9019	9091	9163	9236	9308	9380	9452	9524	
602	9596	9669	9741	9813	9885	9957	..29	.101	.173	.245	
603	780317	0389	0461	0533	0605	0677	0749	0821	0893	0965	
604	1037	1109	1181	1253	1324	1396	1468	1540	1612	1684	
605	1755	1827	1899	1971	2042	2114	2186	2258	2329	2401	
606	2473	2544	2616	2688	2759	2831	2902	2974	3046	3117	
607	3189	3260	3332	3403	3475	3546	3618	3689	3761	3832	71
608	3904	3975	4046	4118	4189	4261	4332	4403	4475	4546	
609	4617	4689	4760	4831	4902	4974	5045	5116	5187	5259	
610	5330	5401	5472	5543	5615	5686	5757	5828	5899	5970	
611	6041	6112	6183	6254	6325	6396	6467	6538	6609	6680	

N.	0	1	2	3	4	5	6	7	8	9	D.
Differences.	77	Propor. Parts. 8	15	23	31	39	46	54	62	69	
	76	8	15	23	30	38	46	53	61	68	
	75	8	15	23	30	38	45	53	60	68	
	74	7	15	22	30	37	44	52	59	67	
	73	7	15	22	29	37	44	51	58	66	
	72	7	14	22	29	36	43	50	58	65	
	71	7	14	21	28	36	43	50	57	64	

N.	0	1	2	3	4	5	6	7	8	9	D.
612	786751	6822	6893	6964	7035	7106	7177	7248	7319	7390	71
613	7460	7531	7602	7673	7744	7815	7885	7956	8027	8098	
614	8168	8239	8310	8381	8451	8522	8593	8663	8734	8804	
615	8875	8946	9016	9087	9157	9228	9299	9369	9440	9510	
616	9581	9651	9722	9792	9863	9933	...4	..74	.144	.215	70
617	790285	0356	0426	0496	0567	0637	0707	0778	0848	0918	
618	0988	1059	1129	1199	1269	1340	1410	1480	1550	1620	
619	1691	1761	1831	1901	1971	2041	2111	2181	2252	2322	
620	2392	2462	2532	2602	2672	2742	2812	2882	2952	3022	
621	3092	3162	3231	3301	3371	3441	3511	3581	3651	3721	
622	3790	3860	3930	4000	4070	4139	4209	4279	4349	4418	
623	4488	4558	4627	4697	4767	4836	4906	4976	5045	5115	
624	5185	5254	5324	5393	5463	5532	5602	5672	5741	5811	
625	5880	5949	6019	6088	6158	6227	6297	6366	6436	6505	69
626	6574	6644	6713	6782	6852	6921	6990	7060	7129	7198	
627	7268	7337	7406	7475	7545	7614	7683	7752	7821	7890	
628	7960	8029	8098	8167	8236	8305	8374	8443	8513	8582	
629	8651	8720	8789	8858	8927	8996	9065	9134	9203	9272	
630	9341	9409	9478	9547	9616	9685	9754	9823	9892	9961	
631	800029	0098	0167	0236	0305	0373	0442	0511	0580	0648	
632	0717	0786	0854	0923	0992	1061	1129	1198	1266	1335	
633	1404	1472	1541	1609	1678	1747	1815	1883	1952	2021	
634	2089	2158	2226	2295	2363	2432	2500	2568	2637	2705	
635	2774	2842	2910	2979	3047	3116	3184	3252	3321	3389	68
636	3457	3525	3594	3662	3730	3798	3867	3935	4003	4071	
637	4139	4208	4276	4344	4412	4480	4548	4616	4685	4753	
638	4821	4889	4957	5025	5093	5161	5229	5297	5365	5433	
639	5501	5569	5637	5705	5773	5841	5908	5976	6044	6112	
640	6180	6248	6316	6384	6451	6519	6587	6655	6723	6790	
641	6858	6926	6994	7061	7129	7197	7264	7332	7400	7467	
642	7535	7603	7670	7738	7806	7873	7941	8008	8076	8143	
643	8211	8279	8346	8414	8481	8549	8616	8684	8751	8818	67
644	8886	8953	9021	9088	9156	9223	9290	9358	9425	9492	
645	9560	9627	9694	9762	9829	9896	9964	..31	..98	.165	
646	810233	0300	0367	0434	0501	0569	0636	0703	0770	0837	
647	0904	0971	1039	1106	1173	1240	1307	1374	1441	1508	
648	1575	1642	1709	1776	1843	1910	1977	2044	2111	2178	
649	2245	2312	2379	2445	2512	2579	2646	2713	2780	2847	
650	2913	2980	3047	3114	3181	3247	3314	3381	3448	3514	
651	3581	3648	3714	3781	3848	3914	3981	4048	4114	4181	
652	4248	4314	4381	4447	4514	4581	4647	4714	4780	4847	
653	4913	4980	5046	5113	5179	5246	5312	5378	5445	5511	66
654	5578	5644	5711	5777	5843	5910	5976	6042	6109	6175	
655	6241	6308	6374	6440	6506	6573	6639	6705	6771	6838	
656	6904	6970	7036	7102	7169	7235	7301	7367	7433	7499	
657	7565	7631	7698	7764	7830	7896	7962	8028	8094	8160	
658	8226	8292	8358	8424	8490	8556	8622	8688	8754	8820	
659	8885	8951	9017	9083	9149	9215	9281	9346	9412	9478	
660	9544	9610	9676	9741	9807	9873	9939	...4	..70	.136	
661	820201	0267	0333	0399	0464	0530	0595	0661	0727	0792	
662	0858	0924	0989	1055	1120	1186	1251	1317	1382	1448	
663	1514	1579	1645	1710	1775	1841	1906	1972	2037	2103	65
664	2168	2233	2299	2364	2430	2495	2560	2626	2691	2756	

N.	0	1	2	3	4	5	6	7	8	9	D.
Differences.	71 Propor. Parts.	7	14	21	28	36	43	50	57	64	
	70	7	14	21	28	35	42	49	56	63	
	69	7	14	21	28	35	41	48	55	62	
	68	7	14	20	27	34	41	48	54	61	
	67	7	13	20	27	34	40	47	54	60	
	66	7	13	20	26	33	40	46	53	59	
	65	7	13	20	26	33	39	46	52	59	

N.	0	1	2	3	4	5	6	7	8	9	D.
665	822822	2887	2952	3018	3083	3148	3213	3279	3344	3409	65
666	3474	3539	3605	3670	3735	3800	3865	3930	3996	4061	
667	4126	4191	4256	4321	4386	4451	4516	4581	4646	4711	
668	4776	4841	4906	4971	5036	5101	5166	5231	5296	5361	
669	5426	5491	5556	5621	5686	5751	5815	5880	5945	6010	
670	6075	6140	6204	6269	6334	6399	6464	6528	6593	6658	
671	6723	6787	6852	6917	6981	7046	7111	7175	7240	7305	
672	7369	7434	7499	7563	7628	7692	7757	7821	7886	7951	
673	8015	8080	8144	8209	8273	8338	8402	8467	8531	8595	64
674	8660	8724	8789	8853	8918	8982	9046	9111	9175	9239	
675	9304	9368	9432	9497	9561	9625	9690	9754	9818	9882	
676	9947	..11	..75	.139	.204	.268	.332	.396	.460	.525	
677	830589	0653	0717	0781	0845	0909	0973	1037	1102	1166	
678	1230	1294	1358	1422	1486	1550	1614	1678	1742	1806	
679	1870	1934	1998	2062	2126	2189	2253	2317	2381	2445	
680	2509	2573	2637	2700	2764	2828	2892	2956	3020	3083	
681	3147	3211	3275	3338	3402	3466	3530	3593	3657	3721	
682	3784	3848	3912	3975	4039	4103	4166	4230	4294	4357	
683	4421	4484	4548	4611	4675	4739	4802	4866	4929	4993	
684	5056	5120	5183	5247	5310	5373	5437	5500	5564	5627	63
685	5691	5754	5817	5881	5944	6007	6071	6134	6197	6261	
686	6324	6387	6451	6514	6577	6641	6704	6767	6830	6894	
687	6957	7020	7083	7146	7210	7273	7336	7399	7462	7525	
688	7588	7652	7715	7778	7841	7904	7967	8030	8093	8156	
689	8219	8282	8345	8408	8471	8534	8597	8660	8723	8786	
690	8849	8912	8975	9038	9101	9164	9227	9289	9352	9415	
691	9478	9541	9604	9667	9729	9792	9855	9918	9981	..43	
692	840106	0169	0232	0294	0357	0420	0482	0545	0608	0671	
693	0733	0796	0859	0921	0984	1046	1109	1172	1234	1297	
694	1359	1422	1485	1547	1610	1672	1735	1797	1860	1922	
695	1985	2047	2110	2172	2235	2297	2360	2422	2484	2547	62
696	2609	2672	2734	2796	2859	2921	2983	3046	3108	3170	
697	3233	3295	3357	3420	3482	3544	3606	3669	3731	3793	
698	3855	3918	3980	4042	4104	4166	4229	4291	4353	4415	
699	4477	4539	4601	4664	4726	4788	4850	4912	4974	5036	
700	5098	5160	5222	5284	5346	5408	5470	5532	5594	5656	
701	5718	5780	5842	5904	5966	6028	6090	6151	6213	6275	
702	6337	6399	6461	6523	6585	6646	6708	6770	6832	6894	
703	6955	7017	7079	7141	7202	7264	7326	7388	7449	7511	
704	7573	7634	7696	7758	7819	7881	7943	8004	8066	8128	
705	8189	8251	8312	8374	8435	8497	8559	8620	8682	8743	
706	8805	8866	8928	8989	9051	9112	9174	9235	9297	9358	61
707	9419	9481	9542	9604	9665	9726	9788	9849	9911	9972	
708	850033	0095	0156	0217	0279	0340	0401	0462	0524	0585	
709	0646	0707	0769	0830	0891	0952	1014	1075	1136	1197	
710	1258	1320	1381	1442	1503	1564	1625	1686	1747	1809	
711	1870	1931	1992	2053	2114	2175	2236	2297	2358	2419	
712	2480	2541	2602	2663	2724	2785	2846	2907	2968	3029	
713	3090	3150	3211	3272	3333	3394	3455	3516	3577	3637	
714	3698	3759	3820	3881	3941	4002	4063	4124	4185	4245	
715	4306	4367	4428	4488	4549	4610	4670	4731	4792	4852	
716	4913	4974	5034	5095	5156	5216	5277	5337	5398	5459	
717	5519	5580	5640	5701	5761	5822	5882	5943	6003	6064	
718	6124	6185	6245	6306	6366	6427	6487	6548	6608	6668	60
719	6729	6789	6850	6910	6970	7031	7091	7152	7212	7272	

N.		0	1	2	3	4	5	6	7	8	9	D.
Differ.	64	Pro. Parts.	6	13	19	26	32	38	45	51	58	
	63		6	13	19	25	32	38	44	50	57	
	62		6	12	19	25	31	37	43	50	56	
	61		6	12	18	24	31	37	43	49	55	
	60		6	12	18	24	30	36	42	48	54	

N.	0	1	2	3	4	5	6	7	8	9	D.
720	857332	7393	7453	7513	7574	7634	7694	7755	7815	7875	60
721	7935	7995	8056	8116	8176	8236	8297	8357	8417	8477	
722	8537	8597	8657	8718	8778	8838	8898	8958	9018	9078	
723	9138	9198	9258	9318	9379	9439	9499	9559	9619	9679	
724	9739	9799	9859	9918	9978	..38	..98	.158	.218	.278	
725	860338	0398	0458	0518	0578	0637	0697	0757	0817	0877	
726	0937	0996	1056	1116	1176	1236	1295	1355	1415	1475	
727	1534	1594	1654	1714	1773	1833	1893	1952	2012	2072	
728	2131	2191	2251	2310	2370	2430	2489	2549	2608	2668	
729	2728	2787	2847	2906	2966	3025	3085	3144	3204	3263	
730	3323	3382	3442	3501	3561	3620	3680	3739	3799	3858	59
731	3917	3977	4036	4096	4155	4214	4274	4333	4392	4452	
732	4511	4570	4630	4689	4748	4808	4867	4926	4985	5045	
733	5104	5163	5222	5282	5341	5400	5459	5519	5578	5637	
734	5696	5755	5814	5874	5933	5992	6051	6110	6169	6228	
735	6287	6346	6405	6465	6524	6583	6642	6701	6760	6819	
736	6878	6937	6996	7055	7114	7173	7232	7291	7350	7409	
737	7467	7526	7585	7644	7703	7762	7821	7880	7939	7998	
738	8056	8115	8174	8233	8292	8350	8409	8468	8527	8586	
739	8644	8703	8762	8821	8879	8938	8997	9056	9114	9173	
740	9232	9290	9349	9408	9466	9525	9584	9642	9701	9760	
741	9818	9877	9935	9994	..53	.111	.170	.228	.287	.345	
742	870404	0462	0521	0579	0638	0696	0755	0813	0872	0930	58
743	0989	1047	1106	1164	1223	1281	1339	1398	1456	1515	
744	1573	1631	1690	1748	1806	1865	1923	1981	2040	2098	
745	2156	2215	2273	2331	2389	2448	2506	2564	2622	2681	
746	2739	2797	2855	2913	2972	3030	3088	3146	3204	3262	
747	3321	3379	3437	3495	3553	3611	3669	3727	3785	3844	
748	3902	3960	4018	4076	4134	4192	4250	4308	4366	4424	
749	4482	4540	4598	4656	4714	4772	4830	4888	4945	5003	
750	5061	5119	5177	5235	5293	5351	5409	5466	5524	5582	
751	5640	5698	5756	5813	5871	5929	5987	6045	6102	6160	
752	6218	6276	6333	6391	6449	6507	6564	6622	6680	6737	
753	6795	6853	6910	6968	7026	7083	7141	7199	7256	7314	
754	7371	7429	7487	7544	7602	7659	7717	7774	7832	7889	
755	7947	8004	8062	8119	8177	8234	8292	8349	8407	8464	57
756	8522	8579	8637	8694	8752	8809	8866	8924	8981	9039	
757	9096	9153	9211	9268	9325	9383	9440	9497	9555	9612	
758	9669	9726	9784	9841	9898	9956	..13	..70	.127	.185	
759	880242	0299	0356	0413	0471	0528	0585	0642	0699	0756	
760	0814	0871	0928	0985	1042	1099	1156	1213	1271	1328	
761	1385	1442	1499	1556	1613	1670	1727	1784	1841	1898	
762	1955	2012	2069	2126	2183	2240	2297	2354	2411	2468	
763	2525	2581	2638	2695	2752	2809	2866	2923	2980	3037	
764	3093	3150	3207	3264	3321	3377	3434	3491	3548	3605	
765	3661	3718	3775	3832	3888	3945	4002	4059	4115	4172	
766	4229	4285	4342	4399	4455	4512	4569	4625	4682	4739	
767	4795	4852	4909	4965	5022	5078	5135	5192	5248	5305	
768	5361	5418	5474	5531	5587	5644	5700	5757	5813	5870	
769	5926	5983	6039	6096	6152	6209	6265	6321	6378	6434	56
770	6491	6547	6604	6660	6716	6773	6829	6885	6942	6998	
771	7054	7111	7167	7223	7280	7336	7392	7449	7505	7561	
772	7617	7674	7730	7786	7842	7898	7955	8011	8067	8123	
773	8179	8236	8292	8348	8404	8460	8516	8573	8629	8685	
774	8741	8797	8853	8909	8965	9021	9077	9134	9190	9246	

N.	0	1	2	3	4	5	6	7	8	9	D.
Differ.	60 Pro. Parts.	6	12	18	24	30	36	42	48	54	
	59	6	12	18	24	30	35	41	47	53	
	58	6	12	17	23	29	35	41	46	52	
	57	6	11	17	23	29	34	40	46	51	
	56	6	11	17	22	28	34	39	45	50	

N.	0	1	2	3	4	5	6	7	8	9	D.
775	889302	9358	9414	9470	9526	9582	9638	9694	9750	9806	56
776	9862	9918	9974	..30	..86	.141	.197	.253	.309	.365	
777	890421	0477	0533	0589	0645	0700	0756	0812	0868	0924	
778	0980	1035	1091	1147	1203	1259	1314	1370	1426	1482	
779	1537	1593	1649	1705	1760	1816	1872	1928	1983	2039	
780	2095	2150	2206	2262	2317	2373	2429	2484	2540	2595	
781	2651	2707	2762	2818	2873	2929	2985	3040	3096	3151	
782	3207	3262	3318	3373	3429	3484	3540	3595	3651	3706	
783	3762	3817	3873	3928	3984	4039	4094	4150	4205	4261	55
784	4316	4371	4427	4482	4538	4593	4648	4704	4759	4814	
785	4870	4925	4980	5036	5091	5146	5201	5257	5312	5367	
786	5423	5478	5533	5588	5644	5699	5754	5809	5864	5920	
787	5975	6030	6085	6140	6195	6251	6306	6361	6416	6471	
788	6526	6581	6636	6692	6747	6802	6857	6912	6967	7022	
789	7077	7132	7187	7242	7297	7352	7407	7462	7517	7572	
790	7627	7682	7737	7792	7847	7902	7957	8012	8067	8122	
791	8176	8231	8286	8341	8396	8451	8506	8561	8615	8670	
792	8725	8780	8835	8890	8944	8999	9054	9109	9164	9218	
793	9273	9328	9383	9437	9492	9547	9602	9656	9711	9766	
794	9821	9875	9930	9985	..39	..94	.149	.203	.258	.312	
795	900367	0422	0476	0531	0586	0640	0695	0749	0804	0859	
796	0913	0968	1022	1077	1131	1186	1240	1295	1349	1404	
797	1458	1513	1567	1622	1676	1731	1785	1840	1894	1948	54
798	2003	2057	2112	2166	2221	2275	2329	2384	2438	2492	
799	2547	2601	2655	2710	2764	2818	2873	2927	2981	3036	
800	3090	3144	3199	3253	3307	3361	3416	3470	3524	3578	
801	3633	3687	3741	3795	3849	3904	3958	4012	4066	4120	
802	4174	4229	4283	4337	4391	4445	4499	4553	4607	4661	
803	4716	4770	4824	4878	4932	4986	5040	5094	5148	5202	
804	5256	5310	5364	5418	5472	5526	5580	5634	5688	5742	
805	5796	5850	5904	5958	6012	6066	6119	6173	6227	6281	
806	6335	6389	6443	6497	6551	6604	6658	6712	6766	6820	
807	6874	6927	6981	7035	7089	7143	7196	7250	7304	7358	
808	7411	7465	7519	7573	7626	7680	7734	7787	7841	7895	
809	7949	8002	8056	8110	8163	8217	8270	8324	8378	8431	
810	8485	8539	8592	8646	8699	8753	8807	8860	8914	8967	
811	9021	9074	9128	9181	9235	9289	9342	9396	9449	9503	
812	9556	9610	9663	9716	9770	9823	9877	9930	9984	..37	53
813	910091	0144	0197	0251	0304	0358	0411	0464	0518	0571	
814	0624	0678	0731	0784	0838	0891	0944	0998	1051	1104	
815	1158	1211	1264	1317	1371	1424	1477	1530	1584	1637	
816	1690	1743	1797	1850	1903	1956	2009	2063	2116	2169	
817	2222	2275	2328	2381	2435	2488	2541	2594	2647	2700	
818	2753	2806	2859	2913	2966	3019	3072	3125	3178	3231	
819	3284	3337	3390	3443	3496	3549	3602	3655	3708	3761	
820	3814	3867	3920	3973	4026	4079	4132	4184	4237	4290	
821	4343	4396	4449	4502	4555	4608	4660	4713	4766	4819	
822	4872	4925	4977	5030	5083	5136	5189	5241	5294	5347	
823	5400	5453	5505	5558	5611	5664	5716	5769	5822	5875	
824	5927	5980	6033	6085	6138	6191	6243	6296	6349	6401	
825	6454	6507	6559	6612	6664	6717	6770	6822	6875	6927	
826	6980	7033	7085	7138	7190	7243	7295	7348	7400	7453	
827	7506	7558	7611	7663	7716	7768	7820	7873	7925	7978	52
828	8030	8083	8135	8188	8240	8293	8345	8397	8450	8502	
829	8555	8607	8659	8712	8764	8816	8869	8921	8973	9026	
830	9078	9130	9183	9235	9287	9340	9392	9444	9496	9549	
N.	0	1	2	3	4	5	6	7	8	9	D.

Differ.	P. Parts.	1	2	3	4	5	6	7	8	9
55		6	11	17	22	28	33	39	44	50
54		5	11	16	22	27	32	38	43	49
53		5	11	16	21	27	32	37	42	48
52		5	10	16	21	26	31	36	42	47

N.	0	1	2	3	4	5	6	7	8	9	D.
831	919601	9653	9706	9758	9810	9862	9914	9967	..19	..71	52
832	920123	0176	0228	0280	0332	0384	0436	0489	0541	0593	
833	0645	0697	0749	0801	0853	0906	0958	1010	1062	1114	
834	1166	1218	1270	1322	1374	1426	1478	1530	1582	1634	
835	1686	1738	1790	1842	1894	1946	1998	2050	2102	2154	
836	2206	2258	2310	2362	2414	2466	2518	2570	2622	2674	
837	2725	2777	2829	2881	2933	2985	3037	3089	3140	3192	
838	3244	3296	3348	3399	3451	3503	3555	3607	3658	3710	
839	3762	3814	3865	3917	3969	4021	4072	4124	4176	4228	
840	4279	4331	4383	4434	4486	4538	4589	4641	4693	4744	
841	4796	4848	4899	4951	5003	5054	5106	5157	5209	5261	
842	5312	5364	5415	5467	5518	5570	5621	5673	5725	5776	
843	5828	5879	5931	5982	6034	6085	6137	6188	6240	6291	51
844	6342	6394	6445	6497	6548	6600	6651	6702	6754	6805	
845	6857	6908	6959	7011	7062	7114	7165	7216	7268	7319	
846	7370	7422	7473	7524	7576	7627	7678	7730	7781	7832	
847	7883	7935	7986	8037	8088	8140	8191	8242	8293	8345	
848	8396	8447	8498	8549	8601	8652	8703	8754	8805	8857	
849	8908	8959	9010	9061	9112	9163	9215	9266	9317	9368	
850	9419	9470	9521	9572	9623	9674	9725	9776	9827	9879	
851	9930	9981	..32	..83	.134	.185	.236	.287	.338	.389	
852	930440	0491	0542	0592	0643	0694	0745	0796	0847	0898	
853	0949	1000	1051	1102	1153	1204	1254	1305	1356	1407	
854	1458	1509	1560	1610	1661	1712	1763	1814	1865	1915	
855	1966	2017	2068	2118	2169	2220	2271	2322	2372	2423	
856	2474	2524	2575	2626	2677	2727	2778	2829	2879	2930	
857	2981	3031	3082	3133	3183	3234	3285	3335	3386	3437	
858	3487	3538	3589	3639	3690	3740	3791	3841	3892	3943	
859	3993	4044	4094	4145	4195	4246	4296	4347	4397	4448	
860	4498	4549	4599	4650	4700	4751	4801	4852	4902	4953	50
861	5003	5054	5104	5154	5205	5255	5306	5356	5406	5457	
862	5507	5558	5608	5658	5709	5759	5809	5860	5910	5960	
863	6011	6061	6111	6162	6212	6262	6313	6363	6413	6463	
864	6514	6564	6614	6665	6715	6765	6815	6865	6916	6966	
865	7016	7066	7117	7167	7217	7267	7317	7367	7418	7468	
866	7518	7568	7618	7668	7718	7769	7819	7869	7919	7969	
867	8019	8069	8119	8169	8219	8269	8320	8370	8420	8470	
868	8520	8570	8620	8670	8720	8770	8820	8870	8920	8970	
869	9020	9070	9120	9170	9220	9270	9320	9369	9419	9469	
870	9519	9569	9619	9669	9719	9769	9819	9869	9918	9968	
871	940018	0068	0118	0168	0218	0267	0317	0367	0417	0467	
872	0516	0566	0616	0666	0716	0765	0815	0865	0915	0964	
873	1014	1064	1114	1163	1213	1263	1313	1362	1412	1462	
874	1511	1561	1611	1660	1710	1760	1809	1859	1909	1958	
875	2008	2058	2107	2157	2207	2256	2306	2355	2405	2455	
876	2504	2554	2603	2653	2702	2752	2801	2851	2901	2950	
877	3000	3049	3099	3148	3198	3247	3297	3346	3396	3445	49
878	3495	3544	3593	3643	3692	3742	3791	3841	3890	3939	
879	3989	4038	4088	4137	4186	4236	4285	4335	4384	4433	
880	4483	4532	4581	4631	4680	4729	4779	4828	4877	4927	
881	4976	5025	5074	5124	5173	5222	5272	5321	5370	5419	
882	5469	5518	5567	5616	5665	5715	5764	5813	5862	5912	
883	5961	6010	6059	6108	6157	6207	6256	6305	6354	6403	
884	6452	6501	6551	6600	6649	6698	6747	6796	6845	6894	
885	6943	6992	7041	7090	7140	7189	7238	7287	7336	7385	
886	7434	7483	7532	7581	7630	7679	7728	7777	7826	7875	
N.	0	1	2	3	4	5	6	7	8	9	D.
Differ.	52	P. Parts. 5	10	16	21	26	31	36	42	47	
	51	5	10	15	20	26	31	36	41	46	
	50	5	10	15	20	25	30	35	40	45	
	49	5	10	15	20	25	29	34	39	44	

N.	0	1	2	3	4	5	6	7	8	9	D.
887	947924	7973	8022	8070	8119	8168	8217	8266	8315	8364	49
888	8413	8462	8511	8560	8609	8657	8706	8755	8804	8853	
889	8902	8951	8999	9048	9097	9146	9195	9244	9292	9341	
890	9390	9439	9488	9536	9585	9634	9683	9731	9780	9829	
891	9878	9926	9975	..24	..73	.121	.170	.219	.267	.316	
892	950365	0414	0462	0511	0560	0608	0657	0706	0754	0803	
893	0851	0900	0949	0997	1046	1095	1143	1192	1240	1289	
894	1338	1386	1435	1483	1532	1580	1629	1677	1726	1775	
895	1823	1872	1920	1969	2017	2066	2114	2163	2211	2260	48
896	2308	2356	2405	2453	2502	2550	2599	2647	2696	2744	
897	2792	2841	2889	2938	2986	3034	3083	3131	3180	3228	
898	3276	3325	3373	3421	3470	3518	3566	3615	3663	3711	
899	3760	3808	3856	3905	3953	4001	4049	4098	4146	4194	
900	4243	4291	4339	4387	4435	4484	4532	4580	4628	4677	
901	4725	4773	4821	4869	4918	4966	5014	5062	5110	5158	
902	5207	5255	5303	5351	5399	5447	5495	5543	5592	5640	
903	5688	5736	5784	5832	5880	5928	5976	6024	6072	6120	
904	6168	6216	6265	6313	6361	6409	6457	6505	6553	6601	
905	6649	6697	6745	6793	6840	6888	6936	6984	7032	7080	
906	7128	7176	7224	7272	7320	7368	7416	7464	7512	7559	
907	7607	7655	7703	7751	7799	7847	7894	7942	7990	8038	
908	8086	8134	8181	8229	8277	8325	8373	8421	8468	8516	
909	8564	8612	8659	8707	8755	8803	8850	8898	8946	8994	
910	9041	9089	9137	9185	9232	9280	9328	9375	9423	9471	
911	9518	9566	9614	9661	9709	9757	9804	9852	9900	9947	
912	9995	..42	..90	.138	.185	.233	.280	.328	.376	.423	
913	960471	0518	0566	0613	0661	0709	0756	0804	0851	0899	
914	0946	0994	1041	1089	1136	1184	1231	1279	1326	1374	47
915	1421	1469	1516	1563	1611	1658	1706	1753	1801	1848	
916	1895	1943	1990	2038	2085	2132	2180	2227	2275	2322	
917	2369	2417	2464	2511	2559	2606	2653	2701	2748	2795	
918	2843	2890	2937	2985	3032	3079	3126	3174	3221	3268	
919	3316	3363	3410	3457	3504	3552	3599	3646	3693	3741	
920	3788	3835	3882	3929	3977	4024	4071	4118	4165	4212	
921	4260	4307	4354	4401	4448	4495	4542	4590	4637	4684	
922	4731	4778	4825	4872	4919	4966	5013	5061	5108	5155	
923	5202	5249	5296	5343	5390	5437	5484	5531	5578	5625	
924	5672	5719	5766	5813	5860	5907	5954	6001	6048	6095	
925	6142	6189	6236	6283	6329	6376	6423	6470	6517	6564	
926	6611	6658	6705	6752	6799	6845	6892	6939	6986	7033	
927	7080	7127	7173	7220	7267	7314	7361	7408	7454	7501	
928	7548	7595	7642	7688	7735	7782	7829	7875	7922	7969	
929	8016	8062	8109	8156	8203	8249	8296	8343	8390	8436	
930	8483	8530	8576	8623	8670	8716	8763	8810	8856	8903	
931	8950	8996	9043	9090	9136	9183	9229	9276	9323	9369	
932	9416	9463	9509	9556	9602	9649	9695	9742	9789	9835	
933	9882	9928	9975	..21	..68	.114	.161	.207	.254	.300	
934	970347	0393	0440	0486	0533	0579	0626	0672	0719	0765	46
935	0812	0858	0904	0951	0997	1044	1090	1137	1183	1229	
936	1276	1322	1369	1415	1461	1508	1554	1601	1647	1693	
937	1740	1786	1832	1879	1925	1971	2018	2064	2110	2157	
938	2203	2249	2295	2342	2388	2434	2481	2527	2573	2619	
939	2666	2712	2758	2804	2851	2897	2943	2989	3035	3082	
940	3128	3174	3220	3266	3313	3359	3405	3451	3497	3543	
941	3590	3636	3682	3728	3774	3820	3866	3913	3959	4005	
942	4051	4097	4143	4189	4235	4281	4327	4374	4420	4466	
943	4512	4558	4604	4650	4696	4742	4788	4834	4880	4926	

N.	0		1	2	3	4	5	6	7	8	9	D.
Differ.	48	P. P's.	5	10	14	19	24	29	34	38	43	
	47		5	9	14	19	24	28	33	38	42	
	46		5	9	14	18	23	28	32	37	41	

N.	0	1	2	3	4	5	6	7	8	9	D.
944	974972	5018	5064	5110	5156	5202	5248	5294	5340	5386	46
945	5432	5478	5524	5570	5616	5662	5707	5753	5799	5845	
946	5891	5937	5983	6029	6075	6121	6167	6212	6258	6304	
947	6350	6396	6442	6488	6533	6579	6625	6671	6717	6763	
948	6808	6854	6900	6946	6992	7037	7083	7129	7175	7220	
949	7266	7312	7358	7403	7449	7495	7541	7586	7632	7678	
950	7724	7769	7815	7861	7906	7952	7998	8043	8089	8135	
951	8181	8226	8272	8317	8363	8409	8454	8500	8546	8591	
952	8637	8683	8728	8774	8819	8865	8911	8956	9002	9047	
953	9093	9138	9184	9230	9275	9321	9366	9412	9457	9503	
954	9548	9594	9639	9685	9730	9776	9821	9867	9912	9958	
955	980003	0049	0094	0140	0185	0231	0276	0322	0367	0412	45
956	0458	0503	0549	0594	0640	0685	0730	0776	0821	0867	
957	0912	0957	1003	1048	1093	1139	1184	1229	1275	1320	
958	1366	1411	1456	1501	1547	1592	1637	1683	1728	1773	
959	1819	1864	1909	1954	2000	2045	2090	2135	2181	2226	
960	2271	2316	2362	2407	2452	2497	2543	2588	2633	2678	
961	2723	2769	2814	2859	2904	2949	2994	3040	3085	3130	
962	3175	3220	3265	3310	3356	3401	3446	3491	3536	3581	
963	3626	3671	3716	3762	3807	3852	3897	3942	3987	4032	
964	4077	4122	4167	4212	4257	4302	4347	4392	4437	4482	
965	4527	4572	4617	4662	4707	4752	4797	4842	4887	4932	
966	4977	5022	5067	5112	5157	5202	5247	5292	5337	5382	
967	5426	5471	5516	5561	5606	5651	5696	5741	5786	5830	
968	5875	5920	5965	6010	6055	6100	6144	6189	6234	6279	
969	6324	6369	6413	6458	6503	6548	6593	6637	6682	6727	
970	6772	6817	6861	6906	6951	6996	7040	7085	7130	7175	
971	7219	7264	7309	7353	7398	7443	7488	7532	7577	7622	
972	7666	7711	7756	7800	7845	7890	7934	7979	8024	8068	
973	8113	8157	8202	8247	8291	8336	8381	8425	8470	8514	
974	8559	8604	8648	8693	8737	8782	8826	8871	8916	8960	
975	9005	9049	9094	9138	9183	9227	9272	9316	9361	9405	
976	9450	9494	9539	9583	9628	9672	9717	9761	9806	9850	44
977	9895	9939	9983	..28	..72	.117	.161	.206	.250	.294	
978	990339	0383	0428	0472	0516	0561	0605	0650	0694	0738	
979	0783	0827	0871	0916	0960	1004	1049	1093	1137	1182	
980	1226	1270	1315	1359	1403	1448	1492	1536	1580	1625	
981	1669	1713	1758	1802	1846	1890	1935	1979	2023	2067	
982	2111	2156	2200	2244	2288	2333	2377	2421	2465	2509	
983	2554	2598	2642	2686	2730	2774	2819	2863	2907	2951	
984	2995	3039	3083	3127	3172	3216	3260	3304	3348	3392	
985	3436	3480	3524	3568	3613	3657	3701	3745	3789	3833	
986	3877	3921	3965	4009	4053	4097	4141	4185	4229	4273	
987	4317	4361	4405	4449	4493	4537	4581	4625	4669	4713	
988	4757	4801	4845	4889	4933	4977	5021	5065	5108	5152	
989	5196	5240	5284	5328	5372	5416	5460	5504	5547	5591	
990	5635	5679	5723	5767	5811	5854	5898	5942	5986	6030	
991	6074	6117	6161	6205	6249	6293	6337	6380	6424	6468	
992	6512	6555	6599	6643	6687	6731	6774	6818	6862	6906	
993	6949	6993	7037	7080	7124	7168	7212	7255	7299	7343	
994	7386	7430	7474	7517	7561	7605	7648	7692	7736	7779	
995	7823	7867	7910	7954	7998	8041	8085	8129	8172	8216	
996	8259	8303	8347	8390	8434	8477	8521	8564	8608	8652	
997	8695	8739	8782	8826	8869	8913	8956	9000	9043	9087	
998	9131	9174	9218	9261	9305	9348	9392	9435	9479	9522	
999	9565	9609	9652	9696	9739	9783	9826	9870	9913	9957	43
N.	0	1	2	3	4	5	6	7	8	9	D.
Differ.	46 P. Parts.	5	9	14	18	23	28	32	37	41	
	45	5	9	14	18	23	27	32	36	41	
	44	4	9	13	18	22	26	31	35	40	
	43	4	9	13	17	22	26	30	34	39	

TABLE

OF

LOGARITHMIC SINES AND TANGENTS

FOR EVERY

TEN SECONDS OF THE QUADRANT.

Min.	Sine of 0 Degree. 0″	10″	20″	30″	40″	50″		P. Part to 1″.
0	Inf. Neg.	5.685575	5.986605	6.162696	6.287635	6.384545	59	
1	6.463726	6.530673	6.588665	639817	685575	726968	58	
2	764756	799518	831703	861666	889695	916024	57	
3	940847	964328	986605	7.007794	7.027997	7.047303	56	
4	7.065786	7.083515	7.100548	116939	132733	147973	55	
5	162696	176936	190725	204089	217054	229643	54	
6	241877	253776	265358	276639	287635	298358	53	
7	308824	319043	329027	338787	348332	357672	52	
8	366816	375771	384544	393145	401578	409850	51	
9	417968	425937	433762	441449	449002	456426	50	
10	463726	470904	477966	484915	491754	498488	49	689.4
11	505118	511649	518083	524423	530672	536832	48	629.4
12	542906	548897	554806	560635	566387	572065	47	579.1
13	577668	583201	588664	594059	599388	604652	46	536.2
14	609853	614993	620072	625093	630056	634964	45	499.2
15	639816	644615	649361	654056	658701	663297	44	467.0
16	667845	672345	676799	681208	685573	689895	43	438.7
17	694173	698410	702606	706762	710879	714957	42	413.6
18	718997	722999	726965	730896	734791	738651	41	391.3
19	742478	746270	750031	753758	757455	761119	40	371.2
20	764754	768358	771932	775477	778994	782482	39	353.1
21	785943	789376	792782	796162	799515	802843	38	336.7
22	806146	809423	812677	815906	819111	822292	37	321.7
23	825451	828586	831700	834791	837860	840907	36	308.0
24	843934	846939	849924	852889	855833	858757	35	295.4
25	861662	864548	867415	870262	873092	875902	34	283.8
26	878695	881470	884228	886968	889690	892396	33	273.1
27	895085	897758	900414	903054	905678	908287	32	263.2
28	910879	913457	916019	918566	921098	923616	31	254.0
29	926119	928608	931082	933543	935989	938422	30	245.4
30	940842	943248	945641	948020	950387	952741	29	237.3
31	955082	957411	959727	962031	964322	966602	28	229.8
32	968870	971126	973370	975603	977824	980034	27	222.7
33	982233	984421	986598	988764	990919	993064	26	216.1
34	995198	997322	999435	8.001538	8.003631	8.005714	25	209.8
35	8.007787	8.009850	8.011903	013947	015981	018005	24	203.9
36	020021	022027	024023	026011	027989	029959	23	198.3
37	031919	033871	035814	037749	039675	041592	22	193.0
38	043501	045401	047294	049178	051054	052922	21	188.0
39	054781	056633	058477	060314	062142	063963	20	183.2
40	065776	067582	069380	071171	072955	074731	19	178.7
41	076500	078261	080016	081764	083504	085238	18	174.4
42	086965	088684	090398	092104	093804	095497	17	170.3
43	097183	098863	100537	102204	103864	105519	16	166.4
44	107167	108809	110444	112074	113697	115315	15	162.6
45	116926	118532	120131	121725	123313	124895	14	159.1
46	126471	128042	129607	131166	132720	134268	13	155.6
47	135810	137348	138879	140406	141927	143443	12	152.4
48	144953	146458	147959	149453	150943	152428	11	149.2
49	153907	155382	156852	158316	159776	161231	10	146.2
50	162681	164126	165566	167002	168433	169859	9	143.3
51	171280	172697	174109	175517	176920	178319	8	140.5
52	179713	181103	182488	183869	185245	186617	7	137.9
53	187985	189348	190707	192062	193413	194760	6	135.3
54	196102	197440	198774	200104	201430	202752	5	132.8
55	204070	205384	206694	208000	209302	210601	4	130.4
56	211895	213185	214472	215755	217034	218309	3	128.1
57	219581	220849	222113	223374	224631	225884	2	125.9
58	227134	228380	229622	230861	232096	233328	1	123.7
59	234557	235782	237003	238221	239436	240647	0	121.6
	60″	50″	40″	30″	20″	10″	Min.	
	Co-sine of 89 Degrees.							

Min.	Tangent of 0 Degree. 0″	10″	20″	30″	40″	50″		P. Part to 1″.
0	Inf. Neg.	5.685575	5.986605	6.162696	6.287635	6.384545	59	
1	6.463726	6.530673	6.588665	639817	685575	726968	58	
2	764756	799518	831703	861666	889695	916024	57	
3	940847	964329	986605	7.007794	7.027998	7.047303	56	
4	7.065786	7.083515	7.100548	116939	132733	147973	55	
5	162696	176937	190725	204089	217054	229643	54	
6	241878	253777	265359	276640	287635	298359	53	
7	308825	319044	329028	338788	348333	357673	52	
8	366817	375772	384546	393146	401579	409852	51	
9	417970	425939	433764	441451	449004	456428	50	
10	463727	470906	477968	484917	491756	498490	49	689.4
11	505120	511651	518085	524426	530675	536835	48	629.4
12	542909	548900	554808	560638	566390	572068	47	579.1
13	577672	583204	588667	594062	599391	604655	46	536.2
14	609857	614996	620076	625097	630060	634968	45	499.2
15	639820	644619	649366	654061	658706	663302	44	467.0
16	667849	672350	676804	681213	685578	689900	43	438.7
17	694179	698416	702612	706768	710885	714963	42	413.6
18	719003	723005	726972	730902	734797	738658	41	391.3
19	742484	746277	750037	753765	757462	761127	40	371.2
20	764761	768365	771940	775485	779002	782490	39	353.1
21	785951	789384	792790	796170	799524	802852	38	336.7
22	806155	809433	812686	815915	819120	822302	37	321.7
23	825460	828596	831710	834801	837870	840918	36	308.0
24	843944	846950	849935	852900	855844	858769	35	295.4
25	861674	864560	867426	870274	873104	875915	34	283.9
26	878708	881483	884240	886981	889704	892410	33	273.2
27	895099	897772	900428	903068	905692	908301	32	263.2
28	910894	913471	916034	918581	921113	923631	31	254.0
29	926134	928623	931098	933559	936006	938439	30	245.4
30	940858	943265	945658	948037	950404	952758	29	237.3
31	955100	957428	959745	962049	964341	966621	28	229.8
32	968889	971145	973389	975622	977844	980054	27	222.7
33	982253	984441	986618	988785	990940	993085	26	216.2
34	995219	997343	999457	8.001560	8.003653	8.005736	25	209.8
35	8.007809	8.009872	8.011926	013970	016004	018029	24	203.9
36	020044	022051	024048	026035	028014	029984	23	198.3
37	031945	033897	035840	037775	039701	041618	22	193.0
38	043527	045428	047321	049205	051081	052949	21	188.0
39	054809	056662	058506	060342	062171	063992	20	183.3
40	065806	067612	069410	071201	072985	074761	19	178.7
41	076531	078293	080047	081795	083536	085270	18	174.4
42	086997	088717	090431	092137	093837	095530	17	170.3
43	097217	098897	100571	102239	103900	105554	16	166.4
44	107203	108845	110481	112110	113734	115352	15	162.7
45	116963	118569	120169	121763	123351	124933	14	159.1
46	126510	128081	129646	131206	132760	134308	13	155.7
47	135851	137389	138921	140447	141969	143485	12	152.4
48	144996	146501	148001	149497	150987	152472	11	149.3
49	153952	155426	156896	158361	159821	161276	10	146.2
50	162727	164172	165613	167049	168480	169906	9	143.4
51	171328	172745	174158	175566	176969	178368	8	140.6
52	179763	181153	182538	183919	185296	186668	7	137.9
53	188036	189400	190760	192115	193466	194813	6	135.3
54	196156	197494	198829	200159	201485	202808	5	132.8
55	204126	205440	206750	208057	209359	210658	4	130.4
56	211953	213243	214530	215814	217093	218369	3	128.1
57	219641	220909	222174	223434	224692	225945	2	125.9
58	227195	228442	229685	230924	232160	233392	1	123.8
59	234621	235846	237068	238286	339502	240713	0	121.7
	60″	50″	40″	30″	20″	10″	Min.	
	Co-tangent of 89 Degrees.							

Min.	Sine of 1 Degree. 0″	10″	20″	30″	40″	50″		P. Part to 1″.
0	8.241855	8.243060	8.244261	8.245459	8.246654	8.247845	59	119.6
1	249033	250218	251400	252578	253753	254925	58	117.7
2	256094	257260	258423	259582	260739	261892	57	115.8
3	263042	264190	265334	266475	267613	268749	56	114.0
4	269881	271010	272137	273260	274381	275499	55	112.2
5	276614	277726	278835	279941	281045	282145	54	110.5
6	283243	284339	285431	286521	287608	288692	53	108.8
7	289773	290852	291928	293002	294073	295141	52	107.2
8	296207	297270	298330	299388	300443	301496	51	105.7
9	302546	303594	304639	305681	306721	307759	50	104.1
10	8.308794	8.309827	8.310857	8.311885	8.312910	8.313933	49	102.6
11	314954	315972	316987	318001	319012	320021	48	101.2
12	321027	322031	323033	324032	325029	326024	47	99.8
13	327016	328007	328995	329980	330964	331945	46	98.5
14	332924	333901	334876	335848	336819	337787	45	97.1
15	338753	339717	340679	341638	342596	343551	44	95.8
16	344504	345456	346405	347352	348297	349240	43	94.6
17	350181	351119	352056	352991	353924	354855	42	93.4
18	355783	356710	357635	358558	359479	360398	41	92.2
19	361315	362230	363143	364055	364964	365871	40	91.0
20	8.366777	8.367681	8.368582	8.369482	8.370380	8.371277	39	89.9
21	372171	373063	373954	374843	375730	376615	38	88.8
22	377499	378380	379260	380138	381015	381889	37	87.7
23	382762	383633	384502	385370	386236	387100	36	86.7
24	387962	388823	389682	390539	391395	392249	35	85.6
25	393101	393951	394800	395647	396493	397337	34	84.6
26	398179	399020	399859	400696	401532	402366	33	83.7
27	403199	404030	404859	405687	406514	407338	32	82.7
28	408161	408983	409803	410621	411438	412254	31	81.8
29	413068	413880	414691	415500	416308	417114	30	80.8
30	8.417919	8.418722	8.419524	8.420325	8.421123	8.421921	29	80.0
31	422717	423511	424304	425096	425886	426675	28	79.1
32	427462	428248	429032	429815	430597	431377	27	78.2
33	432156	432934	433710	434484	435257	436029	26	77.4
34	436800	437569	438337	439103	439868	440632	25	76.6
35	441394	442156	442915	443674	444431	445186	24	75.8
36	445941	446694	447446	448196	448946	449694	23	75.0
37	450440	451186	451930	452673	453414	454154	22	74.2
38	454893	455631	456368	457103	457837	458570	21	73.5
39	459301	460032	460761	461489	462215	462941	20	72.7
40	8.463665	8.464388	8.465110	8.465830	8.466550	8.467268	19	72.0
41	467985	468701	469416	470129	470841	471553	18	71.3
42	472263	472971	473679	474386	475091	475795	17	70.6
43	476498	477200	477901	478601	479299	479997	16	69.9
44	480693	481388	482083	482776	483467	484158	15	69.2
45	484848	485536	486224	486910	487596	488280	14	68.6
46	488963	489645	490326	491006	491685	492363	13	67.9
47	493040	493715	494390	495064	495736	496408	12	67.3
48	497078	497748	498416	499084	499750	500416	11	66.7
49	501080	501743	502405	503067	503727	504386	10	66.1
50	8.505045	8.505702	8.506358	8.507014	8.507668	8.508321	9	65.5
51	508974	509625	510275	510925	511573	512221	8	64.9
52	512867	513513	514157	514801	515444	516086	7	64.3
53	516726	517366	518005	518643	519280	519916	6	63.7
54	520551	521186	521819	522451	523083	523713	5	63.2
55	524343	524972	525599	526226	526852	527477	4	62.6
56	528102	528725	529347	529969	530590	531209	3	62.1
57	531828	532446	533063	533679	534295	534909	2	61.6
58	535523	536136	536747	537358	537969	538578	1	61.1
59	539186	539794	540401	541007	541612	542216	0	60.5
	60″	50″	40″	30″	20″	10″	Min.	
	Co-sine of 88 Degrees.							

Tangent of 1 Degree.

Min.	0″	10″	20″	30″	40″	50″		P. Part to 1″.
0	8.241921	8.243126	8.244328	8.245526	8.246721	8.247913	59	119.7
1	249102	250287	251469	252648	253823	254996	58	117.7
2	256165	257331	258494	259654	260811	261965	57	115.8
3	263115	264263	265408	266549	267688	268824	56	114.0
4	269956	271086	272213	273337	274458	275576	55	112.2
5	276691	277804	278913	280020	281124	282225	54	110.5
6	283323	284419	285512	286602	287689	288774	53	108.9
7	289856	290935	292012	293086	294157	295226	52	107.2
8	296292	297355	298416	299474	300530	301583	51	105.7
9	302634	303682	304727	305770	306811	307849	50	104.2
10	8.308884	8.309917	8.310948	8.311976	8.313002	8.314025	49	102.7
11	315046	316065	317081	318095	319106	320115	48	101.3
12	321122	322127	323129	324129	325126	326121	47	99.8
13	327114	328105	329093	330080	331064	332045	46	98.5
14	333025	334002	334977	335950	336921	337890	45	97.2
15	338856	339821	340783	341743	342701	343657	44	95.9
16	344610	345562	346512	347459	348405	349348	43	94.6
17	350289	351229	352166	353101	354035	354966	42	93.4
18	355895	356823	357748	358671	359593	360512	41	92.2
19	361430	362345	363259	364171	365081	365988	40	91.1
20	8.366895	8.367799	8.368701	8.369601	8.370500	8.371397	39	89.9
21	372292	373185	374076	374965	375853	376738	38	88.8
22	377622	378504	379385	380263	381140	382015	37	87.8
23	382889	383760	384630	385498	386364	387229	36	86.7
24	388092	388953	389813	390670	391526	392381	35	85.7
25	393234	394085	394934	395782	396628	397472	34	84.7
26	398315	399156	399996	400834	401670	402505	33	83.7
27	403338	404170	405000	405828	406655	407480	32	82.8
28	408304	409126	409946	410765	411583	412399	31	81.8
29	413213	414026	414837	415647	416456	417263	30	80.9
30	8.418068	8.418872	8.419674	8.420475	8.421274	8.422072	29	80.0
31	422869	423664	424458	425250	426041	426830	28	79.1
32	427618	428404	429189	429973	430755	431536	27	78.3
33	432315	433093	433870	434645	435419	436191	26	77.5
34	436962	437732	438500	439267	440033	440797	25	76.6
35	441560	442322	443082	443841	444599	445355	24	75.8
36	446110	446864	447616	448368	449117	449866	23	75.0
37	450613	451359	452104	452847	453589	454330	22	74.3
38	455070	455808	456545	457281	458016	458749	21	73.5
39	459481	460212	460942	461670	462398	463124	20	72.8
40	8.463849	8.464572	8.465295	8.466016	8.466736	8.467455	19	72.1
41	468172	468889	469604	470318	471031	471743	18	71.3
42	472454	473163	473872	474579	475285	475990	17	70.7
43	476693	477396	478097	478798	479497	480195	16	70.0
44	480892	481588	482283	482976	483669	484360	15	69.3
45	485050	485740	486428	487115	487801	488486	14	68.6
46	489170	489852	490534	491215	491894	492573	13	68.0
47	493250	493927	494602	495276	495949	496622	12	67.4
48	497293	497963	498632	499300	499967	500633	11	66.8
49	501298	501962	502625	503287	503948	504608	10	66.1
50	8.505267	8.505925	8.506582	8.507238	8.507893	8.508547	9	65.5
51	509200	509852	510503	511153	511802	512451	8	65.0
52	513098	513744	514389	515034	515677	516320	7	64.4
53	516961	517602	518241	518880	519518	520154	6	63.8
54	520790	521425	522059	522692	523324	523956	5	63.3
55	524586	525215	525844	526472	527098	527724	4	62.7
56	528349	528973	529596	530218	530840	531460	3	62.2
57	532080	532698	533316	533933	534549	535164	2	61.6
58	535779	536392	537005	537617	538227	538837	1	61.1
59	539447	540055	540662	541269	541875	542480	0	60.6
	60″	50″	40″	30″	20″	10″	Min.	

Co-tangent of 88 Degrees.

Min.	Sine of 2 Degrees. 0″	10″	20″	30″	40″	50″	
0	8.542819	3422	4023	4624	5224	5823	59
1	6422	7019	7616	8212	8807	9401	58
2	9995	.587	1179	1770	2361	2950	57
3	8 553539	4126	4713	5300	5885	6470	56
4	7054	7637	8219	8801	9381	9961	55
5	8.560540	1119	1696	2273	2849	3425	54
6	3999	4573	5146	5719	6290	6861	53
7	7431	8000	8569	9137	9704	.270	52
8	8.570836	1401	1965	2528	3091	3653	51
9	4214	4774	5334	5893	6451	7009	50
10	7566	8122	8678	9232	9786	.340	49
11	8.580892	1444	1995	2546	3096	3645	48
12	4193	4741	5288	5834	6380	6925	47
13	7469	8013	8556	9098	9640	.181	46
14	8.590721	1260	1799	2338	2875	3412	45
15	3948	4484	5019	5553	6087	6619	44
16	7152	7683	8214	8745	9274	9803	43
17	8.600332	0859	1387	1913	2439	2964	42
18	3489	4012	4536	5058	5580	6102	41
19	6623	7143	7662	8181	8699	9217	40
20	9734	.251	.766	1282	1796	2310	39
21	8.612823	3336	3848	4360	4871	5381	38
22	5891	6400	6909	7417	7924	8431	37
23	8937	9442	9947	.452	.956	1459	36
24	8.621962	2464	2965	3466	3966	4466	35
25	4965	5464	5962	6459	6956	7453	34
26	7948	8444	8938	9432	9926	.419	33
27	8.630911	1403	1894	2385	2875	3365	32
28	3854	4342	4830	5317	5804	6291	31
29	6776	7262	7746	8230	8714	9197	30
30	9680	.162	.643	1124	1604	2084	29
31	8.642563	3042	3520	3998	4475	4952	28
32	5428	5904	6379	6854	7328	7801	27
33	8274	8747	9219	9690	.161	.632	26
34	8.651102	1571	2040	2508	2976	3444	25
35	3911	4377	4843	5308	5773	6238	24
36	6702	7165	7628	8090	8552	9014	23
37	9475	9935	.395	.855	1314	1772	22
38	8.662230	2688	3145	3602	4058	4513	21
39	4968	5423	5877	6331	6784	7237	20
40	7689	8141	8592	9043	9494	9944	19
41	8.670393	0842	1291	1739	2187	2634	18
42	3080	3527	3972	4418	4863	5307	17
43	5751	6194	6638	7080	7522	7964	16
44	8405	8846	9286	9726	.166	.605	15
45	8.681043	1481	1919	2356	2793	3230	14
46	3665	4101	4536	4971	5405	5838	13
47	6272	6705	7137	7569	8001	8432	12
48	8863	9293	9723	.152	.581	1010	11
49	8.691438	1866	2293	2720	3146	3572	10
50	3998	4423	4848	5272	5696	6120	9
51	6543	6966	7388	7810	8232	8653	8
52	9073	9494	9913	.333	.752	1171	7
53	8.701589	2007	2424	2841	3258	3674	6
54	4090	4505	4920	5335	5749	6163	5
55	6577	6990	7402	7815	8226	8638	4
56	9049	9460	9870	.280	.690	1099	3
57	8.711507	1916	2324	2731	3139	3546	2
58	3952	4358	4764	5169	5574	5979	1
59	6383	6787	7190	7593	7996	8398	0
	60″	50″	40″	30″	20″	10″	Min.
	Co-sine of 87 Degrees.						

P. Part { 1″ 2″ 3″ 4″ 5″ 6″ 7″ 8″ 9″ / 48 96 145 193 241 289 338 386 434 }

Min.	Sine of 3 Degrees. 0″	10″	20″	30″	40″	50″	
0	8.718800	9202	9603	...4	.404	.804	59
1	8.721204	1603	2002	2401	2799	3197	58
2	3595	3992	4389	4785	5181	5577	57
3	5972	6367	6762	7156	7550	7943	56
4	8337	8729	9122	9514	9906	.297	55
5	8.730688	1079	1469	1859	2249	2638	54
6	3027	3416	3804	4192	4579	4967	53
7	5354	5740	6126	6512	6898	7283	52
8	7667	8052	8436	8820	9203	9586	51
9	9969	.352	.734	1115	1497	1878	50
10	8.742259	2639	3019	3399	3778	4157	49
11	4536	4914	5293	5670	6048	6425	48
12	6802	7178	7554	7930	8305	8680	47
13	9055	9430	9804	.178	.551	.924	46
14	8.751297	1670	2042	2414	2786	3157	45
15	3528	3898	4269	4639	5008	5378	44
16	5747	6116	6484	6852	7220	7587	43
17	7955	8321	8688	9054	9420	9786	42
18	8.760151	0516	0881	1245	1609	1973	41
19	2337	2700	3063	3425	3787	4149	40
20	4511	4872	5234	5594	5955	6315	39
21	6675	7034	7394	7752	8111	8469	38
22	8828	9185	9543	9900	.257	.613	37
23	8.770970	1326	1681	2037	2392	2747	36
24	3101	3456	3810	4163	4517	4870	35
25	5223	5575	5927	6279	6631	6982	34
26	7333	7684	8035	8385	8735	9085	33
27	9434	9783	.132	.480	.829	1177	32
28	8.781524	1872	2219	2566	2912	3259	31
29	3605	3951	4296	4641	4986	5331	30
30	5675	6019	6363	6707	7050	7393	29
31	7736	8078	8421	8762	9104	9446	28
32	9787	.128	.468	.808	1149	1488	27
33	8.791828	2167	2506	2845	3183	3521	26
34	3859	4197	4534	4872	5208	5545	25
35	5881	6218	6553	6889	7224	7559	24
36	7894	8229	8563	8897	9231	9564	23
37	9897	.230	.563	.896	1228	1560	22
38	8.801892	2223	2554	2885	3216	3546	21
39	3876	4206	4536	4866	5195	5524	20
40	5852	6181	6509	6837	7165	7492	19
41	7819	8146	8473	8799	9126	9451	18
42	9777	.103	.428	.753	1078	1402	17
43	8.811726	2050	2374	2698	3021	3344	16
44	3667	3989	4312	4634	4956	5277	15
45	5599	5920	6241	6561	6882	7202	14
46	7522	7841	8161	8480	8799	9118	13
47	9436	9755	..73	.390	.708	1025	12
48	8.821343	1659	1976	2292	2609	2925	11
49	3240	3556	3871	4186	4501	4816	10
50	5130	5444	5758	6072	6385	6698	9
51	7011	7324	7637	7949	8261	8573	8
52	8884	9196	9507	9818	.129	.439	7
53	8.830749	1060	1369	1679	1988	2298	6
54	2607	2915	3224	3532	3840	4148	5
55	4456	4763	5070	5377	5684	5991	4
56	6297	6603	6909	7215	7520	7825	3
57	8130	8435	8740	9044	9348	9652	2
58	9956	.260	.563	.866	1169	1472	1
59	8.841774	2076	2378	2680	2982	3283	0
	60″	50″	40″	30″	20″	10″	Min.
	Co-sine of 86 Degrees.						

P. Part { 1″ 2″ 3″ 4″ 5″ 6″ 7″ 8″ 9″ / 34 69 103 138 172 207 241 275 310 }

Min.	Tangent of 2 Degrees. 0″	10″	20″	30″	40	50″	
0	8.543084	3687	4289	4891	5492	6092	59
1	6691	7289	7887	8483	9079	9674	58
2	8.550268	0862	1454	2046	2637	3227	57
3	3817	4405	4993	5580	6166	6752	56
4	7336	7920	8503	9085	9667	.248	55
5	8.560828	1407	1985	2563	3140	3716	54
6	4291	4866	5440	6013	6585	7157	53
7	7727	8298	8867	9435	...3	.570	52
8	8.571137	1702	2267	2832	3395	3958	51
9	4520	5081	5642	6201	6760	7319	50
10	7877	8434	8990	9545	.100	.654	49
11	8.581208	1760	2312	2864	3414	3964	48
12	4514	5062	5610	6157	6704	7249	47
13	7795	8339	8883	9426	9968	.510	46
14	8.591051	1591	2131	2670	3208	3746	45
15	4283	4820	5355	5890	6425	6959	44
16	7492	8024	8556	9087	9618	.147	43
17	8.600677	1205	1733	2260	2787	3313	42
18	3839	4363	4887	5411	5934	6456	41
19	6978	7499	8019	8539	9058	9576	40
20	8.610094	0612	1128	1644	2160	2675	39
21	3189	3702	4215	4728	5240	5751	38
22	6262	6772	7281	7790	8298	8806	37
23	9313	9819	.325	.830	1335	1839	36
24	8.622343	2846	3348	3850	4351	4852	35
25	5352	5851	6350	6849	7346	7844	34
26	8340	8836	9332	9827	.321	.815	33
27	8.631308	1801	2293	2785	3276	3766	32
28	4256	4746	5235	5723	6211	6698	31
29	7184	7671	8156	8641	9126	9610	30
30	8.640093	0576	1058	1540	2021	2502	29
31	2982	3462	3941	4420	4898	5376	28
32	5853	6329	6805	7281	7756	8230	27
33	8704	9178	9651	.123	.595	1067	26
34	8.651537	2008	2478	2947	3416	3884	25
35	4352	4820	5286	5753	6219	6684	24
36	7149	7613	8077	8541	9004	9466	23
37	9928	.389	.850	1311	1771	2230	22
38	8.662689	3148	3606	4063	4520	4977	21
39	5433	5889	6344	6799	7253	7707	20
40	8160	8613	9065	9517	9968	.419	19
41	8.670870	1320	1769	2218	2667	3115	18
42	3563	4010	4457	4903	5349	5794	17
43	6239	6684	7128	7572	8015	8457	16
44	8900	9341	9783	.224	.664	1104	15
45	8.681544	1983	2422	2860	3298	3735	14
46	4172	4608	5044	5480	5915	6350	13
47	6784	7218	7652	8085	8517	8950	12
48	9381	9813	.244	.674	1104	1534	11
49	8.691963	2392	2820	3248	3675	4103	10
50	4529	4956	5381	5807	6232	6656	9
51	7081	7504	7928	8351	8773	9195	8
52	9617	..38	.459	.880	1300	1720	7
53	8.702139	2558	2976	3395	3812	4230	6
54	4646	5063	5479	5895	6310	6725	5
55	7140	7554	7967	8381	8794	9206	4
56	9618	..30	.442	.853	1263	1674	3
57	8.712083	2493	2902	3311	3719	4127	2
58	4534	4942	5348	5755	6161	6567	1
59	6972	7377	7781	8186	8589	8993	0
	60″	50″	40″	30″	20″	10″	Min.
	Co-tangent of 87 Degrees.						

P. Part { 1″ 2″ 3″ 4″ 5″ 6″ 7″ 8″ 9″
{ 48 97 145 193 242 290 338 387 435

Min.	Tangent of 3 Degrees. 0″	10″	20″	30″	40″	50″	
0	8.719396	9798	.201	.603	1004	1405	59
1	8.721806	2207	2607	3007	3406	3805	58
2	4204	4602	5000	5397	5794	6191	57
3	6588	6984	7380	7775	8170	8565	56
4	8959	9353	9746	.140	.533	.925	55
5	8.731317	1709	2101	2492	2883	3273	54
6	3663	4053	4442	4831	5220	5608	53
7	5996	6384	6771	7158	7545	7931	52
8	8317	8703	9088	9473	9858	.242	51
9	8.740626	1009	1393	1776	2158	2540	50
10	2922	3304	3685	4066	4447	4827	49
11	5207	5586	5966	6344	6723	7101	48
12	7479	7857	8234	8611	8988	9364	47
13	9740	.116	.491	.866	1241	1615	46
14	8.751989	2363	2736	3109	3482	3855	45
15	4227	4599	4970	5341	5712	6083	44
16	6453	6823	7193	7562	7931	8300	43
17	8668	9036	9404	9771	.139	.505	42
18	8.760872	1238	1604	1970	2335	2700	41
19	3065	3429	3793	4157	4520	4884	40
20	5246	5609	5971	6333	6695	7056	39
21	7417	7778	8139	8499	8859	9218	38
22	9578	9937	.295	.654	1012	1370	37
23	8.771727	2085	2442	2798	3155	3511	36
24	3866	4222	4577	4932	5287	5641	35
25	5995	6349	6702	7056	7409	7761	34
26	8114	8466	8817	9169	9520	9871	33
27	8.780222	0572	0922	1272	1622	1971	32
28	2320	2669	3017	3365	3713	4061	31
29	4408	4755	5102	5448	5794	6140	30
30	6486	6831	7177	7521	7866	8210	29
31	8554	8898	9242	9585	9928	.271	28
32	8.790613	0955	1297	1639	1980	2321	27
33	2662	3003	3343	3683	4023	4362	26
34	4701	5040	5379	5718	6056	6394	25
35	6731	7069	7406	7743	8079	8416	24
36	8752	9088	9423	9759	..94	.429	23
37	8.800763	1098	1432	1765	2099	2432	22
38	2765	3098	3431	3763	4095	4427	21
39	4758	5090	5421	5751	6082	6412	20
40	6742	7072	7402	7731	8060	8389	19
41	8717	9046	9374	9701	..29	.356	18
42	8.810683	1010	1337	1663	1989	2315	17
43	2641	2966	3291	3616	3941	4265	16
44	4589	4913	5237	5560	5884	6207	15
45	6529	6852	7174	7496	7818	8140	14
46	8461	8782	9103	9423	9744	..64	13
47	8.820384	0703	1023	1342	1661	1980	12
48	2298	2617	2935	3253	3570	3888	11
49	4205	4522	4838	5155	5471	5787	10
50	6103	6418	6733	7049	7363	7678	9
51	7992	8307	8621	8934	9248	9561	8
52	9874	.187	.500	.812	1124	1436	7
53	8.831748	2059	2371	2682	2992	3303	6
54	3613	3924	4234	4543	4853	5162	5
55	5471	5780	6089	6397	6705	7013	4
56	7321	7629	7936	8243	8550	8857	3
57	9163	9470	9776	..81	.387	.692	2
58	8.840998	1303	1607	1912	2216	2521	1
59	2825	3128	3432	3735	4038	4341	0
	60″	50″	40″	30″	20″	10″	Min.
	Co-tangent of 86 Degrees.						

P. Part { 1″ 2″ 3″ 4″ 5″ 6″ 7″ 8″ 9″
{ 35 69 104 138 173 207 242 276 311

Min.	Sine of 4 Degrees. 0″	10″	20″	30″	40″	50″	
0	8.843585	3886	4186	4487	4787	5087	59
1	5387	5687	5987	6286	6585	6884	58
2	7183	7481	7780	8078	8376	8673	57
3	8971	9268	9565	9862	.159	.455	56
4	8.850751	1047	1343	1639	1934	2229	55
5	2525	2819	3114	3408	3703	3997	54
6	4291	4584	4878	5171	5464	5757	53
7	6049	6342	6634	6926	7218	7510	52
8	7801	8092	8383	8674	8965	9255	51
9	9546	9836	.126	.415	.705	.994	50
10	8.861283	1572	1861	2149	2438	2726	49
11	3014	3302	3589	3877	4164	4451	48
12	4738	5024	5311	5597	5883	6169	47
13	6455	6740	7025	7310	7595	7880	46
14	8165	8449	8733	9017	9301	9585	45
15	9868	.151	.434	.717	1000	1282	44
16	8.871565	1847	2129	2410	2692	2973	43
17	3255	3536	3817	4097	4378	4658	42
18	4938	5218	5498	5777	6057	6336	41
19	6615	6894	7172	7451	7729	8007	40
20	8285	8563	8841	9118	9395	9672	39
21	9949	.226	.503	.779	1055	1331	38
22	8.881607	1883	2158	2433	2708	2983	37
23	3258	3533	3807	4081	4355	4629	36
24	4903	5177	5450	5723	5996	6269	35
25	6542	6814	7087	7359	7631	7903	34
26	8174	8446	8717	8988	9259	9530	33
27	9801	..71	.341	.612	.882	1151	32
28	8.891421	1690	1960	2229	2498	2767	31
29	3035	3304	3572	3840	4108	4376	30
30	4643	4911	5178	5445	5712	5979	29
31	6246	6512	6778	7044	7310	7576	28
32	7842	8107	8373	8638	8903	9168	27
33	9432	9697	9961	.225	.489	.753	26
34	8.901017	1280	1544	1807	2070	2333	25
35	2596	2858	3121	3383	3645	3907	24
36	4169	4430	4692	4953	5214	5475	23
37	5736	5997	6257	6517	6778	7038	22
38	7297	7557	7817	8076	8335	8595	21
39	8853	9112	9371	9629	9888	.146	20
40	8.910404	0662	0919	1177	1434	1692	19
41	1949	2206	2462	2719	2976	3232	18
42	3488	3744	4000	4256	4511	4767	17
43	5022	5277	5532	5787	6041	6296	16
44	6550	6805	7059	7313	7566	7820	15
45	8073	8327	8580	8833	9086	9338	14
46	9591	9843	..96	.348	.600	.852	13
47	8.921103	1355	1606	1858	2109	2360	12
48	2610	2861	3112	3362	3612	3862	11
49	4112	4362	4612	4861	5111	5360	10
50	5609	5858	6107	6355	6604	6852	9
51	7100	7348	7596	7844	8092	8339	8
52	8587	8834	9081	9328	9575	9821	7
53	8.930068	0314	0560	0806	1052	1298	6
54	1544	1789	2035	2280	2525	2770	5
55	3015	3260	3504	3749	3993	4237	4
56	4481	4725	4969	5212	5456	5699	3
57	5942	6185	6428	6671	6914	7156	2
58	7398	7641	7883	8125	8366	8608	1
59	8850	9091	9332	9573	9814	..55	0
	60″	50″	40″	30″	20″	10″	Min.
	Co-sine of 85 Degrees.						

P. Part { 1″ 2″ 3″ 4″ 5″ 6″ 7″ 8″ 9″ / 27 53 80 107 134 160 187 214 241

P. Part	1″	2″	3″	4″	5″	6″	7″	8″	9″
	27	53	80	107	134	160	187	214	241

Min.	Sine of 5 Degrees. 0″	10″	20″	30″	40″	50″	
0	8.940296	0537	0777	1017	1258	1498	59
1	1738	1977	2217	2457	2696	2935	58
2	3174	3413	3652	3891	4129	4368	57
3	4606	4844	5083	5321	5558	5796	56
4	6034	6271	6508	6745	6982	7219	55
5	7456	7693	7929	8166	8402	8638	54
6	8874	9110	9345	9581	9817	..52	53
7	8.950287	0522	0757	0992	1227	1461	52
8	1696	1930	2164	2398	2632	2866	51
9	3100	3333	3567	3800	4033	4266	50
10	4499	4732	4965	5197	5429	5662	49
11	5894	6126	6358	6590	6821	7053	48
12	7284	7516	7747	7978	8209	8440	47
13	8670	8901	9131	9362	9592	9822	46
14	8.960052	0282	0511	0741	0970	1200	45
15	1429	1658	1887	2116	2344	2573	44
16	2801	3030	3258	3486	3714	3942	43
17	4170	4397	4625	4852	5080	5307	42
18	5534	5761	5987	6214	6441	6667	41
19	6893	7120	7346	7572	7797	8023	40
20	8249	8474	8700	8925	9150	9375	39
21	9600	9825	..49	.274	.498	.723	38
22	8.970947	1171	1395	1619	1842	2066	37
23	2289	2513	2736	2959	3182	3405	36
24	3628	3851	4073	4296	4518	4740	35
25	4962	5184	5406	5628	5850	6071	34
26	6293	6514	6735	6956	7177	7398	33
27	7619	7839	8060	8280	8501	8721	32
28	8941	9161	9381	9600	9820	..39	31
29	8.980259	0478	0697	0916	1135	1354	30
30	1573	1791	2010	2228	2447	2665	29
31	2883	3101	3319	3536	3754	3972	28
32	4189	4406	4623	4840	5057	5274	27
33	5491	5708	5924	6141	6357	6573	26
34	6789	7005	7221	7437	7652	7868	25
35	8083	8299	8514	8729	8944	9159	24
36	9374	9588	9803	..17	.232	.446	23
37	8.990660	0874	1088	1302	1516	1729	22
38	1943	2156	2370	2583	2796	3009	21
39	3222	3435	3647	3860	4072	4285	20
40	4497	4709	4921	5133	5345	5556	19
41	5768	5980	6191	6402	6614	6825	18
42	7036	7247	7457	7668	7879	8089	17
43	8299	8510	8720	8930	9140	9350	16
44	9560	9769	9979	.188	.398	.607	15
45	9.000816	1025	1234	1443	1652	1860	14
46	2069	2277	2486	2694	2902	3110	13
47	3318	3526	3733	3941	4149	4356	12
48	4563	4771	4978	5185	5392	5599	11
49	5805	6012	6218	6425	6631	6837	10
50	7044	7250	7456	7661	7867	8073	9
51	8278	8484	8689	8894	9100	9305	8
52	9510	9715	9919	.124	.329	.533	7
53	9.010737	0942	1146	1350	1554	1758	6
54	1962	2165	2369	2572	2776	2979	5
55	3182	3385	3588	3791	3994	4197	4
56	4400	4602	4805	5007	5209	5411	3
57	5613	5815	6017	6219	6421	6622	2
58	6824	7025	7227	7428	7629	7830	1
59	8031	8232	8433	8633	8834	9034	0
	60″	50″	40″	30″	20″	10″	Min.
	Co-sine of 84 Degrees.						

P. Part	1″	2″	3″	4″	5″	6″	7″	8″	9″
	22	44	66	87	109	131	153	175	197

Min.	Tangent of 4 Degrees. 0″	10″	20″	30″	40″	50″	
0	8.844644	4946	5248	5551	5852	6154	59
1	6455	6757	7058	7358	7659	7959	58
2	8260	8560	8859	9159	9458	9758	57
3	8.850057	0355	0654	0952	1250	1548	56
4	1846	2144	2441	2738	3035	3332	55
5	3628	3925	4221	4517	4813	5108	54
6	5403	5699	5993	6288	6583	6877	53
7	7171	7465	7759	8053	8346	8639	52
8	8932	9225	9517	9810	.102	.394	51
9	8.860686	0977	1269	1560	1851	2142	50
10	2433	2723	3013	3303	3593	3883	49
11	4173	4462	4751	5040	5329	5617	48
12	5906	6194	6482	6769	7057	7344	47
13	7632	7919	8206	8492	8779	9065	46
14	9351	9637	9923	.208	.494	.779	45
15	8.871064	1349	1633	1918	2202	2486	44
16	2770	3054	3337	3620	3904	4187	43
17	4469	4752	5034	5317	5599	5881	42
18	6162	6444	6725	7006	7287	7568	41
19	7849	8129	8409	8689	8969	9249	40
20	9529	9808	..87	.366	.645	.924	39
21	8.881202	1480	1759	2037	2314	2592	38
22	2869	3147	3424	3701	3977	4254	37
23	4530	4807	5083	5358	5634	5910	36
24	6185	6460	6735	7010	7285	7559	35
25	7833	8108	8382	8655	8929	9202	34
26	9476	9749	..22	.295	.567	.840	33
27	8.891112	1384	1656	1928	2199	2471	32
28	2742	3013	3284	3555	3825	4096	31
29	4366	4636	4906	5176	5445	5715	30
30	5984	6253	6522	6791	7060	7328	29
31	7596	7864	8132	8400	8668	8935	28
32	9203	9470	9737	...4	.270	.537	27
33	8.900803	1069	1335	1601	1867	2132	26
34	2398	2663	2928	3193	3458	3722	25
35	3987	4251	4515	4779	5043	5306	24
36	5570	5833	6096	6359	6622	6885	23
37	7147	7410	7672	7934	8196	8457	22
38	8719	8980	9242	9503	9764	..25	21
39	8.910285	0546	0806	1066	1326	1586	20
40	1846	2106	2365	2624	2883	3142	19
41	3401	3660	3918	4177	4435	4693	18
42	4951	5209	5466	5724	5981	6238	17
43	6495	6752	7009	7265	7522	7778	16
44	8034	8290	8546	8801	9057	9312	15
45	9568	9823	..78	.332	.587	.841	14
46	8.921096	1350	1604	1858	2112	2365	13
47	2619	2872	3125	3378	3631	3884	12
48	4136	4389	4641	4893	5145	5397	11
49	5649	5900	6152	6403	6654	6905	10
50	7156	7407	7657	7908	8158	8408	9
51	8658	8908	9158	9407	9657	9906	8
52	8.930155	0404	0653	0902	1150	1399	7
53	1647	1895	2143	2391	2639	2887	6
54	3134	3381	3629	3876	4123	4369	5
55	4616	4862	5109	5355	5601	5847	4
56	6093	6339	6584	6830	7075	7320	3
57	7565	7810	8055	8299	8544	8788	2
58	9032	9276	9520	9764	...7	.251	1
59	8.940494	0738	0981	1224	1467	1709	0
	60″	50″	40″	30″	20″	10″	Min.
	Co-tangent of 85 Degrees.						

P. Part { 1″ 2″ 3″ 4″ 5″ 6″ 7″ 8″ 9″
27 54 81 108 135 162 188 215 242

Min.	Tangent of 5 Degrees. 0″	10″	20″	30″	40″	50″	
0	8.941952	2194	2437	2679	2921	3163	59
1	3404	3646	3888	4129	4370	4611	58
2	4852	5093	5334	5574	5815	6055	57
3	6295	6535	6775	7015	7255	7494	56
4	7734	7973	8212	8451	8690	8929	55
5	9168	9406	9644	9883	.121	.359	54
6	8.950597	0834	1072	1309	1547	1784	53
7	2021	2258	2495	2732	2968	3205	52
8	3441	3677	3913	4149	4385	4621	51
9	4856	5092	5327	5562	5797	6032	50
10	6267	6502	6736	6971	7205	7439	49
11	7674	7908	8141	8375	8609	8842	48
12	9075	9309	9542	9775	...8	.240	47
13	8.960473	0705	0938	1170	1402	1634	46
14	1866	2098	2329	2561	2792	3023	45
15	3255	3486	3716	3947	4178	4408	44
16	4639	4869	5099	5329	5559	5789	43
17	6019	6248	6478	6707	6936	7165	42
18	7394	7623	7852	8081	8309	8538	41
19	8766	8994	9222	9450	9678	9905	40
20	8.970133	0360	0588	0815	1042	1269	39
21	1496	1723	1949	2176	2402	2628	38
22	2855	3081	3307	3532	3758	3984	37
23	4209	4435	4660	4885	5110	5335	36
24	5560	5784	6009	6233	6458	6682	35
25	6906	7130	7354	7578	7801	8025	34
26	8248	8472	8695	8918	9141	9364	33
27	9586	9809	..32	.254	.476	.699	32
28	8.980921	1143	1364	1586	1808	2029	31
29	2251	2472	2693	2914	3135	3356	30
30	3577	3798	4018	4238	4459	4679	29
31	4899	5119	5339	5559	5778	5998	28
32	6217	6437	6656	6875	7094	7313	27
33	7532	7750	7969	8187	8406	8624	26
34	8842	9060	9278	9496	9714	9931	25
35	8.990149	0366	0583	0801	1018	1235	24
36	1451	1668	1885	2101	2318	2534	23
37	2750	2966	3182	3398	3614	3830	22
38	4045	4261	4476	4692	4907	5122	21
39	5337	5552	5766	5981	6196	6410	20
40	6624	6839	7053	7267	7481	7694	19
41	7908	8122	8335	8549	8762	8975	18
42	9188	9401	9614	9827	..40	.252	17
43	9.000465	0677	0889	1102	1314	1526	16
44	1738	1949	2161	2373	2584	2795	15
45	3007	3218	3429	3640	3851	4061	14
46	4272	4483	4693	4904	5114	5324	13
47	5534	5744	5954	6164	6373	6583	12
48	6792	7002	7211	7420	7629	7838	11
49	8047	8256	8465	8673	8882	9090	10
50	9298	9507	9715	9923	.131	.338	9
51	9.010546	0754	0961	1169	1376	1583	8
52	1790	1997	2204	2411	2618	2824	7
53	3031	3237	3444	3650	3856	4062	6
54	4268	4474	4680	4886	5091	5297	5
55	5502	5707	5913	6118	6323	6528	4
56	6732	6937	7142	7346	7551	7755	3
57	7959	8164	8368	8572	8776	8979	2
58	9183	9387	9590	9794	9997	.200	1
59	9.020403	0606	0809	1012	1215	1418	0
	60″	50″	40″	30″	20″	10″	Min.
	Co-tangent of 84 Degrees.						

P. Part { 1″ 2″ 3″ 4″ 5″ 6″ 7″ 8″ 9″
22 44 66 88 110 132 154 177 199

Min.	Sine of 6 Degrees. 0″	10″	20″	30″	40″	50″	
0	9.019235	9435	9635	9835	..35	.235	59
1	9.020435	0635	0834	1034	1233	1433	58
2	1632	1831	2030	2229	2428	2627	57
3	2825	3024	3223	3421	3619	3818	56
4	4016	4214	4412	4610	4807	5005	55
5	5203	5400	5598	5795	5992	6189	54
6	6386	6583	6780	6977	7174	7370	53
7	7567	7763	7960	8156	8352	8548	52
8	8744	8940	9136	9332	9527	9723	51
9	9918	.114	.309	.504	.699	.894	50
10	9.031089	1284	1479	1673	1868	2062	49
11	2257	2451	2645	2839	3033	3227	48
12	3421	3615	3809	4002	4196	4389	47
13	4582	4776	4969	5162	5355	5548	46
14	5741	5933	6126	6319	6511	6703	45
15	6896	7088	7280	7472	7664	7856	44
16	8048	8239	8431	8623	8814	9005	43
17	9197	9388	9579	9770	9961	.152	42
18	9.040342	0533	0724	0914	1105	1295	41
19	1485	1675	1865	2055	2245	2435	40
20	2625	2815	3004	3194	3383	3572	39
21	3762	3951	4140	4329	4518	4707	38
22	4895	5084	5273	5461	5650	5838	37
23	6026	6214	6402	6590	6778	6966	36
24	7154	7342	7529	7717	7904	8091	35
25	8279	8466	8653	8840	9027	9214	34
26	9400	9587	9774	9960	.147	.333	33
27	9.050519	0706	0892	1078	1264	1450	32
28	1635	1821	2007	2192	2378	2563	31
29	2749	2934	3119	3304	3489	3674	30
30	3859	4044	4228	4413	4597	4782	29
31	4966	5150	5335	5519	5703	5887	28
32	6071	6254	6438	6622	6805	6989	27
33	7172	7356	7539	7722	7905	8088	26
34	8271	8454	8637	8820	9002	9185	25
35	9367	9550	9732	9914	..96	.278	24
36	9.060460	0642	0824	1006	1188	1369	23
37	1551	1732	1914	2095	2276	2457	22
38	2639	2820	3001	3181	3362	3543	21
39	3724	3904	4085	4265	4445	4626	20
40	4806	4986	5166	5346	5526	5705	19
41	5885	6065	6244	6424	6603	6783	18
42	6962	7141	7320	7499	7678	7857	17
43	8036	8215	8393	8572	8751	8929	16
44	9107	9286	9464	9642	9820	9998	15
45	9.070176	0354	0532	0709	0887	1065	14
46	1242	1420	1597	1774	1951	2128	13
47	2306	2482	2659	2836	3013	3190	12
48	3366	3543	3719	3896	4072	4248	11
49	4424	4600	4777	4952	5128	5304	10
50	5480	5656	5831	6007	6182	6358	9
51	6533	6708	6883	7058	7233	7408	8
52	7583	7758	7933	8107	8282	8457	7
53	8631	8805	8980	9154	9328	9502	6
54	9676	9850	..24	.198	.372	.545	5
55	9.080719	0892	1066	1239	1413	1586	4
56	1759	1932	2105	2278	2451	2624	3
57	2797	2969	3142	3314	3487	3659	2
58	3832	4004	4176	4348	4520	4692	1
59	4864	5036	5208	5380	5551	5723	0
	60″	50″	40″	30″	20″	10″	Min.
	Co-sine of 83 Degrees.						

P. Part { 1″ 2″ 3″ 4″ 5″ 6″ 7″ 8′ 9″
{ 18 37 55 74 92 111 129 148 166

Min.	Sine of 7 Degrees. 0″	10″	20″	30″	40″	50″	
0	9.085894	6066	6237	6409	6580	6751	59
1	6922	7093	7264	7435	7606	7777	58
2	7947	8118	8288	8459	8629	8800	57
3	8970	9140	9310	9480	9651	9820	56
4	9990	.160	.330	.500	.669	.839	55
5	9.091008	1178	1347	1516	1685	1855	54
6	2024	2193	2362	2530	2699	2868	53
7	3037	3205	3374	3542	3711	3879	52
8	4047	4216	4384	4552	4720	4888	51
9	5056	5223	5391	5559	5726	5894	50
10	6062	6229	6396	6564	6731	6898	49
11	7065	7232	7399	7566	7733	7900	48
12	8066	8233	8399	8566	8732	8899	47
13	9065	9231	9398	9564	9730	9896	46
14	9.100062	0227	0393	0559	0725	0890	45
15	1056	1221	1387	1552	1717	1883	44
16	2048	2213	2378	2543	2708	2873	43
17	3037	3202	3367	3531	3696	3860	42
18	4025	4189	4353	4517	4682	4846	41
19	5010	5174	5337	5501	5665	5829	40
20	5992	6156	6319	6483	6646	6810	39
21	6973	7136	7299	7462	7625	7788	38
22	7951	8114	8277	8439	8602	8765	37
23	8927	9090	9252	9414	9577	9739	36
24	9901	..63	.225	.387	.549	.711	35
25	9.110873	1034	1196	1358	1519	1681	34
26	1842	2003	2165	2326	2487	2648	33
27	2809	2970	3131	3292	3453	3613	32
28	3774	3935	4095	4256	4416	4577	31
29	4737	4897	5057	5218	5378	5538	30
30	5698	5858	6017	6177	6337	6497	29
31	6656	6816	6975	7135	7294	7453	28
32	7613	7772	7931	8090	8249	8408	27
33	8567	8726	8884	9043	9202	9360	26
34	9519	9677	9836	9994	.152	.311	25
35	9.120469	0627	0785	0943	1101	1259	24
36	1417	1574	1732	1890	2047	2205	23
37	2362	2520	2677	2835	2992	3149	22
38	3306	3463	3620	3777	3934	4091	21
39	4248	4404	4561	4718	4874	5031	20
40	5187	5344	5500	5656	5812	5969	19
41	6125	6281	6437	6593	6748	6904	18
42	7060	7216	7371	7527	7682	7838	17
43	7993	8149	8304	8459	8614	8770	16
44	8925	9080	9235	9390	9544	9699	15
45	9854	...9	.163	.318	.472	.627	14
46	9.130781	0936	1090	1244	1398	1552	13
47	1706	1860	2014	2168	2322	2476	12
48	2630	2783	2937	3091	3244	3398	11
49	3551	3704	3858	4011	4164	4317	10
50	4470	4623	4776	4929	5082	5235	9
51	5387	5540	5693	5845	5998	6150	8
52	6303	6455	6607	676[illegible]	6912	7064	7
53	7216	7368	7520	7672	7824	7976	6
54	8128	8279	8431	8582	8734	8886	5
55	9037	9188	9340	9491	9642	9793	4
56	9944	..96	.247	.398	.548	.699	3
57	9.140850	1001	1151	1302	1453	1603	2
58	1754	1904	2055	2205	2355	2505	1
59	2655	2806	2956	3106	3256	3405	0
	60″	50″	40″	30″	20″	10″	Min.
	Co-sine of 82 Degrees.						

P. Part { 1″ 2″ 3″ 4″ 5″ 6″ 7″ 8″ 9″
{ 16 32 48 64 80 96 112 128 144

Min.	Tangent of 6 Degrees. 0″	10″	20″	30″	40″	50″	
0	9.021620	1823	2025	2227	2430	2632	59
1	2834	3036	3238	3439	3641	3843	58
2	4044	4245	4447	4648	4849	5050	57
3	5251	5452	5653	5853	6054	6254	56
4	6455	6655	6855	7055	7255	7455	55
5	7655	7855	8055	8254	8454	8653	54
6	8852	9052	9251	9450	9649	9848	53
7	9.030046	0245	0444	0642	0841	1039	52
8	1237	1435	1633	1831	2029	2227	51
9	2425	2623	2820	3017	3215	3412	50
10	3609	3806	4003	4200	4397	4594	49
11	4791	4987	5184	5380	5576	5773	48
12	5969	6165	6361	6557	6753	6948	47
13	7144	7339	7535	7730	7926	8121	46
14	8316	8511	8706	8901	9095	9290	45
15	9485	9679	9874	..68	.262	.456	44
16	9.040651	0845	1039	1232	1426	1620	43
17	1813	2007	2200	2394	2587	2780	42
18	2973	3166	3359	3552	3745	3937	41
19	4130	4322	4515	4707	4899	5092	40
20	5284	5476	5668	5859	6051	6243	39
21	6434	6626	6817	7009	7200	7391	38
22	7582	7773	7964	8155	8346	8536	37
23	8727	8917	9108	9298	9489	9679	36
24	9869	..59	.249	.439	.629	.818	35
25	9.051008	1197	1387	1576	1766	1955	34
26	2144	2333	2522	2711	2900	3088	33
27	3277	3466	3654	3843	4031	4219	32
28	4407	4596	4784	4972	5159	5347	31
29	5535	5723	5910	6098	6285	6472	30
30	6659	6847	7034	7221	7408	7594	29
31	7781	7968	8155	8341	8528	8714	28
32	8900	9086	9273	9459	9645	9831	27
33	9.060016	0202	0388	0573	0759	0944	26
34	1130	1315	1500	1685	1870	2055	25
35	2240	2425	2610	2795	2979	3164	24
36	3348	3533	3717	3901	4085	4269	23
37	4453	4637	4821	5005	5188	5372	22
38	5556	5739	5922	6106	6289	6472	21
39	6655	6838	7021	7204	7387	7570	20
40	7752	7935	8117	8300	8482	8664	19
41	8846	9029	9211	9393	9575	9756	18
42	9938	.120	.301	.483	.664	.846	17
43	9.071027	1208	1389	1570	1751	1932	16
44	2113	2294	2475	2655	2836	3016	15
45	3197	3377	3558	3738	3918	4098	14
46	4278	4458	4638	4817	4997	5177	13
47	5356	5536	5715	5895	6074	6253	12
48	6432	6611	6790	6969	7148	7327	11
49	7505	7684	7862	8041	8219	8398	10
50	8576	8754	8932	9110	9288	9466	9
51	9644	9822	....	.177	.355	.532	8
52	9.080710	0887	1064	1241	1419	1596	7
53	1773	1950	2126	2303	2480	2657	6
54	2833	3010	3186	3362	3539	3715	5
55	3891	4067	4243	4419	4595	4771	4
56	4947	5122	5298	5473	5649	5824	3
57	6000	6175	6350	6525	6700	6875	2
58	7050	7225	7400	7574	7749	7924	1
59	8098	8273	8447	8621	8795	8970	0
	60″	50″	40″	30″	20″	10″	Min.
	Co-tangent of 83 Degrees.						

P. Part	1″	2″	3″	4″	5″	6″	7″	8″	9″
	19	37	56	75	94	112	131	150	168

Min.	Tangent of 7 Degrees. 0″	10″	20″	30″	40″	50″	
0	9.089144	9318	9492	9666	9839	..13	59
1	9.090187	0361	0534	0708	0881	1054	58
2	1228	1401	1574	1747	1920	2093	57
3	2266	2439	2612	2784	2957	3129	56
4	3302	3474	3647	3819	3991	4163	55
5	4336	4508	4680	4851	5023	5195	54
6	5367	5538	5710	5881	6053	6224	53
7	6395	6567	6738	6909	7080	7251	52
8	7422	7593	7764	7934	8105	8276	51
9	8446	8616	8787	8957	9127	9298	50
10	9468	9638	9808	9978	.148	.317	49
11	9.100487	0657	0827	0996	1166	1335	48
12	1504	1674	1843	2012	2181	2350	47
13	2519	2688	2857	3026	3194	3363	46
14	3532	3700	3869	4037	4205	4374	45
15	4542	4710	4878	5046	5214	5382	44
16	5550	5718	5885	6053	6221	6388	43
17	6556	6723	6890	7058	7225	7392	42
18	7559	7726	7893	8060	8227	8394	41
19	8560	8727	8894	9060	9227	9393	40
20	9559	9726	9892	..58	.224	.390	39
21	9.110556	0722	0888	1054	1219	1385	38
22	1551	1716	1882	2047	2213	2378	37
23	2543	2708	2873	3039	3204	3368	36
24	3533	3698	3863	4028	4192	4357	35
25	4521	4686	4850	5015	5179	5343	34
26	5507	5671	5835	5999	6163	6327	33
27	6491	6655	6818	6982	7145	7309	32
28	7472	7636	7799	7962	8126	8289	31
29	8452	8615	8778	8941	9104	9266	30
30	9429	9592	9754	9917	..79	.242	29
31	9.120404	0567	0729	0891	1053	1215	28
32	1377	1539	1701	1863	2025	2187	27
33	2348	2510	2671	2833	2994	3156	26
34	3317	3478	3640	3801	3962	4123	25
35	4284	4445	4606	4766	4927	5088	24
36	5249	5409	5570	5730	5891	6051	23
37	6211	6371	6532	6692	6852	7012	22
38	7172	7332	7492	7651	7811	7971	21
39	8130	8290	8449	8609	8768	8928	20
40	9087	9246	9405	9564	9723	9882	19
41	9.130041	0200	0359	0518	0676	0835	18
42	0994	1152	1311	1469	1628	1786	17
43	1944	2102	2261	2419	2577	2735	16
44	2893	3050	3208	3366	3524	3681	15
45	3839	3997	4154	4312	4469	4626	14
46	4784	4941	5098	5255	5412	5569	13
47	5726	5883	6040	6197	6353	6510	12
48	6667	6823	6980	7136	7292	7449	11
49	7605	7761	7918	8074	8230	8386	10
50	8542	8698	8854	9009	9165	9321	9
51	9476	9632	9788	9943	..98	.254	8
52	9.140409	0564	0720	0875	1030	1185	7
53	1340	1495	1650	1805	1959	2114	6
54	2269	2424	2578	2733	2887	3042	5
55	3196	3350	3504	3659	3813	3967	4
56	4121	4275	4429	4583	4737	4890	3
57	5044	5198	5351	5505	5659	5812	2
58	5966	6119	6272	6425	6579	6732	1
59	6885	7038	7191	7344	7497	7650	0
	60″	50″	40″	30″	20″	10″	Min.
	Co-tangent of 82 Degrees.						

P. Part	1″	2″	3″	4″	5″	6″	7″	8″	9″
	16	33	49	65	81	98	114	130	146

Min.	Sine of 8 Degrees.						
	0″	10″	20″	30″	40″	50″	
0	9.143555	3705	3855	4005	4154	4304	59
1	4453	4603	4752	4902	5051	5200	58
2	5349	5498	5648	5797	5946	6095	57
3	6243	6392	6541	6690	6839	6987	56
4	7136	7284	7433	7581	7730	7878	55
5	8026	8174	8323	8471	8619	8767	54
6	8915	9063	9211	9358	9506	9654	53
7	9802	9949	..97	.244	.392	.539	52
8	9.150686	0834	0981	1128	1275	1422	51
9	1569	1716	1863	2010	2157	2304	50
10	2451	2597	2744	2891	3037	3184	49
11	3330	3476	3623	3769	3915	4061	48
12	4208	4354	4500	4646	4792	4938	47
13	5083	5229	5375	5521	5666	5812	46
14	5957	6103	6248	6394	6539	6684	45
15	6830	6975	7120	7265	7410	7555	44
16	7700	7845	7990	8135	8279	8424	43
17	8569	8713	8858	9002	9147	9291	42
18	9435	9580	9724	9868	..12	.156	41
19	9.160301	0445	0589	0732	0876	1020	40
20	1164	1308	1451	1595	1738	1882	39
21	2025	2169	2312	2456	2599	2742	38
22	2885	3028	3172	3315	3458	3600	37
23	3743	3886	4029	4172	4314	4457	36
24	4600	4742	4885	5027	5170	5312	35
25	5454	5597	5739	5881	6023	6165	34
26	6307	6449	6591	6733	6875	7017	33
27	7159	7300	7442	7584	7725	7867	32
28	8008	8150	8291	8432	8574	8715	31
29	8856	8997	9138	9279	9420	9561	30
30	9702	9843	9984	.125	.265	.406	29
31	9.170547	0687	0828	0968	1109	1249	28
32	1389	1530	1670	1810	1950	2090	27
33	2230	2370	2510	2650	2790	2930	26
34	3070	3210	3349	3489	3629	3768	25
35	3908	4047	4187	4326	4465	4605	24
36	4744	4883	5022	5161	5300	5439	23
37	5578	5717	5856	5995	6134	6273	22
38	6411	6550	6688	6827	6966	7104	21
39	7242	7381	7519	7657	7796	7934	20
40	8072	8210	8348	8486	8624	8762	19
41	8900	9038	9176	9313	9451	9589	18
42	9726	9864	...2	.139	.276	.414	17
43	9.180551	0689	0826	0963	1100	1237	16
44	1374	1511	1648	1785	1922	2059	15
45	2196	2333	2469	2606	2743	2879	14
46	3016	3152	3289	3425	3562	3698	13
47	3834	3971	4107	4243	4379	4515	12
48	4651	4787	4923	5059	5195	5331	11
49	5466	5602	5738	5874	6009	6145	10
50	6280	6416	6551	6686	6822	6957	9
51	7092	7228	7363	7498	7633	7768	8
52	7903	8038	8173	8308	8442	8577	7
53	8712	8847	8981	9116	9250	9385	6
54	9519	9654	9788	9923	..57	.191	5
55	9.190325	0460	0594	0728	0862	0996	4
56	1130	1264	1398	1532	1665	1799	3
57	1933	2066	2200	2334	2467	2601	2
58	2734	2868	3001	3134	3268	3401	1
59	3534	3667	3800	3933	4066	4199	0
	60″	50″	40″	30″	20″	10″	Min.
	Co-sine of 81 Degrees.						

P. Part { 1″ 2″ 3″ 4″ 5″ 6″ 7″ 8″ 9″ / 14 28 42 56 70 85 99 113 127

Min.	Sine of 9 Degrees.						
	0″	10″	20″	30″	40″	50″	
0	9.194332	4465	4598	4731	4864	4997	59
1	5129	5262	5395	5527	5660	5792	58
2	5925	6057	6189	6322	6454	6586	57
3	6719	6851	6983	7115	7247	7379	56
4	7511	7643	7775	7907	8038	8170	55
5	8302	8434	8565	8697	8828	8960	54
6	9091	9223	9354	9486	9617	9748	53
7	9879	..11	.142	.273	.404	.535	52
8	9.200666	0797	0928	1059	1189	1320	51
9	1451	1582	1712	1843	1973	2104	50
10	2234	2365	2495	2626	2756	2886	49
11	3017	3147	3277	3407	3537	3667	48
12	3797	3927	4057	4187	4317	4447	47
13	4577	4706	4836	4966	5095	5225	46
14	5354	5484	5613	5743	5872	6002	45
15	6131	6260	6389	6519	6648	6777	44
16	6906	7035	7164	7293	7422	7551	43
17	7679	7808	7937	8066	8194	8323	42
18	8452	8580	8709	8837	8966	9094	41
19	9222	9351	9479	9607	9735	9864	40
20	9992	.120	.248	.376	.504	.632	39
21	9.210760	0888	1015	1143	1271	1399	38
22	1526	1654	1781	1909	2037	2164	37
23	2291	2419	2546	2674	2801	2928	36
24	3055	3182	3310	3437	3564	3691	35
25	3818	3945	4071	4198	4325	4452	34
26	4579	4705	4832	4959	5085	5212	33
27	5338	5465	5591	5718	5844	5970	32
28	6097	6223	6349	6475	6601	6728	31
29	6854	6980	7106	7232	7358	7483	30
30	7609	7735	7861	7987	8112	8238	29
31	8363	8489	8615	8740	8866	8991	28
32	9116	9242	9367	9492	9618	9743	27
33	9868	9993	.118	.243	.368	.493	26
34	9.220618	0743	0868	0993	1118	1242	25
35	1367	1492	1616	1741	1866	1990	24
36	2115	2239	2364	2488	2612	2737	23
37	2861	2985	3109	3234	3358	3482	22
38	3606	3730	3854	3978	4102	4226	21
39	4349	4473	4597	4721	4845	4968	20
40	5092	5215	5339	5462	5586	5709	19
41	5833	5956	6080	6203	6326	6449	18
42	6573	6696	6819	6942	7065	7188	17
43	7311	7434	7557	7680	7803	7925	16
44	8048	8171	8294	8416	8539	8661	15
45	8784	8906	9029	9151	9274	9396	14
46	9518	9641	9763	9885	...7	.130	13
47	9.230252	0374	0496	0618	0740	0862	12
48	0984	1106	1228	1349	1471	1593	11
49	1715	1836	1958	2079	2201	2323	10
50	2444	2565	2687	2808	2930	3051	9
51	3172	3293	3415	3536	3657	3778	8
52	3899	4020	4141	4262	4383	4504	7
53	4625	4746	4867	4987	5108	5229	6
54	5349	5470	5591	5711	5832	5952	5
55	6073	6193	6313	6434	6554	6674	4
56	6795	6915	7035	7155	7275	7395	3
57	7515	7635	7755	7875	7995	8115	2
58	8235	8355	8474	8594	8714	8834	1
59	8953	9073	9192	9312	9431	9551	0
	60″	50″	40″	30″	20″	10″	Min.
	Co-sine of 80 Degrees.						

P. Part { 1″ 2″ 3″ 4″ 5″ 6″ 7″ 8″ 9″ / 13 25 38 50 63 75 88 101 113

Tangent of 8 Degrees.

Min.	0″	10″	20″	30″	40″	50″	
0	9.147803	7955	8108	8261	8413	8566	59
1	8718	8871	9023	9175	9328	9480	58
2	9632	9784	9936	..88	.240	.392	57
3	9.150544	0696	0848	0999	1151	1303	56
4	1454	1606	1757	1909	2060	2211	55
5	2363	2514	2665	2816	2967	3118	54
6	3269	3420	3571	3722	3873	4023	53
7	4174	4325	4475	4626	4776	4926	52
8	5077	5227	5377	5528	5678	5828	51
9	5978	6128	6278	6428	6578	6728	50
10	6877	7027	7177	7326	7476	7625	49
11	7775	7924	8074	8223	8372	8521	48
12	8671	8820	8969	9118	9267	9416	47
13	9565	9713	9862	..11	.160	.308	46
14	9.160457	0605	0754	0902	1051	1199	45
15	1347	1496	1644	1792	1940	2088	44
16	2236	2384	2532	2680	2828	2975	43
17	3123	3271	3418	3566	3713	3861	42
18	4008	4156	4303	4450	4598	4745	41
19	4892	5039	5186	5333	5480	5627	40
20	5774	5920	6067	6214	6361	6507	39
21	6654	6800	6947	7093	7240	7386	38
22	7532	7678	7825	7971	8117	8263	37
23	8409	8555	8701	8847	8992	9138	36
24	9284	9430	9575	9721	9866	..12	35
25	9.170157	0303	0448	0593	0739	0884	34
26	1029	1174	1319	1464	1609	1754	33
27	1899	2044	2188	2333	2478	2623	32
28	2767	2912	3056	3201	3345	3489	31
29	3634	3778	3922	4067	4211	4355	30
30	4499	4643	4787	4931	5075	5218	29
31	5362	5506	5650	5793	5937	6080	28
32	6224	6367	6511	6654	6797	6941	27
33	7084	7227	7370	7513	7656	7800	26
34	7942	8085	8228	8371	8514	8657	25
35	8799	8942	9085	9227	9370	9512	24
36	9655	9797	9939	..82	.224	.366	23
37	9.180508	0650	0792	0934	1076	1218	22
38	1360	1502	1644	1786	1927	2069	21
39	2211	2352	2494	2635	2777	2918	20
40	3059	3201	3342	3483	3625	3766	19
41	3907	4048	4189	4330	4471	4612	18
42	4752	4893	5034	5175	5315	5456	17
43	5597	5737	5878	6018	6158	6299	16
44	6439	6579	6720	6860	7000	7140	15
45	7280	7420	7560	7700	7840	7980	14
46	8120	8259	8399	8539	8678	8818	13
47	8958	9097	9236	9376	9515	9655	12
48	9794	9933	..72	.212	.351	.490	11
49	9.190629	0768	0907	1046	1184	1323	10
50	1462	1601	1739	1878	2017	2155	9
51	2294	2432	2571	2709	2848	2986	8
52	3124	3262	3401	3539	3677	3815	7
53	3953	4091	4229	4367	4505	4642	6
54	4780	4918	5056	5193	5331	5468	5
55	5606	5743	5881	6018	6156	6293	4
56	6430	6567	6705	6842	6979	7116	3
57	7253	7390	7527	7664	7801	7938	2
58	8074	8211	8348	8484	8621	8758	1
59	8894	9031	9167	9304	9440	9576	0
	60″	50″	40″	30″	20″	10″	Min.

Co-tangent of 81 Degrees.

P. Part { 1″ 2″ 3″ 4″ 5″ 6″ 7″ 8″ 9″
{ 14 29 43 58 72 86 101 115 130

Tangent of 9 Degrees.

Min.	0″	10″	20″	30″	40″	50″	
0	9.199713	9849	9985	.121	.257	.393	59
1	9.200529	0665	0801	0937	1073	1209	58
2	1345	1481	1616	1752	1888	2023	57
3	2159	2294	2430	2565	2701	2836	56
4	2971	3107	3242	3377	3512	3647	55
5	3782	3918	4053	4188	4322	4457	54
6	4592	4727	4862	4996	5131	5266	53
7	5400	5535	5669	5804	5938	6073	52
8	6207	6342	6476	6610	6744	6878	51
9	7013	7147	7281	7415	7549	7683	50
10	7817	7950	8084	8218	8352	8485	49
11	8619	8753	8886	9020	9153	9287	48
12	9420	9554	9687	9820	9954	..87	47
13	9.210220	0353	0486	0619	0752	0885	46
14	1018	1151	1284	1417	1550	1683	45
15	1815	1948	2081	2213	2346	2478	44
16	2611	2743	2876	3008	3141	3273	43
17	3405	3537	3670	3802	3934	4066	42
18	4198	4330	4462	4594	4726	4858	41
19	4989	5121	5253	5385	5516	5648	40
20	5780	5911	6043	6174	6305	6437	39
21	6568	6700	6831	6962	7093	7225	38
22	7356	7487	7618	7749	7880	8011	37
23	8142	8273	8403	8534	8665	8796	36
24	8926	9057	9188	9318	9449	9579	35
25	9710	9840	9971	.101	.231	.361	34
26	9.220492	0622	0752	0882	1012	1142	33
27	1272	1402	1532	1662	1792	1922	32
28	2052	2182	2311	2441	2571	2700	31
29	2830	2959	3089	3218	3348	3477	30
30	3607	3736	3865	3994	4124	4253	29
31	4382	4511	4640	4769	4898	5027	28
32	5156	5285	5414	5543	5671	5800	27
33	5929	6058	6186	6315	6443	6572	26
34	6700	6829	6957	7086	7214	7342	25
35	7471	7599	7727	7855	7983	8111	24
36	8239	8368	8496	8623	8751	8879	23
37	9007	9135	9263	9390	9518	9646	22
38	9773	9901	..29	.156	.284	.411	21
39	9.230539	0666	0793	0921	1048	1175	20
40	1302	1430	1557	1684	1811	1938	19
41	2065	2192	2319	2446	2573	2699	18
42	2826	2953	3080	3206	3333	3460	17
43	3586	3713	3839	3966	4092	4219	16
44	4345	4471	4598	4724	4850	4976	15
45	5103	5229	5355	5481	5607	5733	14
46	5859	5985	6111	6237	6362	6488	13
47	6614	6740	6865	6991	7117	7242	12
48	7368	7493	7619	7744	7870	7995	11
49	8120	8246	8371	8496	8621	8747	10
50	8872	8997	9122	9247	9372	9497	9
51	9622	9747	9872	9996	.121	.246	8
52	9.240371	0495	0620	0745	0869	0994	7
53	1118	1243	1367	1492	1616	1741	6
54	1865	1989	2114	2238	2362	2486	5
55	2610	2734	2858	2982	3106	3230	4
56	3354	3478	3602	3726	3850	3974	3
57	4097	4221	4345	4468	4592	4715	2
58	4839	4962	5086	5209	5333	5456	1
59	5579	5703	5826	5949	6072	6196	0
	60″	50″	40″	30″	20″	10″	Min.

Co-tangent of 80 Degrees.

P. Part { 1″ 2″ 3″ 4″ 5″ 6″ 7″ 8″ 9″
{ 13 26 39 52 65 78 91 103 116

Sine of 10 Degrees.

Min.	0″	10″	20″	30″	40″	50′	
0	9.239670	9790	9909	..28	.148	.267	59
1	9.240386	0505	0624	0744	0863	0982	58
2	1101	1220	1339	1458	1576	1695	57
3	1814	1933	2052	2170	2289	2408	56
4	2526	2645	2763	2882	3001	3119	55
5	3237	3356	3474	3592	3711	3829	54
6	3947	4065	4184	4302	4420	4538	53
7	4656	4774	4892	5010	5128	5245	52
8	5363	5481	5599	5717	5834	5952	51
9	6069	6187	6305	6422	6540	6657	50
10	6775	6892	7009	7127	7244	7361	49
11	7478	7596	7713	7830	7947	8064	48
12	8181	8298	8415	8532	8649	8766	47
13	8883	8999	9116	9233	9350	9466	46
14	9583	9700	9816	9933	..49	.166	45
15	9.250282	0399	0515	0631	0748	0864	44
16	0980	1097	1213	1329	1445	1561	43
17	1677	1793	1909	2025	2141	2257	42
18	2373	2489	2605	2720	2836	2952	41
19	3067	3183	3299	3414	3530	3645	40
20	3761	3876	3992	4107	4223	4338	39
21	4453	4568	4684	4799	4914	5029	38
22	5144	5259	5374	5490	5604	5719	37
23	5834	5949	6064	6179	6294	6409	36
24	6523	6638	6753	6867	6982	7096	35
25	7211	7326	7440	7554	7669	7783	34
26	7898	8012	8126	8241	8355	8469	33
27	8583	8697	8811	8926	9040	9154	32
28	9268	9382	9495	9609	9723	9837	31
29	9951	..65	.178	.292	.406	.519	30
30	9.260633	0747	0860	0974	1087	1201	29
31	1314	1428	1541	1654	1768	1881	28
32	1994	2107	2220	2334	2447	2560	27
33	2673	2786	2899	3012	3125	3238	26
34	3351	3464	3576	3689	3802	3915	25
35	4027	4140	4253	4365	4478	4590	24
36	4703	4815	4928	5040	5153	5265	23
37	5377	5490	5602	5714	5827	5939	22
38	6051	6163	6275	6387	6499	6611	21
39	6723	6835	6947	7059	7171	7283	20
40	7395	7506	7618	7730	7841	7953	19
41	8065	8176	8288	8399	8511	8622	18
42	8734	8845	8957	9068	9179	9291	17
43	9402	9513	9624	9736	9847	9958	16
44	9.270069	0180	0291	0402	0513	0624	15
45	0735	0846	0957	1067	1178	1289	14
46	1400	1510	1621	1732	1842	1953	13
47	2064	2174	2285	2395	2505	2616	12
48	2726	2837	2947	3057	3168	3278	11
49	3388	3498	3608	3718	3829	3939	10
50	4049	4159	4269	4379	4489	4598	9
51	4708	4818	4928	5038	5148	5257	8
52	5367	5477	5586	5696	5805	5915	7
53	6025	6134	6243	6353	6462	6572	6
54	6681	6790	6900	7009	7118	7227	5
55	7337	7446	7555	7664	7773	7882	4
56	7991	8100	8209	8318	8427	8536	3
57	8645	8753	8862	8971	9080	9188	2
58	9297	9406	9514	9623	9731	9840	1
59	9948	..57	.165	.274	.382	.491	0
	60″	50″	40″	30″	20″	10″	Min.

Co-sine of 79 Degrees.

P. Part	1″	2″	3″	4″	5″	6″	7″	8″	9″
	11	23	34	45	57	68	80	91	102

Sine of 11 Degrees.

Min.	0″	10″	20″	30″	40″	50″	
0	9.280599	0707	0815	0924	1032	1140	59
1	1248	1356	1465	1573	1681	1789	58
2	1897	2005	2113	2220	2328	2436	57
3	2544	2652	2760	2867	2975	3083	56
4	3190	3298	3406	3513	3621	3728	55
5	3836	3943	4051	4158	4266	4373	54
6	4480	4588	4695	4802	4909	5017	53
7	5124	5231	5338	5445	5552	5659	52
8	5766	5873	5980	6087	6194	6301	51
9	6408	6514	6621	6728	6835	6941	50
10	7048	7155	7261	7368	7474	7581	49
11	7688	7794	7900	8007	8113	8220	48
12	8326	8432	8539	8645	8751	8857	47
13	8964	9070	9176	9282	9388	9494	46
14	9600	9706	9812	9918	..24	.130	45
15	9.290236	0342	0447	0553	0659	0765	44
16	0870	0976	1082	1187	1293	1398	43
17	1504	1610	1715	1820	1926	2031	42
18	2137	2242	2347	2453	2558	2663	41
19	2768	2874	2979	3084	3189	3294	40
20	3399	3504	3609	3714	3819	3924	39
21	4029	4134	4239	4344	4448	4553	38
22	4658	4763	4867	4972	5077	5181	37
23	5286	5391	5495	5600	5704	5809	36
24	5913	6017	6122	6226	6330	6435	35
25	6539	6643	6747	6852	6956	7060	34
26	7164	7268	7372	7476	7580	7684	33
27	7788	7892	7996	8100	8204	8308	32
28	8412	8515	8619	8723	8827	8930	31
29	9034	9138	9241	9345	9448	9552	30
30	9655	9759	9862	9966	..69	.172	29
31	9.300276	0379	0482	0586	0689	0792	28
32	0895	0999	1102	1205	1308	1411	27
33	1514	1617	1720	1823	1926	2029	26
34	2132	2235	2337	2440	2543	2646	25
35	2748	2851	2954	3057	3159	3262	24
36	3364	3467	3569	3672	3774	3877	23
37	3979	4082	4184	4287	4389	4491	22
38	4593	4696	4798	4900	5002	5104	21
39	5207	5309	5411	5513	5615	5717	20
40	5819	5921	6023	6125	6227	6328	19
41	6430	6532	6634	6736	6837	6939	18
42	7041	7142	7244	7346	7447	7549	17
43	7650	7752	7853	7955	8056	8158	16
44	8259	8360	8462	8563	8664	8766	15
45	8867	8968	9069	9170	9272	9373	14
46	9474	9575	9676	9777	9878	9979	13
47	9.310080	0181	0282	0382	0483	0584	12
48	0685	0786	0886	0987	1088	1189	11
49	1289	1390	1490	1591	1692	1792	10
50	1893	1993	2094	2194	2294	2395	9
51	2495	2595	2696	2796	2896	2997	8
52	3097	3197	3297	3397	3497	3597	7
53	3698	3798	3898	3998	4098	4198	6
54	4297	4397	4497	4597	4697	4797	5
55	4897	4996	5096	5196	5295	5395	4
56	5495	5594	5694	5793	5893	5993	3
57	6092	6192	6291	6390	6490	6589	2
58	6689	6788	6887	6986	7086	7185	1
59	7284	7383	7482	7582	7681	7780	0
	60″	50″	40″	30″	20″	10″	Min.

Co-sine of 78 Degrees

P. Part	1″	2″	3″	4″	5″	6″	7″	8″	9″
	10	21	31	41	52	62	72	83	93

Min.	Tangent of 10 Degrees. 0″	10″	20″	30″	40″	50″	
0	9.246319	6442	6565	6688	6811	6934	59
1	7057	7180	7303	7426	7548	7671	58
2	7794	7917	8039	8162	8285	8407	57
3	8530	8652	8775	8897	9020	9142	56
4	9264	9387	9509	9631	9753	9876	55
5	9998	.120	.242	.364	.486	.608	54
6	9.250730	0852	0974	1096	1218	1339	53
7	1461	1583	1705	1826	1948	2070	52
8	2191	2313	2434	2556	2677	2799	51
9	2920	3041	3163	3284	3405	3527	50
10	3648	3769	3890	4011	4132	4253	49
11	4374	4495	4616	4737	4858	4979	48
12	5100	5221	5341	5462	5583	5703	47
13	5824	5945	6065	6186	6306	6427	46
14	6547	6668	6788	6908	7029	7149	45
15	7269	7389	7510	7630	7750	7870	44
16	7990	8110	8230	8350	8470	8590	43
17	8710	8830	8950	9069	9189	9309	42
18	9429	9548	9668	9787	9907	..27	41
19	9.260146	0266	0385	0504	0624	0743	40
20	0863	0982	1101	1220	1340	1459	39
21	1578	1697	1816	1935	2054	2173	38
22	2292	2411	2530	2649	2768	2887	37
23	3005	3124	3243	3361	3480	3599	36
24	3717	3836	3954	4073	4191	4310	35
25	4428	4547	4665	4783	4902	5020	34
26	5138	5256	5375	5493	5611	5729	33
27	5847	5965	6083	6201	6319	6437	32
28	6555	6673	6790	6908	7026	7144	31
29	7261	7379	7497	7614	7732	7849	30
30	7967	8084	8202	8319	8437	8554	29
31	8671	8789	8906	9023	9140	9258	28
32	9375	9492	9609	9726	9843	9960	27
33	9.270077	0194	0311	0428	0545	0662	26
34	0779	0895	1012	1129	1246	1362	25
35	1479	1595	1712	1829	1945	2062	24
36	2178	2294	2411	2527	2644	2760	23
37	2876	2992	3109	3225	3341	3457	22
38	3573	3689	3805	3921	4037	4153	21
39	4269	4385	4501	4617	4733	4849	20
40	4964	5080	5196	5312	5427	5543	19
41	5658	5774	5890	6005	6121	6236	18
42	6351	6467	6582	6698	6813	6928	17
43	7043	7159	7274	7389	7504	7619	16
44	7734	7849	7964	8079	8194	8309	15
45	8424	8539	8654	8769	8884	8998	14
46	9113	9228	9342	9457	9572	9686	13
47	9801	9915	..30	.144	.259	.373	12
48	9.280488	0602	0717	0831	0945	1059	11
49	1174	1288	1402	1516	1630	1744	10
50	1858	1973	2087	2201	2314	2428	9
51	2542	2656	2770	2884	2998	3111	8
52	3225	3339	3453	3566	3680	3793	7
53	3907	4021	4134	4248	4361	4474	6
54	4588	4701	4815	4928	5041	5154	5
55	5268	5381	5494	5607	5720	5833	4
56	5947	6060	6173	6286	6399	6512	3
57	6624	6737	6850	6963	7076	7189	2
58	7301	7414	7527	7639	7752	7865	1
59	7977	8090	8202	8315	8427	8540	0
	60″	50″	40″	30″	20″	10″	Min.
	Co-tangent of 79 Degrees.						

P. Part { 1″ 2″ 3″ 4″ 5″ 6″ 7″ 8″ 9″ / 12 23 35 47 59 70 82 94 106 }

Min.	Tangent of 11 Degrees. 0″	10″	20″	30″	40″	50″	
0	9.288652	8765	8877	8989	9102	9214	59
1	9326	9438	9551	9663	9775	9887	58
2	9999	.111	.223	.335	.447	.559	57
3	9.290671	0783	0895	1007	1119	1231	56
4	1342	1454	1566	1678	1789	1901	55
5	2013	2124	2236	2347	2459	2570	54
6	2682	2793	2905	3016	3127	3239	53
7	3350	3461	3572	3684	3795	3906	52
8	4017	4128	4239	4351	4462	4573	51
9	4684	4795	4905	5016	5127	5238	50
10	5349	5460	5571	5681	5792	5903	49
11	6013	6124	6235	6345	6456	6566	48
12	6677	6787	6898	7008	7119	7229	47
13	7339	7450	7560	7670	7781	7891	46
14	8001	8111	8221	8332	8442	8552	45
15	8662	8772	8882	8992	9102	9212	44
16	9322	9431	9541	9651	9761	9871	43
17	9980	..90	.200	.309	.419	.529	42
18	9.300638	0748	0857	0967	1076	1186	41
19	1295	1405	1514	1624	1733	1842	40
20	1951	2061	2170	2279	2388	2497	39
21	2607	2716	2825	2934	3043	3152	38
22	3261	3370	3479	3588	3697	3805	37
23	3914	4023	4132	4241	4349	4458	36
24	4567	4675	4784	4893	5001	5110	35
25	5218	5327	5435	5544	5652	5761	34
26	5869	5977	6086	6194	6302	6410	33
27	6519	6627	6735	6843	6951	7059	32
28	7168	7276	7384	7492	7600	7708	31
29	7816	7923	8031	8139	8247	8355	30
30	8463	8570	8678	8786	8893	9001	29
31	9109	9216	9324	9432	9539	9647	28
32	9754	9862	9969	..76	.184	.291	27
33	9.310399	0506	0613	0720	0828	0935	26
34	1042	1149	1256	1364	1471	1578	25
35	1685	1792	1899	2006	2113	2220	24
36	2327	2433	2540	2647	2754	2861	23
37	2968	3074	3181	3288	3394	3501	22
38	3608	3714	3821	3927	4034	4140	21
39	4247	4353	4460	4566	4672	4779	20
40	4885	4991	5098	5204	5310	5416	19
41	5523	5629	5735	5841	5947	6053	18
42	6159	6265	6371	6477	6583	6689	17
43	6795	6901	7007	7113	7218	7324	16
44	7430	7536	7641	7747	7853	7958	15
45	8064	8170	8275	8381	8486	8592	14
46	8697	8803	8908	9013	9119	9224	13
47	9330	9435	9540	9645	9751	9856	12
48	9961	..66	.171	.277	.382	.487	11
49	9.320592	0697	0802	0907	1012	1117	10
50	1222	1326	1431	1536	1641	1746	9
51	1851	1955	2060	2165	2269	2374	8
52	2479	2583	2688	2793	2897	3002	
53	3106	3211	3315	3420	3524	3628	6
54	3733	3837	3941	4046	4150	4254	5
55	4358	4463	4567	4671	4775	4879	4
56	4983	5087	5191	5295	5399	5503	3
57	5607	5711	5815	5919	6023	6127	2
58	6231	6334	6438	6542	6646	6749	1
59	6853	6957	7060	7164	7267	7371	0
	60″	50″	40″	30″	20″	10″	Min.
	Co-tangent of 78 Degrees.						

P. Part { 1″ 2″ 3″ 4″ 5″ 6″ 7″ 8″ 9″ / 11 22 32 43 54 65 75 86 97 }

Min.	Sine of 12 Degrees. 0″	10″	20″	30″	40″	50″	
0	9.317879	7978	8077	8176	8275	8374	59
1	8473	8572	8671	8769	8868	8967	58
2	9066	9165	9263	9362	9461	9559	57
3	9658	9757	9855	9954	..52	.151	56
4	9.320249	0348	0446	0545	0643	0742	55
5	0840	0938	1037	1135	1233	1332	54
6	1430	1528	1626	1724	1822	1921	53
7	2019	2117	2215	2313	2411	2509	52
8	2607	2705	2802	2900	2998	3096	51
9	3194	3292	3389	3487	3585	3683	50
10	9.323780	3878	3975	4073	4171	4268	49
11	4366	4463	4561	4658	4756	4853	48
12	4950	5048	5145	5243	5340	5437	47
13	5534	5632	5729	5826	5923	6020	46
14	6117	6215	6312	6409	6506	6603	45
15	6700	6797	6894	6991	7087	7184	44
16	7281	7378	7475	7572	7668	7765	43
17	7862	7958	8055	8152	8248	8345	42
18	8442	8538	8635	8731	8828	8924	41
19	9021	9117	9213	9310	9406	9502	40
20	9.329599	9695	9791	9888	9984	..80	39
21	9.330176	0272	0368	0465	0561	0657	38
22	0753	0849	0945	1041	1137	1233	37
23	1329	1424	1520	1616	1712	1808	36
24	1903	1999	2095	2191	2286	2382	35
25	2478	2573	2669	2764	2860	2956	34
26	3051	3147	3242	3337	3433	3528	33
27	3624	3719	3814	3910	4005	4100	32
28	4195	4291	4386	4481	4576	4671	31
29	4767	4862	4957	5052	5147	5242	30
30	9.335337	5432	5527	5622	5716	5811	29
31	5906	6001	6096	6191	6285	6380	28
32	6475	6570	6664	6759	6854	6948	27
33	7043	7137	7232	7326	7421	7515	26
34	7610	7704	7799	7893	7988	8082	25
35	8176	8271	8365	8459	8553	8648	24
36	8742	8836	8930	9024	9118	9212	23
37	9307	9401	9495	9589	9683	9777	22
38	9871	9964	..58	.152	.246	.340	21
39	9.340434	0528	0621	0715	0809	0903	20
40	9.340996	1090	1184	1277	1371	1464	19
41	1558	1652	1745	1839	1932	2026	18
42	2119	2212	2306	2399	2493	2586	17
43	2679	2772	2866	2959	3052	3145	16
44	3239	3332	3425	3518	3611	3704	15
45	3797	3890	3983	4076	4169	4262	14
46	4355	4448	4541	4634	4727	4820	13
47	4912	5005	5098	5191	5283	5376	12
48	5469	5561	5654	5747	5839	5932	11
49	6024	6117	6210	6302	6395	6487	10
50	9.346579	6672	6764	6857	6949	7041	9
51	7134	7226	7318	7410	7503	7595	8
52	7687	7779	7871	7963	8056	8148	7
53	8240	8332	8424	8516	8608	8700	6
54	8792	8884	8976	9067	9159	9251	5
55	9343	9435	9526	9618	9710	9802	4
56	9893	9985	..77	.168	.260	.352	3
57	9.350443	0535	0626	0718	0809	0901	2
58	0992	1084	1175	1266	1358	1449	1
59	1540	1632	1723	1814	1906	1997	0
	60″ Co-sine of 77 Degrees.	50″	40″	30″	20″	10″	Min.

P. Part { 1″ 2″ 3″ 4″ 5″ 6″ 7″ 8″ 9″ / 9 19 28 38 47 57 66 76 85 }

Min.	Sine of 13 Degrees. 0″	10″	20″	30″	40″	50″	
0	9.352088	2179	2270	2362	2453	2544	59
1	2635	2726	2817	2908	2999	3090	58
2	3181	3272	3363	3454	3545	3636	57
3	3726	3817	3908	3999	4090	4180	56
4	4271	4362	4452	4543	4634	4724	55
5	4815	4906	4996	5087	5177	5268	54
6	5358	5449	5539	5630	5720	5810	53
7	5901	5991	6081	6172	6262	6352	52
8	6443	6533	6623	6713	6803	6894	51
9	6984	7074	7164	7254	7344	7434	50
10	9.357524	7614	7704	7794	7884	7974	49
11	8064	8154	8243	8333	8423	8513	48
12	8603	8692	8782	8872	8962	9051	47
13	9141	9231	9320	9410	9499	9589	46
14	9678	9768	9858	9947	..36	.126	45
15	9.360215	0305	0394	0484	0573	0662	44
16	0752	0841	0930	1019	1109	1198	43
17	1287	1376	1465	1554	1644	1733	42
18	1822	1911	2000	2089	2178	2267	41
19	2356	2445	2534	2623	2711	2800	40
20	9.362889	2978	3067	3156	3244	3333	39
21	3422	3511	3599	3688	3777	3865	38
22	3954	4042	4131	4220	4308	4397	37
23	4485	4574	4662	4751	4839	4927	36
24	5016	5104	5193	5281	5369	5457	35
25	5546	5634	5722	5810	5899	5987	34
26	6075	6163	6251	6339	6427	6516	33
27	6604	6692	6780	6868	6956	7044	32
28	7131	7219	7307	7395	7483	7571	31
29	7659	7747	7834	7922	8010	8098	30
30	9.368185	8273	8361	8448	8536	8624	29
31	8711	8799	8886	8974	9061	9149	28
32	9236	9324	9411	9499	9586	9673	27
33	9761	9848	9936	..23	.110	.197	26
34	9.370285	0372	0459	0546	0634	0721	25
35	0808	0895	0982	1069	1156	1243	24
36	1330	1417	1504	1591	1678	1765	23
37	1852	1939	2026	2113	2200	2287	22
38	2373	2460	2547	2634	2721	2807	21
39	2894	2981	3067	3154	3241	3327	20
40	9.373414	3500	3587	3674	3760	3847	19
41	3933	4020	4106	4192	4279	4365	18
42	4452	4538	4624	4711	4797	4883	17
43	4970	5056	5142	5228	5314	5401	16
44	5487	5573	5659	5745	5831	5917	15
45	6003	6089	6175	6261	6347	6433	14
46	6519	6605	6691	6777	6863	6949	13
47	7035	7120	7206	7292	7378	7464	12
48	7549	7635	7721	7806	7892	7978	11
49	8063	8149	8235	8320	8406	8491	10
50	9.378577	8662	8748	8833	8919	9004	9
51	9089	9175	9260	9346	9431	9516	8
52	9601	9687	9772	9857	9942	..28	7
53	9.380113	0198	0283	0368	0454	0539	6
54	0624	0709	0794	0879	0964	1049	5
55	1134	1219	1304	1389	1474	1559	4
56	1643	1728	1813	1898	1983	2068	3
57	2152	2237	2322	2406	2491	2576	2
58	2661	2745	2830	2914	2999	3084	1
59	3168	3253	3337	3422	3506	3591	0
	60″ Co-sine of 76 Degrees.	50″	40″	30″	20″	10″	Min.

P. Part { 1″ 2″ 3″ 4″ 5″ 6″ 7″ 8″ 9″ / 9 18 26 35 44 53 61 70 79 }

Min.	Tangent of 12 Degrees. 0″	10″	20″	30″	40″	50″	
0	9.327475	7578	7682	7785	7888	7992	59
1	8095	8199	8302	8405	8509	8612	58
2	8715	8819	8922	9025	9128	9231	57
3	9334	9438	9541	9644	9747	9850	56
4	9953	..56	.159	.262	.365	.468	55
5	9.330570	0673	0776	0879	0982	1084	54
6	1187	1290	1393	1495	1598	1701	53
7	1803	1906	2008	2111	2213	2316	52
8	2418	2521	2623	2726	2828	2930	51
9	3033	3135	3237	3340	3442	3544	50
10	9.333646	3748	3851	3953	4055	4157	49
11	4259	4361	4463	4565	4667	4769	48
12	4871	4973	5075	5177	5279	5380	47
13	5482	5584	5686	5788	5889	5991	46
14	6093	6194	6296	6398	6499	6601	45
15	6702	6804	6905	7007	7108	7210	44
16	7311	7413	7514	7615	7717	7818	43
17	7919	8021	8122	8223	8324	8426	42
18	8527	8628	8729	8830	8931	9032	41
19	9133	9234	9335	9436	9537	9638	40
20	9.339739	9840	9941	..42	.143	.243	39
21	9.340344	0445	0546	0646	0747	0848	38
22	0948	1049	1150	1250	1351	1451	37
23	1552	1652	1753	1853	1954	2054	36
24	2155	2255	2355	2456	2556	2656	35
25	2757	2857	2957	3057	3158	3258	34
26	3358	3458	3558	3658	3758	3858	33
27	3958	4058	4158	4258	4358	4458	32
28	4558	4658	4758	4858	4957	5057	31
29	5157	5257	5357	5456	5556	5656	30
30	9.345755	5855	5954	6054	6154	6253	29
31	6353	6452	6552	6651	6751	6850	28
32	6949	7049	7148	7248	7347	7446	27
33	7545	7645	7744	7843	7942	8042	26
34	8141	8240	8339	8438	8537	8636	25
35	8735	8834	8933	9032	9131	9230	24
36	9329	9428	9527	9626	9724	9823	23
37	9922	..21	.120	.218	.317	.416	22
38	9.350514	0613	0712	0810	0909	1007	21
39	1106	1204	1303	1401	1500	1598	20
40	9.351697	1795	1894	1992	2090	2189	19
41	2287	2385	2483	2582	2680	2778	18
42	2876	2974	3073	3171	3269	3367	17
43	3465	3563	3661	3759	3857	3955	16
44	4053	4151	4249	4347	4445	4542	15
45	4640	4738	4836	4934	5031	5129	14
46	5227	5324	5422	5520	5617	5715	13
47	5813	5910	6008	6105	6203	6300	12
48	6398	6495	6593	6690	6787	6885	11
49	6982	7079	7177	7274	7371	7469	10
50	9.357566	7663	7760	7857	7954	8052	9
51	8149	8246	8343	8440	8537	8634	8
52	8731	8828	8925	9022	9119	9216	7
53	9313	9409	9506	9603	9700	9797	6
54	9893	9990	..87	.184	.280	.377	5
55	9.360474	0570	0667	0763	0860	0957	4
56	1053	1150	1246	1343	1439	1535	3
57	1632	1728	1825	1921	2017	2114	2
58	2210	2306	2403	2499	2595	2691	1
59	2787	2884	2980	3076	3172	3268	0
	60″	50″	40″	30″	20″	10″	Min.
	Co-tangent of 77 Degrees.						

P. Part	1″	2″	3″	4″	5″	6″	7″	8″	9″
	10	20	30	40	50	60	70	80	90

Min.	Tangent of 13 Degrees. 0″	10″	20″	30″	40″	50″	
0	9.363364	3460	3556	3652	3748	3844	59
1	3940	4036	4132	4228	4324	4420	58
2	4515	4611	4707	4803	4899	4994	57
3	5090	5186	5282	5377	5473	5568	56
4	5664	5760	5855	5951	6046	6142	55
5	6237	6333	6428	6524	6619	6715	54
6	6810	6905	7001	7096	7191	7287	53
7	7382	7477	7572	7668	7763	7858	52
8	7953	8048	8143	8239	8334	8429	51
9	8524	8619	8714	8809	8904	8999	50
10	9.369094	9189	9284	9378	9473	9568	49
11	9663	9758	9853	9947	..42	.137	48
12	9.370232	0326	0421	0516	0610	0705	47
13	0799	0894	0989	1083	1178	1272	46
14	1367	1461	1556	1650	1744	1839	45
15	1933	2028	2122	2216	2311	2405	44
16	2499	2593	2688	2782	2876	2970	43
17	3064	3159	3253	3347	3441	3535	42
18	3629	3723	3817	3911	4005	4099	41
19	4193	4287	4381	4475	4569	4662	40
20	9.374756	4850	4944	5038	5131	5225	39
21	5319	5413	5506	5600	5694	5787	38
22	5881	5975	6068	6162	6255	6349	37
23	6442	6536	6629	6723	6816	6910	36
24	7003	7096	7190	7283	7376	7470	35
25	7563	7656	7750	7843	7936	8029	34
26	8122	8216	8309	8402	8495	8588	33
27	8681	8774	8867	8960	9053	9146	32
28	9239	9332	9425	9518	9611	9704	31
29	9797	9890	9983	..75	.168	.261	30
30	9.380354	0446	0539	0632	0725	0817	29
31	0910	1003	1095	1188	1280	1373	28
32	1466	1558	1651	1743	1836	1928	27
33	2020	2113	2205	2298	2390	2482	26
34	2575	2667	2759	2852	2944	3036	25
35	3129	3221	3313	3405	3497	3589	24
36	3682	3774	3866	3958	4050	4142	23
37	4234	4326	4418	4510	4602	4694	22
38	4786	4878	4970	5062	5153	5245	21
39	5337	5429	5521	5612	5704	5796	20
40	9 385888	5979	6071	6163	6254	6346	19
41	6438	6529	6621	6712	6804	6895	18
42	6987	7078	7170	7261	7353	7444	17
43	7536	7627	7718	7810	7901	7992	16
44	8084	8175	8266	8358	8449	8540	15
45	8631	8722	8814	8905	8996	9087	14
46	9178	9269	9360	9451	9542	9633	13
47	9724	9815	9906	9997	..88	.179	12
48	9.390270	0361	0452	0543	0633	0724	11
49	0815	0906	0997	1087	1178	1269	10
50	9.391360	1450	1541	1632	1722	1813	9
51	1903	1994	2085	2175	2266	2356	8
52	2447	2537	2628	2718	2808	2899	7
53	2989	3080	3170	3260	3351	3441	6
54	3531	3622	3712	3802	3892	3983	5
55	4073	4163	4253	4343	4433	4523	4
56	4614	4704	4794	4884	4974	5064	3
57	5154	5244	5334	5424	5514	5604	2
58	5694	5783	5873	5963	6053	6143	1
59	6233	6322	6412	6502	6592	6681	0
	60″	50″	40″	30″	20″	10″	Min.
	Co-tangent of 76 Degrees.						

P. Part	1″	2″	3″	4″	5″	6″	7″	8″	9″
	9	19	28	37	46	56	65	74	83

Min.	Sine of 14 Degrees. 0″	10″	20″	30″	40″	50″	
0	9.383675	3760	3844	3928	4013	4097	59
1	4182	4266	4350	4435	4519	4603	58
2	4687	4772	4856	4940	5024	5108	57
3	5192	5277	5361	5445	5529	5613	56
4	5697	5781	5865	5949	6033	6117	55
5	6201	6285	6369	6452	6536	6620	54
6	6704	6788	6872	6955	7039	7123	53
7	7207	7290	7374	7458	7541	7625	52
8	7709	7792	7876	7959	8043	8127	51
9	8210	8294	8377	8461	8544	8627	50
10	9.388711	8794	8878	8961	9044	9128	49
11	9211	9294	9378	9461	9544	9627	48
12	9711	9794	9877	9960	..43	.126	47
13	9.390210	0293	0376	0459	0542	0625	46
14	0708	0791	0874	0957	1040	1123	45
15	1206	1289	1371	1454	1537	1620	44
16	1703	1786	1868	1951	2034	2117	43
17	2199	2282	2365	2447	2530	2613	42
18	2695	2778	2860	2943	3025	3108	41
19	3191	3273	3356	3438	3520	3603	40
20	9.393685	3768	3850	3932	4015	4097	39
21	4179	4262	4344	4426	4508	4591	38
22	4673	4755	4837	4919	5002	5084	37
23	5166	5248	5330	5412	5494	5576	36
24	5658	5740	5822	5904	5986	6068	35
25	6150	6232	6314	6395	6477	6559	34
26	6641	6723	6805	6886	6968	7050	33
27	7132	7213	7295	7377	7458	7540	32
28	7621	7703	7785	7866	7948	8029	31
29	8111	8192	8274	8355	8437	8518	30
30	9.398600	8681	8762	8844	8925	9007	29
31	9088	9169	9250	9332	9413	9494	28
32	9575	9657	9738	9819	9900	9981	27
33	9.400062	0144	0225	0306	0387	0468	26
34	0549	0630	0711	0792	0873	0954	25
35	1035	1116	1197	1277	1358	1439	24
36	1520	1601	1682	1762	1843	1924	23
37	2005	2085	2166	2247	2328	2408	22
38	2489	2570	2650	2731	2811	2892	21
39	2972	3053	3133	3214	3294	3375	20
40	9.403455	3536	3616	3697	3777	3857	19
41	3938	4018	4098	4179	4259	4339	18
42	4420	4500	4580	4660	4741	4821	17
43	4901	4981	5061	5141	5221	5302	16
44	5382	5462	5542	5622	5702	5782	15
45	5862	5942	6022	6102	6181	6261	14
46	6341	6421	6501	6581	6661	6740	13
47	6820	6900	6980	7060	7139	7219	12
48	7299	7378	7458	7538	7617	7697	11
49	7777	7856	7936	8015	8095	8174	10
50	9.408254	8333	8413	8492	8572	8651	9
51	8731	8810	8889	8969	9048	9127	8
52	9207	9286	9365	9445	9524	9603	7
53	9682	9762	9841	9920	9999	..78	6
54	9.410157	0237	0316	0395	0474	0553	5
55	0632	0711	0790	0869	0948	1027	4
56	1106	1185	1264	1343	1422	1500	3
57	1579	1658	1737	1816	1895	1973	2
58	2052	2131	2210	2288	2367	2446	1
59	2524	2603	2682	2760	2839	2918	0
	60″	50″	40″	30″	20″	10″	Min.
	Co-sine of 75 Degrees.						

P. Part	1″	2″	3″	4″	5″	6″	7″	8″	9″
	8	16	24	33	41	49	57	65	73

Min.	Sine of 15 Degrees. 0″	10″	20″	30″	40″	50″	
0	9.412996	3075	3153	3232	3310	3389	59
1	3467	3546	3624	3703	3781	3860	58
2	3938	4016	4095	4173	4252	4330	57
3	4408	4486	4565	4643	4721	4800	56
4	4878	4956	5034	5112	5190	5269	55
5	5347	5425	5503	5581	5659	5737	54
6	5815	5893	5971	6049	6127	6205	53
7	6283	6361	6439	6517	6595	6673	52
8	6751	6828	6906	6984	7062	7140	51
9	7217	7295	7373	7451	7528	7606	50
10	9.417684	7761	7839	7917	7994	8072	49
11	8150	8227	8305	8382	8460	8537	48
12	8615	8692	8770	8847	8925	9002	47
13	9079	9157	9234	9312	9389	9466	46
14	9544	9621	9698	9776	9853	9930	45
15	9.420007	0085	0162	0239	0316	0393	44
16	0470	0548	0625	0702	0779	0856	43
17	0933	1010	1087	1164	1241	1318	42
18	1395	1472	1549	1626	1703	1780	41
19	1857	1933	2010	2087	2164	2241	40
20	9.422318	2394	2471	2548	2625	2701	39
21	2778	2855	2931	3008	3085	3161	38
22	3238	3315	3391	3468	3544	3621	37
23	3697	3774	3850	3927	4003	4080	36
24	4156	4233	4309	4386	4462	4538	35
25	4615	4691	4767	4844	4920	4996	34
26	5073	5149	5225	5301	5378	5454	33
27	5530	5606	5682	5758	5835	5911	32
28	5987	6063	6139	6215	6291	6367	31
29	6443	6519	6595	6671	6747	6823	30
30	9.426899	6975	7051	7127	7202	7278	29
31	7354	7430	7506	7582	7657	7733	28
32	7809	7885	7960	8036	8112	8187	27
33	8263	8339	8414	8490	8566	8641	26
34	8717	8792	8868	8944	9019	9095	25
35	9170	9246	9321	9397	9472	9547	24
36	9623	9698	9774	9849	9924	....	23
37	9.430075	0150	0226	0301	0376	0451	22
38	0527	0602	0677	0752	0828	0903	21
39	0978	1053	1128	1203	1278	1354	20
40	9.431429	1504	1579	1654	1729	1804	19
41	1879	1954	2029	2104	2179	2254	18
42	2329	2403	2478	2553	2628	2703	17
43	2778	2853	2927	3002	3077	3152	16
44	3226	3301	3376	3451	3525	3600	15
45	3675	3749	3824	3898	3973	4048	14
46	4122	4197	4271	4346	4420	4495	13
47	4569	4644	4718	4793	4867	4942	12
48	5016	5091	5165	5239	5314	5388	11
49	5462	5537	5611	5685	5760	5834	10
50	9.435908	5982	6056	6131	6205	6279	9
51	6353	6427	6502	6576	6650	6724	8
52	6798	6872	6946	7020	7094	7168	7
53	7242	7316	7390	7464	7538	7612	6
54	7686	7760	7834	7908	7981	8055	5
55	8129	8203	8277	8351	8424	8498	4
56	8572	8646	8719	8793	8867	8941	3
57	9014	9088	9162	9235	9309	9382	2
58	9456	9530	9603	9677	9750	9824	1
59	9897	9971	..44	.118	.191	.265	0
	60″	50″	40″	30″	20″	10″	Min.
	Co-sine of 74 Degrees.						

P. Part	1″	2″	3″	4″	5″	6″	7″	8″	9″
	8	15	23	30	38	46	53	61	68

Min.	Tangent of 14 Degrees. 0″	10″	20″	30″	40″	50″	
0	9.396771	6861	6950	7040	7130	7219	59
1	7309	7399	7488	7578	7667	7757	58
2	7846	7936	8025	8115	8204	8294	57
3	8383	8472	8562	8651	8740	8830	56
4	8919	9008	9098	9187	9276	9365	55
5	9455	9544	9633	9722	9811	9900	54
6	9990	..79	.168	.257	.346	.435	53
7	9.400524	0613	0702	0791	0880	0969	52
8	1058	1147	1236	1325	1413	1502	51
9	1591	1680	1769	1857	1946	2035	50
10	9.402124	2212	2301	2390	2478	2567	49
11	2656	2744	2833	2922	3010	3099	48
12	3187	3276	3364	3453	3541	3630	47
13	3718	3807	3895	3983	4072	4160	46
14	4249	4337	4425	4514	4602	4690	45
15	4778	4867	4955	5043	5131	5219	44
16	5308	5396	5484	5572	5660	5748	43
17	5836	5924	6012	6100	6188	6276	42
18	6364	6452	6540	6628	6716	6804	41
19	6892	6980	7068	7155	7243	7331	40
20	9.407419	7507	7594	7682	7770	7858	39
21	7945	8033	8121	8208	8296	8384	38
22	8471	8559	8646	8734	8821	8909	37
23	8996	9084	9171	9259	9346	9434	36
24	9521	9609	9696	9783	9871	9958	35
25	9.410045	0133	0220	0307	0395	0482	34
26	0569	0656	0743	0831	0918	1005	33
27	1092	1179	1266	1353	1441	1528	32
28	1615	1702	1789	1876	1963	2050	31
29	2137	2224	2310	2397	2484	2571	30
30	9.412658	2745	2832	2919	3005	3092	29
31	3179	3266	3352	3439	3526	3613	28
32	3699	3786	3873	3959	4046	4132	27
33	4219	4306	4392	4479	4565	4652	26
34	4738	4825	4911	4998	5084	5171	25
35	5257	5343	5430	5516	5603	5689	24
36	5775	5862	5948	6034	6120	6207	23
37	6293	6379	6465	6551	6638	6724	22
38	6810	6896	6982	7068	7154	7240	21
39	7326	7413	7499	7585	7671	7757	20
40	9.417842	7928	8014	8100	8186	8272	19
41	8358	8444	8530	8616	8701	8787	18
42	8873	8959	9044	9130	9216	9302	17
43	9387	9473	9559	9644	9730	9816	16
44	9901	9987	..72	.158	.244	.329	15
45	9.420415	0500	0586	0671	0757	0842	14
46	0927	1013	1098	1184	1269	1354	13
47	1440	1525	1610	1696	1781	1866	12
48	1952	2037	2122	2207	2292	2378	11
49	2463	2548	2633	2718	2803	2888	10
50	9.422974	3059	3144	3229	3314	3399	9
51	3484	3569	3654	3739	3824	3909	8
52	3993	4078	4163	4248	4333	4418	7
53	4503	4587	4672	4757	4842	4927	6
54	5011	5096	5181	5265	5350	5435	5
55	5519	5604	5689	5773	5858	5942	4
56	6027	6112	6196	6281	6365	6450	3
57	6534	6619	6703	6788	6872	6956	2
58	7041	7125	7210	7294	7378	7463	1
59	7547	7631	7715	7800	7884	7968	0
	60″	50″	40″	30″	20″	10″	Min.
	Co-tangent of 75 Degrees.						

P. Part	1″	2″	3″	4″	5″	6″	7″	8″	9″
	9	17	26	35	43	52	61	69	78

Min.	Tangent of 15 Degrees. 0″	10″	20″	30″	40″	50″	
0	9.428052	8137	8221	8305	8389	8473	59
1	8558	8642	8726	8810	8894	8978	58
2	9062	9146	9230	9314	9398	9482	57
3	9566	9650	9734	9818	9902	9986	56
4	9.430070	0154	0237	0321	0405	0489	55
5	0573	0657	0740	0824	0908	0992	54
6	1075	1159	1243	1326	1410	1494	53
7	1577	1661	1745	1828	1912	1995	52
8	2079	2162	2246	2329	2413	2496	51
9	2580	2663	2747	2830	2914	2997	50
10	9.433080	3164	3247	3331	3414	3497	49
11	3580	3664	3747	3830	3914	3997	48
12	4080	4163	4246	4330	4413	4496	47
13	4579	4662	4745	4828	4912	4995	46
14	5078	5161	5244	5327	5410	5493	45
15	5576	5659	5742	5825	5907	5990	44
16	6073	6156	6239	6322	6405	6488	43
17	6570	6653	6736	6819	6901	6984	42
18	7067	7150	7232	7315	7398	7480	41
19	7563	7646	7728	7811	7894	7976	40
20	9.438059	8141	8224	8306	8389	8471	39
21	8554	8636	8719	8801	8884	8966	38
22	9048	9131	9213	9296	9378	9460	37
23	9543	9625	9707	9790	9872	9954	36
24	9.440036	0119	0201	0283	0365	0447	35
25	0529	0612	0694	0776	0858	0940	34
26	1022	1104	1186	1268	1350	1432	33
27	1514	1596	1678	1760	1842	1924	32
28	2006	2088	2170	2252	2334	2416	31
29	2497	2579	2661	2743	2825	2907	30
30	9.442988	3070	3152	3234	3315	3397	29
31	3479	3560	3642	3724	3805	3887	28
32	3968	4050	4132	4213	4295	4376	27
33	4458	4539	4621	4702	4784	4865	26
34	4947	5028	5110	5191	5272	5354	25
35	5435	5517	5598	5679	5761	5842	24
36	5923	6005	6086	6167	6248	6330	23
37	6411	6492	6573	6654	6735	6817	22
38	6898	6979	7060	7141	7222	7303	21
39	7384	7465	7546	7627	7708	7789	20
40	9.447870	7951	8032	8113	8194	8275	19
41	8356	8437	8518	8599	8680	8760	18
42	8841	8922	9003	9084	9164	9245	17
43	9326	9407	9487	9568	9649	9730	16
44	9810	9891	9972	..52	.133	.213	15
45	9.450294	0375	0455	0536	0616	0697	14
46	0777	0858	0938	1019	1099	1180	13
47	1260	1341	1421	1502	1582	1662	12
48	1743	1823	1903	1984	2064	2144	11
49	2225	2305	2385	2465	2546	2626	10
50	9.452706	2786	2867	2947	3027	3107	9
51	3187	3267	3347	3428	3508	3588	8
52	3668	3748	3828	3908	3988	4068	7
53	4148	4228	4308	4388	4468	4548	6
54	4628	4708	4787	4867	4947	5027	5
55	5107	5187	5267	5346	5426	5506	4
56	5586	5655	5745	5825	5905	5984	3
57	6064	6144	6223	6303	6383	6462	2
58	6542	6622	6701	6781	6860	6940	1
59	7019	7099	7178	7258	7337	7417	0
	60″	50″	40″	30″	20″	10″	Min.
	Co-tangent of 74 Degrees.						

P. Part	1″	2″	3″	4″	5″	6″	7″	8″	9″
	8	16	25	33	41	49	57	65	74

Min.	Sine of 16 Degrees. 0″	10″	20″	30″	40″	50″	
0	9.440338	0411	0485	0558	0632	0705	59
1	0778	0852	0925	0998	1072	1145	58
2	1218	1292	1365	1438	1511	1584	57
3	1658	1731	1804	1877	1950	2023	56
4	2096	2170	2243	2316	2389	2462	55
5	2535	2608	2681	2754	2827	2900	54
6	2973	3046	3119	3192	3265	3337	53
7	3410	3483	3556	3629	3702	3774	52
8	3847	3920	3993	4066	4138	4211	51
9	4284	4356	4429	4502	4574	4647	50
10	9.444720	4792	4865	4938	5010	5083	49
11	5155	5228	5300	5373	5445	5518	48
12	5590	5663	5735	5808	5880	5953	47
13	6025	6097	6170	6242	6314	6387	46
14	6459	6531	6604	6676	6748	6820	45
15	6893	6965	7037	7109	7182	7254	44
16	7326	7398	7470	7542	7614	7687	43
17	7759	7831	7903	7975	8047	8119	42
18	8191	8263	8335	8407	8479	8551	41
19	8623	8695	8767	8838	8910	8982	40
20	9.449054	9126	9198	9269	9341	9413	39
21	9485	9557	9628	9700	9772	9844	38
22	9915	9987	..59	.130	.202	.274	37
23	9.450345	0417	0488	0560	0632	0703	36
24	0775	0846	0918	0989	1061	1132	35
25	1204	1275	1347	1418	1489	1561	34
26	1632	1704	1775	1846	1918	1989	33
27	2060	2132	2203	2274	2345	2417	32
28	2488	2559	2630	2702	2773	2844	31
29	2915	2986	3057	3129	3200	3271	30
30	9.453342	3413	3484	3555	3626	3697	29
31	3768	3839	3910	3981	4052	4123	28
32	4194	4265	4336	4407	4477	4548	27
33	4619	4690	4761	4832	4903	4973	26
34	5044	5115	5186	5256	5327	5398	25
35	5469	5539	5610	5681	5751	5822	24
36	5893	5963	6034	6104	6175	6246	23
37	6316	6387	6457	6528	6598	6669	22
38	6739	6810	6880	6951	7021	7091	21
39	7162	7232	7303	7373	7443	7514	20
40	9.457584	7654	7725	7795	7865	7936	19
41	8006	8076	8146	8217	8287	8357	18
42	8427	8497	8567	8638	8708	8778	17
43	8848	8918	8988	9058	9128	9198	16
44	9268	9338	9408	9478	9548	9618	15
45	9688	9758	9828	9898	9968	..38	14
46	9.460108	0178	0248	0317	0387	0457	13
47	0527	0597	0667	0736	0806	0876	12
48	0946	1015	1085	1155	1224	1294	11
49	1364	1433	1503	1573	1642	1712	10
50	9.461782	1851	1921	1990	2060	2129	9
51	2199	2268	2338	2407	2477	2546	8
52	2616	2685	2755	2824	2894	2963	7
53	3032	3102	3171	3240	3310	3379	6
54	3448	3518	3587	3656	3725	3795	5
55	3864	3933	4002	4072	4141	4210	4
56	4279	4348	4417	4486	4556	4625	3
57	4694	4763	4832	4901	4970	5039	2
58	5108	5177	5246	5315	5384	5453	1
59	5522	5591	5660	5729	5798	5866	0
	60″	50″	40″	30″	20″	10″	Min.
	Co-sine of 73 Degrees.						

P. Part { 1″ 2″ 3″ 4″ 5″ 6″ 7″ 8″ 9″
P. Part { 7 14 21 28 36 43 50 57 64

Min.	Sine of 17 Degrees. 0″	10″	20″	30″	40″	50″	
0	9.465935	6004	6073	6142	6211	6280	59
1	6348	6417	6486	6555	6623	6692	58
2	6761	6830	6898	6967	7036	7104	57
3	7173	7242	7310	7379	7448	7516	56
4	7585	7653	7722	7790	7859	7928	55
5	7996	8065	8133	8202	8270	8338	54
6	8407	8475	8544	8612	8681	8749	53
7	8817	8886	8954	9022	9091	9159	52
8	9227	9296	9364	9432	9500	9569	51
9	9637	9705	9773	9842	9910	9978	50
10	9.470046	0114	0182	0251	0319	0387	49
11	0455	0523	0591	0659	0727	0795	48
12	0863	0931	0999	1067	1135	1203	47
13	1271	1339	1407	1475	1543	1611	46
14	1679	1746	1814	1882	1950	2018	45
15	2086	2153	2221	2289	2357	2424	44
16	2492	2560	2628	2695	2763	2831	43
17	2898	2966	3034	3101	3169	3237	42
18	3304	3372	3439	3507	3575	3642	41
19	3710	3777	3845	3912	3980	4047	40
20	9.474115	4182	4250	4317	4384	4452	39
21	4519	4587	4654	4721	4789	4856	38
22	4923	4991	5058	5125	5193	5260	37
23	5327	5394	5462	5529	5596	5663	36
24	5730	5798	5865	5932	5999	6066	35
25	6133	6200	6268	6335	6402	6469	34
26	6536	6603	6670	6737	6804	6871	33
27	6938	7005	7072	7139	7206	7273	32
28	7340	7407	7473	7540	7607	7674	31
29	7741	7808	7875	7941	8008	8075	30
30	9.478142	8209	8275	8342	8409	8476	29
31	8542	8609	8676	8742	8809	8876	28
32	8942	9009	9076	9142	9209	9275	27
33	9342	9409	9475	9542	9608	9675	26
34	9741	9808	9874	9941	...7	..74	25
35	9.480140	0207	0273	0339	0406	0472	24
36	0539	0605	0671	0738	0804	0870	23
37	0937	1003	1069	1135	1202	1268	22
38	1334	1400	1467	1533	1599	1665	21
39	1731	1798	1864	1930	1996	2062	20
40	9.482128	2194	2261	2327	2393	2459	19
41	2525	2591	2657	2723	2789	2855	18
42	2921	2987	3053	3119	3185	3251	17
43	3316	3382	3448	3514	3580	3646	16
44	3712	3778	3843	3909	3975	4041	15
45	4107	4172	4238	4304	4370	4435	14
46	4501	4567	4632	4698	4764	4829	13
47	4895	4961	5026	5092	5158	5223	12
48	5289	5354	5420	5485	5551	5617	11
49	5682	5748	5813	5879	5944	6009	10
50	9.486075	6140	6206	6271	6337	6402	9
51	6467	6533	6598	6664	6729	6794	8
52	6860	6925	6990	7055	7121	7186	7
53	7251	7316	7382	7447	7512	7577	6
54	7643	7708	7773	7838	7903	7968	5
55	8034	8099	8164	8229	8294	8359	4
56	8424	8489	8554	8619	8684	8749	3
57	8814	8879	8944	9009	9074	9139	2
58	9204	9269	9334	9399	9464	9528	1
59	9593	9658	9723	9788	9853	9918	0
	60″	50″	40″	30″	20″	10″	Min.
	Co-sine of 72 Degrees.						

P. Part { 1″ 2″ 3″ 4″ 5″ 6″ 7″ 8″ 9″
P. Part { 7 13 20 27 33 40 47 53 60

Min.	Tangent of 16 Degrees. 0″	10″	20″	30″	40″	50″	
0	9.457496	7576	7655	7735	7814	7894	59
1	7973	8052	8132	8211	8290	8370	58
2	8449	8528	8608	8687	8766	8846	57
3	8925	9004	9083	9163	9242	9321	56
4	9400	9479	9558	9638	9717	9796	55
5	9875	9954	..33	.112	.191	.270	54
6	9.460349	0428	0507	0586	0665	0744	53
7	0823	0902	0981	1060	1139	1218	52
8	1297	1376	1454	1533	1612	1691	51
9	1770	1849	1927	2006	2085	2164	50
10	9.462242	2321	2400	2478	2557	2636	49
11	2715	2793	2872	2950	3029	3108	48
12	3186	3265	3343	3422	3501	3579	47
13	3658	3736	3815	3893	3972	4050	46
14	4128	4207	4285	4364	4442	4521	45
15	4599	4677	4756	4834	4912	4991	44
16	5069	5147	5226	5304	5382	5460	43
17	5539	5617	5695	5773	5851	5930	42
18	6008	6086	6164	6242	6320	6398	41
19	6477	6555	6633	6711	6789	6867	40
20	9.466945	7023	7101	7179	7257	7335	39
21	7413	7491	7569	7647	7724	7802	38
22	7880	7958	8036	8114	8192	8269	37
23	8347	8425	8503	8581	8658	8736	36
24	8814	8892	8969	9047	9125	9202	35
25	9280	9358	9435	9513	9591	9668	34
26	9746	9823	9901	9979	..56	.134	33
27	9.470211	0289	0366	0444	0521	0599	32
28	0676	0754	0831	0909	0986	1063	31
29	1141	1218	1295	1373	1450	1528	30
30	9.471605	1682	1759	1837	1914	1991	29
31	2069	2146	2223	2300	2377	2455	28
32	2532	2609	2686	2763	2840	2918	27
33	2995	3072	3149	3226	3303	3380	26
34	3457	3534	3611	3688	3765	3842	25
35	3919	3996	4073	4150	4227	4304	24
36	4381	4458	4535	4612	4688	4765	23
37	4842	4919	4996	5073	5149	5226	22
38	5303	5380	5456	5533	5610	5687	21
39	5763	5840	5917	5993	6070	6147	20
40	9.476223	6300	6377	6453	6530	6606	19
41	6683	6759	6836	6913	6989	7066	18
42	7142	7219	7295	7372	7448	7524	17
43	7601	7677	7754	7830	7906	7983	16
44	8059	8136	8212	8288	8365	8441	15
45	8517	8593	8670	8746	8822	8899	14
46	8975	9051	9127	9203	9280	9356	13
47	9432	9508	9584	9660	9737	9813	12
48	9889	9965	..41	.117	.193	.269	11
49	9.480345	0421	0497	0573	0649	0725	10
50	9.480801	0877	0953	1029	1105	1181	9
51	1257	1333	1408	1484	1560	1636	8
52	1712	1788	1863	1939	2015	2091	7
53	2167	2242	2318	2394	2470	2545	6
54	2621	2697	2772	2848	2924	2999	5
55	3075	3151	3226	3302	3377	3453	4
56	3529	3604	3680	3755	3831	3906	3
57	3982	4057	4133	4208	4284	4359	2
58	4435	4510	4585	4661	4736	4812	1
59	4887	4962	5038	5113	5188	5264	0
	60″	50″	40″	30″	20″	10″	Min.
	Co-tangent of 73 Degrees.						

P. Part { 1″ 2″ 3″ 4″ 5″ 6″ 7″ 8″ 9″
{ 8 15 23 31 39 46 54 62 70

Min.	Tangent of 17 Degrees. 0″	10″	20″	30″	40″	50″	
0	9.485339	5414	5490	5565	5640	5715	59
1	5791	5866	5941	6016	6092	6167	58
2	6242	6317	6392	6467	6543	6618	57
3	6693	6768	6843	6918	6993	7068	56
4	7143	7218	7293	7368	7443	7518	55
5	7593	7668	7743	7818	7893	7968	54
6	8043	8118	8193	8268	8343	8418	53
7	8492	8567	8642	8717	8792	8866	52
8	8941	9016	9091	9166	9240	9315	51
9	9390	9465	9539	9614	9689	9763	50
10	9.489838	9913	9987	..62	.137	.211	49
11	9.490286	0360	0435	0510	0584	0659	48
12	0733	0808	0882	0957	1031	1106	47
13	1180	1255	1329	1404	1478	1552	46
14	1627	1701	1776	1850	1924	1999	45
15	2073	2147	2222	2296	2370	2445	44
16	2519	2593	2668	2742	2816	2890	43
17	2965	3039	3113	3187	3261	3336	42
18	3410	3484	3558	3632	3706	3780	41
19	3854	3929	4003	4077	4151	4225	40
20	9.494299	4373	4447	4521	4595	4669	39
21	4743	4817	4891	4965	5039	5113	38
22	5186	5260	5334	5408	5482	5556	37
23	5630	5704	5777	5851	5925	5999	36
24	6073	6146	6220	6294	6368	6441	35
25	6515	6589	6663	6736	6810	6884	34
26	6957	7031	7105	7178	7252	7326	33
27	7399	7473	7546	7620	7693	7767	32
28	7841	7914	7988	8061	8135	8208	31
29	8282	8355	8429	8502	8575	8649	30
30	9.498722	8796	8869	8943	9016	9089	29
31	9163	9236	9309	9383	9456	9529	28
32	9603	9676	9749	9822	9896	9969	27
33	9.500042	0115	0189	0262	0335	0408	26
34	0481	0555	0628	0701	0774	0847	25
35	0920	0993	1066	1140	1213	1286	24
36	1359	1432	1505	1578	1651	1724	23
37	1797	1870	1943	2016	2089	2162	22
38	2235	2308	2381	2453	2526	2599	21
39	2672	2745	2818	2891	2964	3036	20
40	9.503109	3182	3255	3328	3400	3473	19
41	3546	3619	3691	3764	3837	3910	18
42	3982	4055	4128	4200	4273	4346	17
43	4418	4491	4563	4636	4709	4781	16
44	4854	4926	4999	5072	5144	5217	15
45	5289	5362	5434	5507	5579	5652	14
46	5724	5796	5869	5941	6014	6086	13
47	6159	6231	6303	6376	6448	6520	12
48	6593	6665	6737	6810	6882	6954	11
49	7027	7099	7171	7243	7316	7388	10
50	9.507460	7532	7605	7677	7749	7821	9
51	7893	7965	8038	8110	8182	8254	8
52	8326	8398	8470	8542	8614	8687	7
53	8759	8831	8903	8975	9047	9119	6
54	9191	9263	9335	9407	9479	9551	5
55	9622	9694	9766	9838	9910	9982	4
56	9.510054	0126	0198	0269	0341	0413	3
57	0485	0557	0629	0700	0772	0844	2
58	0916	0987	1059	1131	1203	1274	1
59	1346	1418	1489	1561	1633	1704	0
	60″	50″	40″	30″	20″	10″	Min.
	Co-tangent of 72 Degrees.						

P. Part { 1″ 2″ 3″ 4″ 5″ 6″ 7″ 8″ 9″
{ 7 15 22 29 37 44 51 59 66

Min.	Sine of 18 Degrees. 0″	10″	20″	30″	40″	50″	
0	9.489982	..47	.112	.177	.241	.306	59
1	9.490371	0436	0500	0565	0630	0695	58
2	0759	0824	0889	0953	1018	1082	57
3	1147	1212	1276	1341	1405	1470	56
4	1535	1599	1664	1728	1793	1857	55
5	1922	1986	2051	2115	2179	2244	54
6	2308	2373	2437	2502	2566	2630	53
7	2695	2759	2823	2888	2952	3016	52
8	3081	3145	3209	3273	3338	3402	51
9	3466	3530	3595	3659	3723	3787	50
10	9.493851	3915	3980	4044	4108	4172	49
11	4236	4300	4364	4428	4492	4556	48
12	4621	4685	4749	4813	4877	4941	47
13	5005	5069	5133	5196	5260	5324	46
14	5388	5452	5516	5580	5644	5708	45
15	5772	5835	5899	5963	6027	6091	44
16	6154	6218	6282	6346	6410	6473	43
17	6537	6601	6664	6728	6792	6856	42
18	6919	6983	7047	7110	7174	7237	41
19	7301	7365	7428	7492	7555	7619	40
20	9.497682	7746	7810	7873	7937	8000	39
21	8064	8127	8190	8254	8317	8381	38
22	8444	8508	8571	8634	8698	8761	37
23	8825	8888	8951	9015	9078	9141	36
24	9204	9268	9331	9394	9458	9521	35
25	9584	9647	9710	9774	9837	9900	34
26	9963	..26	..90	.153	.216	.279	33
27	9.500342	0405	0468	0531	0594	0658	32
28	0721	0784	0847	0910	0973	1036	31
29	1099	1162	1225	1288	1351	1414	30
30	9.501476	1539	1602	1665	1728	1791	29
31	1854	1917	1980	2042	2105	2168	28
32	2231	2294	2356	2419	2482	2545	27
33	2607	2670	2733	2796	2858	2921	26
34	2984	3046	3109	3172	3234	3297	25
35	3360	3422	3485	3548	3610	3673	24
36	3735	3798	3860	3923	3985	4048	23
37	4110	4173	4235	4298	4360	4423	22
38	4485	4548	4610	4673	4735	4797	21
39	4860	4922	4985	5047	5109	5172	20
40	9.505234	5296	5359	5421	5483	5545	19
41	5608	5670	5732	5794	5857	5919	18
42	5981	6043	6106	6168	6230	6292	17
43	6354	6416	6478	6541	6603	6665	16
44	6727	6789	6851	6913	6975	7037	15
45	7099	7161	7223	7285	7347	7409	14
46	7471	7533	7595	7657	7719	7781	13
47	7843	7905	7967	8028	8090	8152	12
48	8214	8276	8338	8400	8461	8523	11
49	8585	8647	8709	8770	8832	8894	10
50	9.508956	9017	9079	9141	9202	9264	9
51	9326	9387	9449	9511	9572	9634	8
52	9696	9757	9819	9880	9942	...4	7
53	9.510065	0127	0188	0250	0311	0373	6
54	0434	0496	0557	0619	0680	0742	5
55	0803	0865	0926	0987	1049	1110	4
56	1172	1233	1294	1356	1417	1478	3
57	1540	1601	1662	1724	1785	1846	2
58	1907	1969	2030	2091	2152	2214	1
59	2275	2336	2397	2458	2520	2581	0
	60″	50″	40″	30″	20″	10″	Min.
	Co-sine of 71 Degrees.						

P. Part { 1″ 2″ 3″ 4″ 5″ 6″ 7″ 8″ 9″
{ 6 13 19 25 31 38 44 50 57

Min.	Sine of 19 Degrees. 0″	10″	20″	30″	40″	50″	
0	9.512642	2703	2764	2825	2886	2948	59
1	3009	3070	3131	3192	3253	3314	58
2	3375	3436	3497	3558	3619	3680	57
3	3741	3802	3863	3924	3985	4046	56
4	4107	4168	4229	4289	4350	4411	55
5	4472	4533	4594	4655	4715	4776	54
6	4837	4898	4959	5019	5080	5141	53
7	5202	5262	5323	5384	5445	5505	52
8	5566	5627	5687	5748	5809	5869	51
9	5930	5991	6051	6112	6172	6233	50
10	9 516294	6354	6415	6475	6536	6596	49
11	6657	6717	6778	6838	6899	6959	48
12	7020	7080	7141	7201	7262	7322	47
13	7382	7443	7503	7564	7624	7684	46
14	7745	7805	7865	7926	7986	8046	45
15	8107	8167	8227	8287	8348	8408	44
16	8468	8528	8589	8649	8709	8769	43
17	8829	8890	8950	9010	9070	9130	42
18	9190	9250	9311	9371	9431	9491	41
19	9551	9611	9671	9731	9791	9851	40
20	9.519911	9971	..31	..91	.151	.211	39
21	9.520271	0331	0391	0451	0511	0571	38
22	0631	0691	0750	0810	0870	0930	37
23	0990	1050	1110	1169	1229	1289	36
24	1349	1409	1468	1528	1588	1648	35
25	1707	1767	1827	1887	1946	2006	34
26	2066	2125	2185	2245	2304	2364	33
27	2424	2483	2543	2602	2662	2722	32
28	2781	2841	2900	2960	3019	3079	31
29	3138	3198	3257	3317	3376	3436	30
30	9.523495	3555	3614	3674	3733	3792	29
31	3852	3911	3971	4030	4089	4149	28
32	4208	4267	4327	4386	4445	4505	27
33	4564	4623	4683	4742	4801	4860	26
34	4920	4979	5038	5097	5156	5216	25
35	5275	5334	5393	5452	5512	5571	24
36	5630	5689	5748	5807	5866	5925	23
37	5984	6044	6103	6162	6221	6280	22
38	6339	6398	6457	6516	6575	6634	21
39	6693	6752	6811	6870	6928	6987	20
40	9.527046	7105	7164	7223	7282	7341	19
41	7400	7459	7517	7576	7635	7694	18
42	7753	7811	7870	7929	7988	8047	17
43	8105	8164	8223	8282	8340	8399	16
44	8458	8516	8575	8634	8692	8751	15
45	8810	8868	8927	8986	9044	9103	14
46	9161	9220	9279	9337	9396	9454	13
47	9513	9571	9630	9688	9747	9805	12
48	9864	9922	9981	..39	..98	.156	11
49	9.530215	0273	0331	0390	0448	0507	10
50	9.530565	0623	0682	0740	0798	0857	9
51	0915	0973	1032	1090	1148	1207	8
52	1265	1323	1381	1440	1498	1556	7
53	1614	1673	1731	1789	1847	1905	6
54	1963	2022	2080	2138	2196	2254	5
55	2312	2370	2428	2487	2545	2603	4
56	2661	2719	2777	2835	2893	2951	3
57	3009	3067	3125	3183	3241	3299	2
58	3357	3415	3473	3531	3589	3647	1
59	3704	3762	3820	3878	3936	3994	0
	60″	50″	40″	30″	20″	10″	Min.
	Co-sine of 70 Degrees.						

P. Part { 1″ 2″ 3″ 4″ 5″ 6″ 7″ 8″ 9″
{ 6 12 18 24 30 36 42 48 54

Min.	Tangent of 18 Degrees. 0″	10″	20″	30″	40″	50″	
0	9.511776	1848	1919	1991	2063	2134	59
1	2206	2277	2349	2420	2492	2564	58
2	2635	2707	2778	2850	2921	2993	57
3	3064	3136	3207	3278	3350	3421	56
4	3493	3564	3636	3707	3778	3850	55
5	3921	3992	4064	4135	4206	4278	54
6	4349	4420	4492	4563	4634	4705	53
7	4777	4848	4919	4990	5062	5133	52
8	5204	5275	5346	5417	5489	5560	51
9	5631	5702	5773	5844	5915	5986	50
10	9.516057	6129	6200	6271	6342	6413	49
11	6484	6555	6626	6697	6768	6839	48
12	6910	6981	7052	7123	7193	7264	47
13	7335	7406	7477	7548	7619	7690	46
14	7761	7831	7902	7973	8044	8115	45
15	8186	8256	8327	8398	8469	8539	44
16	8610	8681	8752	8822	8893	8964	43
17	9034	9105	9176	9246	9317	9388	42
18	9458	9529	9600	9670	9741	9811	41
19	9882	9953	..23	..94	.164	.235	40
20	9.520305	0376	0446	0517	0587	0658	39
21	0728	0799	0869	0939	1010	1080	38
22	1151	1221	1292	1362	1432	1503	37
23	1573	1643	1714	1784	1854	1925	36
24	1995	2065	2136	2206	2276	2346	35
25	2417	2487	2557	2627	2698	2768	34
26	2838	2908	2978	3048	3119	3189	33
27	3259	3329	3399	3469	3539	3609	32
28	3680	3750	3820	3890	3960	4030	31
29	4100	4170	4240	4310	4380	4450	30
30	9.524520	4590	4660	4730	4800	4870	29
31	4940	5009	5079	5149	5219	5289	28
32	5359	5429	5499	5568	5638	5708	27
33	5778	5848	5918	5987	6057	6127	26
34	6197	6266	6336	6406	6476	6545	25
35	6615	6685	6754	6824	6894	6963	24
36	7033	7103	7172	7242	7312	7381	23
37	7451	7520	7590	7660	7729	7799	22
38	7868	7938	8007	8077	8146	8216	21
39	8285	8355	8424	8494	8563	8633	20
40	9.528702	8772	8841	8910	8980	9049	19
41	9119	9188	9257	9327	9396	9465	18
42	9535	9604	9673	9743	9812	9881	17
43	9951	..20	..89	.158	.228	.297	16
44	9.530366	0435	0504	0574	0643	0712	15
45	0781	0850	0920	0989	1058	1127	14
46	1196	1265	1334	1403	1473	1542	13
47	1611	1680	1749	1818	1887	1956	12
48	2025	2094	2163	2232	2301	2370	11
49	2439	2508	2577	2646	2715	2784	10
50	9.532853	2921	2990	3059	3128	3197	9
51	3266	3335	3404	3472	3541	3610	8
52	3679	3748	3816	3885	3954	4023	7
53	4092	4160	4229	4298	4367	4435	6
54	4504	4573	4641	4710	4779	4847	5
55	4916	4985	5053	5122	5191	5259	4
56	5328	5396	5465	5534	5602	5671	3
57	5739	5808	5876	5945	6013	6082	2
58	6150	6219	6287	6356	6424	6493	1
59	6561	6630	6698	6767	6835	6903	0
	60″	50″	40″	30″	20″	10″	Min.
	Co-tangent of 71 Degrees.						

P. Part { 1″ 2″ 3″ 4″ 5″ 6″ 7″ 8″ 9″ / 7 14 21 28 35 42 49 56 63 }

Min.	Tangent of 19 Degrees. 0″	10″	20″	30″	40″	50″	
0	9.536972	7040	7109	7177	7245	7314	59
1	7382	7450	7519	7587	7655	7724	58
2	7792	7860	7929	7997	8065	8133	57
3	8202	8270	8338	8406	8475	8543	56
4	8611	8679	8747	8816	8884	8952	55
5	9020	9088	9156	9224	9293	9361	54
6	9429	9497	9565	9633	9701	9769	53
7	9837	9905	9973	..41	.109	.177	52
8	9.540245	0313	0381	0449	0517	0585	51
9	0653	0721	0789	0857	0925	0993	50
10	9.541061	1128	1196	1264	1332	1400	49
11	1468	1536	1603	1671	1739	1807	48
12	1875	1943	2010	2078	2146	2214	47
13	2281	2349	2417	2485	2552	2620	46
14	2688	2755	2823	2891	2958	3026	45
15	3094	3161	3229	3297	3364	3432	44
16	3499	3567	3635	3702	3770	3837	43
17	3905	3972	4040	4107	4175	4242	42
18	4310	4377	4445	4512	4580	4647	41
19	4715	4782	4850	4917	4985	5052	40
20	9.545119	5187	5254	5322	5389	5456	39
21	5524	5591	5658	5726	5793	5860	38
22	5928	5995	6062	6129	6197	6264	37
23	6331	6398	6466	6533	6600	6667	36
24	6735	6802	6869	6936	7003	7071	35
25	7138	7205	7272	7339	7406	7473	34
26	7540	7608	7675	7742	7809	7876	33
27	7943	8010	8077	8144	8211	8278	32
28	8345	8412	8479	8546	8613	8680	31
29	8747	8814	8881	8948	9015	9082	30
30	9.549149	9216	9283	9349	9416	9483	29
31	9550	9617	9684	9751	9817	9884	28
32	9951	..18	..85	.152	.218	.285	27
33	9.550352	0419	0485	0552	0619	0686	26
34	0752	0819	0886	0952	1019	1086	25
35	1153	1219	1286	1353	1419	1486	24
36	1552	1619	1686	1752	1819	1885	23
37	1952	2019	2085	2152	2218	2285	22
38	2351	2418	2484	2551	2617	2684	21
39	2750	2817	2883	2950	3016	3083	20
40	9.553149	3216	3282	3348	3415	3481	19
41	3548	3614	3680	3747	3813	3880	18
42	3946	4012	4079	4145	4211	4278	17
43	4344	4410	4476	4543	4609	4675	16
44	4741	4808	4874	4940	5006	5073	15
45	5139	5205	5271	5337	5404	5470	14
46	5536	5602	5668	5734	5800	5867	13
47	5933	5999	6065	6131	6197	6263	12
48	6329	6395	6461	6527	6593	6659	11
49	6725	6791	6857	6923	6989	7055	10
50	9.557121	7187	7253	7319	7385	7451	9
51	7517	7583	7649	7715	7781	7847	8
52	7913	7978	8044	8110	8176	8242	7
53	8308	8373	8439	8505	8571	8637	6
54	8703	8768	8834	8900	8966	9031	5
55	9097	9163	9229	9294	9360	9426	4
56	9491	9557	9623	9688	9754	9820	3
57	9885	9951	..17	..82	.148	.214	2
58	9.560279	0345	0410	0476	0542	0607	1
59	0673	0738	0804	0869	0935	1000	0
	60″	50″	40″	30″	20″	10″	Min.
	Co-tangent of 70 Degrees.						

P. Part { 1″ 2″ 3″ 4″ 5″ 6″ 7″ 8″ 9″ / 7 13 20 27 33 40 47 54 60 }

Min.	Sine of 20 Degrees. 0″	10″	20″	30″	40″	50″	
0	9.534052	4110	4167	4225	4283	4341	59
1	4399	4456	4514	4572	4630	4687	58
2	4745	4803	4861	4918	4976	5034	57
3	5092	5149	5207	5265	5322	5380	56
4	5438	5495	5553	5610	5668	5726	55
5	5783	5841	5898	5956	6014	6071	54
6	6129	6186	6244	6301	6359	6416	53
7	6474	6531	6589	6646	6704	6761	52
8	6818	6876	6933	6991	7048	7105	51
9	7163	7220	7278	7335	7392	7450	50
10	9.537507	7564	7622	7679	7736	7794	49
11	7851	7908	7965	8023	8080	8137	48
12	8194	8252	8309	8366	8423	8480	47
13	8538	8595	8652	8709	8766	8823	46
14	8880	8938	8995	9052	9109	9166	45
15	9223	9280	9337	9394	9451	9508	44
16	9565	9622	9679	9736	9793	9850	43
17	9907	9964	..21	..78	.135	.192	42
18	9.540249	0306	0363	0420	0477	0533	41
19	0590	0647	0704	0761	0818	0875	40
20	9.540931	0988	1045	1102	1159	1215	39
21	1272	1329	1386	1442	1499	1556	38
22	1613	1669	1726	1783	1839	1896	37
23	1953	2009	2066	2123	2179	2236	36
24	2293	2349	2406	2462	2519	2576	35
25	2632	2689	2745	2802	2858	2915	34
26	2971	3028	3084	3141	3197	3254	33
27	3310	3367	3423	3480	3536	3593	32
28	3649	3705	3762	3818	3875	3931	31
29	3987	4044	4100	4156	4213	4269	30
30	9.544325	4382	4438	4494	4550	4607	29
31	4663	4719	4776	4832	4888	4944	28
32	5000	5057	5113	5169	5225	5281	27
33	5338	5394	5450	5506	5562	5618	26
34	5674	5731	5787	5843	5899	5955	25
35	6011	6067	6123	6179	6235	6291	24
36	6347	6403	6459	6515	6571	6627	23
37	6683	6739	6795	6851	6907	6963	22
38	7019	7075	7131	7187	7242	7298	21
39	7354	7410	7466	7522	7578	7633	20
40	9.547689	7745	7801	7857	7912	7968	19
41	8024	8080	8136	8191	8247	8303	18
42	8359	8414	8470	8526	8581	8637	17
43	8693	8748	8804	8860	8915	8971	16
44	9027	9082	9138	9193	9249	9305	15
45	9360	9416	9471	9527	9582	9638	14
46	9693	9749	9805	9860	9916	9971	13
47	9.550026	0082	0137	0193	0248	0304	12
48	0359	0415	0470	0525	0581	0636	11
49	0692	0747	0802	0858	0913	0968	10
50	9.551024	1079	1134	1190	1245	1300	9
51	1356	1411	1466	1521	1577	1632	8
52	1687	1742	1798	1853	1908	1963	7
53	2018	2074	2129	2184	2239	2294	6
54	2349	2405	2460	2515	2570	2625	5
55	2680	2735	2790	2845	2900	2955	4
56	3010	3065	3121	3176	3231	3286	3
57	3341	3396	3451	3506	3560	3615	2
58	3670	3725	3780	3835	3890	3945	1
59	4000	4055	4110	4165	4219	4274	0
	60″	50″	40″	30″	20″	10″	Min.
	Co-sine of 69 Degrees.						

P. Part { 1″ 2″ 3″ 4″ 5″ 6″ 7″ 8″ 9″ / 6 11 17 23 28 34 39 45 51 }

Min.	Sine of 21 Degrees. 0″	10″	20″	30″	40″	50″	
0	9.554329	4384	4439	4494	4549	4603	59
1	4658	4713	4768	4822	4877	4932	58
2	4987	5042	5096	5151	5206	5260	57
3	5315	5370	5425	5479	5534	5589	56
4	5643	5698	5753	5807	5862	5916	55
5	5971	6026	6080	6135	6190	6244	54
6	6299	6353	6408	6462	6517	6571	53
7	6626	6680	6735	6789	6844	6898	52
8	6953	7007	7062	7116	7171	7225	51
9	7280	7334	7388	7443	7497	7552	50
10	9.557606	7660	7715	7769	7823	7878	49
11	7932	7986	8041	8095	8149	8204	48
12	8258	8312	8366	8421	8475	8529	47
13	8583	8638	8692	8746	8800	8855	46
14	8909	8963	9017	9071	9125	9180	45
15	9234	9288	9342	9396	9450	9504	44
16	9558	9613	9667	9721	9775	9829	43
17	9883	9937	9991	..45	..99	.153	42
18	9.560207	0261	0315	0369	0423	0477	41
19	0531	0585	0639	0693	0747	0801	40
20	9.560855	0908	0962	1016	1070	1124	39
21	1178	1232	1286	1339	1393	1447	38
22	1501	1555	1609	1662	1716	1770	37
23	1824	1878	1931	1985	2039	2093	36
24	2146	2200	2254	2307	2361	2415	35
25	2468	2522	2576	2629	2683	2737	34
26	2790	2844	2898	2951	3005	3058	33
27	3112	3166	3219	3273	3326	3380	32
28	3433	3487	3541	3594	3648	3701	31
29	3755	3808	3862	3915	3969	4022	30
30	9.564075	4129	4182	4236	4289	4343	29
31	4396	4449	4503	4556	4610	4663	28
32	4716	4770	4823	4876	4930	4983	27
33	5036	5090	5143	5196	5250	5303	26
34	5356	5409	5463	5516	5569	5622	25
35	5676	5729	5782	5835	5888	5942	24
36	5995	6048	6101	6154	6207	6261	23
37	6314	6367	6420	6473	6526	6579	22
38	6632	6685	6739	6792	6845	6898	21
39	6951	7004	7057	7110	7163	7216	20
40	9.567269	7322	7375	7428	7481	7534	19
41	7587	7640	7693	7746	7799	7851	18
42	7904	7957	8010	8063	8116	8169	17
43	8222	8275	8327	8380	8433	8486	16
44	8539	8592	8644	8697	8750	8803	15
45	8856	8908	8961	9014	9067	9119	14
46	9172	9225	9277	9330	9383	9436	13
47	9488	9541	9594	9646	9699	9752	12
48	9804	9857	9910	9962	..15	..67	11
49	9.570120	0173	0225	0278	0330	0383	10
50	9.570435	0488	0541	0593	0646	0698	9
51	0751	0803	0856	0908	0961	1013	8
52	1066	1118	1170	1223	1275	1328	7
53	1380	1433	1485	1537	1590	1642	6
54	1695	1747	1799	1852	1904	1956	5
55	2009	2061	2113	2166	2218	2270	4
56	2323	2375	2427	2479	2532	2584	3
57	2636	2688	2741	2793	2845	2897	2
58	2950	3002	3054	3106	3158	3210	1
59	3263	3315	3367	3419	3471	3523	0
	60″	50″	40″	30″	20″	10″	Min.
	Co-sine of 68 Degrees.						

P. Part { 1″ 2″ 3″ 4″ 5″ 6″ 7″ 8″ 9″ / 5 11 16 21 27 32 37 43 48 }

Min.	Tangent of 20 Degrees. 0″	10″	20″	30″	40″	50″	
0	9.561066	1131	1197	1262	1328	1393	59
1	1459	1524	1590	1655	1721	1786	58
2	1851	1917	1982	2048	2113	2178	57
3	2244	2309	2375	2440	2505	2571	56
4	2636	2701	2767	2832	2897	2963	55
5	3028	3093	3158	3224	3289	3354	54
6	3419	3485	3550	3615	3680	3746	53
7	3811	3876	3941	4006	4071	4137	52
8	4202	4267	4332	4397	4462	4527	51
9	4593	4658	4723	4788	4853	4918	50
10	9.564983	5048	5113	5178	5243	5308	49
11	5373	5438	5503	5568	5633	5698	48
12	5763	5828	5893	5958	6023	6088	47
13	6153	6218	6283	6348	6413	6478	46
14	6542	6607	6672	6737	6802	6867	45
15	6932	6996	7061	7126	7191	7256	44
16	7320	7385	7450	7515	7580	7644	43
17	7709	7774	7839	7903	7968	8033	42
18	8098	8162	8227	8292	8356	8421	41
19	8486	8550	8615	8680	8744	8809	40
20	9.568873	8938	9003	9067	9132	9197	39
21	9261	9326	9390	9455	9519	9584	38
22	9648	9713	9777	9842	9906	9971	37
23	9.570035	0100	0164	0229	0293	0358	36
24	0422	0487	0551	0616	0680	0744	35
25	0809	0873	0938	1002	1066	1131	34
26	1195	1259	1324	1388	1452	1517	33
27	1581	1645	1710	1774	1838	1903	32
28	1967	2031	2095	2160	2224	2288	31
29	2352	2417	2481	2545	2609	2673	30
30	9.572738	2802	2866	2930	2994	3059	29
31	3123	3187	3251	3315	3379	3443	28
32	3507	3571	3636	3700	3764	3828	27
33	3892	3956	4020	4084	4148	4212	26
34	4276	4340	4404	4468	4532	4596	25
35	4660	4724	4788	4852	4916	4980	24
36	5044	5108	5172	5236	5299	5363	23
37	5427	5491	5555	5619	5683	5747	22
38	5810	5874	5938	6002	6066	6130	21
39	6193	6257	6321	6385	6449	6512	20
40	9.576576	6640	6704	6767	6831	6895	19
41	6959	7022	7086	7150	7213	7277	18
42	7341	7404	7468	7532	7595	7659	17
43	7723	7786	7850	7914	7977	8041	16
44	8104	8168	8231	8295	8359	8422	15
45	8486	8549	8613	8676	8740	8803	14
46	8867	8930	8994	9057	9121	9184	13
47	9248	9311	5375	9438	9502	9565	12
48	9629	9692	9755	9819	9882	9946	11
49	9.580009	0072	0136	0199	0262	0326	10
50	9.580389	0453	0516	0579	0642	0706	9
51	0769	0832	0896	0959	1022	1086	8
52	1149	1212	1275	1339	1402	1465	7
53	1528	1591	1655	1718	1781	1844	6
54	1907	1971	2034	2097	2160	2223	5
55	2286	2350	2413	2476	2539	2602	4
56	2665	2728	2791	2854	2917	2980	3
57	3044	3107	3170	3233	3296	3359	2
58	3422	3485	3548	3611	3674	3737	1
59	3800	3863	3926	3989	4052	4114	0
	60″	50″	40″	30″	20″	10″	Min.
	Co-tangent of 69 Degrees.						

P. Part { 1″ 2″ 3″ 4″ 5″ 6″ 7″ 8″ 9″ / 6 13 19 26 32 39 45 51 58

Min.	Tangent of 21 Degrees. 0″	10″	20″	30″	40″	50″	
0	9.584177	4240	4303	4366	4429	4492	59
1	4555	4618	4681	4744	4806	4869	58
2	4932	4995	5058	5121	5183	5246	57
3	5309	5372	5435	5498	5560	5623	56
4	5686	5749	5811	5874	5937	6000	55
5	6062	6125	6188	6251	6313	6376	54
6	6439	6501	6564	6627	6689	6752	53
7	6815	6877	6940	7003	7065	7128	52
8	7190	7253	7316	7378	7441	7503	51
9	7566	7629	7691	7754	7816	7879	50
10	9.587941	8004	8066	8129	8191	8254	49
11	8316	8379	8441	8504	8566	8629	48
12	8691	8754	8816	8878	8941	9003	47
13	9066	9128	9191	9253	9315	9378	46
14	9440	9502	9565	9627	9690	9752	45
15	9814	9877	9939	...1	..63	.126	44
16	9.590188	0250	0313	0375	0437	0499	43
17	0562	0624	0686	0748	0811	0873	42
18	0935	0997	1060	1122	1184	1246	41
19	1308	1370	1433	1495	1557	1619	40
20	9.591681	1743	1805	1868	1930	1992	39
21	2054	2116	2178	2240	2302	2364	38
22	2426	2488	2550	2612	2674	2737	37
23	2799	2861	2923	2985	3047	3109	36
24	3171	3232	3294	3356	3418	3480	35
25	3542	3604	3666	3728	3790	3852	34
26	3914	3976	4038	4099	4161	4223	33
27	4285	4347	4409	4471	4532	4594	32
28	4656	4718	4780	4842	4903	4965	31
29	5027	5089	5150	5212	5274	5336	30
30	9.595398	5459	5521	5583	5644	5706	29
31	5768	5830	5891	5953	6015	6076	28
32	6138	6200	6261	6323	6385	6446	27
33	6508	6570	6631	6693	6754	6816	26
34	6878	6939	7001	7062	7124	7185	25
35	7247	7309	7370	7432	7493	7555	24
36	7616	7678	7739	7801	7862	7924	23
37	7985	8047	8108	8170	8231	8293	22
38	8354	8415	8477	8538	8600	8661	21
39	8722	8784	8845	8907	8968	9029	20
40	9.599091	9152	9213	9275	9336	9398	19
41	9459	9520	9581	9643	9704	9765	18
42	9827	9888	9949	..11	..72	.133	17
43	9.600194	0256	0317	0378	0439	0500	16
44	0562	0623	0684	0745	0806	0868	15
45	0929	0990	1051	1112	1174	1235	14
46	1296	1357	1418	1479	1540	1601	13
47	1663	1724	1785	1846	1907	1968	12
48	2029	2090	2151	2212	2273	2334	11
49	2395	2456	2517	2578	2639	2700	10
50	9.602761	2822	2883	2944	3005	3066	9
51	3127	3188	3249	3310	3371	3432	8
52	3493	3554	3615	3675	3736	3797	7
53	3858	3919	3980	4041	4102	4162	6
54	4223	4284	4345	4406	4467	4527	5
55	4588	4649	4710	4771	4831	4892	4
56	4953	5014	5074	5135	5196	5257	3
57	5317	5378	5439	5500	5560	5621	2
58	5682	5742	5803	5864	5924	5985	1
59	6046	6106	6167	6228	6288	6349	0
	60″	50″	40″	30″	20″	10″	Min.
	Co-tangent of 68 Degrees.						

P. Part { 1″ 2″ 3″ 4″ 5″ 6″ 7″ 8″ 9″ / 6 12 19 25 31 37 43 49 56

Min.	Sine of 22 Degrees. 0″	10″	20″	30″	40″	50″	
0	9.573575	3628	3680	3732	3784	3836	59
1	3888	3940	3992	4044	4096	4148	58
2	4200	4252	4304	4356	4408	4460	57
3	4512	4564	4616	4668	4720	4772	56
4	4824	4876	4928	4980	5032	5084	55
5	5136	5187	5239	5291	5343	5395	54
6	5447	5499	5550	5602	5654	5706	53
7	5758	5810	5861	5913	5965	6017	52
8	6069	6120	6172	6224	6276	6327	51
9	6379	6431	6482	6534	6586	6638	50
10	9.576689	6741	6793	6844	6896	6948	49
11	6999	7051	7102	7154	7206	7257	48
12	7309	7360	7412	7464	7515	7567	47
13	7618	7670	7721	7773	7824	7876	46
14	7927	7979	8030	8082	8133	8185	45
15	8236	8288	8339	8391	8442	8494	44
16	8545	8596	8648	8699	8751	8802	43
17	8853	8905	8956	9008	9059	9110	42
18	9162	9213	9264	9316	9367	9418	41
19	9470	9521	9572	9623	9675	9726	40
20	9.579777	9828	9880	9931	9982	..33	39
21	9.580085	0136	0187	0238	0289	0341	38
22	0392	0443	0494	0545	0596	0647	37
23	0699	0750	0801	0852	0903	0954	36
24	1005	1056	1107	1158	1209	1261	35
25	1312	1363	1414	1465	1516	1567	34
26	1618	1669	1720	1771	1822	1873	33
27	1924	1975	2025	2076	2127	2178	32
28	2229	2280	2331	2382	2433	2484	31
29	2535	2585	2636	2687	2738	2789	30
30	9.582840	2890	2941	2992	3043	3094	29
31	3145	3195	3246	3297	3348	3398	28
32	3449	3500	3551	3601	3652	3703	27
33	3754	3804	3855	3906	3956	4007	26
34	4058	4108	4159	4210	4260	4311	25
35	4361	4412	4463	4513	4564	4615	24
36	4665	4716	4766	4817	4867	4918	23
37	4968	5019	5070	5120	5171	5221	22
38	5272	5322	5373	5423	5474	5524	21
39	5574	5625	5675	5726	5776	5827	20
40	9.585877	5927	5978	6028	6079	6129	19
41	6179	6230	6280	6331	6381	6431	18
42	6482	6532	6582	6633	6683	6733	17
43	6783	6834	6884	6934	6985	7035	16
44	7085	7135	7186	7236	7286	7336	15
45	7386	7437	7487	7537	7587	7637	14
46	7688	7738	7788	7838	7888	7938	13
47	7989	8039	8089	8139	8189	8239	12
48	8289	8339	8389	8439	8489	8540	11
49	8590	8640	8690	8740	8790	8840	10
50	9.588890	8940	8990	9040	9090	9140	9
51	9190	9240	9290	9340	9389	9439	8
52	9489	9539	9589	9639	9689	9739	7
53	9789	9839	9889	9938	9988	..38	6
54	9.590088	0138	0188	0237	0287	0337	5
55	0387	0437	0487	0536	0586	0636	4
56	0686	0735	0785	0835	0885	0934	3
57	0984	1034	1084	1133	1183	1233	2
58	1282	1332	1382	1431	1481	1531	1
59	1580	1630	1680	1729	1779	1828	0
	60″	50″	40″	30″	20″	10″	Min.
	Co-sine of 67 Degrees.						

P. Part	1″	2″	3″	4″	5″	6″	7″	8″	9″
	5	10	15	20	25	31	36	41	46

Min.	Sine of 23 Degrees. 0″	10″	20″	30″	40″	50″	
0	9.591878	1928	1977	2027	2076	2126	59
1	2176	2225	2275	2324	2374	2423	58
2	2473	2522	2572	2621	2671	2720	57
3	2770	2819	2869	2918	2968	3017	56
4	3067	3116	3165	3215	3264	3314	55
5	3363	3412	3462	3511	3561	3610	54
6	3659	3709	3758	3807	3857	3906	53
7	3955	4005	4054	4103	4153	4202	52
8	4251	4301	4350	4399	4448	4498	51
9	4547	4596	4645	4695	4744	4793	50
10	9.594842	4891	4941	4990	5039	5088	49
11	5137	5186	5236	5285	5334	5383	48
12	5432	5481	5530	5580	5629	5678	47
13	5727	5776	5825	5874	5923	5972	46
14	6021	6070	6119	6168	6217	6266	45
15	6315	6364	6413	6462	6511	6560	44
16	6609	6658	6707	6756	6805	6854	43
17	6903	6952	7001	7050	7099	7148	42
18	7196	7245	7294	7343	7392	7441	41
19	7490	7539	7587	7636	7685	7734	40
20	9.597783	7831	7880	7929	7978	8027	39
21	8075	8124	8173	8222	8270	8319	38
22	8368	8417	8465	8514	8563	8612	37
23	8660	8709	8758	8806	8855	8904	36
24	8952	9001	9050	9098	9147	9195	35
25	9244	9293	9341	9390	9438	9487	34
26	9536	9584	9633	9681	9730	9778	33
27	9827	9876	9924	9973	..21	..70	32
28	9.600118	0167	0215	0264	0312	0361	31
29	0409	0457	0506	0554	0603	0651	30
30	9.600700	0748	0797	0845	0893	0942	29
31	0990	1038	1087	1135	1184	1232	28
32	1280	1329	1377	1425	1474	1522	27
33	1570	1619	1667	1715	1763	1812	26
34	1860	1908	1957	2005	2053	2101	25
35	2150	2198	2246	2294	2342	2391	24
36	2439	2487	2535	2583	2632	2680	23
37	2728	2776	2824	2872	2920	2969	22
38	3017	3065	3113	3161	3209	3257	21
39	3305	3353	3401	3449	3497	3546	20
40	9.603594	3642	3690	3738	3786	3834	19
41	3882	3930	3978	4026	4074	4122	18
42	4170	4218	4266	4313	4361	4409	17
43	4457	4505	4553	4601	4649	4697	16
44	4745	4793	4841	4888	4936	4984	15
45	5032	5080	5128	5176	5223	5271	14
46	5319	5367	5415	5462	5510	5558	13
47	5606	5654	5701	5749	5797	5845	12
48	5892	5940	5988	6035	6083	6131	11
49	6179	6226	6274	6322	6369	6417	10
50	9.606465	6512	6560	6608	6655	6703	9
51	6751	6798	6846	6893	6941	6989	8
52	7036	7084	7131	7179	7227	7274	7
53	7322	7369	7417	7464	7512	7559	6
54	7607	7654	7702	7749	7797	7844	5
55	7892	7939	7987	8034	8082	8129	4
56	8177	8224	8271	8319	8366	8414	3
57	8461	8508	8556	8603	8651	8698	2
58	8745	8793	8840	8887	8935	8982	1
59	9029	9077	9124	9171	9219	9266	0
	60″	50″	40″	30″	20″	10″	Min.
	Co-sine of 66 Degrees.						

P. Part	1″	2″	3″	4″	5″	6″	7″	8″	9″
	5	10	15	19	24	29	34	39	44

Min.	Tangent of 22 Degrees. 0″	10″	20″	30″	40″	50″	
0	9.606410	6470	6531	6591	6652	6713	59
1	6773	6834	6894	6955	7015	7076	58
2	7137	7197	7258	7318	7379	7439	57
3	7500	7560	7621	7681	7742	7802	56
4	7863	7923	7984	8044	8105	8165	55
5	8225	8286	8346	8407	8467	8528	54
6	8588	8648	8709	8769	8830	8890	53
7	8950	9011	9071	9131	9192	9252	52
8	9312	9373	9433	9493	9554	9614	51
9	9674	9735	9795	9855	9915	9976	50
10	9.610036	0096	0156	0217	0277	0337	49
11	0397	0458	0518	0578	0638	0698	48
12	0759	0819	0879	0939	0999	1059	47
13	1120	1180	1240	1300	1360	1420	46
14	1480	1540	1601	1661	1721	1781	45
15	1841	1901	1961	2021	2081	2141	44
16	2201	2261	2321	2381	2441	2501	43
17	2561	2621	2681	2741	2801	2861	42
18	2921	2981	3041	3101	3161	3221	41
19	3281	3341	3401	3461	3521	3581	40
20	9.613641	3701	3760	3820	3880	3940	39
21	4000	4060	4120	4180	4239	4299	38
22	4359	4419	4479	4539	4598	4658	37
23	4718	4778	4838	4897	4957	5017	36
24	5077	5136	5196	5256	5316	5375	35
25	5435	5495	5555	5614	5674	5734	34
26	5793	5853	5913	5972	6032	6092	33
27	6151	6211	6271	6330	6390	6450	32
28	6509	6569	6628	6688	6748	6807	31
29	6867	6926	6986	7046	7105	7165	30
30	9 617224	7284	7343	7403	7462	7522	29
31	7582	7641	7701	7760	7820	7879	28
32	7939	7998	8057	8117	8176	8236	27
33	8295	8355	8414	8474	8533	8593	26
34	8652	8711	8771	8830	8890	8949	25
35	9008	9068	9127	9186	9246	9305	24
36	9364	9424	9483	9543	9602	9661	23
37	9720	9780	9839	9898	9958	..17	22
38	9.620076	0136	0195	0254	0313	0373	21
39	0432	0491	0550	0610	0669	0728	20
40	9.620787	0846	0906	0965	1024	1083	19
41	1142	1201	1261	1320	1379	1438	18
42	1497	1556	1616	1675	1734	1793	17
43	1852	1911	1970	2029	2088	2147	16
44	2207	2266	2325	2384	2443	2502	15
45	2561	2620	2679	2738	2797	2856	14
46	2915	2974	3033	3092	3151	3210	13
47	3269	3328	3387	3446	3505	3564	12
48	3623	3682	3741	3800	3858	3917	11
49	3976	4035	4094	4153	4212	4271	10
50	9.624330	4388	4447	4506	4565	4624	9
51	4683	4742	4800	4859	4918	4977	8
52	5036	5094	5153	5212	5271	5330	7
53	5388	5447	5506	5565	5623	5682	6
54	5741	5800	5858	5917	5976	6035	5
55	6093	6152	6211	6269	6328	6387	4
56	6445	6504	6563	6621	6680	6739	3
57	6797	6856	6915	6973	7032	7090	2
58	7149	7208	7266	7325	7383	7442	1
59	7501	7559	7618	7676	7735	7793	0
	60″	50″	40″	30″	20″	10″	Min.
	Co-tangent of 67 Degrees.						

P. Part { 1″ 2″ 3″ 4″ 5″ 6″ 7″ 8″ 9″
{ 6 12 18 24 30 36 42 48 54

Min.	Tangent of 23 Degrees. 0″	10″	20″	30″	40″	50″	
0	9.627852	7910	7969	8028	8086	8145	59
1	8203	8262	8320	8379	8437	8496	58
2	8554	8612	8671	8729	8788	8846	57
3	8905	8963	9022	9080	9138	9197	56
4	9255	9314	9372	9431	9489	9547	55
5	9606	9664	9722	9781	9839	9897	54
6	9956	..14	..73	.131	.189	.247	53
7	9.630306	0364	0422	0481	0539	0597	52
8	0656	0714	0772	0830	0889	0947	51
9	1005	1063	1122	1180	1238	1296	50
10	9.631355	1413	1471	1529	1587	1646	49
11	1704	1762	1820	1878	1936	1995	48
12	2053	2111	2169	2227	2285	2343	47
13	2402	2460	2518	2576	2634	2692	46
14	2750	2808	2866	2924	2982	3040	45
15	3099	3157	3215	3273	3331	3389	44
16	3447	3505	3563	3621	3679	3737	43
17	3795	3853	3911	3969	4027	4085	42
18	4143	4201	4259	4316	4374	4432	41
19	4490	4548	4606	4664	4722	4780	40
20	9.634838	4896	4954	5011	5069	5127	39
21	5185	5243	5301	5359	5416	5474	38
22	5532	5590	5648	5706	5763	5821	37
23	5879	5937	5995	6052	6110	6168	36
24	6226	6283	6341	6399	6457	6514	35
25	6572	6630	6688	6745	6803	6861	34
26	6919	6976	7034	7092	7149	7207	33
27	7265	7322	7380	7438	7495	7553	32
28	7611	7668	7726	7783	7841	7899	31
29	7956	8014	8072	8129	8187	8244	30
30	9.638302	8359	8417	8475	8532	8590	29
31	8647	8705	8762	8820	8877	8935	28
32	8992	9050	9107	9165	9222	9280	27
33	9337	9395	9452	9510	9567	9625	26
34	9682	9740	9797	9855	9912	9969	25
35	9.640027	0084	0142	0199	0257	0314	24
36	0371	0429	0486	0544	0601	0658	23
37	0716	0773	0830	0888	0945	1002	22
38	1060	1117	1174	1232	1289	1346	21
39	1404	1461	1518	1575	1633	1690	20
40	9.641747	1805	1862	1919	1976	2034	19
41	2091	2148	2205	2263	2320	2377	18
42	2434	2491	2549	2606	2663	2720	17
43	2777	2834	2892	2949	3006	3063	16
44	3120	3177	3235	3292	3349	3406	15
45	3463	3520	3577	3634	3691	3749	14
46	3806	3863	3920	3977	4034	4091	13
47	4148	4205	4262	4319	4376	4433	12
48	4490	4547	4604	4661	4718	4775	11
49	4832	4889	4946	5003	5060	5117	10
50	9.645174	5231	5288	5345	5402	5459	9
51	5516	5573	5630	5687	5744	5801	8
52	5857	5914	5971	6028	6085	6142	7
53	6199	6256	6313	6369	6426	6483	6
54	6540	6597	6654	6710	6767	6824	5
55	6881	6938	6995	7051	7108	7165	4
56	7222	7279	7335	7392	7449	7506	3
57	7562	7619	7676	7733	7789	7846	2
58	7903	7960	8016	8073	8130	8186	1
59	8243	8300	8356	8413	8470	8526	0
	60″	50″	40″	30″	20″	10″	Min.
	Co-tangent of 66 Degrees.						

P. Part { 1″ 2″ 3″ 4″ 5″ 6″ 7″ 8″ 9″
{ 6 12 17 23 29 35 40 46 52

Min.	Sine of 24 Degrees. 0″	10″	20″	30″	40″	50″	
0	9.609313	9361	9408	9455	9502	9550	59
1	9597	9644	9691	9739	9786	9833	58
2	9880	9928	9975	..22	..69	.116	57
3	9.610164	0211	0258	0305	0352	0399	56
4	0447	0494	0541	0588	0635	0682	55
5	0729	0776	0823	0871	0918	0965	54
6	1012	1059	1106	1153	1200	1247	53
7	1294	1341	1388	1435	1482	1529	52
8	1576	1623	1670	1717	1764	1811	51
9	1858	1905	1952	1999	2046	2093	50
10	9.612140	2187	2234	2280	2327	2374	49
11	2421	2468	2515	2562	2609	2655	48
12	2702	2749	2796	2843	2890	2936	47
13	2983	3030	3077	3124	3171	3217	46
14	3264	3311	3358	3404	3451	3498	45
15	3545	3591	3638	3685	3732	3778	44
16	3825	3872	3918	3965	4012	4058	43
17	4105	4152	4198	4245	4292	4338	42
18	4385	4432	4478	4525	4571	4618	41
19	4665	4711	4758	4804	4851	4898	40
20	9.614944	4991	5037	5084	5130	5177	39
21	5223	5270	5316	5363	5409	5456	38
22	5502	5549	5595	5642	5688	5735	37
23	5781	5828	5874	5921	5967	6013	36
24	6060	6106	6153	6199	6245	6292	35
25	6338	6385	6431	6477	6524	6570	34
26	6616	6663	6709	6755	6802	6848	33
27	6894	6941	6987	7033	7080	7126	32
28	7172	7218	7265	7311	7357	7403	31
29	7450	7496	7542	7588	7635	7681	30
30	9.617727	7773	7819	7866	7912	7958	29
31	8004	8050	8096	8143	8189	8235	28
32	8281	8327	8373	8419	8465	8512	27
33	8558	8604	8650	8696	8742	8788	26
34	8834	8880	8926	8972	9018	9064	25
35	9110	9156	9202	9248	9294	9340	24
36	9386	9432	9478	9524	9570	9616	23
37	9662	9708	9754	9800	9846	9892	22
38	9938	9984	..30	..76	.121	.167	21
39	9.620213	0259	0305	0351	0397	0443	20
40	9.620488	0534	0580	0626	0672	0718	19
41	0763	0809	0855	0901	0947	0992	18
42	1038	1084	1130	1175	1221	1267	17
43	1313	1358	1404	1450	1496	1541	16
44	1587	1633	1678	1724	1770	1816	15
45	1861	1907	1953	1998	2044	2089	14
46	2135	2181	2226	2272	2318	2363	13
47	2409	2454	2500	2546	2591	2637	12
48	2682	2728	2773	2819	2865	2910	11
49	2956	3001	3047	3092	3138	3183	10
50	9.623229	3274	3320	3365	3411	3456	9
51	3502	3547	3593	3638	3683	3729	8
52	3774	3820	3865	3911	3956	4001	7
53	4047	4092	4138	4183	4228	4274	6
54	4319	4364	4410	4455	4500	4546	5
55	4591	4636	4682	4727	4772	4818	4
56	4863	4908	4954	4999	5044	5089	3
57	5135	5180	5225	5270	5316	5361	2
58	5406	5451	5496	5542	5587	5632	1
59	5677	5722	5768	5813	5858	5903	0
	60″	50″	40″	30″	20″	10″	Min.
	Co-sine of 65 Degrees.						

P. Part { 1″ 2″ 3″ 4″ 5″ 6″ 7″ 8″ 9″ / 5 9 14 18 23 28 32 37 42

Min.	Sine of 25 Degrees. 0″	10″	20″	30″	40″	50″	
0	9.625948	5993	6039	6084	6129	6174	59
1	6219	6264	6309	6354	6400	6445	58
2	6490	6535	6580	6625	6670	6715	57
3	6760	6805	6850	6895	6940	6985	56
4	7030	7075	7120	7165	7210	7255	55
5	7300	7345	7390	7435	7480	7525	54
6	7570	7615	7660	7705	7750	7795	53
7	7840	7885	7929	7974	8019	8064	52
8	8109	8154	8199	8244	8289	8333	51
9	8378	8423	8468	8513	8558	8602	50
10	9.628647	8692	8737	8782	8826	8871	49
11	8916	8961	9006	9050	9095	9140	48
12	9185	9229	9274	9319	9363	9408	47
13	9453	9498	9542	9587	9632	9676	46
14	9721	9766	9810	9855	9900	9944	45
15	9989	..34	..78	.123	.168	.212	44
16	9.630257	0301	0346	0391	0435	0480	43
17	0524	0569	0613	0658	0703	0747	42
18	0792	0836	0881	0925	0970	1014	41
19	1059	1103	1148	1192	1237	1281	40
20	9.631326	1370	1415	1459	1504	1548	39
21	1593	1637	1681	1726	1770	1815	38
22	1859	1904	1948	1992	2037	2081	37
23	2125	2170	2214	2259	2303	2347	36
24	2392	2436	2480	2525	2569	2613	35
25	2658	2702	2746	2790	2835	2879	34
26	2923	2968	3012	3056	3100	3145	33
27	3189	3233	3277	3322	3366	3410	32
28	3454	3498	3543	3587	3631	3675	31
29	3719	3764	3808	3852	3896	3940	30
30	9.633984	4028	4073	4117	4161	4205	29
31	4249	4293	4337	4381	4426	4470	28
32	4514	4558	4602	4646	4690	4734	27
33	4778	4822	4866	4910	4954	4998	26
34	5042	5086	5130	5174	5218	5262	25
35	5306	5350	5394	5438	5482	5526	24
36	5570	5614	5658	5702	5746	5790	23
37	5834	5877	5921	5965	6009	6053	22
38	6097	6141	6185	6229	6272	6316	21
39	6360	6404	6448	6492	6535	6579	20
40	9.636623	6667	6711	6754	6798	6842	19
41	6886	6930	6973	7017	7061	7105	18
42	7148	7192	7236	7280	7323	7367	17
43	7411	7455	7498	7542	7586	7629	16
44	7673	7717	7760	7804	7848	7891	15
45	7935	7979	8022	8066	8110	8153	14
46	8197	8240	8284	8328	8371	8415	13
47	8458	8502	8546	8589	8633	8676	12
48	8720	8763	8807	8851	8894	8938	11
49	8981	9025	9068	9112	9155	9199	10
50	9.639242	9286	9329	9373	9416	9460	9
51	9503	9546	9590	9633	9677	9720	8
52	9764	9807	9851	9894	9937	9981	7
53	9.640024	0068	0111	0154	0198	0241	6
54	0284	0328	0371	0414	0458	0501	5
55	0544	0588	0631	0674	0718	0761	4
56	0804	0848	0891	0934	0978	1021	3
57	1064	1107	1151	1194	1237	1280	2
58	1324	1367	1410	1453	1496	1540	1
59	1583	1626	1669	1712	1756	1799	0
	60″	50″	40″	30″	20″	10″	Min.
	Co-sine of 64 Degrees.						

P. Part { 1″ 2″ 3″ 4″ 5″ 6″ 7″ 8″ 9″ / 4 9 13 18 22 26 31 35 40

Min.	Tangent of 24 Degrees. 0″	10″	20″	30″	40″	50″	
0	9.648583	8640	8696	8753	8810	8866	59
1	8923	8980	9036	9093	9150	9206	58
2	9263	9319	9376	9433	9489	9546	57
3	9602	9659	9715	9772	9829	9885	56
4	9942	9998	..55	.111	.168	.224	55
5	9.650281	0337	0394	0450	0507	0563	54
6	0620	0676	0733	0789	0846	0902	53
7	0959	1015	1072	1128	1185	1241	52
8	1297	1354	1410	1467	1523	1579	51
9	1636	1692	1749	1805	1861	1918	50
10	9.651974	2031	2087	2143	2200	2256	49
11	2312	2369	2425	2481	2538	2594	48
12	2650	2707	2763	2819	2875	2932	47
13	2988	3044	3101	3157	3213	3269	46
14	3326	3382	3438	3494	3551	3607	45
15	3663	3719	3776	3832	3888	3944	44
16	4000	4057	4113	4169	4225	4281	43
17	4337	4394	4450	4506	4562	4618	42
18	4674	4731	4787	4843	4899	4955	41
19	5011	5067	5123	5179	5236	5292	40
20	9.655348	5404	5460	5516	5572	5628	39
21	5684	5740	5796	5852	5908	5964	38
22	6020	6076	6132	6188	6244	6300	37
23	6356	6412	6468	6524	6580	6636	36
24	6692	6748	6804	6860	6916	6972	35
25	7028	7084	7140	7196	7252	7308	34
26	7364	7419	7475	7531	7587	7643	33
27	7699	7755	7811	7867	7922	7978	32
28	8034	8090	8146	8202	8258	8313	31
29	8369	8425	8481	8537	8592	8648	30
30	9.658704	8760	8816	8871	8927	8983	29
31	9039	9095	9150	9206	9262	9318	28
32	9373	9429	9485	9540	9596	9652	27
33	9708	9763	9819	9875	9930	9986	26
34	9.660042	0098	0153	0209	0265	0320	25
35	0376	0431	0487	0543	0598	0654	24
36	0710	0765	0821	0877	0932	0988	23
37	1043	1099	1155	1210	1266	1321	22
38	1377	1432	1488	1544	1599	1655	21
39	1710	1766	1821	1877	1932	1988	20
40	9.662043	2099	2154	2210	2265	2321	19
41	2376	2432	2487	2543	2598	2654	18
42	2709	2765	2820	2876	2931	2987	17
43	3042	3097	3153	3208	3264	3319	16
44	3375	3430	3485	3541	3596	3651	15
45	3707	3762	3818	3873	3928	3984	14
46	4039	4094	4150	4205	4260	4316	13
47	4371	4426	4482	4537	4592	4648	12
48	4703	4758	4814	4869	4924	4979	11
49	5035	5090	5145	5200	5256	5311	10
50	9.665366	5421	5477	5532	5587	5642	9
51	5698	5753	5808	5863	5918	5974	8
52	6029	6084	6139	6194	6249	6305	7
53	6360	6415	6470	6525	6580	6636	6
54	6691	6746	6801	6856	6911	6966	5
55	7021	7076	7132	7187	7242	7297	4
56	7352	7407	7462	7517	7572	7627	3
57	7682	7737	7792	7847	7903	7958	2
58	8013	8068	8123	8178	8233	8288	1
59	8343	8398	8453	8508	8563	8618	0
	60″	50″	40″	30″	20″	10″	Min.
	Co-tangent of 65 Degrees.						

P. Part { 1″ 2″ 3″ 4″ 5″ 6″ 7″ 8″ 9″ / 6 11 17 22 28 33 39 45 50

Min.	Tangent of 25 Degrees. 0″	10″	20″	30″	40″	50″	
0	9.668673	8728	8782	8837	8892	8947	59
1	9002	9057	9112	9167	9222	9277	58
2	9332	9387	9442	9497	9552	9606	57
3	9661	9716	9771	9826	9881	9936	56
4	9991	..45	.100	.155	.210	.265	55
5	9.670320	0375	0429	0484	0539	0594	54
6	0649	0703	0758	0813	0868	0923	53
7	0977	1032	1087	1142	1197	1251	52
8	1306	1361	1416	1470	1525	1580	51
9	1635	1689	1744	1799	1853	1908	50
10	9.671963	2018	2072	2127	2182	2236	49
11	2291	2346	2400	2455	2510	2564	48
12	2619	2674	2728	2783	2838	2892	47
13	2947	3001	3056	3111	3165	3220	46
14	3274	3329	3384	3438	3493	3547	45
15	3602	3657	3711	3766	3820	3875	44
16	3929	3984	4038	4093	4148	4202	43
17	4257	4311	4366	4420	4475	4529	42
18	4584	4638	4693	4747	4802	4856	41
19	4911	4965	5019	5074	5128	5183	40
20	9.675237	5292	5346	5401	5455	5509	39
21	5564	5618	5673	5727	5781	5836	38
22	5890	5945	5999	6053	6108	6162	37
23	6217	6271	6325	6380	6434	6488	36
24	6543	6597	6651	6706	6760	6814	35
25	6869	6923	6977	7032	7086	7140	34
26	7194	7249	7303	7357	7412	7466	33
27	7520	7574	7629	7683	7737	7791	32
28	7846	7900	7954	8008	8062	8117	31
29	8171	8225	8279	8334	8388	8442	30
30	9.678496	8550	8604	8659	8713	8767	29
31	8821	8875	8929	8984	9038	9092	28
32	9146	9200	9254	9308	9363	9417	27
33	9471	9525	9579	9633	9687	9741	26
34	9795	9849	9904	9958	..12	..66	25
35	9.680120	0174	0228	0282	0336	0390	24
36	0444	0498	0552	0606	0660	0714	23
37	0768	0822	0876	0930	0984	1038	22
38	1092	1146	1200	1254	1308	1362	21
39	1416	1470	1524	1578	1632	1686	20
40	9.681740	1794	1847	1901	1955	2009	19
41	2063	2117	2171	2225	2279	2333	18
42	2387	2440	2494	2548	2602	2656	17
43	2710	2764	2817	2871	2925	2979	16
44	3033	3087	3140	3194	3248	3302	15
45	3356	3410	3463	3517	3571	3625	14
46	3679	3732	3786	3840	3894	3947	13
47	4001	4055	4109	4162	4216	4270	12
48	4324	4377	4431	4485	4539	4592	11
49	4646	4700	4753	4807	4861	4914	10
50	9.684968	5022	5075	5129	5183	5236	9
51	5290	5344	5397	5451	5505	5558	8
52	5612	5666	5719	5773	5827	5880	7
53	5934	5987	6041	6095	6148	6202	6
54	6255	6309	6363	6416	6470	6523	5
55	6577	6630	6684	6737	6791	6845	4
56	6898	6952	7005	7059	7112	7166	3
57	7219	7273	7326	7380	7433	7487	2
58	7540	7594	7647	7701	7754	7808	1
59	7861	7915	7968	8021	8075	8128	0
	60″	50″	40″	30″	20″	10″	Min.
	Co-tangent of 64 Degrees.						

P. Part { 1″ 2″ 3″ 4″ 5″ 6″ 7″ 8″ 9″ / 5 11 16 22 27 33 38 43 49

Min.	Sine of 26 Degrees.						
	0″	10″	20″	30″	40″	50″	
0	9.641842	1885	1928	1971	2015	[illegible]	59
1	2101	2144	2187	2230	2273	[illegible]	58
2	2360	2403	2446	2489	2532	2575	57
3	2618	2661	2704	2747	2790	2833	56
4	2877	2920	2963	3006	3049	[illegible]	55
5	3135	3178	3221	3264	3307	3350	54
6	3393	3436	3479	3522	3565	3607	53
7	3650	3693	3736	3779	3822	3865	52
8	3908	3951	3994	4037	4080	4123	51
9	4165	4208	4251	4294	4337	4380	50
10	9.644423	4465	4508	4551	4594	4637	49
11	4680	4722	4765	4808	4851	4894	48
12	4936	4979	5022	5065	5108	5150	47
13	5193	5236	5279	5321	5364	5407	46
14	5450	5492	5535	5578	5620	5663	45
15	5706	5749	5791	5834	5877	5919	44
16	5962	6005	6047	6090	6133	6175	43
17	6218	6260	6303	6346	6388	6431	42
18	6474	6516	6559	6601	6644	6686	41
19	6729	6772	6814	6857	6899	6942	40
20	9.646984	7027	7069	7112	7154	7197	39
21	7240	7282	7325	7367	7409	7452	38
22	7494	7537	7579	7622	7664	7707	37
23	7749	7792	7834	7877	7919	7961	36
24	8004	8046	8089	8131	8173	8216	35
25	8258	8301	8343	8385	8428	8470	34
26	8512	8555	8597	8639	8682	8724	33
27	8766	8809	8851	8893	8936	8978	32
28	9020	9063	9105	9147	9189	9232	31
29	9274	9316	9358	9401	9443	9485	30
30	9.649527	9570	9612	9654	9696	9739	29
31	9781	9823	9865	9907	9949	9992	28
32	9.650034	0076	0118	0160	0202	0245	27
33	0287	0329	0371	0413	0455	0497	26
34	0539	0582	0624	0666	0708	0750	25
35	0792	0834	0876	0918	0960	1002	24
36	1044	1086	1128	1171	1213	1255	23
37	1297	1339	1381	1423	1465	1507	22
38	1549	1591	1633	1675	1716	1758	21
39	1800	1842	1884	1926	1968	2010	20
40	9.652052	2094	2136	2178	2220	2262	19
41	2304	2345	2387	2429	2471	2513	18
42	2555	2597	2638	2680	2722	2764	17
43	2806	2848	2890	2931	2973	3015	16
44	3057	3099	3140	3182	3224	3266	15
45	3308	3349	3391	3433	3475	3516	14
46	3558	3600	3642	3683	3725	3767	13
47	3808	3850	3892	3934	3975	4017	12
48	4059	4100	4142	4184	4225	4267	11
49	4309	4350	4392	4434	4475	4517	10
50	9.654558	4600	4642	4683	4725	4766	9
51	4808	4850	4891	4933	4974	5016	8
52	5058	5099	5141	5182	5224	5265	7
53	5307	5348	5390	5431	5473	5514	6
54	5556	5597	5639	5680	5722	5763	5
55	5805	5846	5888	5929	5971	6012	4
56	6054	6095	6136	6178	6219	6261	3
57	6302	6344	6385	6426	6468	6509	2
58	6551	6592	6633	6675	6716	6757	1
59	6799	6840	6881	6923	6964	7005	0
	60″	50″	40″	30″	20″	10″	Min.
	Co-sine of 63 Degrees.						

P. Part	1″	2″	3″	4″	5″	6″	7″	8″	9″
	4	8	13	17	21	25	30	34	38

Min.	Sine of 27 Degrees.						
	0″	10″	20″	30″	40″	50″	
0	9.657047	7088	7129	7171	7212	7253	59
1	7295	7336	7377	7418	7460	7501	58
2	7542	7584	7625	7666	7707	7749	57
3	7790	7831	7872	7913	7955	7996	56
4	8037	8078	8119	8161	8202	8243	55
5	8284	8325	8367	8408	8449	8490	54
6	8531	8572	8613	8655	8696	8737	53
7	8778	8819	8860	8901	8942	8983	52
8	9025	9066	9107	9148	9189	9230	51
9	9271	9312	9353	9394	9435	9476	50
10	9.659517	9558	9599	9640	9681	9722	49
11	9763	9804	9845	9886	9927	9968	48
12	9.660009	0050	0091	0132	0173	0214	47
13	0255	0296	0337	0378	0419	0460	46
14	0501	0541	0582	0623	0664	0705	45
15	0746	0787	0828	0869	0909	0950	44
16	0991	1032	1073	1114	1154	1195	43
17	1236	1277	1318	1359	1399	1440	42
18	1481	1522	1563	1603	1644	1685	41
19	1726	1766	1807	1848	1889	1929	40
20	9.661970	2011	2052	2092	2133	2174	39
21	2214	2255	2296	2337	2377	2418	38
22	2459	2499	2540	2581	2621	2662	37
23	2703	2743	2784	2825	2865	2906	36
24	2946	2987	3028	3068	3109	3149	35
25	3190	3231	3271	3312	3352	3393	34
26	3433	3474	3515	3555	3596	3636	33
27	3677	3717	3758	3798	3839	3879	32
28	3920	3960	4001	4041	4082	4122	31
29	4163	4203	4244	4284	4325	4365	30
30	9.664406	4446	4486	4527	4567	4608	29
31	4648	4689	4729	4769	4810	4850	28
32	4891	4931	4971	5012	5052	5093	27
33	5133	5173	5214	5254	5294	5335	26
34	5375	5415	5456	5496	5536	5577	25
35	5617	5657	5697	5738	5778	5818	24
36	5859	5899	5939	5979	6020	6060	23
37	6100	6140	6181	6221	6261	6301	22
38	6342	6382	6422	6462	6502	6543	21
39	6583	6623	6663	6703	6743	6784	20
40	9.666824	6864	6904	6944	6984	7025	19
41	7065	7105	7145	7185	7225	7265	18
42	7305	7346	7386	7426	7466	7506	17
43	7546	7586	7626	7666	7706	7746	16
44	7786	7826	7866	7906	7946	7986	15
45	8027	8067	8107	8147	8187	8227	14
46	8267	8307	8347	8386	8426	8466	13
47	8506	8546	8586	8626	8666	8706	12
48	8746	8786	8826	8866	8906	8946	11
49	8986	9026	9065	9105	9145	9185	10
50	9.669225	9265	9305	9345	9384	9424	9
51	9464	9504	9544	9584	9624	9663	8
52	9703	9743	9783	9823	9862	9902	7
53	9942	9982	..22	..61	.101	.141	6
54	9.670181	0220	0260	0300	0340	0379	5
55	0419	0459	0499	0538	0578	0618	4
56	0658	0697	0737	0777	0816	0856	3
57	0896	0935	0975	1015	1054	1094	2
58	1134	1173	1213	1253	1292	1332	1
59	1372	1411	1451	1490	1530	1570	0
	60″	50″	40″	30″	20″	10″	Min.
	Co-sine of 62 Degrees.						

P. Part	1″	2″	3″	4″	5″	6″	7″	8″	9″
	4	8	12	16	20	24	28	32	36

Min.	Tangent of 26 Degrees. 0″	10″	20″	30″	40″	50″	
0	9.688182	8235	8289	8342	8395	8449	59
1	8502	8556	8609	8663	8716	8769	58
2	8823	8876	8930	8983	9036	9090	57
3	9143	9196	9250	9303	9356	9410	56
4	9463	9516	9570	9623	9676	9730	55
5	9783	9836	9890	9943	9996	..50	54
6	9.690103	0156	0210	0263	0316	0369	53
7	0423	0476	0529	0582	0636	0689	52
8	0742	0795	0849	0902	0955	1008	51
9	1062	1115	1168	1221	1274	1328	50
10	9.691381	1434	1487	1540	1594	1647	49
11	1700	1753	1806	1859	1913	1966	48
12	2019	2072	2125	2178	2232	2285	47
13	2338	2391	2444	2497	2550	2603	46
14	2656	2710	2763	2816	2869	2922	45
15	2975	3028	3081	3134	3187	3240	44
16	3293	3346	3400	3453	3506	3559	43
17	3612	3665	3718	3771	3824	3877	42
18	3930	3983	4036	4089	4142	4195	41
19	4248	4301	4354	4407	4460	4513	40
20	9.694566	4619	4672	4724	4777	4830	39
21	4883	4936	4989	5042	5095	5148	38
22	5201	5254	5307	5360	5412	5465	37
23	5518	5571	5624	5677	5730	5783	36
24	5836	5888	5941	5994	6047	6100	35
25	6153	6206	6258	6311	6364	6417	34
26	6470	6522	6575	6628	6681	6734	33
27	6787	6839	6892	6945	6998	7050	32
28	7103	7156	7209	7262	7314	7367	31
29	7420	7473	7525	7578	7631	7684	30
30	9.697736	7789	7842	7894	7947	8000	29
31	8053	8105	8158	8211	8263	8316	28
32	8369	8421	8474	8527	8579	8632	27
33	8685	8737	8790	8843	8895	8948	26
34	9001	9053	9106	9159	9211	9264	25
35	9316	9369	9422	9474	9527	9579	24
36	9632	9685	9737	9790	9842	9895	23
37	9947	....	..53	.105	.158	.210	22
38	9.700263	0315	0368	0420	0473	0525	21
39	0578	0630	0683	0736	0788	0841	20
40	9.700893	0946	0998	1051	1103	1155	19
41	1208	1260	1313	1365	1418	1470	18
42	1523	1575	1628	1680	1733	1785	17
43	1837	1890	1942	1995	2047	2100	16
44	2152	2204	2257	2309	2362	2414	15
45	2466	2519	2571	2623	2676	2728	14
46	2781	2833	2885	2938	2990	3042	13
47	3095	3147	3199	3252	3304	3356	12
48	3409	3461	3513	3566	3618	3670	11
49	3722	3775	3827	3879	3932	3984	10
50	9.704036	4088	4141	4193	4245	4297	9
51	4350	4402	4454	4506	4559	4611	8
52	4663	4715	4768	4820	4872	4924	7
53	4976	5029	5081	5133	5185	5237	6
54	5290	5342	5394	5446	5498	5551	5
55	5603	5655	5707	5759	5811	5863	4
56	5916	5968	6020	6072	6124	6176	3
57	6228	6280	6333	6385	6437	6489	2
58	6541	6593	6645	6697	6749	6801	1
59	6854	6906	6958	7010	7062	7114	0
	60″	50″	40″	30″	20″	10″	Min.
	Co-tangent of 63 Degrees.						

P. Part { 1″ 2″ 3″ 4″ 5″ 6″ 7″ 8″ 9″ / 5 11 16 21 26 32 37 42 47

Min.	Tangent of 27 Degrees. 0″	10″	20″	30″	40″	50″	
0	9.707166	7218	7270	7322	7374	7426	59
1	7478	7530	7582	7634	7686	7738	58
2	7790	7842	7894	7946	7998	8050	57
3	8102	8154	8206	8258	8310	8362	56
4	8414	8466	8518	8570	8622	8674	55
5	8726	8778	8830	8882	8934	8985	54
6	9037	9089	9141	9193	9245	9297	53
7	9349	9401	9453	9504	9556	9608	52
8	9660	9712	9764	9816	9868	9919	51
9	9971	..23	..75	.127	.179	.231	50
10	9.710282	0334	0386	0438	0490	0542	49
11	0593	0645	0697	0749	0801	0852	48
12	0904	0956	1008	1059	1111	1163	47
13	1215	1267	1318	1370	1422	1474	46
14	1525	1577	1629	1681	1732	1784	45
15	1836	1887	1939	1991	2043	2094	44
16	2146	2198	2249	2301	2353	2405	43
17	2456	2508	2560	2611	2663	2715	42
18	2766	2818	2870	2921	2973	3025	41
19	3076	3128	3179	3231	3283	3334	40
20	9.713386	3438	3489	3541	3592	3644	39
21	3696	3747	3799	3850	3902	3954	38
22	4005	4057	4108	4160	4211	4263	37
23	4314	4366	4418	4469	4521	4572	36
24	4624	4675	4727	4778	4830	4881	35
25	4933	4984	5036	5087	5139	5190	34
26	5242	5293	5345	5396	5448	5499	33
27	5551	5602	5654	5705	5757	5808	32
28	5860	5911	5962	6014	6065	6117	31
29	6168	6220	6271	6322	6374	6425	30
30	9.716477	6528	6579	6631	6682	6734	29
31	6785	6836	6888	6939	6991	7042	28
32	7093	7145	7196	7247	7299	7350	27
33	7401	7453	7504	7555	7607	7658	26
34	7709	7761	7812	7863	7915	7966	25
35	8017	8069	8120	8171	8223	8274	24
36	8325	8376	8428	8479	8530	8581	23
37	8633	8684	8735	8786	8838	8889	22
38	8940	8991	9043	9094	9145	9196	21
39	9248	9299	9350	9401	9452	9504	20
40	9.719555	9606	9657	9708	9760	9811	19
41	9862	9913	9964	..16	..67	.118	18
42	9.720169	0220	0271	0322	0374	0425	17
43	0476	0527	0578	0629	0680	0732	16
44	0783	0834	0885	0936	0987	1038	15
45	1089	1140	1191	1243	1294	1345	14
46	1396	1447	1498	1549	1600	1651	13
47	1702	1753	1804	1855	1906	1957	12
48	2009	2060	2111	2162	2213	2264	11
49	2315	2366	2417	2468	2519	2570	10
50	9.722621	2672	2723	2774	2825	2876	9
51	2927	2978	3029	3080	3130	3181	8
52	3232	3283	3334	3385	3436	3487	7
53	3538	3589	3640	3691	3742	3793	6
54	3844	3895	3945	3996	4047	4098	5
55	4149	4200	4251	4302	4353	4403	4
56	4454	4505	4556	4607	4658	4709	3
57	4760	4810	4861	4912	4963	5014	2
58	5065	5115	5166	5217	5268	5319	1
59	5370	5420	5471	5522	5573	5624	0
	60″	50″	40″	30″	20″	10″	Min.
	Co-tangent of 62 Degrees.						

P. Part { 1″ 2″ 3″ 4″ 5″ 6″ 7″ 8″ 9″ / 5 10 15 21 26 31 36 41 46

Min.	Sine of 28 Degrees. 0″	10″	20″	30″	40″	50″	
0	9.671609	1649	1688	1728	1768	1807	59
1	1847	1886	1926	1965	2005	2045	58
2	2084	2124	2163	2203	2242	2282	57
3	2321	2361	2400	2440	2479	2519	56
4	2558	2598	2637	2677	2716	2756	55
5	2795	2835	2874	2914	2953	2992	54
6	3032	3071	3111	3150	3190	3229	53
7	3268	3308	3347	3387	3426	3465	52
8	3505	3544	3583	3623	3662	3702	51
9	3741	3780	3820	3859	3898	3938	50
10	9.673977	4016	4056	4095	4134	4173	49
11	4213	4252	4291	4331	4370	4409	48
12	4448	4488	4527	4566	4606	4645	47
13	4684	4723	4762	4802	4841	4880	46
14	4919	4959	4998	5037	5076	5115	45
15	5155	5194	5233	5272	5311	5350	44
16	5390	5429	5468	5507	5546	5585	43
17	5624	5664	5703	5742	5781	5820	42
18	5859	5898	5937	5976	6016	6055	41
19	6094	6133	6172	6211	6250	6289	40
20	9.676328	6367	6406	6445	6484	6523	39
21	6562	6601	6640	6679	6718	6757	38
22	6796	6835	6874	6913	6952	6991	37
23	7030	7069	7108	7147	7186	7225	36
24	7264	7303	7342	7381	7420	7459	35
25	7498	7536	7575	7614	7653	7692	34
26	7731	7770	7809	7848	7886	7925	33
27	7964	8003	8042	8081	8120	8158	32
28	8197	8236	8275	8314	8353	8391	31
29	8430	8469	8508	8547	8585	8624	30
30	9.678663	8702	8740	8779	8818	8857	29
31	8895	8934	8973	9012	9050	9089	28
32	9128	9167	9205	9244	9283	9321	27
33	9360	9399	9438	9476	9515	9554	26
34	9592	9631	9670	9708	9747	9786	25
35	9824	9863	9902	9940	9979	..17	24
36	9.680056	0095	0133	0172	0210	0249	23
37	0288	0326	0365	0403	0442	0481	22
38	0519	0558	0596	0635	0673	0712	21
39	0750	0789	0828	0866	0905	0943	20
40	9.680982	1020	1059	1097	1136	1174	19
41	1213	1251	1290	1328	1366	1405	18
42	1443	1482	1520	1559	1597	1636	17
43	1674	1713	1751	1789	1828	1866	16
44	1905	1943	1981	2020	2058	2097	15
45	2135	2173	2212	2250	2288	2327	14
46	2365	2403	2442	2480	2519	2557	13
47	2595	2633	2672	2710	2748	2787	12
48	2825	2863	2902	2940	2978	3016	11
49	3055	3093	3131	3170	3208	3246	10
50	9.683284	3323	3361	3399	3437	3475	9
51	3514	3552	3590	3628	3667	3705	8
52	3743	3781	3819	3858	3896	3934	7
53	3972	4010	4048	4087	4125	4163	6
54	4201	4239	4277	4315	4353	4392	5
55	4430	4468	4506	4544	4582	4620	4
56	4658	4696	4735	4773	4811	4849	3
57	4887	4925	4963	5001	5039	5077	2
58	5115	5153	5191	5229	5267	5305	1
59	5343	5381	5419	5457	5495	5533	0
	60″	50″	40″	30″	20″	10″	Min.
	Co-sine of 61 Degrees.						

P. Part	1″	2″	3″	4″	5″	6″	7″	8″	9″
	4	8	12	16	19	23	27	31	35

Min.	Sine of 29 Degrees. 0″	10″	20″	30″	40″	50″	
0	9.685571	5609	5647	5685	5723	5761	59
1	5799	5837	5875	5913	5951	5989	58
2	6027	6065	6103	6141	6178	6216	57
3	6254	6292	6330	6368	6406	6444	56
4	6482	6519	6557	6595	6633	6671	55
5	6709	6747	6785	6822	6860	6898	54
6	6936	6974	7012	7049	7087	7125	53
7	7163	7201	7238	7276	7314	7352	52
8	7389	7427	7465	7503	7541	7578	51
9	7616	7654	7692	7729	7767	7805	50
10	9.687843	7880	7918	7956	7993	8031	49
11	8069	8106	8144	8182	8220	8257	48
12	8295	8333	8370	8408	8446	8483	47
13	8521	8559	8596	8634	8671	8709	46
14	8747	8784	8822	8860	8897	8935	45
15	8972	9010	9048	9085	9123	9160	44
16	9198	9235	9273	9311	9348	9386	43
17	9423	9461	9498	9536	9573	9611	42
18	9648	9686	9723	9761	9798	9836	41
19	9873	9911	9948	9986	..23	..61	40
20	9.690098	0136	0173	0211	0248	0286	39
21	0323	0361	0398	0435	0473	0510	38
22	0548	0585	0622	0660	0697	0735	37
23	0772	0809	0847	0884	0922	0959	36
24	0996	1034	1071	1108	1146	1183	35
25	1220	1258	1295	1332	1370	1407	34
26	1444	1482	1519	1556	1594	1631	33
27	1668	1706	1743	1780	1817	1855	32
28	1892	1929	1966	2004	2041	2078	31
29	2115	2153	2190	2227	2264	2302	30
30	9.692339	2376	2413	2450	2488	2525	29
31	2562	2599	2636	2674	2711	2748	28
32	2785	2822	2859	2897	2934	2971	27
33	3008	3045	3082	3119	3157	3194	26
34	3231	3268	3305	3342	3379	3416	25
35	3453	3490	3528	3565	3602	3639	24
36	3676	3713	3750	3787	3824	3861	23
37	3898	3935	3972	4009	4046	4083	22
38	4120	4157	4194	4231	4268	4305	21
39	4342	4379	4416	4453	4490	4527	20
40	9.694564	4601	4638	4675	47.2	4749	19
41	4786	4823	4860	4897	4934	4971	18
42	5007	5044	5081	5118	5155	5192	17
43	5229	5266	5303	5339	5376	5413	16
44	5450	5487	5524	5561	5598	5634	15
45	5671	5708	5745	5782	5819	5855	14
46	5892	5929	5966	6003	6039	6076	13
47	6113	6150	6187	6223	6260	6297	12
48	6334	6370	6407	6444	6481	6517	11
49	6554	6591	6628	6664	6701	6738	10
50	9.696775	6811	6848	6885	6921	6958	9
51	6995	7031	7068	7105	7141	7178	8
52	7215	7251	7288	7325	7361	7398	7
53	7435	7471	7508	7545	7581	7618	6
54	7654	7691	7728	7764	7801	7838	5
55	7874	7911	7947	7984	8020	8057	4
56	8094	8130	8167	8203	8240	8276	3
57	8313	8349	8386	8423	8459	8496	2
58	8532	8569	8605	8642	8678	8715	1
59	8751	8788	8824	8861	8897	8934	0
	60″	50″	40″	30″	20″	10″	Min.
	Co-sine of 60 Degrees.						

P. Part	1″	2″	3″	4″	5″	6″	7″	8″	9″
	4	7	11	15	19	22	26	30	33

Min.	Tangent of 28 Degrees. 0″	10″	20″	30″	40″	50″	
0	9.725674	5725	5776	5827	5878	5928	59
1	5979	6030	6081	6131	6182	6233	58
2	6284	6334	6385	6436	6487	6537	57
3	6588	6639	6690	6740	6791	6842	56
4	6892	6943	6994	7045	7095	7146	55
5	7197	7247	7298	7349	7399	7450	54
6	7501	7551	7602	7653	7703	7754	53
7	7805	7855	7906	7957	8007	8058	52
8	8109	8159	8210	8261	8311	8362	51
9	8412	8463	8514	8564	8615	8665	50
10	9.728716	8767	8817	8868	8918	8969	49
11	9020	9070	9121	9171	9222	9272	48
12	9323	9374	9424	9475	9525	9576	47
13	9626	9677	9727	9778	9828	9879	46
14	9929	9980	..30	..81	.132	.182	45
15	9.730233	0283	0333	0384	0434	0485	44
16	0535	0586	0636	0687	0737	0788	43
17	0838	0889	0939	0990	1040	1091	42
18	1141	1191	1242	1292	1343	1393	41
19	1444	1494	1544	1595	1645	1696	40
20	9.731746	1796	1847	1897	1948	1998	39
21	2048	2099	2149	2200	2250	2300	38
22	2351	2401	2451	2502	2552	2602	37
23	2653	2703	2753	2804	2854	2904	36
24	2955	3005	3055	3106	3156	3206	35
25	3257	3307	3357	3408	3458	3508	34
26	3558	3609	3659	3709	3760	3810	33
27	3860	3910	3961	4011	4061	4111	32
28	4162	4212	4262	4312	4363	4413	31
29	4463	4513	4564	4614	4664	4714	30
30	9.734764	4815	4865	4915	4965	5015	29
31	5066	5116	5166	5216	5266	5317	28
32	5367	5417	5467	5517	5567	5618	27
33	5668	5718	5768	5818	5868	5918	26
34	5969	6019	6069	6119	6169	6219	25
35	6269	6319	6370	6420	6470	6520	24
36	6570	6620	6670	6720	6770	6820	23
37	6870	6921	6971	7021	7071	7121	22
38	7171	7221	7271	7321	7371	7421	21
39	7471	7521	7571	7621	7671	7721	20
40	9.737771	7821	7871	7921	7971	8021	19
41	8071	8121	8171	8221	8271	8321	18
42	8371	8421	8471	8521	8571	8621	17
43	8671	8721	8771	8821	8871	8921	16
44	8971	9021	9071	9121	9171	9221	15
45	9271	9321	9371	9420	9470	9520	14
46	9570	9620	9670	9720	9770	9820	13
47	9870	9920	9969	..19	..69	.119	12
48	9.740169	0219	0269	0319	0368	0418	11
49	0468	0518	0568	0618	0668	0717	10
50	9.740767	0817	0867	0917	0967	1016	9
51	1066	1116	1166	1216	1265	1315	8
52	1365	1415	1465	1514	1564	1614	7
53	1664	1714	1763	1813	1863	1913	6
54	1962	2012	2062	2112	2161	2211	5
55	2261	2311	2360	2410	2460	2510	4
56	2559	2609	2659	2709	2758	2808	3
57	2858	2907	2957	3007	3056	3106	2
58	3156	3206	3255	3305	3355	3404	1
59	3454	3504	3553	3603	3653	3702	0
	60″	50″	40″	30″	20″	10″	Min.
	Co-tangent of 61 Degrees.						

P. Part { 1″ 2″ 3″ 4″ 5″ 6″ 7″ 8″ 9″ / 5 10 15 20 25 30 35 40 45

Min.	Tangent of 29 Degrees. 0″	10″	20″	30″	40″	50″	
0	9.743752	3802	3851	3901	3951	4000	59
1	4050	4099	4149	4199	4248	4298	58
2	4348	4397	4447	4496	4546	4596	57
3	4645	4695	4744	4794	4844	4893	56
4	4943	4992	5042	5092	5141	5191	55
5	5240	5290	5339	5389	5439	5488	54
6	5538	5587	5637	5686	5736	5785	53
7	5835	5884	5934	5983	6033	6082	52
8	6132	6182	6231	6281	6330	6380	51
9	6429	6479	6528	6577	6627	6676	50
10	9.746726	6775	6825	6874	6924	6973	49
11	7023	7072	7122	7171	7221	7270	48
12	7319	7369	7418	7468	7517	7567	47
13	7616	7665	7715	7764	7814	7863	46
14	7913	7962	8011	8061	8110	8160	45
15	8209	8258	8308	8357	8406	8456	44
16	8505	8555	8604	8653	8703	8752	43
17	8801	8851	8900	8949	8999	9048	42
18	9097	9147	9196	9245	9295	9344	41
19	9393	9443	9492	9541	9591	9640	40
20	9.749689	9739	9788	9837	9886	9936	39
21	9985	..34	..84	.133	.182	.231	38
22	9.750281	0330	0379	0428	0478	0527	37
23	0576	0625	0675	0724	0773	0822	36
24	0872	0921	0970	1019	1069	1118	35
25	1167	1216	1265	1315	1364	1413	34
26	1462	1511	1561	1610	1659	1708	33
27	1757	1806	1856	1905	1954	2003	32
28	2052	2101	2151	2200	2249	2298	31
29	2347	2396	2446	2495	2544	2593	30
30	9.752642	2691	2740	2789	2839	2888	29
31	2937	2986	3035	3084	3133	3182	28
32	3231	3280	3330	3379	3428	3477	27
33	3526	3575	3624	3673	3722	3771	26
34	3820	3869	3918	3967	4016	4066	25
35	4115	4164	4213	4262	4311	4360	24
36	4409	4458	4507	4556	4605	4654	23
37	4703	4752	4801	4850	4899	4948	22
38	4997	5046	5095	5144	5193	5242	21
39	5291	5340	5389	5438	5487	5536	20
40	9.755585	5634	5682	5731	5780	5829	19
41	5878	5927	5976	6025	6074	6123	18
42	6172	6221	6270	6319	6368	6416	17
43	6465	6514	6563	6612	6661	6710	16
44	6759	6808	6857	6905	6954	7003	15
45	7052	7101	7150	7199	7247	7296	14
46	7345	7394	7443	7492	7541	7589	13
47	7638	7687	7736	7785	7834	7882	12
48	7931	7980	8029	8078	8127	8175	11
49	8224	8273	8322	8371	8419	8468	10
50	9.758517	8566	8615	8663	8712	8761	9
51	8810	8858	8907	8956	9005	9053	8
52	9102	9151	9200	9248	9297	9346	7
53	9395	9443	9492	9541	9590	9638	6
54	9687	9736	9785	9833	9882	9931	5
55	9979	..28	..77	.126	.174	.223	4
56	9.760272	0320	0369	0418	0466	0515	3
57	0564	0612	0661	0710	0758	0807	2
58	0856	0904	0953	1002	1050	1099	1
59	1148	1196	1245	1293	1342	1391	0
	60″	50″	40″	30″	20″	10″	Min.
	Co-tangent of 60 Degrees.						

P. Part { 1″ 2″ 3″ 4″ 5″ 6″ 7″ 8″ 9″ / 5 10 15 20 25 29 34 39 44

Min.	Sine of 30 Degrees. 0″	10″	20″	30″	40″	50″	
0	9.698970	9006	9043	9079	9116	9152	59
1	9189	9225	9262	9298	9334	9371	58
2	9407	9444	9480	9517	9553	9589	57
3	9626	9662	9699	9735	9771	9808	56
4	9844	9880	9917	9953	9990	..26	55
5	9.700062	0099	0135	0171	0208	0244	54
6	0280	0317	0353	0389	0425	0462	53
7	0498	0534	0571	0607	0643	0680	52
8	0716	0752	0788	0825	0861	0897	51
9	0933	0970	1006	1042	1078	1115	50
10	9.701151	1187	1223	1259	1296	1332	49
11	1368	1404	1440	1477	1513	1549	48
12	1585	1621	1658	1694	1730	1766	47
13	1802	1838	1874	1911	1947	1983	46
14	2019	2055	2091	2127	2164	2200	45
15	2236	2272	2308	2344	2380	2416	44
16	2452	2488	2524	2561	2597	2633	43
17	2669	2705	2741	2777	2813	2849	42
18	2885	2921	2957	2993	3029	3065	41
19	3101	3137	3173	3209	3245	3281	40
20	9.703317	3353	3389	3425	3461	3497	39
21	3533	3569	3605	3641	3677	3713	38
22	3749	3784	3820	3856	3892	3928	37
23	3964	4000	4036	4072	4108	4144	36
24	4179	4215	4251	4287	4323	4359	35
25	4395	4431	4466	4502	4538	4574	34
26	4610	4646	4682	4717	4753	4789	33
27	4825	4861	4896	4932	4968	5004	32
28	5040	5075	5111	5147	5183	5219	31
29	5254	5290	5326	5362	5397	5433	30
30	9.705469	5505	5540	5576	5612	5648	29
31	5683	5719	5755	5790	5826	5862	28
32	5898	5933	5969	6005	6040	6076	27
33	6112	6147	6183	6219	6254	6290	26
34	6326	6361	6397	6433	6468	6504	25
35	6539	6575	6611	6646	6682	6718	24
36	6753	6789	6824	6860	6895	6931	23
37	6967	7002	7038	7073	7109	7145	22
38	7180	7216	7251	7287	7322	7358	21
39	7393	7429	7464	7500	7535	7571	20
40	9.707606	7642	7677	7713	7748	7784	19
41	7819	7855	7890	7926	7961	7997	18
42	8032	8068	8103	8139	8174	8210	17
43	8245	8280	8316	8351	8387	8422	16
44	8458	8493	8528	8564	8599	8635	15
45	8670	8705	8741	8776	8811	8847	14
46	8882	8918	8953	8988	9024	9059	13
47	9094	9130	9165	9200	9236	9271	12
48	9306	9342	9377	9412	9448	9483	11
49	9518	9553	9589	9624	9659	9695	10
50	9.709730	9765	9800	9836	9871	9906	9
51	9941	9977	..12	..47	..82	.118	8
52	9.710153	0188	0223	0259	0294	0329	7
53	0364	0399	0435	0470	0505	0540	6
54	0575	0611	0646	0681	0716	0751	5
55	0786	0822	0857	0892	0927	0962	4
56	0997	1032	1067	1103	1138	1173	3
57	1208	1243	1278	1313	1348	1383	2
58	1419	1454	1489	1524	1559	1594	1
59	1629	1664	1699	1734	1769	1804	0
	60″	50″	40″	30″	20″	10″	Min.
	Co-sine of 59 Degrees.						

P. Part { 1″ 2″ 3″ 4″ 5″ 6″ 7″ 8″ 9″
{ 4 7 11 14 18 21 25 29 32

Min.	Sine of 31 Degrees. 0″	10″	20″	30″	40″	50″	
0	9.711839	1874	1909	1944	1979	2014	59
1	2050	2085	2120	2155	2190	2225	58
2	2260	2295	2330	2365	2400	2434	57
3	2469	2504	2539	2574	2609	2644	56
4	2679	2714	2749	2784	2819	2854	55
5	2889	2924	2959	2994	3029	3063	54
6	3098	3133	3168	3203	3238	3273	53
7	3308	3343	3377	3412	3447	3482	52
8	3517	3552	3587	3621	3656	3691	51
9	3726	3761	3796	3830	3865	3900	50
10	9.713935	3970	4005	4039	4074	4109	49
11	4144	4179	4213	4248	4283	4318	48
12	4352	4387	4422	4457	4491	4526	47
13	4561	4596	4630	4665	4700	4735	46
14	4769	4804	4839	4873	4908	4943	45
15	4978	5012	5047	5082	5116	5151	44
16	5186	5220	5255	5290	5324	5359	43
17	5394	5428	5463	5498	5532	5567	42
18	5602	5636	5671	5705	5740	5775	41
19	5809	5844	5878	5913	5948	5982	40
20	9.716017	6051	6086	6121	6155	6190	39
21	6224	6259	6293	6328	6362	6397	38
22	6432	6466	6501	6535	6570	6604	37
23	6639	6673	6708	6742	6777	6811	36
24	6846	6880	6915	6949	6984	7018	35
25	7053	7087	7122	7156	7191	7225	34
26	7259	7294	7328	7363	7397	7432	33
27	7466	7500	7535	7569	7604	7638	32
28	7673	7707	7741	7776	7810	7844	31
29	7879	7913	7948	7982	8016	8051	30
30	9.718085	8119	8154	8188	8223	8257	29
31	8291	8326	8360	8394	8429	8463	28
32	8497	8531	8566	8600	8634	8669	27
33	8703	8737	8772	8806	8840	8874	26
34	8909	8943	8977	9011	9046	9080	25
35	9114	9148	9183	9217	9251	9285	24
36	9320	9354	9388	9422	9456	9491	23
37	9525	9559	9593	9627	9662	9696	22
38	9730	9764	9798	9833	9867	9901	21
39	9935	9969	...3	..38	..72	.106	20
40	9.720140	0174	0208	0242	0276	0311	19
41	0345	0379	0413	0447	0481	0515	18
42	0549	0583	0617	0652	0686	0720	17
43	0754	0788	0822	0856	0890	0924	16
44	0958	0992	1026	1060	1094	1128	15
45	1162	1196	1230	1264	1298	1332	14
46	1366	1400	1434	1468	1502	1536	13
47	1570	1604	1638	1672	1706	1740	12
48	1774	1808	1842	1876	1910	1944	11
49	1978	2012	2046	2080	2114	2148	10
50	9.722181	2215	2249	2283	2317	2351	9
51	2385	2419	2453	2487	2520	2554	8
52	2588	2622	2656	2690	2724	2757	7
53	2791	2825	2859	2893	2927	2960	6
54	2994	3028	3062	3096	3130	3163	5
55	3197	3231	3265	3299	3332	3366	4
56	3400	3434	3468	3501	3535	3569	3
57	3603	3636	3670	3704	3738	3771	2
58	3805	3839	3873	3906	3940	3974	1
59	4007	4041	4075	4109	4142	4176	0
	60″	50″	40″	30″	20″	10″	Min.
	Co-sine of 58 Degrees.						

P. Part { 1″ 2″ 3″ 4″ 5″ 6″ 7″ 8″ 9″
{ 3 7 10 14 17 21 24 27 31

Min.	Tangent of 30 Degrees. 0″	10″	20″	30″	40″	50″	
0	9·761439	1488	1537	1585	1634	1682	59
1	1731	1780	1828	1877	1925	1974	58
2	2023	2071	2120	2168	2217	2266	57
3	2314	2363	2411	2460	2508	2557	56
4	2606	2654	2703	2751	2800	2848	55
5	2897	2945	2994	3043	3091	3140	54
6	3188	3237	3285	3334	3382	3431	53
7	3479	3528	3576	3625	3673	3722	52
8	3770	3819	3867	3916	3964	4013	51
9	4061	4110	4158	4207	4255	4304	50
10	9·764352	4400	4449	4497	4546	4594	49
11	4643	4691	4740	4788	4836	4885	48
12	4933	4982	5030	5079	5127	5175	47
13	5224	5272	5321	5369	5418	5466	46
14	5514	5563	5611	5660	5708	5756	45
15	5805	5853	5901	5950	5998	6047	44
16	6095	6143	6192	6240	6288	6337	43
17	6385	6433	6482	6530	6578	6627	42
18	6675	6723	6772	6820	6868	6917	41
19	6965	7013	7062	7110	7158	7207	40
20	9·767255	7303	7352	7400	7448	7496	39
21	7545	7593	7641	7690	7738	7786	38
22	7834	7883	7931	7979	8027	8076	37
23	8124	8172	8221	8269	8317	8365	36
24	8414	8462	8510	8558	8606	8655	35
25	8703	8751	8799	8848	8896	8944	34
26	8992	9040	9089	9137	9185	9233	33
27	9281	9330	9378	9426	9474	9522	32
28	9571	9619	9667	9715	9763	9811	31
29	9860	9908	9956	...4	..52	.100	30
30	9·770148	0197	0245	0293	0341	0389	29
31	0437	0485	0534	0582	0630	0678	28
32	0726	0774	0822	0870	0919	0967	27
33	1015	1063	1111	1159	1207	1255	26
34	1303	1351	1399	1448	1496	1544	25
35	1592	1640	1688	1736	1784	1832	24
36	1880	1928	1976	2024	2072	2120	23
37	2168	2216	2264	2312	2361	2409	22
38	2457	2505	2553	2601	2649	2697	21
39	2745	2793	2841	2889	2937	2985	20
40	9·773033	3081	3129	3177	3225	3273	19
41	3321	3369	3417	3465	3512	3560	18
42	3608	3656	3704	3752	3800	3848	17
43	3896	3944	3992	4040	4088	4136	16
44	4184	4232	4280	4328	4375	4423	15
45	4471	4519	4567	4615	4663	4711	14
46	4759	4807	4855	4902	4950	4998	13
47	5046	5094	5142	5190	5238	5286	12
48	5333	5381	5429	5477	5525	5573	11
49	5621	5668	5716	5764	5812	5860	10
50	9·775908	5956	6003	6051	6099	6147	9
51	6195	6243	6290	6338	6386	6434	8
52	6482	6529	6577	6625	6673	6721	7
53	6768	6816	6864	6912	6960	7007	6
54	7055	7103	7151	7199	7246	7294	5
55	7342	7390	7437	7485	7533	7581	4
56	7628	7676	7724	7772	7819	7867	3
57	7915	7963	8010	8058	8106	8154	2
58	8201	8249	8297	8344	8392	8440	1
59	8488	8535	8583	8631	8678	8726	0
	60″	50″	40″	30″	20″	10″	Min.
	Co-tangent of 59 Degrees.						

P. Part { 1″ 2″ 3″ 4″ 5″ 6″ 7″ 8″ 9″ / 5 10 14 19 24 29 34 39 43 }

Min.	Tangent of 31 Degrees. 0″	10″	20″	30″	40″	50″	
0	9·778774	8821	8869	8917	8964	9012	59
1	9060	9108	9155	9203	9251	9298	58
2	9346	9394	9441	9489	9537	9584	57
3	9632	9679	9727	9775	9822	9870	56
4	9918	9965	..13	..61	.108	.156	55
5	9·780203	0251	0299	0346	0394	0441	54
6	0489	0537	0584	0632	0679	0727	53
7	0775	0822	0870	0917	0965	1013	52
8	1060	1108	1155	1203	1250	1298	51
9	1346	1393	1441	1488	1536	1583	50
10	9·781631	1678	1726	1774	1821	1869	49
11	1916	1964	2011	2059	2106	2154	48
12	2201	2249	2296	2344	2391	2439	47
13	2486	2534	2581	2629	2676	2724	46
14	2771	2819	2866	2914	2961	3009	45
15	3056	3104	3151	3199	3246	3294	44
16	3341	3388	3436	3483	3531	3578	43
17	3626	3673	3721	3768	3816	3863	42
18	3910	3958	4005	4053	4100	4148	41
19	4195	4242	4290	4337	4385	4432	40
20	9·784479	4527	4574	4622	4669	4716	39
21	4764	4811	4859	4906	4953	5001	38
22	5048	5095	5143	5190	5238	5285	37
23	5332	5380	5427	5474	5522	5569	36
24	5616	5664	5711	5758	5806	5853	35
25	5900	5948	5995	6042	6090	6137	34
26	6184	6232	6279	6326	6374	6421	33
27	6468	6516	6563	6610	6657	6705	32
28	6752	6799	6847	6894	6941	6988	31
29	7036	7083	7130	7178	7225	7272	30
30	9·787319	7367	7414	7461	7508	7556	29
31	7603	7650	7697	7745	7792	7839	28
32	7886	7934	7981	8028	8075	8122	27
33	8170	8217	8264	8311	8359	8406	26
34	8453	8500	8547	8595	8642	8689	25
35	8736	8783	8830	8878	8925	8972	24
36	9019	9066	9114	9161	9208	9255	23
37	9302	9349	9397	9444	9491	9538	22
38	9585	9632	9679	9727	9774	9821	21
39	9868	9915	9962	...9	..57	.104	20
40	9·790151	0198	0245	0292	0339	0386	19
41	0434	0481	0528	0575	0622	0669	18
42	0716	0763	0810	0857	0905	0952	17
43	0999	1046	1093	1140	1187	1234	16
44	1281	1328	1375	1422	1469	1516	15
45	1563	1611	1658	1705	1752	1799	14
46	1846	1893	1940	1987	2034	2081	13
47	2128	2175	2222	2269	2316	2363	12
48	2410	2457	2504	2551	2598	2645	11
49	2692	2739	2786	2833	2880	2927	10
50	9·792974	3021	3068	3115	3162	3209	9
51	3256	3303	3350	3397	3444	3491	8
52	3538	3585	3632	3679	3726	3773	7
53	3819	3866	3913	3960	4007	4054	6
54	4101	4148	4195	4242	4289	4336	5
55	4383	4430	4476	4523	4570	4617	4
56	4664	4711	4758	4805	4852	4899	3
57	4946	4992	5039	5086	5133	5180	2
58	5227	5274	5321	5367	5414	5461	1
59	5508	5555	5602	5649	5696	5742	0
	60″	50″	40″	30″	20″	10″	Min.
	Co-tangent of 58 Degrees.						

P. Part { 1″ 2″ 3″ 4″ 5″ 6″ 7″ 8″ 9″ / 5 9 14 19 24 28 33 38 43 }

Min.	Sine of 32 Degrees. 0″	10″	20″	30″	40″	50″	
0	9.724210	4243	4277	4311	4344	4378	59
1	4412	4445	4479	4513	4546	4580	58
2	4614	4647	4681	4715	4748	4782	57
3	4816	4849	4883	4917	4950	4984	56
4	5017	5051	5085	5118	5152	5185	55
5	5219	5253	5286	5320	5353	5387	54
6	5420	5454	5488	5521	5555	5588	53
7	5622	5655	5689	5722	5756	5789	52
8	5823	5856	5890	5923	5957	5990	51
9	6024	6057	6091	6124	6158	6191	50
10	9.726225	6258	6292	6325	6359	6392	49
11	6426	6459	6493	6526	6560	6593	48
12	6626	6660	6693	6727	6760	6794	47
13	6827	6860	6894	6927	6961	6994	46
14	7027	7061	7094	7128	7161	7194	45
15	7228	7261	7294	7328	7361	7394	44
16	7428	7461	7494	7528	7561	7594	43
17	7628	7661	7694	7728	7761	7794	42
18	7828	7861	7894	7928	7961	7994	41
19	8027	8061	8094	8127	8161	8194	40
20	9.728227	8260	8294	8327	8360	8393	39
21	8427	8460	8493	8526	8560	8593	38
22	8626	8659	8692	8726	8759	8792	37
23	8825	8858	8892	8925	8958	8991	36
24	9024	9058	9091	9124	9157	9190	35
25	9223	9257	9290	9323	9356	9389	34
26	9422	9455	9489	9522	9555	9588	33
27	9621	9654	9687	9720	9753	9787	32
28	9820	9853	9886	9919	9952	9985	31
29	9.730018	0051	0084	0117	0150	0183	30
30	9.730217	0250	0283	0316	0349	0382	29
31	0415	0448	0481	0514	0547	0580	28
32	0613	0646	0679	0712	0745	0778	27
33	0811	0844	0877	0910	0943	0976	26
34	1009	1042	1075	1108	1141	1173	25
35	1206	1239	1272	1305	1338	1371	24
36	1404	1437	1470	1503	1536	1569	23
37	1602	1634	1667	1700	1733	1766	22
38	1799	1832	1865	1897	1930	1963	21
39	1996	2029	2062	2095	2127	2160	20
40	9.732193	2226	2259	2292	2325	2357	19
41	2390	2423	2456	2489	2521	2554	18
42	2587	2620	2653	2685	2718	2751	17
43	2784	2816	2849	2882	2915	2948	16
44	2980	3013	3046	3079	3111	3144	15
45	3177	3210	3242	3275	3308	3340	14
46	3373	3406	3439	3471	3504	3537	13
47	3569	3602	3635	3667	3700	3733	12
48	3765	3798	3831	3863	3896	3929	11
49	3961	3994	4027	4059	4092	4125	10
50	9.734157	4190	4222	4255	4288	4320	9
51	4353	4386	4418	4451	4483	4516	8
52	4549	4581	4614	4646	4679	4711	7
53	4744	4777	4809	4842	4874	4907	6
54	4939	4972	5004	5037	5069	5102	5
55	5135	5167	5200	5232	5265	5297	4
56	5330	5362	5395	5427	5460	5492	3
57	5525	5557	5590	5622	5655	5687	2
58	5719	5752	578[illegible]	5817	5849	5882	1
59	5914	5947	5979	6011	6044	6076	0
	60″	50″	40″	30″	20″	10″	Min.
	Co-sine of 57 Degrees.						

P. Part { 1″ 2″ 3″ 4″ 5″ 6″ 7″ 8″ 9″ / 3 7 10 13 17 20 23 26 30

Min.	Sine of 33 Degrees. 0″	10″	20″	30″	40″	50″	
0	9.736109	6141	6174	6206	6238	6271	59
1	6303	6336	6368	6400	6433	6465	58
2	6498	6530	6562	6595	6627	6659	57
3	6692	6724	6757	6789	6821	6854	56
4	6886	6918	6951	6983	7015	7048	55
5	7080	7112	7145	7177	7209	7241	54
6	7274	7306	7338	7371	7403	7435	53
7	7467	7500	7532	7564	7597	7629	52
8	7661	7693	7726	7758	7790	7822	51
9	7855	7887	7919	7951	7983	8016	50
10	9.738048	8080	8112	8145	8177	8209	49
11	8241	8273	8306	8338	8370	8402	48
12	8434	8466	8499	8531	8563	8595	47
13	8627	8659	8692	8724	8756	8788	46
14	8820	8852	8884	8917	8949	8981	45
15	9013	9045	9077	9109	9141	9173	44
16	9206	9238	9270	9302	9334	9366	43
17	9398	9430	9462	9494	9526	9558	42
18	9590	9622	9654	9687	9719	9751	41
19	9783	9815	9847	9879	9911	9943	40
20	9.739975	...7	..39	..71	.103	.135	39
21	9.740167	0199	0231	0263	0295	0327	38
22	0359	0391	0423	0455	0487	0519	37
23	0550	0582	0614	0646	0678	0710	36
24	0742	0774	0806	0838	0870	0902	35
25	0934	0966	0997	1029	1061	1093	34
26	1125	1157	1189	1221	1253	1284	33
27	1316	1348	1380	1412	1444	1476	32
28	1508	1539	1571	1603	1635	1667	31
29	1699	1730	1762	1794	1826	1858	30
30	9.741889	1921	1953	1985	2017	2049	29
31	2080	2112	2144	2176	2207	2239	28
32	2271	2303	2335	2366	2398	2430	27
33	2462	2493	2525	2557	2589	2620	26
34	2652	2684	2715	2747	2779	2811	25
35	2842	2874	2906	2937	2969	3001	24
36	3033	3064	3096	3128	3159	3191	23
37	3223	3254	3286	3318	3349	3381	22
38	3413	3444	3476	3508	3539	3571	21
39	3602	3634	3666	3697	3729	3761	20
40	9.743792	3824	3855	3887	3919	3950	19
41	3982	4013	4045	4077	4108	4140	18
42	4171	4203	4234	4266	4297	4329	17
43	4361	4392	4424	4455	4487	4518	16
44	4550	4581	4613	4644	4676	4707	15
45	4739	4770	4802	4833	4865	4896	14
46	4928	4959	4991	5022	5054	5085	13
47	5117	5148	5180	5211	5243	5274	12
48	5306	5337	5369	5400	5431	5463	11
49	5494	5526	5557	5589	5620	5651	10
50	9.745683	5714	5746	5777	5808	5840	9
51	5871	5903	5934	5965	5997	6028	8
52	6060	6091	6122	6154	6185	6216	7
53	6248	6279	6310	6342	6373	6404	6
54	6436	6467	6498	6530	6561	6592	5
55	6624	6655	6686	6718	6749	6780	4
56	6812	6843	6874	6905	6937	6968	3
57	6999	7031	7062	7093	7124	7156	2
58	7187	7218	7249	7281	7312	7343	:
59	7374	7406	7437	7468	7499	7530	0
	60″	50″	40″	30″	20″	10″	Min.
	Co-sine of 56 Degrees.						

P. Part { 1″ 2″ 3″ 4″ 5″ 6″ 7″ 8″ 9″ / 3 6 10 13 16 19 22 25 29

Min.	Tangent of 32 Degrees. 0″	10″	20″	30″	40″	50″	
0	9.795789	5836	5883	5930	5977	6023	59
1	6070	6117	6164	6211	6258	6304	58
2	6351	6398	6445	6492	6539	6585	57
3	6632	6679	6726	6773	6819	6866	56
4	6913	6960	7007	7053	7100	7147	55
5	7194	7241	7287	7334	7381	7428	54
6	7474	7521	7568	7615	7662	7708	53
7	7755	7802	7849	7895	7942	7989	52
8	8036	8082	8129	8176	8223	8269	51
9	8316	8363	8409	8456	8503	8550	50
10	9.798596	8643	8690	8737	8783	8830	49
11	8877	8923	8970	9017	9063	9110	48
12	9157	9204	9250	9297	9344	9390	47
13	9437	9484	9530	9577	9624	9670	46
14	9717	9764	9810	9857	9904	9950	45
15	9997	..44	..90	.137	.184	.230	44
16	9.800277	0324	0370	0417	0463	0510	43
17	0557	0603	0650	0697	0743	0790	42
18	0836	0883	0930	0976	1023	1070	41
19	1116	1163	1209	1256	1303	1349	40
20	9.801396	1442	1489	1535	1582	1629	39
21	1675	1722	1768	1815	1862	1908	38
22	1955	2001	2048	2094	2141	2187	37
23	2234	2281	2327	2374	2420	2467	36
24	2513	2560	2606	2653	2699	2746	35
25	2792	2839	2886	2932	2979	3025	34
26	3072	3118	3165	3211	3258	3304	33
27	3351	3397	3444	3490	3537	3583	32
28	3630	3676	3723	3769	3816	3862	31
29	3909	3955	4001	4048	4094	4141	30
30	9.804187	4234	4280	4327	4373	4420	29
31	4466	4513	4559	4605	4652	4698	28
32	4745	4791	4838	4884	4930	4977	27
33	5023	5070	5116	5163	5209	5255	26
34	5302	5348	5395	5441	5487	5534	25
35	5580	5627	5673	5719	5766	5812	24
36	5859	5905	5951	5998	6044	6091	23
37	6137	6183	6230	6276	6322	6369	22
38	6415	6462	6508	6554	6601	6647	21
39	6693	6740	6786	6832	6879	6925	20
40	9 806971	7018	7064	7110	7157	7203	19
41	7249	7296	7342	7388	7435	7481	18
42	7527	7574	7620	7666	7713	7759	17
43	7805	7851	7898	7944	7990	8037	16
44	8083	8129	8176	8222	8268	8314	15
45	8361	8407	8453	8499	8546	8592	14
46	8638	8685	8731	8777	8823	8870	13
47	8916	8962	9008	9055	9101	9147	12
48	9193	9240	9286	9332	9378	9424	11
49	9471	9517	9563	9609	9656	9702	10
50	9.809748	9794	9840	9887	9933	9979	9
51	9.810025	0071	0118	0164	0210	0256	8
52	0302	0349	0395	0441	0487	0533	7
53	0580	0626	0672	0718	0764	0810	6
54	0857	0903	0949	0995	1041	1087	5
55	1134	1180	1226	1272	1318	1364	4
56	1410	1457	1503	1549	1595	1641	3
57	1687	1733	1780	1826	1872	1918	2
58	1964	2010	2056	2102	2149	2195	1
59	2241	2287	2333	2379	2425	2471	0
	60″	50″	40″	30″	20″	10″	Min.
	Co-tangent of 57 Degrees.						

P. Part { 1″ 2″ 3″ 4″ 5″ 6″ 7″ 8″ 9″ / 5 9 14 19 23 28 33 37 42 }

Min.	Tangent of 33 Degrees. 0″	10″	20″	30″	40″	50″	
0	9.812517	2563	2610	2656	2702	2748	59
1	2794	2840	2886	2932	2978	3024	58
2	3070	3116	3163	3209	3255	3301	57
3	3347	3393	3439	3485	3531	3577	56
4	3623	3669	3715	3761	3807	3853	55
5	3899	3945	3991	4037	4083	4129	54
6	4176	4222	4268	4314	4360	4406	53
7	4452	4498	4544	4590	4636	4682	52
8	4728	4774	4820	4866	4912	4958	51
9	5004	5050	5096	5142	5188	5234	50
10	9.815280	5326	5371	5417	5463	5509	49
11	5555	5601	5647	5693	5739	5785	48
12	5831	5877	5923	5969	6015	6061	47
13	6107	6153	6199	6245	6291	6336	46
14	6382	6428	6474	6520	6566	6612	45
15	6658	6704	6750	6796	6842	6888	44
16	6933	6979	7025	7071	7117	7163	43
17	7209	7255	7301	7347	7392	7438	42
18	7484	7530	7576	7622	7668	7714	41
19	7759	7805	7851	7897	7943	7989	40
20	9.818035	8081	8126	8172	8218	8264	39
21	8310	8356	8402	8447	8493	8539	38
22	8585	8631	8677	8722	8768	8814	37
23	8860	8906	8952	8997	9043	9089	36
24	9135	9181	9226	9272	9318	9364	35
25	9410	9455	9501	9547	9593	9639	34
26	9684	9730	9776	9822	9868	9913	33
27	9959	...5	..51	..96	.142	.188	32
28	9.820234	0280	0325	0371	0417	0463	31
29	0508	0554	0600	0646	0691	0737	30
30	9.820783	0829	0874	0920	0966	1012	29
31	1057	1103	1149	1195	1240	1286	28
32	1332	1377	1423	1469	1515	1560	27
33	1606	1652	1697	1743	1789	1835	26
34	1880	1926	1972	2017	2063	2109	25
35	2154	2200	2246	2292	2337	2383	24
36	2429	2474	2520	2566	2611	2657	23
37	2703	2748	2794	2840	2885	2931	22
38	2977	3022	3068	3114	3159	3205	21
39	3251	3296	3342	3387	3433	3479	20
40	9.823524	3570	3616	3661	3707	3753	19
41	3798	3844	3889	3935	3981	4026	18
42	4072	4117	4163	4209	4254	4300	17
43	4345	4391	4437	4482	4528	4573	16
44	4619	4665	4710	4756	4801	4847	15
45	4893	4938	4984	5029	5075	5120	14
46	5166	5212	5257	5303	5348	5394	13
47	5439	5485	5531	5576	5622	5667	12
48	5713	5758	5804	5849	5895	5940	11
49	5986	6032	6077	6123	6168	6214	10
50	9.826259	6305	6350	6396	6441	6487	9
51	6532	6578	6623	6669	6714	6760	8
52	6805	6851	6896	6942	6987	7033	7
53	7078	7124	7169	7215	7260	7306	6
54	7351	7397	7442	7488	7533	7579	5
55	7624	7670	7715	7761	7806	7851	4
56	7897	7942	7988	8033	8079	8124	3
57	8170	8215	8261	8306	8351	8397	2
58	8442	8488	8533	8579	8624	8669	1
59	8715	8760	8806	8851	8897	8942	0
	60″	50″	40″	30″	20″	10″	Min.
	Co-tangent of 56 Degrees.						

P. Part { 1″ 2″ 3″ 4″ 5″ 6″ 7″ 8″ 9″ / 5 9 14 18 23 27 32 37 41 }

Min.	Sine of 34 Degrees. 0″	10″	20″	30″	40″	50″	
0	9.747562	7593	7624	7655	7686	7718	59
1	7749	7780	7811	7842	7874	7905	58
2	7936	7967	7998	8030	8061	8092	57
3	8123	8154	8185	8216	8248	8279	56
4	8310	8341	8372	8403	8434	8466	55
5	8497	8528	8559	8590	8621	8652	54
6	8683	8714	8745	8777	8808	8839	53
7	8870	8901	8932	8963	8994	9025	52
8	9056	9087	9118	9149	9180	9212	51
9	9243	9274	9305	9336	9367	9398	50
10	9.749429	9460	9491	9522	9553	9584	49
11	9615	9646	9677	9708	9739	9770	48
12	9801	9832	9863	9894	9925	9956	47
13	9987	..18	..48	..79	.110	.141	46
14	9.750172	0203	0234	0265	0296	0327	45
15	0358	0389	0420	0451	0482	0512	44
16	0543	0574	0605	0636	0667	0698	43
17	0729	0760	0791	0821	0852	0883	42
18	0914	0945	0976	1007	1037	1068	41
19	1099	1130	1161	1192	1222	1253	40
20	9.751284	1315	1346	1377	1407	1438	39
21	1469	1500	1531	1561	1592	1623	38
22	1654	1685	1715	1746	1777	1808	37
23	1839	1869	1900	1931	1962	1992	36
24	2023	2054	2085	2115	2146	2177	35
25	2208	2238	2269	2300	2330	2361	34
26	2392	2423	2453	2484	2515	2545	33
27	2576	2607	2637	2668	2699	2729	32
28	2760	2791	2822	2852	2883	2914	31
29	2944	2975	3005	3036	3067	3097	30
30	9.753128	3159	3189	3220	3251	3281	29
31	3312	3342	3373	3404	3434	3465	28
32	3495	3526	3557	3587	3618	3648	27
33	3679	3710	3740	3771	3801	3832	26
34	3862	3893	3923	3954	3985	4015	25
35	4046	4076	4107	4137	4168	4198	24
36	4229	4259	4290	4320	4351	4381	23
37	4412	4442	4473	4503	4534	4564	22
38	4595	4625	4656	4686	4717	4747	21
39	4778	4808	4839	4869	4900	4930	20
40	9.754960	4991	5021	5052	5082	5113	19
41	5143	5173	5204	5234	5265	5295	18
42	5326	5356	5386	5417	5447	5478	17
43	5508	5538	5569	5599	5629	5660	16
44	5690	5721	5751	5781	5812	5842	15
45	5872	5903	5933	5963	5994	6024	14
46	6054	6085	6115	6145	6176	6206	13
47	6236	6267	6297	6327	6358	6388	12
48	6418	6448	6479	6509	6539	6570	11
49	6600	6630	6660	6691	6721	6751	10
50	9.756782	6812	6842	6872	6903	6933	9
51	6963	6993	7023	7054	7084	7114	8
52	7144	7175	7205	7235	7265	7295	7
53	7326	7356	7386	7416	7446	7477	6
54	7507	7537	7567	7597	7627	7658	5
55	7688	7718	7748	7778	7808	7839	4
56	7869	7899	7929	7959	7989	8019	3
57	8050	8080	8110	8140	8170	8200	2
58	8230	8260	8290	8321	8351	8381	1
59	8411	8441	8471	8501	8531	8561	0
	60″	50″	40″	30″	20″	10″	Min.
	Co-sine of 55 Degrees.						

P. Part { 1″ 2″ 3″ 4″ 5″ 6″ 7″ 8″ 9″
{ 3 6 9 12 15 18 21 25 28

Min.	Sine of 35 Degrees. 0″	10″	20″	30″	40″	50″	
0	9.758591	8621	8651	8681	8712	8742	59
1	8772	8802	8832	8862	8892	8922	58
2	8952	8982	9012	9042	9072	9102	57
3	9132	9162	9192	9222	9252	9282	56
4	9312	9342	9372	9402	9432	9462	55
5	9492	9522	9552	9582	9612	9642	54
6	9672	9702	9732	9762	9792	9822	53
7	9852	9881	9911	9941	9971	...1	52
8	9.760031	0061	0091	0121	0151	0181	51
9	0211	0240	0270	0300	0330	0360	50
10	9.760390	0420	0450	0480	0509	0539	49
11	0569	0599	0629	0659	0689	0718	48
12	0748	0778	0808	0838	0868	0898	47
13	0927	0957	0987	1017	1047	1076	46
14	1106	1136	1166	1196	1225	1255	45
15	1285	1315	1345	1374	1404	1434	44
16	1464	1494	1523	1553	1583	1613	43
17	1642	1672	1702	1732	1761	1791	42
18	1821	1851	1880	1910	1940	1969	41
19	1999	2029	2059	2088	2118	2148	40
20	9.762177	2207	2237	2267	2296	2326	39
21	2356	2385	2415	2445	2474	2504	38
22	2534	2563	2593	2623	2652	2682	37
23	2712	2741	2771	2801	2830	2860	36
24	2889	2919	2949	2978	3008	3038	35
25	3067	3097	3126	3156	3186	3215	34
26	3245	3274	3304	3333	3363	3393	33
27	3422	3452	3481	3511	3540	3570	32
28	3600	3629	3659	3688	3718	3747	31
29	3777	3806	3836	3865	3895	3925	30
30	9.763954	3984	4013	4043	4072	4102	29
31	4131	4161	4190	4220	4249	4279	28
32	4308	4338	4367	4396	4426	4455	27
33	4485	4514	4544	4573	4603	4632	26
34	4662	4691	4720	4750	4779	4809	25
35	4838	4868	4897	4926	4956	4985	24
36	5015	5044	5074	5103	5132	5162	23
37	5191	5221	5250	5279	5309	5338	22
38	5367	5397	5426	5456	5485	5514	21
39	5544	5573	5602	5632	5661	5690	20
40	9.765720	5749	5778	5808	5837	5866	19
41	5896	5925	5954	5984	6013	6042	18
42	6072	6101	6130	6159	6189	6218	17
43	6247	6277	6306	6335	6364	6394	16
44	6423	6452	6481	6511	6540	6569	15
45	6598	6628	6657	6686	6715	6745	14
46	6774	6803	6832	6862	6891	6920	13
47	6949	6978	7008	7037	7066	7095	12
48	7124	7154	7183	7212	7241	7270	11
49	7300	7329	7358	7387	7416	7445	10
50	9.767475	7504	7533	7562	7591	7620	9
51	7649	7679	7708	7737	7766	7795	8
52	7824	7853	7882	7912	7941	7970	7
53	7999	8028	8057	8086	8115	8144	6
54	8173	8203	8232	8261	8290	8319	5
55	8348	8377	8406	8435	8464	8493	4
56	8522	8551	8580	8609	8638	8668	3
57	8697	8726	8755	8784	8813	8842	2
58	8871	8900	8929	8958	8987	9016	1
59	9045	9074	9103	9132	9161	9190	0
	60″	50″	40″	30″	20″	10″	Min.
	Co-sine of 54 Degrees.						

P. Part { 1″ 2″ 3″ 4″ 5″ 6″ 7″ 8″ 9″
{ 3 6 9 12 15 18 21 24 27

Min.	Tangent of 34 Degrees. 0″	10″	20″	30″	40″	50″	
0	9.828987	9033	9078	9124	9169	9215	59
1	9260	9305	9351	9396	9442	9487	58
2	9532	9578	9623	9669	9714	9759	57
3	9805	9850	9895	9941	9986	..32	56
4	9.830077	0122	0168	0213	0258	0304	55
5	0349	0395	0440	0485	0531	0576	54
6	0621	0667	0712	0757	0803	0848	53
7	0893	0939	0984	1029	1075	1120	52
8	1165	1211	1256	1301	1347	1392	51
9	1437	1483	1528	1573	1619	1664	50
10	9.831709	1755	1800	1845	1891	1936	49
11	1981	2026	2072	2117	2162	2208	48
12	2253	2298	2343	2389	2434	2479	47
13	2525	2570	2615	2660	2706	2751	46
14	2796	2842	2887	2932	2977	3023	45
15	3068	3113	3158	3204	3249	3294	44
16	3339	3385	3430	3475	3520	3566	43
17	3611	3656	3701	3747	3792	3837	42
18	3882	3927	3973	4018	4063	4108	41
19	4154	4199	4244	4289	4334	4380	40
20	9.834425	4470	4515	4561	4606	4651	39
21	4696	4741	4787	4832	4877	4922	38
22	4967	5012	5058	5103	5148	5193	37
23	5238	5284	5329	5374	5419	5464	36
24	5509	5555	5600	5645	5690	5735	35
25	5780	5826	5871	5916	5961	6006	34
26	6051	6096	6142	6187	6232	6277	33
27	6322	6367	6412	6458	6503	6548	32
28	6593	6638	6683	6728	6773	6819	31
29	6864	6909	6954	6999	7044	7089	30
30	9.837134	7179	7225	7270	7315	7360	29
31	7405	7450	7495	7540	7585	7630	28
32	7675	7721	7766	7811	7856	7901	27
33	7946	7991	8036	8081	8126	8171	26
34	8216	8261	8307	8352	8397	8442	25
35	8487	8532	8577	8622	8667	8712	24
36	8757	8802	8847	8892	8937	8982	23
37	9027	9072	9117	9162	9207	9252	22
38	9297	9343	9388	9433	9478	9523	21
39	9568	9613	9658	9703	9748	9793	20
40	9.839838	9883	9928	9973	..18	..63	19
41	9.840108	0153	0198	0243	0288	0333	18
42	0378	0423	0468	0513	0558	0603	17
43	0648	0693	0737	0782	0827	0872	16
44	0917	0962	1007	1052	1097	1142	15
45	1187	1232	1277	1322	1367	1412	14
46	1457	1502	1547	1592	1637	1682	13
47	1727	1771	1816	1861	1906	1951	12
48	1996	2041	2086	2131	2176	2221	11
49	2266	2311	2355	2400	2445	2490	10
50	9.842535	2580	2625	2670	2715	2760	9
51	2805	2849	2894	2939	2984	3029	8
52	3074	3119	3164	3209	3253	3298	7
53	3343	3388	3433	3478	3523	3568	6
54	3612	3657	3702	3747	3792	3837	5
55	3882	3927	3971	4016	4061	4106	4
56	4151	4196	4241	4285	4330	4375	3
57	4420	4465	4510	4554	4599	4644	2
58	4689	4734	4779	4823	4868	4913	1
59	4958	5003	5048	5092	5137	5182	0
	60″	50″	40″	30″	20″	10″	Min.
	Co-tangent of 55 Degrees.						

P. Part { 1″ 2″ 3″ 4″ 5″ 6″ 7″ 8″ 9″ / 5 9 14 18 23 27 32 36 41 }

Min.	Tangent of 35 Degrees. 0″	10″	20″	30″	40″	50″	
0	9.845227	5272	5316	5361	5406	5451	59
1	5496	5540	5585	5630	5675	5720	58
2	5764	5809	5854	5899	5944	5988	57
3	6033	6078	6123	6168	6212	6257	56
4	6302	6347	6391	6436	6481	6526	55
5	6570	6615	6660	6705	6750	6794	54
6	6839	6884	6929	6973	7018	7063	53
7	7108	7152	7197	7242	7287	7331	52
8	7376	7421	7465	7510	7555	7600	51
9	7644	7689	7734	7779	7823	7868	50
10	9.847913	7957	8002	8047	8092	8136	49
11	8181	8226	8270	8315	8360	8405	48
12	8449	8494	8539	8583	8628	8673	47
13	8717	8762	8807	8851	8896	8941	46
14	8986	9030	9075	9120	9164	9209	45
15	9254	9298	9343	9388	9432	9477	44
16	9522	9566	9611	9656	9700	9745	43
17	9790	9834	9879	9924	9968	..13	42
18	9.850057	0102	0147	0191	0236	0281	41
19	0325	0370	0415	0459	0504	0548	40
20	9.850593	0638	0682	0727	0772	0816	39
21	0861	0905	0950	0995	1039	1084	38
22	1129	1173	1218	1262	1307	1352	37
23	1396	1441	1485	1530	1575	1619	36
24	1664	1708	1753	1797	1842	1887	35
25	1931	1976	2020	2065	2110	2154	34
26	2199	2243	2288	2332	2377	2422	33
27	2466	2511	2555	2600	2644	2689	32
28	2733	2778	2823	2867	2912	2956	31
29	3001	3045	3090	3134	3179	3223	30
30	9.853268	3313	3357	3402	3446	3491	29
31	3535	3580	3624	3669	3713	3758	28
32	3802	3847	3891	3936	3980	4025	27
33	4069	4114	4158	4203	4247	4292	26
34	4336	4381	4425	4470	4514	4559	25
35	4603	4648	4692	4737	4781	4826	24
36	4870	4915	4959	5004	5048	5093	23
37	5137	5182	5226	5271	5315	5360	22
38	5404	5449	5493	5537	5582	5626	21
39	5671	5715	5760	5804	5849	5893	20
40	9.855938	5982	6026	6071	6115	6160	19
41	6204	6249	6293	6338	6382	6426	18
42	6471	6515	6560	6604	6649	6693	17
43	6737	6782	6826	6871	6915	6959	16
44	7004	7048	7093	7137	7182	7226	15
45	7270	7315	7359	7404	7448	7492	14
46	7537	7581	7626	7670	7714	7759	13
47	7803	7848	7892	7936	7981	8025	12
48	8069	8114	8158	8203	8247	8291	11
49	8336	8380	8424	8469	8513	8558	10
50	9.858602	8646	8691	8735	8779	8824	9
51	8868	8912	8957	9001	9045	9090	8
52	9134	9178	9223	9267	9311	9356	7
53	9400	9444	9489	9533	9577	9622	6
54	9666	9710	9755	9799	9843	9888	5
55	9932	9976	..21	..65	.109	.154	4
56	9.860198	0242	0287	0331	0375	0420	3
57	0464	0508	0552	0597	0641	0685	2
58	0730	0774	0818	0862	0907	0951	1
59	0995	1040	1084	1128	1172	1217	0
	60″	50″	40″	30″	20″	10″	Min.
	Co-tangent of 54 Degrees.						

P. Part { 1″ 2″ 3″ 4″ 5″ 6″ 7″ 8″ 9″ / 4 9 13 18 22 27 31 36 40 }

Min.	Sine of 36 Degrees. 0″	10″	20″	30″	40″	50″	
0	9·769219	9248	9277	9306	9335	9364	59
1	9393	9421	9450	9479	9508	9537	58
2	9566	9595	9624	9653	9682	9711	57
3	9740	9769	9798	9827	9856	9884	56
4	9913	9942	9971	....	..29	..58	55
5	9·770087	0116	0145	0173	0202	0231	54
6	0260	0289	0318	0347	0376	0404	53
7	0433	0462	0491	0520	0549	0577	52
8	0606	0635	0664	0693	0722	0750	51
9	0779	0808	0837	0866	0895	0923	50
10	9·770952	0981	1010	1039	1067	1096	49
11	1125	1154	1183	1211	1240	1269	48
12	1298	1326	1355	1384	1413	1441	47
13	1470	1499	1528	1556	1585	1614	46
14	1643	1671	1700	1729	1758	1786	45
15	1815	1844	1872	1901	1930	1959	44
16	1987	2016	2045	2073	2102	2131	43
17	2159	2188	2217	2245	2274	2303	42
18	2331	2360	2389	2417	2446	2475	41
19	2503	2532	2561	2589	2618	2646	40
20	9·772675	2704	2732	2761	2790	2818	39
21	2847	2875	2904	2933	2961	2990	38
22	3018	3047	3076	3104	3133	3161	37
23	3190	3219	3247	3276	3304	3333	36
24	3361	3390	3418	3447	3476	3504	35
25	3533	3561	3590	3618	3647	3675	34
26	3704	3732	3761	3789	3818	3846	33
27	3875	3903	3932	3960	3989	4017	32
28	4046	4074	4103	4131	4160	4188	31
29	4217	4245	4274	4302	4331	4359	30
30	9·774388	4416	4445	4473	4501	4530	29
31	4558	4587	4615	4644	4672	4700	28
32	4729	4757	4786	4814	4842	4871	27
33	4899	4928	4956	4985	5013	5041	26
34	5070	5098	5126	5155	5183	5212	25
35	5240	5268	5297	5325	5353	5382	24
36	5410	5438	5467	5495	5523	5552	23
37	5580	5608	5637	5665	5693	5722	22
38	5750	5778	5807	5835	5863	5892	21
39	5920	5948	5977	6005	6033	6061	20
40	9·776090	6118	6146	6175	6203	6231	19
41	6259	6288	6316	6344	6372	6401	18
42	6429	6457	6485	6514	6542	6570	17
43	6598	6627	6655	6683	6711	6739	16
44	6768	6796	6824	6852	6880	6909	15
45	6937	6965	6993	7021	7050	7078	14
46	7106	7134	7162	7191	7219	7247	13
47	7275	7303	7331	7359	7388	7416	12
48	7444	7472	7500	7528	7556	7585	11
49	7613	7641	7669	7697	7725	7753	10
50	9·777781	7810	7838	7866	7894	7922	9
51	7950	7978	8006	8034	8062	8091	8
52	8119	8147	8175	8203	8231	8259	7
53	8287	8315	8343	8371	8399	8427	6
54	8455	8483	8511	8539	8567	8595	5
55	8624	8652	8680	8708	8736	8764	4
56	8792	8820	8848	8876	8904	8932	3
57	8960	8988	9016	9044	9072	9100	2
58	9128	9156	9183	9211	9239	9267	1
59	9295	9323	9351	9379	9407	9435	0
	60″	50″	40″	30″	20″	10″	Min.
	Co-sine of 53 Degrees.						

P. Part	1″	2″	3″	4″	5″	6″	7″	8″	9″
	3	6	9	11	14	17	20	23	26

Min.	Sine of 37 Degrees. 0″	10″	20″	30″	40″	50″	
0	9·779463	9491	9519	9547	9575	9603	59
1	9631	9659	9686	9714	9742	9770	58
2	9798	9826	9854	9882	9910	9938	57
3	9966	9993	..21	..49	..77	.105	56
4	9·780133	0161	0189	0216	0244	0272	55
5	0300	0328	0356	0384	0411	0439	54
6	0467	0495	0523	0551	0578	0606	53
7	0634	0662	0690	0718	0745	0773	52
8	0801	0829	0857	0884	0912	0940	51
9	0968	0996	1023	1051	1079	1107	50
10	9·781134	1162	1190	1218	1246	1273	49
11	1301	1329	1357	1384	1412	1440	48
12	1468	1495	1523	1551	1578	1606	47
13	1634	1662	1689	1717	1745	1772	46
14	1800	1828	1856	1883	1911	1939	45
15	1966	1994	2022	2049	2077	2105	44
16	2132	2160	2188	2215	2243	2271	43
17	2298	2326	2354	2381	2409	2437	42
18	2464	2492	2520	2547	2575	2602	41
19	2630	2658	2685	2713	2741	2768	40
20	9·782796	2823	2851	2879	2906	2934	39
21	2961	2989	3017	3044	3072	3099	38
22	3127	3154	3182	3210	3237	3265	37
23	3292	3320	3347	3375	3402	3430	36
24	3458	3485	3513	3540	3568	3595	35
25	3623	3650	3678	3705	3733	3760	34
26	3788	3815	3843	3870	3898	3925	33
27	3953	3980	4008	4035	4063	4090	32
28	4118	4145	4173	4200	4228	4255	31
29	4282	4310	4337	4365	4392	4420	30
30	9·784447	4475	4502	4529	4557	4584	29
31	4612	4639	4667	4694	4721	4749	28
32	4776	4804	4831	4858	4886	4913	27
33	4941	4968	4995	5023	5050	5078	26
34	5105	5132	5160	5187	5214	5242	25
35	5269	5296	5324	5351	5378	5406	24
36	5433	5461	5488	5515	5543	5570	23
37	5597	5624	5652	5679	5706	5734	22
38	5761	5788	5816	5843	5870	5898	21
39	5925	5952	5979	6007	6034	6061	20
40	9·786089	6116	6143	6170	6198	6225	19
41	6252	6279	6307	6334	6361	6388	18
42	6416	6443	6470	6497	6525	6552	17
43	6579	6606	6634	6661	6688	6715	16
44	6742	6770	6797	6824	6851	6878	15
45	6906	6933	6960	6987	7014	7042	14
46	7069	7096	7123	7150	7177	7205	13
47	7232	7259	7286	7313	7340	7367	12
48	7395	7422	7449	7476	7503	7530	11
49	7557	7585	7612	7639	7666	7693	10
50	9·787720	7747	7774	7801	7829	7856	9
51	7883	7910	7937	7964	7991	8018	8
52	8045	8072	8099	8127	8154	8181	7
53	8208	8235	8262	8289	8316	8343	6
54	8370	8397	8424	8451	8478	8505	5
55	8532	8559	8586	8613	8640	8667	4
56	8694	8721	8748	8775	8802	8829	3
57	8856	8883	8910	8937	8964	8991	2
58	9018	9045	9072	9099	9126	9153	1
59	9180	9207	9234	9261	9288	9315	0
	60″	50″	40″	30″	20″	10″	Min.
	Co-sine of 52 Degrees.						

P. Part	1″	2″	3″	4″	5″	6″	7″	8″	9″
	3	5	8	11	14	16	19	22	25

Min.	Tangent of 36 Degrees. 0″	10″	20″	30″	40″	50″	
0	9.861261	1305	1350	1394	1438	1482	59
1	1527	1571	1615	1659	1704	1748	58
2	1792	1837	1881	1925	1969	2014	57
3	2058	2102	2146	2191	2235	2279	56
4	2323	2368	2412	2456	2500	2545	55
5	2589	2633	2677	2721	2766	2810	54
6	2854	2898	2943	2987	3031	3075	53
7	3119	3164	3208	3252	3296	3341	52
8	3385	3429	3473	3517	3562	3606	51
9	3650	3694	3738	3783	3827	3871	50
10	9.863915	3959	4004	4048	4092	4136	49
11	4180	4225	4269	4313	4357	4401	48
12	4445	4490	4534	4578	4622	4666	47
13	4710	4755	4799	4843	4887	4931	46
14	4975	5020	5064	5108	5152	5196	45
15	5240	5285	5329	5373	5417	5461	44
16	5505	5549	5594	5638	5682	5726	43
17	5770	5814	5858	5903	5947	5991	42
18	6035	6079	6123	6167	6211	6256	41
19	6300	6344	6388	6432	6476	6520	40
20	9.866564	6609	6653	6697	6741	6785	39
21	6829	6873	6917	6961	7006	7050	38
22	7094	7138	7182	7226	7270	7314	37
23	7358	7402	7446	7491	7535	7579	36
24	7623	7667	7711	7755	7799	7843	35
25	7887	7931	7975	8019	8064	8108	34
26	8152	8196	8240	8284	8328	8372	33
27	8416	8460	8504	8548	8592	8636	32
28	8680	8724	8768	8813	8857	8901	31
29	8945	8989	9033	9077	9121	9165	30
30	9.869209	9253	9297	9341	9385	9429	29
31	9473	9517	9561	9605	9649	9693	28
32	9737	9781	9825	9869	9913	9957	27
33	9.870001	0045	0089	0133	0177	0221	26
34	0265	0309	0353	0397	0441	0485	25
35	0529	0573	0617	0661	0705	0749	24
36	0793	0837	0881	0925	0969	1013	23
37	1057	1101	1145	1189	1233	1277	22
38	1321	1365	1409	1453	1497	1541	21
39	1585	1629	1673	1717	1761	1805	20
40	9.871849	1893	1937	1980	2024	2068	19
41	2112	2156	2200	2244	2288	2332	18
42	2376	2420	2464	2508	2552	2596	17
43	2640	2684	2727	2771	2815	2859	16
44	2903	2947	2991	3035	3079	3123	15
45	3167	3211	3255	3299	3342	3386	14
46	3430	3474	3518	3562	3606	3650	13
47	3694	3738	3781	3825	3869	3913	12
48	3957	4001	4045	4089	4133	4177	11
49	4220	4264	4308	4352	4396	4440	10
50	9.874484	4528	4572	4615	4659	4703	9
51	4747	4791	4835	4879	4923	4966	8
52	5010	5054	5098	5142	5186	5230	7
53	5273	5317	5361	5405	5449	5493	6
54	5537	5580	5624	5668	5712	5756	5
55	5800	5843	5887	5931	5975	6019	4
56	6063	6107	6150	6194	6238	6282	3
57	6326	6370	6413	6457	6501	6545	2
58	6589	6632	6676	6720	6764	6808	1
59	6852	6895	6939	6983	7027	7071	0
	60″	50″	40″	30″	20″	10″	Min.
	Co-tangent of 53 Degrees.						

P. Part { 1″ 2″ 3″ 4″ 5″ 6″ 7″ 8″ 9″
{ 4 9 13 18 22 26 31 35 40

Min.	Tangent of 37 Degrees. 0″	10″	20″	30″	40″	50″	
0	9.877114	7158	7202	7246	7290	7333	59
1	7377	7421	7465	7509	7552	7596	58
2	7640	7684	7728	7771	7815	7859	57
3	7903	7947	7990	8034	8078	8122	56
4	8165	8209	8253	8297	8341	8384	55
5	8428	8472	8516	8559	8603	8647	54
6	8691	8734	8778	8822	8866	8909	53
7	8953	8997	9041	9085	9128	9172	52
8	9216	9260	9303	9347	9391	9435	51
9	9478	9522	9566	9609	9653	9697	50
10	9.879741	9784	9828	9872	9916	9959	49
11	9.880003	0047	0091	0134	0178	0222	48
12	0265	0309	0353	0397	0440	0484	47
13	0528	0571	0615	0659	0703	0746	46
14	0790	0834	0877	0921	0965	1008	45
15	1052	1096	1140	1183	1227	1271	44
16	1314	1358	1402	1445	1489	1533	43
17	1577	1620	1664	1708	1751	1795	42
18	1839	1882	1926	1970	2013	2057	41
19	2101	2144	2188	2232	2275	2319	40
20	9.882363	2406	2450	2494	2537	2581	39
21	2625	2668	2712	2756	2799	2843	38
22	2887	2930	2974	3018	3061	3105	37
23	3148	3192	3236	3279	3323	3367	36
24	3410	3454	3498	3541	3585	3628	35
25	3672	3716	3759	3803	3847	3890	34
26	3934	3977	4021	4065	4108	4152	33
27	4196	4239	4283	4326	4370	4414	32
28	4457	4501	4544	4588	4632	4675	31
29	4719	4762	4806	4850	4893	4937	30
30	9.884980	5024	5068	5111	5155	5198	29
31	5242	5286	5329	5373	5416	5460	28
32	5504	5547	5591	5634	5678	5721	27
33	5765	5809	5852	5896	5939	5983	26
34	6026	6070	6114	6157	6201	6244	25
35	6288	6331	6375	6419	6462	6506	24
36	6549	6593	6636	6680	6723	6767	23
37	6811	6854	6898	6941	6985	7028	22
38	7072	7115	7159	7202	7246	7289	21
39	7333	7377	7420	7464	7507	7551	20
40	9.887594	7638	7681	7725	7768	7812	19
41	7855	7899	7942	7986	8029	8073	18
42	8116	8160	8203	8247	8291	8334	17
43	8378	8421	8465	8508	8552	8595	16
44	8639	8682	8726	8769	8813	8856	15
45	8900	8943	8987	9030	9074	9117	14
46	9161	9204	9248	9291	9334	9378	13
47	9421	9465	9508	9552	9595	9639	12
48	9682	9726	9769	9813	9856	9900	11
49	9943	9987	..30	..74	.117	.160	10
50	9.890204	0247	0291	0334	0378	0421	9
51	0465	0508	0552	0595	0639	0682	8
52	0725	0769	0812	0856	0899	0943	7
53	0986	1030	1073	1116	1160	1203	6
54	1247	1290	1334	1377	1421	1464	5
55	1507	1551	1594	1638	1681	1725	4
56	1768	1811	1855	1898	1942	1985	3
57	2028	2072	2115	2159	2202	2246	2
58	2289	2332	2376	2419	2463	2506	1
59	2549	2593	2636	2680	2723	2766	0
	60″	50″	40″	30″	20″	10″	Min.
	Co-tangent of 52 Degrees.						

P. Part { 1″ 2″ 3″ 4″ 5″ 6″ 7″ 8″ 9″
{ 4 9 13 17 22 26 31 35 39

Min.	Sine of 38 Degrees. 0″	10″	20″	30″	40″	50″	
0	9.789342	9369	9396	9423	9450	9477	59
1	9504	9531	9557	9584	9611	9638	58
2	9665	9692	9719	9746	9773	9800	57
3	9827	9854	9880	9907	9934	9961	56
4	9988	..15	..42	..69	..96	.122	55
5	9.790149	0176	0203	0230	0257	0284	54
6	0310	0337	0364	0391	0418	0445	53
7	0471	0498	0525	0552	0579	0606	52
8	0632	0659	0686	0713	0740	0767	51
9	0793	0820	0847	0874	0901	0927	50
10	9.790954	0981	1008	1034	1061	1088	49
11	1115	1142	1168	1195	1222	1249	48
12	1275	1302	1329	1356	1382	1409	47
13	1436	1463	1489	1516	1543	1570	46
14	1596	1623	1650	1676	1703	1730	45
15	1757	1783	1810	1837	1863	1890	44
16	1917	1943	1970	1997	2024	2050	43
17	2077	2104	2130	2157	2184	2210	42
18	2237	2264	2290	2317	2344	2370	41
19	2397	2423	2450	2477	2503	2530	40
20	9.792557	2583	2610	2636	2663	2690	39
21	2716	2743	2770	2796	2823	2849	38
22	2876	2903	2929	2956	2982	3009	37
23	3035	3062	3089	3115	3142	3168	36
24	3195	3222	3248	3275	3301	3328	35
25	3354	3381	3407	3434	3460	3487	34
26	3514	3540	3567	3593	3620	3646	33
27	3673	3699	3726	3752	3779	3805	32
28	3832	3858	3885	3911	3938	3964	31
29	3991	4017	4044	4070	4097	4123	30
30	9.794150	4176	4203	4229	4255	4282	29
31	4308	4335	4361	4388	4414	4441	28
32	4467	4493	4520	4546	4573	4599	27
33	4626	4652	4678	4705	4731	4758	26
34	4784	4810	4837	4863	4890	4916	25
35	4942	4969	4995	5022	5048	5074	24
36	5101	5127	5154	5180	5206	5233	23
37	5259	5285	5312	5338	5364	5391	22
38	5417	5443	5470	5496	5522	5549	21
39	5575	5601	5628	5654	5680	5707	20
40	9.795733	5759	5786	5812	5838	5865	19
41	5891	5917	5943	5970	5996	6022	18
42	6049	6075	6101	6127	6154	6180	17
43	6206	6233	6259	6285	6311	6338	16
44	6364	6390	6416	6443	6469	6495	15
45	6521	6547	6574	6600	6626	6652	14
46	6679	6705	6731	6757	6783	6810	13
47	6836	6862	6888	6914	6941	6967	12
48	6993	7019	7045	7072	7098	7124	11
49	7150	7176	7202	7229	7255	7281	10
50	9.797307	7333	7359	7386	7412	7438	9
51	7464	7490	7516	7542	7569	7595	8
52	7621	7647	7673	7699	7725	7751	7
53	7777	7804	7830	7856	7882	7908	6
54	7934	7960	7986	8012	8038	8065	5
55	8091	8117	8143	8169	8195	8221	4
56	8247	8273	8299	8325	8351	8377	3
57	8403	8429	8455	8481	8508	8534	2
58	8560	8586	8612	8638	8664	8690	1
59	8716	8742	8768	8794	8820	8846	0
	60″	50″	40″	30″	20″	10″	Min.
	Co-sine of 51 Degrees.						

P. Part	1″	2″	3″	4″	5″	6″	7″	8″	9″
	3	5	8	11	13	16	19	21	24

Min.	Sine of 39 Degrees. 0″	10″	20″	30″	40″	50″	
0	9.798872	8898	8924	8950	8976	9002	59
1	9028	9054	9080	9106	9132	9158	58
2	9184	9210	9236	9262	9287	9313	57
3	9339	9365	9391	9417	9443	9469	56
4	9495	9521	9547	9573	9599	9625	55
5	9651	9677	9703	9728	9754	9780	54
6	9806	9832	9858	9884	9910	9936	53
7	9962	9987	..13	..39	..65	..91	52
8	9.800117	0143	0169	[illegible]195	0220	0246	51
9	0272	0298	0324	0350	0376	0401	50
10	9.800427	0453	0479	0505	0531	0556	49
11	0582	0608	0634	0660	0686	0711	48
12	0737	0763	0789	0815	0840	0866	47
13	0892	0918	0944	0969	0995	1021	46
14	1047	1073	1098	1124	1150	1176	45
15	1201	1227	1253	1279	1305	1330	44
16	1356	1382	1408	1433	1459	1485	43
17	1511	1536	1562	1588	1613	1639	42
18	1665	1691	1716	1742	1768	1794	41
19	1819	1845	1871	1896	1922	1948	40
20	9.801973	1999	2025	2051	2076	2102	39
21	2128	2153	2179	2205	2230	2256	38
22	2282	2307	2333	2359	2384	2410	37
23	2436	2461	2487	2512	2538	2564	36
24	2589	2615	2641	2666	2692	2718	35
25	2743	2769	2794	2820	2846	2871	34
26	2897	2922	2948	2974	2999	3025	33
27	3050	3076	3102	3127	3153	3178	32
28	3204	3229	3255	3281	3306	3332	31
29	3357	3383	3408	3434	3459	3485	30
30	9.803511	3536	3562	3587	3613	3638	29
31	3664	3689	3715	3740	3766	3791	28
32	3817	3842	3868	3893	3919	3944	27
33	3970	3995	4021	4046	4072	4097	26
34	4123	4148	4174	4199	4225	4250	25
35	4276	4301	4327	4352	4377	4403	24
36	4428	4454	4479	4505	4530	4556	23
37	4581	4607	4632	4657	4683	4708	22
38	4734	4759	4784	4810	4835	4861	21
39	4886	4912	4937	4962	4988	5013	20
40	9.805039	5064	5089	5115	5140	5165	19
41	5191	5216	5242	5267	5292	5318	18
42	5343	5368	5394	5419	5444	5470	17
43	5495	5520	5546	5571	5597	5622	16
44	5647	5673	5698	5723	5748	5774	15
45	5799	5824	5850	5875	5900	5926	14
46	5951	5976	6002	6027	6052	6077	13
47	6103	6128	6153	6179	6204	6229	12
48	6254	6280	6305	6330	6355	6381	11
49	6406	6431	6456	6482	6507	6532	10
50	9.806557	6583	6608	6633	6658	6684	9
51	6709	6734	6759	6785	6810	6835	8
52	6860	6885	6911	6936	6961	6986	7
53	7011	7037	7062	7087	7112	7137	6
54	7163	7188	7213	7238	7263	7288	5
55	7314	7339	7364	7389	7414	7439	4
56	7465	7490	7515	7540	7565	7590	3
57	7615	7641	7666	7691	7716	7741	2
58	7766	7791	7816	7842	7867	7892	1
59	7917	7942	7967	7992	8017	8042	0
	60″	50″	40″	30″	20″	10″	Min.
	Co-sine of 50 Degrees.						

P. Part	1″	2″	3″	4″	5″	6″	7″	8″	9″
	3	5	8	10	13	15	18	20	23

Min.	Tangent of 38 Degrees. 0″	10″	20″	30″	40″	50″	
0	9.892810	2853	2897	2940	2983	3027	59
1	3070	3114	3157	3200	3244	3287	58
2	3331	3374	3417	3461	3504	3547	57
3	3591	3634	3678	3721	3764	3808	56
4	3851	3894	3938	3981	4025	4068	55
5	4111	4155	4198	4241	4285	4328	54
6	4372	4415	4458	4502	4545	4588	53
7	4632	4675	4718	4762	4805	4848	52
8	4892	4935	4979	5022	5065	5109	51
9	5152	5195	5239	5282	5325	5369	50
10	9.895412	5455	5499	5542	5585	5629	49
11	5672	5715	5759	5802	5845	5889	48
12	5932	5975	6019	6062	6105	6149	47
13	6192	6235	6278	6322	6365	6408	46
14	6452	6495	6538	6582	6625	6668	45
15	6712	6755	6798	6842	6885	6928	44
16	6971	7015	7058	7101	7145	7188	43
17	7231	7275	7318	7361	7404	7448	42
18	7491	7534	7578	7621	7664	7707	41
19	7751	7794	7837	7881	7924	7967	40
20	9.898010	8054	8097	8140	8183	8227	39
21	8270	8313	8357	8400	8443	8486	38
22	8530	8573	8616	8659	8703	8746	37
23	8789	8832	8876	8919	8962	9005	36
24	9049	9092	9135	9178	9222	9265	35
25	9308	9351	9395	9438	9481	9524	34
26	9568	9611	9654	9697	9741	9784	33
27	9827	9870	9914	9957	....	..43	32
28	9.900087	0130	0173	0216	0259	0303	31
29	0346	0389	0432	0476	0519	0562	30
30	9.900605	0648	0692	0735	0778	0821	29
31	0864	0908	0951	0994	1037	1081	28
32	1124	1167	1210	1253	1297	1340	27
33	1383	1426	1469	1513	1556	1599	26
34	1642	1685	1729	1772	1815	1858	25
35	1901	1944	1988	2031	2074	2117	24
36	2160	2204	2247	2290	2333	2376	23
37	2420	2463	2506	2549	2592	2635	22
38	2679	2722	2765	2808	2851	2894	21
39	2938	2981	3024	3067	3110	3153	20
40	9.903197	3240	3283	3326	3369	3412	19
41	3456	3499	3542	3585	3628	3671	18
42	3714	3758	3801	3844	3887	3930	17
43	3973	4016	4060	4103	4146	4189	16
44	4232	4275	4318	4362	4405	4448	15
45	4491	4534	4577	4620	4663	4707	14
46	4750	4793	4836	4879	4922	4965	13
47	5008	5052	5095	5138	5181	5224	12
48	5267	5310	5353	5397	5440	5483	11
49	5526	5569	5612	5655	5698	5741	10
50	9.905785	5828	5871	5914	5957	6000	9
51	6043	6086	6129	6172	6216	6259	8
52	6302	6345	6388	6431	6474	6517	7
53	6560	6603	6646	6690	6733	6776	6
54	6819	6862	6905	6948	6991	7034	5
55	7077	7120	7163	7207	7250	7293	4
56	7336	7379	7422	7465	7508	7551	3
57	7594	7637	7680	7723	7766	7809	2
58	7853	7896	7939	7982	8025	8068	1
59	8111	8154	8197	8240	8283	8326	0
	60″	50″	40″	30″	20″	10″	Min.
	Co-tangent of 51 Degrees.						

P. Part { 1″ 2″ 3″ 4″ 5″ 6″ 7″ 8″ 9″ / 4 9 13 17 22 26 30 35 39 }

Min.	Tangent of 39 Degrees. 0″	10″	20″	30″	40″	50″	
0	9.908369	8412	8455	8498	8541	8584	59
1	8628	8671	8714	8757	8800	8843	58
2	8886	8929	8972	9015	9058	9101	57
3	9144	9187	9230	9273	9316	9359	56
4	9402	9445	9488	9531	9574	9617	55
5	9660	9703	9746	9789	9832	9875	54
6	9918	9961	...5	..48	..91	.134	53
7	9.910177	0220	0263	0306	0349	0392	52
8	0435	0478	0521	0564	0607	0650	51
9	0693	0736	0779	0822	0865	0908	50
10	9.910951	0994	1037	1080	1123	1166	49
11	1209	1252	1295	1338	1381	1424	48
12	1467	1510	1553	1596	1639	1682	47
13	1725	1768	1810	1853	1896	1939	46
14	1982	2025	2068	2111	2154	2197	45
15	2240	2283	2326	2369	2412	2455	44
16	2498	2541	2584	2627	2670	2713	43
17	2756	2799	2842	2885	2928	2971	42
18	3014	3057	3100	3143	3185	3228	41
19	3271	3314	3357	3400	3443	3486	40
20	9.913529	3572	3615	3658	3701	3744	39
21	3787	3830	3873	3916	3959	4001	38
22	4044	4087	4130	4173	4216	4259	37
23	4302	4345	4388	4431	4474	4517	36
24	4560	4603	4645	4688	4731	4774	35
25	4817	4860	4903	4946	4989	5032	34
26	5075	5118	5161	5203	5246	5289	33
27	5332	5375	5418	5461	5504	5547	32
28	5590	5633	5675	5718	5761	5804	31
29	5847	5890	5933	5976	6019	6062	30
30	9.916104	6147	6190	6233	6276	6319	29
31	6362	6405	6448	6491	6533	6576	28
32	6619	6662	6705	6748	6791	6834	27
33	6877	6919	6962	7005	7048	7091	26
34	7134	7177	7220	7262	7305	7348	25
35	7391	7434	7477	7520	7563	7605	24
36	7648	7691	7734	7777	7820	7863	23
37	7906	7948	7991	8034	8077	8120	22
38	8163	8206	8248	8291	8334	8377	21
39	8420	8463	8506	8548	8591	8634	20
40	9.918677	8720	8763	8805	8848	8891	19
41	8934	8977	9020	9063	9105	9148	18
42	9191	9234	9277	9320	9362	9405	17
43	9448	9491	9534	9577	9619	9662	16
44	9705	9748	9791	9834	9876	9919	15
45	9962	...5	. 48	..91	.133	.176	14
46	9.920219	0262	0305	0348	0390	0433	13
47	0476	0519	0562	0604	0647	0690	12
48	0733	0776	0819	0861	0904	0947	11
49	0990	1033	1075	1118	1161	1204	10
50	9.921247	1289	1332	1375	1418	1461	9
51	1503	1546	1589	1632	1675	1717	8
52	1760	1803	1846	1889	1931	1974	7
53	2017	2060	2103	2145	2188	2231	6
54	2274	2316	2359	2402	2445	2488	5
55	2530	2573	2616	2659	2702	2744	4
56	2787	2830	2873	2915	2958	3001	3
57	3044	3087	3129	3172	3215	3258	2
58	3300	3343	3386	3429	3471	3514	1
59	3557	3600	3642	3685	3728	3771	0
	60″	50″	40″	30″	20″	10″	Min.
	Co-tangent of 50 Degrees.						

P. Part { 1″ 2″ 3″ 4″ 5″ 6″ 7″ 8″ 9″ / 4 9 13 17 21 26 30 34 39 }

Min.	Sine of 40 Degrees. 0″	10″	20″	30″	40″	50″	
0	9.808067	8093	8118	8143	8168	8193	59
1	8218	8243	8268	8293	8318	8343	58
2	8368	8393	8419	8444	8469	8494	57
3	8519	8544	8569	8594	8619	8644	56
4	8669	8694	8719	8744	8769	8794	55
5	8819	8844	8869	8894	8919	8944	54
6	8969	8994	9019	9044	9069	9094	53
7	9119	9144	9169	9194	9219	9244	52
8	9269	9294	9319	9344	9369	9394	51
9	9419	9444	9469	9494	9519	9544	50
10	9.809569	9594	9619	9643	9668	9693	49
11	9718	9743	9768	9793	9818	9843	48
12	9868	9893	9918	9943	9967	9992	47
13	9.810017	0042	0067	0092	0117	0142	46
14	0167	0191	0216	0241	0266	0291	45
15	0316	0341	0366	0390	0415	0440	44
16	0465	0490	0515	0540	0564	0589	43
17	0614	0639	0664	0689	0713	0738	42
18	0763	0788	0813	0838	0862	0887	41
19	0912	0937	0962	0986	1011	1036	40
20	9.811061	1086	1110	1135	1160	1185	39
21	1210	1234	1259	1284	1309	1334	38
22	1358	1383	1408	1433	1457	1482	37
23	1507	1532	1556	1581	1606	1631	36
24	1655	1680	1705	1730	1754	1779	35
25	1804	1828	1853	1878	1903	1927	34
26	1952	1977	2001	2026	2051	2076	33
27	2100	2125	2150	2174	2199	2224	32
28	2248	2273	2298	2322	2347	2372	31
29	2396	2421	2446	2470	2495	2520	30
30	9.812544	2569	2594	2618	2643	2668	29
31	2692	2717	2742	2766	2791	2815	28
32	2840	2865	2889	2914	2939	2963	27
33	2988	3012	3037	3062	3086	3111	26
34	3135	3160	3185	3209	3234	3258	25
35	3283	3307	3332	3357	3381	3406	24
36	3430	3455	3479	3504	3529	3553	23
37	3578	3602	3627	3651	3676	3700	22
38	3725	3749	3774	3799	3823	3848	21
39	3872	3897	3921	3946	3970	3995	20
40	9.814019	4044	4068	4093	4117	4142	19
41	4166	4191	4215	4240	4264	4289	18
42	4313	4338	4362	4387	4411	4436	17
43	4460	4484	4509	4533	4558	4582	16
44	4607	4631	4656	4680	4704	4729	15
45	4753	4778	4802	4827	4851	4876	14
46	4900	4924	4949	4973	4998	5022	13
47	5046	5071	5095	5120	5144	5168	12
48	5193	5217	5242	5266	5290	5315	11
49	5339	5364	5388	5412	5437	5461	10
50	9.815485	5510	5534	5558	5583	5607	9
51	5632	5656	5680	5705	5729	5753	8
52	5778	5802	5826	5851	5875	5899	7
53	5924	5948	5972	5996	6021	6045	6
54	6069	6094	6118	6142	6167	6191	5
55	6215	6240	6264	6288	6312	6337	4
56	6361	6385	6409	6434	6458	6482	3
57	6507	6531	6555	6579	6604	6628	2
58	6652	6676	6701	6725	6749	6773	1
59	6798	6822	6846	6870	6894	6919	0
	60″ Co-sine of 49 Degrees.	50″	40″	30″	20″	10″	Min.

P. Part { 1″ 2″ 3″ 4″ 5″ 6″ 7″ 8″ 9″ / 2 5 7 10 12 15 17 20 22

Min.	Sine of 41 Degrees. 0″	10″	20″	30″	40″	50″	
0	9.816943	6967	6991	7016	7040	7064	59
1	7088	7112	7137	7161	7185	7209	58
2	7233	7258	7282	7306	7330	7354	57
3	7379	7403	7427	7451	7475	7499	56
4	7524	7548	7572	7596	7620	7644	55
5	7668	7693	7717	7741	7765	7789	54
6	7813	7837	7862	7886	7910	7934	53
7	7958	7982	8006	8030	8055	8079	52
8	8103	8127	8151	8175	8199	8223	51
9	8247	8272	8296	8320	8344	8368	50
10	9.818392	8416	8440	8464	8488	8512	49
11	8536	8560	8584	8609	8633	8657	48
12	8681	8705	8729	8753	8777	8801	47
13	8825	8849	8873	8897	8921	8945	46
14	8969	8993	9017	9041	9065	9089	45
15	9113	9137	9161	9185	9209	9233	44
16	9257	9281	9305	9329	9353	9377	43
17	9401	9425	9449	9473	9497	9521	42
18	9545	9569	9593	9617	9641	9665	41
19	9689	9713	9737	9761	9785	9809	40
20	9.819832	9856	9880	9904	9928	9952	39
21	9976	....	..24	..48	..72	..96	38
22	9.820120	0143	0167	0191	0215	0239	37
23	0263	0287	0311	0335	0359	0382	36
24	0406	0430	0454	0478	0502	0526	35
25	0550	0573	0597	0621	0645	0669	34
26	0693	0717	0740	0764	0788	0812	33
27	0836	0860	0883	0907	0931	0955	32
28	0979	1003	1026	1050	1074	1098	31
29	1122	1146	1169	1193	1217	1241	30
30	9.821265	1288	1312	1336	1360	1384	29
31	1407	1431	1455	1479	1502	1526	28
32	1550	1574	1598	1621	1645	1669	27
33	1693	1716	1740	1764	1788	1811	26
34	1835	1859	1883	1906	1930	1954	25
35	1977	2001	2025	2049	2072	2096	24
36	2120	2144	2167	2191	2215	2238	23
37	2262	2286	2309	2333	2357	2381	22
38	2404	2428	2452	2475	2499	2523	21
39	2546	2570	2594	2617	2641	2665	20
40	9.822688	2712	2736	2759	2783	2807	19
41	2830	2854	2878	2901	2925	2948	18
42	2972	2996	3019	3043	3067	3090	17
43	3114	3137	3161	3185	3208	3232	16
44	3255	3279	3303	3326	3350	3373	15
45	3397	3421	3444	3468	3491	3515	14
46	3539	3562	3586	3609	3633	3656	13
47	3680	3704	3727	3751	3774	3798	12
48	3821	3845	3868	3892	3915	3939	11
49	3963	3986	4010	4033	4057	4080	10
50	9.824104	4127	4151	4174	4198	4221	9
51	4245	4268	4292	4315	4339	4362	8
52	4386	4409	4433	4456	4480	4503	7
53	4527	4550	4574	4597	4621	4644	6
54	4668	4691	4715	4738	4761	4785	5
55	4808	4832	4855	4879	4902	4926	4
56	4949	4972	4996	5019	5043	5066	3
57	5090	5113	5136	5160	5183	5207	2
58	5230	5254	5277	5300	5324	5347	1
59	5371	5394	5417	5441	5464	5488	0
	60″ Co-sine of 48 Degrees.	50″	40″	30″	20″	10″	Min.

P. Part { 1″ 2″ 3″ 4″ 5″ 6″ 7″ 8″ 9″ / 2 5 7 10 12 14 17 19 21

Min.	Tangent of 40 Degrees. 0″	10″	20″	30″	40″	50″	
0	9.923814	3856	3899	3942	3985	4027	59
1	4070	4113	4156	4198	4241	4284	58
2	4327	4369	4412	4455	4498	4540	57
3	4583	4626	4669	4711	4754	4797	56
4	4840	4882	4925	4968	5011	5053	55
5	5096	5139	5181	5224	5267	5310	54
6	5352	5395	5438	5481	5523	5566	53
7	5609	5652	5694	5737	5780	5822	52
8	5865	5908	5951	5993	6036	6079	51
9	6122	6164	6207	6250	6292	6335	50
10	9.926378	6421	6463	6506	6549	6591	49
11	6634	6677	6720	6762	6805	6848	48
12	6890	6933	6976	7019	7061	7104	47
13	7147	7189	7232	7275	7317	7360	46
14	7403	7446	7488	7531	7574	7616	45
15	7659	7702	7744	7787	7830	7872	44
16	7915	7958	8001	8043	8086	8129	43
17	8171	8214	8257	8299	8342	8385	42
18	8427	8470	8513	8555	8598	8641	41
19	8684	8726	8769	8812	8854	8897	40
20	9.928940	8982	9025	9068	9110	9153	39
21	9196	9238	9281	9324	9366	9409	38
22	9452	9494	9537	9580	9622	9665	37
23	9708	9750	9793	9836	9878	9921	36
24	9964	...6	..49	..92	.134	.177	35
25	9.930220	0262	0305	0348	0390	0433	34
26	0475	0518	0561	0603	0646	0689	33
27	0731	0774	0817	0859	0902	0945	32
28	0987	1030	1073	1115	1158	1200	31
29	1243	1286	1328	1371	1414	1456	30
30	9.931499	1542	1584	1627	1669	1712	29
31	1755	1797	1840	1883	1925	1968	28
32	2010	2053	2096	2138	2181	2224	27
33	2266	2309	2351	2394	2437	2479	26
34	2522	2565	2607	2650	2692	2735	25
35	2778	2820	2863	2906	2948	2991	24
36	3033	3076	3119	3161	3204	3246	23
37	3289	3332	3374	3417	3459	3502	22
38	3545	3587	3630	3672	3715	3758	21
39	3800	3843	3885	3928	3971	4013	20
40	9.934056	4098	4141	4184	4226	4269	19
41	4311	4354	4397	4439	4482	4524	18
42	4567	4610	4652	4695	4737	4780	17
43	4822	4865	4908	4950	4993	5035	16
44	5078	5121	5163	5206	5248	5291	15
45	5333	5376	5419	5461	5504	5546	14
46	5589	5632	5674	5717	5759	5802	13
47	5844	5887	5930	5972	6015	6057	12
48	6100	6142	6185	6227	6270	6313	11
49	6355	6398	6440	6483	6525	6568	10
50	9.936611	6653	6696	6738	6781	6823	9
51	6866	6908	6951	6994	7036	7079	8
52	7121	7164	7206	7249	7291	7334	7
53	7377	7419	7462	7504	7547	7589	6
54	7632	7674	7717	7759	7802	7845	5
55	7887	7930	7972	8015	8057	8100	4
56	8142	8185	8227	8270	8312	8355	3
57	8398	8440	8483	8525	8568	8610	2
58	8653	8695	8738	8780	8823	8865	1
59	8908	8950	8993	9035	9078	9121	0
	60″	50″	40″	30″	20″	10″	Min.
	Co-tangent of 49 Degrees.						

P. Part { 1″ 2″ 3″ 4″ 5″ 6″ 7″ 8″ 9″
{ 4 9 13 17 21 26 30 34 38

Min.	Tangent of 41 Degrees. 0″	10″	20″	30″	40″	50″	
0	9.939163	9206	9248	9291	9333	9376	59
1	9418	9461	9503	9546	9588	9631	58
2	9673	9716	9758	9801	9843	9886	57
3	9928	9971	..13	..56	..98	.141	56
4	9.940183	0226	0268	0311	0354	0396	55
5	0439	0481	0524	0566	0609	0651	54
6	0694	0736	0779	0821	0864	0906	53
7	0949	0991	1034	1076	1119	1161	52
8	1204	1246	1289	1331	1374	1416	51
9	1459	1501	1544	1586	1628	1671	50
10	9.941713	1756	1798	1841	1883	1926	49
11	1968	2011	2053	2096	2138	2181	48
12	2223	2266	2308	2351	2393	2436	47
13	2478	2521	2563	2606	2648	2691	46
14	2733	2776	2818	2861	2903	2945	45
15	2988	3030	3073	3115	3158	3200	44
16	3243	3285	3328	3370	3413	3455	43
17	3498	3540	3583	3625	3667	3710	42
18	3752	3795	3837	3880	3922	3965	41
19	4007	4050	4092	4135	4177	4219	40
20	9.944262	4304	4347	4389	4432	4474	39
21	4517	4559	4602	4644	4686	4729	38
22	4771	4814	4856	4899	4941	4984	37
23	5026	5069	5111	5153	5196	5238	36
24	5281	5323	5366	5408	5451	5493	35
25	5535	5578	5620	5663	5705	5748	34
26	5790	5832	5875	5917	5960	6002	33
27	6045	6087	6130	6172	6214	6257	32
28	6299	6342	6384	6427	6469	6511	31
29	6554	6596	6639	6681	6724	6766	30
30	9.946808	6851	6893	6936	6978	7021	29
31	7063	7105	7148	7190	7233	7275	28
32	7318	7360	7402	7445	7487	7530	27
33	7572	7614	7657	7699	7742	7784	26
34	7827	7869	7911	7954	7996	8039	25
35	8081	8123	8166	8208	8251	8293	24
36	8335	8378	8420	8463	8505	8548	23
37	8590	8632	8675	8717	8760	8802	22
38	8844	8887	8929	8972	9014	9056	21
39	9099	9141	9184	9226	9268	9311	20
40	9.949353	9396	9438	9480	9523	9565	19
41	9608	9650	9692	9735	9777	9819	18
42	9862	9904	9947	9989	..31	..74	17
43	9.950116	0159	0201	0243	0286	0328	16
44	0371	0413	0455	0498	0540	0582	15
45	0625	0667	0710	0752	0794	0837	14
46	0879	0921	0964	1006	1049	1091	13
47	1133	1176	1218	1261	1303	1345	12
48	1388	1430	1472	1515	1557	1600	11
49	1642	1684	1727	1769	1811	1854	10
50	9.951896	1938	1981	2023	2066	2108	9
51	2150	2193	2235	2277	2320	2362	8
52	2405	2447	2489	2532	2574	2616	7
53	2659	2701	2743	2786	2828	2870	6
54	2913	2955	2998	3040	3082	3125	5
55	3167	3209	3252	3294	3336	3379	4
56	3421	3463	3506	3548	3591	3633	3
57	3675	3718	3760	3802	3845	3887	2
58	3929	3972	4014	4056	4099	4141	1
59	4183	4226	4268	4310	4353	4395	0
	60″	50″	40″	30″	20″	10″	Min.
	Co-tangent of 48 Degrees.						

P. Part { 1″ 2″ 3″ 4″ 5″ 6″ 7″ 8″ 9″
{ 4 8 13 17 21 25 30 34 38

Min.	Sine of 42 Degrees. 0″	10″	20″	30″	40″	50″	
0	9.825511	5534	5558	5581	5604	5628	59
1	5651	5675	5698	5721	5745	5768	58
2	5791	5815	5838	5861	5885	5908	57
3	5931	5955	5978	6001	6025	6048	56
4	6071	6095	6118	6141	6165	6188	55
5	6211	6235	6258	6281	6305	6328	54
6	6351	6375	6398	6421	6444	6468	53
7	6491	6514	6538	6561	6584	6607	52
8	6631	6654	6677	6701	6724	6747	51
9	6770	6794	6817	6840	6863	6887	50
10	9.826910	6933	6956	6980	7003	7026	49
11	7049	7073	7096	7119	7142	7165	48
12	7189	7212	7235	7258	7282	7305	47
13	7328	7351	7374	7398	7421	7444	46
14	7467	7490	7514	7537	7560	7583	45
15	7606	7629	7653	7676	7699	7722	44
16	7745	7768	7792	7815	7838	7861	43
17	7884	7907	7931	7954	7977	8000	42
18	8023	8046	8069	8093	8116	8139	41
19	8162	8185	8208	8231	8254	8278	40
20	9.828301	8324	8347	8370	8393	8416	39
21	8439	8462	8485	8509	8532	8555	38
22	8578	8601	8624	8647	8670	8693	37
23	8716	8739	8762	8786	8809	8832	36
24	8855	8878	8901	8924	8947	8970	35
25	8993	9016	9039	9062	9085	9108	34
26	9131	9154	9177	9200	9223	9246	33
27	9269	9292	9315	9338	9361	9384	32
28	9407	9430	9453	9476	9499	9522	31
29	9545	9568	9591	9614	9637	9660	30
30	9.829683	9706	9729	9752	9775	9798	29
31	9821	9844	9867	9890	9913	9936	28
32	9959	9982	...5	..28	..51	..74	27
33	9.830097	0120	0142	0165	0188	0211	26
34	0234	0257	0280	0303	0326	0349	25
35	0372	0395	0417	0440	0463	0486	24
36	0509	0532	0555	0578	0601	0624	23
37	0646	0669	0692	0715	0738	0761	22
38	0784	0807	0829	0852	0875	0898	21
39	0921	0944	0967	0989	1012	1035	20
40	9.831058	1081	1104	1127	1149	1172	19
41	1195	1218	1241	1263	1286	1309	18
42	1332	1355	1378	1400	1423	1446	17
43	1469	1492	1514	1537	1560	1583	16
44	1606	1628	1651	1674	1697	1720	15
45	1742	1765	1788	1811	1833	1856	14
46	1879	1902	1924	1947	1970	1993	13
47	2015	2038	2061	2084	2106	2129	12
48	2152	2175	2197	2220	2243	2266	11
49	2288	2311	2334	2356	2379	2402	10
50	9.832425	2447	2470	2493	2515	2538	9
51	2561	2584	2606	2629	2652	2674	8
52	2697	2720	2742	2765	2788	2810	7
53	2833	2856	2878	2901	2924	2946	6
54	2969	2992	3014	3037	3060	3082	5
55	3105	3128	3150	3173	3196	3218	4
56	3241	3263	3286	3309	3331	3354	3
57	3377	3399	3422	3444	3467	3490	2
58	3512	3535	3557	3580	3603	3625	1
59	3648	3670	3693	3716	3738	3761	0
	60″	50″	40″	30″	20″	10″	Min.
	Co-sine of 47 Degrees.						

P. Part { 1″ 2″ 3″ 4″ 5″ 6″ 7″ 8″ 9″ / 2 5 7 9 11 14 16 18 21

Min.	Sine of 43 Degrees. 0″	10″	20″	30″	40″	50″	
0	9.833783	3806	3828	3851	3874	3896	59
1	3919	3941	3964	3986	4009	4032	58
2	4054	4077	4099	4122	4144	4167	57
3	4189	4212	4234	4257	4280	4302	56
4	4325	4347	4370	4392	4415	4437	55
5	4460	4482	4505	4527	4550	4572	54
6	4595	4617	4640	4662	4685	4707	53
7	4730	4752	4775	4797	4820	4842	52
8	4865	4887	4910	4932	4954	4977	51
9	4999	5022	5044	5067	5089	5112	50
10	9.835134	5157	5179	5201	5224	5246	49
11	5269	5291	5314	5336	5358	5381	48
12	5403	5426	5448	5471	5493	5515	47
13	5538	5560	5583	5605	5627	5650	46
14	5672	5695	5717	5739	5762	5784	45
15	5807	5829	5851	5874	5896	5918	44
16	5941	5963	5986	6008	6030	6053	43
17	6075	6097	6120	6142	6164	6187	42
18	6209	6231	6254	6276	6298	6321	41
19	6343	6365	6388	6410	6432	6455	40
20	9.836477	6499	6522	6544	6566	6589	39
21	6611	6633	6656	6678	6700	6722	38
22	6745	6767	6789	6812	6834	6856	37
23	6878	6901	6923	6945	6968	6990	36
24	7012	7034	7057	7079	7101	7123	35
25	7146	7168	7190	7212	7235	7257	34
26	7279	7301	7324	7346	7368	7390	33
27	7412	7435	7457	7479	7501	7524	32
28	7546	7568	7590	7612	7635	7657	31
29	7679	7701	7723	7746	7768	7790	30
30	9.837812	7834	7857	7879	7901	7923	29
31	7945	7967	7990	8012	8034	8056	28
32	8078	8100	8123	8145	8167	8189	27
33	8211	8233	8256	8278	8300	8322	26
34	8344	8366	8388	8410	8433	8455	25
35	8477	8499	8521	8543	8565	8587	24
36	8610	8632	8654	8676	8698	8720	23
37	8742	8764	8786	8808	8831	8853	22
38	8875	8897	8919	8941	8963	8985	21
39	9007	9029	9051	9073	9095	9118	20
40	9.839140	9162	9184	9206	9228	9250	19
41	9272	9294	9316	9338	9360	9382	18
42	9404	9426	9448	9470	9492	9514	17
43	9536	9558	9580	9602	9624	9646	16
44	9668	9690	9712	9734	9756	9778	15
45	9800	9822	9844	9866	9888	9910	14
46	9932	9954	9976	9998	..20	..42	13
47	9.840064	0086	0108	0130	0152	0174	12
48	0196	0218	0240	0262	0284	0306	11
49	0328	0350	0372	0393	0415	0437	10
50	9.840459	0481	0503	0525	0547	0569	9
51	0591	0613	0635	0657	0678	0700	8
52	0722	0744	0766	0788	0810	0832	7
53	0854	0876	0897	0919	0941	0963	6
54	0985	1007	1029	1051	1072	1094	5
55	1116	1138	1160	1182	1204	1226	4
56	1247	1269	1291	1313	1335	1357	3
57	1378	1400	1422	1444	1466	1488	2
58	1509	1531	1553	1575	1597	1619	1
59	1640	1662	1684	1706	1728	1749	0
	60″	50″	40″	30″	20″	10″	Min.
	Co-sine of 46 Degrees.						

P. Part { 1″ 2″ 3″ 4″ 5″ 6″ 7″ 8″ 9″ / 2 4 7 9 11 13 16 18 20

Min.	Tangent of 42 Degrees.						
	0″	10″	20″	30″	40″	50″	
0	9.954437	4480	4522	4564	4607	4649	59
1	4691	4734	4776	4819	4861	4903	58
2	4946	4988	5030	5073	5115	5157	57
3	5200	5242	5284	5327	5369	5411	56
4	5454	5496	5538	5581	5623	5665	55
5	5708	5750	5792	5835	5877	5919	54
6	5961	6004	6046	6088	6131	6173	53
7	6215	6258	6300	6342	6385	6427	52
8	6469	6512	6554	6596	6639	6681	51
9	6723	6766	6808	6850	6893	6935	50
10	9.956977	7020	7062	7104	7146	7189	49
11	7231	7273	7316	7358	7400	7443	48
12	7485	7527	7570	7612	7654	7697	47
13	7739	7781	7823	7866	7908	7950	46
14	7993	8035	8077	8120	8162	8204	45
15	8247	8289	8331	8373	8416	8458	44
16	8500	8543	8585	8627	8670	8712	43
17	8754	8796	8839	8881	8923	8966	42
18	9008	9050	9093	9135	9177	9219	41
19	9262	9304	9346	9389	9431	9473	40
20	9.959516	9558	9600	9642	9685	9727	39
21	9769	9812	9854	9896	9938	9981	38
22	9.960023	0065	0108	0150	0192	0234	37
23	0277	0319	0361	0404	0446	0488	36
24	0530	0573	0615	0657	0700	0742	35
25	0784	0826	0869	0911	0953	0996	34
26	1038	1080	1122	1165	1207	1249	33
27	1292	1334	1376	1418	1461	1503	32
28	1545	1587	1630	1672	1714	1757	31
29	1799	1841	1883	1926	1968	2010	30
30	9.962052	2095	2137	2179	2222	2264	29
31	2306	2348	2391	2433	2475	2517	28
32	2560	2602	2644	2686	2729	2771	27
33	2813	2856	2898	2940	2982	3025	26
34	3067	3109	3151	3194	3236	3278	25
35	3320	3363	3405	3447	3489	3532	24
36	3574	3616	3659	3701	3743	3785	23
37	3828	3870	3912	3954	3997	4039	22
38	4081	4123	4166	4208	4250	4292	21
39	4335	4377	4419	4461	4504	4546	20
40	9.964588	4630	4673	4715	4757	4799	19
41	4842	4884	4926	4968	5011	5053	18
42	5095	5137	5180	5222	5264	5306	17
43	5349	5391	5433	5475	5518	5560	16
44	5602	5644	5687	5729	5771	5813	15
45	5855	5898	5940	5982	6024	6067	14
46	6109	6151	6193	6236	6278	6320	13
47	6362	6405	6447	6489	6531	6574	12
48	6616	6658	6700	6742	6785	6827	11
49	6869	6911	6954	6996	7038	7080	10
50	9.967123	7165	7207	7249	7291	7334	9
51	7376	7418	7460	7503	7545	7587	8
52	7629	7672	7714	7756	7798	7840	7
53	7883	7925	7967	8009	8052	8094	6
54	8136	8178	8220	8263	8305	8347	5
55	8389	8432	8474	8516	8558	8600	4
56	8643	8685	8727	8769	8812	8854	3
57	8896	8938	8980	9023	9065	9107	2
58	9149	9192	9234	9276	9318	9360	1
59	9403	9445	9487	9529	9571	9614	0
	60″	50″	40″	30″	20″	10″	Min.
	Co-tangent of 47 Degrees.						

P. Part	1″	2″	3″	4″	5″	6″	7″	8″	9″
	4	8	13	17	21	25	30	34	38

Min.	Tangent of 43 Degrees.						
	0″	10″	20″	30″	40″	50″	
0	9.969656	9698	9740	9783	9825	9867	59
1	9909	9951	9994	..36	..78	.120	58
2	9.970162	0205	0247	0289	0331	0373	57
3	0416	0458	0500	0542	0584	0627	56
4	0669	0711	0753	0796	0838	0880	55
5	0922	0964	1007	1049	1091	1133	54
6	1175	1218	1260	1302	1344	1386	53
7	1429	1471	1513	1555	1597	1640	52
8	1682	1724	1766	1808	1851	1893	51
9	1935	1977	2019	2062	2104	2146	50
10	9.972188	2230	2273	2315	2357	2399	49
11	2441	2484	2526	2568	2610	2652	48
12	2695	2737	2779	2821	2863	2905	47
13	2948	2990	3032	3074	3116	3159	46
14	3201	3243	3285	3327	3370	3412	45
15	3454	3496	3538	3581	3623	3665	44
16	3707	3749	3791	3834	3876	3918	43
17	3960	4002	4045	4087	4129	4171	42
18	4213	4255	4298	4340	4382	4424	41
19	4466	4509	4551	4593	4635	4677	40
20	9.974720	4762	4804	4846	4888	4930	39
21	4973	5015	5057	5099	5141	5183	38
22	5226	5268	5310	5352	5394	5437	37
23	5479	5521	5563	5605	5647	5690	36
24	5732	5774	5816	5858	5901	5943	35
25	5985	6027	6069	6111	6154	6196	34
26	6238	6280	6322	6364	6407	6449	33
27	6491	6533	6575	6617	6660	6702	32
28	6744	6786	6828	6870	6913	6955	31
29	6997	7039	7081	7123	7166	7208	30
30	9.977250	7292	7334	7377	7419	7461	29
31	7503	7545	7587	7630	7672	7714	28
32	7756	7798	7840	7882	7925	7967	27
33	8009	8051	8093	8135	8178	8220	26
34	8262	8304	8346	8388	8431	8473	25
35	8515	8557	8599	8641	8684	8726	24
36	8768	8810	8852	8894	8937	8979	23
37	9021	9063	9105	9147	9190	9232	22
38	9274	9316	9358	9400	9442	9485	21
39	9527	9569	9611	9653	9695	9738	20
40	9.979780	9822	9864	9906	9948	9990	19
41	9.980033	0075	0117	0159	0201	0243	18
42	0286	0328	0370	0412	0454	0496	17
43	0538	0581	0623	0665	0707	0749	16
44	0791	0834	0876	0918	0960	1002	15
45	1044	1086	1129	1171	1213	1255	14
46	1297	1339	1382	1424	1466	1508	13
47	1550	1592	1634	1677	1719	1761	12
48	1803	1845	1887	1929	1972	2014	11
49	2056	2098	2140	2182	2224	2267	10
50	9.982309	2351	2393	2435	2477	2519	9
51	2562	2604	2646	2688	2730	2772	8
52	2814	2857	2899	2941	2983	3025	7
53	3067	3109	3152	3194	3236	3278	6
54	3320	3362	3404	3447	3489	3531	5
55	3573	3615	3657	3699	3742	3784	4
56	3826	3868	3910	3952	3994	4037	3
57	4079	4121	4163	4205	4247	4289	2
58	4332	4374	4416	4458	4500	4542	1
59	4584	4627	4669	4711	4753	4795	0
	60″	50″	40″	30″	20″	10″	Min.
	Co-tangent of 46 Degrees.						

P. Part	1″	2″	3″	4″	5″	6″	7″	8″	9″
	4	8	13	17	21	25	30	34	38

Min.	Sine of 44 Degrees.						
	0″	10″	20″	30″	40″	50″	
0	9.841771	1793	1815	1837	1858	1880	59
1	1902	1924	1946	1967	1989	2011	58
2	2033	2055	2076	2098	2120	2142	57
3	2163	2185	2207	2229	2250	2272	56
4	2294	2316	2337	2359	2381	2403	55
5	2424	2446	2468	2490	2511	2533	54
6	2555	2577	2598	2620	2642	2663	53
7	2685	2707	2729	2750	2772	2794	52
8	2815	2837	2859	2880	2902	2924	51
9	2946	2967	2989	3011	3032	3054	50
10	9.843076	3097	3119	3141	3162	3184	49
11	3206	3227	3249	3271	3292	3314	48
12	3336	3357	3379	3401	3422	3444	47
13	3466	3487	3509	3530	3552	3574	46
14	3595	3617	3639	3660	3682	3703	45
15	3725	3747	3768	3790	3811	3833	44
16	3855	3876	3898	3919	3941	3963	43
17	3984	4006	4027	4049	4071	4092	42
18	4114	4135	4157	4178	4200	4222	41
19	4243	4265	4286	4308	4329	4351	40
20	9.844372	4394	4416	4437	4459	4480	39
21	4502	4523	4545	4566	4588	4609	38
22	4631	4652	4674	4696	4717	4739	37
23	4760	4782	4803	4825	4846	4868	36
24	4889	4911	4932	4954	4975	4997	35
25	5018	5040	5061	5083	5104	5126	34
26	5147	5168	5190	5211	5233	5254	33
27	5276	5297	5319	5340	5362	5383	32
28	5405	5426	5447	5469	5490	5512	31
29	5533	5555	5576	5598	5619	5640	30
30	9.845662	5683	5705	5726	5747	5769	29
31	5790	5812	5833	5855	5876	5897	28
32	5919	5940	5962	5983	6004	6026	27
33	6047	6069	6090	6111	6133	6154	26
34	6175	6197	6218	6240	6261	6282	25
35	6304	6325	6346	6368	6389	6410	24
36	6432	6453	6474	6496	6517	6539	23
37	6560	6581	6603	6624	6645	6667	22
38	6688	6709	6731	6752	6773	6794	21
39	6816	6837	6858	6880	6901	6922	20
40	9.846944	6965	6986	7008	7029	7050	19
41	7071	7093	7114	7135	7157	7178	18
42	7199	7220	7242	7263	7284	7305	17
43	7327	7348	7369	7391	7412	7433	16
44	7454	7476	7497	7518	7539	7561	15
45	7582	7603	7624	7645	7667	7688	14
46	7709	7730	7752	7773	7794	7815	13
47	7836	7858	7879	7900	7921	7943	12
48	7964	7985	8006	8027	8049	8070	11
49	8091	8112	8133	8154	8176	8197	10
50	9.848218	8239	8260	8282	8303	8324	9
51	8345	8366	8387	8409	8430	8451	8
52	8472	8493	8514	8535	8557	8578	7
53	8599	8620	8641	8662	8683	8705	6
54	8726	8747	8768	8789	8810	8831	5
55	8852	8874	8895	8916	8937	8958	4
56	8979	9000	9021	9042	9063	9085	3
57	9106	9127	9148	9169	9190	9211	2
58	9232	9253	9274	9295	9316	9338	1
59	9359	9380	9401	9422	9443	9464	0
	60″	50″	40″	30″	20″	10″	Min.
	Co-sine of 45 Degrees.						

P. Part	1″	2″	3″	4″	5″	6″	7″	8″	9″
	2	4	6	9	11	13	15	17	19

Min.	Sine of 45 Degrees.						
	0″	10″	20″	30″	40″	50″	
0	9.849485	9506	9527	9548	9569	9590	59
1	9611	9632	9653	9674	9695	9716	58
2	9738	9759	9780	9801	9822	9843	57
3	9864	9885	9906	9927	9948	9969	56
4	9990	..11	..32	..53	..74	..95	55
5	9.850116	0137	0158	0179	0200	0221	54
6	0242	0263	0284	0305	0326	0347	53
7	0368	0388	0409	0430	0451	0472	52
8	0493	0514	0535	0556	0577	0598	51
9	0619	0640	0661	0682	0703	0724	50
10	9.850745	0766	0787	0807	0828	0849	49
11	0870	0891	0912	0933	0954	0975	48
12	0996	1017	1038	1058	1079	1100	47
13	1121	1142	1163	1184	1205	1226	46
14	1246	1267	1288	1309	1330	1351	45
15	1372	1393	1413	1434	1455	1476	44
16	1497	1518	1539	1559	1580	1601	43
17	1622	1643	1664	1685	1705	1726	42
18	1747	1768	1789	1810	1830	1851	41
19	1872	1893	1914	1935	1955	1976	40
20	9.851997	2018	2039	2059	2080	2101	39
21	2122	2143	2163	2184	2205	2226	38
22	2247	2267	2288	2309	2330	2350	37
23	2371	2392	2413	2434	2454	2475	36
24	2496	2517	2537	2558	2579	2600	35
25	2620	2641	2662	2683	2703	2724	34
26	2745	2766	2786	2807	2828	2849	33
27	2869	2890	2911	2931	2952	2973	32
28	2994	3014	3035	3056	3076	3097	31
29	3118	3139	3159	3180	3201	3221	30
30	9.853242	3263	3283	3304	3325	3345	29
31	3366	3387	3408	3428	3449	3470	28
32	3490	3511	3532	3552	3573	3594	27
33	3614	3635	3655	3676	3697	3717	26
34	3738	3759	3779	3800	3821	3841	25
35	3862	3883	3903	3924	3944	3965	24
36	3986	4006	4027	4047	4068	4089	23
37	4109	4130	4151	4171	4192	4212	22
38	4233	4254	4274	4295	4315	4336	21
39	4356	4377	4398	4418	4439	4459	20
40	9.854480	4500	4521	4542	4562	4583	19
41	4603	4624	4644	4665	4686	4706	18
42	4727	4747	4768	4788	4809	4829	17
43	4850	4870	4891	4911	4932	4953	16
44	4973	4994	5014	5035	5055	5076	15
45	5096	5117	5137	5158	5178	5199	14
46	5219	5240	5260	5281	5301	5322	13
47	5342	5363	5383	5404	5424	5445	12
48	5465	5485	5506	5526	5547	5567	11
49	5588	5608	5629	5649	5670	5690	10
50	9.855711	5731	5751	5772	5792	5813	9
51	5833	5854	5874	5895	5915	5935	8
52	5956	5976	5997	6017	6038	6058	7
53	6078	6099	6119	6140	6160	6180	6
54	6201	6221	6242	6262	6282	6303	5
55	6323	6344	6364	6384	6405	6425	4
56	6446	6466	6486	6507	6527	6547	3
57	6568	6588	6609	6629	6649	6670	2
58	6690	6710	6731	6751	6771	6792	1
59	6812	6832	6853	6873	6893	6914	0
	60″	50″	40″	30″	20″	10″	Min.
	Co-sine of 44 Degrees.						

P. Part	1″	2″	3″	4″	5″	6″	7″	8″	9″
	2	4	6	8	10	12	14	17	19

Min.	Tangent of 44 Degrees. 0″	10″	20″	30″	40″	50″	
0	9.984837	4879	4921	4964	5006	5048	59
1	5090	5132	5174	5216	5259	5301	58
2	5343	5385	5427	5469	5511	5553	57
3	5596	5638	5680	5722	5764	5806	56
4	5848	5891	5933	5975	6017	6059	55
5	6101	6143	6185	6228	6270	6312	54
6	6354	6396	6438	6480	6523	6565	53
7	6607	6649	6691	6733	6775	6817	52
8	6860	6902	6944	6986	7028	7070	51
9	7112	7154	7197	7239	7281	7323	50
10	9.987365	7407	7449	7491	7534	7576	49
11	7618	7660	7702	7744	7786	7829	48
12	7871	7913	7955	7997	8039	8081	47
13	8123	8166	8208	8250	8292	8334	46
14	8376	8418	8460	8503	8545	8587	45
15	8629	8671	8713	8755	8797	8840	44
16	8882	8924	8966	9008	9050	9092	43
17	9134	9177	9219	9261	9303	9345	42
18	9387	9429	9471	9513	9556	9598	41
19	9640	9682	9724	9766	9808	9850	40
20	9.989893	9935	9977	..19	..61	.103	39
21	9.990145	0187	0230	0272	0314	0356	38
22	0398	0440	0482	0524	0567	0609	37
23	0651	0693	0735	0777	0819	0861	36
24	0903	0946	0988	1030	1072	1114	35
25	1156	1198	1240	1283	1325	1367	34
26	1409	1451	1493	1535	1577	1620	33
27	1662	1704	1746	1788	1830	1872	32
28	1914	1956	1999	2041	2083	2125	31
29	2167	2209	2251	2293	2336	2378	30
30	9.992420	2462	2504	2546	2588	2630	29
31	2672	2715	2757	2799	2841	2883	28
32	2925	2967	3009	3051	3094	3136	27
33	3178	3220	3262	3304	3346	3388	26
34	3431	3473	3515	3557	3599	3641	25
35	3683	3725	3767	3810	3852	3894	24
36	3936	3978	4020	4062	4104	4146	23
37	4189	4231	4273	4315	4357	4399	22
38	4441	4483	4526	4568	4610	4652	21
39	4694	4736	4778	4820	4862	4905	20
40	9.994947	4989	5031	5073	5115	5157	19
41	5199	5241	5284	5326	5368	5410	18
42	5452	5494	5536	5578	5620	5663	17
43	5705	5747	5789	5831	5873	5915	16
44	5957	5999	6042	6084	6126	6168	15
45	6210	6252	6294	6336	6378	6421	14
46	6463	6505	6547	6589	6631	6673	13
47	6715	6757	6800	6842	6884	6926	12
48	6968	7010	7052	7094	7136	7179	11
49	7221	7263	7305	7347	7389	7431	10
50	9.997473	7515	7558	7600	7642	7684	9
51	7726	7768	7810	7852	7894	7937	8
52	7979	8021	8063	8105	8147	8189	7
53	8231	8273	8316	8358	8400	8442	6
54	8484	8526	8568	8610	8652	8695	5
55	8737	8779	8821	8863	8905	8947	4
56	8989	9031	9074	9116	9158	9200	3
57	9242	9284	9326	9368	9410	9453	2
58	9495	9537	9579	9621	9663	9705	1
59	9747	9789	9832	9874	9916	9958	0
	60″	50″	40″	30″	20″	10″	Min.
	Co-tangent of 45 Degrees.						

P. Part { 1″ 2″ 3″ 4″ 5″ 6″ 7″ 8″ 9″ / 4 8 13 17 21 25 29 34 38

Min.	Tangent of 45 Degrees. 0″	10″	20″	30″	40″	50″	
0	10.000000	0042	0084	0126	0168	0211	59
1	0253	0295	0337	0379	0421	0463	58
2	0505	0547	0590	0632	0674	0716	57
3	0758	0800	0842	0884	0926	0969	56
4	1011	1053	1095	1137	1179	1221	55
5	1263	1305	1348	1390	1432	1474	54
6	1516	1558	1600	1642	1684	1727	53
7	1769	1811	1853	1895	1937	1979	52
8	2021	2063	2106	2148	2190	2232	51
9	2274	2316	2358	2400	2442	2485	50
10	10.002527	2569	2611	2653	2695	2737	49
11	2779	2821	2864	2906	2948	2990	48
12	3032	3074	3116	3158	3200	3243	47
13	3285	3327	3369	3411	3453	3495	46
14	3537	3579	3622	3664	3706	3748	45
15	3790	3832	3874	3916	3958	4001	44
16	4043	4085	4127	4169	4211	4253	43
17	4295	4337	4380	4422	4464	4506	42
18	4548	4590	4632	4674	4716	4759	41
19	4801	4843	4885	4927	4969	5011	40
20	10.005053	5095	5138	5180	5222	5264	39
21	5306	5348	5390	5432	5474	5517	38
22	5559	5601	5643	5685	5727	5769	37
23	5811	5854	5896	5938	5980	6022	36
24	6064	6106	6148	6190	6233	6275	35
25	6317	6359	6401	6443	6485	6527	34
26	6569	6612	6654	6696	6738	6780	33
27	6822	6864	6906	6949	6991	7033	32
28	7075	7117	7159	7201	7243	7285	31
29	7328	7370	7412	7454	7496	7538	30
30	10.007580	7622	7664	7707	7749	7791	29
31	7833	7875	7917	7959	8001	8044	28
32	8086	8128	8170	8212	8254	8296	27
33	8338	8380	8423	8465	8507	8549	26
34	8591	8633	8675	8717	8760	8802	25
35	8844	8886	8928	8970	9012	9054	24
36	9097	9139	9181	9223	9265	9307	23
37	9349	9391	9433	9476	9518	9560	22
38	9602	9644	9686	9728	9770	9813	21
39	9855	9897	9939	9981	..23	..65	20
40	10.010107	0150	0192	0234	0276	0318	19
41	0360	0402	0444	0487	0529	0571	18
42	0613	0655	0697	0739	0781	0823	17
43	0866	0908	0950	0992	1034	1076	16
44	1118	1160	1203	1245	1287	1329	15
45	1371	1413	1455	1497	1540	1582	14
46	1624	1666	1708	1750	1792	1834	13
47	1877	1919	1961	2003	2045	2087	12
48	2129	2171	2214	2256	2298	2340	11
49	2382	2424	2466	2509	2551	2593	10
50	10.012635	2677	2719	2761	2803	2846	9
51	2888	2930	2972	3014	3056	3098	8
52	3140	3183	3225	3267	3309	3351	7
53	3393	3435	3477	3520	3562	3604	6
54	3646	3688	3730	3772	3815	3857	5
55	3899	3941	3983	4025	4067	4109	4
56	4152	4194	4236	4278	4320	4362	3
57	4404	4447	4489	4531	4573	4615	2
58	4657	4699	4741	4784	4826	4868	1
59	4910	4952	4994	5036	5079	5121	0
	60″	50″	40″	30″	20″	10″	Min.
	Co-tangent of 44 Degrees.						

P. Part { 1″ 2″ 3″ 4″ 5″ 6″ 7″ 8″ 9″ / 4 8 13 17 21 25 29 34 38

Sine of 46 Degrees.

Min.	0″	10″	20″	30″	40″	50″	
0	9.856934	6954	6975	6995	7015	7036	59
1	7056	7076	7097	7117	7137	7158	58
2	7178	7198	7219	7239	7259	7279	57
3	7300	7320	7340	7361	7381	7401	56
4	7422	7442	7462	7482	7503	7523	55
5	7543	7563	7584	7604	7624	7645	54
6	7665	7685	7705	7726	7746	7766	53
7	7786	7807	7827	7847	7867	7888	52
8	7908	7928	7948	7968	7989	8009	51
9	8029	8049	8070	8090	8110	8130	50
10	9.858151	8171	8191	8211	8231	8252	49
11	8272	8292	8312	8332	8353	8373	48
12	8393	8413	8433	8454	8474	8494	47
13	8514	8534	8554	8575	8595	8615	46
14	8635	8655	8675	8696	8716	8736	45
15	8756	8776	8796	8817	8837	8857	44
16	8877	8897	8917	8937	8958	8978	43
17	8998	9018	9038	9058	9078	9098	42
18	9119	9139	9159	9179	9199	9219	41
19	9239	9259	9279	9300	9320	9340	40
20	9.859360	9380	9400	9420	9440	9460	39
21	9480	9501	9521	9541	9561	9581	38
22	9601	9621	9641	9661	9681	9701	37
23	9721	9741	9761	9781	9802	9822	36
24	9842	9862	9882	9902	9922	9942	35
25	9962	9982	...2	..22	..42	..62	34
26	9.860082	0102	0122	0142	0162	0182	33
27	0202	0222	0242	0262	0282	0302	32
28	0322	0342	0362	0382	0402	0422	31
29	0442	0462	0482	0502	0522	0542	30
30	9.860562	0582	0602	0622	0642	0662	29
31	0682	0702	0722	0742	0762	0782	28
32	0802	0822	0842	0862	0882	0902	27
33	0922	0941	0961	0981	1001	1021	26
34	1041	1061	1081	1101	1121	1141	25
35	1161	1181	1201	1221	1240	1260	24
36	1280	1300	1320	1340	1360	1380	23
37	1400	1420	1439	1459	1479	1499	22
38	1519	1539	1559	1579	1599	1618	21
39	1638	1658	1678	1698	1718	1738	20
40	9.861758	1777	1797	1817	1837	1857	19
41	1877	1897	1916	1936	1956	1976	18
42	1996	2016	2035	2055	2075	2095	17
43	2115	2135	2154	2174	2194	2214	16
44	2234	2254	2273	2293	2313	2333	15
45	2353	2372	2392	2412	2432	2452	14
46	2471	2491	2511	2531	2551	2570	13
47	2590	2610	2630	2650	2669	2689	12
48	2709	2729	2748	2768	2788	2808	11
49	2827	2847	2867	2887	2906	2926	10
50	9.862946	2966	2985	3005	3025	3045	9
51	3064	3084	3104	3124	3143	3163	8
52	3183	3203	3222	3242	3262	3281	7
53	3301	3321	3341	3360	3380	3400	6
54	3419	3439	3459	3478	3498	3518	5
55	3538	3557	3577	3597	3616	3636	4
56	3656	3675	3695	3715	3734	3754	3
57	3774	3793	3813	3833	3852	3872	2
58	3892	3911	3931	3951	3970	3990	1
59	4010	4029	4049	4069	4088	4108	0
	60″	50″	40″	30″	20″	10″	Min.

Co-sine of 43 Degrees.

P. Part	1″	2″	3″	4″	5″	6″	7″	8″	9″
	2	4	6	8	10	12	14	16	18

Sine of 47 Degrees.

Min.	0″	10″	20″	30″	40″	50″	
0	9.864127	4147	4167	4186	4206	4226	59
1	4245	4265	4284	4304	4324	4343	58
2	4363	4383	4402	4422	4441	4461	57
3	4481	4500	4520	4539	4559	4579	56
4	4598	4618	4637	4657	4676	4696	55
5	4716	4735	4755	4774	4794	4813	54
6	4833	4853	4872	4892	4911	4931	53
7	4950	4970	4990	5009	5029	5048	52
8	5068	5087	5107	5126	5146	5165	51
9	5185	5204	5224	5244	5263	5283	50
10	9.865302	5322	5341	5361	5380	5400	49
11	5419	5439	5458	5478	5497	5517	48
12	5536	5556	5575	5595	5614	5634	47
13	5653	5673	5692	5712	5731	5751	46
14	5770	5790	5809	5828	5848	5867	45
15	5887	5906	5926	5945	5965	5984	44
16	6004	6023	6042	6062	6081	6101	43
17	6120	6140	6159	6179	6198	6217	42
18	6237	6256	6276	6295	6315	6334	41
19	6353	6373	6392	6412	6431	6450	40
20	9.866470	6489	6509	6528	6547	6567	39
21	6586	6606	6625	6644	6664	6683	38
22	6703	6722	6741	6761	6780	6800	37
23	6819	6838	6858	6877	6896	6916	36
24	6935	6954	6974	6993	7013	7032	35
25	7051	7071	7090	7109	7129	7148	34
26	7167	7187	7206	7225	7245	7264	33
27	7283	7303	7322	7341	7361	7380	32
28	7399	7419	7438	7457	7476	7496	31
29	7515	7534	7554	7573	7592	7612	30
30	9.867631	7650	7669	7689	7708	7727	29
31	7747	7766	7785	7804	7824	7843	28
32	7862	7882	7901	7920	7939	7959	27
33	7978	7997	8016	8036	8055	8074	26
34	8093	8113	8132	8151	8170	8190	25
35	8209	8228	8247	8267	8286	8305	24
36	8324	8343	8363	8382	8401	8420	23
37	8440	8459	8478	8497	8516	8536	22
38	8555	8574	8593	8612	8632	8651	21
39	8670	8689	8708	8728	8747	8766	20
40	9.868785	8804	8823	8843	8862	8881	19
41	8900	8919	8939	8958	8977	8996	18
42	9015	9034	9053	9073	9092	9111	17
43	9130	9149	9168	9188	9207	9226	16
44	9245	9264	9283	9302	9321	9341	15
45	9360	9379	9398	9417	9436	9455	14
46	9474	9494	9513	9532	9551	9570	13
47	9589	9608	9627	9646	9665	9685	12
48	9704	9723	9742	9761	9780	9799	11
49	9818	9837	9856	9875	9894	9914	10
50	9.869933	9952	9971	9990	...9	..28	9
51	9.870047	0066	0085	0104	0123	0142	8
52	0161	0180	0199	0218	0238	0257	7
53	0276	0295	0314	0333	0352	0371	6
54	0390	0409	0428	0447	0466	0485	5
55	0504	0523	0542	0561	0580	0599	4
56	0618	0637	0656	0675	0694	0713	3
57	0732	0751	0770	0789	0808	0827	2
58	0846	0865	0884	0903	0922	0941	1
59	0960	0979	0998	1017	1036	1054	0
	60″	50″	40″	30″	20″	10″	Min.

Co-sine of 42 Degrees.

P. Part	1″	2″	3″	4″	5″	6″	7″	8″	9″
	2	4	6	8	10	12	14	15	17

Min.	Tangent of 46 Degrees. 0″	10″	20″	30″	40″	50″	
0	10.015163	5205	5247	5289	5331	5373	59
1	5416	5458	5500	5542	5584	5626	58
2	5668	5711	5753	5795	5837	5879	57
3	5921	5963	6006	6048	6090	6132	56
4	6174	6216	6258	6301	6343	6385	55
5	6427	6469	6511	6553	6596	6638	54
6	6680	6722	6764	6806	6848	6891	53
7	6933	6975	7017	7059	7101	7143	52
8	7186	7228	7270	7312	7354	7396	51
9	7438	7481	7523	7565	7607	7649	50
10	10.017691	7733	7776	7818	7860	7902	49
11	7944	7986	8028	8071	8113	8155	48
12	8197	8239	8281	8323	8366	8408	47
13	8450	8492	8534	8576	8618	8661	46
14	8703	8745	8787	8829	8871	8914	45
15	8956	8998	9040	9082	9124	9166	44
16	9209	9251	9293	9335	9377	9419	43
17	9462	9504	9546	9588	9630	9672	42
18	9714	9757	9799	9841	9883	9925	41
19	9967	..10	..52	..94	.136	.178	40
20	10.020220	0262	0305	0347	0389	0431	39
21	0473	0515	0558	0600	0642	0684	38
22	0726	0768	0810	0853	0895	0937	37
23	0979	1021	1063	1106	1148	1190	36
24	1232	1274	1316	1359	1401	1443	35
25	1485	1527	1569	1612	1654	1696	34
26	1738	1780	1822	1865	1907	1949	33
27	1991	2033	2075	2118	2160	2202	32
28	2244	2286	2328	2370	2413	2455	31
29	2497	2539	2581	2623	2666	2708	30
30	10.022750	2792	2834	2877	2919	2961	29
31	3003	3045	3087	3130	3172	3214	28
32	3256	3298	3340	3383	3425	3467	27
33	3509	3551	3593	3636	3678	3720	26
34	3762	3804	3846	3889	3931	3973	25
35	4015	4057	4099	4142	4184	4226	24
36	4268	4310	4353	4395	4437	4479	23
37	4521	4563	4606	4648	4690	4732	22
38	4774	4817	4859	4901	4943	4985	21
39	5027	5070	5112	5154	5196	5238	20
40	10.025280	5323	5365	5407	5449	5491	19
41	5534	5576	5618	5660	5702	5745	18
42	5787	5829	5871	5913	5955	5998	17
43	6040	6082	6124	6166	6209	6251	16
44	6293	6335	6377	6419	6462	6504	15
45	6546	6588	6630	6673	6715	6757	14
46	6799	6841	6884	6926	6968	7010	13
47	7052	7095	7137	7179	7221	7263	12
48	7305	7348	7390	7432	7474	7516	11
49	7559	7601	7643	7685	7727	7770	10
50	10.027812	7854	7896	7938	7981	8023	9
51	8065	8107	8149	8192	8234	8276	8
52	8318	8360	8403	8445	8487	8529	7
53	8571	8614	8656	8698	8740	8782	6
54	8825	8867	8909	8951	8993	9036	5
55	9078	9120	9162	9204	9247	9289	4
56	9331	9373	9416	9458	9500	9542	3
57	9584	9627	9669	9711	9753	9795	2
58	9838	9880	9922	9964	...6	..49	1
59	10.030091	0133	0175	0217	0260	0302	0
	60″	50″	40″	30″	20″	10″	Min.
	Co-tangent of 43 Degrees.						

P. Part { 1″ 2″ 3″ 4″ 5″ 6″ 7″ 8″ 9″ / 4 8 13 17 21 25 30 34 38 }

Min.	Tangent of 47 Degrees. 0″	10″	20″	30″	40″	50″	
0	10.030344	0386	0429	0471	0513	0555	59
1	0597	0640	0682	0724	0766	0808	58
2	0851	0893	0935	0977	1020	1062	57
3	1104	1146	1188	1231	1273	1315	56
4	1357	1400	1442	1484	1526	1568	55
5	1611	1653	1695	1737	1780	1822	54
6	1864	1906	1948	1991	2033	2075	53
7	2117	2160	2202	2244	2286	2328	52
8	2371	2413	2455	2497	2540	2582	51
9	2624	2666	2709	2751	2793	2835	50
10	10.032877	2920	2962	3004	3046	3089	49
11	3131	3173	3215	3258	3300	3342	48
12	3384	3426	3469	3511	3553	3595	47
13	3638	3680	3722	3764	3807	3849	46
14	3891	3933	3976	4018	4060	4102	45
15	4145	4187	4229	4271	4313	4356	44
16	4398	4440	4482	4525	4567	4609	43
17	4651	4694	4736	4778	4820	4863	42
18	4905	4947	4989	5032	5074	5116	41
19	5158	5201	5243	5285	5327	5370	40
20	10.035412	5454	5496	5539	5581	5623	39
21	5665	5708	5750	5792	5834	5877	38
22	5919	5961	6003	6046	6088	6130	37
23	6172	6215	6257	6299	6341	6384	36
24	6426	6468	6511	6553	6595	6637	35
25	6680	6722	6764	6806	6849	6891	34
26	6933	6975	7018	7060	7102	7144	33
27	7187	7229	7271	7314	7356	7398	32
28	7440	7483	7525	7567	7609	7652	31
29	7694	7736	7778	7821	7863	7905	30
30	10.037948	7990	8032	8074	8117	8159	29
31	8201	8243	8286	8328	8370	8413	28
32	8455	8497	8539	8582	8624	8666	27
33	8708	8751	8793	8835	8878	8920	26
34	8962	9004	9047	9089	9131	9174	25
35	9216	9258	9300	9343	9385	9427	24
36	9470	9512	9554	9596	9639	9681	23
37	9723	9766	9808	9850	9892	9935	22
38	9977	..19	..62	.104	.146	.188	21
39	10.040231	0273	0315	0358	0400	0442	20
40	10.040484	0527	0569	0611	0654	0696	19
41	0738	0781	0823	0865	0907	0950	18
42	0992	1034	1077	1119	1161	1204	17
43	1246	1288	1330	1373	1415	1457	16
44	1500	1542	1584	1627	1669	1711	15
45	1753	1796	1833	1880	1923	1965	14
46	2007	2050	2092	2134	2177	2219	13
47	2261	2303	2346	2388	2430	2473	12
48	2515	2557	2600	2642	2684	2727	11
49	2769	2811	2854	2896	2938	2980	10
50	10.043023	3065	3107	3150	3192	3234	9
51	3277	3319	3361	3404	3446	3488	8
52	3531	3573	3615	3658	3700	3742	7
53	3785	3827	3869	3912	3954	3996	6
54	4039	4081	4123	4165	4208	4250	5
55	4292	4335	4377	4419	4462	4504	4
56	4546	4589	4631	4673	4716	4758	3
57	4800	4843	4885	4927	4970	5012	2
58	5054	5097	5139	5181	5224	5266	1
59	5309	5351	5393	5436	5478	5520	0
	60″	50″	40″	30″	20″	10″	Min.
	Co-tangent of 42 Degrees.						

P. Part { 1″ 2″ 3″ 4″ 5″ 6″ 7″ 8″ 9″ / 4 8 13 17 21 25 30 34 38 }

Sine of 48 Degrees.

Min.	0″	10″	20″	30″	40″	50″	
0	9.871073	1092	1111	1130	1149	1168	59
1	1187	1206	1225	1244	1263	1282	58
2	1301	1320	1339	1358	1377	1395	57
3	1414	1433	1452	1471	1490	1509	56
4	1528	1547	1566	1585	1604	1622	55
5	1641	1660	1679	1698	1717	1736	54
6	1755	1774	1793	1811	1830	1849	53
7	1868	1887	1906	1925	1944	1962	52
8	1981	2000	2019	2038	2057	2076	51
9	2095	2113	2132	2151	2170	2189	50
10	9.872208	2226	2245	2264	2283	2302	49
11	2321	2340	2358	2377	2396	2415	48
12	2434	2452	2471	2490	2509	2528	47
13	2547	2565	2584	2603	2622	2641	46
14	2659	2678	2697	2716	2735	2753	45
15	2772	2791	2810	2829	2847	2866	44
16	2885	2904	2923	2941	2960	2979	43
17	2998	3016	3035	3054	3073	3091	42
18	3110	3129	3148	3166	3185	3204	41
19	3223	3241	3260	3279	3298	3316	40
20	9.873335	3354	3373	3391	3410	3429	39
21	3448	3466	3485	3504	3522	3541	38
22	3560	3579	3597	3616	3635	3653	37
23	3672	3691	3710	3728	3747	3766	36
24	3784	3803	3822	3840	3859	3878	35
25	3896	3915	3934	3953	3971	3990	34
26	4009	4027	4046	4065	4083	4102	33
27	4121	4139	4158	4177	4195	4214	32
28	4232	4251	4270	4288	4307	4326	31
29	4344	4363	4382	4400	4419	4438	30
30	9.874456	4475	4493	4512	4531	4549	29
31	4568	4586	4605	4624	4642	4661	28
32	4680	4698	4717	4735	4754	4773	27
33	4791	4810	4828	4847	4866	4884	26
34	4903	4921	4940	4958	4977	4996	25
35	5014	5033	5051	5070	5088	5107	24
36	5126	5144	5163	5181	5200	5218	23
37	5237	5255	5274	5293	5311	5330	22
38	5348	5367	5385	5404	5422	5441	21
39	5459	5478	5496	5515	5534	5552	20
40	9.875571	5589	5608	5626	5645	5663	19
41	5682	5700	5719	5737	5756	5774	18
42	5793	5811	5830	5848	5867	5885	17
43	5904	5922	5941	5959	5978	5996	16
44	6014	6033	6051	6070	6088	6107	15
45	6125	6144	6162	6181	6199	6218	14
46	6236	6255	6273	6291	6310	6328	13
47	6347	6365	6384	6402	6421	6439	12
48	6457	6476	6494	6513	6531	6550	11
49	6568	6586	6605	6623	6642	6660	10
50	9.876678	6697	6715	6734	6752	6770	9
51	6789	6807	6826	6844	6862	6881	8
52	6899	6918	6936	6954	6973	6991	7
53	7010	7028	7046	7065	7083	7101	6
54	7120	7138	7157	7175	7193	7212	5
55	7230	7248	7267	7285	7303	7322	4
56	7340	7358	7377	7395	7413	7432	3
57	7450	7468	7487	7505	7523	7542	2
58	7560	7578	7597	7615	7633	7652	1
59	7670	7688	7707	7725	7743	7762	0
	60″	50″	40″	30″	20″	10″	Min.

Co-sine of 41 Degrees.

P. Part	1″	2″	3″	4″	5″	6″	7″	8″	9″
	2	4	6	7	9	11	13	15	17

Sine of 49 Degrees.

Min.	0″	10″	20″	30″	40″	50″	
0	9.877780	7798	7816	7835	7853	7871	59
1	7890	7908	7926	7945	7963	7981	58
2	7999	8018	8036	8054	8072	8091	57
3	8109	8127	8146	8164	8182	8200	56
4	8219	8237	8255	8273	8292	8310	55
5	8328	8346	8365	8383	8401	8419	54
6	8438	8456	8474	8492	8511	8529	53
7	8547	8565	8583	8602	8620	8638	52
8	8656	8675	8693	8711	8729	8747	51
9	8766	8784	8802	8820	8838	8857	50
10	9.878875	8893	8911	8929	8948	8966	49
11	8984	9002	9020	9039	9057	9075	48
12	9093	9111	9129	9148	9166	9184	47
13	9202	9220	9238	9257	9275	9293	46
14	9311	9329	9347	9365	9384	9402	45
15	9420	9438	9456	9474	9492	9511	44
16	9529	9547	9565	9583	9601	9619	43
17	9637	9656	9674	9692	9710	9728	42
18	9746	9764	9782	9800	9819	9837	41
19	9855	9873	9891	9909	9927	9945	40
20	9.879963	9981	....	..18	..36	..54	39
21	9.880072	0090	0108	0126	0144	0162	38
22	0180	0198	0216	0234	0253	0271	37
23	0289	0307	0325	0343	0361	0379	36
24	0397	0415	0433	0451	0469	0487	35
25	0505	0523	0541	0559	0577	0595	34
26	0613	0631	0649	0667	0686	0704	33
27	0722	0740	0758	0776	0794	0812	32
28	0830	0848	0866	0884	0902	0920	31
29	0938	0956	0974	0992	1010	1028	30
30	9.881046	1063	1081	1099	1117	1135	29
31	1153	1171	1189	1207	1225	1243	28
32	1261	1279	1297	1315	1333	1351	27
33	1369	1387	1405	1423	1441	1459	26
34	1477	1495	1512	1530	1548	1566	25
35	1584	1602	1620	1638	1656	1674	24
36	1692	1710	1728	1746	1763	1781	23
37	1799	1817	1835	1853	1871	1889	22
38	1907	1925	1942	1960	1978	1996	21
39	2014	2032	2050	2068	2086	2103	20
40	9.882121	2139	2157	2175	2193	2211	19
41	2229	2246	2264	2282	2300	2318	18
42	2336	2354	2371	2389	2407	2425	17
43	2443	2461	2479	2496	2514	2532	16
44	2550	2568	2586	2603	2621	2639	15
45	2657	2675	2692	2710	2728	2746	14
46	2764	2782	2799	2817	2835	2853	13
47	2871	2888	2906	2924	2942	2960	12
48	2977	2995	3013	3031	3049	3066	11
49	3084	3102	3120	3137	3155	3173	10
50	9.883191	3209	3226	3244	3262	3280	9
51	3297	3315	3333	3351	3368	3386	8
52	3404	3422	3439	3457	3475	3493	7
53	3510	3528	3546	3564	3581	3599	6
54	3617	3635	3652	3670	3688	3705	5
55	3723	3741	3759	3776	3794	3812	4
56	3829	3847	3865	3883	3900	3918	3
57	3936	3953	3971	3989	4006	4024	2
58	4042	4060	4077	4095	4113	4130	1
59	4148	4166	4183	4201	4219	4236	0
	60″	50″	40″	30″	20″	10″	Min.

Co-sine of 40 Degrees.

P. Part	1″	2″	3″	4″	5″	6″	7″	8″	9″
	2	4	5	7	9	11	13	14	16

Min.	Tangent of 48 Degrees. 0″	10″	20″	30″	40″	50″	
0	10.045563	5605	5647	5690	5732	5774	59
1	5817	5859	5901	5944	5986	6028	58
2	6071	6113	6155	6198	6240	6282	57
3	6325	6367	6409	6452	6494	6537	56
4	6579	6621	6664	6706	6748	6791	55
5	6833	6875	6918	6960	7002	7045	54
6	7087	7130	7172	7214	7257	7299	53
7	7341	7384	7426	7468	7511	7553	52
8	7595	7638	7680	7723	7765	7807	51
9	7850	7892	7934	7977	8019	8062	50
10	10.048104	8146	8189	8231	8273	8316	49
11	8358	8400	8443	8485	8528	8570	48
12	8612	8655	8697	8739	8782	8824	47
13	8867	8909	8951	8994	9036	9079	46
14	9121	9163	9206	9248	9290	9333	45
15	9375	9418	9460	9502	9545	9587	44
16	9629	9672	9714	9757	9799	9841	43
17	9884	9926	9969	..11	..53	..96	42
18	10.050138	0181	0223	0265	0308	0350	41
19	0392	0435	0477	0520	0562	0604	40
20	10.050647	0689	0732	0774	0816	0859	39
21	0901	0944	0986	1028	1071	1113	38
22	1156	1198	1240	1283	1325	1368	37
23	1410	1452	1495	1537	1580	1622	36
24	1665	1707	1749	1792	1834	1877	35
25	1919	1961	2004	2046	2089	2131	34
26	2173	2216	2258	2301	2343	2386	33
27	2428	2470	2513	2555	2598	2640	32
28	2682	2725	2767	2810	2852	2895	31
29	2937	2979	3022	3064	3107	3149	30
30	10.053192	3234	3276	3319	3361	3404	29
31	3446	3489	3531	3573	3616	3658	28
32	3701	3743	3786	3828	3870	3913	27
33	3955	3998	4040	4083	4125	4168	26
34	4210	4252	4295	4337	4380	4422	25
35	4465	4507	4549	4592	4634	4677	24
36	4719	4762	4804	4847	4889	4931	23
37	4974	5016	5059	5101	5144	5186	22
38	5229	5271	5314	5356	5398	5441	21
39	5483	5526	5568	5611	5653	5696	20
40	10.055738	5781	5823	5865	5908	5950	19
41	5993	6035	6078	6120	6163	6205	18
42	6248	6290	6333	6375	6417	6460	17
43	6502	6545	6587	6630	6672	6715	16
44	6757	6800	6842	6885	6927	6970	15
45	7012	7055	7097	7139	7182	7224	14
46	7267	7309	7352	7394	7437	7479	13
47	7522	7564	7607	7649	7692	7734	12
48	7777	7819	7862	7904	7947	7989	11
49	8032	8074	8117	8159	8202	8244	10
50	10.058287	8329	8372	8414	8456	8499	9
51	8541	8584	8626	8669	8711	8754	8
52	8796	8839	8881	8924	8966	9009	7
53	9051	9094	9136	9179	9221	9264	6
54	9306	9349	9391	9434	9476	9519	5
55	9561	9604	9646	9689	9732	9774	4
56	9817	9859	9902	9944	9987	..29	3
57	10.060072	0114	0157	0199	0242	0284	2
58	0327	0369	0412	0454	0497	0539	1
59	0582	0624	0667	0709	0752	0794	0
	60″	50″	40″	30″	20″	10″	Min.
	Co-tangent of 41 Degrees.						

P. Part { 1″ 2″ 3″ 4″ 5″ 6″ 7″ 8″ 9″ / 4 8 13 17 21 25 30 34 38 }

1″	2″	3″	4″	5″	6″	7″	8″	9″
4	8	13	17	21	25	30	34	38

Min.	Tangent of 49 Degrees. 0″	10″	20″	30″	40″	50″	
0	10.060837	0879	0922	0965	1007	1050	59
1	1092	1135	1177	1220	1262	1305	58
2	1347	1390	1432	1475	1517	1560	57
3	1602	1645	1688	1730	1773	1815	56
4	1858	1900	1943	1985	2028	2070	55
5	2113	2155	2198	2241	2283	2326	54
6	2368	2411	2453	2496	2538	2581	53
7	2623	2666	2709	2751	2794	2836	52
8	2879	2921	2964	3006	3049	3092	51
9	3134	3177	3219	3262	3304	3347	50
10	10.063389	3432	3475	3517	3560	3602	49
11	3645	3687	3730	3773	3815	3858	48
12	3900	3943	3985	4028	4070	4113	47
13	4156	4198	4241	4283	4326	4368	46
14	4411	4454	4496	4539	4581	4624	45
15	4667	4709	4752	4794	4837	4879	44
16	4922	4965	5007	5050	5092	5135	43
17	5178	5220	5263	5305	5348	5390	42
18	5433	5476	5518	5561	5603	5646	41
19	5689	5731	5774	5816	5859	5902	40
20	10.065944	5987	6029	6072	6115	6157	39
21	6200	6242	6285	6328	6370	6413	38
22	6455	6498	6541	6583	6626	6668	37
23	6711	6754	6796	6839	6881	6924	36
24	6967	7009	7052	7094	7137	7180	35
25	7222	7265	7308	7350	7393	7435	34
26	7478	7521	7563	7606	7649	7691	33
27	7734	7776	7819	7862	7904	7947	32
28	7990	8032	8075	8117	8160	8203	31
29	8245	8288	8331	8373	8416	8458	30
30	10.068501	8544	8586	8629	8672	8714	29
31	8757	8800	8842	8885	8927	8970	28
32	9013	9055	9098	9141	9183	9226	27
33	9269	9311	9354	9397	9439	9482	26
34	9525	9567	9610	9652	9695	9738	25
35	9780	9823	9866	9908	9951	9994	24
36	10.070036	0079	0122	0164	0207	0250	23
37	0292	0335	0378	0420	0463	0506	22
38	0548	0591	0634	0676	0719	0762	21
39	0804	0847	0890	0932	0975	1018	20
40	10.071060	1103	1146	1188	1231	1274	19
41	1316	1359	1402	1445	1487	1530	18
42	1573	1615	1658	1701	1743	1786	17
43	1829	1871	1914	1957	1999	2042	16
44	2085	2128	2170	2213	2256	2298	15
45	2341	2384	2426	2469	2512	2554	14
46	2597	2640	2683	2725	2768	2811	13
47	2853	2896	2939	2981	3024	3067	12
48	3110	3152	3195	3238	3280	3323	11
49	3366	3409	3451	3494	3537	3579	10
50	10.073622	3665	3708	3750	3793	3836	9
51	3878	3921	3964	4007	4049	4092	8
52	4135	4178	4220	4263	4306	4348	7
53	4391	4434	4477	4519	4562	4605	6
54	4648	4690	4733	4776	4819	4861	5
55	4904	4947	4989	5032	5075	5118	4
56	5160	5203	5246	5289	5331	5374	3
57	5417	5460	5502	5545	5588	5631	2
58	5673	5716	5759	5802	5844	5887	1
59	5930	5973	6015	6058	6101	6144	0
	60″	50″	40″	30″	20″	10″	Min.
	Co-tangent of 40 Degrees.						

P. Part

1″	2″	3″	4″	5″	6″	7″	8″	9″
4	9	13	17	21	26	30	34	38

Min.	Sine of 50 Degrees. 0″	10″	20″	30″	40″	50″	
0	9.884254	4272	4289	4307	4325	4342	59
1	4360	4378	4395	4413	4431	4448	58
2	4466	4483	4501	4519	4536	4554	57
3	4572	4589	4607	4625	4642	4660	56
4	4677	4695	4713	4730	4748	4766	55
5	4783	4801	4818	4836	4854	4871	54
6	4889	4906	4924	4942	4959	4977	53
7	4994	5012	5030	5047	5065	5082	52
8	5100	5118	5135	5153	5170	5188	51
9	5205	5223	5241	5258	5276	5293	50
10	9.885311	5328	5346	5364	5381	5399	49
11	5416	5434	5451	5469	5486	5504	48
12	5522	5539	5557	5574	5592	5609	47
13	5627	5644	5662	5679	5697	5714	46
14	5732	5749	5767	5784	5802	5819	45
15	5837	5855	5872	5890	5907	5925	44
16	5942	5960	5977	5995	6012	6030	43
17	6047	6065	6082	6099	6117	6134	42
18	6152	6169	6187	6204	6222	6239	41
19	6257	6274	6292	6309	6327	6344	40
20	9.886362	6379	6396	6414	6431	6449	39
21	6466	6484	6501	6519	6536	6554	38
22	6571	6588	6606	6623	6641	6658	37
23	6676	6693	6710	6728	6745	6763	36
24	6780	6798	6815	6832	6850	6867	35
25	6885	6902	6919	6937	6954	6972	34
26	6989	7006	7024	7041	7059	7076	33
27	7093	7111	7128	7146	7163	7180	32
28	7198	7215	7232	7250	7267	7285	31
29	7302	7319	7337	7354	7371	7389	30
30	9.887406	7423	7441	7458	7475	7493	29
31	7510	7528	7545	7562	7580	7597	28
32	7614	7632	7649	7666	7684	7701	27
33	7718	7736	7753	7770	7787	7805	26
34	7822	7839	7857	7874	7891	7909	25
35	7926	7943	7961	7978	7995	8012	24
36	8030	8047	8064	8082	8099	8116	23
37	8134	8151	8168	8185	8203	8220	22
38	8237	8254	8272	8289	8306	8324	21
39	8341	8358	8375	8393	8410	8427	20
40	9.888444	8462	8479	8496	8513	8531	19
41	8548	8565	8582	8600	8617	8634	18
42	8651	8669	8686	8703	8720	8737	17
43	8755	8772	8789	8806	8824	8841	16
44	8858	8875	8892	8910	8927	8944	15
45	8961	8978	8996	9013	9030	9047	14
46	9064	9082	9099	9116	9133	9150	13
47	9168	9185	9202	9219	9236	9253	12
48	9271	9288	9305	9322	9339	9356	11
49	9374	9391	9408	9425	9442	9459	10
50	9.889477	9494	9511	9528	9545	9562	9
51	9579	9597	9614	9631	9648	9665	8
52	9682	9699	9716	9734	9751	9768	7
53	9785	9802	9819	9836	9853	9871	6
54	9888	9905	9922	9939	9956	9973	5
55	9990	...7	..25	..42	..59	..76	4
56	9.890093	0110	0127	0144	0161	0178	3
57	0195	0212	0230	0247	0264	0281	2
58	0298	0315	0332	0349	0366	0383	1
59	0400	0417	0434	0451	0468	0486	0
	60″	50″	40″	30″	20″	10″	Min.
	Co-sine of 39 Degrees.						
P. Part	1″ 2	2″ 3	3″ 5	4″ 7	5″ 9	6″ 10	7″ 12 · 8″ 14 · 9″ 16

Min.	Sine of 51 Degrees. 0″	10″	20″	30″	40″	50″	
0	9.890503	0520	0537	0554	0571	0588	59
1	0605	0622	0639	0656	0673	0690	58
2	0707	0724	0741	0758	0775	0792	57
3	0809	0826	0843	0860	0877	0894	56
4	0911	0928	0945	0962	0979	0996	55
5	1013	1030	1047	1064	1081	1098	54
6	1115	1132	1149	1166	1183	1200	53
7	1217	1234	1251	1268	1285	1302	52
8	1319	1336	1353	1370	1387	1404	51
9	1421	1438	1455	1472	1489	1506	50
10	9.891523	1540	1556	1573	1590	1607	49
11	1624	1641	1658	1675	1692	1709	48
12	1726	1743	1760	1777	1794	1810	47
13	1827	1844	1861	1878	1895	1912	46
14	1929	1946	1963	1980	1996	2013	45
15	2030	2047	2064	2081	2098	2115	44
16	2132	2149	2165	2182	2199	2216	43
17	2233	2250	2267	2284	2300	2317	42
18	2334	2351	2368	2385	2402	2419	41
19	2435	2452	2469	2486	2503	2520	40
20	9.892536	2553	2570	2587	2604	2621	39
21	2638	2654	2671	2688	2705	2722	38
22	2739	2755	2772	2789	2806	2823	37
23	2839	2856	2873	2890	2907	2924	36
24	2940	2957	2974	2991	3008	3024	35
25	3041	3058	3075	3092	3108	3125	34
26	3142	3159	3176	3192	3209	3226	33
27	3243	3259	3276	3293	3310	3327	32
28	3343	3360	3377	3394	3410	3427	31
29	3444	3461	3477	3494	3511	3528	30
30	9.893544	3561	3578	3595	3611	3628	29
31	3645	3662	3678	3695	3712	3728	28
32	3745	3762	3779	3795	3812	3829	27
33	3846	3862	3879	3896	3912	3929	26
34	3946	3963	3979	3996	4013	4029	25
35	4046	4063	4079	4096	4113	4130	24
36	4146	4163	4180	4196	4213	4230	23
37	4246	4263	4280	4296	4313	4330	22
38	4346	4363	4380	4396	4413	4430	21
39	4446	4463	4480	4496	4513	4530	20
40	9.894546	4563	4580	4596	4613	4629	19
41	4646	4663	4679	4696	4713	4729	18
42	4746	4763	4779	4796	4812	4829	17
43	4846	4862	4879	4896	4912	4929	16
44	4945	4962	4979	4995	5012	5028	15
45	5045	5062	5078	5095	5111	5128	14
46	5145	5161	5178	5194	5211	5227	13
47	5244	5261	5277	5294	5310	5327	12
48	5343	5360	5377	5393	5410	5426	11
49	5443	5459	5476	5493	5509	5526	10
50	9.895542	5559	5575	5592	5608	5625	9
51	5641	5658	5675	5691	5708	5724	8
52	5741	5757	5774	5790	5807	5823	7
53	5840	5856	5873	5889	5906	5922	6
54	5939	5955	5972	5988	6005	6021	5
55	6038	6054	6071	6087	6104	6120	4
56	6137	6153	6170	6186	6203	6219	3
57	6236	6252	6269	6285	6302	6318	2
58	6335	6351	6368	6384	6400	6417	1
59	6433	6450	6466	6483	6499	6516	0
	60″	50″	40″	30″	20″	10″	Min.
	Co-sine of 38 Degrees.						
P. Part	1″ 2	2″ 3	3″ 5	4″ 7	5″ 8	6″ 10	7″ 12 · 8″ 13 · 9″ 15

Min.	Tangent of 50 Degrees. 0″	10″	20″	30″	40″	50″	
0	10.076186	6229	6272	6315	6358	6400	59
1	6443	6486	6529	6571	6614	6657	58
2	6700	6742	6785	7828	6871	6913	57
3	6956	6999	7042	7085	7127	7170	56
4	7213	7256	7298	7341	7384	7427	55
5	7470	7512	7555	7598	7641	7684	54
6	7726	7769	7812	7855	7897	7940	53
7	7983	8026	8069	8111	8154	8197	52
8	8240	8283	8325	8368	8411	8454	51
9	8497	8539	8582	8625	8668	8711	50
10	10.078753	8796	8839	8882	8925	8967	49
11	9010	9053	9096	9139	9181	9224	48
12	9267	9310	9353	9396	9438	9481	47
13	9524	9567	9610	9652	9695	9738	46
14	9781	9824	9867	9909	9952	9995	45
15	10.080038	0081	0124	0166	0209	0252	44
16	0295	0338	0381	0423	0466	0509	43
17	0552	0595	0638	0680	0723	0766	42
18	0809	0852	0895	0937	0980	1023	41
19	1066	1109	1152	1195	1237	1280	40
20	10.081323	1366	1409	1452	1494	1537	39
21	1580	1623	1666	1709	1752	1794	38
22	1837	1880	1923	1966	2009	2052	37
23	2094	2137	2180	2223	2266	2309	36
24	2352	2395	2437	2480	2523	2566	35
25	2609	2652	2695	2738	2780	2823	34
26	2866	2909	2952	2995	3038	3081	33
27	3123	3166	3209	3252	3295	3338	32
28	3381	3424	3467	3509	3552	3595	31
29	3638	3681	3724	3767	3810	3853	30
30	10.083896	3938	3981	4024	4067	4110	29
31	4153	4196	4239	4282	4325	4367	28
32	4410	4453	4496	4539	4582	4625	27
33	4668	4711	4754	4797	4839	4882	26
34	4925	4968	5011	5054	5097	5140	25
35	5183	5226	5269	5312	5355	5397	24
36	5440	5483	5526	5569	5612	5655	23
37	5698	5741	5784	5827	5870	5913	22
38	5956	5999	6041	6084	6127	6170	21
39	6213	6256	6299	6342	6385	6428	20
40	10.086471	6514	6557	6600	6643	6686	19
41	6729	6772	6815	6857	6900	6943	18
42	6986	7029	7072	7115	7158	7201	17
43	7244	7287	7330	7373	7416	7459	16
44	7502	7545	7588	7631	7674	7717	15
45	7760	7803	7846	7889	7932	7975	14
46	8018	8061	8104	8147	8190	8232	13
47	8275	8318	8361	8404	8447	8490	12
48	8533	8576	8619	8662	8705	8748	11
49	8791	8834	8877	8920	8963	9006	10
50	10.089049	9092	9135	9178	9221	9264	9
51	9307	9350	9393	9436	9479	9522	8
52	9565	9608	9651	9694	9737	9780	7
53	9823	9866	9909	9952	9995	..39	6
54	10.090082	0125	0168	0211	0254	0297	5
55	0340	0383	0426	0469	0512	0555	4
56	0598	0641	0684	0727	0770	0813	3
57	0856	0899	0942	0985	1028	1071	2
58	1114	1157	1200	1243	1286	1329	1
59	1372	1416	1459	1502	1545	1588	0
	60″	50″	40″	30″	20″	10″	Min.
	Co-tangent of 39 Degrees.						

P. Part { 1″ 2″ 3″ 4″ 5″ 6″ 7″ 8″ 9″
{ 4 9 13 17 21 26 30 34 39

Min.	Tangent of 51 Degrees. 0″	10″	20″	30″	40″	50″	
0	10.091631	1674	1717	1760	1803	1846	59
1	1889	1932	1975	2018	2061	2104	58
2	2147	2191	2234	2277	2320	2363	57
3	2406	2449	2492	2535	2578	2621	56
4	2664	2707	2750	2793	2837	2880	55
5	2923	2966	3009	3052	3095	3138	54
6	3181	3224	3267	3310	3354	3397	53
7	3440	3483	3526	3569	3612	3655	52
8	3698	3741	3784	3828	3871	3914	51
9	3957	4000	4043	4086	4129	4172	50
10	10.094215	4259	4302	4345	4388	4431	49
11	4474	4517	4560	4603	4647	4690	48
12	4733	4776	4819	4862	4905	4948	47
13	4992	5035	5078	5121	5164	5207	46
14	5250	5293	5337	5380	5423	5466	45
15	5509	5552	5595	5638	5682	5725	44
16	5768	5811	5854	5897	5940	5984	43
17	6027	6070	6113	6156	6199	6242	42
18	6286	6329	6372	6415	6458	6501	41
19	6544	6588	6631	6674	6717	6760	40
20	10.096803	6847	6890	6933	6976	7019	39
21	7062	7106	7149	7192	7235	7278	38
22	7321	7365	7408	7451	7494	7537	37
23	7580	7624	7667	7710	7753	7796	36
24	7840	7883	7926	7969	8012	8056	35
25	8099	8142	8185	8228	8271	8315	34
26	8358	8401	8444	8487	8531	8574	33
27	8617	8660	8703	8747	8790	8833	32
28	8876	8919	8963	9006	9049	9092	31
29	9136	9179	9222	9265	9308	9352	30
30	10.099395	9438	9481	9524	9568	9611	29
31	9654	9697	9741	9784	9827	9870	28
32	9913	9957	....	..43	..86	.130	27
33	10.100173	0216	0259	0303	0346	0389	26
34	0432	0476	0519	0562	0605	0649	25
35	0692	0735	0778	0822	0865	0908	24
36	0951	0995	1038	1081	1124	1168	23
37	1211	1254	1297	1341	1384	1427	22
38	1470	1514	1557	1600	1643	1687	21
39	1730	1773	1817	1860	1903	1946	20
40	10.101990	2033	2076	2119	2163	2206	19
41	2249	2293	2336	2379	2422	2466	18
42	2509	2552	2596	2639	2682	2725	17
43	2769	2812	2855	2899	2942	2985	16
44	3029	3072	3115	3158	3202	3245	15
45	3288	3332	3375	3418	3462	3505	14
46	3548	3592	3635	3678	3722	3765	13
47	3808	3851	3895	3938	3981	4025	12
48	4068	4111	4155	4198	4241	4285	11
49	4328	4371	4415	4458	4501	4545	10
50	10.104588	4631	4675	4718	4761	4805	9
51	4848	4891	4935	4978	5021	5065	8
52	5108	5152	5195	5238	5282	5325	7
53	5368	5412	5455	5498	5542	5585	6
54	5628	5672	5715	5759	5802	5845	5
55	5889	5932	5975	6019	6062	6106	4
56	6149	6192	6236	6279	6322	6366	3
57	6409	6453	6496	6539	6583	6626	2
58	6669	6713	6756	6800	6843	6886	1
59	6930	6973	7017	7060	7103	7147	0
	60″	50″	40″	30″	20″	10″	Min.
	Co-tangent of 38 Degrees.						

P. Part { 1″ 2″ 3″ 4″ 5″ 6″ 7″ 8″ 9″
{ 4 9 13 17 22 26 30 35 39

Min.	Sine of 52 Degrees. 0″	10″	20″	30″	40″	50″	
0	9.896532	6549	6565	6581	6598	6614	59
1	6631	6647	6664	6680	6697	6713	58
2	6729	6746	6762	6779	6795	6812	57
3	6828	6844	6861	6877	6894	6910	56
4	6926	6943	6959	6976	6992	7009	55
5	7025	7041	7058	7074	7090	7107	54
6	7123	7140	7156	7172	7189	7205	53
7	7222	7238	7254	7271	7287	7303	52
8	7320	7336	7353	7369	7385	7402	51
9	7418	7434	7451	7467	7483	7500	50
10	9.897516	7533	7549	7565	7582	7598	49
11	7614	7631	7647	7663	7680	7696	48
12	7712	7729	7745	7761	7778	7794	47
13	7810	7827	7843	7859	7876	7892	46
14	7908	7924	7941	7957	7973	7990	45
15	8006	8022	8039	8055	8071	8088	44
16	8104	8120	8136	8153	8169	8185	43
17	8202	8218	8234	8250	8267	8283	42
18	8299	8315	8332	8348	8364	8381	41
19	8397	8413	8429	8446	8462	8478	40
20	9.898494	8511	8527	8543	8559	8576	39
21	8592	8608	8624	8641	8657	8673	38
22	8689	8706	8722	8738	8754	8770	37
23	8787	8803	8819	8835	8852	8868	36
24	8884	8900	8916	8933	8949	8965	35
25	8981	8997	9014	9030	9046	9062	34
26	9078	9095	9111	9127	9143	9159	33
27	9176	9192	9208	9224	9240	9256	32
28	9273	9289	9305	9321	9337	9354	31
29	9370	9386	9402	9418	9434	9450	30
30	9.899467	9483	9499	9515	9531	9547	29
31	9564	9580	9596	9612	9628	9644	28
32	9660	9677	9693	9709	9725	9741	27
33	9757	9773	9789	9806	9822	9838	26
34	9854	9870	9886	9902	9918	9935	25
35	9951	9967	9983	9999	..15	..31	24
36	9.900047	0063	0079	0096	0112	0128	23
37	0144	0160	0176	0192	0208	0224	22
38	0240	0256	0272	0289	0305	0321	21
39	0337	0353	0369	0385	0401	0417	20
40	9.900433	0449	0465	0481	0497	0513	19
41	0529	0545	0562	0578	0594	0610	18
42	0626	0642	0658	0674	0690	0706	17
43	0722	0738	0754	0770	0786	0802	16
44	0818	0834	0850	0866	0882	0898	15
45	0914	0930	0946	0962	0978	0994	14
46	1010	1026	1042	1058	1074	1090	13
47	1106	1122	1138	1154	1170	1186	12
48	1202	1218	1234	1250	1266	1282	11
49	1298	1314	1330	1346	1362	1378	10
50	9.901394	1410	1426	1442	1458	1474	9
51	1490	1505	1521	1537	1553	1569	8
52	1585	1601	1617	1633	1649	1665	7
53	1681	1697	1713	1729	1745	1760	6
54	1776	1792	1808	1824	1840	1856	5
55	1872	1888	1904	1920	1936	1951	4
56	1967	1983	1999	2015	2031	2047	3
57	2063	2079	2095	2110	2126	2142	2
58	2158	2174	2190	2206	2222	2238	1
59	2253	2269	2285	2301	2317	2333	0
	60″	50″	40″	30″	20″	10″	Min.
	Co-sine of 37 Degrees.						

P. Part { 1″ 2″ 3″ 4″ 5″ 6″ 7″ 8″ 9″ / 2 3 5 6 8 10 11 13 15 }

Min.	Sine of 53 Degrees. 0″	10″	20″	30″	40″	50″	
0	9.902349	2364	2380	2396	2412	2428	59
1	2444	2460	2475	2491	2507	2523	58
2	2539	2555	2571	2586	2602	2618	57
3	2634	2650	2666	2681	2697	2713	56
4	2729	2745	2761	2776	2792	2808	55
5	2824	2840	2856	2871	2887	2903	54
6	2919	2935	2950	2966	2982	2998	53
7	3014	3029	3045	3061	3077	3093	52
8	3108	3124	3140	3156	3171	3187	51
9	3203	3219	3235	3250	3266	3282	50
10	9.903298	3313	3329	3345	3361	3377	49
11	3392	3408	3424	3440	3455	3471	48
12	3487	3503	3518	3534	3550	3566	47
13	3581	3597	3613	3629	3644	3660	46
14	3676	3691	3707	3723	3739	3754	45
15	3770	3786	3802	3817	3833	3849	44
16	3864	3880	3896	3912	3927	3943	43
17	3959	3974	3990	4006	4021	4037	42
18	4053	4069	4084	4100	4116	4131	41
19	4147	4163	4178	4194	4210	4225	40
20	9.904241	4257	4272	4288	4304	4319	39
21	4335	4351	4366	4382	4398	4413	38
22	4429	4445	4460	4476	4492	4507	37
23	4523	4539	4554	4570	4586	4601	36
24	4617	4632	4648	4664	4679	4695	35
25	4711	4726	4742	4757	4773	4789	34
26	4804	4820	4836	4851	4867	4882	33
27	4898	4914	4929	4945	4960	4976	32
28	4992	5007	5023	5038	5054	5070	31
29	5085	5101	5116	5132	5148	5163	30
30	9.905179	5194	5210	5225	5241	5257	29
31	5272	5288	5303	5319	5334	5350	28
32	5366	5381	5397	5412	5428	5443	27
33	5459	5474	5490	5506	5521	5537	26
34	5552	5568	5583	5599	5614	5630	25
35	5645	5661	5676	5692	5708	5723	24
36	5739	5754	5770	5785	5801	5816	23
37	5832	5847	5863	5878	5894	5909	22
38	5925	5940	5956	5971	5987	6002	21
39	6018	6033	6049	6064	6080	6095	20
40	9.906111	6126	6142	6157	6173	6188	19
41	6204	6219	6235	6250	6265	6281	18
42	6296	6312	6327	6343	6358	6374	17
43	6389	6405	6420	6436	6451	6466	16
44	6482	6497	6513	6528	6544	6559	15
45	6575	6590	6605	6621	6636	6652	14
46	6667	6683	6698	6713	6729	6744	13
47	6760	6775	6791	6806	6821	6837	12
48	6852	6868	6883	6898	6914	6929	11
49	6945	6960	6975	6991	7006	7022	10
50	9.907037	7052	7068	7083	7099	7114	9
51	7129	7145	7160	7175	7191	7206	8
52	7222	7237	7252	7268	7283	7298	7
53	7314	7329	7344	7360	7375	7391	6
54	7406	7421	7437	7452	7467	7483	5
55	7498	7513	7529	7544	7559	7575	4
56	7590	7605	7621	7636	7651	7667	3
57	7682	7697	7713	7728	7743	7759	2
58	7774	7789	7805	7820	7835	7851	1
59	7866	7881	7896	7912	7927	7942	0
	60″	50″	40″	30″	20″	10″	Min.
	Co-sine of 36 Degrees.						

P. Part { 1″ 2″ 3″ 4″ 5″ 6″ 7″ 8″ 9″ / 2 3 5 6 8 9 11 12 14 }

Min.	Tangent of 52 Degrees. 0″	10″	20″	30″	40″	50″	
0	10.107190	7234	7277	7320	7364	7407	59
1	7451	7494	7537	7581	7624	7668	58
2	7711	7754	7798	7841	7885	7928	57
3	7972	8015	8058	8102	8145	8189	56
4	8232	8275	8319	8362	8406	8449	55
5	8493	8536	8579	8623	8666	8710	54
6	8753	8797	8840	8884	8927	8970	53
7	9014	9057	9101	9144	9188	9231	52
8	9275	9318	9361	9405	9448	9492	51
9	9535	9579	9622	9666	9709	9753	50
10	10.109796	9840	9883	9926	9970	..13	49
11	10.110057	0100	0144	0187	0231	0274	48
12	0318	0361	0405	0448	0492	0535	47
13	0579	0622	0666	0709	0752	0796	46
14	0839	0883	0926	0970	1013	1057	45
15	1100	1144	1187	1231	1274	1318	44
16	1361	1405	1448	1492	1535	1579	43
17	1622	1666	1709	1753	1797	1840	42
18	1884	1927	1971	2014	2058	2101	41
19	2145	2188	2232	2275	2319	2362	40
20	10.112406	2449	2493	2536	2580	2623	39
21	2667	2711	2754	2798	2841	2885	38
22	2928	2972	3015	3059	3102	3146	37
23	3189	3233	3277	3320	3364	3407	36
24	3451	3494	3538	3581	3625	3669	35
25	3712	3756	3799	3843	3886	3930	34
26	3974	4017	4061	4104	4148	4191	33
27	4235	4279	4322	4366	4409	4453	32
28	4496	4540	4584	4627	4671	4714	31
29	4758	4802	4845	4889	4932	4976	30
30	10.115020	5063	5107	5150	5194	5238	29
31	5281	5325	5368	5412	5456	5499	28
32	5543	5586	5630	5674	5717	5761	27
33	5804	5848	5892	5935	5979	6023	26
34	6066	6110	6153	6197	6241	6284	25
35	6328	6372	6415	6459	6502	6546	24
36	6590	6633	6677	6721	6764	6808	23
37	6852	6895	6939	6982	7026	7070	22
38	7113	7157	7201	7244	7288	7332	21
39	7375	7419	7463	7506	7550	7594	20
40	10.117637	7681	7725	7768	7812	7856	19
41	7899	7943	7987	8030	8074	8118	18
42	8161	8205	8249	8292	8336	8380	17
43	8423	8467	8511	8555	8598	8642	16
44	8686	8729	8773	8817	8860	8904	15
45	8948	8992	9035	9079	9123	9166	14
46	9210	9254	9297	9341	9385	9429	13
47	9472	9516	9560	9603	9647	9691	12
48	9735	9778	9822	9866	9909	9953	11
49	9997	..41	..84	.128	.172	.216	10
50	10.120259	0303	0347	0391	0434	0478	9
51	0522	0565	0609	0653	0697	0740	8
52	0784	0828	0872	0915	0959	1003	7
53	1047	1091	1134	1178	1222	1266	6
54	1309	1353	1397	1441	1484	1528	5
55	1572	1616	1659	1703	1747	1791	4
56	1835	1878	1922	1966	2010	2053	3
57	2097	2141	2185	2229	2272	2316	2
58	2360	2404	2448	2491	2535	2579	1
59	2623	2667	2710	2754	2798	2842	0
	60″ Co-tangent of 37 Degrees.	50″	40″	30″	20″	10″	Min.

P. Part	1″	2″	3″	4″	5″	6″	7″	8″	9″
	4	9	13	17	22	26	31	35	39

Min.	Tangent of 53 Degrees. 0″	10″	20″	30″	40″	50″	
0	10.122886	2929	2973	3017	3061	3105	59
1	3148	3192	3236	3280	3324	3368	58
2	3411	3455	3499	3543	3587	3630	57
3	3674	3718	3762	3806	3850	3893	56
4	3937	3981	4025	4069	4113	4157	55
5	4200	4244	4288	4332	4376	4420	54
6	4463	4507	4551	4595	4639	4683	53
7	4727	4770	4814	4858	4902	4946	52
8	4990	5034	5077	5121	5165	5209	51
9	5253	5297	5341	5385	5428	5472	50
10	10.125516	5560	5604	5648	5692	5736	49
11	5780	5823	5867	5911	5955	5999	48
12	6043	6087	6131	6175	6219	6262	47
13	6306	6350	6394	6438	6482	6526	46
14	6570	6614	6658	6701	6745	6789	45
15	6833	6877	6921	6965	7009	7053	44
16	7097	7141	7185	7229	7273	7316	43
17	7360	7404	7448	7492	7536	7580	42
18	7624	7668	7712	7756	7800	7844	41
19	7888	7932	7976	8020	8063	8107	40
20	10.128151	8195	8239	8283	8327	8371	39
21	8415	8459	8503	8547	8591	8635	38
22	8679	8723	8767	8811	8855	8899	37
23	8943	8987	9031	9075	9119	9163	36
24	9207	9251	9295	9339	9383	9427	35
25	9471	9515	9559	9603	9647	9691	34
26	9735	9779	9823	9867	9911	9955	33
27	9999	..43	..87	.131	.175	.219	32
28	10.130263	0307	0351	0395	0439	0483	31
29	0527	0571	0615	0659	0703	0747	30
30	10.130791	0835	0879	0923	0967	1011	29
31	1055	1099	1143	1187	1232	1276	28
32	1320	1364	1408	1452	1496	1540	27
33	1584	1628	1672	1716	1760	1804	26
34	1848	1892	1936	1981	2025	2069	25
35	2113	2157	2201	2245	2289	2333	24
36	2377	2421	2465	2509	2554	2598	23
37	2642	2686	2730	2774	2818	2862	22
38	2906	2950	2994	3039	3083	3127	21
39	3171	3215	3259	3303	3347	3391	20
40	10.133436	3480	3524	3568	3612	3656	19
41	3700	3744	3789	3833	3877	3921	18
42	3965	4009	4053	4097	4142	4186	17
43	4230	4274	4318	4362	4406	4451	16
44	4495	4539	4583	4627	4671	4715	15
45	4760	4804	4848	4892	4936	4980	14
46	5025	5069	5113	5157	5201	5245	13
47	5290	5334	5378	5422	5466	5510	12
48	5555	5599	5643	5687	5731	5775	11
49	5820	5864	5908	5952	5996	6041	10
50	10.136085	6129	6173	6217	6262	6306	9
51	6350	6394	6438	6483	6527	6571	8
52	6615	6659	6704	6748	6792	6836	7
53	6881	6925	6969	7013	7057	7102	6
54	7146	7190	7234	7279	7323	7367	5
55	7411	7455	7500	7544	7588	7632	4
56	7677	7721	7765	7809	7854	7898	3
57	7942	7986	8031	8075	8119	8163	2
58	8208	8252	8296	8341	8385	8429	1
59	8473	8518	8562	8606	8650	8695	0
	60″ Co-tangent of 36 Degrees.	50″	40″	30″	20″	10″	Min.

P. Part	1″	2″	3″	4″	5″	6″	7″	8″	9″
	4	9	13	18	22	26	31	35	40

Min.	Sine of 54 Degrees. 0″	10″	20″	30″	40″	50″	
0	9.907958	7973	7988	8004	8019	8034	59
1	8049	8065	8080	8095	8111	8126	58
2	8141	8156	8172	8187	8202	8217	57
3	8233	8248	8263	8279	8294	8309	56
4	8324	8340	8355	8370	8385	8401	55
5	8416	8431	8446	8462	8477	8492	54
6	8507	8523	8538	8553	8568	8584	53
7	8599	8614	8629	8644	8660	8675	52
8	8690	8705	8721	8736	8751	8766	51
9	8781	8797	8812	8827	8842	8857	50
10	9.908873	8888	8903	8918	8933	8949	49
11	8964	8979	8994	9009	9025	9040	48
12	9055	9070	9085	9101	9116	9131	47
13	9146	9161	9176	9192	9207	9222	46
14	9237	9252	9267	9283	9298	9313	45
15	9328	9343	9358	9374	9389	9404	44
16	9419	9434	9449	9464	9480	9495	43
17	9510	9525	9540	9555	9570	9586	42
18	9601	9616	9631	9646	9661	9676	41
19	9691	9707	9722	9737	9752	9767	40
20	9.909782	9797	9812	9827	9843	9858	39
21	9873	9888	9903	9918	9933	9948	38
22	9963	9978	9994	...9	..24	..39	37
23	9.910054	0069	0084	0099	0114	0129	36
24	0144	0159	0175	0190	0205	0220	35
25	0235	0250	0265	0280	0295	0310	34
26	0325	0340	0355	0370	0385	0400	33
27	0415	0430	0446	0461	0476	0491	32
28	0506	0521	0536	0551	0566	0581	31
29	0596	0611	0626	0641	0656	0671	30
30	9.910686	0701	0716	0731	0746	0761	29
31	0776	0791	0806	0821	0836	0851	28
32	0866	0881	0896	0911	0926	0941	27
33	0956	0971	0986	1001	1016	1031	26
34	1046	1061	1076	1091	1106	1121	25
35	1136	1151	1166	1181	1196	1211	24
36	1226	1241	1256	1271	1286	1300	23
37	1315	1330	1345	1360	1375	1390	22
38	1405	1420	1435	1450	1465	1480	21
39	1495	1510	1525	1540	1555	1569	20
40	9.911584	1599	1614	1629	1644	1659	19
41	1674	1689	1704	1719	1734	1748	18
42	1763	1778	1793	1808	1823	1838	17
43	1853	1868	1883	1897	1912	1927	16
44	1942	1957	1972	1987	2002	2017	15
45	2031	2046	2061	2076	2091	2106	14
46	2121	2136	2150	2165	2180	2195	13
47	2210	2225	2240	2255	2269	2284	12
48	2299	2314	2329	2344	2358	2373	11
49	2388	2403	2418	2433	2448	2462	10
50	9.912477	2492	2507	2522	2537	2551	9
51	2566	2581	2596	2611	2625	2640	8
52	2655	2670	2685	2700	2714	2729	7
53	2744	2759	2774	2788	2803	2818	6
54	2833	2848	2862	2877	2892	2907	5
55	2922	2936	2951	2966	2981	2995	4
56	3010	3025	3040	3055	3069	3084	3
57	3099	3114	3128	3143	3158	3173	2
58	3187	3202	3217	3232	3247	3261	1
59	3276	3291	3306	3320	3335	3350	0
	60″	50″	40″	30″	20″	10″	Min.
	Co-sine of 35 Degrees.						

P. Part { 1″ 2″ 3″ 4″ 5″ 6″ 7″ 8″ 9″ / 2 3 5 6 8 9 11 12 14

Min.	Sine of 55 Degrees. 0″	10″	20″	30″	40″	50″	
0	9.913365	3379	3394	3409	3423	3438	59
1	3453	3468	3482	3497	3512	3527	58
2	3541	3556	3571	3585	3600	3615	57
3	3630	3644	3659	3674	3688	3703	56
4	3718	3733	3747	3762	3777	3791	55
5	3806	3821	3836	3850	3865	3880	54
6	3894	3909	3924	3938	3953	3968	53
7	3982	3997	4012	4026	4041	4056	52
8	4070	4085	4100	4114	4129	4144	51
9	4158	4173	4188	4202	4217	4232	50
10	9.914246	4261	4276	4290	4305	4320	49
11	4334	4349	4364	4378	4393	4407	48
12	4422	4437	4451	4466	4481	4495	47
13	4510	4524	4539	4554	4568	4583	46
14	4598	4612	4627	4641	4656	4671	45
15	4685	4700	4714	4729	4744	4758	44
16	4773	4787	4802	4817	4831	4846	43
17	4860	4875	4890	4904	4919	4933	42
18	4948	4962	4977	4992	5006	5021	41
19	5035	5050	5064	5079	5094	5108	40
20	9.915123	5137	5152	5166	5181	5196	39
21	5210	5225	5239	5254	5268	5283	38
22	5297	5312	5326	5341	5356	5370	37
23	5385	5399	5414	5428	5443	5457	36
24	5472	5486	5501	5515	5530	5544	35
25	5559	5573	5588	5602	5617	5631	34
26	5646	5660	5675	5689	5704	5718	33
27	5733	5747	5762	5776	5791	5805	32
28	5820	5834	5849	5863	5878	5892	31
29	5907	5921	5936	5950	5965	5979	30
30	9.915994	6008	6023	6037	6052	6066	29
31	6081	6095	6109	6124	6138	6153	28
32	6167	6182	6196	6211	6225	6240	27
33	6254	6268	6283	6297	6312	6326	26
34	6341	6355	6369	6384	6398	6413	25
35	6427	6442	6456	6470	6485	6499	24
36	6514	6528	6543	6557	6571	6586	23
37	6600	6615	6629	6643	6658	6672	22
38	6687	6701	6715	6730	6744	6759	21
39	6773	6787	6802	6816	6830	6845	20
40	9.916859	6874	6888	6902	6917	6931	19
41	6946	6960	6974	6989	7003	7017	18
42	7032	7046	7060	7075	7089	7104	17
43	7118	7132	7147	7161	7175	7190	16
44	7204	7218	7233	7247	7261	7276	15
45	7290	7304	7319	7333	7347	7362	14
46	7376	7390	7405	7419	7433	7448	13
47	7462	7476	7491	7505	7519	7534	12
48	7548	7562	7576	7591	7605	7619	11
49	7634	7648	7662	7677	7691	7705	10
50	9.917719	7734	7748	7762	7777	7791	9
51	7805	7819	7834	7848	7862	7877	8
52	7891	7905	7919	7934	7948	7962	7
53	7976	7991	8005	8019	8033	8048	6
54	8062	8076	8090	8105	8119	8133	5
55	8147	8162	8176	8190	8204	8219	4
56	8233	8247	8261	8276	8290	8304	3
57	8318	8333	8347	8361	8375	8389	2
58	8404	8418	8432	8446	8461	8475	1
59	8489	8503	8517	8532	8546	8560	0
	60″	50″	40″	30″	20″	10″	Min.
	Co-sine of 34 Degrees.						

P. Part { 1″ 2″ 3″ 4″ 5″ 6″ 7″ 8″ 9″ / 1 3 4 6 7 9 10 12 13

Min.	Tangent of 54 Degrees. 0″	10″	20″	30″	40″	50″	
0	10.138739	8783	8828	8872	8916	8960	59
1	9005	9049	9093	9138	9182	9226	58
2	9270	9315	9359	9403	9448	9492	57
3	9536	9580	9625	9669	9713	9758	56
4	9802	9846	9891	9935	9979	..24	55
5	10.140068	0112	0157	0201	0245	0290	54
6	0334	0378	0423	0467	0511	0556	53
7	0600	0644	0689	0733	0777	0822	52
8	0866	0910	0955	0999	1043	1088	51
9	1132	1176	1221	1265	1309	1354	50
10	10.141398	1442	1487	1531	1576	1620	49
11	1664	1709	1753	1797	1842	1886	48
12	1931	1975	2019	2064	2108	2152	47
13	2197	2241	2286	2330	2374	2419	46
14	2463	2508	2552	2596	2641	2685	45
15	2730	2774	2818	2863	2907	2952	44
16	2996	3041	3085	3129	3174	3218	43
17	3263	3307	3351	3396	3440	3485	42
18	3529	3574	3618	3662	3707	3751	41
19	3796	3840	3885	3929	3974	4018	40
20	10.144062	4107	4151	4196	4240	4285	39
21	4329	4374	4418	4463	4507	4551	38
22	4596	4640	4685	4729	4774	4818	37
23	4863	4907	4952	4996	5041	5085	36
24	5130	5174	5219	5263	5308	5352	35
25	5397	5441	5486	5530	5575	5619	34
26	5664	5708	5753	5797	5842	5886	33
27	5931	5975	6020	6064	6109	6153	32
28	6198	6242	6287	6331	6376	6420	31
29	6465	6509	6554	6598	6643	6687	30
30	10.146732	6777	6821	6866	6910	6955	29
31	6999	7044	7088	7133	7177	7222	28
32	7267	7311	7356	7400	7445	7489	27
33	7534	7578	7623	7668	7712	7757	26
34	7801	7846	7890	7935	7980	8024	25
35	8069	8113	8158	8203	8247	8292	24
36	8336	8381	8425	8470	8515	8559	23
37	8604	8648	8693	8738	8782	8827	22
38	8871	8916	8961	9005	9050	9095	21
39	9139	9184	9228	9273	9318	9362	20
40	10.149407	9452	9496	9541	9585	9630	19
41	9675	9719	9764	9809	9853	9898	18
42	9943	9987	..32	..76	.121	.166	17
43	10.150210	0255	0300	0344	0389	0434	16
44	0478	0523	0568	0612	0657	0702	15
45	0746	0791	0836	0880	0925	0970	14
46	1014	1059	1104	1149	1193	1238	13
47	1283	1327	1372	1417	1461	1506	12
48	1551	1595	1640	1685	1730	1774	11
49	1819	1864	1908	1953	1998	2043	10
50	10.152087	2132	2177	2221	2266	2311	9
51	2356	2400	2445	2490	2535	2579	8
52	2624	2669	2713	2758	2803	2848	7
53	2892	2937	2982	3027	3071	3116	6
54	3161	3206	3250	3295	3340	3385	5
55	3430	3474	3519	3564	3609	3653	4
56	3698	3743	3788	3832	3877	3922	3
57	3967	4012	4056	4101	4146	4191	2
58	4236	4280	4325	4370	4415	4460	1
59	4504	4549	4594	4639	4684	4728	0
	60″	50″	40″	30″	20″	10″	Min.
	Co-tangent of 35 Degrees.						

P. Part	1″	2″	3″	4″	5″	6″	7″	8″	9″
	4	9	13	18	22	27	31	36	40

Min.	Tangent of 55 Degrees. 0″	10″	20″	30″	40″	50″	
0	10.154773	4818	4863	4908	4952	4997	59
1	5042	5087	5132	5177	5221	5266	58
2	5311	5356	5401	5446	5490	5535	57
3	5580	5625	5670	5715	5759	5804	56
4	5849	5894	5939	5984	6029	6073	55
5	6118	6163	6208	6253	6298	6343	54
6	6388	6432	6477	6522	6567	6612	53
7	6657	6702	6747	6791	6836	6881	52
8	6926	6971	7016	7061	7106	7151	51
9	7195	7240	7285	7330	7375	7420	50
10	10.157465	7510	7555	7600	7645	7689	49
11	7734	7779	7824	7869	7914	7959	48
12	8004	8049	8094	8139	8184	8229	47
13	8273	8318	8363	8408	8453	8498	46
14	8543	8588	8633	8678	8723	8768	45
15	8813	8858	8903	8948	8993	9038	44
16	9083	9128	9173	9218	9263	9307	43
17	9352	9397	9442	9487	9532	9577	42
18	9622	9667	9712	9757	9802	9847	41
19	9892	9937	9982	..27	..72	.117	40
20	10.160162	0207	0252	0297	0342	0387	39
21	0432	0477	0522	0567	0612	0657	38
22	0703	0748	0793	0838	0883	0928	37
23	0973	1018	1063	1108	1153	1198	36
24	1243	1288	1333	1378	1423	1468	35
25	1513	1558	1603	1648	1693	1739	34
26	1784	1829	1874	1919	1964	2009	33
27	2054	2099	2144	2189	2234	2279	32
28	2325	2370	2415	2460	2505	2550	31
29	2595	2640	2685	2730	2775	2821	30
30	10.162866	2911	2956	3001	3046	3091	29
31	3136	3181	3227	3272	3317	3362	28
32	3407	3452	3497	3542	3588	3633	27
33	3678	3723	3768	3813	3858	3904	26
34	3949	3994	4039	4084	4129	4174	25
35	4220	4265	4310	4355	4400	4445	24
36	4491	4536	4581	4626	4671	4716	23
37	4762	4807	4852	4897	4942	4988	22
38	5033	5078	5123	5168	5213	5259	21
39	5304	5349	5394	5439	5485	5530	20
40	10.165575	5620	5666	5711	5756	5801	19
41	5846	5892	5937	5982	6027	6073	18
42	6118	6163	6208	6253	6299	6344	17
43	6389	6434	6480	6525	6570	6615	16
44	6661	6706	6751	6796	6842	6887	15
45	6932	6977	7023	7068	7113	7158	14
46	7204	7249	7294	7340	7385	7430	13
47	7475	7521	7566	7611	7657	7702	12
48	7747	7792	7838	7883	7928	7974	11
49	8019	8064	8109	8155	8200	8245	10
50	10.168291	8336	8381	8427	8472	8517	9
51	8563	8608	8653	8699	8744	8789	8
52	8835	8880	8925	8971	9016	9061	7
53	9107	9152	9197	9243	9288	9333	6
54	9379	9424	9469	9515	9560	9605	5
55	9651	9696	9742	9787	9832	9878	4
56	9923	9968	..14	..59	.105	.150	3
57	10.170195	0241	0286	0331	0377	0422	2
58	0468	0513	0558	0604	0649	0695	1
59	0740	0785	0831	0876	0922	0967	0
	60″	50″	40″	30″	20″	10″	Min.
	Co-tangent of 34 Degrees.						

P. Part	1″	2″	3″	4″	5″	6″	7″	8″	9″
	5	9	14	18	23	27	32	36	41

Min.	Sine of 56 Degrees. 0″	10″	20″	30″	40″	50″	
0	9.918574	8588	8603	8617	8631	8645	59
1	8659	8674	8688	8702	8716	8730	58
2	8745	8759	8773	8787	8801	8815	57
3	8830	8844	8858	8872	8886	8900	56
4	8915	8929	8943	8957	8971	8985	55
5	9000	9014	9028	9042	9056	9070	54
6	9085	9099	9113	9127	9141	9155	53
7	9169	9184	9198	9212	9226	9240	52
8	9254	9268	9282	9297	9311	9325	51
9	9339	9353	9367	9381	9395	9410	50
10	9.919424	9438	9452	9466	9480	9494	49
11	9508	9522	9537	9551	9565	9579	48
12	9593	9607	9621	9635	9649	9663	47
13	9677	9692	9706	9720	9734	9748	46
14	9762	9776	9790	9804	9818	9832	45
15	9846	9860	9875	9889	9903	9917	44
16	9931	9945	9959	9973	9987	...1	43
17	9.920015	0029	0043	0057	0071	0085	42
18	0099	0113	0127	0141	0156	0170	41
19	0184	0198	0212	0226	0240	0254	40
20	9.920268	0282	0296	0310	0324	0338	39
21	0352	0366	0380	0394	0408	0422	38
22	0436	0450	0464	0478	0492	0506	37
23	0520	0534	0548	0562	0576	0590	36
24	0604	0618	0632	0646	0660	0674	35
25	0688	0702	0716	0730	0744	0758	34
26	0772	0786	0800	0814	0828	0842	33
27	0856	0869	0883	0897	0911	0925	32
28	0939	0953	0967	0981	0995	1009	31
29	1023	1037	1051	1065	1079	1093	30
30	9.921107	1121	1134	1148	1162	1176	29
31	1190	1204	1218	1232	1246	1260	28
32	1274	1288	1302	1315	1329	1343	27
33	1357	1371	1385	1399	1413	1427	26
34	1441	1455	1468	1482	1496	1510	25
35	1524	1538	1552	1566	1580	1593	24
36	1607	1621	1635	1649	1663	1677	23
37	1691	1704	1718	1732	1746	1760	22
38	1774	1788	1802	1815	1829	1843	21
39	1857	1871	1885	1899	1912	1926	20
40	9.921940	1954	1968	1982	1995	2009	19
41	2023	2037	2051	2065	2079	2092	18
42	2106	2120	2134	2148	2162	2175	17
43	2189	2203	2217	2231	2244	2258	16
44	2272	2286	2300	2313	2327	2341	15
45	2355	2369	2383	2396	2410	2424	14
46	2438	2452	2465	2479	2493	2507	13
47	2520	2534	2548	2562	2576	2589	12
48	2603	2617	2631	2644	2658	2672	11
49	2686	2700	2713	2727	2741	2755	10
50	9.922768	2782	2796	2810	2823	2837	9
51	2851	2865	2878	2892	2906	2920	8
52	2933	2947	2961	2975	2988	3002	7
53	3016	3030	3043	3057	3071	3084	6
54	3098	3112	3126	3139	3153	3167	5
55	3181	3194	3208	3222	3235	3249	4
56	3263	3277	3290	3304	3318	3331	3
57	3345	3359	3372	3386	3400	3414	2
58	3427	3441	3455	3468	3482	3496	1
59	3509	3523	3537	3550	3564	3578	0
	60″	50″	40″	30″	20″	10″	Min.
	Co-sine of 33 Degrees.						

P. Part { 1″ 2″ 3″ 4″ 5″ 6″ 7″ 8″ 9″ / 1 3 4 6 7 8 10 11 13 }

Min.	Sine of 57 Degrees. 0″	10″	20″	30″	40″	50″	
0	9.923591	3605	3619	3632	3646	3660	59
1	3673	3687	3701	3714	3728	3742	58
2	3755	3769	3783	3796	3810	3824	57
3	3837	3851	3865	3878	3892	3906	56
4	3919	3933	3946	3960	3974	3987	55
5	4001	4015	4028	4042	4055	4069	54
6	4083	4096	4110	4124	4137	4151	53
7	4164	4178	4192	4205	4219	4232	52
8	4246	4260	4273	4287	4300	4314	51
9	4328	4341	4355	4368	4382	4396	50
10	9.924409	4423	4436	4450	4464	4477	49
11	4491	4504	4518	4531	4545	4559	48
12	4572	4586	4599	4613	4626	4640	47
13	4654	4667	4681	4694	4708	4721	46
14	4735	4748	4762	4776	4789	4803	45
15	4816	4830	4843	4857	4870	4884	44
16	4897	4911	4924	4938	4952	4965	43
17	4979	4992	5006	5019	5033	5046	42
18	5060	5073	5087	5100	5114	5127	41
19	5141	5154	5168	5181	5195	5208	40
20	9.925222	5235	5249	5262	5276	5289	39
21	5303	5316	5330	5343	5357	5370	38
22	5384	5397	5411	5424	5438	5451	37
23	5465	5478	5491	5505	5518	5532	36
24	5545	5559	5572	5586	5599	5613	35
25	5626	5640	5653	5667	5680	5693	34
26	5707	5720	5734	5747	5761	5774	33
27	5788	5801	5814	5828	5841	5855	32
28	5868	5882	5895	5908	5922	5935	31
29	5949	5962	5976	5989	6002	6016	30
30	9.926029	6043	6056	6069	6083	6096	29
31	6110	6123	6136	6150	6163	6177	28
32	6190	6203	6217	6230	6244	6257	27
33	6270	6284	6297	6311	6324	6337	26
34	6351	6364	6377	6391	6404	6418	25
35	6431	6444	6458	6471	6484	6498	24
36	6511	6525	6538	6551	6565	6578	23
37	6591	6605	6618	6631	6645	6658	22
38	6671	6685	6698	6711	6725	6738	21
39	6751	6765	6778	6791	6805	6818	20
40	9.926831	6845	6858	6871	6885	6898	19
41	6911	6925	6938	6951	6965	6978	18
42	6991	7005	7018	7031	7044	7058	17
43	7071	7084	7098	7111	7124	7138	16
44	7151	7164	7177	7191	7204	7217	15
45	7231	7244	7257	7270	7284	7297	14
46	7310	7324	7337	7350	7363	7377	13
47	7390	7403	7416	7430	7443	7456	12
48	7470	7483	7496	7509	7523	7536	11
49	7549	7562	7576	7589	7602	7615	10
50	9.927629	7642	7655	7668	7681	7695	9
51	7708	7721	7734	7748	7761	7774	8
52	7787	7801	7814	7827	7840	7853	7
53	7867	7880	7893	7906	7920	7933	6
54	7946	7959	7972	7986	7999	8012	5
55	8025	8038	8052	8065	8078	8091	4
56	8104	8118	8131	8144	8157	8170	3
57	8183	8197	8210	8223	8236	8249	2
58	8263	8276	8289	8302	8315	8328	1
59	8342	8355	8368	8381	8394	8407	0
	60″	50″	40″	30″	20″	10″	Min.
	Co-sine of 32 Degrees.						

P. Part { 1′ 2″ 3″ 4″ 5″ 6″ 7″ 8″ 9″ / 1 3 4 5 7 8 9 11 12 }

Min.	Tangent of 56 Degrees. 0″	10″	20″	30″	40″	50″	
0	10.171013	1058	1103	1149	1194	1240	59
1	1285	1331	1376	1421	1467	1512	58
2	1558	1603	1649	1694	1739	1785	57
3	1830	1876	1921	1967	2012	2058	56
4	2103	2149	2194	2239	2285	2330	55
5	2376	2421	2467	2512	2558	2603	54
6	2649	2694	2740	2785	2831	2876	53
7	2922	2967	3013	3058	3104	3149	52
8	3195	3240	3286	3331	3377	3422	51
9	3468	3513	3559	3604	3650	3695	50
10	10.173741	3786	3832	3877	3923	3968	49
11	4014	4060	4105	4151	4196	4242	48
12	4287	4333	4378	4424	4469	4515	47
13	4561	4606	4652	4697	4743	4788	46
14	4834	4880	4925	4971	5016	5062	45
15	5107	5153	5199	5244	5290	5335	44
16	5381	5427	5472	5518	5563	5609	43
17	5655	5700	5746	5791	5837	5883	42
18	5928	5974	6019	6065	6111	6156	41
19	6202	6247	6293	6339	6384	6430	40
20	10.176476	6521	6567	6613	6658	6704	39
21	6749	6795	6841	6886	6932	6978	38
22	7023	7069	7115	7160	7206	7252	37
23	7297	7343	7389	7434	7480	7526	36
24	7571	7617	7663	7708	7754	7800	35
25	7846	7891	7937	7983	8028	8074	34
26	8120	8165	8211	8257	8303	8348	33
27	8394	8440	8485	8531	8577	8623	32
28	8668	8714	8760	8805	8851	8897	31
29	8943	8988	9034	9080	9126	9171	30
30	10.179217	9263	9309	9354	9400	9446	29
31	9492	9537	9583	9629	9675	9720	28
32	9766	9812	9858	9904	9949	9995	27
33	10.180041	0087	0132	0178	0224	0270	26
34	0316	0361	0407	0453	0499	0545	25
35	0590	0636	0682	0728	0774	0819	24
36	0865	0911	0957	1003	1048	1094	23
37	1140	1186	1232	1278	1323	1369	22
38	1415	1461	1507	1553	1598	1644	21
39	1690	1736	1782	1828	1874	1919	20
40	10.181965	2011	2057	2103	2149	2195	19
41	2241	2286	2332	2378	2424	2470	18
42	2516	2562	2608	2653	2699	2745	17
43	2791	2837	2883	2929	2975	3021	16
44	3067	3112	3158	3204	3250	3296	15
45	3342	3388	3434	3480	3526	3572	14
46	3618	3664	3709	3755	3801	3847	13
47	3893	3939	3985	4031	4077	4123	12
48	4169	4215	4261	4307	4353	4399	11
49	4445	4491	4537	4583	4629	4674	10
50	10.184720	4766	4812	4858	4904	4950	9
51	4996	5042	5088	5134	5180	5226	8
52	5272	5318	5364	5410	5456	5502	7
53	5548	5594	5640	5686	5732	5778	6
54	5824	5871	5917	5963	6009	6055	5
55	6101	6147	6193	6239	6285	6331	4
56	6377	6423	6469	6515	6561	6607	3
57	6653	6699	6745	6791	6837	6884	2
58	6930	6976	7022	7068	7114	7160	1
59	7206	7252	7298	7344	7390	7437	0
	60″	50″	40″	30″	20″	10″	Min.
	Co-tangent of 33 Degrees.						

P. Part { 1″ 2″ 3″ 4″ 5″ 6″ 7″ 8″ 9″ / 5 9 14 18 23 27 32 37 41 }

Min.	Tangent of 57 Degrees. 0″	10″	20″	30″	40″	50″	
0	10.187483	7529	7575	7621	7667	7713	59
1	7759	7805	7851	7898	7944	7990	58
2	8036	8082	8128	8174	8220	8267	57
3	8313	8359	8405	8451	8497	8543	56
4	8590	8636	8682	8728	8774	8820	55
5	8866	8913	8959	9005	9051	9097	54
6	9143	9190	9236	9282	9328	9374	53
7	9420	9467	9513	9559	9605	9651	52
8	9698	9744	9790	9836	9882	9929	51
9	9975	..21	..67	.113	.160	.206	50
10	10.190252	0298	0344	0391	0437	0483	49
11	0529	0576	0622	0668	0714	0760	48
12	0807	0853	0899	0945	0992	1038	47
13	1084	1130	1177	1223	1269	1315	46
14	1362	1408	1454	1501	1547	1593	45
15	1639	1686	1732	1778	1824	1871	44
16	1917	1963	2010	2056	2102	2149	43
17	2195	2241	2287	2334	2380	2426	42
18	2473	2519	2565	2612	2658	2704	41
19	2751	2797	2843	2890	2936	2982	40
20	10.193029	3075	3121	3168	3214	3260	39
21	3307	3353	3399	3446	3492	3538	38
22	3585	3631	3678	3724	3770	3817	37
23	3863	3909	3956	4002	4049	4095	36
24	4141	4188	4234	4281	4327	4373	35
25	4420	4466	4513	4559	4605	4652	34
26	4698	4745	4791	4837	4884	4930	33
27	4977	5023	5070	5116	5162	5209	32
28	5255	5302	5348	5395	5441	5487	31
29	5534	5580	5627	5673	5720	5766	30
30	10.195813	5859	5906	5952	5999	6045	29
31	6091	6138	6184	6231	6277	6324	28
32	6370	6417	6463	6510	6556	6603	27
33	6649	6696	6742	6789	6835	6882	26
34	6928	6975	7021	7068	7114	7161	25
35	7208	7254	7301	7347	7394	7440	24
36	7487	7533	7580	7626	7673	7719	23
37	7766	7813	7859	7906	7952	7999	22
38	8045	8092	8138	8185	8232	8278	21
39	8325	8371	8418	8465	8511	8558	20
40	10.198604	8651	8697	8744	8791	8837	19
41	8884	8930	8977	9024	9070	9117	18
42	9164	9210	9257	9303	9350	9397	17
43	9443	9490	9537	9583	9630	9676	16
44	9723	9770	9816	9863	9910	9956	15
45	10.200003	0050	0096	0143	0190	0236	14
46	0283	0330	0376	0423	0470	0516	13
47	0563	0610	0656	0703	0750	0796	12
48	0843	0890	0937	0983	1030	1077	11
49	1123	1170	1217	1263	1310	1357	10
50	10.201404	1450	1497	1544	1591	1637	9
51	1684	1731	1777	1824	1871	1918	8
52	1964	2011	2058	2105	2151	2198	7
53	2245	2292	2338	2385	2432	2479	6
54	2526	2572	2619	2666	2713	2759	5
55	2806	2853	2900	2947	2993	3040	4
56	3087	3134	3181	3227	3274	3321	3
57	3368	3415	3461	3508	3555	3602	2
58	3649	3696	3742	3789	3836	3883	1
59	3930	3977	4023	4070	4117	4164	0
	60″	50″	40″	30″	20″	10″	Min.
	Co-tangent of 32 Degrees.						

P. Part { 1″ 2″ 3″ 4″ 5″ 6″ 7″ 8″ 9″ / 5 9 14 19 23 28 33 37 42 }

Min.	Sine of 58 Degrees. 0″	10″	20″	30″	40″	50″	
0	9.928420	8434	8447	8460	8473	8486	59
1	8499	8513	8526	8539	8552	8565	58
2	8578	8591	8605	8618	8631	8644	57
3	8657	8670	8683	8696	8710	8723	56
4	8736	8749	8762	8775	8788	8801	55
5	8815	8828	8841	8854	8867	8880	54
6	8893	8906	8919	8933	8946	8959	53
7	8972	8985	8998	9011	9024	9037	52
8	9050	9063	9077	9090	9103	9116	51
9	9129	9142	9155	9168	9181	9194	50
10	9.929207	9220	9233	9247	9260	9273	49
11	9286	9299	9312	9325	9338	9351	48
12	9364	9377	9390	9403	9416	9429	47
13	9442	9455	9468	9482	9495	9508	46
14	9521	9534	9547	9560	9573	9586	45
15	9599	9612	9625	9638	9651	9664	44
16	9677	9690	9703	9716	9729	9742	43
17	9755	9768	9781	9794	9807	9820	42
18	9833	9846	9859	9872	9885	9898	41
19	9911	9924	9937	9950	9963	9976	40
20	9.929989	...2	..15	..28	..41	..54	39
21	9.930067	0080	0093	0106	0119	0132	38
22	0145	0158	0171	0184	0197	0210	37
23	0223	0236	0249	0262	0274	0287	36
24	0300	0313	0326	0339	0352	0365	35
25	0378	0391	0404	0417	0430	0443	34
26	0456	0469	0482	0495	0507	0520	33
27	0533	0546	0559	0572	0585	0598	32
28	0611	0624	0637	0650	0663	0675	31
29	0688	0701	0714	0727	0740	0753	30
30	9.930766	0779	0792	0804	0817	0830	29
31	0843	0856	0869	0882	0895	0908	28
32	0921	0933	0946	0959	0972	0985	27
33	0998	1011	1024	1036	1049	1062	26
34	1075	1088	1101	1114	1127	1139	25
35	1152	1165	1178	1191	1204	1217	24
36	1229	1242	1255	1268	1281	1294	23
37	1306	1319	1332	1345	1358	1371	22
38	1383	1396	1409	1422	1435	1448	21
39	1460	1473	1486	1499	1512	1525	20
40	9.931537	1550	1563	1576	1589	1601	19
41	1614	1627	1640	1653	1666	1678	18
42	1691	1704	1717	1730	1742	1755	17
43	1768	1781	1794	1806	1819	1832	16
44	1845	1857	1870	1883	1896	1909	15
45	1921	1934	1947	1960	1972	1985	14
46	1998	2011	2024	2036	2049	2062	13
47	2075	2087	2100	2113	2126	2138	12
48	2151	2164	2177	2189	2202	2215	11
49	2228	2240	2253	2266	2279	2291	10
50	9.932304	2317	2329	2342	2355	2368	9
51	2380	2393	2406	2419	2431	2444	8
52	2457	2469	2482	2495	2508	2520	7
53	2533	2546	2558	2571	2584	2597	6
54	2609	2622	2635	2647	2660	2673	5
55	2685	2698	2711	2724	2736	2749	4
56	2762	2774	2787	2800	2812	2825	3
57	2838	2850	2863	2876	2888	2901	2
58	2914	2926	2939	2952	2964	2977	1
59	2990	3002	3015	3028	3040	3053	0
	60″	50″	40″	30″	20″	10″	Min.
	Co-sine of 31 Degrees.						

P. Part	1″	2″	3″	4″	5″	6″	7″	8″	9″
	1	3	4	5	6	8	9	10	12

Min.	Sine of 59 Degrees. 0″	10″	20″	30″	40″	50″	
0	9.933066	3078	3091	3104	3116	3129	59
1	3141	3154	3167	3179	3192	3205	58
2	3217	3230	3243	3255	3268	3280	57
3	3293	3306	3318	3331	3344	3356	56
4	3369	3381	3394	3407	3419	3432	55
5	3445	3457	3470	3482	3495	3508	54
6	3520	3533	3545	3558	3571	3583	53
7	3596	3608	3621	3633	3646	3659	52
8	3671	3684	3696	3709	3722	3734	51
9	3747	3759	3772	3784	3797	3810	50
10	9.933822	3835	3847	3860	3872	3885	49
11	3898	3910	3923	3935	3948	3960	48
12	3973	3985	3998	4011	4023	4036	47
13	4048	4061	4073	4086	4098	4111	46
14	4123	4136	4148	4161	4174	4186	45
15	4199	4211	4224	4236	4249	4261	44
16	4274	4286	4299	4311	4324	4336	43
17	4349	4361	4374	4386	4399	4411	42
18	4424	4436	4449	4461	4474	4486	41
19	4499	4511	4524	4536	4549	4561	40
20	9.934574	4586	4599	4611	4624	4636	39
21	4649	4661	4674	4686	4699	4711	38
22	4723	4736	4748	4761	4773	4786	37
23	4798	4811	4823	4836	4848	4861	36
24	4873	4885	4898	4910	4923	4935	35
25	4948	4960	4973	4985	4997	5010	34
26	5022	5035	5047	5060	5072	5084	33
27	5097	5109	5122	5134	5147	5159	32
28	5171	5184	5196	5209	5221	5234	31
29	5246	5258	5271	5283	5296	5308	30
30	9.935320	5333	5345	5358	5370	5382	29
31	5395	5407	5420	5432	5444	5457	28
32	5469	5482	5494	5506	5519	5531	27
33	5543	5556	5568	5581	5593	5605	26
34	5618	5630	5642	5655	5667	5679	25
35	5692	5704	5717	5729	5741	5754	24
36	5766	5778	5791	5803	5815	5828	23
37	5840	5852	5865	5877	5889	5902	22
38	5914	5926	5939	5951	5963	5976	21
39	5988	6000	6013	6025	6037	6050	20
40	9.936062	6074	6087	6099	6111	6124	19
41	6136	6148	6161	6173	6185	6198	18
42	6210	6222	6234	6247	6259	6271	17
43	6284	6296	6308	6320	6333	6345	16
44	6357	6370	6382	6394	6406	6419	15
45	6431	6443	6456	6468	6480	6492	14
46	6505	6517	6529	6542	6554	6566	13
47	6578	6591	6603	6615	6627	6640	12
48	6652	6664	6676	6689	6701	6713	11
49	6725	6738	6750	6762	6774	6787	10
50	9.936799	6811	6823	6836	6848	6860	9
51	6872	6884	6897	6909	6921	6933	8
52	6946	6958	6970	6982	6994	7007	7
53	7019	7031	7043	7056	7068	7080	6
54	7092	7104	7117	7129	7141	7153	5
55	7165	7178	7190	7202	7214	7226	4
56	7238	7251	7263	7275	7287	7299	3
57	7312	7324	7336	7348	7360	7372	2
58	7385	7397	7409	7421	7433	7446	1
59	7458	7470	7482	7494	7506	7518	0
	60″	50″	40″	30″	20″	10″	Min.
	Co-sine of 30 Degrees.						

P. Part	1″	2″	3″	4″	5″	6″	7″	8″	9″
	1	2	4	5	6	7	9	10	11

Min.	Tangent of 58 Degrees. 0″	10″	20″	30″	40″	50″	
0	10.204211	4258	4304	4351	4398	4445	59
1	4492	4539	4586	4633	4679	4726	58
2	4773	4820	4867	4914	4961	5008	57
3	5054	5101	5148	5195	5242	5289	56
4	5336	5383	5430	5477	5524	5570	55
5	5617	5664	5711	5758	5805	5852	54
6	5899	5946	5993	6040	6087	6134	53
7	6181	6227	6274	6321	6368	6415	52
8	6462	6509	6556	6603	6650	6697	51
9	6744	6791	6838	6885	6932	6979	50
10	10.207026	7073	7120	7167	7214	7261	49
11	7308	7355	7402	7449	7496	7543	48
12	7590	7637	7684	7731	7778	7825	47
13	7872	7919	7966	8013	8060	8107	46
14	8154	8201	8248	8295	8342	8389	45
15	8437	8484	8531	8578	8625	8672	44
16	8719	8766	8813	8860	8907	8954	43
17	9001	9048	9095	9143	9190	9237	42
18	9284	9331	9378	9425	9472	9519	41
19	9566	9614	9661	9708	9755	9802	40
20	10.209849	9896	9943	9991	..38	..85	39
21	10.210132	0179	0226	0273	0321	0368	38
22	0415	0462	0509	0556	0603	0651	37
23	0698	0745	0792	0839	0886	0934	36
24	0981	1028	1075	1122	1170	1217	35
25	1264	1311	1358	1405	1453	1500	34
26	1547	1594	1641	1689	1736	1783	33
27	1830	1878	1925	1972	2019	2066	32
28	2114	2161	2208	2255	2303	2350	31
29	2397	2444	2492	2539	2586	2633	30
30	10.212681	2728	2775	2822	2870	2917	29
31	2964	3012	3059	3106	3153	3201	28
32	3248	3295	3343	3390	3437	3484	27
33	3532	3579	3626	3674	3721	3768	26
34	3816	3863	3910	3958	4005	4052	25
35	4100	4147	4194	4242	4289	4336	24
36	4384	4431	4478	4526	4573	4620	23
37	4668	4715	4762	4810	4857	4905	22
38	4952	4999	5047	5094	5141	5189	21
39	5236	5284	5331	5378	5426	5473	20
40	10.215521	5568	5615	5663	5710	5758	19
41	5805	5852	5900	5947	5995	6042	18
42	6090	6137	6184	6232	6279	6327	17
43	6374	6422	6469	6517	6564	6612	16
44	6659	6706	6754	6801	6849	6896	15
45	6944	6991	7039	7086	7134	7181	14
46	7229	7276	7324	7371	7419	7466	13
47	7514	7561	7609	7656	7704	7751	12
48	7799	7846	7894	7941	7989	8036	11
49	8084	8131	8179	8226	8274	8322	10
50	10.218369	8417	8464	8512	8559	8607	9
51	8654	8702	8750	8797	8845	8892	8
52	8940	8987	9035	9083	9130	9178	7
53	9225	9273	9321	9368	9416	9463	6
54	9511	9559	9606	9654	9701	9749	5
55	9797	9844	9892	9939	9987	..35	4
56	10.220082	0130	0178	0225	0273	0321	3
57	0368	0416	0463	0511	0559	0606	2
58	0654	0702	0749	0797	0845	0892	1
59	0940	0988	1036	1083	1131	1179	0
	60″	50″	40″	30″	20″	10″	Min.
	Co-tangent of 31 Degrees.						

P. Part { 1″ 2″ 3″ 4″ 5″ 6″ 7″ 8″ 9″ / 5 9 14 19 24 28 33 38 43 }

Min.	Tangent of 59 Degrees. 0″	10″	20″	30″	40″	50″	
0	10.221226	1274	1322	1369	1417	1465	59
1	1512	1560	1608	1656	1703	1751	58
2	1799	1846	1894	1942	1990	2037	57
3	2085	2133	2181	2228	2276	2324	56
4	2372	2419	2467	2515	2563	2610	55
5	2658	2706	2754	2801	2849	2897	54
6	2945	2993	3040	3088	3136	3184	53
7	3232	3279	3327	3375	3423	3471	52
8	3518	3566	3614	3662	3710	3757	51
9	3805	3853	3901	3949	3997	4044	50
10	10.224092	4140	4188	4236	4284	4332	49
11	4379	4427	4475	4523	4571	4619	48
12	4667	4714	4762	4810	4858	4906	47
13	4954	5002	5050	5098	5145	5193	46
14	5241	5289	5337	5385	5433	5481	45
15	5529	5577	5625	5672	5720	5768	44
16	5816	5864	5912	5960	6008	6056	43
17	6104	6152	6200	6248	6296	6344	42
18	6392	6440	6488	6535	6583	6631	41
19	6679	6727	6775	6823	6871	6919	40
20	10.226967	7015	7063	7111	7159	7207	39
21	7255	7303	7351	7399	7447	7495	38
22	7543	7591	7639	7688	7736	7784	37
23	7832	7880	7928	7976	8024	8072	36
24	8120	8168	8216	8264	8312	8360	35
25	8408	8456	8504	8552	8601	8649	34
26	8697	8745	8793	8841	8889	8937	33
27	8985	9033	9081	9130	9178	9226	32
28	9274	9322	9370	9418	9466	9515	31
29	9563	9611	9659	9707	9755	9803	30
30	10.229852	9900	9948	9996	..44	..92	29
31	10.230140	0189	0237	0285	0333	0381	28
32	0429	0478	0526	0574	0622	0670	27
33	0719	0767	0815	0863	0911	0960	26
34	1008	1056	1104	1152	1201	1249	25
35	1297	1345	1394	1442	1490	1538	24
36	1586	1635	1683	1731	1779	1828	23
37	1876	1924	1973	2021	2069	2117	22
38	2166	2214	2262	2310	2359	2407	21
39	2455	2504	2552	2600	2648	2697	20
40	10.232745	2793	2842	2890	2938	2987	19
41	3035	3083	3132	3180	3228	3277	18
42	3325	3373	3422	3470	3518	3567	17
43	3615	3663	3712	3760	3808	3857	16
44	3905	3953	4002	4050	4099	4147	15
45	4195	4244	4292	4340	4389	4437	14
46	4486	4534	4582	4631	4679	4728	13
47	4776	4825	4873	4921	4970	5018	12
48	5067	5115	5164	5212	5260	5309	11
49	5357	5406	5454	5503	5551	5600	10
50	10.235648	5696	5745	5793	5842	5890	9
51	5939	5987	6036	6084	6133	6181	8
52	6230	6278	6327	6375	6424	6472	7
53	6521	6569	6618	6666	6715	6763	6
54	6812	6860	6909	6957	7006	7055	5
55	7103	7152	7200	7249	7297	7346	4
56	7394	7443	7492	7540	7589	7637	3
57	7686	7734	7783	7832	7880	7929	2
58	7977	8026	8075	8123	8172	8220	1
59	8269	8318	8366	8415	8463	8512	0
	60″	50″	40″	30″	20″	10″	Min.
	Co-tangent of 30 Degrees.						

P. Part { 1″ 2″ 3″ 4″ 5″ 6″ 7″ 8″ 9″ / 5 10 14 19 24 29 34 39 43 }

Min.	Sine of 60 Degrees. 0″	10″	20″	30″	40″	50″	
0	9.937531	7543	7555	7567	7579	7591	59
1	7604	7616	7628	7640	7652	7664	58
2	7676	7689	7701	7713	7725	7737	57
3	7749	7761	7773	7786	7798	7810	56
4	7822	7834	7846	7858	7870	7883	55
5	7895	7907	7919	7931	7943	7955	54
6	7967	7979	7992	8004	8016	8028	53
7	8040	8052	8064	8076	8088	8100	52
8	8113	8125	8137	8149	8161	8173	51
9	8185	8197	8209	8221	8233	8245	50
10	9.938258	8270	8282	8294	8306	8318	49
11	8330	8342	8354	8366	8378	8390	48
12	8402	8414	8426	8439	8451	8463	47
13	8475	8487	8499	8511	8523	8535	46
14	8547	8559	8571	8583	8595	8607	45
15	8619	8631	8643	8655	8667	8679	44
16	8691	8703	8715	8727	8739	8751	43
17	8763	8776	8788	8800	8812	8824	42
18	8836	8848	8860	8872	8884	8896	41
19	8908	8920	8932	8944	8956	8968	40
20	9.938980	8992	9004	9016	9028	9040	39
21	9052	9064	9076	9087	9099	9111	38
22	9123	9135	9147	9159	9171	9183	37
23	9195	9207	9219	9231	9243	9255	36
24	9267	9279	9291	9303	9315	9327	35
25	9339	9351	9363	9375	9387	9399	34
26	9410	9422	9434	9446	9458	9470	33
27	9482	9494	9506	9518	9530	9542	32
28	9554	9566	9578	9590	9601	9613	31
29	9625	9637	9649	9661	9673	9685	30
30	9.939697	9709	9721	9733	9744	9756	29
31	9768	9780	9792	9804	9816	9828	28
32	9840	9852	9863	9875	9887	9899	27
33	9911	9923	9935	9947	9959	9970	26
34	9982	9994	...6	..18	..30	..42	25
35	9.940054	0065	0077	0089	0101	0113	24
36	0125	0137	0148	0160	0172	0184	23
37	0196	0208	0220	0231	0243	0255	22
38	0267	0279	0291	0303	0314	0326	21
39	0338	0350	0362	0374	0385	0397	20
40	9.940409	0421	0433	0445	0456	0468	19
41	0480	0492	0504	0516	0527	0539	18
42	0551	0563	0575	0586	0598	0610	17
43	0622	0634	0645	0657	0669	0681	16
44	0693	0704	0716	0728	0740	0752	15
45	0763	0775	0787	0799	0811	0822	14
46	0834	0846	0858	0870	0881	0893	13
47	0905	0917	0928	0940	0952	0964	12
48	0975	0987	0999	1011	1023	1034	11
49	1046	1058	1070	1081	1093	1105	10
50	9.941117	1128	1140	1152	1164	1175	9
51	1187	1199	1211	1222	1234	1246	8
52	1258	1269	1281	1293	1304	1316	7
53	1328	1340	1351	1363	1375	1387	6
54	1398	1410	1422	1433	1445	1457	5
55	1469	1480	1492	1504	1515	1527	4
56	1539	1550	1562	1574	1586	1597	3
57	1609	1621	1632	1644	1656	1667	2
58	1679	1691	1702	1714	1726	1738	1
59	1749	1761	1773	1784	1796	1808	0
	60″ Co-sine of 29 Degrees.	50″	40″	30″	20″	10″	Min.

P. Part { 1″ 2″ 3″ 4″ 5″ 6″ 7″ 8″ 9″ / 1 2 4 5 6 7 8 10 11

Min.	Sine of 61 Degrees. 0″	10″	20″	30″	40″	50″	
0	9.941819	1831	1843	1854	1866	1878	59
1	1889	1901	1913	1924	1936	1948	58
2	1959	1971	1983	1994	2006	2017	57
3	2029	2041	2052	2064	2076	2087	56
4	2099	2111	2122	2134	2146	2157	55
5	2169	2180	2192	2204	2215	2227	54
6	2239	2250	2262	2273	2285	2297	53
7	2308	2320	2331	2343	2355	2366	52
8	2378	2390	2401	2413	2424	2436	51
9	2448	2459	2471	2482	2494	2506	50
10	9.942517	2529	2540	2552	2563	2575	49
11	2587	2598	2610	2621	2633	2645	48
12	2656	2668	2679	2691	2702	2714	47
13	2726	2737	2749	2760	2772	2783	46
14	2795	2806	2818	2830	2841	2853	45
15	2864	2876	2887	2899	2910	2922	44
16	2934	2945	2957	2968	2980	2991	43
17	3003	3014	3026	3037	3049	3060	42
18	3072	3083	3095	3107	3118	3130	41
19	3141	3153	3164	3176	3187	3199	40
20	9.943210	3222	3233	3245	3256	3268	39
21	3279	3291	3302	3314	3325	3337	38
22	3348	3360	3371	3383	3394	3406	37
23	3417	3429	3440	3452	3463	3475	36
24	3486	3498	3509	3521	3532	3543	35
25	3555	3566	3578	3589	3601	3612	34
26	3624	3635	3647	3658	3670	3681	33
27	3693	3704	3715	3727	3738	3750	32
28	3761	3773	3784	3796	3807	3818	31
29	3830	3841	3853	3864	3876	3887	30
30	9.943899	3910	3921	3933	3944	3956	29
31	3967	3978	3990	4001	4013	4024	28
32	4036	4047	4058	4070	4081	4093	27
33	4104	4115	4127	4138	4150	4161	26
34	4172	4184	4195	4207	4218	4229	25
35	4241	4252	4264	4275	4286	4298	24
36	4309	4321	4332	4343	4355	4366	23
37	4377	4389	4400	4412	4423	4434	22
38	4446	4457	4468	4480	4491	4503	21
39	4514	4525	4537	4548	4559	4571	20
40	9.944582	4593	4605	4616	4627	4639	19
41	4650	4661	4673	4684	4696	4707	18
42	4718	4730	4741	4752	4764	4775	17
43	4786	4798	4809	4820	4831	4843	16
44	4854	4865	4877	4888	4899	4911	15
45	4922	4933	4945	4956	4967	4979	14
46	4990	5001	5013	5024	5035	5046	13
47	5058	5069	5080	5092	5103	5114	12
48	5125	5137	5148	5159	5171	5182	11
49	5193	5204	5216	5227	5238	5250	10
50	9.945261	5272	5283	5295	5306	5317	9
51	5328	5340	5351	5362	5374	5385	8
52	5396	5407	5419	5430	5441	5452	7
53	5464	5475	5486	5497	5509	5520	6
54	5531	5542	5554	5565	5576	5587	5
55	5598	5610	5621	5632	5643	5655	4
56	5666	5677	5688	5700	5711	5722	3
57	5733	5744	5756	5767	5778	5789	2
58	5800	5812	5823	5834	5845	5857	1
59	5868	5879	5890	5901	5913	5924	0
	60″ Co-sine of 28 Degrees.	50″	40″	30″	20″	10″	Min.

P. Part { 1″ 2″ 3″ 4″ 5″ 6″ 7″ 8″ 9″ / 1 2 3 5 6 7 8 9 10

Min.	Tangent of 60 Degrees. 0″	10″	20″	30″	40″	50″	
0	10.238561	8609	8658	8707	8755	8804	59
1	8852	8901	8950	8998	9047	9096	58
2	9144	9193	9242	9290	9339	9388	57
3	9436	9485	9534	9582	9631	9680	56
4	9728	9777	9826	9874	9923	9972	55
5	10.240021	0069	0118	0167	0215	0264	54
6	0313	0362	0410	0459	0508	0557	53
7	0605	0654	0703	0752	0800	0849	52
8	0898	0947	0995	1044	1093	1142	51
9	1190	1239	1288	1337	1385	1434	50
10	10.241483	1532	1581	1629	1678	1727	49
11	1776	1825	1873	1922	1971	2020	48
12	2069	2118	2166	2215	2264	2313	47
13	2362	2411	2459	2508	2557	2606	46
14	2655	2704	2753	2801	2850	2899	45
15	2948	2997	3046	3095	3143	3192	44
16	3241	3290	3339	3388	3437	3486	43
17	3535	3584	3632	3681	3730	3779	42
18	3828	3877	3926	3975	4024	4073	41
19	4122	4171	4220	4269	4318	4366	40
20	10.244415	4464	4513	4562	4611	4660	39
21	4709	4758	4807	4856	4905	4954	38
22	5003	5052	5101	5150	5199	5248	37
23	5297	5346	5395	5444	5493	5542	36
24	5591	5640	5689	5738	5787	5836	35
25	5885	5934	5984	6033	6082	6131	34
26	6180	6229	6278	6327	6376	6425	33
27	6474	6523	6572	6621	6670	6720	32
28	6769	6818	6867	6916	6965	7014	31
29	7063	7112	7161	7211	7260	7309	30
30	10.247358	7407	7456	7505	7554	7604	29
31	7653	7702	7751	7800	7849	7899	28
32	7948	7997	8046	8095	8144	8194	27
33	8243	8292	8341	8390	8439	8489	26
34	8538	8587	8636	8685	8735	8784	25
35	8833	8882	8931	8981	9030	9079	24
36	9128	9178	9227	9276	9325	9375	23
37	9424	9473	9522	9572	9621	9670	22
38	9719	9769	9818	9867	9916	9966	21
39	10.250015	0064	0114	0163	0212	0261	20
40	10.250311	0360	0409	0459	0508	0557	19
41	0607	0656	0705	0755	0804	0853	18
42	0903	0952	1001	1051	1100	1149	17
43	1199	1248	1297	1347	1396	1445	16
44	1495	1544	1594	1643	1692	1742	15
45	1791	1840	1890	1939	1989	2038	14
46	2087	2137	2186	2236	2285	2335	13
47	2384	2433	2483	2532	2582	2631	12
48	2681	2730	2779	2829	2878	2928	11
49	2977	3027	3076	3126	3175	3225	10
50	10.253274	3324	3373	3423	3472	3521	9
51	3571	3620	3670	3719	3769	3818	8
52	3868	3918	3967	4017	4066	4116	7
53	4165	4215	4264	4314	4363	4413	6
54	4462	4512	4561	4611	4661	4710	5
55	4760	4809	4859	4908	4958	5008	4
56	5057	5107	5156	5206	5256	5305	3
57	5355	5404	5454	5504	5553	5603	2
58	5652	5702	5752	5801	5851	5901	1
59	5950	6000	6049	6099	6149	6198	0
	60″	50″	40″	30″	20″	10″	Min.
	Co-tangent of 29 Degrees.						

P. Part { 1″ 2″ 3″ 4″ 5″ 6″ 7″ 8″ 9″ / 5 10 15 20 25 29 34 39 44

Min.	Tangent of 61 Degrees. 0″	10″	20″	30″	40″	50″	
0	10.256248	6298	6347	6397	6447	6496	59
1	6546	6596	6645	6695	6745	6794	58
2	6844	6894	6944	6993	7043	7093	57
3	7142	7192	7242	7291	7341	7391	56
4	7441	7490	7540	7590	7640	7689	55
5	7739	7789	7839	7888	7938	7988	54
6	8038	8087	8137	8187	8237	8286	53
7	8336	8386	8436	8486	8535	8585	52
8	8635	8685	8735	8784	8834	8884	51
9	8934	8984	9033	9083	9133	9183	50
10	10.259233	9283	9332	9382	9432	9482	49
11	9532	9582	9632	9681	9731	9781	48
12	9831	9881	9931	9981	..31	..80	47
13	10.260130	0180	0230	0280	0330	0380	46
14	0430	0480	0530	0580	0629	0679	45
15	0729	0779	0829	0879	0929	0979	44
16	1029	1079	1129	1179	1229	1279	43
17	1329	1379	1429	1479	1529	1579	42
18	1629	1679	1729	1779	1829	1879	41
19	1929	1979	2029	2079	2129	2179	40
20	10.262229	2279	2329	2379	2429	2479	39
21	2529	2579	2629	2679	2729	2779	38
22	2829	2879	2929	2979	3029	3079	37
23	3130	3180	3230	3280	3330	3380	36
24	3430	3480	3530	3580	3630	3681	35
25	3731	3781	3831	3881	3931	3981	34
26	4031	4082	4132	4182	4232	4282	33
27	4332	4382	4433	4483	4533	4583	32
28	4633	4683	4734	4784	4834	4884	31
29	4934	4985	5035	5085	5135	5185	30
30	10.265236	5286	5336	5386	5436	5487	29
31	5537	5587	5637	5688	5738	5788	28
32	5838	5889	5939	5989	6039	6090	27
33	6140	6190	6240	6291	6341	6391	26
34	6442	6492	6542	6592	6643	6693	25
35	6743	6794	6844	6894	6945	6995	24
36	7045	7096	7146	7196	7247	7297	23
37	7347	7398	7448	7498	7549	7599	22
38	7649	7700	7750	7800	7851	7901	21
39	7952	8002	8052	8103	8153	8204	20
40	10.268254	8304	8355	8405	8456	8506	19
41	8556	8607	8657	8708	8758	8809	18
42	8859	8909	8960	9010	9061	9111	17
43	9162	9212	9263	9313	9364	9414	16
44	9465	9515	9566	9616	9667	9717	15
45	9767	9818	9868	9919	9970	..20	14
46	10.270071	0121	0172	0222	0273	0323	13
47	0374	0424	0475	0525	0576	0626	12
48	0677	0728	0778	0829	0879	0930	11
49	0980	1031	1082	1132	1183	1233	10
50	10.271284	1335	1385	1436	1486	1537	9
51	1588	1638	1689	1739	1790	1841	8
52	1891	1942	1993	2043	2094	2145	7
53	2195	2246	2297	2347	2398	2449	6
54	2499	2550	2601	2651	2702	2753	5
55	2803	2854	2905	2955	3006	3057	4
56	3108	3158	3209	3260	3310	3361	3
57	3412	3463	3513	3564	3615	3666	2
58	3716	3767	3818	3869	3919	3970	1
59	4021	4072	4122	4173	4224	4275	0
	60″	50″	40″	30″	20″	10″	Min.
	Co-tangent of 28 Degrees.						

P. Part { 1″ 2″ 3″ 4″ 5″ 6″ 7″ 8″ 9″ / 5 10 15 20 25 30 35 40 45

Min.	Sine of 62 Degrees. 0″	10″	20″	30″	40″	50″	
0	9·945935	5946	5957	5969	5980	5991	59
1	6002	6013	6024	6036	6047	6058	58
2	6069	6080	6092	6103	6114	6125	57
3	6136	6147	6159	6170	6181	6192	56
4	6203	6214	6226	6237	6248	6259	55
5	6270	6281	6293	6304	6315	6326	54
6	6337	6348	6359	6371	6382	6393	53
7	6404	6415	6426	6437	6449	6460	52
8	6471	6482	6493	6504	6515	6526	51
9	6538	6549	6560	6571	6582	6593	50
10	9·946604	6615	6627	6638	6649	6660	49
11	6671	6682	6693	6704	6715	6726	48
12	6738	6749	6760	6771	6782	6793	47
13	6804	6815	6826	6837	6849	6860	46
14	6871	6882	6893	6904	6915	6926	45
15	6937	6948	6959	6970	6982	6993	44
16	7004	7015	7026	7037	7048	7059	43
17	7070	7081	7092	7103	7114	7125	42
18	7136	7147	7158	7170	7181	7192	41
19	7203	7214	7225	7236	7247	7258	40
20	9·947269	7280	7291	7302	7313	7324	39
21	7335	7346	7357	7368	7379	7390	38
22	7401	7412	7423	7434	7445	7456	37
23	7467	7478	7489	7500	7511	7522	36
24	7533	7545	7556	7567	7578	7589	35
25	7600	7611	7622	7633	7644	7655	34
26	7665	7676	7687	7698	7709	7720	33
27	7731	7742	7753	7764	7775	7786	32
28	7797	7808	7819	7830	7841	7852	31
29	7863	7874	7885	7896	7907	7918	30
30	9·947929	7940	7951	7962	7973	7984	29
31	7995	8006	8017	8028	8038	8049	28
32	8060	8071	8082	8093	8104	8115	27
33	8126	8137	8148	8159	8170	8181	26
34	8192	8203	8213	8224	8235	8246	25
35	8257	8268	8279	8290	8301	8312	24
36	8323	8334	8344	8355	8366	8377	23
37	8388	8399	8410	8421	8432	8443	22
38	8454	8464	8475	8486	8497	8508	21
39	8519	8530	8541	8552	8562	8573	20
40	9·948584	8595	8606	8617	8628	8639	19
41	8650	8660	8671	8682	8693	8704	18
42	8715	8726	8736	8747	8758	8769	17
43	8780	8791	8802	8812	8823	8834	16
44	8845	8856	8867	8878	8888	8899	15
45	8910	8921	8932	8943	8954	8964	14
46	8975	8986	8997	9008	9019	9029	13
47	9040	9051	9062	9073	9083	9094	12
48	9105	9116	9127	9138	9148	9159	11
49	9170	9181	9192	9202	9213	9224	10
50	9·949235	9246	9256	9267	9278	9289	9
51	9300	9310	9321	9332	9343	9354	8
52	9364	9375	9386	9397	9408	9418	7
53	9429	9440	9451	9462	9472	9483	6
54	9494	9505	9515	9526	9537	9548	5
55	9558	9569	9580	9591	9602	9612	4
56	9623	9634	9645	9655	9666	9677	3
57	9688	9698	9709	9720	9731	9741	2
58	9752	9763	9774	9784	9795	9806	1
59	9816	9827	9838	9849	9859	9870	0
	60″	50″	40″	30″	20″	10″	Min.
	Co-sine of 27 Degrees.						

P. Part { 1″ 2″ 3″ 4″ 5″ 6″ 7″ 8″ 9″ / 1 2 3 4 5 7 8 9 10 }

Min.	Sine of 63 Degrees. 0″	10″	20″	30″	40″	50″	
0	9·949881	9892	9902	9913	9924	9935	59
1	9945	9956	9967	9977	9988	9999	58
2	9·950010	0020	0031	0042	0052	0063	57
3	0074	0084	0095	0106	0117	0127	56
4	0138	0149	0159	0170	0181	0191	55
5	0202	0213	0224	0234	0245	0256	54
6	0266	0277	0288	0298	0309	0320	53
7	0330	0341	0352	0362	0373	0384	52
8	0394	0405	0416	0426	0437	0448	51
9	0458	0469	0480	0490	0501	0512	50
10	9·950522	0533	0544	0554	0565	0576	49
11	0586	0597	0607	0618	0629	0639	48
12	0650	0661	0671	0682	0693	0703	47
13	0714	0724	0735	0746	0756	0767	46
14	0778	0788	0799	0809	0820	0831	45
15	0841	0852	0862	0873	0884	0894	44
16	0905	0915	0926	0937	0947	0958	43
17	0968	0979	0990	1000	1011	1021	42
18	1032	1043	1053	1064	1074	1085	41
19	1096	1106	1117	1127	1138	1148	40
20	9·951159	1170	1180	1191	1201	1212	39
21	1222	1233	1244	1254	1265	1275	38
22	1286	1296	1307	1317	1328	1339	37
23	1349	1360	1370	1381	1391	1402	36
24	1412	1423	1434	1444	1455	1465	35
25	1476	1486	1497	1507	1518	1528	34
26	1539	1549	1560	1570	1581	1591	33
27	1602	1613	1623	1634	1644	1655	32
28	1665	1676	1686	1697	1707	1718	31
29	1728	1739	1749	1760	1770	1781	30
30	9·951791	1802	1812	1823	1833	1844	29
31	1854	1865	1875	1886	1896	1907	28
32	1917	1928	1938	1949	1959	1969	27
33	1980	1990	2001	2011	2022	2032	26
34	2043	2053	2064	2074	2085	2095	25
35	2106	2116	2126	2137	2147	2158	24
36	2168	2179	2189	2200	2210	2221	23
37	2231	2241	2252	2262	2273	2283	22
38	2294	2304	2314	2325	2335	2346	21
39	2356	2367	2377	2387	2398	2408	20
40	9·952419	2429	2440	2450	2460	2471	19
41	2481	2492	2502	2512	2523	2533	18
42	2544	2554	2565	2575	2585	2596	17
43	2606	2617	2627	2637	2648	2658	16
44	2669	2679	2689	2700	2710	2720	15
45	2731	2741	2752	2762	2772	2783	14
46	2793	2803	2814	2824	2835	2845	13
47	2855	2866	2876	2886	2897	2907	12
48	2918	2928	2938	2949	2959	2969	11
49	2980	2990	3000	3011	3021	3031	10
50	9·953042	3052	3062	3073	3083	3093	9
51	3104	3114	3124	3135	3145	3155	8
52	3166	3176	3186	3197	3207	3217	7
53	3228	3238	3248	3259	3269	3279	6
54	3290	3300	3310	3321	3331	3341	5
55	3352	3362	3372	3382	3393	3403	4
56	3413	3424	3434	3444	3455	3465	3
57	3475	3485	3496	3506	3516	3527	2
58	3537	3547	3557	3568	3578	3588	1
59	3599	3609	3619	3629	3640	3650	0
	60″	50″	40″	30″	20″	10″	Min.
	Co-sine of 26 Degrees.						

P. Part { 1″ 2″ 3″ 4″ 5″ 6″ 7″ 8″ 9″ / 1 2 3 4 5 6 7 8 9 }

Tangent of 62 Degrees.

Min.	0″	10″	20″	30″	40″	50″	
0	10.274326	4376	4427	4478	4529	4580	59
1	4630	4681	4732	4783	4834	4885	58
2	4935	4986	5037	5088	5139	5190	57
3	5240	5291	5342	5393	5444	5495	56
4	5546	5597	5647	5698	5749	5800	55
5	5851	5902	5953	6004	6055	6105	54
6	6156	6207	6258	6309	6360	6411	53
7	6462	6513	6564	6615	6666	6717	52
8	6768	6819	6870	6920	6971	7022	51
9	7073	7124	7175	7226	7277	7328	50
10	10.277379	7430	7481	7532	7583	7634	49
11	7685	7736	7787	7838	7889	7940	48
12	7991	8043	8094	8145	8196	8247	47
13	8298	8349	8400	8451	8502	8553	46
14	8604	8655	8706	8757	8809	8860	45
15	8911	8962	9013	9064	9115	9166	44
16	9217	9268	9320	9371	9422	9473	43
17	9524	9575	9626	9678	9729	9780	42
18	9831	9882	9933	9984	..36	..87	41
19	10.280138	0189	0240	0292	0343	0394	40
20	10.280445	0496	0548	0599	0650	0701	39
21	0752	0804	0855	0906	0957	1009	38
22	1060	1111	1162	1214	1265	1316	37
23	1367	1419	1470	1521	1572	1624	36
24	1675	1726	1777	1829	1880	1931	35
25	1983	2034	2085	2137	2188	2239	34
26	2291	2342	2393	2445	2496	2547	33
27	2599	2650	2701	2753	2804	2855	32
28	2907	2958	3009	3061	3112	3164	31
29	3215	3266	3318	3369	3421	3472	30
30	10.283523	3575	3626	3678	3729	3780	29
31	3832	3883	3935	3986	4038	4089	28
32	4140	4192	4243	4295	4346	4398	27
33	4449	4501	4552	4604	4655	4707	26
34	4758	4810	4861	4913	4964	5016	25
35	5067	5119	5170	5222	5273	5325	24
36	5376	5428	5479	5531	5582	5634	23
37	5686	5737	5789	5840	5892	5943	22
38	5995	6046	6098	6150	6201	6253	21
39	6304	6356	6408	6459	6511	6562	20
40	10.286614	6666	6717	6769	6821	6872	19
41	6924	6975	7027	7079	7130	7182	18
42	7234	7285	7337	7389	7440	7492	17
43	7544	7595	7647	7699	7751	7802	16
44	7854	7906	7957	8009	8061	8113	15
45	8164	8216	8268	8319	8371	8423	14
46	8475	8526	8578	8630	8682	8733	13
47	8785	8837	8889	8941	8992	9044	12
48	9096	9148	9199	9251	9303	9355	11
49	9407	9458	9510	9562	9614	9666	10
50	10.289718	9769	9821	9873	9925	9977	9
51	10.290029	0081	0132	0184	0236	0288	8
52	0340	0392	0444	0496	0547	0599	7
53	0651	0703	0755	0807	0859	0911	6
54	0963	1015	1066	1118	1170	1222	5
55	1274	1326	1378	1430	1482	1534	4
56	1586	1638	1690	1742	1794	1846	3
57	1898	1950	2002	2054	2106	2158	2
58	2210	2262	2314	2366	2418	2470	1
59	2522	2574	2626	2678	2730	2782	0
	60″	50″	40″	30″	20″	10″	Min.

Co-tangent of 27 Degrees.

P. Part	1″	2″	3″	4″	5″	6″	7″	8″	9″
	5	10	15	21	26	31	36	41	46

Tangent of 63 Degrees.

Min.	0″	10″	20″	30″	40″	50″	
0	10.292834	2886	2938	2990	3042	3094	59
1	3146	3199	3251	3303	3355	3407	58
2	3459	3511	3563	3615	3667	3720	57
3	3772	3824	3876	3928	3980	4032	56
4	4084	4137	4189	4241	4293	4345	55
5	4397	4449	4502	4554	4606	4658	54
6	4710	4763	4815	4867	4919	4971	53
7	5024	5076	5128	5180	5232	5285	52
8	5337	5389	5441	5494	5546	5598	51
9	5650	5703	5755	5807	5859	5912	50
10	10.295964	6016	6068	6121	6173	6225	49
11	6278	6330	6382	6434	6487	6539	48
12	6591	6644	6696	6748	6801	6853	47
13	6905	6958	7010	7062	7115	7167	46
14	7219	7272	7324	7377	7429	7481	45
15	7534	7586	7638	7691	7743	7796	44
16	7848	7900	7953	8005	8058	8110	43
17	8163	8215	8267	8320	8372	8425	42
18	8477	8530	8582	8635	8687	8740	41
19	8792	8845	8897	8949	9002	9054	40
20	10.299107	9159	9212	9264	9317	9370	39
21	9422	9475	9527	9580	9632	9685	38
22	9737	9790	9842	9895	9947	....	37
23	10.300053	0105	0158	0210	0263	0315	36
24	0368	0421	0473	0526	0578	0631	35
25	0684	0736	0789	0841	0894	0947	34
26	0999	1052	1105	1157	1210	1263	33
27	1315	1368	1421	1473	1526	1579	32
28	1631	1684	1737	1789	1842	1895	31
29	1947	2000	2053	2106	2158	2211	30
30	10.302264	2316	2369	2422	2475	2527	29
31	2580	2633	2686	2738	2791	2844	28
32	2897	2950	3002	3055	3108	3161	27
33	3213	3266	3319	3372	3425	3478	26
34	3530	3583	3636	3689	3742	3794	25
35	3847	3900	3953	4006	4059	4112	24
36	4164	4217	4270	4323	4376	4429	23
37	4482	4535	4588	4640	4693	4746	22
38	4799	4852	4905	4958	5011	5064	21
39	5117	5170	5223	5276	5328	5381	20
40	10.305434	5487	5540	5593	5646	5699	19
41	5752	5805	5858	5911	5964	6017	18
42	6070	6123	6176	6229	6282	6335	17
43	6388	6441	6494	6547	6600	6654	16
44	6707	6760	6813	6866	6919	6972	15
45	7025	7078	7131	7184	7237	7290	14
46	7344	7397	7450	7503	7556	7609	13
47	7662	7715	7768	7822	7875	7928	12
48	7981	8034	8087	8141	8194	8247	11
49	8300	8353	8406	8460	8513	8566	10
50	10.308619	8672	8726	8779	8832	8885	9
51	8938	8992	9045	9098	9151	9205	8
52	9258	9311	9364	9418	9471	9524	7
53	9577	9631	9684	9737	9790	9844	6
54	9897	9950	...4	..57	.110	.164	5
55	10.310217	0270	0324	0377	0430	0484	4
56	0537	0590	0644	0697	0750	0804	3
57	0857	0910	0964	1017	1070	1124	2
58	1177	1231	1284	1337	1391	1444	1
59	1498	1551	1605	1658	1711	1765	0
	60″	50″	40″	30″	20″	10″	Min.

Co-tangent of 26 Degrees.

P. Part	1″	2″	3″	4″	5″	6″	7″	8″	9″
	5	11	16	21	26	32	37	42	47

Sine of 64 Degrees.

Min.	0″	10″	20″	30″	40″	50″	
0	9.953660	3670	3681	3691	3701	3712	59
1	3722	3732	3742	3753	3763	3773	58
2	3783	3794	3804	3814	3824	3835	57
3	3845	3855	3865	3876	3886	3896	56
4	3906	3917	3927	3937	3947	3957	55
5	3968	3978	3988	3998	4009	4019	54
6	4029	4039	4050	4060	4070	4080	53
7	4090	4101	4111	4121	4131	4141	52
8	4152	4162	4172	4182	4192	4203	51
9	4213	4223	4233	4243	4254	4264	50
10	9.954274	4284	4294	4305	4315	4325	49
11	4335	4345	4356	4366	4376	4386	48
12	4396	4406	4417	4427	4437	4447	47
13	4457	4468	4478	4488	4498	4508	46
14	4518	4529	4539	4549	4559	4569	45
15	4579	4589	4600	4610	4620	4630	44
16	4640	4650	4661	4671	4681	4691	43
17	4701	4711	4721	4732	4742	4752	42
18	4762	4772	4782	4792	4802	4813	41
19	4823	4833	4843	4853	4863	4873	40
20	9.954883	4894	4904	4914	4924	4934	39
21	4944	4954	4964	4974	4985	4995	38
22	5005	5015	5025	5035	5045	5055	37
23	5065	5075	5086	5096	5106	5116	36
24	5126	5136	5146	5156	5166	5176	35
25	5186	5196	5207	5217	5227	5237	34
26	5247	5257	5267	5277	5287	5297	33
27	5307	5317	5327	5337	5348	5358	32
28	5368	5378	5388	5398	5408	5418	31
29	5428	5438	5448	5458	5468	5478	30
30	9.955488	5498	5508	5518	5528	5538	29
31	5548	5559	5569	5579	5589	5599	28
32	5609	5619	5629	5639	5649	5659	27
33	5669	5679	5689	5699	5709	5719	26
34	5729	5739	5749	5759	5769	5779	25
35	5789	5799	5809	5819	5829	5839	24
36	5849	5859	5869	5879	5889	5899	23
37	5909	5919	5929	5939	5949	5959	22
38	5969	5979	5989	5999	6009	6019	21
39	6029	6039	6049	6059	6069	6079	20
40	9.956089	6099	6108	6118	6128	6138	19
41	6148	6158	6168	6178	6188	6198	18
42	6208	6218	6228	6238	6248	6258	17
43	6268	6278	6288	6298	6308	6317	16
44	6327	6337	6347	6357	6367	6377	15
45	6387	6397	6407	6417	6427	6437	14
46	6447	6457	6466	6476	6486	6496	13
47	6506	6516	6526	6536	6546	6556	12
48	6566	6575	6585	6595	6605	6615	11
49	6625	6635	6645	6655	6665	6674	10
50	9.956684	6694	6704	6714	6724	6734	9
51	6744	6754	6763	6773	6783	6793	8
52	6803	6813	6823	6833	6843	6852	7
53	6862	6872	6882	6892	6902	6912	6
54	6921	6931	6941	6951	6961	6971	5
55	6981	6990	7000	7010	7020	7030	4
56	7040	7050	7059	7069	7079	7089	3
57	7099	7109	7118	7128	7138	7148	2
58	7158	7168	7177	7187	7197	7207	1
59	7217	7227	7236	7246	7256	7266	0
	60″	50″	40″	30″	20″	10″	Min.

Co-sine of 25 Degrees.

P. Part	1″	2″	3″	4″	5″	6″	7″	8″	9″
	1	2	3	4	5	6	7	8	9

Sine of 65 Degrees.

Min.	0″	10″	20″	30″	40″	50″	
0	9.957276	7286	7295	7305	7315	7325	59
1	7335	7344	7354	7364	7374	7384	58
2	7393	7403	7413	7423	7433	7442	57
3	7452	7462	7472	7482	7491	7501	56
4	7511	7521	7531	7540	7550	7560	55
5	7570	7579	7589	7599	7609	7619	54
6	7628	7638	7648	7658	7667	7677	53
7	7687	7697	7707	7716	7726	7736	52
8	7746	7755	7765	7775	7785	7794	51
9	7804	7814	7824	7833	7843	7853	50
10	9.957863	7872	7882	7892	7902	7911	49
11	7921	7931	7940	7950	7960	7970	48
12	7979	7989	7999	8009	8018	8028	47
13	8038	8047	8057	8067	8077	8086	46
14	8096	8106	8115	8125	8135	8145	45
15	8154	8164	8174	8183	8193	8203	44
16	8213	8222	8232	8242	8251	8261	43
17	8271	8280	8290	8300	8309	8319	42
18	8329	8339	8348	8358	8368	8377	41
19	8387	8397	8406	8416	8426	8435	40
20	9.958445	8455	8464	8474	8484	8493	39
21	8503	8513	8522	8532	8542	8551	38
22	8561	8571	8580	8590	8600	8609	37
23	8619	8628	8638	8648	8657	8667	36
24	8677	8686	8696	8706	8715	8725	35
25	8734	8744	8754	8763	8773	8783	34
26	8792	8802	8812	8821	8831	8840	33
27	8850	8860	8869	8879	8888	8898	32
28	8908	8917	8927	8937	8946	8956	31
29	8965	8975	8985	8994	9004	9013	30
30	9.959023	9033	9042	9052	9061	9071	29
31	9080	9090	9100	9109	9119	9128	28
32	9138	9148	9157	9167	9176	9186	27
33	9195	9205	9215	9224	9234	9243	26
34	9253	9262	9272	9282	9291	9301	25
35	9310	9320	9329	9339	9348	9358	24
36	9368	9377	9387	9396	9406	9415	23
37	9425	9434	9444	9453	9463	9473	22
38	9482	9492	9501	9511	9520	9530	21
39	9539	9549	9558	9568	9577	9587	20
40	9.959596	9606	9615	9625	9634	9644	19
41	9654	9663	9673	9682	9692	9701	18
42	9711	9720	9730	9739	9749	9758	17
43	9768	9777	9787	9796	9806	9815	16
44	9825	9834	9844	9853	9863	9872	15
45	9882	9891	9900	9910	9919	9929	14
46	9938	9948	9957	9967	9976	9986	13
47	9995	...5	..14	..24	..33	..43	12
48	9.960052	0061	0071	0080	0090	0099	11
49	0109	0118	0128	0137	0147	0156	10
50	9.960165	0175	0184	0194	0203	0213	9
51	0222	0232	0241	0250	0260	0269	8
52	0279	0288	0298	0307	0317	0326	7
53	0335	0345	0354	0364	0373	0382	6
54	0392	0401	0411	0420	0430	0439	5
55	0448	0458	0467	0477	0486	0495	4
56	0505	0514	0524	0533	0542	0552	3
57	0561	0571	0580	0589	0599	0608	2
58	0618	0627	0636	0646	0655	0665	1
59	0674	0683	0693	0702	0711	0721	0
	60″	50″	40″	30″	20″	10″	Min.

Co-sine of 24 Degrees.

P. Part	1″	2″	3″	4″	5″	6″	7″	8″	9″
	1	2	3	4	5	6	7	8	9

Min.	Tangent of 64 Degrees. 0″	10″	20″	30″	40″	50″	
0	10.311818	1872	1925	1979	2032	2085	59
1	2139	2192	2246	2299	2353	2406	58
2	2460	2513	2567	2620	2674	2727	57
3	2781	2834	2888	2941	2995	3048	56
4	3102	3155	3209	3263	3316	3370	55
5	3423	3477	3530	3584	3637	3691	54
6	3745	3798	3852	3905	3959	4013	53
7	4066	4120	4173	4227	4281	4334	52
8	4388	4442	4495	4549	4603	4656	51
9	4710	4764	4817	4871	4925	4978	50
10	10.315032	5086	5139	5193	5247	5300	49
11	5354	5408	5461	5515	5569	5623	48
12	5676	5730	5784	5838	5891	5945	47
13	5999	6053	6106	6160	6214	6268	46
14	6321	6375	6429	6483	6537	6590	45
15	6644	6698	6752	6806	6860	6913	44
16	6967	7021	7075	7129	7183	7236	43
17	7290	7344	7398	7452	7506	7560	42
18	7613	7667	7721	7775	7829	7883	41
19	7937	7991	8045	8099	8153	8206	40
20	10.318260	8314	8368	8422	8476	8530	39
21	8584	8638	8692	8746	8800	8854	38
22	8908	8962	9016	9070	9124	9178	37
23	9232	9286	9340	9394	9448	9502	36
24	9556	9610	9664	9718	9772	9826	35
25	9880	9934	9988	..42	..96	.151	34
26	10.320205	0259	0313	0367	0421	0475	33
27	0529	0583	0637	0692	0746	0800	32
28	0854	0908	0962	1016	1071	1125	31
29	1179	1233	1287	1341	1396	1450	30
30	·o 321504	1558	1612	1666	1721	1775	29
31	1829	1883	1938	1992	2046	2100	28
32	2154	2209	2263	2317	2371	2426	27
33	2480	2534	2588	2643	2697	2751	26
34	2806	2860	2914	2968	3023	3077	25
35	3131	3186	3240	3294	3349	3403	24
36	3457	3512	3566	3620	3675	3729	23
37	3783	3838	3892	3947	4001	4055	22
38	4110	4164	4219	4273	4327	4382	21
39	4436	4491	4545	4599	4654	4708	20
40	10.324763	4817	4872	4926	4981	5035	19
41	5089	5144	5198	5253	5307	5362	18
42	5416	5471	5525	5580	5634	5689	17
43	5743	5798	5852	5907	5962	6016	16
44	6071	6125	6180	6234	6289	6343	15
45	6398	6453	6507	6562	6616	6671	14
46	6726	6780	6835	6889	6944	6999	13
47	7053	7108	7162	7217	7272	7326	12
48	7381	7436	7490	7545	7600	7654	11
49	7709	7764	7818	7873	7928	7982	10
50	10.328037	8092	8147	8201	8256	8311	9
51	8365	8420	8475	8530	8584	8639	8
52	8694	8749	8803	8858	8913	8968	7
53	9023	9077	9132	9187	9242	9297	6
54	9351	9406	9461	9516	9571	9625	5
55	9680	9735	9790	9845	9900	9955	4
56	10.330009	0064	0119	0174	0229	0284	3
57	0339	0394	0448	0503	0558	0613	2
58	0668	0723	0778	0833	0888	0943	1
59	0998	1053	1108	1163	1218	1272	0
	60″	50″	40″	30″	20″	10″	Min.
	Co-tangent of 25 Degrees.						

P. Part { 1″ 2″ 3″ 4″ 5″ 6″ 7″ 8″ 9″ / 5 11 16 22 27 33 38 43 49 }

Min.	Tangent of 65 Degrees. 0″	10″	20″	30″	40″	50″	
0	10.331327	1382	1437	1492	1547	1602	59
1	1657	1712	1767	1822	1877	1932	58
2	1987	2042	2097	2153	2208	2263	57
3	2318	2373	2428	2483	2538	2593	56
4	2648	2703	2758	2813	2868	2924	55
5	2979	3034	3089	3144	3199	3254	54
6	3309	3364	3420	3475	3530	3585	53
7	3640	3695	3751	3806	3861	3916	52
8	3971	4026	4082	4137	4192	4247	51
9	4302	4358	4413	4468	4523	4579	50
10	10.334634	4689	4744	4800	4855	4910	49
11	4965	5021	5076	5131	5186	5242	48
12	5297	5352	5408	5463	5518	5574	47
13	5629	5684	5740	5795	5850	5906	46
14	5961	6016	6072	6127	6182	6238	45
15	6293	6349	6404	6459	6515	6570	44
16	6625	6681	6736	6792	6847	6903	43
17	6958	7013	7069	7124	7180	7235	42
18	7291	7346	7402	7457	7513	7568	41
19	7624	7679	7735	7790	7846	7901	40
20	10.337957	8012	8068	8123	8179	8234	39
21	8290	8345	8401	8456	8512	8568	38
22	8623	8679	8734	8790	8845	8901	37
23	8957	9012	9068	9123	9179	9235	36
24	9290	9346	9402	9457	9513	9569	35
25	9624	9680	9735	9791	9847	9902	34
26	9958	..14	..70	.125	.181	.237	33
27	10.340292	0348	0404	0460	0515	0571	32
28	0627	0682	0738	0794	0850	0905	31
29	0961	1017	1073	1129	1184	1240	30
30	10.341296	1352	1408	1463	1519	1575	29
31	1631	1687	1742	1798	1854	1910	28
32	1966	2022	2078	2133	2189	2245	27
33	2301	2357	2413	2469	2525	2581	26
34	2636	2692	2748	2804	2860	2916	25
35	2972	3028	3084	3140	3196	3252	24
36	3308	3364	3420	3476	3532	3588	23
37	3644	3700	3756	3812	3868	3924	22
38	3980	4036	4092	4148	4204	4260	21
39	4316	4372	4428	4484	4540	4596	20
40	10.344652	4708	4764	4821	4877	4933	19
41	4989	5045	5101	5157	5213	5269	18
42	5326	5382	5438	5494	5550	5606	17
43	5663	5719	5775	5831	5887	5943	16
44	6000	6056	6112	6168	6224	6281	15
45	6337	6393	6449	6506	6562	6618	14
46	6674	6731	6787	6843	6899	6956	13
47	7012	7068	7125	7181	7237	7293	12
48	7350	7406	7462	7519	7575	7631	11
49	7688	7744	7800	7857	7913	7969	10
50	10.348026	8082	8139	8195	8251	8308	9
51	8364	8421	8477	8533	8590	8646	8
52	8703	8759	8815	8872	8928	8985	7
53	9041	9098	9154	9211	9267	9324	6
54	9380	9437	9493	9550	9606	9663	5
55	9719	9776	9832	9889	9945	...2	4
56	10.350058	0115	0171	0228	0285	0341	3
57	0398	0454	0511	0567	0624	0681	2
58	0737	0794	0850	0907	0964	1020	1
59	1077	1134	1190	1247	1304	1360	0
	60″	50″	40″	30″	20″	10″	Min.
	Co-tangent of 24 Degrees.						

P. Part { 1″ 2″ 3″ 4″ 5″ 6″ 7″ 8″ 9″ / 6 11 17 22 28 33 39 45 50 }

Min.	Sine of 66 Degrees. 0″	10″	20″	30″	40″	50″	
0	9.960730	0740	0749	0758	0768	0777	59
1	0786	0796	0805	0814	0824	0833	58
2	0843	0852	0861	0871	0880	0889	57
3	0899	0908	0917	0927	0936	0945	56
4	0955	0964	0973	0983	0992	1002	55
5	1011	1020	1030	1039	1048	1058	54
6	1067	1076	1086	1095	1104	1113	53
7	1123	1132	1141	1151	1160	1169	52
8	1179	1188	1197	1207	1216	1225	51
9	1235	1244	1253	1263	1272	1281	50
10	9.961290	1300	1309	1318	1328	1337	49
11	1346	1356	1365	1374	1383	1393	48
12	1402	1411	1421	1430	1439	1448	47
13	1458	1467	1476	1485	1495	1504	46
14	1513	1523	1532	1541	1550	1560	45
15	1569	1578	1587	1597	1606	1615	44
16	1624	1634	1643	1652	1661	1671	43
17	1680	1689	1698	1708	1717	1726	42
18	1735	1745	1754	1763	1772	1782	41
19	1791	1800	1809	1819	1828	1837	40
20	9.961846	1856	1865	1874	1883	1892	39
21	1902	1911	1920	1929	1939	1948	38
22	1957	1966	1975	1985	1994	2003	37
23	2012	2021	2031	2040	2049	2058	36
24	2067	2077	2086	2095	2104	2113	35
25	2123	2132	2141	2150	2159	2169	34
26	2178	2187	2196	2205	2214	2224	33
27	2233	2242	2251	2260	2269	2279	32
28	2288	2297	2306	2315	2325	2334	31
29	2343	2352	2361	2370	2379	2389	30
30	9.962398	2407	2416	2425	2434	2444	29
31	2453	2462	2471	2480	2489	2498	28
32	2508	2517	2526	2535	2544	2553	27
33	2562	2572	2581	2590	2599	2608	26
34	2617	2626	2635	2645	2654	2663	25
35	2672	2681	2690	2699	2708	2717	24
36	2727	2736	2745	2754	2763	2772	23
37	2781	2790	2799	2809	2818	2827	22
38	2836	2845	2854	2863	2872	2881	21
39	2890	2899	2909	2918	2927	2936	20
40	9.962945	2954	2963	2972	2981	2990	19
41	2999	3008	3018	3027	3036	3045	18
42	3054	3063	3072	3081	3090	3099	17
43	3108	3117	3126	3135	3144	3153	16
44	3163	3172	3181	3190	3199	3208	15
45	3217	3226	3235	3244	3253	3262	14
46	3271	3280	3289	3298	3307	3316	13
47	3325	3334	3343	3352	3361	3370	12
48	3379	3388	3398	3407	3416	3425	11
49	3434	3443	3452	3461	3470	3479	10
50	9.963488	3497	3506	3515	3524	3533	9
51	3542	3551	3560	3569	3578	3587	8
52	3596	3605	3614	3623	3632	3641	7
53	3650	3659	3668	3677	3686	3695	6
54	3704	3713	3722	3730	3739	3748	5
55	3757	3766	3775	3784	3793	3802	4
56	3811	3820	3829	3838	3847	3856	3
57	3865	3874	3883	3892	3901	3910	2
58	3919	3928	3937	3946	3955	3963	1
59	3972	3981	3990	3999	4008	4017	0
	60″	50″	40″	30″	20″	10″	Min.
	Co-sine of 23 Degrees.						

P. Part	1″	2″	3″	4″	5″	6″	7″	8″	9″
	1	2	3	4	5	5	6	7	8

Min.	Sine of 67 Degrees. 0″	10″	20″	30″	40″	50″	
0	9.964026	4035	4044	4053	4062	4071	59
1	4080	4089	4098	4106	4115	4124	58
2	4133	4142	4151	4160	4169	4178	57
3	4187	4196	4205	4214	4222	4231	56
4	4240	4249	4258	4267	4276	4285	55
5	4294	4303	4311	4320	4329	4338	54
6	4347	4356	4365	4374	4383	4392	53
7	4400	4409	4418	4427	4436	4445	52
8	4454	4463	4471	4480	4489	4498	51
9	4507	4516	4525	4534	4542	4551	50
10	9.964560	4569	4578	4587	4596	4604	49
11	4613	4622	4631	4640	4649	4658	48
12	4666	4675	4684	4693	4702	4711	47
13	4720	4728	4737	4746	4755	4764	46
14	4773	4781	4790	4799	4808	4817	45
15	4826	4834	4843	4852	4861	4870	44
16	4879	4887	4896	4905	4914	4923	43
17	4931	4940	4949	4958	4967	4975	42
18	4984	4993	5002	5011	5020	5028	41
19	5037	5046	5055	5064	5072	5081	40
20	9.965090	5099	5107	5116	5125	5134	39
21	5143	5151	5160	5169	5178	5187	38
22	5195	5204	5213	5222	5230	5239	37
23	5248	5257	5266	5274	5283	5292	36
24	5301	5309	5318	5327	5336	5344	35
25	5353	5362	5371	5379	5388	5397	34
26	5406	5414	5423	5432	5441	5449	33
27	5458	5467	5476	5484	5493	5502	32
28	5511	5519	5528	5537	5546	5554	31
29	5563	5572	5580	5589	5598	5607	30
30	9.965615	5624	5633	5642	5650	5659	29
31	5668	5676	5685	5694	5702	5711	28
32	5720	5729	5737	5746	5755	5763	27
33	5772	5781	5790	5798	5807	5816	26
34	5824	5833	5842	5850	5859	5868	25
35	5876	5885	5894	5902	5911	5920	24
36	5929	5937	5946	5955	5963	5972	23
37	5981	5989	5998	6007	6015	6024	22
38	6033	6041	6050	6059	6067	6076	21
39	6085	6093	6102	6111	6119	6128	20
40	9.966136	6145	6154	6162	6171	6180	19
41	6188	6197	6206	6214	6223	6232	18
42	6240	6249	6257	6266	6275	6283	17
43	6292	6301	6309	6318	6326	6335	16
44	6344	6352	6361	6370	6378	6387	15
45	6395	6404	6413	6421	6430	6438	14
46	6447	6456	6464	6473	6482	6490	13
47	6499	6507	6516	6525	6533	6542	12
48	6550	6559	6567	6576	6585	6593	11
49	6602	6610	6619	6628	6636	6645	10
50	9.966653	6662	6670	6679	6688	6696	9
51	6705	6713	6722	6730	6739	6748	8
52	6756	6765	6773	6782	6790	6799	7
53	6808	6816	6825	6833	6842	6850	6
54	6859	6867	6876	6884	6893	6902	5
55	6910	6919	6927	6936	6944	6953	4
56	6961	6970	6978	6987	6995	7004	3
57	7013	7021	7030	7038	7047	7055	2
58	7064	7072	7081	7089	7098	7106	1
59	7115	7123	7132	7140	7149	7157	0
	60″	50″	40″	30″	20″	10″	Min.
	Co-sine of 22 Degrees.						

P. Part	1″	2″	3″	4″	5″	6″	7″	8″	9″
	1	2	3	3	4	5	6	7	8

Min.	Tangent of 66 Degrees. 0″	10″	20″	30″	40″	50″	
0	10.351417	1474	1530	1587	1644	1700	59
1	1757	1814	1870	1927	1984	2040	58
2	2097	2154	2211	2267	2324	2381	57
3	2438	2494	2551	2608	2665	2721	56
4	2778	2835	2892	2949	3005	3062	55
5	3119	3176	3233	3290	3346	3403	54
6	3460	3517	3574	3631	3687	3744	53
7	3801	3858	3915	3972	4029	4086	52
8	4143	4199	4256	4313	4370	4427	51
9	4484	4541	4598	4655	4712	4769	50
10	10.354826	4883	4940	4997	5054	5111	49
11	5168	5225	5282	5339	5396	5453	48
12	5510	5567	5624	5681	5738	5795	47
13	5852	5909	5966	6023	6080	6137	46
14	6194	6251	6309	6366	6423	6480	45
15	6537	6594	6651	6708	6765	6823	44
16	6880	6937	6994	7051	7108	7166	43
17	7223	7280	7337	7394	7451	7509	42
18	7566	7623	7680	7737	7795	7852	41
19	7909	7966	8024	8081	8138	8195	40
20	10.358253	8310	8367	8425	8482	8539	39
21	8596	8654	8711	8768	8826	8883	38
22	8940	8998	9055	9112	9170	9227	37
23	9284	9342	9399	9456	9514	9571	36
24	9629	9686	9743	9801	9858	9916	35
25	9973	..31	..88	.145	.203	.260	34
26	10.360318	0375	0433	0490	0548	0605	33
27	0663	0720	0778	0835	0893	0950	32
28	1008	1065	1123	1180	1238	1295	31
29	1353	1410	1468	1525	1583	1641	30
30	10.361698	1756	1813	1871	1928	1986	29
31	2044	2101	2159	2217	2274	2332	28
32	2389	2447	2505	2562	2620	2678	27
33	2735	2793	2851	2908	2966	3024	26
34	3081	3139	3197	3255	3312	3370	25
35	3428	3486	3543	3601	3659	3717	24
36	3774	3832	3890	3948	4005	4063	23
37	4121	4179	4237	4294	4352	4410	22
38	4468	4526	4584	4641	4699	4757	21
39	4815	4873	4931	4989	5046	5104	20
40	10.365162	5220	5278	5336	5394	5452	19
41	5510	5568	5626	5684	5741	5799	18
42	5857	5915	5973	6031	6089	6147	17
43	6205	6263	6321	6379	6437	6495	16
44	6553	6611	6669	6727	6785	6843	15
45	6901	6960	7018	7076	7134	7192	14
46	7250	7308	7366	7424	7482	7540	13
47	7598	7657	7715	7773	7831	7889	12
48	7947	8005	8064	8122	8180	8238	11
49	8296	8354	8413	8471	8529	8587	10
50	10.368645	8704	8762	8820	8878	8937	9
51	8995	9053	9111	9170	9228	9286	8
52	9344	9403	9461	9519	9578	9636	7
53	9694	9753	9811	9869	9927	9986	6
54	10.370044	0103	0161	0219	0278	0336	5
55	0394	0453	0511	0569	0628	0686	4
56	0745	0803	0862	0920	0978	1037	3
57	1095	1154	1212	1271	1329	1388	2
58	1446	1504	1563	1621	1680	1738	1
59	1797	1855	1914	1972	2031	2090	0
	60″	50″	40″	30″	20″	10″	Min.
	Co-tangent of 23 Degrees.						

P. Part	1″	2″	3″	4″	5″	6″	7″	8″	9″
	6	12	17	23	29	35	40	46	52

Min.	Tangent of 67 Degrees. 0″	10″	20″	30″	40″	50″	
0	10.372148	2207	2265	2324	2382	2441	59
1	2499	2558	2617	2675	2734	2792	58
2	2851	2910	2968	3027	3085	3144	57
3	3203	3261	3320	3379	3437	3496	56
4	3555	3613	3672	3731	3789	3848	55
5	3907	3965	4024	4083	4142	4200	54
6	4259	4318	4377	4435	4494	4553	53
7	4612	4670	4729	4788	4847	4906	52
8	4964	5023	5082	5141	5200	5258	51
9	5317	5376	5435	5494	5553	5612	50
10	10.375670	5729	5788	5847	5906	5965	49
11	6024	6083	6142	6200	6259	6318	48
12	6377	6436	6495	6554	6613	6672	47
13	6731	6790	6849	6908	6967	7026	46
14	7085	7144	7203	7262	7321	7380	45
15	7439	7498	7557	7616	7675	7734	44
16	7793	7853	7912	7971	8030	8089	43
17	8148	8207	8266	8325	8384	8444	42
18	8503	8562	8621	8680	8739	8799	41
19	8858	8917	8976	9035	9094	9154	40
20	10.379213	9272	9331	9390	9450	9509	39
21	9568	9627	9687	9746	9805	9864	38
22	9924	9983	..42	.102	.161	.220	37
23	10.380280	0339	0398	0457	0517	0576	36
24	0636	0695	0754	0814	0873	0932	35
25	0992	1051	1110	1170	1229	1289	34
26	1348	1407	1467	1526	1586	1645	33
27	1705	1764	1824	1883	1943	2002	32
28	2061	2121	2180	2240	2299	2359	31
29	2418	2478	2538	2597	2657	2716	30
30	10.382776	2835	2895	2954	3014	3074	29
31	3133	3193	3252	3312	3372	3431	28
32	3491	3550	3610	3670	3729	3789	27
33	3849	3908	3968	4028	4087	4147	26
34	4207	4266	4326	4386	4445	4505	25
35	4565	4625	4684	4744	4804	4864	24
36	4923	4983	5043	5103	5162	5222	23
37	5282	5342	5402	5461	5521	5581	22
38	5641	5701	5761	5820	5880	5940	21
39	6000	6060	6120	6180	6240	6299	20
40	10.386359	6419	6479	6539	6599	6659	19
41	6719	6779	6839	6899	6959	7019	18
42	7079	7139	7199	7259	7319	7379	17
43	7439	7499	7559	7619	7679	7739	16
44	7799	7859	7919	7979	8039	8099	15
45	8159	8219	8279	8339	8399	8460	14
46	8520	8580	8640	8700	8760	8820	13
47	8880	8941	9001	9061	9121	9181	12
48	9241	9302	9362	9422	9482	9542	11
49	9603	9663	9723	9783	9844	9904	10
50	10.389964	..24	..85	.145	.205	.265	9
51	10.390326	0386	0446	0507	0567	0627	8
52	0688	0748	0808	0869	0929	0989	7
53	1050	1110	1170	1231	1291	1352	6
54	1412	1472	1533	1593	1654	1714	5
55	1775	1835	1895	1956	2016	2077	4
56	2137	2198	2258	2319	2379	2440	3
57	2500	2561	2621	2682	2742	2803	2
58	2863	2924	2985	3045	3106	3166	1
59	3227	3287	3348	3409	3469	3530	0
	60″	50″	40″	30″	20″	10″	Min.
	Co-tangent of 22 Degrees.						

P. Part	1″	2″	3″	4″	5″	6″	7″	8″	9″
	6	12	18	24	30	36	42	48	54

Min.	Sine of 68 Degrees. 0″	10″	20″	30″	40″	50″	
0	9.967166	7174	7183	7191	7200	7208	59
1	7217	7225	7234	7242	7251	7259	58
2	7268	7276	7285	7293	7302	7310	57
3	7319	7327	7336	7344	7353	7361	56
4	7370	7378	7387	7395	7404	7412	55
5	7421	7429	7437	7446	7454	7463	54
6	7471	7480	7488	7497	7505	7514	53
7	7522	7531	7539	7547	7556	7564	52
8	7573	7581	7590	7598	7607	7615	51
9	7624	7632	7640	7649	7657	7666	50
10	9.967674	7683	7691	7699	7708	7716	49
11	7725	7733	7742	7750	7758	7767	48
12	7775	7784	7792	7801	7809	7817	47
13	7826	7834	7843	7851	7859	7868	46
14	7876	7885	7893	7901	7910	7918	45
15	7927	7935	7943	7952	7960	7969	44
16	7977	7985	7994	8002	8011	8019	43
17	8027	8036	8044	8053	8061	8069	42
18	8078	8086	8094	8103	8111	8120	41
19	8128	8136	8145	8153	8161	8170	40
20	9.968178	8187	8195	8203	8212	8220	39
21	8228	8237	8245	8253	8262	8270	38
22	8278	8287	8295	8303	8312	8320	37
23	8329	8337	8345	8354	8362	8370	36
24	8379	8387	8395	8404	8412	8420	35
25	8429	8437	8445	8454	8462	8470	34
26	8479	8487	8495	8503	8512	8520	33
27	8528	8537	8545	8553	8562	8570	32
28	8578	8587	8595	8603	8612	8620	31
29	8628	8636	8645	8653	8661	8670	30
30	9.968678	8686	8694	8703	8711	8719	29
31	8728	8736	8744	8752	8761	8769	28
32	8777	8786	8794	8802	8810	8819	27
33	8827	8835	8844	8852	8860	8868	26
34	8877	8885	8893	8901	8910	8918	25
35	8926	8934	8943	8951	8959	8967	24
36	8976	8984	8992	9000	9009	9017	23
37	9025	9033	9042	9050	9058	9066	22
38	9075	9083	9091	9099	9108	9116	21
39	9124	9132	9141	9149	9157	9165	20
40	9.969173	9182	9190	9198	9206	9215	19
41	9223	9231	9239	9247	9256	9264	18
42	9272	9280	9288	9297	9305	9313	17
43	9321	9329	9338	9346	9354	9362	16
44	9370	9379	9387	9395	9403	9411	15
45	9420	9428	9436	9444	9452	9461	14
46	9469	9477	9485	9493	9501	9510	13
47	9518	9526	9534	9542	9550	9559	12
48	9567	9575	9583	9591	9599	9608	11
49	9616	9624	9632	9640	9648	9657	10
50	9.969665	9673	9681	9689	9697	9705	9
51	9714	9722	9730	9738	9746	9754	8
52	9762	9771	9779	9787	9795	9803	7
53	9811	9819	9828	9836	9844	9852	6
54	9860	9868	9876	9884	9893	9901	5
55	9909	9917	9925	9933	9941	9949	4
56	9957	9966	9974	9982	9990	9998	3
57	9.970006	0014	0022	0030	0038	0047	2
58	0055	0063	0071	0079	0087	0095	1
59	0103	0111	0119	0127	0136	0144	0
	60″	50″	40″	30″	20″	10″	Min.
	Co-sine of 21 Degrees.						

P. Part { 1″ 2″ 3″ 4″ 5″ 6″ 7″ 8″ 9″ / 1 2 2 3 4 5 6 7 7

Min.	Sine of 69 Degrees. 0″	10″	20″	30″	40″	50″	
0	9 970152	0160	0168	0176	0184	0192	59
1	0200	0208	0216	0224	0233	0241	58
2	0249	0257	0265	0273	0281	0289	57
3	0297	0305	0313	0321	0329	0337	56
4	0345	0353	0361	0370	0378	0386	55
5	0394	0402	0410	0418	0426	0434	54
6	0442	0450	0458	0466	0474	0482	53
7	0490	0498	0506	0514	0522	0530	52
8	0538	0546	0554	0562	0570	0578	51
9	0586	0594	0603	0611	0619	0627	50
10	9.970635	0643	0651	0659	0667	0675	49
11	0683	0691	0699	0707	0715	0723	48
12	0731	0739	0747	0755	0763	0771	47
13	0779	0787	0795	0803	0811	0819	46
14	0827	0835	0842	0850	0858	0866	45
15	0874	0882	0890	0898	0906	0914	44
16	0922	0930	0938	0946	0954	0962	43
17	0970	0978	0986	0994	1002	1010	42
18	1018	1026	1034	1042	1050	1058	41
19	1066	1073	1081	1089	1097	1105	40
20	9.971113	1121	1129	1137	1145	1153	39
21	1161	1169	1177	1185	1193	1200	38
22	1208	1216	1224	1232	1240	1248	37
23	1256	1264	1272	1280	1288	1296	36
24	1303	1311	1319	1327	1335	1343	35
25	1351	1359	1367	1375	1383	1390	34
26	1398	1406	1414	1422	1430	1438	33
27	1446	1454	1462	1469	1477	1485	32
28	1493	1501	1509	1517	1525	1532	31
29	1540	1548	1556	1564	1572	1580	30
30	9.971588	1595	1603	1611	1619	1627	29
31	1635	1643	1651	1658	1666	1674	28
32	1682	1690	1698	1706	1713	1721	27
33	1729	1737	1745	1753	1761	1768	26
34	1776	1784	1792	1800	1808	1815	25
35	1823	1831	1839	1847	1855	1862	24
36	1870	1878	1886	1894	1902	1909	23
37	1917	1925	1933	1941	1949	1956	22
38	1964	1972	1980	1988	1995	2003	21
39	2011	2019	2027	2034	2042	2050	20
40	9.972058	2066	2073	2081	2089	2097	19
41	2105	2112	2120	2128	2136	2144	18
42	2151	2159	2167	2175	2183	2190	17
43	2198	2206	2214	2221	2229	2237	16
44	2245	2253	2260	2268	2276	2284	15
45	2291	2299	2307	2315	2322	2330	14
46	2338	2346	2354	2361	2369	2377	13
47	2385	2392	2400	2408	2416	2423	12
48	2431	2439	2447	2454	2462	2470	11
49	2478	2485	2493	2501	2508	2516	10
50	9.972524	2532	2539	2547	2555	2563	9
51	2570	2578	2586	2593	2601	2609	8
52	2617	2624	2632	2640	2648	2655	7
53	2663	2671	2678	2686	2694	2701	6
54	2709	2717	2725	2732	2740	2748	5
55	2755	2763	2771	2778	2786	2794	4
56	2802	2809	2817	2825	2832	2840	3
57	2848	2855	2863	2871	2878	2886	2
58	2894	2901	2909	2917	2924	2932	1
59	2940	2947	2955	2963	2970	2978	0
	60″	50″	40″	30″	20″	10″	Min.
	Co-sine of 20 Degrees.						

P. Part { 1″ 2″ 3″ 4″ 5″ 6″ 7″ 8″ 9″ / 1 2 2 3 4 5 6 6 7

Min.	Tangent of 68 Degrees. 0″	10″	20″	30″	40″	50″	
0	10.393590	3651	3712	3772	3833	3894	59
1	3954	4015	4076	4136	4197	4258	58
2	4318	4379	4440	4500	4561	4622	57
3	4683	4743	4804	4865	4926	4986	56
4	5047	5108	5169	5229	5290	5351	55
5	5412	5473	5533	5594	5655	5716	54
6	5777	5838	5898	5959	6020	6081	53
7	6142	6203	6264	6325	6385	6446	52
8	6507	6568	6629	6690	6751	6812	51
9	6873	6934	6995	7056	7117	7178	50
10	10.397239	7300	7361	7422	7483	7544	49
11	7605	7666	7727	7788	7849	7910	48
12	7971	8032	8093	8154	8215	8276	47
13	8337	8399	8460	8521	8582	8643	46
14	8704	8765	8826	8888	8949	9010	45
15	9071	9132	9194	9255	9316	9377	44
16	9438	9500	9561	9622	9683	9744	43
17	9806	9867	9928	9989	..51	.112	42
18	10.400173	0235	0296	0357	0419	0480	41
19	0541	0602	0664	0725	0787	0848	40
20	10.400909	0971	1032	1093	1155	1216	39
21	1278	1339	1400	1462	1523	1585	38
22	1646	1707	1769	1830	1892	1953	37
23	2015	2076	2138	2199	2261	2322	36
24	2384	2445	2507	2568	2630	2691	35
25	2753	2815	2876	2938	2999	3061	34
26	3122	3184	3246	3307	3369	3430	33
27	3492	3554	3615	3677	3739	3800	32
28	3862	3924	3985	4047	4109	4170	31
29	4232	4294	4356	4417	4479	4541	30
30	10.404602	4664	4726	4788	4850	4911	29
31	4973	5035	5097	5158	5220	5282	28
32	5344	5406	5468	5529	5591	5653	27
33	5715	5777	5839	5901	5962	6024	26
34	6086	6148	6210	6272	6334	6396	25
35	6458	6520	6582	6644	6706	6768	24
36	6829	6891	6953	7015	7077	7139	23
37	7201	7263	7326	7388	7450	7512	22
38	7574	7636	7698	7760	7822	7884	21
39	7946	8008	8070	8132	8195	8257	20
40	10.408319	8381	8443	8505	8567	8630	19
41	8692	8754	8816	8878	8940	9003	18
42	9065	9127	9189	9252	9314	9376	17
43	9438	9501	9563	9625	9687	9750	16
44	9812	9874	9937	9999	..61	.123	15
45	10.410186	0248	0310	0373	0435	0498	14
46	0560	0622	0685	0747	0809	0872	13
47	0934	0997	1059	1122	1184	1246	12
48	1309	1371	1434	1496	1559	1621	11
49	1684	1746	1809	1871	1934	1996	10
50	10.412059	2121	2184	2246	2309	2371	9
51	2434	2497	2559	2622	2684	2747	8
52	2810	2872	2935	2997	3060	3123	7
53	3185	3248	3311	3373	3436	3499	6
54	3561	3624	3687	3749	3812	3875	5
55	3938	4000	4063	4126	4189	4251	4
56	4314	4377	4440	4502	4565	4628	3
57	4691	4754	4817	4879	4942	5005	2
58	5068	5131	5194	5256	5319	5382	1
59	5445	5508	5571	5634	5697	5760	0
	60″	50″	40″	30″	20″	10″	Min.
	Co-tangent of 21 Degrees.						

P. Part { 1″ 2″ 3″ 4″ 5″ 6″ 7″ 8″ 9″ / 6 12 19 25 31 37 43 49 56 }

Min.	Tangent of 69 Degrees. 0″	10″	20″	30″	40″	50″	
0	10.415823	5886	5948	6011	6074	6137	59
1	6200	6263	6326	6389	6452	6515	58
2	6578	6641	6704	6767	6830	6893	57
3	6956	7020	7083	7146	7209	7272	56
4	7335	7398	7461	7524	7587	7650	55
5	7714	7777	7840	7903	7966	8029	54
6	8093	8156	8219	8282	8345	8409	53
7	8472	8535	8598	8661	8725	8788	52
8	8851	8914	8978	9041	9104	9168	51
9	9231	9294	9358	9421	9484	9547	50
10	10.419611	9674	9738	9801	9864	9928	49
11	9991	..54	.118	.181	.245	.308	48
12	10.420371	0435	0498	0562	0625	0689	47
13	0752	0816	0879	0943	1006	1070	46
14	1133	1197	1260	1324	1387	1451	45
15	1514	1578	1641	1705	1769	1832	44
16	1896	1959	2023	2086	2150	2214	43
17	2277	2341	2405	2468	2532	2596	42
18	2659	2723	2787	2850	2914	2978	41
19	3041	3105	3169	3233	3296	3360	40
20	10.423424	3488	3551	3615	3679	3743	39
21	3807	3870	3934	3998	4062	4126	38
22	4190	4253	4317	4381	4445	4509	37
23	4573	4637	4701	4764	4828	4892	36
24	4956	5020	5084	5148	5212	5276	35
25	5340	5404	5468	5532	5596	5660	34
26	5724	5788	5852	5916	5980	6044	33
27	6108	6172	6236	6300	6364	6429	32
28	6493	6557	6621	6685	6749	6813	31
29	6877	6941	7006	7070	7134	7198	30
30	10.427262	7327	7391	7455	7519	7583	29
31	7648	7712	7776	7840	7905	7969	28
32	8033	8097	8162	8226	8290	8355	27
33	8419	8483	8548	8612	8676	8741	26
34	8805	8869	8934	8998	9062	9127	25
35	9191	9256	9320	9384	9449	9513	24
36	9578	9642	9707	9771	9836	9900	23
37	9965	..29	..94	.158	.223	.287	22
38	10.430352	0416	0481	0545	0610	0674	21
39	0739	0803	0868	0933	0997	1062	20
40	10.431127	1191	1256	1320	1385	1450	19
41	1514	1579	1644	1708	1773	1838	18
42	1902	1967	2032	2097	2161	2226	17
43	2291	2356	2420	2485	2550	2615	16
44	2680	2744	2809	2874	2939	3004	15
45	3068	3133	3198	3263	3328	3393	14
46	3458	3522	3587	3652	3717	3782	13
47	3847	3912	3977	4042	4107	4172	12
48	4237	4302	4367	4432	4497	4562	11
49	4627	4692	4757	4822	4887	4952	10
50	10.435017	5082	5147	5212	5277	5342	9
51	5407	5473	5538	5603	5668	5733	8
52	5798	5863	5929	5994	6059	6124	7
53	6189	6254	6320	6385	6450	6515	6
54	6581	6646	6711	6776	6842	6907	5
55	6972	7037	7103	7168	7233	7299	4
56	7364	7429	7495	7560	7625	7691	3
57	7756	7822	7887	7952	8018	8083	2
58	8149	8214	8279	8345	8410	8476	1
59	8541	8607	8672	8738	8803	8869	0
	60″	50″	40″	30″	20″	10″	Min.
	Co-tangent of 20 Degrees.						

P. Part { 1″ 2″ 3″ 4″ 5″ 6″ 7″ 8″ 9″ / 6 13 19 26 32 39 45 51 58 }

Min.	Sine of 70 Degrees. 0″	10″	20″	30″	40″	50″	
0	9·972986	2993	3001	3009	3016	3024	59
1	3032	3039	3047	3055	3062	3070	58
2	3078	3085	3093	3101	3108	3116	57
3	3124	3131	3139	3146	3154	3162	56
4	3169	3177	3185	3192	3200	3208	55
5	3215	3223	3230	3238	3246	3253	54
6	3261	3269	3276	3284	3291	3299	53
7	3307	3314	3322	3330	3337	3345	52
8	3352	3360	3368	3375	3383	3390	51
9	3398	3406	3413	3421	3428	3436	50
10	9·973444	3451	3459	3466	3474	3482	49
11	3489	3497	3504	3512	3519	3527	48
12	3535	3542	3550	3557	3565	3572	47
13	3580	3588	3595	3603	3610	3618	46
14	3625	3633	3641	3648	3656	3663	45
15	3671	3678	3686	3694	3701	3709	44
16	3716	3724	3731	3739	3746	3754	43
17	3761	3769	3777	3784	3792	3799	42
18	3807	3814	3822	3829	3837	3844	41
19	3852	3859	3867	3875	3882	3890	40
20	9·973897	3905	3912	3920	3927	3935	39
21	3942	3950	3957	3965	3972	3980	38
22	3987	3995	4002	4010	4017	4025	37
23	4032	4040	4047	4055	4062	4070	36
24	4077	4085	4092	4100	4107	4115	35
25	4122	4130	4137	4145	4152	4160	34
26	4167	4175	4182	4190	4197	4205	33
27	4212	4220	4227	4235	4242	4250	32
28	4257	4264	4272	4279	4287	4294	31
29	4302	4309	4317	4324	4332	4339	30
30	9·974347	4354	4361	4369	4376	4384	29
31	4391	4399	4406	4414	4421	4428	28
32	4436	4443	4451	4458	4466	4473	27
33	4481	4488	4495	4503	4510	4518	26
34	4525	4533	4540	4547	4555	4562	25
35	4570	4577	4585	4592	4599	4607	24
36	4614	4622	4629	4636	4644	4651	23
37	4659	4666	4674	4681	4688	4696	22
38	4703	4711	4718	4725	4733	4740	21
39	4748	4755	4762	4770	4777	4784	20
40	9·974792	4799	4807	4814	4821	4829	19
41	4836	4844	4851	4858	4866	4873	18
42	4880	4888	4895	4903	4910	4917	17
43	4925	4932	4939	4947	4954	4961	16
44	4969	4976	4984	4991	4998	5006	15
45	5013	5020	5028	5035	5042	5050	14
46	5057	5064	5072	5079	5086	5094	13
47	5101	5108	5116	5123	5130	5138	12
48	5145	5152	5160	5167	5174	5182	11
49	5189	5196	5204	5211	5218	5226	10
50	9·975233	5240	5248	5255	5262	5270	9
51	5277	5284	5292	5299	5306	5313	8
52	5321	5328	5335	5343	5350	5357	7
53	5365	5372	5379	5386	5394	5401	6
54	5408	5416	5423	5430	5437	5445	5
55	5452	5459	5467	5474	5481	5488	4
56	5496	5503	5510	5518	5525	5532	3
57	5539	5547	5554	5561	5568	5576	2
58	5583	5590	5598	5605	5612	5619	1
59	5627	5634	5641	5648	5656	5663	0
	60″	50″	40″	30″	20″	10″	Min.
	Co-sine of 19 Degrees.						

P. Part { 1″ 2″ 3″ 4″ 5″ 6″ 7″ 8″ 9″ / 1 1 2 3 4 4 5 6 7 }

Min.	Sine of 71 Degrees. 0″	10″	20″	30″	40″	50″	
0	9·975670	5677	5685	5692	5699	5706	59
1	5714	5721	5728	5735	5743	5750	58
2	5757	5764	5771	5779	5786	5793	57
3	5800	5808	5815	5822	5829	5837	56
4	5844	5851	5858	5865	5873	5880	55
5	5887	5894	5901	5909	5916	5923	54
6	5930	5938	5945	5952	5959	5966	53
7	5974	5981	5988	5995	6002	6010	52
8	6017	6024	6031	6038	6046	6053	51
9	6060	6067	6074	6081	6089	6096	50
10	9·976103	6110	6117	6125	6132	6139	49
11	6146	6153	6160	6168	6175	6182	48
12	6189	6196	6203	6211	6218	6225	47
13	6232	6239	6246	6254	6261	6268	46
14	6275	6282	6289	6296	6304	6311	45
15	6318	6325	6332	6339	6347	6354	44
16	6361	6368	6375	6382	6389	6396	43
17	6404	6411	6418	6425	6432	6439	42
18	6446	6454	6461	6468	6475	6482	41
19	6489	6496	6503	6510	6518	6525	40
20	9·976532	6539	6546	6553	6560	6567	39
21	6574	6582	6589	6596	6603	6610	38
22	6617	6624	6631	6638	6646	6653	37
23	6660	6667	6674	6681	6688	6695	36
24	6702	6709	6716	6723	6731	6738	35
25	6745	6752	6759	6766	6773	6780	34
26	6787	6794	6801	6808	6815	6823	33
27	6830	6837	6844	6851	6858	6865	32
28	6872	6879	6886	6893	6900	6907	31
29	6914	6921	6928	6935	6942	6950	30
30	9·976957	6964	6971	6978	6985	6992	29
31	6999	7006	7013	7020	7027	7034	28
32	7041	7048	7055	7062	7069	7076	27
33	7083	7090	7097	7104	7111	7118	26
34	7125	7132	7139	7146	7153	7160	25
35	7167	7174	7181	7188	7195	7202	24
36	7209	7216	7223	7230	7237	7244	23
37	7251	7258	7265	7272	7279	7286	22
38	7293	7300	7307	7314	7321	7328	21
39	7335	7342	7349	7356	7363	7370	20
40	9·977377	7384	7391	7398	7405	7412	19
41	7419	7426	7433	7440	7447	7454	18
42	7461	7468	7475	7482	7489	7496	17
43	7503	7510	7517	7524	7530	7537	16
44	7544	7551	7558	7565	7572	7579	15
45	7586	7593	7600	7607	7614	7621	14
46	7628	7635	7642	7648	7655	7662	13
47	7669	7676	7683	7690	7697	7704	12
48	7711	7718	7725	7732	7739	7745	11
49	7752	7759	7766	7773	7780	7787	10
50	9·977794	7801	7808	7815	7821	7828	9
51	7835	7842	7849	7856	7863	7870	8
52	7877	7884	7890	7897	7904	7911	7
53	7918	7925	7932	7939	7946	7952	6
54	7959	7966	7973	7980	7987	7994	5
55	8001	8007	8014	8021	8028	8035	4
56	8042	8049	8056	8062	8069	8076	3
57	8083	8090	8097	8104	8110	8117	2
58	8124	8131	8138	8145	8152	8158	1
59	8165	8172	8179	8186	8193	8199	0
	60″	50″	40″	30″	20″	10″	Min.
	Co-sine of 18 Degrees.						

P. Part { 1″ 2″ 3″ 4″ 5″ 6″ 7″ 8″ 9″ / 1 1 2 3 4 4 5 6 6 }

Tangent of 70 Degrees.

Min.	0″	10″	20″	30″	40″	50″	
0	10.438934	9000	9065	9131	9196	9262	59
1	9327	9393	9458	9524	9590	9655	58
2	9721	9786	9852	9918	9983	..49	57
3	10.440115	0180	0246	0312	0377	0443	56
4	0509	0574	0640	0706	0771	0837	55
5	0903	0969	1034	1100	1166	1232	54
6	1297	1363	1429	1495	1561	1627	53
7	1692	1758	1824	1890	1956	2022	52
8	2087	2153	2219	2285	2351	2417	51
9	2483	2549	2615	2681	2747	2813	50
10	10.442879	2945	3011	3077	3143	3209	49
11	3275	3341	3407	3473	3539	3605	48
12	3671	3737	3803	3869	3935	4001	47
13	4067	4133	4200	4266	4332	4398	46
14	4464	4530	4596	4663	4729	4795	45
15	4861	4927	4994	5060	5126	5192	44
16	5259	5325	5391	5457	5524	5590	43
17	5656	5722	5789	5855	5921	5988	42
18	6054	6120	6187	6253	6320	6386	41
19	6452	6519	6585	6652	6718	6784	40
20	10.446851	6917	6984	7050	7117	7183	39
21	7250	7316	7383	7449	7516	7582	38
22	7649	7715	7782	7848	7915	7981	37
23	8048	8115	8181	8248	8314	8381	36
24	8448	8514	8581	8647	8714	8781	35
25	8847	8914	8981	9048	9114	9181	34
26	9248	9314	9381	9448	9515	9581	33
27	9648	9715	9782	9848	9915	9982	32
28	10.450049	0116	0183	0249	0316	0383	31
29	0450	0517	0584	0651	0717	0784	30
30	10.450851	0918	0985	1052	1119	1186	29
31	1253	1320	1387	1454	1521	1588	28
32	1655	1722	1789	1856	1923	1990	27
33	2057	2124	2191	2258	2325	2392	26
34	2460	2527	2594	2661	2728	2795	25
35	2862	2929	2997	3064	3131	3198	24
36	3265	3333	3400	3467	3534	3602	23
37	3669	3736	3803	3871	3938	4005	22
38	4072	4140	4207	4274	4342	4409	21
39	4476	4544	4611	4678	4746	4813	20
40	10.454881	4948	5015	5083	5150	5218	19
41	5285	5353	5420	5488	5555	5623	18
42	5690	5758	5825	5893	5960	6028	17
43	6095	6163	6230	6298	6365	6433	16
44	6501	6568	6636	6703	6771	6839	15
45	6906	6974	7042	7109	7177	7245	14
46	7312	7380	7448	7515	7583	7651	13
47	7719	7786	7854	7922	7990	8057	12
48	8125	8193	8261	8329	8397	8464	11
49	8532	8600	8668	8736	8804	8872	10
50	10.458939	9007	9075	9143	9211	9279	9
51	9347	9415	9483	9551	9619	9687	8
52	9755	9823	9891	9959	..27	..95	7
53	10.460163	0231	0299	0367	0435	0503	6
54	0571	0639	0707	0776	0844	0912	5
55	0980	1048	1116	1184	1253	1321	4
56	1389	1457	1525	1594	1662	1730	3
57	1798	1867	1935	2003	2071	2140	2
58	2208	2276	2345	2413	2481	2550	1
59	2618	2686	2755	2823	2891	2960	0
	60″	50″	40″	30″	20″	10″	Min.

Co-tangent of 19 Degrees.

P. Part	1″	2″	3″	4″	5″	6″	7″	8″	9″
	7	13	20	27	33	40	47	54	60

Tangent of 71 Degrees.

Min.	0″	10″	20″	30″	40″	50′	
0	10.463028	3097	3165	3233	3302	3370	59
1	3439	3507	3576	3644	3713	3781	58
2	3850	3918	3987	4055	4124	4192	57
3	4261	4329	4398	4466	4535	4604	56
4	4672	4741	4809	4878	4947	5015	55
5	5084	5153	5221	5290	5359	5427	54
6	5496	5565	5633	5702	5771	5840	53
7	5908	5977	6046	6115	6184	6252	52
8	6321	6390	6459	6528	6596	6665	51
9	6734	6803	6872	6941	7010	7079	50
10	10.467147	7216	7285	7354	7423	7492	49
11	7561	7630	7699	7768	7837	7906	48
12	7975	8044	8113	8182	8251	8320	47
13	8389	8458	8527	8597	8666	8735	46
14	8804	8873	8942	9011	9080	9150	45
15	9219	9288	9357	9426	9496	9565	44
16	9634	9703	9772	9842	9911	9980	43
17	10.470049	0119	0188	0257	0327	0396	42
18	0465	0535	0604	0673	0743	0812	41
19	0881	0951	1020	1090	1159	1228	40
20	10.471298	1367	1437	1506	1576	1645	39
21	1715	1784	1854	1923	1993	2062	38
22	2132	2201	2271	2340	2410	2480	37
23	2549	2619	2688	2758	2828	2897	36
24	2967	3037	3106	3176	3246	3315	35
25	3385	3455	3524	3594	3664	3734	34
26	3803	3873	3943	4013	4082	4152	33
27	4222	4292	4362	4432	4501	4571	32
28	4641	4711	4781	4851	4921	4991	31
29	5060	5130	5200	5270	5340	5410	30
30	10.475480	5550	5620	5690	5760	5830	29
31	5900	5970	6040	6110	6180	6250	28
32	6320	6391	6461	6531	6601	6671	27
33	6741	6811	6881	6952	7022	7092	26
34	7162	7232	7302	7373	7443	7513	25
35	7583	7654	7724	7794	7864	7935	24
36	8005	8075	8146	8216	8286	8357	23
37	8427	8497	8568	8638	8708	8779	22
38	8849	8920	8990	9061	9131	9201	21
39	9272	9342	9413	9483	9554	9624	20
40	10.479695	9765	9836	9906	9977	..47	19
41	10.480118	0189	0259	0330	0400	0471	18
42	0542	0612	0683	0754	0824	0895	17
43	0966	1036	1107	1178	1248	1319	16
44	1390	1461	1531	1602	1673	1744	15
45	1814	1885	1956	2027	2098	2169	14
46	2239	2310	2381	2452	2523	2594	13
47	2665	2736	2807	2877	2948	3019	12
48	3090	3161	3232	3303	3374	3445	11
49	3516	3587	3658	3729	3800	3871	10
50	10.483943	4014	4085	4156	4227	4298	9
51	4369	4440	4511	4583	4654	4725	8
52	4796	4867	4938	5010	5081	5152	7
53	5223	5295	5366	5437	5508	5580	6
54	5651	5722	5794	5865	5936	6008	5
55	6079	6150	6222	6293	6364	6436	4
56	6507	6579	6650	6722	6793	6864	3
57	6936	7007	7079	7150	7222	7293	2
58	7365	7436	7508	7580	7651	7723	1
59	7794	7866	7937	8009	8081	8152	0
	60″	50″	40″	30″	20″	10″	Min.

Co-tangent of 18 Degrees.

P. Part	1″	2″	3″	4″	5″	6″	7″	8″	9″
	7	14	21	28	35	42	49	56	63

Min.	Sine of 72 Degrees. 0″	10″	20″	30″	40″	50″	
0	9.978206	8213	8220	8227	8234	8241	59
1	8247	8254	8261	8268	8275	8282	58
2	8288	8295	8302	8309	8316	8322	57
3	8329	8336	8343	8350	8357	8363	56
4	8370	8377	8384	8391	8397	8404	55
5	8411	8418	8425	8431	8438	8445	54
6	8452	8459	8465	8472	8479	8486	53
7	8493	8499	8506	8513	8520	8527	52
8	8533	8540	8547	8554	8561	8567	51
9	8574	8581	8588	8594	8601	8608	50
10	9.978615	8622	8628	8635	8642	8649	49
11	8655	8662	8669	8676	8682	8689	48
12	8696	8703	8709	8716	8723	8730	47
13	8737	8743	8750	8757	8764	8770	46
14	8777	8784	8791	8797	8804	8811	45
15	8817	8824	8831	8838	8844	8851	44
16	8858	8865	8871	8878	8885	8892	43
17	8898	8905	8912	8918	8925	8932	42
18	8939	8945	8952	8959	8965	8972	41
19	8979	8986	8992	8999	9006	9012	40
20	9.979019	9026	9033	9039	9046	9053	39
21	9059	9066	9073	9079	9086	9093	38
22	9100	9106	9113	9120	9126	9133	37
23	9140	9146	9153	9160	9166	9173	36
24	9180	9186	9193	9200	9206	9213	35
25	9220	9227	9233	9240	9247	9253	34
26	9260	9267	9273	9280	9287	9293	33
27	9300	9306	9313	9320	9326	9333	32
28	9340	9346	9353	9360	9366	9373	31
29	9380	9386	9393	9400	9406	9413	30
30	9.979420	9426	9433	9439	9446	9453	29
31	9459	9466	9473	9479	9486	9492	28
32	9499	9506	9512	9519	9526	9532	27
33	9539	9545	9552	9559	9565	9572	26
34	9579	9585	9592	9598	9605	9612	25
35	9618	9625	9631	9638	9645	9651	24
36	9658	9664	9671	9678	9684	9691	23
37	9697	9704	9711	9717	9724	9730	22
38	9737	9743	9750	9757	9763	9770	21
39	9776	9783	9790	9796	9803	9809	20
40	9.979816	9822	9829	9836	9842	9849	19
41	9855	9862	9868	9875	9881	9888	18
42	9895	9901	9908	9914	9921	9927	17
43	9934	9940	9947	9954	9960	9967	16
44	9973	9980	9986	9993	9999	...6	15
45	9.980012	0019	0026	0032	0039	0045	14
46	0052	0058	0065	0071	0078	0084	13
47	0091	0097	0104	0110	0117	0123	12
48	0130	0136	0143	0149	0156	0163	11
49	0169	0176	0182	0189	0195	0202	10
50	9.980208	0215	0221	0228	0234	0241	9
51	0247	0254	0260	0267	0273	0280	8
52	0286	0293	0299	0306	0312	0318	7
53	0325	0331	0338	0344	0351	0357	6
54	0364	0370	0377	0383	0390	0396	5
55	0403	0409	0416	0422	0429	0435	4
56	0442	0448	0454	0461	0467	0474	3
57	0480	0487	0493	0500	0506	0513	2
58	0519	0525	0532	0538	0545	0551	1
59	0558	0564	0571	0577	0583	0590	0
	60″	50″	40″	30″	20″	10″	Min.
	Co-sine of 17 Degrees.						

P. Part { 1″ 2″ 3″ 4″ 5″ 6″ 7″ 8″ 9″ / 1 1 2 3 3 4 5 5 6 }

Min.	Sine of 73 Degrees. 0″	10″	20″	30″	40″	50″	
0	9.980596	0603	0609	0616	0622	0628	59
1	0635	0641	0648	0654	0661	0667	58
2	0673	0680	0686	0693	0699	0706	57
3	0712	0718	0725	0731	0738	0744	56
4	0750	0757	0763	0770	0776	0783	55
5	0789	0795	0802	0808	0815	0821	54
6	0827	0834	0840	0847	0853	0859	53
7	0866	0872	0878	0885	0891	0898	52
8	0904	0910	0917	0923	0930	0936	51
9	0942	0949	0955	0961	0968	0974	50
10	9.980981	0987	0993	1000	1006	1012	49
11	1019	1025	1031	1038	1044	1051	48
12	1057	1063	1070	1076	1082	1089	47
13	1095	1101	1108	1114	1120	1127	46
14	1133	1139	1146	1152	1158	1165	45
15	1171	1177	1184	1190	1196	1203	44
16	1209	1215	1222	1228	1234	1241	43
17	1247	1253	1260	1266	1272	1279	42
18	1285	1291	1298	1304	1310	1317	41
19	1323	1329	1336	1342	1348	1354	40
20	9.981361	1367	1373	1380	1386	1392	39
21	1399	1405	1411	1417	1424	1430	38
22	1436	1443	1449	1455	1461	1468	37
23	1474	1480	1487	1493	1499	1505	36
24	1512	1518	1524	1531	1537	1543	35
25	1549	1556	1562	1568	1574	1581	34
26	1587	1593	1599	1606	1612	1618	33
27	1625	1631	1637	1643	1650	1656	32
28	1662	1668	1675	1681	1687	1693	31
29	1700	1706	1712	1718	1724	1731	30
30	9 981737	1743	1749	1756	1762	1768	29
31	1774	1781	1787	1793	1799	1806	28
32	1812	1818	1824	1830	1837	1843	27
33	1849	1855	1861	1868	1874	1880	26
34	1886	1893	1899	1905	1911	1917	25
35	1924	1930	1936	1942	1948	1955	24
36	1961	1967	1973	1979	1986	1992	23
37	1998	2004	2010	2016	2023	2029	22
38	2035	2041	2047	2054	2060	2066	21
39	2072	2078	2084	2091	2097	2103	20
40	9.982109	2115	2122	2128	2134	2140	19
41	2146	2152	2159	2165	2171	2177	18
42	2183	2189	2195	2202	2208	2214	17
43	2220	2226	2232	2239	2245	2251	16
44	2257	2263	2269	2275	2282	2288	15
45	2294	2300	2306	2312	2318	2324	14
46	2331	2337	2343	2349	2355	2361	13
47	2367	2373	2380	2386	2392	2398	12
48	2404	2410	2416	2422	2429	2435	11
49	2441	2447	2453	2459	2465	2471	10
50	9.982477	2484	2490	2496	2502	2508	9
51	2514	2520	2526	2532	2538	2544	8
52	2551	2557	2563	2569	2575	2581	7
53	2587	2593	2599	2605	2611	2617	6
54	2624	2630	2636	2642	2648	2654	5
55	2660	2666	2672	2678	2684	2690	4
56	2696	2702	2709	2715	2721	2727	3
57	2733	2739	2745	2751	2757	2763	2
58	2769	2775	2781	2787	2793	2799	1
59	2805	2811	2817	2824	2830	2836	0
	60″	50″	40″	30″	20″	10″	Min.
	Co-sine of 16 Degrees.						

P. Part { 1″ 2″ 3″ 4″ 5″ 6″ 7″ 8″ 9″ / 1 1 2 2 3 4 4 5 6 }

Min.	Tangent of 72 Degrees.						
	0″	10″	20″	30″	40″	50″	
0	10.488224	8296	8367	8439	8511	8582	59
1	8654	8726	8797	8869	8941	9013	58
2	9084	9156	9228	9300	9371	9443	57
3	9515	9587	9659	9731	9802	9874	56
4	9946	..18	..90	.162	.234	.306	55
5	10.490378	0449	0521	0593	0665	0737	54
6	0809	0881	0953	1025	1097	1169	53
7	1241	1313	1386	1458	1530	1602	52
8	1674	1746	1818	1890	1962	2035	51
9	2107	2179	2251	2323	2395	2468	50
10	10.492540	2612	2684	2757	2829	2901	49
11	2973	3046	3118	3190	3263	3335	48
12	3407	3480	3552	3624	3697	3769	47
13	3841	3914	3986	4059	4131	4204	46
14	4276	4348	4421	4493	4566	4638	45
15	4711	4783	4856	4928	5001	5074	44
16	5146	5219	5291	5364	5437	5509	43
17	5582	5654	5727	5800	5872	5945	42
18	6018	6090	6163	6236	6309	6381	41
19	6454	6527	6600	6672	6745	6818	40
20	10.496891	6964	7036	7109	7182	7255	39
21	7328	7401	7474	7547	7619	6792	38
22	7765	7838	7911	7984	8057	8130	37
23	8203	8276	8349	8422	8495	8568	36
24	8641	8714	8787	8860	8934	9007	35
25	9080	9153	9226	9299	9372	9445	34
26	9519	9592	9665	9738	9811	9885	33
27	9958	..31	.104	.178	.251	.324	32
28	10.500397	0471	0544	0617	0691	0764	31
29	0837	0911	0984	1057	1131	1204	30
30	10.501278	1351	1425	1498	1571	1645	29
31	1718	1792	1865	1939	2012	2086	28
32	2159	2233	2307	2380	2454	2527	27
33	2601	2674	2748	2822	2895	2969	26
34	3043	3116	3190	3264	3337	3411	25
35	3485	3559	3632	3706	3780	3854	24
36	3927	4001	4075	4149	4223	4296	23
37	4370	4444	4518	4592	4666	4740	22
38	4814	4887	4961	5035	5109	5183	21
39	5257	5331	5405	5479	5553	5627	20
40	10.505701	5775	5849	5923	5997	6071	19
41	6146	6220	6294	6368	6442	6516	18
42	6590	6664	6739	6813	6887	6961	17
43	7035	7110	7184	7258	7332	7407	16
44	7481	7555	7630	7704	7778	7853	15
45	7927	8001	8076	8150	8224	8299	14
46	8373	8448	8522	8596	8671	8745	13
47	8820	8894	8969	9043	9118	9192	12
48	9267	9341	9416	9490	9565	9640	11
49	9714	9789	9863	9938	..13	..87	10
50	10.510162	0237	0311	0386	0461	0535	9
51	0610	0685	0760	0834	0909	0984	8
52	1059	1134	1208	1283	1358	1433	7
53	1508	1582	1657	1732	1807	1882	6
54	1957	2032	2107	2182	2257	2332	5
55	2407	2482	2557	2632	2707	2782	4
56	2857	2932	3007	3082	3157	3232	3
57	3307	3382	3457	3533	3608	3683	2
58	3758	3833	3908	3984	4059	4134	1
59	4209	4285	4360	4435	4510	4586	0
	60″	50″	40″	30″	20″	10″	Min.
	Co-tangent of 17 Degrees.						

P. Part { 1″ 2″ 3″ 4″ 5″ 6″ 7″ 8″ 9″
{ 7 15 22 29 37 44 51 59 66

Min.	Tangent of 73 Degrees.						
	0″	10″	20″	30″	40″	50″	
0	10.514661	4736	4812	4887	4962	5038	59
1	5113	5188	5264	5339	5415	5490	58
2	5565	5641	5716	5792	5867	5943	57
3	6018	6094	6169	6245	6320	6396	56
4	6471	6547	6623	6698	6774	6849	55
5	6925	7001	7076	7152	7228	7303	54
6	7379	7455	7530	7606	7682	7758	53
7	7833	7909	7985	8061	8137	8212	52
8	8288	8364	8440	8516	8592	8667	51
9	8743	8819	8895	8971	9047	9123	50
10	10.519199	9275	9351	9427	9503	9579	49
11	9655	9731	9807	9883	9959	..35	48
12	10.520111	0187	0263	0340	0416	0492	47
13	0568	0644	0720	0797	0873	0949	46
14	1025	1101	1178	1254	1330	1407	45
15	1483	1559	1635	1712	1788	1864	44
16	1941	2017	2094	2170	2246	2323	43
17	2399	2476	2552	2628	2705	2781	42
18	2858	2934	3011	3087	3164	3241	41
19	3317	3394	3470	3547	3623	3700	40
20	10.523777	3853	3930	4007	4083	4160	39
21	4237	4313	4390	4467	4544	4620	38
22	4697	4774	4851	4927	5004	5081	37
23	5158	5235	5312	5388	5465	5542	36
24	5619	5696	5773	5850	5927	6004	35
25	6081	6158	6235	6312	6389	6466	34
26	6543	6620	6697	6774	6851	6928	33
27	7005	7082	7160	7237	7314	7391	32
28	7468	7545	7623	7700	7777	7854	31
29	7931	8009	8086	8163	8241	8318	30
30	10.528395	8472	8550	8627	8705	8782	29
31	8859	8937	9014	9091	9169	9246	28
32	9324	9401	9479	9556	9634	9711	27
33	9789	9866	9944	..21	..99	.177	26
34	10.530254	0332	0409	0487	0565	0642	25
35	0720	0798	0875	0953	1031	1108	24
36	1186	1264	1342	1419	1497	1575	23
37	1653	1731	1808	1886	1964	2042	22
38	2120	2198	2276	2353	2431	2509	21
39	2587	2665	2743	2821	2899	2977	20
40	10.533055	3133	3211	3289	3367	3445	19
41	3523	3602	3680	3758	3836	3914	18
42	3992	4070	4149	4227	4305	4383	17
43	4461	4540	4618	4696	4774	4853	16
44	4931	5009	5088	5166	5244	5323	15
45	5401	5479	5558	5636	5715	5793	14
46	5872	5950	6028	6107	6185	6264	13
47	6342	6421	6499	6578	6657	6735	12
48	6814	6892	6971	7050	7128	7207	11
49	7285	7364	7443	7522	7600	7679	10
50	10.537758	7836	7915	7994	8073	8151	9
51	8230	8309	8388	8467	8546	8624	8
52	8703	8782	8861	8940	9019	9098	7
53	9177	9256	9335	9414	9493	9572	6
54	9651	9730	9809	9888	9967	..46	5
55	10.540125	0204	0283	0362	0442	0521	4
56	0600	0679	0758	0837	0917	0996	3
57	1075	1154	1234	1313	1392	1472	2
58	1551	1630	1710	1789	1868	1948	1
59	2027	2106	2186	2265	2345	2424	0
	60″	50″	40″	30″	20″	10″	Min.
	Co-tangent of 16 Degrees.						

P. Part { 1″ 2″ 3″ 4″ 5″ 6″ 7″ 8″ 9″
{ 8 15 23 31 39 46 54 62 70

Min.	Sine of 74 Degrees. 0″	10″	20″	30″	40″	50″	
0	9.982842	2848	2854	2860	2866	2872	59
1	2878	2884	2890	2896	2902	2908	58
2	2914	2920	2926	2932	2938	2944	57
3	2950	2956	2962	2968	2974	2980	56
4	2986	2992	2998	3004	3010	3016	55
5	3022	3028	3034	3040	3046	3052	54
6	3058	3064	3070	3076	3082	3088	53
7	3094	3100	3106	3112	3118	3124	52
8	3130	3136	3142	3148	3154	3160	51
9	3166	3172	3178	3184	3190	3196	50
10	9.983202	3208	3214	3220	3226	3232	49
11	3238	3244	3250	3256	3262	3268	48
12	3273	3279	3285	3291	3297	3303	47
13	3309	3315	3321	3327	3333	3339	46
14	3345	3351	3357	3363	3369	3375	45
15	3381	3386	3392	3398	3404	3410	44
16	3416	3422	3428	3434	3440	3446	43
17	3452	3458	3464	3469	3475	3481	42
18	3487	3493	3499	3505	3511	3517	41
19	3523	3529	3535	3540	3546	3552	40
20	9.983558	3564	3570	3576	3582	3588	39
21	3594	3599	3605	3611	3617	3623	38
22	3629	3635	3641	3647	3653	3658	37
23	3664	3670	3676	3682	3688	3694	36
24	3700	3705	3711	3717	3723	3729	35
25	3735	3741	3747	3752	3758	3764	34
26	3770	3776	3782	3788	3794	3799	33
27	3805	3811	3817	3823	3829	3835	32
28	3840	3846	3852	3858	3864	3870	31
29	3875	3881	3887	3893	3899	3905	30
30	9.983911	3916	3922	3928	3934	3940	29
31	3946	3951	3957	3963	3969	3975	28
32	3981	3986	3992	3998	4004	4010	27
33	4015	4021	4027	4033	4039	4045	26
34	4050	4056	4062	4068	4074	4079	25
35	4085	4091	4097	4103	4108	4114	24
36	4120	4126	4132	4137	4143	4149	23
37	4155	4161	4166	4172	4178	4184	22
38	4190	4195	4201	4207	4213	4218	21
39	4224	4230	4236	4242	4247	4253	20
40	9.984259	4265	4270	4276	4282	4288	19
41	4294	4299	4305	4311	4317	4322	18
42	4328	4334	4340	4345	4351	4357	17
43	4363	4368	4374	4380	4386	4391	16
44	4397	4403	4409	4414	4420	4426	15
45	4432	4437	4443	4449	4455	4460	14
46	4466	4472	4477	4483	4489	4495	13
47	4500	4506	4512	4518	4523	4529	12
48	4535	4540	4546	4552	4558	4563	11
49	4569	4575	4580	4586	4592	4598	10
50	9.984603	4609	4615	4620	4626	4632	9
51	4638	4643	4649	4655	4660	4666	8
52	4672	4677	4683	4689	4694	4700	7
53	4706	4712	4717	4723	4729	4734	6
54	4740	4746	4751	4757	4763	4768	5
55	4774	4780	4785	4791	4797	4802	4
56	4808	4814	4819	4825	4831	4836	3
57	4842	4848	4853	4859	4865	4870	2
58	4876	4882	4887	4893	4899	4904	1
59	4910	4916	4921	4927	4932	4938	0
	60″	50″	40″	30″	20″	10″	Min.
	Co-sine of 15 Degrees.						

P. Part { 1″ 2″ 3″ 4″ 5″ 6″ 7″ 8″ 9″ / 1 1 2 2 3 3 4 5 5 }

Min.	Sine of 75 Degrees. 0″	10″	20″	30″	40″	50″	
0	9.984944	4949	4955	4961	4966	4972	59
1	4978	4983	4989	4995	5000	5006	58
2	5011	5017	5023	5028	5034	5040	57
3	5045	5051	5056	5062	5068	5073	56
4	5079	5084	5090	5096	5101	5107	55
5	5113	5118	5124	5129	5135	5141	54
6	5146	5152	5157	5163	5169	5174	53
7	5180	5185	5191	5197	5202	5208	52
8	5213	5219	5224	5230	5236	5241	51
9	5247	5252	5258	5264	5269	5275	50
10	9.985280	5286	5291	5297	5303	5308	49
11	5314	5319	5325	5330	5336	5342	48
12	5347	5353	5358	5364	5369	5375	47
13	5381	5386	5392	5397	5403	5408	46
14	5414	5419	5425	5430	5436	5442	45
15	5447	5453	5458	5464	5469	5475	44
16	5480	5486	5491	5497	5502	5508	43
17	5514	5519	5525	5530	5536	5541	42
18	5547	5552	5558	5563	5569	5574	41
19	5580	5585	5591	5596	5602	5607	40
20	9.985613	5618	5624	5629	5635	5640	39
21	5646	5651	5657	5662	5668	5673	38
22	5679	5684	5690	5695	5701	5706	37
23	5712	5717	5723	5728	5734	5739	36
24	5745	5750	5756	5761	5767	5772	35
25	5778	5783	5789	5794	5800	5805	34
26	5811	5816	5822	5827	5832	5838	33
27	5843	5849	5854	5860	5865	5871	32
28	5876	5882	5887	5893	5898	5903	31
29	5909	5914	5920	5925	5931	5936	30
30	9.985942	5947	5952	5958	5963	5969	29
31	5974	5980	5985	5991	5996	6001	28
32	6007	6012	6018	6023	6029	6034	27
33	6039	6045	6050	6056	6061	6067	26
34	6072	6077	6083	6088	6094	6099	25
35	6104	6110	6115	6121	6126	6132	24
36	6137	6142	6148	6153	6159	6164	23
37	6169	6175	6180	6186	6191	6196	22
38	6202	6207	6212	6218	6223	6229	21
39	6234	6239	6245	6250	6256	6261	20
40	9.986266	6272	6277	6282	6288	6293	19
41	6299	6304	6309	6315	6320	6325	18
42	6331	6336	6342	6347	6352	6358	17
43	6363	6368	6374	6379	6384	6390	16
44	6395	6401	6406	6411	6417	6422	15
45	6427	6433	6438	6443	6449	6454	14
46	6459	6465	6470	6475	6481	6486	13
47	6491	6497	6502	6507	6513	6518	12
48	6523	6529	6534	6539	6545	6550	11
49	6555	6561	6566	6571	6577	6582	10
50	9.986587	6593	6598	6603	6608	6614	9
51	6619	6624	6630	6635	6640	6646	8
52	6651	6656	6661	6667	6672	6677	7
53	6683	6688	6693	6699	6704	6709	6
54	6714	6720	6725	6730	6736	6741	5
55	6746	6751	6757	6762	6767	6773	4
56	6778	6783	6788	6794	6799	6804	3
57	6809	6815	6820	6825	6831	6836	2
58	6841	6846	6852	6857	6862	6867	1
59	6873	6878	6883	6888	6894	6899	0
	60″	50″	40″	30″	20″	10″	Min.
	Co-sine of 14 Degrees.						

P. Part { 1″ 2″ 3″ 4″ 5″ 6″ 7″ 8″ 9″ / 1 1 2 2 3 3 4 4 5 }

Min.	Tangent of 74 Degrees.						
	0″	10″	20″	30″	40″	50″	
0	10.542504	2583	2663	2742	2822	2901	59
1	2981	3060	3140	3219	3299	3378	58
2	3458	3538	3617	3697	3777	3856	57
3	3936	4016	4095	4175	4255	4335	56
4	4414	4494	4574	4654	4733	4813	55
5	4893	4973	5053	5133	5213	5292	54
6	5372	5452	5532	5612	5692	5772	53
7	5852	5932	6012	6092	6172	6252	52
8	6332	6412	6492	6572	6653	6733	51
9	6813	6893	6973	7053	7133	7214	50
10	10.547294	7374	7454	7535	7615	7695	49
11	7775	7856	7936	8016	8097	8177	48
12	8257	8338	8418	8498	8579	8659	47
13	8740	8820	8901	8981	9062	9142	46
14	9223	9303	9384	9464	9545	9625	45
15	9706	9787	9867	9948	..28	.109	44
16	10.550190	0270	0351	0432	0513	0593	43
17	0674	0755	0836	0916	0997	1078	42
18	1159	1240	1320	1401	1482	1563	41
19	1644	1725	1806	1887	1968	2049	40
20	10.552130	2211	2292	2373	2454	2535	39
21	2616	2697	2778	2859	2940	3021	38
22	3102	3183	3265	3346	3427	3508	37
23	3589	3670	3752	3833	3914	3995	36
24	4077	4158	4239	4321	4402	4483	35
25	4565	4646	4728	4809	4890	4972	34
26	5053	5135	5216	5298	5379	5461	33
27	5542	5624	5705	5787	5868	5950	32
28	6032	6113	6195	6276	6358	6440	31
29	6521	6603	6685	6766	6848	6930	30
30	10.557012	7093	7175	7257	7339	7421	29
31	7503	7584	7666	7748	7830	7912	28
32	7994	8076	8158	8240	8322	8404	27
33	8486	8568	8650	8732	8814	8896	26
34	8978	9060	9142	9224	9306	9388	25
35	9471	9553	9635	9717	9799	9881	24
36	9964	..46	.128	.210	.293	.375	23
37	10.560457	0540	0622	0704	0787	0869	22
38	0952	1034	1116	1199	1281	1364	21
39	1446	1529	1611	1694	1776	1859	20
40	10.561941	2024	2106	2189	2272	2354	19
41	2437	2520	2602	2685	2768	2850	18
42	2933	3016	3099	3181	3264	3347	17
43	3430	3512	3595	3678	3761	3844	16
44	3927	4010	4093	4175	4258	4341	15
45	4424	4507	4590	4673	4756	4839	14
46	4922	5005	5088	5172	5255	5338	13
47	5421	5504	5587	5670	5754	5837	12
48	5920	6003	6086	6170	6253	6336	11
49	6420	6503	6586	6669	6753	6836	10
50	10.566920	7003	7086	7170	7253	7337	9
51	7420	7504	7587	7671	7754	7838	8
52	7921	8005	8088	8172	8255	8339	7
53	8423	8506	8590	8674	8757	8841	6
54	8925	9008	9092	9176	9260	9343	5
55	9427	9511	9595	9679	9763	9846	4
56	9930	..14	..98	.182	.266	.350	3
57	10.570434	0518	0602	0686	0770	0854	2
58	0938	1022	1106	1190	1274	1358	1
59	1442	1527	1611	1695	1779	1863	0
	60″	50″	40″	30″	20″	10″	Min.
	Co-tangent of 15 Degrees.						

P. Part { 1″ 2″ 3″ 4″ 5″ 6″ 7″ 8″ 9″ / 8 16 25 33 41 49 57 65 74 }

Min.	Tangent of 75 Degrees.						
	0″	10″	20″	30″	40″	50″	
0	10.571948	2032	2116	2200	2285	2369	59
1	2453	2537	2622	2706	2790	2875	58
2	2959	3044	3128	3212	3297	3381	57
3	3466	3550	3635	3719	3804	3888	56
4	3973	4058	4142	4227	4311	4396	55
5	4481	4565	4650	4735	4819	4904	54
6	4989	5073	5158	5243	5328	5413	53
7	5497	5582	5667	5752	5837	5922	52
8	6007	6091	6176	6261	6346	6431	51
9	6516	6601	6686	6771	6856	6941	50
10	10.577026	7112	7197	7282	7367	7452	49
11	7537	7622	7708	7793	7878	7963	48
12	8048	8134	8219	8304	8390	8475	47
13	8560	8646	8731	8816	8902	8987	46
14	9073	9158	9243	9329	9414	9500	45
15	9585	9671	9756	9842	9928	..13	44
16	10.580099	0184	0270	0356	0441	0527	43
17	0613	0698	0784	0870	0956	1041	42
18	1127	1213	1299	1384	1470	1556	41
19	1642	1728	1814	1900	1986	2072	40
20	10.582158	2243	2329	2415	2501	2587	39
21	2674	2760	2846	2932	3018	3104	38
22	3190	3276	3362	3449	3535	3621	37
23	3707	3793	3880	3966	4052	4138	36
24	4225	4311	4397	4484	4570	4657	35
25	4743	4829	4916	5002	5089	5175	34
26	5262	5348	5435	5521	5608	5694	33
27	5781	5868	5954	6041	6127	6214	32
28	6301	6387	6474	6561	6648	6734	31
29	6821	6908	6995	7081	7168	7255	30
30	10.587342	7429	7516	7603	7690	7776	29
31	7863	7950	8037	8124	8211	8298	28
32	8385	8472	8559	8647	8734	8821	27
33	8908	8995	9082	9169	9257	9344	26
34	9431	9518	9605	9693	9780	9867	25
35	9955	..42	.129	.217	.304	.391	24
36	10.590479	0566	0654	0741	0829	0916	23
37	1004	1091	1179	1266	1354	1441	22
38	1529	1616	1704	1792	1879	1967	21
39	2055	2142	2230	2318	2406	2493	20
40	10.592581	2669	2757	2845	2932	3020	19
41	3108	3196	3284	3372	3460	3548	18
42	3636	3724	3812	3900	3988	4076	17
43	4164	4252	4340	4428	4516	4604	16
44	4692	4781	4869	4957	5045	5133	15
45	5222	5310	5398	5486	5575	5663	14
46	5751	5840	5928	6017	6105	6193	13
47	6282	6370	6459	6547	6636	6724	12
48	6813	6901	6990	7078	7167	7256	11
49	7344	7433	7522	7610	7699	7788	10
50	10.597876	7965	8054	8143	8231	8320	9
51	8409	8498	8587	8675	8764	8853	8
52	8942	9031	9120	9209	9298	9387	7
53	9476	9565	9654	9743	9832	9921	6
54	10.600010	0100	0189	0278	0367	0456	5
55	0545	0635	0724	0813	0902	0992	4
56	1081	1170	1260	1349	1438	1528	3
57	1617	1706	1796	1885	1975	2064	2
58	2154	2243	2333	2422	2512	2601	1
59	2691	2781	2870	2960	3050	3139	0
	60″	50″	40″	30″	20″	10″	Min.
	Co-tangent of 14 Degrees.						

P. Part { 1″ 2″ 3″ 4″ 5″ 6″ 7″ 8″ 9″ / 9 17 26 35 43 52 61 69 78 }

Min.	Sine of 76 Degrees. 0″	10″	20″	30″	40″	50″	
0	9.986904	6909	6915	6920	6925	6930	59
1	6936	6941	6946	6951	6957	6962	58
2	6967	6972	6978	6983	6988	6993	57
3	6998	7004	7009	7014	7019	7025	56
4	7030	7035	7040	7045	7051	7056	55
5	7061	7066	7072	7077	7082	7087	54
6	7092	7098	7103	7108	7113	7118	53
7	7124	7129	7134	7139	7144	7150	52
8	7155	7160	7165	7170	7176	7181	51
9	7186	7191	7196	7202	7207	7212	50
10	9.987217	7222	7228	7233	7238	7243	49
11	7248	7253	7259	7264	7269	7274	48
12	7279	7284	7290	7295	7300	7305	47
13	7310	7315	7321	7326	7331	7336	46
14	7341	7346	7352	7357	7362	7367	45
15	7372	7377	7383	7388	7393	7398	44
16	7403	7408	7413	7419	7424	7429	43
17	7434	7439	7444	7449	7454	7460	42
18	7465	7470	7475	7480	7485	7490	41
19	7496	7501	7506	7511	7516	7521	40
20	9.987526	7531	7537	7542	7547	7552	39
21	7557	7562	7567	7572	7577	7583	38
22	7588	7593	7598	7603	7608	7613	37
23	7618	7623	7628	7634	7639	7644	36
24	7649	7654	7659	7664	7669	7674	35
25	7679	7684	7690	7695	7700	7705	34
26	7710	7715	7720	7725	7730	7735	33
27	7740	7745	7750	7756	7761	7766	32
28	7771	7776	7781	7786	7791	7796	31
29	7801	7806	7811	7816	7821	7826	30
30	9.987832	7837	7842	7847	7852	7857	29
31	7862	7867	7872	7877	7882	7887	28
32	7892	7897	7902	7907	7912	7917	27
33	7922	7927	7932	7937	7942	7947	26
34	7953	7958	7963	7968	7973	7978	25
35	7983	7988	7993	7998	8003	8008	24
36	8013	8018	8023	8028	8033	8038	23
37	8043	8048	8053	8058	8063	8068	22
38	8073	8078	8083	8088	8093	8098	21
39	8103	8108	8113	8118	8123	8128	20
40	9.988133	8138	8143	8148	8153	8158	19
41	8163	8168	8173	8178	8183	8188	18
42	8193	8198	8203	8208	8213	8218	17
43	8223	8227	8232	8237	8242	8247	16
44	8252	8257	8262	8267	8272	8277	15
45	8282	8287	8292	8297	8302	8307	14
46	8312	8317	8322	8327	8332	8337	13
47	8342	8346	8351	8356	8361	8366	12
48	8371	8376	8381	8386	8391	8396	11
49	8401	8406	8411	8416	8420	8425	10
50	9.988430	8435	8440	8445	8450	8455	9
51	8460	8465	8470	8475	8480	8484	8
52	8489	8494	8499	8504	8509	8514	7
53	8519	8524	8529	8534	8538	8543	6
54	8548	8553	8558	8563	8568	8573	5
55	8578	8583	8587	8592	8597	8602	4
56	8607	8612	8617	8622	8626	8631	3
57	8636	8641	8646	8651	8656	8661	2
58	8666	8670	8675	8680	8685	8690	1
59	8695	8700	8704	8709	8714	8719	0
	60″	50″	40″	30″	20″	10″	Min.
	Co-sine of 13 Degrees.						

P. Part { 1″ 2″ 3″ 4″ 5″ 6″ 7″ 8″ 9″ / 1 1 2 2 3 3 4 4 5 }

Min.	Sine of 77 Degrees. 0″	10″	20″	30″	40″	50″	
0	9.988724	8729	8734	8739	8743	8748	59
1	8753	8758	8763	8768	8772	8777	58
2	8782	8787	8792	8797	8802	8806	57
3	8811	8816	8821	8826	8831	8835	56
4	8840	8845	8850	8855	8860	8864	55
5	8869	8874	8879	8884	8889	8893	54
6	8898	8903	8908	8913	8918	8922	53
7	8927	8932	8937	8942	8946	8951	52
8	8956	8961	8966	8970	8975	8980	51
9	8985	8990	8994	8999	9004	9009	50
10	9.989014	9018	9023	9028	9033	9038	49
11	9042	9047	9052	9057	9062	9066	48
12	9071	9076	9081	9085	9090	9095	47
13	9100	9105	9109	9114	9119	9124	46
14	9128	9133	9138	9143	9148	9152	45
15	9157	9162	9167	9171	9176	9181	44
16	9186	9190	9195	9200	9205	9209	43
17	9214	9219	9224	9228	9233	9238	42
18	9243	9247	9252	9257	9262	9266	41
19	9271	9276	9281	9285	9290	9295	40
20	9.989300	9304	9309	9314	9318	9323	39
21	9328	9333	9337	9342	9347	9352	38
22	9356	9361	9366	9370	9375	9380	37
23	9385	9389	9394	9399	9403	9408	36
24	9413	9417	9422	9427	9432	9436	35
25	9441	9446	9450	9455	9460	9464	34
26	9469	9474	9479	9483	9488	9493	33
27	9497	9502	9507	9511	9516	9521	32
28	9525	9530	9535	9539	9544	9549	31
29	9553	9558	9563	9568	9572	9577	30
30	9.989582	9586	9591	9596	9600	9605	29
31	9610	9614	9619	9623	9628	9633	28
32	9637	9642	9647	9651	9656	9661	27
33	9665	9670	9675	9679	9684	9689	26
34	9693	9698	9703	9707	9712	9716	25
35	9721	9726	9730	9735	9740	9744	24
36	9749	9753	9758	9763	9767	9772	23
37	9777	9781	9786	9790	9795	9800	22
38	9804	9809	9814	9818	9823	9827	21
39	9832	9837	9841	9846	9850	9855	20
40	9.989860	9864	9869	9873	9878	9883	19
41	9887	9892	9896	9901	9906	9910	18
42	9915	9919	9924	9929	9933	9938	17
43	9942	9947	9952	9956	9961	9965	16
44	9970	9974	9979	9984	9988	9993	15
45	9997	...2	...6	..11	..16	..20	14
46	9.990025	0029	0034	0038	0043	0048	13
47	0052	0057	0061	0066	0070	0075	12
48	0079	0084	0088	0093	0098	0102	11
49	0107	0111	0116	0120	0125	0129	10
50	9.990134	0138	0143	0148	0152	0157	9
51	0161	0166	0170	0175	0179	0184	8
52	0188	0193	0197	0202	0206	0211	7
53	0215	0220	0225	0229	0234	0238	6
54	0243	0247	0252	0256	0261	0265	5
55	0270	0274	0279	0283	0288	0292	4
56	0297	0301	0306	0310	0315	0319	3
57	0324	0328	0333	0337	0342	0346	2
58	0351	0355	0360	0364	0369	0373	1
59	0378	0382	0386	0391	0395	0400	0
	60″	50″	40″	30″	20″	10″	Min.
	Co-sine of 12 Degrees.						

P. Part { 1″ 2″ 3″ 4″ 5″ 6″ 7″ 8″ 9″ / 0 1 1 2 2 3 3 4 4 }

Tangent of 76 Degrees.

Min.	0″	10″	20″	30″	40″	50″	
0	10.603229	3319	3408	3498	3588	3678	59
1	3767	3857	3947	4037	4127	4217	58
2	4306	4396	4486	4576	4666	4756	57
3	4846	4936	5026	5116	5206	5296	56
4	5386	5477	5567	5657	5747	5837	55
5	5927	6017	6108	6198	6288	6378	54
6	6469	6559	6649	6740	6830	6920	53
7	7011	7101	7192	7282	7372	7463	52
8	7553	7644	7734	7825	7915	8006	51
9	8097	8187	8278	8368	8459	8550	50
10	10.608640	8731	8822	8913	9003	9094	49
11	9185	9276	9367	9457	9548	9639	48
12	9730	9821	9912	...3	..94	.185	47
13	10.610276	0367	0458	0549	0640	0731	46
14	0822	0913	1004	1095	1186	1278	45
15	1369	1460	1551	1642	1734	1825	44
16	1916	2008	2099	2190	2282	2373	43
17	2464	2556	2647	2739	2830	2922	42
18	3013	3105	3196	3288	3379	3471	41
19	3562	3654	3746	3837	3929	4021	40
20	10.614112	4204	4296	4388	4479	4571	39
21	4663	4755	4847	4938	5030	5122	38
22	5214	5306	5398	5490	5582	5674	37
23	5766	5858	5950	6042	6134	6226	36
24	6318	6411	6503	6595	6687	6779	35
25	6871	6964	7056	7148	7241	7333	34
26	7425	7518	7610	7702	7795	7887	33
27	7980	8072	8164	8257	8349	8442	32
28	8534	8627	8720	8812	8905	8997	31
29	9090	9183	9275	9368	9461	9554	30
30	10.619646	9739	9832	9925	..17	.110	29
31	10.620203	0296	0389	0482	0575	0668	28
32	0761	0854	0947	1040	1133	1226	27
33	1319	1412	1505	1598	1691	1784	26
34	1878	1971	2064	2157	2250	2344	25
35	2437	2530	2624	2717	2810	2904	24
36	2997	3090	3184	3277	3371	3464	23
37	3558	3651	3745	3838	3932	4025	22
38	4119	4213	4306	4400	4494	4587	21
39	4681	4775	4869	4962	5056	5150	20
40	10.625244	5338	5431	5525	5619	5713	19
41	5807	5901	5995	6089	6183	6277	18
42	6371	6465	6559	6653	6747	6841	17
43	6936	7030	7124	7218	7312	7407	16
44	7501	7595	7689	7784	7878	7972	15
45	8067	8161	8256	8350	8444	8539	14
46	8633	8728	8822	8917	9011	9106	13
47	9201	9295	9390	9484	9579	9674	12
48	9768	9863	9958	..53	.147	.242	11
49	10.630337	0432	0527	0622	0716	0811	10
50	10.630906	1001	1096	1191	1286	1381	9
51	1476	1571	1666	1761	1857	1952	8
52	2047	2142	2237	2332	2428	2523	7
53	2618	2713	2809	2904	2999	3095	6
54	3190	3285	3381	3476	3572	3667	5
55	3763	3858	3954	4049	4145	4240	4
56	4336	4432	4527	4623	4718	4814	3
57	4910	5006	5101	5197	5293	5389	2
58	5485	5580	5676	5772	5868	5964	1
59	6060	6156	6252	6348	6444	6540	0
	60″	50″	40″	30″	20″	10″	Min.

Co-tangent of 13 Degrees.

P. Part	1″	2″	3″	4″	5″	6″	7″	8″	9″
	9	19	28	37	46	56	65	74	83

Tangent of 77 Degrees.

Min.	0″	10″	20″	30″	40″	50″	
0	10.636636	6732	6828	6924	7020	7116	59
1	7213	7309	7405	7501	7597	7694	58
2	7790	7886	7983	8079	8175	8272	57
3	8368	8465	8561	8657	8754	8850	56
4	8947	9043	9140	9237	9333	9430	55
5	9526	9623	9720	9816	9913	..10	54
6	10.640107	0203	0300	0397	0494	0591	53
7	0687	0784	0881	0978	1075	1172	52
8	1269	1366	1463	1560	1657	1754	51
9	1851	1948	2046	2143	2240	2337	50
10	10.642434	2531	2629	2726	2823	2921	49
11	3018	3115	3213	3310	3407	3505	48
12	3602	3700	3797	3895	3992	4090	47
13	4187	4285	4383	4480	4578	4676	46
14	4773	4871	4969	5066	5164	5262	45
15	5360	5458	5555	5653	5751	5849	44
16	5947	6045	6143	6241	6339	6437	43
17	6535	6633	6731	6829	6927	7026	42
18	7124	7222	7320	7418	7517	7615	41
19	7713	7811	7910	8008	8106	8205	40
20	10.648303	8402	8500	8599	8697	8796	39
21	8894	8993	9091	9190	9288	9387	38
22	9486	9584	9683	9782	9880	9979	37
23	10.650078	0177	0276	0374	0473	0572	36
24	0671	0770	0869	0968	1067	1166	35
25	1265	1364	1463	1562	1661	1760	34
26	1859	1958	2058	2157	2256	2355	33
27	4455	2554	2653	2752	2852	2951	32
28	3051	3150	3249	3349	3448	3548	31
29	3647	3747	3846	3946	4046	4145	30
30	10.654245	4344	4444	4544	4643	4743	29
31	4843	4943	5043	5142	5242	5342	28
32	5442	5542	5642	5742	5842	5942	27
33	6042	6142	6242	6342	6442	6542	26
34	6642	6742	6842	6943	7043	7143	25
35	7243	7344	7444	7544	7645	7745	24
36	7845	7946	8046	8147	8247	8348	23
37	8448	8549	8649	8750	8850	8951	22
38	9052	9152	9253	9354	9454	9555	21
39	9656	9757	9857	9958	..59	.160	20
40	10.660261	0362	0463	0564	0665	0766	19
41	0867	0968	1069	1170	1271	1372	18
42	1473	1574	1676	1777	1878	1979	17
43	2081	2182	2283	2385	2486	2587	16
44	2689	2790	2892	2993	3095	3196	15
45	3298	3399	3501	3602	3704	3806	14
46	3907	4009	4111	4212	4314	4416	13
47	4518	4620	4721	4823	4925	5027	12
48	5129	5231	5333	5435	5537	5639	11
49	5741	5843	5945	6047	6149	6252	10
50	10.666354	6456	6558	6660	6763	6865	9
51	6967	7070	7172	7274	7377	7479	8
52	7582	7684	7787	7889	7992	8094	7
53	8197	8299	8402	8505	8607	8710	6
54	8813	8916	9018	9121	9224	9327	5
55	9430	9532	9635	9738	9841	9944	4
56	10.670047	0150	0253	0356	0459	0562	3
57	0666	0769	0872	0975	1078	1181	2
58	1285	1388	1491	1595	1698	1801	1
59	1905	2008	2112	2215	2318	2422	0
	60″	50″	40″	30″	20″	10″	Min.

Co-tangent of 12 Degrees.

P. Part	1″	2″	3″	4″	5″	6″	7″	8″	9″
	10	20	30	40	50	60	70	80	90

Min.	Sine of 78 Degrees. 0″	10″	20″	30″	40″	50″	
0	9.990404	0409	0413	0418	0422	0427	59
1	0431	0436	0440	0445	0449	0454	58
2	0458	0462	0467	0471	0476	0480	57
3	0485	0489	0494	0498	0503	0507	56
4	0511	0516	0520	0525	0529	0534	55
5	0538	0543	0547	0552	0556	0560	54
6	0565	0569	0574	0578	0583	0587	53
7	0591	0596	0600	0605	0609	0614	52
8	0618	0622	0627	0631	0636	0640	51
9	0645	0649	0653	0658	0662	0667	50
10	9.990671	0675	0680	0684	0689	0693	49
11	0697	0702	0706	0711	0715	0719	48
12	0724	0728	0733	0737	0741	0746	47
13	0750	0755	0759	0763	0768	0772	46
14	0777	0781	0785	0790	0794	0798	45
15	0803	0807	0812	0816	0820	0825	44
16	0829	0833	0838	0842	0847	0851	43
17	0855	0860	0864	0868	0873	0877	42
18	0882	0886	0890	0895	0899	0903	41
19	0908	0912	0916	0921	0925	0929	40
20	9.990934	0938	0942	0947	0951	0955	39
21	0960	0964	0969	0973	0977	0982	38
22	0986	0990	0995	0999	1003	1008	37
23	1012	1016	1021	1025	1029	1033	36
24	1038	1042	1046	1051	1055	1059	35
25	1064	1068	1072	1077	1081	1085	34
26	1090	1094	1098	1103	1107	1111	33
27	1115	1120	1124	1128	1133	1137	32
28	1141	1146	1150	1154	1158	1163	31
29	1167	1171	1176	1180	1184	1188	30
30	9.991193	1197	1201	1206	1210	1214	29
31	1218	1223	1227	1231	1235	1240	28
32	1244	1248	1253	1257	1261	1265	27
33	1270	1274	1278	1282	1287	1291	26
34	1295	1299	1304	1308	1312	1316	25
35	1321	1325	1329	1333	1338	1342	24
36	1346	1350	1355	1359	1363	1367	23
37	1372	1376	1380	1384	1389	1393	22
38	1397	1401	1406	1410	1414	1418	21
39	1422	1427	1431	1435	1439	1444	20
40	9.991448	1452	1456	1460	1465	1469	19
41	1473	1477	1482	1486	1490	1494	18
42	1498	1503	1507	1511	1515	1519	17
43	1524	1528	1532	1536	1540	1545	16
44	1549	1553	1557	1561	1566	1570	15
45	1574	1578	1582	1586	1591	1595	14
46	1599	1603	1607	1612	1616	1620	13
47	1624	1628	1632	1637	1641	1645	12
48	1649	1653	1657	1662	1666	1670	11
49	1674	1678	1682	1687	1691	1695	10
50	9.991699	1703	1707	1712	1716	1720	9
51	1724	1728	1732	1736	1741	1745	8
52	1749	1753	1757	1761	1765	1770	7
53	1774	1778	1782	1786	1790	1794	6
54	1799	1803	1807	1811	1815	1819	5
55	1823	1827	1832	1836	1840	1844	4
56	1848	1852	1856	1860	1865	1869	3
57	1873	1877	1881	1885	1889	1893	2
58	1897	1901	1906	1910	1914	1918	1
59	1922	1926	1930	1934	1938	1942	0
	60″	50″	40″	30″	20″	10″	Min.
	Co-sine of 11 Degrees.						

P. Part { 1″ 2″ 3″ 4″ 5″ 6″ 7″ 8″ 9″ / 0 1 1 2 2 3 3 3 4 }

Min.	Sine of 79 Degrees. 0″	10″	20″	30″	40″	50″	
0	9.991947	1951	1955	1959	1963	1967	59
1	1971	1975	1979	1983	1987	1992	58
2	1996	2000	2004	2008	2012	2016	57
3	2020	2024	2028	2032	2036	2040	56
4	2044	2049	2053	2057	2061	2065	55
5	2069	2073	2077	2081	2085	2089	54
6	2093	2097	2101	2105	2109	2113	53
7	2118	2122	2126	2130	2134	2138	52
8	2142	2146	2150	2154	2158	2162	51
9	2166	2170	2174	2178	2182	2186	50
10	9.992190	2194	2198	2202	2206	2210	49
11	2214	2218	2222	2226	2230	2234	48
12	2239	2243	2247	2251	2255	2259	47
13	2263	2267	2271	2275	2279	2283	46
14	2287	2291	2295	2299	2303	2307	45
15	2311	2315	2319	2323	2327	2331	44
16	2335	2339	2343	2347	2351	2355	43
17	2359	2363	2366	2370	2374	2378	42
18	2382	2386	2390	2394	2398	2402	41
19	2406	2410	2414	2418	2422	2426	40
20	9.992430	2434	2438	2442	2446	2450	39
21	2454	2458	2462	2466	2470	2474	38
22	2478	2482	2485	2489	2493	2497	37
23	2501	2505	2509	2513	2517	2521	36
24	2525	2529	2533	2537	2541	2545	35
25	2549	2553	2556	2560	2564	2568	34
26	2572	2576	2580	2584	2588	2592	33
27	2596	2600	2604	2607	2611	2615	32
28	2619	2623	2627	2631	2635	2639	31
29	2643	2647	2651	2654	2658	2662	30
30	9.992666	2670	2674	2678	2682	2686	29
31	2690	2693	2697	2701	2705	2709	28
32	2713	2717	2721	2725	2728	2732	27
33	2736	2740	2744	2748	2752	2756	26
34	2759	2763	2767	2771	2775	2779	25
35	2783	2787	2790	2794	2798	2802	24
36	2806	2810	2814	2818	2821	2825	23
37	2829	2833	2837	2841	2845	2848	22
38	2852	2856	2860	2864	2868	2871	21
39	2875	2879	2883	2887	2891	2895	20
40	9.992898	2902	2906	2910	2914	2918	19
41	2921	2925	2929	2933	2937	2941	18
42	2944	2948	2952	2956	2960	2963	17
43	2967	2971	2975	2979	2983	2986	16
44	2990	2994	2998	3002	3005	3009	15
45	3013	3017	3021	3024	3028	3032	14
46	3036	3040	3043	3047	3051	3055	13
47	3059	3062	3066	3070	3074	3078	12
48	3081	3085	3089	3093	3097	3100	11
49	3104	3108	3112	3115	3119	3123	10
50	9.993127	3131	3134	3138	3142	3146	9
51	3149	3153	3157	3161	3165	3168	8
52	3172	3176	3180	3183	3187	3191	7
53	3195	3198	3202	3206	3210	3213	6
54	3217	3221	3225	3228	3232	3236	5
55	3240	3243	3247	3251	3255	3258	4
56	3262	3266	3270	3273	3277	3281	3
57	3284	3288	3292	3296	3299	3303	2
58	3307	3311	3314	3318	3322	3325	1
59	3329	3333	3337	3340	3344	3348	0
	60″	50″	40″	30″	20″	10″	Min.
	Co-sine of 10 Degrees.						

P. Part { 1″ 2″ 3″ 4″ 5″ 6″ 7″ 8″ 9″ / 0 1 1 2 2 2 3 3 4 }

Min.	Tangent of 78 Degrees.						
	0″	10″	20″	30″	40″	50″	
0	10.672525	2629	2733	2836	2940	3043	59
1	3147	3251	3354	3458	3562	3666	58
2	3769	3873	3977	4081	4185	4289	57
3	4393	4497	4601	4705	4809	4913	56
4	5017	5121	5225	5329	5433	5537	55
5	5642	5746	5850	5954	6059	6163	54
6	6267	6372	6476	6580	6685	6789	53
7	6894	6998	7103	7207	7312	7417	52
8	7521	7626	7731	7835	7940	8045	51
9	8149	8254	8359	8464	8569	8674	50
10	8778	8883	8988	9093	9198	9303	49
11	9408	9513	9618	9723	9829	9934	48
12	10.680039	0144	0249	0355	0460	0565	47
13	0670	0776	0881	0987	1092	1197	46
14	1303	1408	1514	1619	1725	1830	45
15	1936	2042	2147	2253	2359	2464	44
16	2570	2676	2782	2887	2993	3099	43
17	3205	3311	3417	3523	3629	3735	42
18	3841	3947	4053	4159	4265	4371	41
19	4477	4584	4690	4796	4902	5009	40
20	5115	5221	5328	5434	5540	5647	39
21	5753	5860	5966	6073	6179	6286	38
22	6392	6499	6606	6712	6819	6926	37
23	7032	7139	7246	7353	7460	7567	36
24	7673	7780	7887	7994	8101	8208	35
25	8315	8422	8529	8636	8744	8851	34
26	8958	9065	9172	9280	9387	9494	33
27	9601	9709	9816	9924	..31	.138	32
28	10.690246	0353	0461	0568	0676	0784	31
29	0891	0999	1107	1214	1322	1430	30
30	1537	1645	1753	1861	1969	2077	29
31	2184	2292	2400	2508	2616	2724	28
32	2832	2941	3049	3157	3265	3373	27
33	3481	3590	3698	3806	3914	4023	26
34	4131	4239	4348	4456	4565	4673	25
35	4782	4890	4999	5107	5216	5325	24
36	5433	5542	5651	5759	5868	5977	23
37	6086	6195	6303	6412	6521	6630	22
38	6739	6848	6957	7066	7175	7284	21
39	7393	7503	7612	7721	7830	7939	20
40	8049	8158	8267	8376	8486	8595	19
41	8705	8814	8924	9033	9143	9252	18
42	9362	9471	9581	9691	9800	9910	17
43	10.700020	0129	0239	0349	0459	0569	16
44	0678	0788	0898	1008	1118	1228	15
45	1338	1448	1558	1668	1779	1889	14
46	1999	2109	2219	2330	2440	2550	13
47	2661	2771	2881	2992	3102	3213	12
48	3323	3434	3544	3655	3765	3876	11
49	3987	4097	4208	4319	4429	4540	10
50	4651	4762	4873	4984	5095	5205	9
51	5316	5427	5538	5649	5761	5872	8
52	5983	6094	6205	6316	6428	6539	7
53	6650	6761	6873	6984	7095	7207	6
54	7318	7430	7541	7653	7764	7876	5
55	7987	8099	8211	8322	8434	8546	4
56	8658	8769	8881	8993	9105	9217	3
57	9329	9441	9553	9665	9777	9889	2
58	10.710001	0113	0225	0337	0449	0562	1
59	0674	0786	0898	1011	1123	1235	0
	60″	50″	40″	30″	20″	10″	Min.
	Co-tangent of 11 Degrees.						

P. Part	1″	2″	3″	4″	5″	6″	7″	8″	9″
	11	22	32	43	54	65	75	86	97

Min.	Tangent of 79 Degrees.						
	0″	10″	20″	30″	40″	50″	
0	10.711348	1460	1573	1685	1798	1910	59
1	2023	2135	2248	2361	2473	2586	58
2	2699	2811	2924	3037	3150	3263	57
3	3376	3488	3601	3714	3827	3940	56
4	4053	4167	4280	4393	4506	4619	55
5	4732	4846	4959	5072	5185	5299	54
6	5412	5526	5639	5752	5866	5979	53
7	6093	6207	6320	6434	6547	6661	52
8	6775	6889	7002	7116	7230	7344	51
9	7458	7572	7686	7799	7913	8027	50
10	8142	8256	8370	8484	8598	8712	49
11	8826	8941	9055	9169	9283	9398	48
12	9512	9627	9741	9856	9970	..85	47
13	10.720199	0314	0428	0543	0658	0772	46
14	0887	1002	1116	1231	1346	1461	45
15	1576	1691	1806	1921	2036	2151	44
16	2266	2381	2496	2611	2726	2841	43
17	2957	3072	3187	3302	3418	3533	42
18	3649	3764	3879	3995	4110	4226	41
19	4342	4457	4573	4688	4804	4920	40
20	5036	5151	5267	5383	5499	5615	39
21	5731	5847	5963	6079	6195	6311	38
22	6427	6543	6659	6775	6891	7008	37
23	7124	7240	7356	7473	7589	7706	36
24	7822	7938	8055	8171	8288	8405	35
25	8521	8638	8754	8871	8988	9105	34
26	9221	9338	9455	9572	9689	9806	33
27	9923	..40	.157	.274	.391	.508	32
28	10.730625	0742	0860	0977	1094	1211	31
29	1329	1446	1563	1681	1798	1916	30
30	2033	2151	2268	2386	2503	2621	29
31	2739	2856	2974	3092	3210	3327	28
32	3445	3563	3681	3799	3917	4035	27
33	4153	4271	4389	4507	4625	4744	26
34	4862	4980	5098	5217	5335	5453	25
35	5572	5690	5809	5927	6046	6164	24
36	6283	6401	6520	6639	6757	6876	23
37	6995	7113	7232	7351	7470	7589	22
38	7708	7827	7946	8065	8184	8303	21
39	8422	8541	8660	8780	8899	9018	20
40	9137	9257	9376	9496	9615	9734	19
41	9854	9973	..93	.213	.332	.452	18
42	10.740571	0691	0811	0931	1050	1170	17
43	1290	1410	1530	1650	1770	1890	16
44	2010	2130	2250	2370	2490	2611	15
45	2731	2851	2971	3092	3212	3332	14
46	3453	3573	3694	3814	3935	4055	13
47	4176	4297	4417	4538	4659	4779	12
48	4900	5021	5142	5263	5384	5505	11
49	5626	5747	5868	5989	6110	6231	10
50	6352	6473	6595	6716	6837	6959	9
51	7080	7201	7323	7444	7566	7687	8
52	7809	7930	8052	8174	8295	8417	7
53	8539	8661	8782	8904	9026	9148	6
54	9270	9392	9514	9636	9758	9880	5
55	10.750002	0124	0247	0369	0491	0613	4
56	0736	0858	0980	1103	1225	1348	3
57	1470	1593	1715	1838	1961	2083	2
58	2206	2329	2452	2574	2697	2820	1
59	2943	3066	3189	3312	3435	3558	0
	60″	50″	40″	30″	20″	10″	Min.
	Co-tangent of 10 Degrees.						

P. Part	1″	2″	3″	4″	5″	6″	7″	8″	9″
	12	23	35	47	59	70	82	94	106

Min.	Sine of 80 Degrees. 0″	10″	20″	30″	40″	50″	
0	9·993351	3355	3359	3363	3366	3370	59
1	3374	3377	3381	3385	3389	3392	58
2	3396	3400	3403	3407	3411	3414	57
3	3418	3422	3426	3429	3433	3437	56
4	3440	3444	3448	3451	3455	3459	55
5	3462	3466	3470	3473	3477	3481	54
6	3484	3488	3492	3495	3499	3503	53
7	3506	3510	3514	3517	3521	3525	52
8	3528	3532	3536	3539	3543	3547	51
9	3550	3554	3558	3561	3565	3569	50
10	9·993572	3576	3580	3583	3587	3591	49
11	3594	3598	3601	3605	3609	3612	48
12	3616	3620	3623	3627	3631	3634	47
13	3638	3641	3645	3649	3652	3656	46
14	3660	3663	3667	3670	3674	3678	45
15	3681	3685	3689	3692	3696	3699	44
16	3703	3707	3710	3714	3717	3721	43
17	3725	3728	3732	3735	3739	3743	42
18	3746	3750	3753	3757	3761	3764	41
19	3768	3771	3775	3779	3782	3786	40
20	9·993789	3793	3797	3800	3804	3807	39
21	3811	3814	3818	3822	3825	3829	38
22	3832	3836	3840	3843	3847	3850	37
23	3854	3857	3861	3864	3868	3872	36
24	3875	3879	3882	3886	3889	3893	35
25	3897	3900	3904	3907	3911	3914	34
26	3918	3921	3925	3928	3932	3936	33
27	3939	3943	3946	3950	3953	3957	32
28	3960	3964	3967	3971	3974	3978	31
29	3982	3985	3989	3992	3996	3999	30
30	9·994003	4006	4010	4013	4017	4020	29
31	4024	4027	4031	4034	4038	4041	28
32	4045	4048	4052	4055	4059	4062	27
33	4066	4069	4073	4076	4080	4083	26
34	4087	4090	4094	4097	4101	4104	25
35	4108	4111	4115	4118	4122	4125	24
36	4129	4132	4136	4139	4143	4146	23
37	4150	4153	4157	4160	4164	4167	22
38	4171	4174	4178	4181	4184	4188	21
39	4191	4195	4198	4202	4205	4209	20
40	9·994212	4216	4219	4223	4226	4230	19
41	4233	4236	4240	4243	4247	4250	18
42	4254	4257	4261	4264	4267	4271	17
43	4274	4278	4281	4285	4288	4292	16
44	4295	4298	4302	4305	4309	4312	15
45	4316	4319	4322	4326	4329	4333	14
46	4336	4340	4343	4346	4350	4353	13
47	4357	4360	4363	4367	4370	4374	12
48	4377	4381	4384	4387	4391	4394	11
49	4398	4401	4404	4408	4411	4415	10
50	9·994418	4421	4425	4428	4432	4435	9
51	4438	4442	4445	4448	4452	4455	8
52	4459	4462	4465	4469	4472	4476	7
53	4479	4482	4486	4489	4492	4496	6
54	4499	4503	4506	4509	4513	4516	5
55	4519	4523	4526	4530	4533	4536	4
56	4540	4543	4546	4550	4553	4556	3
57	4560	4563	4566	4570	4573	4576	2
58	4580	4583	4587	4590	4593	4597	1
59	4600	4603	4607	4610	4613	4617	0
	60″	50″	40″	30″	20″	10″	Min.
	Co-sine of 9 Degrees.						

P. Part { 1″ 2″ 3″ 4″ 5″ 6″ 7″ 8″ 9″ / 0 1 1 1 2 2 2 3 3

Min.	Sine of 81 Degrees. 0″	10″	20″	30″	40″	50″	
0	9·994620	4623	4627	4630	4633	4637	59
1	4640	4643	4647	4650	4653	4657	58
2	4660	4663	4667	4670	4673	4676	57
3	4680	4683	4686	4690	4693	4696	56
4	4700	4703	4706	4710	4713	4716	55
5	4720	4723	4726	4729	4733	4736	54
6	4739	4743	4746	4749	4752	4756	53
7	4759	4762	4766	4769	4772	4776	52
8	4779	4782	4785	4789	4792	4795	51
9	4798	4802	4805	4808	4812	4815	50
10	9·994818	4821	4825	4828	4831	4834	49
11	4838	4841	4844	4848	4851	4854	48
12	4857	4861	4864	4867	4870	4874	47
13	4877	4880	4883	4887	4890	4893	46
14	4896	4900	4903	4906	4909	4913	45
15	4916	4919	4922	4926	4929	4932	44
16	4935	4938	4942	4945	4948	4951	43
17	4955	4958	4961	4964	4968	4971	42
18	4974	4977	4980	4984	4987	4990	41
19	4993	4997	5000	5003	5006	5009	40
20	9·995013	5016	5019	5022	5025	5029	39
21	5032	5035	5038	5041	5045	5048	38
22	5051	5054	5057	5061	5064	5067	37
23	5070	5073	5077	5080	5083	5086	36
24	5089	5092	5096	5099	5102	5105	35
25	5108	5112	5115	5118	5121	5124	34
26	5127	5131	5134	5137	5140	5143	33
27	5146	5150	5153	5156	5159	5162	32
28	5165	5169	5172	5175	5178	5181	31
29	5184	5188	5191	5194	5197	5200	30
30	9·995203	5206	5210	5213	5216	5219	29
31	5222	5225	5228	5232	5235	5238	28
32	5241	5244	5247	5250	5253	5257	27
33	5260	5263	5266	5269	5272	5275	26
34	5278	5282	5285	5288	5291	5294	25
35	5297	5300	5303	5307	5310	5313	24
36	5316	5319	5322	5325	5328	5331	23
37	5334	5338	5341	5344	5347	5350	22
38	5353	5356	5359	5362	5365	5369	21
39	5372	5375	5378	5381	5384	5387	20
40	9·995390	5393	5396	5399	5403	5406	19
41	5409	5412	5415	5418	5421	5424	18
42	5427	5430	5433	5436	5439	5442	17
43	5446	5449	5452	5455	5458	5461	16
44	5464	5467	5470	5473	5476	5479	15
45	5482	5485	5488	5491	5494	5497	14
46	5501	5504	5507	5510	5513	5516	13
47	5519	5522	5525	5528	5531	5534	12
48	5537	5540	5543	5546	5549	5552	11
49	5555	5558	5561	5564	5567	5570	10
50	9·995573	5576	5579	5582	5585	5588	9
51	5591	5594	5597	5601	5604	5607	8
52	5610	5613	5616	5619	5622	5625	7
53	5628	5631	5634	5637	5640	5643	6
54	5646	5649	5652	5655	5658	5661	5
55	5664	5667	5670	5672	5675	5678	4
56	5681	5684	5687	5690	5693	5696	3
57	5699	5702	5705	5708	5711	5714	2
58	5717	5720	5723	5726	5729	5732	1
59	5735	5738	5741	5744	5747	5750	0
	60″	50″	40″	30″	20″	10″	Min.
	Co-sine of 8 Degrees.						

P. Part { 1″ 2″ 3″ 4″ 5″ 6″ 7″ 8″ 9″ / 0 1 1 1 2 2 2 3 3

Min.	Tangent of 80 Degrees. 0″	10″	20″	30″	40″	50″	
0	10.753681	3804	3928	4051	4174	4297	59
1	4421	4544	4667	4791	4914	5038	58
2	5161	5285	5408	5532	5655	5779	57
3	5903	6026	6150	6274	6398	6522	56
4	6646	6770	6894	7018	7142	7266	55
5	7390	7514	7638	7762	7886	8011	54
6	8135	8259	8384	8508	8633	8757	53
7	8882	9006	9131	9255	9380	9505	52
8	9629	9754	9879	...4	.128	.253	51
9	10.760378	0503	0628	0753	0878	1003	50
10	1128	1253	1379	1504	1629	1754	49
11	1880	2005	2130	2256	2381	2507	48
12	2632	2758	2883	3009	3135	3260	47
13	3386	3512	3638	3763	3889	4015	46
14	4141	4267	4393	4519	4645	4771	45
15	4897	5024	5150	5276	5402	5529	44
16	5655	5781	5908	6034	6161	6287	43
17	6414	6540	6667	6794	6920	7047	42
18	7174	7301	7427	7554	7681	7808	41
19	7935	8062	8189	8316	8443	8570	40
20	8698	8825	8952	9079	9207	9334	39
21	9461	9589	9716	9844	9971	..99	38
22	10.770227	0354	0482	0610	0737	0865	37
23	0993	1121	1249	1377	1504	1632	36
24	1761	1889	2017	2145	2273	2401	35
25	2529	2658	2786	2914	3043	3171	34
26	3300	3428	3557	3685	3814	3942	33
27	4071	4200	4329	4457	4586	4715	32
28	4844	4973	5102	5231	5360	5489	31
29	5618	5747	5876	6006	6135	6264	30
30	6393	6523	6652	6782	6911	7041	29
31	7170	7300	7429	7559	7689	7818	28
32	7948	8078	8208	8338	8468	8598	27
33	8728	8858	8988	9118	9248	9378	26
34	9508	9639	9769	9899	..29	.160	25
35	10.780290	0421	0551	0682	0812	0943	24
36	1074	1204	1335	1466	1597	1727	23
37	1858	1989	2120	2251	2382	2513	22
38	2644	2775	2907	3038	3169	3300	21
39	3432	3563	3695	3826	3957	4089	20
40	4220	4352	4484	4615	4747	4879	19
41	5011	5142	5274	5406	5538	5670	18
42	5802	5934	6066	6198	6330	6463	17
43	6595	6727	6859	6992	7124	7257	16
44	7389	7522	7654	7787	7919	8052	15
45	8185	8317	8450	8583	8716	8849	14
46	8982	9115	9248	9381	9514	9647	13
47	9780	9913	..46	.180	.313	.446	12
48	10.790580	0713	0847	0980	1114	1247	11
49	1381	1515	1648	1782	1916	2050	10
50	2183	2317	2451	2585	2719	2853	9
51	2987	3122	3256	3390	3524	3658	8
52	3793	3927	4062	4196	4331	4465	7
53	4600	4734	4869	5004	5138	5273	6
54	5408	5543	5678	5812	5947	6082	5
55	6218	6353	6488	6623	6758	6893	4
56	7029	7164	7299	7435	7570	7706	3
57	7841	7977	8112	8248	8384	8519	2
58	8655	8791	8927	9063	9199	9335	1
59	9471	9607	9743	9879	..15	.151	0
	60″	50″	40″	30″	20″	10″	Min.
	Co-tangent of 9 Degrees						

P. Part { 1″ 2″ 3″ 4″ 5″ 6″ 7″ 8″ 9′
{ 13 26 39 52 65 78 91 103 116

Min.	Tangent of 81 Degrees. 0″	10″	20″	30″	40″	50″	
0	10.800287	0424	0560	0696	0833	0969	59
1	1106	1242	1379	1516	1652	1789	58
2	1926	2062	2199	2336	2473	2610	57
3	2747	2884	3021	3158	3295	3433	56
4	3570	3707	3844	3982	4119	4257	55
5	4394	4532	4669	4807	4944	5082	54
6	5220	5358	5495	5633	5771	5909	53
7	6047	6185	6323	6461	6599	6738	52
8	6876	7014	7152	7291	7429	7568	51
9	7706	7845	7983	8122	8261	8399	50
10	8538	8677	8816	8954	9093	9232	49
11	9371	9510	9649	9788	9928	..67	48
12	10.810206	0345	0485	0624	0764	0903	47
13	1042	1182	1322	1461	1601	1741	46
14	1880	2020	2160	2300	2440	2580	45
15	2720	2860	3000	3140	3280	3421	44
16	3561	3701	3842	3982	4122	4263	43
17	4403	4544	4685	4825	4966	5107	42
18	5248	5388	5529	5670	5811	5952	41
19	6093	6234	6375	6517	6658	6799	40
20	6941	7082	7223	7365	7506	7648	39
21	7789	7931	8073	8214	8356	8498	38
22	8640	8782	8924	9066	9208	9350	37
23	9492	9634	9776	9918	..61	.203	36
24	10.820345	0488	0630	0773	0915	1058	35
25	1201	1343	1486	1629	1772	1915	34
26	2058	2200	2344	2487	2630	2773	33
27	2916	3059	3203	3346	3489	3633	32
28	3776	3920	4063	4207	4350	4494	31
29	4638	4782	4925	5069	5213	5357	30
30	5501	5645	5789	5933	6078	6222	29
31	6366	6511	6655	6799	6944	7088	28
32	7233	7377	7522	7667	7812	7956	27
33	8101	8246	8391	8536	8681	8826	26
34	8971	9116	9261	9407	9552	9697	25
35	9843	9988	.134	.279	.425	.570	24
36	10.830716	0862	1008	1153	1299	1445	23
37	1591	1737	1883	2029	2175	2322	22
38	2468	2614	2760	2907	3053	3200	21
39	3346	3493	3639	3786	3933	4080	20
40	4226	4373	4520	4667	4814	4961	19
41	5108	5255	5402	5550	5697	5844	18
42	5992	6139	6287	6434	6582	6729	17
43	6877	7025	7172	7320	7468	7616	16
44	7764	7912	8060	8208	8356	8504	15
45	8653	8801	8949	9098	9246	9395	14
46	9543	9692	9840	9989	.138	.287	13
47	10.840435	0584	0733	0882	1031	1180	12
48	1329	1479	1628	1777	1926	2076	11
49	2225	2375	2524	2674	2823	2973	10
50	3123	3272	3422	3572	3722	3872	9
51	4022	4172	4322	4472	4623	4773	8
52	4923	5074	5224	5374	5525	5675	7
53	5826	5977	6127	6278	6429	6580	6
54	6731	6882	7033	7184	7335	7486	5
55	7637	7789	7940	8091	8243	8394	4
56	8546	8697	8849	9001	9152	9304	3
57	9456	9608	9760	9912	..64	.216	2
58	10.850368	0520	0672	0825	0977	1129	1
59	1282	1434	1587	1739	1892	2045	0
	60″	50″	40″	30″	20″	10″	Min.
	Co-tangent of 8 Degrees.						

P. Part { 1″ 2″ 3″ 4″ 5″ 6″ 7″ 8″ 9″
{ 14 29 43 58 72 86 101 115 130

Min.	Sine of 82 Degrees. 0″	10″	20″	30″	40″	50″	
0	9·995753	5756	5759	5762	5765	5768	59
1	5771	5773	5776	5779	5782	5785	58
2	5788	5791	5794	5797	5800	5803	57
3	5806	5809	5812	5815	5818	5821	56
4	5823	5826	5829	5832	5835	5838	55
5	5841	5844	5847	5850	5853	5856	54
6	5859	5862	5864	5867	5870	5873	53
7	5876	5879	5882	5885	5888	5891	52
8	5894	5897	5899	5902	5905	5908	51
9	5911	5914	5917	5920	5923	5926	50
10	9·995928	5931	5934	5937	5940	5943	49
11	5946	5949	5952	5954	5957	5960	48
12	5963	5966	5969	5972	5975	5978	47
13	5980	5983	5986	5989	5992	5995	46
14	5998	6001	6003	6006	6009	6012	45
15	6015	6018	6021	6023	6026	6029	44
16	6032	6035	6038	6041	6043	6046	43
17	6049	6052	6055	6058	6061	6063	42
18	6066	6069	6072	6075	6078	6081	41
19	6083	6086	6089	6092	6095	6098	40
20	9·996100	6103	6106	6109	6112	6115	39
21	6117	6120	6123	6126	6129	6131	38
22	6134	6137	6140	6143	6146	6148	37
23	6151	6154	6157	6160	6162	6165	36
24	6168	6171	6174	6177	6179	6182	35
25	6185	6188	6191	6193	6196	6199	34
26	6202	6205	6207	6210	6213	6216	33
27	6219	6221	6224	6227	6230	6232	32
28	6235	6238	6241	6244	6246	6249	31
29	6252	6255	6257	6260	6263	6266	30
30	9·996269	6271	6274	6277	6280	6282	29
31	6285	6288	6291	6293	6296	6299	28
32	6302	6305	6307	6310	6313	6316	27
33	6318	6321	6324	6327	6329	6332	26
34	6335	6338	6340	6343	6346	6349	25
35	6351	6354	6357	6359	6362	6365	24
36	6368	6370	6373	6376	6379	6381	23
37	6384	6387	6390	6392	6395	6398	22
38	6400	6403	6406	6409	6411	6414	21
39	6417	6419	6422	6425	6428	6430	20
40	9·996433	6436	6438	6441	6444	6447	19
41	6449	6452	6455	6457	6460	6463	18
42	6465	6468	6471	6474	6476	6479	17
43	6482	6484	6487	6490	6492	6495	16
44	6498	6500	6503	6506	6508	6511	15
45	6514	6517	6519	6522	6525	6527	14
46	6530	6533	6535	6538	6541	6543	13
47	6546	6549	6551	6554	6557	6559	12
48	6562	6565	6567	6570	6573	6575	11
49	6578	6580	6583	6586	6588	6591	10
50	9·996594	6596	6599	6602	6604	6607	9
51	6610	6612	6615	6618	6620	6623	8
52	6625	6628	6631	6633	6636	6639	7
53	6641	6644	6646	6649	6652	6654	6
54	6657	6660	6662	6665	6667	6670	5
55	6673	6675	6678	6681	6683	6686	4
56	6688	6691	6694	6696	6699	6701	3
57	6704	6707	6709	6712	6714	6717	2
58	6720	6722	6725	6727	6730	6733	1
59	6735	6738	6740	6743	6746	6748	0
	60″	50″	40″	30″	20″	10″	Min.
	Co-sine of 7 Degrees.						

P. Part { 1″ 2″ 3″ 4″ 5″ 6″ 7″ 8″ 9″
{ 0 1 1 1 1 2 2 2 2

Min.	Sine of 83 Degrees. 0″	10″	20″	30″	40″	50″	
0	9·996751	6753	6756	6758	6761	6764	59
1	6766	6769	6771	6774	6777	6779	58
2	6782	6784	6787	6789	6792	6795	57
3	6797	6800	6802	6805	6807	6810	56
4	6812	6815	6818	6820	6823	6825	55
5	6828	6830	6833	6835	6838	6841	54
6	6843	6846	6848	6851	6853	6856	53
7	6858	6861	6863	6866	6869	6871	52
8	6874	6876	6879	6881	6884	6886	51
9	6889	6891	6894	6896	6899	6901	50
10	9·996904	6906	6909	6912	6914	6917	49
11	6919	6922	6924	6927	6929	6932	48
12	6934	6937	6939	6942	6944	6947	47
13	6949	6952	6954	6957	6959	6962	46
14	6964	6967	6969	6972	6974	6977	45
15	6979	6982	6984	6987	6989	6992	44
16	6994	6997	6999	7002	7004	7007	43
17	7009	7011	7014	7016	7019	7021	42
18	7024	7026	7029	7031	7034	7036	41
19	7039	7041	7044	7046	7049	7051	40
20	9·997053	7056	7058	7061	7063	7066	39
21	7068	7071	7073	7076	7078	7080	38
22	7083	7085	7088	7090	7093	7095	37
23	7098	7100	7102	7105	7107	7110	36
24	7112	7115	7117	7120	7122	7124	35
25	7127	7129	7132	7134	7137	7139	34
26	7141	7144	7146	7149	7151	7154	33
27	7156	7158	7161	7163	7166	7168	32
28	7170	7173	7175	7178	7180	7182	31
29	7185	7187	7190	7192	7194	7197	30
30	9·997199	7202	7204	7206	7209	7211	29
31	7214	7216	7218	7221	7223	7226	28
32	7228	7230	7233	7235	7238	7240	27
33	7242	7245	7247	7249	7252	7254	26
34	7257	7259	7261	7264	7266	7268	25
35	7271	7273	7276	7278	7280	7283	24
36	7285	7287	7290	7292	7294	7297	23
37	7299	7301	7304	7306	7309	7311	22
38	7313	7316	7318	7320	7323	7325	21
39	7327	7330	7332	7334	7337	7339	20
40	9·997341	7344	7346	7348	7351	7353	19
41	7355	7358	7360	7362	7365	7367	18
42	7369	7372	7374	7376	7379	7381	17
43	7383	7386	7388	7390	7393	7395	16
44	7397	7399	7402	7404	7406	7409	15
45	7411	7413	7416	7418	7420	7423	14
46	7425	7427	7429	7432	7434	7436	13
47	7439	7441	7443	7445	7448	7450	12
48	7452	7455	7457	7459	7461	7464	11
49	7466	7468	7471	7473	7475	7477	10
50	9·997480	7482	7484	7487	7489	7491	9
51	7493	7496	7498	7500	7502	7505	8
52	7507	7509	7511	7514	7516	7518	7
53	7520	7523	7525	7527	7530	7532	6
54	7534	7536	7539	7541	7543	7545	5
55	7547	7550	7552	7554	7556	7559	4
56	7561	7563	7565	7568	7570	7572	3
57	7574	7577	7579	7581	7583	7585	2
58	7588	7590	7592	7594	7597	7599	1
59	7601	7603	7605	7608	7610	7612	0
	60″	50″	40″	30″	20″	10″	Min.
	Co-sine of 6 Degrees.						

P. Part { 1″ 2″ 3″ 4″ 5″ 6″ 7″ 8 9″
{ 0 0 1 1 1 1 2 2 2

Tangent of 82 Degrees.

Min.	0″	10″	20″	30″	40″	50″	
0	10.852197	2350	2503	2656	2809	2962	59
1	3115	3268	3421	3575	3728	3881	58
2	4034	4188	4341	4495	4649	4802	57
3	4956	5110	5263	5417	5571	5725	56
4	5879	6033	6187	6341	6496	6650	55
5	6804	6958	7113	7267	7422	7576	54
6	7731	7886	8041	8195	8350	8505	53
7	8660	8815	8970	9125	9280	9436	52
8	9591	9746	9902	..57	.212	.368	51
9	10.860524	0679	0835	0991	1146	1302	50
10	1458	1614	1770	1926	2082	2239	49
11	2395	2551	2708	2864	3020	3177	48
12	3333	3490	3647	3803	3960	4117	47
13	4274	4431	4588	4745	4902	5059	46
14	5216	5374	5531	5688	5846	6003	45
15	6161	6319	6476	6634	6792	6950	44
16	7107	7265	7423	7581	7739	7898	43
17	8056	8214	8372	8531	8689	8848	42
18	9006	9165	9324	9482	9641	9800	41
19	9959	.118	.277	.436	.595	.754	40
20	10.870913	1072	1232	1391	1551	1710	39
21	1870	2029	2189	2349	2508	2668	38
22	2828	2988	3148	3308	3468	3629	37
23	3789	3949	4109	4270	4430	4591	36
24	4751	4912	5073	5234	5394	5555	35
25	5716	5877	6038	6199	6360	6522	34
26	6683	6844	7006	7167	7329	7490	33
27	7652	7813	7975	8137	8299	8461	32
28	8623	8785	8947	9109	9271	9433	31
29	9596	9758	9921	..83	.246	.408	30
30	10.880571	0734	0896	1059	1222	1385	29
31	1548	1711	1874	2038	2201	2364	28
32	2528	2691	2855	3018	3182	3345	27
33	3509	3673	3837	4001	4165	4329	26
34	4493	4657	4821	4985	5150	5314	25
35	5479	5643	5808	5972	6137	6302	24
36	6467	6632	6796	6961	7127	7292	23
37	7457	7622	7787	7953	8118	8284	22
38	8449	8615	8781	8946	9112	9278	21
39	9444	9610	9776	9942	.108	.274	20
40	10.890441	0607	0773	0940	1106	1273	19
41	1440	1606	1773	1940	2107	2274	18
42	2441	2608	2775	2942	3110	3277	17
43	3444	3612	3779	3947	4115	4282	16
44	4450	4618	4786	4954	5122	5290	15
45	5458	5626	5795	5963	6131	6300	14
46	6468	6637	6806	6974	7143	7312	13
47	7481	7650	7819	7988	8157	8326	12
48	8496	8665	8834	9004	9173	9343	11
49	9513	9683	9852	..22	.192	.362	10
50	10.900532	0702	0873	1043	1213	1384	9
51	1554	1724	1895	2066	2236	2407	8
52	2578	2749	2920	3091	3262	3433	7
53	3605	3776	3947	4119	4290	4462	6
54	4633	4805	4977	5149	5320	5492	5
55	5664	5837	6009	6181	6353	6526	4
56	6698	6871	7043	7216	7388	7561	3
57	7734	7907	8080	8253	8426	8599	2
58	8772	8946	9119	9292	9466	9639	1
59	9813	9987	.161	.334	.508	.682	0
	60″	50″	40″	30″	20″	10″	Min.

Co-tangent of 7 Degrees.

P. Part { 1″ 2″ 3″ 4″ 5″ 6″ 7″ 8″ 9″ / 16 33 49 65 81 98 114 130 146

Tangent of 83 Degrees.

Min.	0″	10″	20″	30″	40″	50″	
0	10.910856	1030	1205	1379	1553	1727	59
1	1902	2076	2251	2426	2600	2775	58
2	2950	3125	3300	3475	3650	3825	57
3	4000	4176	4351	4527	4702	4878	56
4	5053	5229	5405	5581	5757	5933	55
5	6109	6285	6461	6638	6814	6990	54
6	7167	7343	7520	7697	7874	8050	53
7	8227	8404	8581	8759	8936	9113	52
8	9290	9468	9645	9823	....	.178	51
9	10.920356	0534	0712	0890	1068	1246	50
10	1424	1602	1781	1959	2138	2316	49
11	2495	2673	2852	3031	3210	3389	48
12	3568	3747	3926	4105	4285	4464	47
13	4644	4823	5003	5183	5362	5542	46
14	5722	5902	6082	6262	6442	6623	45
15	6803	6984	7164	7345	7525	7706	44
16	7887	8068	8249	8430	8611	8792	43
17	8973	9154	9336	9517	9699	9880	42
18	10.930062	0244	0425	0607	0789	0971	41
19	1154	1336	1518	1700	1883	2065	40
20	2248	2430	2613	2796	2979	3162	39
21	3345	3528	3711	3894	4078	4261	38
22	4444	4628	4812	4995	5179	5363	37
23	5547	5731	5915	6099	6283	6467	36
24	6652	6836	7021	7205	7390	7575	35
25	7760	7945	8130	8315	8500	8685	34
26	8870	9056	9241	9427	9612	9798	33
27	9984	.169	.355	.541	.727	.914	32
28	10.941100	1286	1472	1659	1845	2032	31
29	2219	2406	2592	2779	2966	3153	30
30	3341	3528	3715	3902	4090	4277	29
31	4465	4653	4841	5028	5216	5404	28
32	5593	5781	5969	6157	6346	6534	27
33	6723	6912	7100	7289	7478	7667	26
34	7856	8045	8234	8424	8613	8803	25
35	8992	9182	9371	9561	9751	9941	24
36	10.950131	0321	0511	0702	0892	1083	23
37	1273	1464	1654	1845	2036	2227	22
38	2418	2509	2800	2991	3183	3374	21
39	3566	3757	3949	4141	4332	4524	20
40	4716	4908	5101	5293	5485	5678	19
41	5870	6063	6255	6448	6641	6834	18
42	7027	7220	7413	7606	7800	7993	17
43	8187	8380	8574	8768	8961	9155	16
44	9349	9544	9738	9932	.126	.321	15
45	10.960515	0710	0905	1099	1294	1489	14
46	1684	1879	2074	2270	2465	2661	13
47	2856	3052	3247	3443	3639	3835	12
48	4031	4227	4424	4620	4816	5013	11
49	5209	5406	5603	5800	5997	6194	10
50	6391	6588	6785	6983	7180	7377	9
51	7575	7773	7971	8169	8367	8565	8
52	8763	8961	9159	9358	9556	9755	7
53	9954	.152	.351	.550	.749	.948	6
54	10.971148	1347	1546	1746	1945	2145	5
55	2345	2545	2745	2945	3145	3345	4
56	3545	3746	3946	4147	4347	4548	3
57	4749	4950	5151	5352	5553	5755	2
58	5956	6157	6359	6561	6762	6964	1
59	7166	7368	7570	7773	7975	8177	0
	60″	50″	40″	30″	20″	10″	Min.

Co-tangent of 6 Degrees.

P. Part { 1″ 2″ 3″ 4″ 5″ 6″ 7″ 8″ 9″ / 19 37 56 75 94 112 131 150 168

Min.	Sine of 84 Degrees. 0″	10″	20″	30″	40″	50″	
0	9·997614	7617	7619	7621	7623	7625	59
1	7628	7630	7632	7634	7636	7639	58
2	7641	7643	7645	7647	7650	7652	57
3	7654	7656	7658	7661	7663	7665	56
4	7667	7669	7672	7674	7676	7678	55
5	7680	7682	7685	7687	7689	7691	54
6	7693	7696	7698	7700	7702	7704	53
7	7706	7709	7711	7713	7715	7717	52
8	7719	7722	7724	7726	7728	7730	51
9	7732	7735	7737	7739	7741	7743	50
10	9·997745	7747	7750	7752	7754	7756	49
11	7758	7760	7762	7765	7767	7769	48
12	7771	7773	7775	7777	7780	7782	47
13	7784	7786	7788	7790	7792	7794	46
14	7797	7799	7801	7803	7805	7807	45
15	7809	7811	7814	7816	7818	7820	44
16	7822	7824	7826	7828	7830	7833	43
17	7835	7837	7839	7841	7843	7845	42
18	7847	7849	7852	7854	7856	7858	41
19	7860	7862	7864	7866	7868	7870	40
20	9·997872	7875	7877	7879	7881	7883	39
21	7885	7887	7889	7891	7893	7895	38
22	7897	7900	7902	7904	7906	7908	37
23	7910	7912	7914	7916	7918	7920	36
24	7922	7924	7926	7929	7931	7933	35
25	7935	7937	7939	7941	7943	7945	34
26	7947	7949	7951	7953	7955	7957	33
27	7959	7961	7963	7965	7967	7970	32
28	7972	7974	7976	7978	7980	7982	31
29	7984	7986	7988	7990	7992	7994	30
30	9·997996	7998	8000	8002	8004	8006	29
31	8008	8010	8012	8014	8016	8018	28
32	8020	8022	8024	8026	8028	8030	27
33	8032	8034	8036	8038	8040	8042	26
34	8044	8046	8048	8050	8052	8054	25
35	8056	8058	8060	8062	8064	8066	24
36	8068	8070	8072	8074	8076	8078	23
37	8080	8082	8084	8086	8088	8090	22
38	8092	8094	8096	8098	8100	8102	21
39	8104	8106	8108	8110	8112	8114	20
40	9·998116	8118	8120	8122	8124	8126	19
41	8128	8130	8131	8133	8135	8137	18
42	8139	8141	8143	8145	8147	8149	17
43	8151	8153	8155	8157	8159	8161	16
44	8163	8165	8167	8168	8170	8172	15
45	8174	8176	8178	8180	8182	8184	14
46	8186	8188	8190	8192	8194	8195	13
47	8197	8199	8201	8203	8205	8207	12
48	8209	8211	8213	8215	8217	8218	11
49	8220	8222	8224	8226	8228	8230	10
50	9·998232	8234	8236	8238	8239	8241	9
51	8243	8245	8247	8249	8251	8253	8
52	8255	8257	8258	8260	8262	8264	7
53	8266	8268	8270	8272	8273	8275	6
54	8277	8279	8281	8283	8285	8287	5
55	8289	8290	8292	8294	8296	8298	4
56	8300	8302	8303	8305	8307	8309	3
57	8311	8313	8315	8316	8318	8320	2
58	8322	8324	8326	8328	8329	8331	1
59	8333	8335	8337	8339	8341	8342	0
	60″	50″	40″	30″	20″	10″	Min.
	Co-sine of 5 Degrees.						

P. Part	1″	2″	3″	4″	5″	6″	7″	8″	9″
	0	0	1	1	1	1	1	2	2

Min.	Sine of 85 Degrees. 0″	10″	20″	30″	40″	50″	
0	9·998344	8346	8348	8350	8352	8353	59
1	8355	8357	8359	8361	8363	8364	58
2	8366	8368	8370	8372	8374	8375	57
3	8377	8379	8381	8383	8385	8386	56
4	8388	8390	8392	8394	8395	8397	55
5	8399	8401	8403	8404	8406	8408	54
6	8410	8412	8413	8415	8417	8419	53
7	8421	8422	8424	8426	8428	8430	52
8	8431	8433	8435	8437	8439	8440	51
9	8442	8444	8446	8448	8449	8451	50
10	9·998453	8455	8456	8458	8460	8462	49
11	8464	8465	8467	8469	8471	8472	48
12	8474	8476	8478	8479	8481	8483	47
13	8485	8487	8488	8490	8492	8494	46
14	8495	8497	8499	8501	8502	8504	45
15	8506	8508	8509	8511	8513	8515	44
16	8516	8518	8520	8522	8523	8525	43
17	8527	8529	8530	8532	8534	8535	42
18	8537	8539	8541	8542	8544	8546	41
19	8548	8549	8551	8553	8554	8556	40
20	9·998558	8560	8561	8563	8565	8566	39
21	8568	8570	8572	8573	8575	8577	38
22	8578	8580	8582	8584	8585	8587	37
23	8589	8590	8592	8594	8595	8597	36
24	8599	8601	8602	8604	8606	8607	35
25	8609	8611	8612	8614	8616	8617	34
26	8619	8621	8622	8624	8626	8627	33
27	8629	8631	8633	8634	8636	8638	32
28	8639	8641	8643	8644	8646	8648	31
29	8649	8651	8653	8654	8656	8657	30
30	9·998659	8661	8662	8664	8666	8667	29
31	8669	8671	8672	8674	8676	8677	28
32	8679	8681	8682	8684	8686	8687	27
33	8689	8690	8692	8694	8695	8697	26
34	8699	8700	8702	8704	8705	8707	25
35	8708	8710	8712	8713	8715	8717	24
36	8718	8720	8721	8723	8725	8726	23
37	8728	8729	8731	8733	8734	8736	22
38	8738	8739	8741	8742	8744	8746	21
39	8747	8749	8750	8752	8754	8755	20
40	9·998757	8758	8760	8762	8763	8765	19
41	8766	8768	8769	8771	8773	8774	18
42	8776	8777	8779	8781	8782	8784	17
43	8785	8787	8788	8790	8792	8793	16
44	8795	8796	8798	8799	8801	8803	15
45	8804	8806	8807	8809	8810	8812	14
46	8813	8815	8817	8818	8820	8821	13
47	8823	8824	8826	8827	8829	8831	12
48	8832	8834	8835	8837	8838	8840	11
49	8841	8843	8844	8846	8848	8849	10
50	9·998851	8852	8854	8855	8857	8858	9
51	8860	8861	8863	8864	8866	8867	8
52	8869	8870	8872	8873	8875	8877	7
53	8878	8880	8881	8883	8884	8886	6
54	8887	8889	8890	8892	8893	8895	5
55	8896	8898	8899	8901	8902	8904	4
56	8905	8907	8908	8910	8911	8913	3
57	8914	8916	8917	8919	8920	8922	2
58	8923	8925	8926	8927	8929	8930	1
59	8932	8933	8935	8936	8938	8939	0
	60″	50″	40″	30″	20″	10″	Min.
	Co-sine of 4 Degrees.						

P. Part	1″	2″	3″	4″	5″	6″	7″	8″	9″
	0	0	0	1	1	1	1	1	1

Min.	Tangent of 84 Degrees. 0″	10″	20″	30″	40″	50″	
0	10.978380	8582	8785	8988	9191	9394	59
1	9597	9800	...3	.206	.410	.613	58
2	10.980817	1021	1224	1428	1632	1836	57
3	2041	2245	2449	2654	2858	3063	56
4	3268	3472	3677	3882	4087	4293	55
5	4498	4703	4909	5114	5320	5526	54
6	5732	5938	6144	6350	6556	6763	53
7	6969	7176	7382	7589	7796	8003	52
8	8210	8417	8624	8831	9039	9246	51
9	9454	9662	9869	..77	.285	.493	50
10	10.990702	0910	1118	1327	1535	1744	49
11	1953	2162	2371	2580	2789	2998	48
12	3208	3417	3627	3836	4046	4256	47
13	4466	4676	4886	5096	5307	5517	46
14	5728	5939	6149	6360	6571	6782	45
15	6993	7205	7416	7627	7839	8051	44
16	8262	8474	8686	8898	9111	9323	43
17	9535	9748	9960	.173	.386	.599	42
18	11.000812	1025	1238	1451	1665	1878	41
19	2092	2306	2519	2733	2947	3161	40
20	3376	3590	3804	4019	4234	4448	39
21	4663	4878	5093	5308	5524	5739	38
22	5955	6170	6386	6602	6818	7034	37
23	7250	7466	7682	7899	8115	8332	36
24	8549	8765	8982	9199	9417	9634	35
25	9851	..69	.286	.504	.722	.940	34
26	11.011158	1376	1594	1813	2031	2250	33
27	2468	2687	2906	3125	3344	3563	32
28	3783	4002	4222	4441	4661	4881	31
29	5101	5321	5541	5762	5982	6202	30
30	6423	6644	6865	7086	7307	7528	29
31	7749	7971	8192	8414	8636	8857	28
32	9079	9301	9524	9746	9968	.191	27
33	11.020414	0636	0859	1082	1305	1528	26
34	1752	1975	2199	2422	2646	2870	25
35	3094	3318	3542	3767	3991	4216	24
36	4440	4665	4890	5115	5340	5565	23
37	5791	6016	6242	6468	6693	6919	22
38	7145	7372	7598	7824	8051	8277	21
39	8504	8731	8958	9185	9412	9640	20
40	9867	..95	.322	.550	.778	1006	19
41	11.031234	1462	1691	1919	2148	2377	18
42	2606	2835	3064	3293	3522	3752	17
43	3981	4211	4441	4671	4901	5131	16
44	5361	5592	5822	6053	6284	6514	15
45	6745	6977	7208	7439	7671	7902	14
46	8134	8366	8598	8830	9062	9295	13
47	9527	9760	9992	.225	.458	.691	12
48	11.040925	1158	1391	1625	1859	2092	11
49	2326	2561	2795	3029	3264	3498	10
50	3733	3968	4203	4438	4673	4908	9
51	5144	5379	5615	5851	6087	6323	8
52	6559	6795	7032	7268	7505	7742	7
53	7979	8216	8453	8691	8928	9166	6
54	9403	9641	9879	.117	.356	.594	5
55	11.050832	1071	1310	1549	1788	2027	4
56	2266	2506	2745	2985	3225	3465	3
57	3705	3945	4185	4426	4666	4907	2
58	5148	5389	5630	5871	6112	6354	1
59	6596	6837	7079	7321	7563	7806	0
	60″	50″	40″	30″	20″	10″	Min.
	Co-tangent of 5 Degrees.						

P. Part { 1″ 2″ 3″ 4″ 5″ 6″ 7″ 8″ 9″ / 22 44 66 88 110 132 154 177 199

Min.	Tangent of 85 Degrees. 0″	10″	20″	30″	40″	50″	
0	11.058048	8291	8533	8776	9019	9262	59
1	9506	9749	9993	.236	.480	.724	58
2	11.060968	1212	1456	1701	1945	2190	57
3	2435	2680	2925	3170	3416	3661	56
4	3907	4153	4399	4645	4891	5138	55
5	5384	5631	5877	6124	6371	6619	54
6	6866	7113	7361	7609	7857	8105	53
7	8353	8601	8850	9098	9347	9596	52
8	9845	..94	.343	.593	.842	1092	51
9	11.071342	1592	1842	2092	2343	2593	50
10	2844	3095	3346	3597	3848	4100	49
11	4351	4603	4855	5107	5359	5611	48
12	5864	6116	6369	6622	6875	7128	47
13	7381	7635	7888	8142	8396	8650	46
14	8904	9159	9413	9668	9922	.177	45
15	11.080432	0688	0943	1199	1454	1710	44
16	1966	2222	2478	2735	2991	3248	43
17	3505	3762	4019	4276	4534	4791	42
18	5049	5307	5565	5823	6082	6340	41
19	6599	6858	7117	7376	7635	7894	40
20	8154	8414	8674	8934	9194	9454	39
21	9715	9975	.236	.497	.758	1020	38
22	11.091281	1543	1804	2066	2328	2590	37
23	2853	3115	3378	3641	3904	4167	36
24	4430	4694	4957	5221	5485	5749	35
25	6013	6278	6542	6807	7072	7337	34
26	7602	7868	8133	8399	8665	8931	33
27	9197	9463	9730	9996	.263	.530	32
28	11.100797	1065	1332	1600	1868	2136	31
29	2404	2672	2940	3209	3478	3747	30
30	4016	4285	4555	4824	5094	5364	29
31	5634	5904	6175	6445	6716	6987	28
32	7258	7529	7801	8072	8344	8616	27
33	8888	9160	9433	9705	9978	.251	26
34	11.110524	0798	1071	1345	1618	1892	25
35	2167	2441	2715	2990	3265	3540	24
36	3815	4090	4366	4642	4917	5193	23
37	5470	5746	6023	6299	6576	6853	22
38	7131	7408	7686	7963	8241	8520	21
39	8798	9076	9355	9634	9913	.192	20
40	11.120471	0751	1031	1311	1591	1871	19
41	2151	243[illegible]	2713	2994	3275	3556	18
42	3838	4119	4401	4683	4966	5248	17
43	5531	5813	6096	6380	6663	6946	16
44	7230	7514	7798	8082	8367	8651	15
45	8936	9221	9506	9792	..77	.363	14
46	11.130649	0935	1221	1508	1794	2081	13
47	2368	2656	2943	3231	3518	3806	12
48	4094	4383	4671	4960	5249	5538	11
49	5827	6117	6407	6697	6987	7277	10
50	7567	7858	8149	8440	8731	9023	9
51	9314	9606	9898	.190	.483	.775	8
52	11.141068	1361	1654	1947	2241	2535	7
53	2829	3123	3417	3712	4007	4301	6
54	4597	4892	5187	5483	5779	6075	5
55	6372	6668	6965	7262	7559	7856	4
56	8154	8452	8750	9048	9346	9645	3
57	9943	.242	.542	.841	1141	1440	2
58	11.151740	2041	2341	2642	2942	3243	1
59	3545	3846	4148	4449	4752	5054	0
	60″	50″	40″	30″	20″	10″	Min.
	Co-tangent of 4 Degrees.						

P. Part { 1″ 2″ 3″ 4″ 5″ 6″ 7″ 8″ 9″ / 27 54 81 108 135 162 188 215 242

Min.	Sine of 86 Degrees. 0″	10″	20″	30″	40″	50″	
0	9·998941	8942	8944	8945	8947	8948	59
1	8950	8951	8953	8954	8955	8957	58
2	8958	8960	8961	8963	8964	8966	57
3	8967	8969	8970	8971	8973	8974	56
4	8976	8977	8979	8980	8982	8983	55
5	8984	8986	8987	8989	8990	8992	54
6	8993	8995	8996	8997	8999	9000	53
7	9002	9003	9005	9006	9007	9009	52
8	9010	9012	9013	9015	9016	9017	51
9	9019	9020	9022	9023	9024	9026	50
10	9·999027	9029	9030	9032	9033	9034	49
11	9036	9037	9039	9040	9041	9043	48
12	9044	9046	9047	9048	9050	9051	47
13	9053	9054	9055	9057	9058	9059	46
14	9061	9062	9064	9065	9066	9068	45
15	9069	9071	9072	9073	9075	9076	44
16	9077	9079	9080	9082	9083	9084	43
17	9086	9087	9088	9090	9091	9092	42
18	9094	9095	9097	9098	9099	9101	41
19	9102	9103	9105	9106	9107	9109	40
20	9·999110	9111	9113	9114	9115	9117	39
21	9118	9120	9121	9122	9124	9125	38
22	9126	9128	9129	9130	9132	9133	37
23	9134	9136	9137	9138	9140	9141	36
24	9142	9143	9145	9146	9147	9149	35
25	9150	9151	9153	9154	9155	9157	34
26	9158	9159	9161	9162	9163	9165	33
27	9166	9167	9168	9170	9171	9172	32
28	9174	9175	9176	9178	9179	9180	31
29	9181	9183	9184	9185	9187	9188	30
30	9·999189	9190	9192	9193	9194	9196	29
31	9197	9198	9199	9201	9202	9203	28
32	9205	9206	9207	9208	9210	9211	27
33	9212	9213	9215	9216	9217	9219	26
34	9220	9221	9222	9224	9225	9226	25
35	9227	9229	9230	9231	9232	9234	24
36	9235	9236	9237	9239	9240	9241	23
37	9242	9244	9245	9246	9247	9249	22
38	9250	9251	9252	9254	9255	9256	21
39	9257	9258	9260	9261	9262	9263	20
40	9·999265	9266	9267	9268	9270	9271	19
41	9272	9273	9274	9276	9277	9278	18
42	9279	9280	9282	9283	9284	9285	17
43	9287	9288	9289	9290	9291	9293	16
44	9294	9295	9296	9297	9299	9300	15
45	9301	9302	9303	9305	9306	9307	14
46	9308	9309	9310	9312	9313	9314	13
47	9315	9316	9318	9319	9320	9321	12
48	9322	9323	9325	9326	9327	9328	11
49	9329	9331	9332	9333	9334	9335	10
50	9·999336	9338	9339	9340	9341	9342	9
51	9343	9344	9346	9347	9348	9349	8
52	9350	9351	9353	9354	9355	9356	7
53	9357	9358	9359	9361	9362	9363	6
54	9364	9365	9366	9367	9369	9370	5
55	9371	9372	9373	9374	9375	9377	4
56	9378	9379	9380	9381	9382	9383	3
57	9384	9385	9387	9388	9389	9390	2
58	9391	9392	9393	9394	9396	9397	1
59	9398	9399	9400	9401	9402	9403	0
	60″	50″	40″	30″	20″	10″	Min.
	Co-sine of 3 Degrees.						

P. Part	1″	2″	3″	4″	5″	6″	7″	8″	9″
	0	0	0	1	1	1	1	1	1

Min.	Sine of 87 Degrees. 0″	10″	20″	30″	40″	50″	
0	9·999404	9406	9407	9408	9409	9410	59
1	9411	9412	9413	9414	9415	9416	58
2	9418	9419	9420	9421	9422	9423	57
3	9424	9425	9426	9427	9428	9430	56
4	9431	9432	9433	9434	9435	9436	55
5	9437	9438	9439	9440	9441	9442	54
6	9443	9445	9446	9447	9448	9449	53
7	9450	9451	9452	9453	9454	9455	52
8	9456	9457	9458	9459	9460	9461	51
9	9463	9464	9465	9466	9467	9468	50
10	9·999469	9470	9471	9472	9473	9474	49
11	9475	9476	9477	9478	9479	9480	48
12	9481	9482	9483	9484	9485	9486	47
13	9487	9488	9489	9490	9491	9492	46
14	9493	9495	9496	9497	9498	9499	45
15	9500	9501	9502	9503	9504	9505	44
16	9506	9507	9508	9509	9510	9511	43
17	9512	9513	9514	9515	9516	9517	42
18	9518	9519	9520	9521	9522	9523	41
19	9524	9525	9526	9527	9527	9528	40
20	9·999529	9530	9531	9532	9533	9534	39
21	9535	9536	9537	9538	9539	9540	38
22	9541	9542	9543	9544	9545	9546	37
23	9547	9548	9549	9550	9551	9552	36
24	9553	9554	9555	9556	9557	9557	35
25	9558	9559	9560	9561	9562	9563	34
26	9564	9565	9566	9567	9568	9569	33
27	9570	9571	9572	9573	9573	9574	32
28	9575	9576	9577	9578	9579	9580	31
29	9581	9582	9583	9584	9585	9586	30
30	9·999586	9587	9588	9589	9590	9591	29
31	9592	9593	9594	9595	9596	9597	28
32	9597	9598	9599	9600	9601	9602	27
33	9603	9604	9605	9606	9606	9607	26
34	9608	9609	9610	9611	9612	9613	25
35	9614	9614	9615	9616	9617	9618	24
36	9619	9620	9621	9622	9622	9623	23
37	9624	9625	9626	9627	9628	9629	22
38	9629	9630	9631	9632	9633	9634	21
39	9635	9635	9636	9637	9638	9639	20
40	9·999640	9641	9641	9642	9643	9644	19
41	9645	9646	9647	9647	9648	9649	18
42	9650	9651	9652	9653	9653	9654	17
43	9655	9656	9657	9658	9658	9659	16
44	9660	9661	9662	9663	9663	9664	15
45	9665	9666	9667	9668	9668	9669	14
46	9670	9671	9672	9672	9673	9674	13
47	9675	9676	9677	9677	9678	9679	12
48	9680	9681	9681	9682	9683	9684	11
49	9685	9685	9686	9687	9688	9689	10
50	9·999689	9690	9691	9692	9693	9693	9
51	9694	9695	9696	9697	9697	9698	8
52	9699	9700	9700	9701	9702	9703	7
53	9704	9704	9705	9706	9707	9707	6
54	9708	9709	9710	9711	9711	9712	5
55	9713	9714	9714	9715	9716	9717	4
56	9717	9718	9719	9720	9720	9721	3
57	9722	9723	9723	9724	9725	9726	2
58	9726	9727	9728	9729	9729	9730	1
59	9731	9732	9732	9733	9734	9735	0
	60″	50″	40″	30″	20″	10″	Min.
	Co-sine of 2 Degrees.						

P. Part	1″	2″	3″	4″	5″	6″	7″	8″	9″
	0	0	0	0	0	1	1	1	1

Min.	Tangent of 86 Degrees. 0″	10″	20″	30″	40″	50″	
0	11.155356	5659	5962	6265	6568	6872	59
1	7175	7479	7784	8088	8393	8697	58
2	9002	9308	9613	9919	.224	.530	57
3	11.160837	1143	1450	1757	2064	2371	56
4	2679	2987	3295	3603	3911	4220	55
5	4529	4838	5147	5457	5766	6076	54
6	6387	6697	7008	7318	7629	7941	53
7	8252	8564	8876	9188	9500	9813	52
8	11.170126	0439	0752	1066	1379	1693	51
9	2008	2322	2637	2951	3267	3582	50
10	3897	4213	4529	4845	5162	5478	49
11	5795	6112	6430	6747	7065	7383	48
12	7702	8020	8339	8658	8977	9297	47
13	9616	9936	.256	.577	.897	1218	46
14	11.181539	1860	2182	2504	2826	3148	45
15	3471	3793	4116	4440	4763	5087	44
16	5411	5735	6059	6384	6709	7034	43
17	7359	7685	8011	8337	8663	8990	42
18	9317	9644	9971	.299	.626	.954	41
19	11.191283	1611	1940	2269	2598	2928	40
20	3258	3588	3918	4249	4579	4910	39
21	5242	5573	5905	6237	6569	6902	38
22	7235	7568	7901	8235	8568	8902	37
23	9237	9571	9906	.241	.577	.912	36
24	11.201248	1584	1921	2257	2594	2931	35
25	3269	3606	3944	4282	4621	4960	34
26	5299	5638	5977	6317	6657	6997	33
27	7338	7679	8020	8361	8703	9045	32
28	9387	9729	..72	.415	.758	1102	31
29	11.211446	1790	2134	2479	2823	3169	30
30	3514	3860	4206	4552	4898	5245	29
31	5592	5939	6287	6635	6983	7331	28
32	7680	8029	8378	8728	9078	9428	27
33	9778	.129	.480	.831	1183	1534	26
34	11.221886	2239	2591	2944	3298	3651	25
35	4005	4359	4713	5068	5423	5778	24
36	6134	6489	6845	7202	7558	7915	23
37	8273	8630	8988	9346	9705	..63	22
38	11.230422	0782	1141	1501	1861	2222	21
39	2583	2944	3305	3667	4029	4391	20
40	4754	5116	5480	5843	6207	6571	19
41	6935	7300	7665	8030	8396	8762	18
42	9128	9495	9861	.229	.596	.964	17
43	11.241332	1700	2069	2438	2807	3177	16
44	3547	3917	4288	4659	5030	5401	15
45	5773	6145	6518	6891	7264	7637	14
46	8011	8385	8759	9134	9509	9884	13
47	11.250260	0636	1012	1389	1766	2143	12
48	2521	2899	3277	3656	4034	4414	11
49	4793	5173	5553	5934	6315	6696	10
50	7078	7460	7842	8224	8607	8991	9
51	9374	9758	.142	.527	.912	1297	8
52	11.261683	2069	2455	2842	3229	3616	7
53	4004	4392	4780	5169	5558	5947	6
54	6337	6727	7117	7508	7899	8291	5
55	8683	9075	9467	9860	.254	.647	4
56	11.271041	1435	1830	2225	2620	3016	3
57	3412	3809	4206	4603	5000	5398	2
58	5796	6195	6594	6993	7393	7793	1
59	8194	8595	8996	9397	9799	.202	0
	60″	50″	40″	30″	20″	10″	Min.
	Co-tangent of 3 Degrees.						

P. Part { 1″ 2″ 3″ 4″ 5″ 6″ 7″ 8″ 9″
{ 35 69 104 138 173 207 242 276 311

Min.	Tangent of 87 Degrees. 0″	10″	20″	30″	40″	50″	
0	11.280604	1007	1411	1814	2219	2623	59
1	3028	3433	3839	4245	4652	5058	58
2	5466	5873	6281	6689	7098	7507	57
3	7917	8326	8737	9147	9558	9970	56
4	11.290382	0794	1206	1619	2033	2446	55
5	2860	3275	3690	4105	4521	4937	54
6	5354	5770	6188	6605	7024	7442	53
7	7861	8280	8700	9120	9541	9962	52
8	11.300383	0805	1227	1649	2072	2496	51
9	2919	3344	3768	4193	4619	5044	50
10	5471	5897	6325	6752	7180	7608	49
11	8037	8466	8896	9326	9756	.187	48
12	11.310619	1050	1483	1915	2348	2782	47
13	3216	3650	4085	4520	4956	5392	46
14	5828	6265	6702	7140	7578	8017	45
15	8456	8896	9336	9776	.217	.659	44
16	11.321100	1543	1985	2428	2872	3316	43
17	3761	4206	4651	5097	5543	5990	42
18	6437	6885	7333	7782	8231	8680	41
19	9130	9581	..32	.483	.935	1387	40
20	11.331840	2293	2747	3201	3656	4111	39
21	4567	5023	5480	5937	6394	6852	38
22	7311	7770	8229	8689	9150	9611	37
23	11.340072	0534	0996	1459	1923	2387	36
24	2851	3316	3781	4247	4714	5180	35
25	5648	6116	6584	7053	7522	7992	34
26	8463	8933	9405	9877	.349	.822	33
27	11.351296	1770	2244	2719	3195	3671	32
28	4147	4624	5102	5580	6059	6538	31
29	7018	7498	7979	8460	8942	9424	30
30	9907	.390	.874	1359	1844	2329	29
31	11.362816	3302	3789	4277	4765	5254	28
32	5744	6234	6724	7215	7707	8199	27
33	8692	9185	9679	.173	.668	1164	26
34	11.371660	2156	2654	3151	3650	4149	25
35	4648	5148	5649	6150	6652	7154	24
36	7657	8161	8665	9170	9675	.181	23
37	11.380687	1194	1702	2210	2719	3228	22
38	3738	4249	4760	5272	5785	6298	21
39	6811	7325	7840	8356	8872	9388	20
40	9906	.424	.942	1461	1981	2501	19
41	11.393022	3544	4066	4589	5113	5637	18
42	6161	6687	7213	7740	8267	8795	17
43	9323	9853	.382	.913	1444	1976	16
44	11.402508	3041	3575	4110	4645	5180	15
45	5717	6254	6792	7330	7869	8409	14
46	8949	9490	..32	.574	1117	1661	13
47	11.412205	2751	3296	3843	4390	4938	12
48	5486	6036	6586	7136	7688	8240	11
49	8792	9346	9900	.455	1010	1566	10
50	11.422123	2681	3240	3799	4358	4919	9
51	5480	6042	6605	7168	7733	8298	8
52	8863	9430	9997	.565	1133	1702	7
53	11.432273	2843	3415	3987	4560	5134	6
54	5709	6284	6860	7437	8015	8593	5
55	9172	9752	.333	.915	1497	2080	4
56	11.442664	3248	3834	4420	5007	5595	3
57	6183	6773	7363	7954	8546	9138	2
58	9732	.326	.921	1517	2113	2711	1
59	11.453309	3908	4508	5109	5711	6313	0
	60″	50″	40″	30″	20″	10″	Min.
	Co-tangent of 2 Degrees.						

P. Part { 1″ 2″ 3″ 4″ 5″ 6″ 7″ 8″ 9″
{ 48 97 145 193 242 290 338 387 435

Min.	Sine of 88 Degrees. 0″	10″	20″	30″	40″	50″	
0	9·999735	9736	9737	9738	9738	9739	59
1	9740	9740	9741	9742	9743	9743	58
2	9744	9745	9746	9746	9747	9748	57
3	9748	9749	9750	9751	9751	9752	56
4	9753	9753	9754	9755	9756	9756	55
5	9757	9758	9758	9759	9760	9760	54
6	9761	9762	9763	9763	9764	9765	53
7	9765	9766	9767	9767	9768	9769	52
8	9769	9770	9771	9772	9772	9773	51
9	9774	9774	9775	9776	9776	9777	50
10	9·999778	9778	9779	9780	9780	9781	49
11	9782	9782	9783	9784	9784	9785	48
12	9786	9786	9787	9788	9788	9789	47
13	9790	9790	9791	9792	9792	9793	46
14	9794	9794	9795	9795	9796	9797	45
15	9797	9798	9799	9799	9800	9801	44
16	9801	9802	9803	9803	9804	9804	43
17	9805	9806	9806	9807	9808	9808	42
18	9809	9809	9810	9811	9811	9812	41
19	9813	9813	9814	9814	9815	9816	40
20	9·999816	9817	9817	9818	9819	9819	39
21	9820	9820	9821	9822	9822	9823	38
22	9824	9824	9825	9825	9826	9827	37
23	9827	9828	9828	9829	9829	9830	36
24	9831	9831	9832	9832	9833	9834	35
25	9834	9835	9835	9836	9836	9837	34
26	9838	9838	9839	9839	9840	9840	33
27	9841	9842	9842	9843	9843	9844	32
28	9844	9845	9846	9846	9847	9847	31
29	9848	9848	9849	9849	9850	9851	30
30	9·999851	9852	9852	9853	9853	9854	29
31	9854	9855	9856	9856	9857	9857	28
32	9858	9858	9859	9859	9860	9860	27
33	9861	9861	9862	9863	9863	9864	26
34	9864	9865	9865	9866	9866	9867	25
35	9867	9868	9868	9869	9869	9870	24
36	9870	9871	9871	9872	9872	9873	23
37	9873	9874	9874	9875	9875	9876	22
38	9876	9877	9877	9878	9878	9879	21
39	9879	9880	9880	9881	9881	9882	20
40	9·999882	9883	9883	9884	9884	9885	19
41	9885	9886	9886	9887	9887	9888	18
42	9888	9889	9889	9890	9890	9891	17
43	9891	9892	9892	9892	9893	9893	16
44	9894	9894	9895	9895	9896	9896	15
45	9897	9897	9898	9898	9898	9899	14
46	9899	9900	9900	9901	9901	9902	13
47	9902	9903	9903	9903	9904	9904	12
48	9905	9905	9906	9906	9906	9907	11
49	9907	9908	9908	9909	9909	9910	10
50	9·999910	9910	9911	9911	9912	9912	9
51	9913	9913	9913	9914	9914	9915	8
52	9915	9915	9916	9916	9917	9917	7
53	9918	9918	9918	9919	9919	9920	6
54	9920	9920	9921	9921	9922	9922	5
55	9922	9923	9923	9924	9924	9924	4
56	9925	9925	9926	9926	9926	9927	3
57	9927	9927	9928	9928	9929	9929	2
58	9929	9930	9930	9931	9931	9931	1
59	9932	9932	9932	9933	9933	9933	0
	60″	50″	40″	30″	20″	10″	Min.
	Co-sine of 1 Degree.						

P. Part { 1″ 2″ 3″ 4″ 5″ 6″ 7″ 8″ 9″ / 0 0 0 0 0 0 0 0 1 }

Min.	Sine of 89 Degrees. 0″	10″	20″	30″	40″	50″	
0	9·999934	9934	9935	9935	9935	9936	59
1	9936	9936	9937	9937	9937	9938	58
2	9938	9939	9939	9939	9940	9940	57
3	9940	9941	9941	9941	9942	9942	56
4	9942	9943	9943	9943	9944	9944	55
5	9944	9945	9945	9945	9946	9946	54
6	9946	9947	9947	9947	9948	9948	53
7	9948	9949	9949	9949	9950	9950	52
8	9950	9951	9951	9951	9952	9952	51
9	9952	9953	9953	9953	9953	9954	50
10	9·999954	9954	9955	9955	9955	9956	49
11	9956	9956	9956	9957	9957	9957	48
12	9958	9958	9958	9959	9959	9959	47
13	9959	9960	9960	9960	9961	9961	46
14	9961	9961	9962	9962	9962	9963	45
15	9963	9963	9963	9964	9964	9064	44
16	9964	9965	9965	9965	9965	9966	43
17	9966	9966	9967	9967	9967	9967	42
18	9968	9968	9968	9968	9969	9969	41
19	9969	9969	9970	9970	9970	9970	40
20	9·999971	9971	9971	9971	9972	9972	39
21	9972	9972	9973	9973	9973	9973	38
22	9973	9974	9974	9974	9974	9975	37
23	9975	9975	9975	9976	9976	9976	36
24	9976	9976	9977	9977	9977	9977	35
25	9977	9978	9978	9978	9978	9979	34
26	9979	9979	9979	9979	9980	9980	33
27	9980	9980	9980	9981	9981	9981	32
28	9981	9981	9982	9982	9982	9982	31
29	9982	9983	9983	9983	9983	9983	30
30	9·999983	9984	9984	9984	9984	9984	29
31	9985	9985	9985	9985	9985	9985	28
32	9986	9986	9986	9986	9986	9986	27
33	9987	9987	9987	9987	9987	9987	26
34	9988	9988	9988	9988	9988	9988	25
35	9989	9989	9989	9989	9989	9989	24
36	9989	9990	9990	9990	9990	9990	23
37	9990	9990	9991	9991	9991	9991	22
38	9991	9991	9991	9992	9992	9992	21
39	9992	9992	9992	9992	9992	9993	20
40	9·999993	9993	9993	9993	9993	9993	19
41	9993	9993	9994	9994	9994	9994	18
42	9994	9994	9994	9994	9994	9995	17
43	9995	9995	9995	9995	9995	9995	16
44	9995	9995	9995	9996	9996	9996	15
45	9996	9996	9996	9996	9996	9996	14
46	9996	9996	9997	9997	9997	9997	13
47	9997	9997	9997	9997	9997	9997	12
48	9997	9997	9997	9998	9998	9998	11
49	9998	9998	9998	9998	9998	9998	10
50	9·999998	9998	9998	9998	9998	9998	9
51	9999	9999	9999	9999	9999	9999	8
52	9999	9999	9999	9999	9999	9999	7
53	9999	9999	9999	9999	9999	9999	6
54	9999	9999	9999	9999	9999	....	5
55	0.000000	0000	0000	0000	0000	0000	4
56	0000	0000	0000	0000	0000	0000	3
57	0000	0000	0000	0000	0000	0000	2
58	0000	0000	0000	0000	0000	0000	1
59	0000	0000	0000	0000	0000	0000	0
	60″	50″	40″	30″	20″	10″	Min.
	Co-sine of 0 Degree.						

P. Part { 1″ 2″ 3″ 4″ 5″ 6″ 7″ 8″ 9″ / 0 0 0 0 0 0 0 0 0 }

Min.	Tangent of 88 Degrees. 0″	10″	20″	30″	40″	50″		P. Part to 1″.
0	11.456916	11.457520	11.458125	11.458731	11.459338	11.459945	59	60.6
1	460553	461163	461773	462383	462995	463608	58	61.1
2	464221	464836	465451	466067	466684	467302	57	61.6
3	467920	468540	469160	469782	470404	471027	56	62.2
4	471651	472276	472902	473528	474156	474785	55	62.7
5	475414	476044	476676	477308	477941	478575	54	63.3
6	479210	479846	480482	481120	481759	482398	53	63.8
7	483039	483680	484323	484966	485611	486256	52	64.4
8	486902	487549	488198	488847	489497	490148	51	65.0
9	490800	491453	492107	492762	493418	494075	50	65.5
10	11.494733	11.495392	11.496052	11.496713	11.497375	11.498038	49	66.1
11	498702	499367	500033	500700	501368	502037	48	66.8
12	502707	503378	504051	504724	505398	506073	47	67.4
13	506750	507427	508106	508785	509466	510148	46	68.0
14	510830	511514	512199	512885	513572	514260	45	68.6
15	514950	515640	516331	517024	517717	518412	44	69.3
16	519108	519805	520503	521202	521903	522604	43	70.0
17	523307	524010	524715	525421	526128	526837	42	70.7
18	527546	528257	528969	529682	530396	531111	41	71.3
19	531828	532545	533264	533984	534705	535428	40	72.1
20	11.536151	11.536876	11.537602	11.538330	11.539058	11.539788	39	72.8
21	540519	541251	541984	542719	543455	544192	38	73.5
22	544930	545670	546411	547153	547896	548641	37	74.3
23	549387	550134	550883	551632	552384	553136	36	75.0
24	553890	554645	555401	556159	556918	557678	35	75.8
25	558440	559203	559967	560733	561500	562268	34	76.6
26	563038	563809	564581	565355	566130	566907	33	77.5
27	567685	568464	569245	570027	570811	571596	32	78.3
28	572382	573170	573959	574750	575542	576336	31	79.1
29	577131	577928	578726	579525	580326	581128	30	80.0
30	11.581932	11.582737	11.583544	11.584353	11.585163	11.585974	29	80.9
31	586787	587601	588417	589235	590054	590874	28	81.8
32	591696	592520	593345	594172	595000	595830	27	82.8
33	596662	597495	598330	599166	600004	600844	26	83.7
34	601685	602528	603372	604218	605066	605915	25	84.7
35	606766	607619	608474	609330	610187	611047	24	85.7
36	611908	612771	613636	614502	615370	616240	23	86.7
37	617111	617985	618860	619737	620615	621496	22	87.8
38	622378	623262	624147	625035	625924	626815	21	88.8
39	627708	628603	629500	630399	631299	632201	20	89.9
40	11.633105	11.634012	11.634919	11.635829	11.636741	11.637655	19	91.1
41	638570	639488	640407	641329	642252	643177	18	92.2
42	644105	645034	645965	646899	647834	648771	17	93.4
43	649711	650652	651595	652541	653488	654438	16	94.6
44	655390	656343	657299	658257	659217	660179	15	95.9
45	661144	662110	663079	664050	665023	665998	14	97.2
46	666975	667955	668936	669920	670907	671895	13	98.5
47	672886	673879	674874	675871	676871	677873	12	99.8
48	678878	679885	680894	681905	682919	683935	11	101.3
49	684954	685975	686998	688024	689052	690083	10	102.7
50	11.691116	11.692151	11.693189	11.694230	11.695273	11.696318	9	104.2
51	697366	698417	699470	700526	701584	702645	8	105.7
52	703708	704774	705843	706914	707988	709065	7	107.2
53	710144	711226	712311	713398	714488	715581	6	108.9
54	716677	717775	718876	719980	721087	722196	5	110.5
55	723309	724424	725542	726663	727787	728914	4	112 2
56	730044	731176	732312	733451	734592	735737	3	114.0
57	736885	738035	739189	740346	741506	742669	2	115.8
58	743835	745004	746177	747352	748531	749713	1	117.7
59	750898	752087	753279	754474	755672	756874	0	119.7
	60″	50″	40″	30″	20″	10″	Min.	
	Co-tangent of 1 Degree.							

Seconds.	Minutes.	0 Degree. log. sin. A— log. A″.	log. tan. A— log. A″.	log. cot. A+ log. A″.		Seconds.	Minutes.	1 Degree. log. sin. A— log. A″.	log. tan. A— log. A″.	log. cot. A+ log. A″.	
0	0	4.685575	4.685575	15.314425	60	3600	0	4.685553	4.685619	15.314381	60
60	1	575	575	425	59	3660	1	552	620	380	59
120	2	575	575	425	58	3720	2	551	622	378	58
180	3	575	575	425	57	3780	3	551	623	377	57
240	4	575	575	425	56	3840	4	550	625	375	56
300	5	575	575	425	55	3900	5	549	627	373	55
360	6	575	575	425	54	3960	6	548	628	372	54
420	7	575	575	425	53	4020	7	547	630	370	53
480	8	574	576	424	52	4080	8	547	632	368	52
540	9	574	576	424	51	4140	9	546	633	367	51
600	10	4.685574	4.685576	15.314424	50	4200	10	4.685545	4.685635	15.314365	50
660	11	574	576	424	49	4260	11	544	637	363	49
720	12	574	577	423	48	4320	12	543	638	362	48
780	13	574	577	423	47	4380	13	542	640	360	47
840	14	574	577	423	46	4440	14	541	642	358	46
900	15	573	578	422	45	4500	15	540	644	356	45
960	16	573	578	422	44	4560	16	539	646	354	44
1020	17	573	578	422	43	4620	17	539	647	353	43
1080	18	573	579	421	42	4680	18	538	649	351	42
1140	19	573	579	421	41	4740	19	537	651	349	41
1200	20	4.685572	4.685580	15.314420	40	4800	20	4.685536	4.685653	15.314347	40
1260	21	572	580	420	39	4860	21	535	655	345	39
1320	22	572	581	419	38	4920	22	534	657	343	38
1380	23	572	581	419	37	4980	23	533	659	341	37
1440	24	571	582	418	36	5040	24	532	661	339	36
1500	25	571	583	417	35	5100	25	531	663	337	35
1560	26	571	583	417	34	5160	26	530	665	335	34
1620	27	570	584	416	33	5220	27	529	668	332	33
1680	28	570	584	416	32	5280	28	527	670	330	32
1740	29	570	585	415	31	5340	29	526	672	328	31
1800	30	4.685569	4.685586	15.314414	30	5400	30	4.685525	4.685674	15.314326	30
1860	31	569	587	413	29	5460	31	524	676	324	29
1920	32	569	587	413	28	5520	32	523	679	321	28
1980	33	568	588	412	27	5580	33	522	681	319	27
2040	34	568	589	411	26	5640	34	521	683	317	26
2100	35	567	590	410	25	5700	35	520	685	315	25
2160	36	567	591	409	24	5760	36	518	688	312	24
2220	37	566	592	408	23	5820	37	517	690	310	23
2280	38	566	593	407	22	5880	38	516	693	307	22
2340	39	566	593	407	21	5940	39	515	695	305	21
2400	40	4.685565	4.685594	15.314406	20	6000	40	4.685514	4.685697	15.314303	20
2460	41	565	595	405	19	6060	41	512	700	300	19
2520	42	564	596	404	18	6120	42	511	702	298	18
2580	43	564	598	402	17	6180	43	510	705	295	17
2640	44	563	599	401	16	6240	44	509	707	293	16
2700	45	562	600	400	15	6300	45	507	710	290	15
2760	46	562	601	399	14	6360	46	506	713	287	14
2820	47	561	602	398	13	6420	47	505	715	285	13
2880	48	561	603	397	12	6480	48	503	718	282	12
2940	49	560	604	396	11	6540	49	502	720	280	11
3000	50	4.685560	4.685605	15.314395	10	6600	50	4.685501	4.685723	15.314277	10
3060	51	559	607	393	9	6660	51	499	726	274	9
3120	52	558	608	392	8	6720	52	498	729	271	8
3180	53	558	609	391	7	6780	53	497	731	269	7
3240	54	557	611	389	6	6840	54	495	734	266	6
3300	55	556	612	388	5	6900	55	494	737	263	5
3360	56	556	613	387	4	6960	56	492	740	260	4
3420	57	555	615	385	3	7020	57	491	743	257	3
3480	58	554	616	384	2	7080	58	490	745	255	2
3540	59	554	618	382	1	7140	59	488	748	252	1
		log. cos. A— log. c. A″.	log. cot. A— log. c. A″.	log. tan. A+ log. c. A″.	Minutes.			log. cos. A— log. c. A″.	log. cot. A— log. c. A″.	log. tan. A+ log. c. A″.	Minutes.
		89 Degrees.						88 Degrees.			

Min.	Tangent of 89 Degrees. 0″	10″	20″	30″	40″	50″		P. Part to 1″.
0	11.758079	11.759287	11.760498	11.761714	11.762932	11.764154	59	121.7
1	765379	766608	767840	769076	770315	771558	58	123.8
2	772805	774055	775308	776566	777826	779091	57	125.9
3	780359	781631	782907	784186	785470	786757	56	128.1
4	788047	789342	790641	791943	793250	794560	55	130.4
5	795874	797192	798515	799841	801171	802506	54	132.8
6	803844	805187	806534	807885	809240	810600	53	135.3
7	811964	813332	814704	816081	817462	818847	52	137.9
8	820237	821632	823031	824434	825842	827255	51	140.6
9	828672	830094	831520	832951	834387	835828	50	143.4
10	11.837273	11.838724	11.840179	11.841639	11.843104	11.844574	49	146.2
11	846048	847528	849013	850503	851999	853499	48	149.3
12	855004	856515	858031	859553	861079	862611	47	152.4
13	864149	865692	867240	868794	870354	871919	46	155.7
14	873490	875067	876649	878237	879831	881431	45	159.1
15	883037	884648	886266	887890	889519	891155	44	162.7
16	892797	894446	896100	897761	899429	901103	43	166.4
17	902783	904470	906163	907863	909569	911283	42	170.3
18	913003	914730	916464	918205	919953	921707	41	174.4
19	923469	925239	927015	928799	930590	932388	40	178.7
20	11.934194	11.936008	11.937829	11.939658	11.941494	11.943338	39	183.3
21	945191	947051	948919	950795	952679	954572	38	188.0
22	956473	958382	960299	962225	964160	966103	37	193.0
23	968055	970016	971986	973965	975952	977949	36	198.3
24	979956	981971	983996	986030	988074	990128	35	203.9
25	992191	994264	996347	998440	12.000543	12.002657	34	209.8
26	12.004781	12.006915	12.009060	12.011215	013382	015559	33	216.2
27	017747	019946	022156	024378	026611	028855	32	222.7
28	031111	033379	035659	037951	040255	042572	31	229.8
29	044900	047242	049596	051963	054342	056735	30	237.3
30	12.059142	12.061561	12.063994	12.066441	12.068902	12.071377	29	245.4
31	073866	076369	078887	081419	083966	086529	28	254.0
32	089106	091699	094308	096932	099572	102228	27	263.2
33	104901	107590	110296	113019	115760	118517	26	273.2
34	121292	124085	126896	129726	132574	135440	25	283.9
35	138326	141231	144156	147100	150065	153050	24	295.4
36	156056	159082	162130	165199	168290	171404	23	308.0
37	174540	177698	180880	184085	187314	190567	22	321.7
38	193845	197148	200476	203830	207210	210616	21	336.7
39	214049	217510	220998	224515	228060	231635	20	353.1
40	12.235239	12.238873	12.242538	12.246235	12.249963	12.253723	19	371.2
41	257516	261342	265203	269098	273028	276995	18	391.3
42	280997	285037	289115	293232	297388	301584	17	413.6
43	305821	310100	314422	318787	323196	327650	16	438.7
44	332151	336698	341294	345939	350634	355381	15	467.0
45	360180	365032	369940	374903	379924	385004	14	499.2
46	390143	395345	400609	405938	411333	416796	13	536.2
47	422328	427932	433610	439362	445192	451100	12	579.1
48	457091	463165	469325	475574	481915	488349	11	629.4
49	494880	501510	508244	515083	522032	529094	10	689.4
50	12.536273	12.543572	12.550996	12.558549	12.566236	12.574061	9	
51	582030	590148	598421	606854	615454	624228	8	
52	633183	642327	651667	661212	670972	680956	7	
53	691175	701641	712365	723360	734641	746223	6	
54	758122	770357	782946	795911	809275	823063	5	
55	837304	852027	867267	883061	899452	916485	4	
56	934214	952697	972002	992206	13.013395	13.035671	3	
57	13.059153	13.083976	13.110305	13.138334	168297	200482	2	
58	235244	273032	314425	360183	411335	469327	1	
59	536274	615455	712365	837304	14.013395	14.314425	0	
	60″	50″	40″	30″	20″	10″	Min.	
	Co-tangent of 0 Degree.							

Min.	0°	1°	2°	3°	4°	5°	6°	7°	8°	9°	
0	000000	017452	034899	052336	069756	087156	104528	121869	139173	156434	60
1	0291	7743	5190	2626	070047	7446	4818	2158	9461	6722	59
2	0582	8034	5481	2917	0337	7735	5107	2447	9749	7009	58
3	0873	8325	5772	3207	0627	8025	5396	2735	140037	7296	57
4	1164	8616	6062	3498	0917	8315	5686	3024	0325	7584	56
5	1454	8907	6353	3788	1207	8605	5975	3313	0613	7871	55
6	1745	9197	6644	4079	1497	8894	6264	3601	0901	8158	54
7	2036	9488	6934	4369	1788	9184	6553	3890	1189	8445	53
8	2327	9779	7225	4660	2078	9474	6843	4179	1477	8732	52
9	2618	020070	7516	4950	2368	9763	7132	4467	1765	9020	51
10	002909	020361	037806	055241	072658	090053	107421	124756	142053	159307	50
11	3200	0652	8097	5531	2948	0343	7710	5045	2341	9594	49
12	3491	0942	8388	5822	3238	0633	7999	5333	2629	9881	48
13	3782	1233	8678	6112	3528	0922	8289	5622	2917	160168	47
14	4072	1524	8969	6402	3818	1212	8578	5910	3205	0455	46
15	4363	1815	9260	6693	4108	1502	8867	6199	3493	0743	45
16	4654	2106	9550	6983	4399	1791	9156	6488	3780	1030	44
17	4945	2397	9841	7274	4689	2081	9445	6776	4068	1317	43
18	5236	2687	040132	7564	4979	2371	9734	7065	4356	1604	42
19	5527	2978	0422	7854	5269	2660	110023	7353	4644	1891	41
20	005818	023269	040713	058145	075559	092950	110313	127642	144932	162178	40
21	6109	3560	1004	8435	5849	3239	0602	7930	5220	2465	39
22	6399	3851	1294	8726	6139	3529	0891	8219	5507	2752	38
23	6690	4141	1585	9016	6429	3819	1180	8507	5795	3039	37
24	6981	4432	1876	9306	6719	4108	1469	8796	6083	3326	36
25	7272	4723	2166	9597	7009	4398	1758	9084	6371	3613	35
26	7563	5014	2457	9887	7299	4687	2047	9373	6659	3900	34
27	7854	5305	2748	060177	7589	4977	2336	9661	6946	4187	33
28	8145	5595	3038	0468	7879	5267	2625	9949	7234	4474	32
29	8436	5886	3329	0758	8169	5556	2914	130238	7522	4761	31
30	008727	026177	043619	061049	078459	095846	113203	130526	147809	165048	30
31	9017	6468	3910	1339	8749	6135	3492	0815	8097	5334	29
32	9308	6759	4201	1629	9039	6425	3781	1103	8385	5621	28
33	9599	7049	4491	1920	9329	6714	4070	1391	8672	5908	27
34	9890	7340	4782	2210	9619	7004	4359	1680	8960	6195	26
35	010181	7631	5072	2500	9909	7293	4648	1968	9248	6482	25
36	0472	7922	5363	2791	080199	7583	4937	2256	9535	6769	24
37	0763	8212	5654	3081	0489	7872	5226	2545	9823	7056	23
38	1054	8503	5944	3371	0779	8162	5515	2833	150111	7342	22
39	1344	8794	6235	3661	1069	8451	5804	3121	0398	7629	21
40	011635	029085	046525	063952	081359	098741	116093	133410	150686	167916	20
41	1926	9375	6816	4242	1649	9030	6382	3698	0973	8203	19
42	2217	9666	7106	4532	1939	9320	6671	3986	1261	8489	18
43	2508	9957	7397	4823	2228	9609	6960	4274	1548	8776	17
44	2799	030248	7688	5113	2518	9899	7249	4563	1836	9063	16
45	3090	0539	7978	5403	2808	100188	7537	4851	2123	9350	15
46	3380	0829	8269	5693	3098	0477	7826	5139	2411	9636	14
47	3671	1120	8559	5984	3388	0767	8115	5427	2698	9923	13
48	3962	1411	8850	6274	3678	1056	8404	5716	2986	170209	12
49	4253	1702	9140	6564	3968	1346	8693	6004	3273	0496	11
50	014544	031992	049431	066854	084258	101635	118982	136292	153561	170783	10
51	4835	2283	9721	7145	4547	1924	9270	6580	3848	1069	9
52	5126	2574	050012	7435	4837	2214	9559	6868	4136	1356	8
53	5416	2864	0302	7725	5127	2503	9848	7156	4423	1643	7
54	5707	3155	0593	8015	5417	2793	120137	7445	4710	1929	6
55	5998	3446	0883	8306	5707	3082	0426	7733	4998	2216	5
56	6289	3737	1174	8596	5997	3371	0714	8021	5285	2502	4
57	6580	4027	1464	8886	6286	3661	1003	8309	5572	2789	3
58	6871	4318	1755	9176	6576	3950	1292	8597	5860	3075	2
59	7162	4609	2045	9466	6866	4239	1581	8885	6147	3362	1
	89°	88°	87°	86°	85°	84°	83°	82°	81°	80°	Min.
	Natural Co-sines.										
P. P. to 1″.	4.85	4.85	4.84	4.84	4.83	4.83	4.82	4.81	4.80	4.78	

Min.	0°	1°	2°	3°	4°	5°	6°	7°	8°	9°	
0	000000	017455	034921	052408	069927	087489	105104	122785	140541	158384	60
1	0291	7746	5212	2699	070219	7782	5398	3080	0837	8683	59
2	0582	8037	5503	2991	0511	8075	5692	3375	1134	8981	58
3	0873	8328	5795	3283	0804	8368	5987	3670	1431	9279	57
4	1164	8619	6086	3575	1096	8661	6281	3966	1728	9577	56
5	1454	8910	6377	3866	1389	8954	6575	4261	2024	9876	55
6	1745	9201	6668	4158	1681	9248	6869	4557	2321	160174	54
7	2036	9492	6960	4450	1973	9541	7163	4852	2618	0472	53
8	2327	9783	7251	4742	2266	9834	7458	5147	2915	0771	52
9	2618	020074	7542	5033	2558	090127	7752	5443	3212	1069	51
10	002909	020365	037834	055325	072851	090421	108046	125738	143508	161368	50
11	3200	0656	8125	5617	3143	0714	8340	6034	3805	1666	49
12	3491	0947	8416	5909	3435	1007	8635	6329	4102	1965	48
13	3782	1238	8707	6200	3728	1300	8929	6625	4399	2263	47
14	4072	1529	8999	6492	4020	1594	9223	6920	4696	2562	46
15	4363	1820	9290	6784	4313	1887	9518	7216	4993	2860	45
16	4654	2111	9581	7076	4605	2180	9812	7512	5290	3159	44
17	4945	2402	9873	7368	4898	2474	110107	7807	5587	3458	43
18	5236	2693	040164	7660	5190	2767	0401	8103	5884	3756	42
19	5527	2984	0456	7951	5483	3061	0695	8399	6181	4055	41
20	005818	023275	040747	058243	075775	093354	110990	128694	146478	164354	40
21	6109	3566	1038	8535	6068	3647	1284	8990	6776	4652	39
22	6400	3857	1330	8827	6361	3941	1579	9286	7073	4951	38
23	6691	4148	1621	9119	6653	4234	1873	9582	7370	5250	37
24	6981	4439	1912	9411	6946	4528	2168	9877	7667	5549	36
25	7272	4731	2204	9703	7238	4821	2463	130173	7964	5848	35
26	7563	5022	2495	9995	7531	5115	2757	0469	8262	6147	34
27	7854	5313	2787	060287	7824	5408	3052	0765	8559	6446	33
28	8145	5604	3078	0579	8116	5702	3346	1061	8856	6745	32
29	8436	5895	3370	0871	8409	5995	3641	1357	9154	7044	31
30	008727	026186	043661	061163	078702	096289	113936	131652	149451	167343	30
31	9018	6477	3952	1455	8994	6583	4230	1948	9748	7642	29
32	9309	6768	4244	1747	9287	6876	4525	2244	150046	7941	28
33	9600	7059	4535	2039	9580	7170	4820	2540	0343	8240	27
34	9891	7350	4827	2331	9873	7464	5114	2836	0641	8539	26
35	010181	7641	5118	2623	080165	7757	5409	3132	0938	8838	25
36	0472	7933	5410	2915	0458	8051	5704	3428	1236	9137	24
37	0763	8224	5701	3207	0751	8345	5999	3725	1533	9437	23
38	1054	8515	5993	3499	1044	8638	6294	4021	1831	9736	22
39	1345	8806	6284	3791	1336	8932	6588	4317	2129	170035	21
40	011636	029097	046576	064083	081629	099226	116883	134613	152426	170334	20
41	1927	9388	6867	4375	1922	9519	7178	4909	2724	0634	19
42	2218	9679	7159	4667	2215	9813	7473	5205	3022	0933	18
43	2509	9970	7450	4959	2508	100107	7768	5502	3319	1233	17
44	2800	030262	7742	5251	2801	0401	8063	5798	3617	1532	16
45	3091	0553	8033	5543	3094	0695	8358	6094	3915	1831	15
46	3382	0844	8325	5836	3386	0989	8653	6390	4213	2131	14
47	3673	1135	8617	6128	3679	1282	8948	6687	4510	2430	13
48	3964	1426	8908	6420	3972	1576	9243	6983	4808	2730	12
49	4254	1717	9200	6712	4265	1870	9538	7279	5106	3030	11
50	014545	032009	049491	067004	084558	102164	119833	137576	155404	173329	10
51	4836	2300	9783	7296	4851	2458	120128	7872	5702	3629	9
52	5127	2591	050075	7589	5144	2752	0423	8169	6000	3929	8
53	5418	2882	0366	7881	5437	3046	0718	8465	6298	4228	7
54	5709	3173	0658	8173	5730	3340	1013	8761	6596	4528	6
55	6000	3465	0949	8465	6023	3634	1308	9058	6894	4828	5
56	6291	3756	1241	8758	6316	3928	1604	9354	7192	5127	4
57	6582	4047	1533	9050	6609	4222	1899	9651	7490	5427	3
58	6873	4338	1824	9342	6902	4516	2194	9948	7788	5727	2
59	7164	4630	2116	9635	7196	4810	2489	140244	8086	6027	1
	89°	88°	87°	86°	85°	84°	83°	82°	81°	80°	Min.
	Natural Co-tangents.										
P. P. to 1″.	4.85	4.85	4.86	4.87	4.88	4.89	4.91	4.93	4.96	4.98	

Min.	10°	11°	12°	13°	14°	15°	16°	17°	18°	19°	
0	173648	190809	207912	224951	241922	258819	275637	292372	309017	325568	60
1	3935	1095	8196	5234	2204	9100	5917	2650	9294	5843	59
2	4221	1380	8481	5518	2486	9381	6197	2928	9570	6118	58
3	4508	1666	8765	5801	2769	9662	6476	3206	9847	6393	57
4	4794	1951	9050	6085	3051	9943	6756	3484	310123	6668	56
5	5080	2237	9334	6368	3333	260224	7035	3762	0400	6943	55
6	5367	2522	9619	6651	3615	0505	7315	4040	0676	7218	54
7	5653	2807	9903	6935	3897	0785	7594	4318	0953	7493	53
8	5939	3093	210187	7218	4179	1066	7874	4596	1229	7768	52
9	6226	3378	0472	7501	4461	1347	8153	4874	1506	8042	51
10	176512	193664	210756	227784	244743	261628	278432	295152	311782	328317	50
11	6798	3949	1040	8068	5025	1908	8712	5430	2059	8592	49
12	7085	4234	1325	8351	5307	2189	8991	5708	2335	8867	48
13	7371	4520	1609	8634	5589	2470	9270	5986	2611	9141	47
14	7657	4805	1893	8917	5871	2751	9550	6264	2888	9416	46
15	7944	5090	2178	9200	6153	3031	9829	6542	3164	9691	45
16	8230	5376	2462	9484	6435	3312	280108	6819	3440	9965	44
17	8516	5661	2746	9767	6717	3592	0388	7097	3716	330240	43
18	8802	5946	3030	230050	6999	3873	0667	7375	3992	0514	42
19	9088	6231	3315	0333	7281	4154	0946	7653	4269	0789	41
20	179375	196517	213599	230616	247563	264434	281225	297930	314545	331063	40
21	9661	6802	3883	0899	7845	4715	1504	8208	4821	1338	39
22	9947	7087	4167	1182	8126	4995	1783	8486	5097	1612	38
23	180233	7372	4451	1465	8408	5276	2062	8763	5373	1887	37
24	0519	7657	4735	1748	8690	5556	2341	9041	5649	2161	36
25	0805	7942	5019	2031	8972	5837	2620	9318	5925	2435	35
26	1091	8228	5303	2314	9253	6117	2900	9596	6201	2710	34
27	1377	8513	5588	2597	9535	6397	3179	9873	6477	2984	33
28	1663	8798	5872	2880	9817	6678	3457	300151	6753	3258	32
29	1950	9083	6156	3163	250098	6958	3736	0428	7029	3533	31
30	182236	199368	216440	233445	250380	267238	284015	300706	317305	333807	30
31	2522	9653	6724	3728	0662	7519	4294	0983	7580	4081	29
32	2808	9938	7008	4011	0943	7799	4573	1261	7856	4355	28
33	3094	200223	7292	4294	1225	8079	4852	1538	8132	4629	27
34	3379	0508	7575	4577	1506	8359	5131	1815	8408	4903	26
35	3665	0793	7859	4859	1788	8640	5410	2093	8684	5178	25
36	3951	1078	8143	5142	2069	8920	5688	2370	8959	5452	24
37	4237	1363	8427	5425	2351	9200	5967	2647	9235	5726	23
38	4523	1648	8711	5708	2632	9480	6246	2924	9511	6000	22
39	4809	1933	8995	5990	2914	9760	6525	3202	9786	6274	21
40	185095	202218	219279	236273	253195	270040	286803	303479	320062	336547	20
41	5381	2502	9562	6556	3477	0320	7082	3756	0337	6821	19
42	5667	2787	9846	6838	3758	0600	7361	4033	0613	7095	18
43	5952	3072	220130	7121	4039	0880	7639	4310	0889	7369	17
44	6238	3357	0414	7403	4321	1160	7918	4587	1164	7643	16
45	6524	3642	0697	7686	4602	1440	8196	4864	1439	7917	15
46	6810	3927	0981	7968	4883	1720	8475	5141	1715	8190	14
47	7096	4211	1265	8251	5165	2000	8753	5418	1990	8464	13
48	7381	4496	1548	8533	5446	2280	9032	5695	2266	8738	12
49	7667	4781	1832	8816	5727	2560	9310	5972	2541	9012	11
50	187953	205065	222116	239098	256008	272840	289589	306249	322816	339285	10
51	8238	5350	2399	9381	6289	3120	9867	6526	3092	9559	9
52	8524	5635	2683	9663	6571	3400	290145	6803	3367	9832	8
53	8810	5920	2967	9946	6852	3679	0424	7080	3642	340106	7
54	9095	6204	3250	240228	7133	3959	0702	7357	3917	0380	6
55	9381	6489	3534	0510	7414	4239	0981	7633	4193	0653	5
56	9667	6773	3817	0793	7695	4519	1259	7910	4468	0927	4
57	9952	7058	4101	1075	7976	4798	1537	8187	4743	1200	3
58	190238	7343	4384	1357	8257	5078	1815	8464	5018	1473	2
59	0523	7627	4668	1640	8538	5358	2094	8740	5293	1747	1
	79°	78°	77°	76°	75°	74°	73°	72°	71°	70°	Min.
	Natural Co-sines.										
P. P. to 1″.	4.77	4.75	4.73	4.71	4.69	4.67	4.65	4.62	4.60	4.57	

Min.	10°	11°	12°	13°	14°	15°	16°	17°	18°	19°	
0	176327	194380	212557	230868	249328	267949	286745	305731	324920	344328	60
1	6627	4682	2861	1175	9637	8261	7060	6049	5241	4653	59
2	6927	4984	3165	1481	9946	8573	7375	6367	5563	4978	58
3	7227	5286	3469	1788	250255	8885	7690	6685	5885	5304	57
4	7527	5588	3773	2094	0564	9197	8005	7003	6207	5630	56
5	7827	5890	4077	2401	0873	9509	8320	7322	6528	5955	55
6	8127	6192	4381	2707	1183	9821	8635	7640	6850	6281	54
7	8427	6494	4686	3014	1492	270133	8950	7959	7172	6607	53
8	8727	6796	4990	3321	1801	0445	9266	8277	7494	6933	52
9	9028	7099	5294	3627	2111	0757	9581	8596	7817	7259	51
10	179328	197401	215599	233934	252420	271069	289896	308914	328139	347585	50
11	9628	7703	5903	4241	2729	1382	290211	9233	8461	7911	49
12	9928	8005	6208	4548	3039	1694	0527	9552	8783	8237	48
13	180229	8308	6512	4855	3348	2006	0842	9871	9106	8563	47
14	0529	8610	6817	5162	3658	2319	1158	310189	9428	8889	46
15	0829	8912	7121	5469	3968	2631	1473	0508	9751	9216	45
16	1130	9215	7426	5776	4277	2944	1789	0827	330073	9542	44
17	1430	9517	7731	6083	4587	3256	2105	1146	0396	9868	43
18	1731	9820	8035	6390	4897	3569	2420	1465	0718	350195	42
19	2031	200122	8340	6697	5207	3882	2736	1784	1041	0522	41
20	182332	200425	218645	237004	255516	274194	293052	312104	331364	350848	40
21	2632	0727	8950	7312	5826	4507	3368	2423	1687	1175	39
22	2933	1030	9254	7619	6136	4820	3684	2742	2010	1502	38
23	3234	1333	9559	7926	6446	5133	4000	3062	2333	1829	37
24	3534	1635	9864	8234	6756	5446	4316	3381	2656	2156	36
25	3835	1938	220169	8541	7066	5759	4632	3700	2979	2483	35
26	4136	2241	0474	8848	7377	6072	4948	4020	3302	2810	34
27	4437	2544	0779	9156	7687	6385	5265	4340	3625	3137	33
28	4737	2847	1084	9464	7997	6698	5581	4659	3949	3464	32
29	5038	3149	1389	9771	8307	7011	5897	4979	4272	3791	31
30	185339	203452	221695	240079	258618	277325	296213	315299	334595	354119	30
31	5640	3755	2000	0386	8928	7638	6530	5619	4919	4446	29
32	5941	4058	2305	0694	9238	7951	6846	5939	5242	4773	28
33	6242	4361	2610	1002	9549	8265	7163	6258	5566	5101	27
34	6543	4664	2916	1310	9859	8578	7480	6578	5890	5429	26
35	6844	4967	3221	1618	260170	8891	7796	6899	6213	5756	25
36	7145	5271	3526	1925	0480	9205	8113	7219	6537	6084	24
37	7446	5574	3832	2233	0791	9519	8430	7539	6861	6412	23
38	7747	5877	4137	2541	1102	9832	8747	7859	7185	6740	22
39	8048	6180	4443	2849	1413	280146	9063	8179	7509	7068	21
40	188349	206483	224748	243157	261723	280460	299380	318500	337833	357396	20
41	8651	6787	5054	3466	2034	0773	9697	8820	8157	7724	19
42	8952	7090	5360	3774	2345	1087	300014	9141	8481	8052	18
43	9253	7393	5665	4082	2656	1401	0331	9461	8806	8380	17
44	9555	7697	5971	4390	2967	1715	0649	9782	9130	8708	16
45	9856	8000	6277	4698	3278	2029	0966	320103	9454	9037	15
46	190157	8304	6583	5007	3589	2343	1283	0423	9779	9365	14
47	0459	8607	6889	5315	3900	2657	1600	0744	340103	9694	13
48	0760	8911	7194	5624	4211	2971	1918	1065	0428	360022	12
49	1062	9214	7500	5932	4523	3286	2235	1386	0752	0351	11
50	191363	209518	227806	246241	264834	283600	302553	321707	341077	360679	10
51	1665	9822	8112	6549	5145	3914	2870	2028	1402	1008	9
52	1966	210126	8418	6858	5457	4229	3188	2349	1727	1337	8
53	2268	0429	8724	7166	5768	4543	3506	2670	2052	1666	7
54	2570	0733	9031	7475	6079	4857	3823	2991	2377	1995	6
55	2871	1037	9337	7784	6391	5172	4141	3312	2702	2324	5
56	3173	1341	9643	8092	6702	5487	4459	3634	3027	2653	4
57	3475	1645	9949	8401	7014	5801	4777	3955	3352	2982	3
58	3777	1949	230255	8710	7326	6116	5095	4277	3677	3312	2
59	4078	2253	0562	9019	7637	6431	5413	4598	4002	3641	1
	79°	78°	77°	76°	75°	74°	73°	72°	71°	70°	Min.
	Natural Co-tangents.										
P. P. to 1″.	5.01	5.05	5.09	5.13	5.17	5.22	5.27	5.33	5.39	5.46	

Min.	20°	21°	22°	23°	24°	25°	26°	27°	28°	29°	
0	342020	358368	374607	390731	406737	422618	438371	453990	469472	484810	60
1	2293	8640	4876	0999	7002	2882	8633	4250	9728	5064	59
2	2567	8911	5146	1267	7268	3145	8894	4509	9985	5318	58
3	2840	9183	5416	1534	7534	3409	9155	4768	470242	5573	57
4	3113	9454	5685	1802	7799	3673	9417	5027	0499	5827	56
5	3387	9725	5955	2070	8065	3936	9678	5286	0755	6081	55
6	3660	9997	6224	2337	8330	4199	9939	5545	1012	6335	54
7	3933	360268	6494	2605	8596	4463	440200	5804	1268	6590	53
8	4206	0540	6763	2872	8861	4726	0462	6063	1525	6844	52
9	4479	0811	7033	3140	9127	4990	0723	6322	1782	7098	51
10	344752	361082	377302	393407	409392	425253	440984	456580	472038	487352	50
11	5025	1353	7571	3675	9658	5516	1245	6839	2294	7606	49
12	5298	1625	7841	3942	9923	5779	1506	7098	2551	7860	48
13	5571	1896	8110	4209	410188	6042	1767	7357	2807	8114	47
14	5844	2167	8379	4477	0454	6306	2028	7615	3063	8367	46
15	6117	2438	8649	4744	0719	6569	2289	7874	3320	8621	45
16	6390	2709	8918	5011	0984	6832	2550	8133	3576	8875	44
17	6663	2980	9187	5278	1249	7095	2810	8391	3832	9129	43
18	6936	3251	9456	5546	1514	7358	3071	8650	4088	9382	42
19	7208	3522	9725	5813	1779	7621	3332	8908	4344	9636	41
20	347481	363793	379994	396080	412045	427884	443593	459166	474600	489890	40
21	7754	4064	380263	6347	2310	8147	3853	9425	4856	490143	39
22	8027	4335	0532	6614	2575	8410	4114	9683	5112	0397	38
23	8299	4606	0801	6881	2840	8672	4375	9942	5368	0650	37
24	8572	4877	1070	7148	3104	8935	4635	460200	5624	0904	36
25	8845	5148	1339	7415	3369	9198	4896	0458	5880	1157	35
26	9117	5418	1608	7682	3634	9461	5156	0716	6136	1411	34
27	9390	5689	1877	7949	3899	9723	5417	0974	6392	1664	33
28	9662	5960	2146	8215	4164	9986	5677	1232	6647	1917	32
29	9935	6231	2415	8482	4429	430249	5937	1491	6903	2170	31
30	350207	366501	382683	398749	414693	430511	446198	461749	477159	492424	30
31	0480	6772	2952	9016	4958	0774	6458	2007	7414	2677	29
32	0752	7042	3221	9283	5223	1036	6718	2265	7670	2930	28
33	1025	7313	3490	9549	5487	1299	6979	2523	7925	3183	27
34	1297	7584	3758	9816	5752	1561	7239	2780	8181	3436	26
35	1569	7854	4027	400082	6016	1823	7499	3038	8436	3689	25
36	1842	8125	4295	0349	6281	2086	7759	3296	8692	3942	24
37	2114	8395	4564	0616	6545	2348	8019	3554	8947	4195	23
38	2386	8665	4832	0882	6810	2610	8279	3812	9203	4448	22
39	2658	8936	5101	1149	7074	2873	8539	4069	9458	4700	21
40	352931	369206	385369	401415	417338	433135	448799	464327	479713	494953	20
41	3203	9476	5638	1681	7603	3397	9059	4584	9968	5206	19
42	3475	9747	5906	1948	7867	3659	9319	4842	480223	5459	18
43	3747	370017	6174	2214	8131	3921	9579	5100	0479	5711	17
44	4019	0287	6443	2480	8396	4183	9839	5357	0734	5964	16
45	4291	0557	6711	2747	8660	4445	450098	5615	0989	6217	15
46	4563	0828	6979	3013	8924	4707	0358	5872	1244	6469	14
47	4835	1098	7247	3279	9188	4969	0618	6129	1499	6722	13
48	5107	1368	7516	3545	9452	5231	0878	6387	1754	6974	12
49	5379	1638	7784	3811	9716	5493	1137	6644	2009	7226	11
50	355651	371908	388052	404078	419980	435755	451397	466901	482263	497479	10
51	5923	2178	8320	4344	420244	6017	1656	7158	2518	7731	9
52	6194	2448	8588	4610	0508	6278	1916	7416	2773	7983	8
53	6466	2718	8856	4876	0772	6540	2175	7673	3028	8236	7
54	6738	2988	9124	5142	1036	6802	2435	7930	3282	8488	6
55	7010	3258	9392	5408	1300	7063	2694	8187	3537	8740	5
56	7281	3528	9660	5673	1563	7325	2953	8444	3792	8992	4
57	7553	3797	9928	5939	1827	7587	3213	8701	4046	9244	3
58	7825	4067	390196	6205	2091	7848	3472	8958	4301	9496	2
59	8096	4337	0463	6471	2355	8110	3731	9215	4555	9748	1
	69°	68°	67°	66°	65°	64°	63°	62°	61°	60°	Min.
	Natural Co-sines.										
P. P. to 1″.	4.54	4.51	4.48	4.45	4.41	4.38	4.34	4.30	4.26	4.22	

Min.	20°	21°	22°	23°	24°	25°	26°	27°	28°	29°	
0	363970	383864	404026	424475	445229	466308	487733	509525	531709	554309	60
1	4300	4198	4365	4818	5577	6662	8093	9892	2083	4689	59
2	4629	4532	4703	5162	5926	7016	8453	510258	2456	5070	58
3	4959	4866	5042	5505	6275	7371	8813	0625	2829	5450	57
4	5288	5200	5380	5849	6624	7725	9174	0992	3203	5831	56
5	5618	5534	5719	6192	6973	8080	9534	1359	3577	6212	55
6	5948	5868	6058	6536	7322	8434	9895	1726	3950	6593	54
7	6278	6202	6397	6880	7671	8789	490256	2093	4324	6974	53
8	6608	6536	6736	7224	8020	9144	0617	2460	4698	7355	52
9	6938	6871	7075	7568	8369	9499	0978	2828	5072	7736	51
10	367268	387205	407414	427912	448719	469854	491339	513195	535446	558118	50
11	7598	7540	7753	8256	9068	470209	1700	3563	5821	8499	49
12	7928	7874	8092	8601	9418	0564	2061	3930	6195	8881	48
13	8259	8209	8432	8945	9768	0920	2422	4298	6570	9263	47
14	8589	8544	8771	9289	450117	1275	2784	4666	6945	9645	46
15	8919	8879	9111	9634	0467	1631	3145	5034	7319	560027	45
16	9250	9214	9450	9979	0817	1986	3507	5402	7694	0409	44
17	9581	9549	9790	430323	1167	2342	3869	5770	8069	0791	43
18	9911	9884	410130	0668	1517	2698	4231	6138	8445	1174	42
19	370242	390219	0470	1013	1868	3054	4593	6507	8820	1556	41
20	370573	390554	410810	431358	452218	473410	494955	516875	539195	561939	40
21	0904	0889	1150	1703	2568	3766	5317	7244	9571	2322	39
22	1235	1225	1490	2048	2919	4122	5679	7613	9946	2705	38
23	1566	1560	1830	2393	3269	4478	6042	7982	540322	3088	37
24	1897	1896	2170	2739	3620	4835	6404	8351	0698	3471	36
25	2228	2231	2511	3084	3971	5191	6767	8720	1074	3854	35
26	2559	2567	2851	3430	4322	5548	7130	9089	1450	4238	34
27	2890	2903	3192	3775	4673	5905	7492	9458	1826	4621	33
28	3222	3239	3532	4121	5024	6262	7855	9828	2203	5005	32
29	3553	3574	3873	4467	5375	6619	8218	520197	2579	5389	31
30	373885	393910	414214	434812	455726	476976	498582	520567	542956	565773	30
31	4216	4247	4554	5158	6078	7333	8945	0937	3332	6157	29
32	4548	4583	4895	5504	6429	7690	9308	1307	3709	6541	28
33	4880	4919	5236	5850	6781	8047	9672	1677	4086	6925	27
34	5211	5255	5577	6197	7132	8405	500035	2047	4463	7310	26
35	5543	5592	5919	6543	7484	8762	0399	2417	4840	7694	25
36	5875	5928	6260	6889	7836	9120	0763	2787	5218	8079	24
37	6207	6265	6601	7236	8188	9477	1127	3158	5595	8464	23
38	6539	6601	6943	7582	8540	9835	1491	3528	5973	8849	22
39	6872	6938	7284	7929	8892	480193	1855	3899	6350	9234	21
40	377204	397275	417626	438276	459244	480551	502219	524270	546728	569619	20
41	7536	7611	7967	8622	9596	0909	2583	4641	7106	570004	19
42	7869	7948	8309	8969	9949	1267	2948	5012	7484	0390	18
43	8201	8285	8651	9316	460301	1626	3312	5383	7862	0776	17
44	8534	8622	8993	9663	0654	1984	3677	5754	8240	1161	16
45	8866	8960	9335	440011	1006	2343	4041	6125	8619	1547	15
46	9199	9297	9677	0358	1359	2701	4406	6497	8997	1933	14
47	9532	9634	420019	0705	1712	3060	4771	6868	9376	2319	13
48	9864	9971	0361	1053	2065	3419	5136	7240	9755	2705	12
49	380197	400309	0704	1400	2418	3778	5502	7612	550134	3092	11
50	380530	400646	421046	441748	462771	484137	505867	527984	550513	573478	10
51	0863	0984	1389	2095	3124	4496	6232	8356	0892	3865	9
52	1196	1322	1731	2443	3478	4855	6598	8728	1271	4252	8
53	1530	1660	2074	2791	3831	5214	6963	9100	1650	4638	7
54	1863	1997	2417	3139	4185	5574	7329	9473	2030	5026	6
55	2196	2335	2759	3487	4538	5933	7695	9845	2409	5413	5
56	2530	2673	3102	3835	4892	6293	8061	530218	2789	5800	4
57	2863	3011	3445	4183	5246	6653	8427	0591	3169	6187	3
58	3197	3350	3788	4532	5600	7013	8793	0963	3549	6575	2
59	3530	3688	4132	4880	5954	7373	9159	1336	3929	6962	1
	69°	68°	67°	66°	65°	64°	63°	62°	61°	60°	Min.
	Natural Co-tangents.										
P. P. to 1″.	5.53	5.60	5.68	5.76	5.85	5.95	6.05	6 16	6.28	6.40	

Min.	30°	31°	32°	33°	34°	35°	36°	37°	38°	39°	
0	500000	515038	529919	544639	559193	573576	587785	601815	615661	629320	60
1	0252	5287	530166	4883	9434	3815	8021	2047	5891	9546	59
2	0504	5537	0413	5127	9675	4053	8256	2280	6120	9772	58
3	0756	5786	0659	5371	9916	4291	8491	2512	6349	9998	57
4	1007	6035	0906	5615	560157	4529	8726	2744	6578	630224	56
5	1259	6284	1152	5858	0398	4767	8961	2976	6807	0450	55
6	1511	6533	1399	6102	0639	5005	9196	3208	7036	0676	54
7	1762	6782	1645	6346	0880	5243	9431	3440	7265	0902	53
8	2014	7031	1891	6589	1121	5481	9666	3672	7494	1127	52
9	2266	7280	2138	6833	1361	5719	9901	3904	7722	1353	51
10	502517	517529	532384	547076	561602	575957	590136	604136	617951	631578	50
11	2769	7778	2630	7320	1843	6195	0371	4367	8180	1804	49
12	3020	8027	2876	7563	2083	6432	0606	4599	8408	2029	48
13	3271	8276	3122	7807	2324	6670	0840	4831	8637	2255	47
14	3523	8525	3368	8050	2564	6908	1075	5062	8865	2480	46
15	3774	8773	3615	8293	2805	7145	1310	5294	9094	2705	45
16	4025	9022	3861	8536	3045	7383	1544	5526	9322	2931	44
17	4276	9271	4106	8780	3286	7620	1779	5757	9551	3156	43
18	4528	9519	4352	9023	3526	7858	2013	5988	9779	3381	42
19	4779	9768	4598	9266	3766	8095	2248	6220	620007	3606	41
20	505030	520016	534844	549509	564007	578332	592482	606451	620235	633831	40
21	5281	0265	5090	9752	4247	8570	2716	6682	0464	4056	39
22	5532	0513	5335	9995	4487	8807	2951	6914	0692	4281	38
23	5783	0761	5581	550238	4727	9044	3185	7145	0920	4506	37
24	6034	1010	5827	0481	4967	9281	3419	7376	1148	4731	36
25	6285	1258	6072	0724	5207	9518	3653	7607	1376	4955	35
26	6535	1506	6318	0966	5447	9755	3887	7838	1604	5180	34
27	6786	1754	6563	1209	5687	9992	4121	8069	1831	5405	33
28	7037	2002	6809	1452	5927	580229	4355	8300	2059	5629	32
29	7288	2251	7054	1694	6166	0466	4589	8531	2287	5854	31
30	507538	522499	537300	551937	566406	580703	594823	608761	622515	636078	30
31	7789	2747	7545	2180	6646	0940	5057	8992	2742	6303	29
32	8040	2995	7790	2422	6886	1176	5290	9223	2970	6527	28
33	8290	3242	8035	2664	7125	1413	5524	9454	3197	6751	27
34	8541	3490	8281	2907	7365	1650	5758	9684	3425	6976	26
35	8791	3738	8526	3149	7604	1886	5991	9915	3652	7200	25
36	9041	3986	8771	3392	7844	2123	6225	610145	3880	7424	24
37	9292	4234	9016	3634	8083	2359	6458	0376	4107	7648	23
38	9542	4481	9261	3876	8323	2596	6692	0606	4334	7872	22
39	9792	4729	9506	4118	8562	2832	6925	0836	4561	8096	21
40	510043	524977	539751	554360	568801	583069	597159	611067	624789	638320	20
41	0293	5224	9996	4602	9040	3305	7392	1297	5016	8544	19
42	0543	5472	540240	4844	9280	3541	7625	1527	5243	8768	18
43	0793	5719	0485	5086	9519	3777	7858	1757	5470	8992	17
44	1043	5967	0730	5328	9758	4014	8092	1987	5697	9215	16
45	1293	6214	0974	5570	9997	4250	8325	2217	5923	9439	15
46	1543	6461	1219	5812	570236	4486	8558	2447	6150	9663	14
47	1793	6709	1464	6054	0475	4722	8791	2677	6377	9886	13
48	2043	6956	1708	6296	0714	4958	9024	2907	6604	640110	12
49	2293	7203	1953	6537	0952	5194	9256	3137	6830	0333	11
50	512543	527450	542197	556779	571191	585429	599489	613367	627057	640557	10
51	2792	7697	2442	7021	1430	5665	9722	3596	7284	0780	9
52	3042	7944	2686	7262	1669	5901	9955	3826	7510	1003	8
53	3292	8191	2930	7504	1907	6137	600188	4056	7737	1226	7
54	3541	8438	3174	7745	2146	6372	0420	4285	7963	1450	6
55	3791	8685	3419	7987	2384	6608	0653	4515	8189	1673	5
56	4040	8932	3663	8228	2623	6844	0885	4744	8416	1896	4
57	4290	9179	3907	8469	2861	7079	1118	4974	8642	2119	3
58	4539	9426	4151	8710	3100	7314	1350	5203	8868	2342	2
59	4789	9673	4395	8952	3338	7550	1583	5432	9094	2565	1
	59°	58°	57°	56°	55°	54°	53°	52°	51°	50°	Min.
	Natural Co-sines.										
P. P. to 1″.	4.18	4.13	4.09	4.04	4.00	3.95	3.90	3.85	3.80	3.74	

Min.	30°	31°	32°	33°	34°	35°	36°	37°	38°	39°	
0	577350	600861	624869	649408	674509	700208	726543	753554	781286	809784	60
1	7738	1257	5274	9821	4932	0641	6987	4010	1754	810266	59
2	8126	1653	5679	650235	5355	1075	7432	4467	2223	0748	58
3	8514	2049	6083	0649	5779	1509	7877	4923	2692	1230	57
4	8903	2445	6488	1063	6203	1943	8322	5380	3161	1712	56
5	9291	2842	6894	1477	6627	2377	8767	5837	3631	2195	55
6	9680	3239	7299	1892	7051	2812	9213	6294	4100	2678	54
7	580068	3635	7704	2306	7475	3246	9658	6751	4570	3161	53
8	0457	4032	8110	2721	7900	3681	730104	7209	5040	3644	52
9	0846	4429	8516	3136	8324	4116	0550	7667	5510	4128	51
10	581235	604827	628921	653551	678749	704551	730996	758125	785981	814612	50
11	1625	5224	9327	3966	9174	4987	1443	8583	6451	5096	49
12	2014	5622	9734	4382	9599	5422	1889	9041	6922	5580	48
13	2403	6019	630140	4797	680025	5858	2336	9500	7394	6065	47
14	2793	6417	0546	5213	0450	6294	2783	9959	7865	6549	46
15	3183	6815	0953	5629	0876	6730	3230	760418	8336	7034	45
16	3573	7213	1360	6045	1302	7166	3678	0877	8808	7519	44
17	3963	7611	1767	6461	1728	7603	4125	1336	9280	8005	43
18	4353	8010	2174	6877	2154	8039	4573	1796	9752	8491	42
19	4743	8408	2581	7294	2580	8476	5021	2256	790225	8976	41
20	585134	608807	632988	657710	683007	708913	735469	762716	790697	819463	40
21	5524	9205	3396	8127	3433	9350	5917	3176	1170	9949	39
22	5915	9604	3804	8544	3860	9788	6366	3636	1643	820435	38
23	6306	610003	4211	8961	4287	710225	6815	4097	2117	0922	37
24	6697	0403	4619	9379	4714	0663	7264	4558	2590	1409	36
25	7088	0802	5027	9796	5142	1101	7713	5019	3064	1897	35
26	7479	1201	5436	660214	5569	1539	8162	5480	3538	2384	34
27	7870	1601	5844	0631	5997	1977	8611	5941	4012	2872	33
28	8262	2001	6253	1049	6425	2416	9061	6403	4486	3360	32
29	8653	2401	6661	1467	6853	2854	9511	6865	4961	3848	31
30	589045	612801	637070	661886	687281	713293	739961	767327	795436	824336	30
31	9437	3201	7479	2304	7709	3732	740411	7789	5911	4825	29
32	9829	3601	7888	2723	8138	4171	0862	8252	6386	5314	28
33	590221	4002	8298	3141	8567	4611	1312	8714	6862	5803	27
34	0613	4402	8707	3560	8995	5050	1763	9177	7337	6292	26
35	1006	4803	9117	3979	9425	5490	2214	9640	7813	6782	25
36	1398	5204	9527	4398	9854	5930	2666	770104	8290	7272	24
37	1791	5605	9937	4818	690283	6370	3117	0567	8766	7762	23
38	2184	6006	640347	5237	0713	6810	3569	1031	9242	8252	22
39	2577	6408	0757	5657	1143	7250	4020	1495	9719	8743	21
40	592970	616809	641167	666077	691572	717691	744472	771959	800196	829234	20
41	3363	7211	1578	6497	2003	8132	4925	2423	0674	9725	19
42	3757	7613	1989	6917	2433	8573	5377	2888	1151	830216	18
43	4150	8015	2399	7337	2863	9014	5830	3353	1629	0707	17
44	4544	8417	2810	7758	3294	9455	6282	3818	2107	1199	16
45	4937	8819	3222	8179	3725	9897	6735	4283	2585	1691	15
46	5331	9221	3633	8599	4156	720339	7189	4748	3063	2183	14
47	5725	9624	4044	9020	4587	0781	7642	5214	3542	2676	13
48	6120	620026	4456	9442	5018	1223	8096	5680	4021	3169	12
49	6514	0429	4868	9863	5450	1665	8549	6146	4500	3662	11
50	596908	620832	645280	670284	695881	722108	749003	776612	804979	834155	10
51	7303	1235	5692	0706	6313	2550	9458	7078	5458	4648	9
52	7698	1638	6104	1128	6745	2993	9912	7545	5938	5142	8
53	8093	2042	6516	1550	7177	3436	750366	8012	6418	5636	7
54	8488	2445	6929	1972	7610	3879	0821	8479	6898	6130	6
55	8883	2849	7342	2394	8042	4323	1276	8946	7379	6624	5
56	9278	3253	7755	2817	8475	4766	1731	9414	7859	7119	4
57	9674	3657	8168	3240	8908	5210	2187	9881	8340	7614	3
58	600069	4061	8581	3662	9341	5654	2642	780349	8821	8109	2
59	0465	4465	8994	4085	9774	6098	3098	0817	9303	8604	1
	59°	58°	57°	56°	55°	54°	53°	52°	51°	50°	Min.
	Natural Co-tangents.										
P. P. to 1″.	6.53	6.67	6.82	6.97	7.14	7.31	7.50	7.70	7.92	8.:4	

Min.	40°	41°	42°	43°	44°	45°	46°	47°	48°	49°	
0	642788	656059	669131	681998	694658	707107	719340	731354	743145	754710	60
1	3010	6279	9347	2211	4868	7312	9542	1552	3339	4900	59
2	3233	6498	9563	2424	5077	7518	9744	1750	3534	5091	58
3	3456	6717	9779	2636	5286	7724	9946	1949	3728	5282	57
4	3679	6937	9995	2849	5495	7929	720148	2147	3923	5472	56
5	3901	7156	670211	3061	5704	8134	0349	2345	4117	5663	55
6	4124	7375	0427	3274	5913	8340	0551	2543	4312	5853	54
7	4346	7594	0642	3486	6122	8545	0753	2741	4506	6044	53
8	4569	7814	0858	3698	6330	8750	0954	2939	4700	6234	52
9	4791	8033	1074	3911	6539	8956	1156	3137	4894	6425	51
10	645013	658252	671289	684123	696748	709161	721357	733334	745088	756615	50
11	5236	8471	1505	4335	6957	9366	1559	3532	5282	6805	49
12	5458	8689	1721	4547	7165	9571	1760	3730	5476	6995	48
13	5680	8908	1936	4759	7374	9776	1962	3927	5670	7185	47
14	5902	9127	2151	4971	7582	9981	2163	4125	5864	7375	46
15	6124	9346	2367	5183	7790	710185	2364	4323	6057	7565	45
16	6346	9565	2582	5395	7999	0390	2565	4520	6251	7755	44
17	6568	9783	2797	5607	8207	0595	2766	4717	6445	7945	43
18	6790	660002	3013	5818	8415	0799	2967	4915	6638	8134	42
19	7012	0220	3228	6030	8623	1004	3168	5112	6832	8324	41
20	647233	660439	673443	686242	698832	711209	723369	735309	747025	758514	40
21	7455	0657	3658	6453	9040	1413	3570	5506	7218	8703	39
22	7677	0875	3873	6665	9248	1617	3771	5703	7412	8893	38
23	7898	1094	4088	6876	9455	1822	3971	5900	7605	9082	37
24	8120	1312	4302	7088	9663	2026	4172	6097	7798	9271	36
25	8341	1530	4517	7299	9871	2230	4372	6294	7991	9461	35
26	8563	1748	4732	7510	700079	2434	4573	6491	8184	9650	34
27	8784	1966	4947	7721	0287	2639	4773	6687	8377	9839	33
28	9006	2184	5161	7932	0494	2843	4974	6884	8570	760028	32
29	9227	2402	5376	8144	0702	3047	5174	7081	8763	0217	31
30	649448	662620	675590	688355	700909	713250	725374	737277	748956	760406	30
31	9669	2838	5805	8566	1117	3454	5575	7474	9148	0595	29
32	9890	3056	6019	8776	1324	3658	5775	7670	9341	0784	28
33	650111	3273	6233	8987	1531	3862	5975	7867	9534	0972	27
34	0332	3491	6448	9198	1739	4066	6175	8063	9726	1161	26
35	0553	3709	6662	9409	1946	4269	6375	8259	9919	1350	25
36	0774	3926	6876	9620	2153	4473	6575	8455	750111	1538	24
37	0995	4144	7090	9830	2360	4676	6775	8651	0303	1727	23
38	1216	4361	7304	690041	2567	4880	6974	8848	0496	1915	22
39	1437	4579	7518	0251	2774	5083	7174	9043	0688	2104	21
40	1657	664796	677732	690462	702981	715286	727374	739239	750880	762292	20
41	1878	5013	7946	0672	3188	5490	7573	9435	1072	2480	19
42	2098	5230	8160	0882	3395	5693	7773	9631	1264	2668	18
43	2319	5448	8373	1093	3601	5896	7972	9827	1456	2856	17
44	2539	5665	8587	1303	3808	6099	8172	740023	1648	3044	16
45	2760	5882	8801	1513	4015	6302	8371	0218	1840	3232	15
46	2980	6099	9014	1723	4221	6505	8570	0414	2032	3420	14
47	3200	6316	9228	1933	4428	6708	8769	0609	2223	3608	13
48	3421	6532	9441	2143	4634	6911	8969	0805	2415	3796	12
49	3641	6749	9655	2353	4841	7113	9168	1000	2606	3984	11
50	653861	666966	679868	692563	705047	717316	729367	741195	752798	764171	10
51	4081	7183	680081	2773	5253	7519	9566	1391	2989	4359	9
52	4301	7399	0295	2983	5459	7721	9765	1586	3181	4547	8
53	4521	7616	0508	3192	5665	7924	9963	1781	3372	4734	7
54	4741	7833	0721	3402	5872	8126	730162	1976	3563	4921	6
55	4961	8049	0934	3611	6078	8329	0361	2171	3755	5109	5
56	5180	8265	1147	3821	6284	8531	0560	2366	3946	5296	4
57	5400	8482	1360	4030	6489	8733	0758	2561	4137	5483	3
58	5620	8698	1573	4240	6695	8936	0957	2755	4328	5670	2
59	5839	8914	1786	4449	6901	9138	1155	2950	4519	5857	1
	49°	48°	47°	46°	45°	44°	43°	42°	41°	40°	Min.
	Natural Co-sines.										
P. P. to 1″.	3.69	3.63	3.57	3.52	3.46	3.40	3.34	3.27	3.21	3.15	

Min.	40°	41°	42°	43°	44°	45°	46°	47°	48°	49°	
0	839100	869287	900404	932515	965689	1.00000	1.03553	1.07237	1.11061	1.15037	60
1	9595	9798	0931	3059	6251	0058	3613	7299	1126	5104	59
2	840092	870309	1458	3603	6814	0116	3674	7362	1191	5172	58
3	0588	0820	1985	4148	7377	0175	3734	7425	1256	5240	57
4	1084	1332	2513	4693	7940	0233	3794	7487	1321	5308	56
5	1581	1843	3041	5238	8504	0291	3855	7550	1387	5375	55
6	2078	2356	3569	5783	9067	0350	3915	7613	1452	5443	54
7	2575	2868	4098	6329	9632	0408	3976	7676	1517	5511	53
8	3073	3381	4627	6875	970196	0467	4036	7738	1582	5579	52
9	3571	3894	5156	7422	0761	0525	4097	7801	1648	5647	51
10	844069	874407	905685	937968	971326	1.00583	1.04158	1.07864	1.11713	1.15715	50
11	4567	4920	6215	8515	1892	0642	4218	7927	1778	5783	49
12	5066	5434	6745	9063	2458	0701	4279	7990	1844	5851	48
13	5564	5948	7275	9610	3024	0759	4340	8053	1909	5919	47
14	6063	6462	7805	940158	3590	0818	4401	8116	1975	5987	46
15	6562	6976	8336	0706	4157	0876	4461	8179	2041	6056	45
16	7062	7491	8867	1255	4724	0935	4522	8243	2106	6124	44
17	7562	8006	9398	1803	5291	0994	4583	8306	2172	6192	43
18	8062	8521	9930	2352	5859	1053	4644	8369	2238	6261	42
19	8562	9037	910462	2902	6427	1112	4705	8432	2303	6329	41
20	849062	879553	910994	943451	976996	1.01170	1.04766	1.08496	1.12369	1.16398	40
21	9563	880069	1526	4001	7564	1229	4827	8559	2435	6466	39
22	850064	0585	2059	4552	8133	1288	4888	8622	2501	6535	38
23	0565	1102	2592	5102	8703	1347	4949	8686	2567	6603	37
24	1067	1619	3125	5653	9272	1406	5010	8749	2633	6672	36
25	1568	2136	3659	6204	9842	1465	5072	8813	2699	6741	35
26	2070	2653	4193	6756	980413	1524	5133	8876	2765	6809	34
27	2573	3171	4727	7307	0983	1583	5194	8940	2831	6878	33
28	3075	3689	5261	7859	1554	1642	5255	9003	2897	6947	32
29	3578	4207	5796	8412	2126	1702	5317	9067	2963	7016	31
30	854081	884725	916331	948965	982697	1.01761	1.05378	1.09131	1.13029	1.17085	30
31	4584	5244	6866	9518	3269	1820	5439	9195	3096	7154	29
32	5087	5763	7402	950071	3842	1879	5501	9258	3162	7223	28
33	5591	6282	7938	0624	4414	1939	5562	9322	3228	7292	27
34	6095	6802	8474	1178	4987	1998	5624	9386	3295	7361	26
35	6599	7321	9010	1733	5560	2057	5685	9450	3361	7430	25
36	7104	7842	9547	2287	6134	2117	5747	9514	3428	7500	24
37	7608	8362	920084	2842	6708	2176	5809	9578	3494	7569	23
38	8113	8882	0621	3397	7282	2236	5870	9642	3561	7638	22
39	8619	9403	1159	3953	7857	2295	5932	9706	3627	7708	21
40	859124	889924	921697	954508	988432	1.02355	1.05994	1.09770	1.13694	1.17777	20
41	9630	890446	2235	5064	9007	2414	6056	9834	3761	7846	19
42	860136	0967	2773	5621	9582	2474	6117	9899	3828	7916	18
43	0642	1489	3312	6177	990158	2533	6179	0963	3894	7986	17
44	1148	2012	3851	6734	0735	2593	6241	1.10027	3961	8055	16
45	1655	2534	4390	7292	1311	2653	6303	0091	4028	8125	15
46	2162	3057	4930	7849	1888	2713	6365	0156	4095	8194	14
47	2669	3580	5470	8407	2465	2772	6427	0220	4162	8264	13
48	3177	4103	6010	8966	3043	2832	6489	0285	4229	8334	12
49	3685	4627	6551	9524	3621	2892	6551	0349	4296	8404	11
50	864193	895151	927091	960083	994199	1.02952	1.06613	1.10414	1.14363	1.18474	10
51	4701	5675	7632	0642	4778	3012	6676	0478	4430	8544	9
52	5209	6199	8174	1202	5357	3072	6738	0543	4498	8614	8
53	5718	6724	8715	1761	5936	3132	6800	0607	4565	8684	7
54	6227	7249	9257	2322	6515	3192	6862	0672	4632	8754	6
55	6736	7774	9800	2882	7095	3252	6925	0737	4699	8824	5
56	7246	8299	930342	3443	7676	3312	6987	0802	4767	8894	4
57	7756	8825	0885	4004	8256	3372	7049	0867	4834	8964	3
58	8266	9351	1428	4565	8837	3433	7112	0931	4902	9035	2
59	8776	9877	1971	5127	9418	3493	7174	0996	4969	9105	1
	49°	48°	47°	46°	45°	44°	43°	42°	41°	40°	Min.
	Natural Co-tangents.										
P. P. to 1″.	8.38	8.64	8.92	9 21	9.53	0.99	1.02	1.06	1.10	1.15	

Min.	50°	51°	52°	53°	54°	55°	56°	57°	58°	59°	
0	766044	777146	788011	798636	809017	819152	829038	838671	848048	857167	60
1	6231	7329	8190	8811	9188	9319	9200	8829	8202	7317	59
2	6418	7512	8369	8985	9359	9486	9363	8987	8356	7467	58
3	6605	7695	8548	9160	9530	9652	9525	9146	8510	7616	57
4	6792	7878	8727	9335	9700	9819	9688	9304	8664	7766	56
5	6979	8060	8905	9510	9871	9985	9850	9462	8818	7915	55
6	7165	8243	9084	9685	810042	820152	830012	9620	8972	8065	54
7	7352	8426	9263	9859	0212	0318	0174	9778	9125	8214	53
8	7538	8608	9441	800034	0383	0485	0337	9936	9279	8364	52
9	7725	8791	9620	0208	0553	0651	0499	840094	9433	8513	51
10	767911	778973	789798	800383	810723	820817	830661	840251	849586	858662	50
11	8097	9156	9977	0557	0894	0983	0823	0409	9739	8811	49
12	8284	9338	790155	0731	1064	1149	0984	0567	9893	8960	48
13	8470	9520	0333	0906	1234	1315	1146	0724	850046	9109	47
14	8656	9702	0511	1080	1404	1481	1308	0882	0199	9258	46
15	8842	9884	0690	1254	1574	1647	1470	1039	0352	9406	45
16	9028	780067	0868	1428	1744	1813	1631	1196	0505	9555	44
17	9214	0249	1046	1602	1914	1978	1793	1354	0658	9704	43
18	9400	0430	1224	1776	2084	2144	1954	1511	0811	9852	42
19	9585	0612	1401	1949	2253	2310	2115	1668	0964	860001	41
20	769771	780794	791579	802123	812423	822475	832277	841825	851117	860149	40
21	9957	0976	1757	2297	2592	2641	2438	1982	1269	0297	39
22	770142	1157	1935	2470	2762	2806	2599	2139	1422	0446	38
23	0328	1339	2112	2644	2931	2971	2760	2296	1575	0594	37
24	0513	1520	2290	2817	3101	3136	2921	2452	1727	0742	36
25	0699	1702	2467	2991	3270	3302	3082	2609	1879	0890	35
26	0884	1883	2644	3164	3439	3467	3243	2766	2032	1038	34
27	1069	2065	2822	3337	3608	3632	3404	2922	2184	1186	33
28	1254	2246	2999	3511	3778	3797	3565	3079	2336	1334	32
29	1440	2427	3176	3684	3947	3961	3725	3235	2488	1481	31
30	771625	782608	793353	803857	814116	824126	833886	843391	852640	861629	30
31	1810	2789	3530	4030	4284	4291	4046	3548	2792	1777	29
32	1995	2970	3707	4203	4453	4456	4207	3704	2944	1924	28
33	2179	3151	3884	4376	4622	4620	4367	3860	3096	2072	27
34	2364	3332	4061	4548	4791	4785	4527	4016	3248	2219	26
35	2549	3513	4238	4721	4959	4949	4688	4172	3399	2366	25
36	2734	3693	4415	4894	5128	5113	4848	4328	3551	2514	24
37	2918	3874	4591	5066	5296	5278	5008	4484	3702	2661	23
38	3103	4055	4768	5239	5465	5442	5168	4640	3854	2808	22
39	3287	4235	4944	5411	5633	5606	5328	4795	4005	2955	21
40	773472	784416	795121	805584	815801	825770	835488	844951	854156	863102	20
41	3656	4596	5297	5756	5969	5934	5648	5106	4308	3249	19
42	3840	4776	5473	5928	6138	6098	5807	5262	4459	3396	18
43	4024	4957	5650	6100	6306	6262	5967	5417	4610	3542	17
44	4209	5137	5826	6273	6474	6426	6127	5573	4761	3689	16
45	4393	5317	6002	6445	6642	6590	6286	5728	4912	3836	15
46	4577	5497	6178	6617	6809	6753	6446	5883	5063	3982	14
47	4761	5677	6354	6788	6977	6917	6605	6038	5214	4128	13
48	4944	5857	6530	6960	7145	7081	6764	6193	5364	4275	12
49	5128	6037	6706	7132	7313	7244	6924	6348	5515	4421	11
50	775312	786217	796882	807304	817480	827407	837083	846503	855665	864567	10
51	5496	6396	7057	7475	7648	7571	7242	6658	5816	4713	9
52	5679	6576	7233	7647	7815	7734	7401	6813	5966	4860	8
53	5863	6756	7408	7818	7982	7897	7560	6967	6117	5006	7
54	6046	6935	7584	7990	8150	8060	7719	7122	6267	5151	6
55	6230	7114	7759	8161	8317	8223	7878	7277	6417	5297	5
56	6413	7294	7935	8333	8484	8386	8036	7431	6567	5443	4
57	6596	7473	8110	8504	8651	8549	8195	7585	6718	5589	3
58	6780	7652	8285	8675	8818	8712	8354	7740	6868	5734	2
59	6963	7832	8460	8846	8985	8875	8512	7894	7017	5880	1
	39°	38°	37°	36°	35°	34°	33°	32°	31°	30°	Min.
	Natural Co-sines.										
P. P. to 1″.	3.08	3.02	2.95	2.88	2.81	2.75	2.68	2.60	2.53	2.46	

Min.	50°	51°	52°	53°	54°	55°	56°	57°	58°	59°	
0	1.19175	1.23490	1.27994	1.32704	1.37638	1.42815	1.48256	1.53986	1.60033	1.66428	60
1	9246	3563	8071	2785	7722	2903	8349	4085	0137	6538	59
2	9316	3637	8148	2865	7807	2992	8442	4183	0241	6647	58
3	9387	3710	8225	2946	7891	3080	8536	4281	0345	6757	57
4	9457	3784	8302	3026	7976	3169	8629	4379	0449	6867	56
5	9528	3858	8379	3107	8060	3258	8722	4478	0553	6978	55
6	9599	3931	8456	3187	8145	3347	8816	4576	0657	7088	54
7	9669	4005	8533	3268	8229	3436	8909	4675	0761	7198	53
8	9740	4079	8610	3349	8314	3525	9003	4774	0865	7309	52
9	9811	4153	8687	3430	8399	3614	9097	4873	0970	7419	51
10	1.19882	1.24227	1.28764	1.33511	1.38484	1.43703	1.49190	1.54972	1.61074	1.67530	50
11	9953	4301	8842	3592	8568	3792	9284	5071	1179	7641	49
12	1.20024	4375	8919	3673	8653	3881	9378	5170	1283	7752	48
13	0095	4449	8997	3754	8738	3970	9472	5269	1388	7863	47
14	0166	4523	9074	3835	8824	4060	9566	5368	1493	7974	46
15	0237	4597	9152	3916	8909	4149	9661	5467	1598	8085	45
16	0308	4672	9229	3998	8994	4239	9755	5567	1703	8196	44
17	0379	4746	9307	4079	9079	4329	9849	5666	1808	8308	43
18	0451	4820	9385	4160	9165	4418	9944	5766	1914	8419	42
19	0522	4895	9463	4242	9250	4508	1.50038	5866	2019	8531	41
20	1.20593	1.24969	1.29541	1.34323	1.39336	1.44598	1.50133	1.55966	1.62125	1.68643	40
21	0665	5044	9618	4405	9421	4688	0228	6065	2230	8754	39
22	0736	5118	9696	4487	9507	4778	0322	6165	2336	8866	38
23	0808	5193	9775	4568	9593	4868	0417	6265	2442	8979	37
24	0879	5268	9853	4650	9679	4958	0512	6366	2548	9091	36
25	0951	5343	9931	4732	9764	5049	0607	6466	2654	9203	35
26	1023	5417	1.30009	4814	9850	5139	0702	6566	2760	9316	34
27	1094	5492	0087	4896	9936	5229	0797	6667	2866	9428	33
28	1166	5567	0166	4978	1.40022	5320	0893	6767	2972	9541	32
29	1238	5642	0244	5060	0109	5410	0988	6868	3079	9653	31
30	1.21310	1.25717	1.30323	1.35142	1.40195	1.45501	1.51084	1.56969	1.63185	1.69766	30
31	1382	5792	0401	5224	0281	5592	1179	7069	3292	9879	29
32	1454	5867	0480	5307	0367	5682	1275	7170	3398	9992	28
33	1526	5943	0558	5389	0454	5773	1370	7271	3505	1.70106	27
34	1598	6018	0637	5472	0540	5864	1466	7372	3612	0219	26
35	1670	6093	0716	5554	0627	5955	1562	7474	3719	0332	25
36	1742	6169	0795	5637	0714	6046	1658	7575	3826	0446	24
37	1814	6244	0873	5719	0800	6137	1754	7676	3934	0560	23
38	1886	6319	0952	5802	0887	6229	1850	7778	4041	0673	22
39	1959	6395	1031	5885	0974	6320	1946	7879	4148	0787	21
40	1.22031	1.26471	1.31110	1.35968	1.41061	1.46411	1.52043	1.57981	1.64256	1.70901	20
41	2104	6546	1190	6051	1148	6503	2139	8083	4363	1015	19
42	2176	6622	1269	6134	1235	6595	2235	8184	4471	1129	18
43	2249	6698	1348	6217	1322	6686	2332	8286	4579	1244	17
44	2321	6774	1427	6300	1409	6778	2429	8388	4687	1358	16
45	2394	6849	1507	6383	1497	6870	2525	8490	4795	1473	15
46	2467	6925	1586	6466	1584	6962	2622	8593	4903	1588	14
47	2539	7001	1666	6549	1672	7053	2719	8695	5011	1702	13
48	2612	7077	1745	6633	1759	7146	2816	8797	5120	1817	12
49	2685	7153	1825	6716	1847	7238	2913	8900	5228	1932	11
50	1.22758	1.27230	1.31904	1.36800	1.41934	1.47330	1.53010	1.59002	1.65337	1.72047	10
51	2831	7306	1984	6883	2022	7422	3107	9105	5445	2163	9
52	2904	7382	2064	6967	2110	7514	3205	9208	5554	2278	8
53	2977	7458	2144	7050	2198	7607	3302	9311	5663	2393	7
54	3050	7535	2224	7134	2286	7699	3400	9414	5772	2509	6
55	3123	7611	2304	7218	2374	7792	3497	9517	5881	2625	5
56	3196	7688	2384	7302	2462	7885	3595	9620	5990	2741	4
57	3270	7764	2464	7386	2550	7977	3693	9723	6099	2857	3
58	3343	7841	2544	7470	2638	8070	3791	9826	6209	2973	2
59	3416	7917	2624	7554	2726	8163	3888	9930	6318	3089	1
	39°	38°	37°	36°	35°	34°	33°	32°	31°	30°	Min.
	Natural Co-tangents.										
P. P. to 1″.	1.20	1.25	1.31	1.37	1.44	1.51	1.59	1.68	1.78	1.88	

Min.	60°	61°	62°	63°	64°	65°	66°	67°	68°	69°	
0	866025	874620	882948	891007	898794	906308	913545	920505	927184	933580	60
1	6171	4761	3084	1139	8922	6431	3664	0618	7293	3685	59
2	6316	4902	3221	1270	9049	6554	3782	0732	7402	3789	58
3	6461	5042	3357	1402	9176	6676	3900	0846	7510	3893	57
4	6607	5183	3493	1534	9304	6799	4018	0959	7619	3997	56
5	6752	5324	3629	1666	9431	6922	4136	1072	7728	4101	55
6	6897	5465	3766	1798	9558	7044	4254	1185	7836	4204	54
7	7042	5605	3902	1929	9685	7166	4372	1299	7945	4308	53
8	7187	5746	4038	2061	9812	7289	4490	1412	8053	4412	52
9	7331	5886	4174	2192	9939	7411	4607	1525	8161	4515	51
10	867476	876026	884309	892323	900065	907533	914725	921638	928270	934619	50
11	7621	6167	4445	2455	0192	7655	4842	1750	8378	4722	49
12	7765	6307	4581	2586	0319	7777	4960	1863	8486	4826	48
13	7910	6447	4717	2717	0445	7899	5077	1976	8594	4929	47
14	8054	6587	4852	2848	0572	8021	5194	2088	8702	5032	46
15	8199	6727	4988	2979	0698	8143	5311	2201	8810	5135	45
16	8343	6867	5123	3110	0825	8265	5429	2313	8917	5238	44
17	8487	7006	5258	3241	0951	8387	5546	2426	9025	5341	43
18	8632	7146	5394	3371	1077	8508	5663	2538	9133	5444	42
19	8776	7286	5529	3502	1203	8630	5779	2650	9240	5547	41
20	868920	877425	885664	893633	901329	908751	915896	922762	929348	935650	40
21	9064	7565	5799	3763	1455	8872	6013	2875	9455	5752	39
22	9207	7704	5934	3894	1581	8994	6130	2986	9562	5855	38
23	9351	7844	6069	4024	1707	9115	6246	3098	9669	5957	37
24	9495	7983	6204	4154	1833	9236	6363	3210	9776	6060	36
25	9639	8122	6338	4284	1958	9357	6479	3322	9884	6162	35
26	9782	8261	6473	4415	2084	9478	6595	3434	9990	6264	34
27	9926	8400	6608	4545	2209	9599	6712	3545	930097	6366	33
28	870069	8539	6742	4675	2335	9720	6828	3657	0204	6468	32
29	0212	8678	6876	4805	2460	9841	6944	3768	0311	6570	31
30	870356	878817	887011	894934	902585	909961	917060	923880	930418	936672	30
31	0499	8956	7145	5064	2710	910082	7176	3991	0524	6774	29
32	0642	9095	7279	5194	2836	0202	7292	4102	0631	6876	28
33	0785	9233	7413	5323	2961	0323	7408	4213	0737	6977	27
34	0928	9372	7548	5453	3086	0443	7523	4324	0843	7079	26
35	1071	9510	7681	5582	3210	0563	7639	4435	0950	7181	25
36	1214	9649	7815	5712	3335	0684	7755	4546	1056	7282	24
37	1357	9787	7949	5841	3460	0804	7870	4657	1162	7383	23
38	1499	9925	8083	5970	3585	0924	7986	4768	1268	7485	22
39	1642	880063	8217	6099	3709	1044	8101	4878	1374	7586	21
40	871784	880201	888350	896229	903834	911164	918216	924989	931480	937687	20
41	1927	0339	8484	6358	3958	1284	8331	5099	1586	7788	19
42	2069	0477	8617	6486	4083	1403	8446	5210	1691	7889	18
43	2212	0615	8751	6615	4207	1523	8561	5320	1797	7990	17
44	2354	0753	8884	6744	4331	1643	8676	5430	1902	8091	16
45	2496	0891	9017	6873	4455	1762	8791	5541	2008	8191	15
46	2638	1028	9150	7001	4579	1881	8906	5651	2113	8292	14
47	2780	1166	9283	7130	4703	2001	9021	5761	2219	8393	13
48	2922	1303	9416	7258	4827	2120	9135	5871	2324	8493	12
49	3064	1441	9549	7387	4951	2239	9250	5980	2429	8593	11
50	873206	881578	889682	897515	905075	912358	919364	926090	932534	938694	10
51	3347	1716	9815	7643	5198	2477	9479	6200	2639	8794	9
52	3489	1853	9948	7771	5322	2596	9593	6310	2744	8894	8
53	3631	1990	890080	7900	5445	2715	9707	6419	2849	8994	7
54	3772	2127	0213	8028	5569	2834	9821	6529	2954	9094	6
55	3914	2264	0345	8156	5692	2953	9936	6638	3058	9194	5
56	4055	2401	0478	8283	5815	3072	920050	6747	3163	9294	4
57	4196	2538	0610	8411	5939	3190	0164	6857	3267	9394	3
58	4338	2674	0742	8539	6062	3309	0277	6966	3372	9493	2
59	4479	2811	0874	8666	6185	3427	0391	7075	3476	9593	1
	29°	28°	27°	26°	25°	24°	23°	22°	21°	20°	Min.
	Natural Co-sines.										
P. P. to 1″.	2.39	2.31	2.24	2.16	2.09	2.01	1.93	1.86	1.78	1.70	

Min.	60°	61°	62°	63°	64°	65°	66°	67°	68°	69°	
0	1.73205	1.80405	1.88073	1.96261	2.05030	2.14451	2.24604	2.35585	2.47509	2.60509	60
1	3321	0529	8205	6402	5182	4614	4780	5776	7716	0736	59
2	3438	0653	8337	6544	5333	4777	4956	5967	7924	0963	58
3	3555	0777	8469	6685	5485	4940	5132	6158	8132	1190	57
4	3671	0901	8602	6827	5637	5104	5309	6349	8340	1418	56
5	3788	1025	8734	6969	5790	5268	5486	6541	8549	1646	55
6	3905	1150	8867	7111	5942	5432	5663	6733	8758	1874	54
7	4022	1274	9000	7253	6094	5596	5840	6925	8967	2103	53
8	4140	1399	9133	7395	6247	5760	6018	7118	9177	2332	52
9	4257	1524	9266	7538	6400	5925	6196	7311	9386	2561	51
10	1.74375	1.81649	1.89400	1.97681	2.06553	2.16090	2.26374	2.37504	2.49597	2.62791	50
11	4492	1774	9533	7823	6706	6255	6552	7697	9807	3021	49
12	4610	1899	9667	7966	6860	6420	6730	7891	2.50018	3252	48
13	4728	2025	9801	8110	7014	6585	6909	8084	0229	3483	47
14	4846	2150	9935	8253	7167	6751	7088	8279	0440	3714	46
15	4964	2276	1.90069	8396	7321	6917	7267	8473	0652	3945	45
16	5082	2402	0203	8540	7476	7083	7447	8668	0864	4177	44
17	5200	2528	0337	8684	7630	7249	7626	8863	1076	4410	43
18	5319	2654	0472	8828	7785	7416	7806	9058	1289	4642	42
19	5437	2780	0607	8972	7939	7582	7987	9253	1502	4875	41
20	1.75556	1.82906	1.90741	1.99116	2.08094	2.17749	2.28167	2.39449	2.51715	2.65109	40
21	5675	3033	0876	9261	8250	7916	8348	9645	1929	5342	39
22	5794	3159	1012	9406	8405	8084	8528	9841	2142	5576	38
23	5913	3286	1147	9550	8560	8251	8710	2.40038	2357	5811	37
24	6032	3413	1282	9695	8716	8419	8891	0235	2571	6046	36
25	6151	3540	1418	9841	8872	8587	9073	0432	2786	6281	35
26	6271	3667	1554	9986	9028	8755	9254	0629	3001	6516	34
27	6390	3794	1690	2.00131	9184	8923	9437	0827	3217	6752	33
28	6510	3922	1826	0277	9341	9092	9619	1025	3432	6989	32
29	6630	4049	1962	0423	9498	9261	9801	1223	3648	7225	31
30	1.76749	1.84177	1.92098	2.00569	2.09654	2.19430	2.29984	2.41421	2.53865	2.67462	30
31	6869	4305	2235	0715	9811	9599	2.30167	1620	4082	7700	29
32	6990	4433	2371	0862	9969	9769	0351	1819	4299	7937	28
33	7110	4561	2508	1008	2.10126	9938	0534	2019	4516	8175	27
34	7230	4689	2645	1155	0284	2.20108	0718	2218	4734	8414	26
35	7351	4818	2782	1302	0442	0278	0902	2418	4952	8653	25
36	7471	4946	2920	1449	0600	0449	1086	2618	5170	8892	24
37	7592	5075	3057	1596	0758	0619	1271	2819	5389	9131	23
38	7713	5204	3195	1743	0916	0790	1456	3019	5608	9371	22
39	7834	5333	3332	1891	1075	0961	1641	3220	5827	9612	21
40	1.77955	1.85462	1.93470	2.02039	2.11233	2.21132	2.31826	2.43422	2.56046	2.69853	20
41	8077	5591	3608	2187	1392	1304	2012	3623	6266	2.70094	19
42	8198	5720	3746	2335	1552	1475	2197	3825	6487	0335	18
43	8319	5850	3885	2483	1711	1647	2383	4027	6707	0577	17
44	8441	5979	4023	2631	1871	1819	2570	4230	6928	0819	16
45	8563	6109	4162	2780	2030	1992	2756	4433	7150	1062	15
46	8685	6239	4301	2929	2190	2164	2943	4636	7371	1305	14
47	8807	6369	4440	3078	2350	2337	3130	4839	7593	1548	13
48	8929	6499	4579	3227	2511	2510	3317	5043	7815	1792	12
49	9051	6630	4718	3376	2671	2683	3505	5246	8038	2036	11
50	1.79174	1.86760	1.94858	2.03526	2.12832	2.22857	2.33693	2.45451	2.58261	2.72281	10
51	9296	6891	4997	3675	2993	3030	3881	5655	8484	2526	9
52	9419	7021	5137	3825	3154	3204	4069	5860	8708	2771	8
53	9542	7152	5277	3975	3316	3378	4258	6065	8932	3017	7
54	9665	7283	5417	4125	3477	3553	4447	6270	9156	3263	6
55	9788	7415	5557	4276	3639	3727	4636	6476	9381	3509	5
56	9911	7546	5698	4426	3801	3902	4825	6682	9606	3756	4
57	1.80034	7677	5838	4577	3963	4077	5015	6888	9831	4004	3
58	0158	7809	5979	4728	4125	4252	5205	7095	2.60057	4251	2
59	0281	7941	6120	4879	4288	4428	5395	7302	0283	4499	1
	29°	28°	27°	26°	25°	24°	23°	22°	21°	20°	Min.
	Natural Co-tangents.										
P. P. to 1″.	2.00	2.13	2.27	2.44	2.62	2.82	3.05	3.31	3.61	3.95	

Min.	70°	71°	72°	73°	74°	75°	76°	77°	78°	79°	
0	939693	945519	951057	956305	961262	965926	970296	974370	978148	981627	60
1	9792	5613	1146	6390	1342	6001	0366	4435	8208	1683	59
2	9891	5708	1236	6475	1422	6076	0436	4501	8268	1738	58
3	9991	5802	1326	6560	1502	6151	0506	4566	8329	1793	57
4	940090	5897	1415	6644	1582	6226	0577	4631	8389	1849	56
5	0189	5991	1505	6729	1662	6301	0647	4696	8449	1904	55
6	0288	6085	1594	6814	1741	6376	0716	4761	8509	1959	54
7	0387	6180	1684	6898	1821	6451	0786	4826	8569	2014	53
8	0486	6274	1773	6983	1901	6526	0856	4891	8629	2069	52
9	0585	6368	1862	7067	1980	6600	0926	4956	8689	2123	51
10	940684	946462	951951	957151	962059	966675	970995	975020	978748	982178	50
11	0782	6555	2040	7235	2139	6749	1065	5085	8808	2233	49
12	0881	6649	2129	7319	2218	6823	1134	5149	8867	2287	48
13	0979	6743	2218	7404	2297	6898	1204	5214	8927	2342	47
14	1078	6837	2307	7487	2376	6972	1273	5278	8986	2396	46
15	1176	6930	2396	7571	2455	7046	1342	5342	9045	2450	45
16	1274	7024	2484	7655	2534	7120	1411	5406	9105	2505	44
17	1372	7117	2573	7739	2613	7194	1480	5471	9164	2559	43
18	1471	7210	2661	7822	2692	7268	1549	5535	9223	2613	42
19	1569	7304	2750	7906	2770	7342	1618	5598	9282	2667	41
20	941666	947397	952838	957990	962849	967415	971687	975662	979341	982721	40
21	1764	7490	2926	8073	2928	7489	1755	5726	9399	2774	39
22	1862	7583	3015	8156	3006	7562	1824	5790	9458	2828	38
23	1960	7676	3103	8239	3084	7636	1893	5853	9517	2882	37
24	2057	7768	3191	8323	3163	7709	1961	5917	9575	2935	36
25	2155	7861	3279	8406	3241	7782	2029	5980	9634	2989	35
26	2252	7954	3366	8489	3319	7856	2098	6044	9692	3042	34
27	2350	8046	3454	8572	3397	7929	2166	6107	9750	3096	33
28	2447	8139	3542	8654	3475	8002	2234	6170	9809	3149	32
29	2544	8231	3629	8737	3553	8075	2302	6233	9867	3202	31
30	942641	948324	953717	958820	963630	968148	972370	976296	979925	983255	30
31	2739	8416	3804	8902	3708	8220	2438	6359	9983	3308	29
32	2836	8508	3892	8985	3786	8293	2506	6422	980041	3361	28
33	2932	8600	3979	9067	3863	8366	2573	6485	0098	3414	27
34	3029	8692	4066	9150	3941	8438	2641	6547	0156	3466	26
35	3126	8784	4153	9232	4018	8511	2708	6610	0214	3519	25
36	3223	8876	4240	9314	4095	8583	2776	6672	0271	3571	24
37	3319	8968	4327	9396	4173	8656	2843	6735	0329	3624	23
38	3416	9059	4414	9478	4250	8728	2911	6797	0386	3676	22
39	3512	9151	4501	9560	4327	8800	2978	6859	0443	3729	21
40	943609	949243	954588	959642	964404	968872	973045	976921	980500	983781	20
41	3705	9334	4674	9724	4481	8944	3112	6984	0558	3833	19
42	3801	9425	4761	9805	4557	9016	3179	7046	0615	3885	18
43	3897	9517	4847	9887	4634	9088	3246	7108	0672	3937	17
44	3993	9608	4934	9968	4711	9159	3313	7169	0728	3989	16
45	4089	9699	5020	960050	4787	9231	3379	7231	0785	4041	15
46	4185	9790	5106	0131	4864	9302	3446	7293	0842	4092	14
47	4281	9881	5192	0212	4940	9374	3512	7354	0899	4144	13
48	4376	9972	5278	0294	5016	9445	3579	7416	0955	4196	12
49	4472	950063	5364	0375	5093	9517	3645	7477	1012	4247	11
50	944568	950154	955450	960456	965169	969588	973712	977539	981068	984298	10
51	4663	0244	5536	0537	5245	9659	3778	7600	1124	4350	9
52	4758	0335	5622	0618	5321	9730	3844	7661	1181	4401	8
53	4854	0425	5707	0698	5397	9801	3910	7722	1237	4452	7
54	4949	0516	5793	0779	5473	9872	3976	7783	1293	4503	6
55	5044	0606	5879	0860	5548	9943	4042	7844	1349	4554	5
56	5139	0696	5964	0940	5624	970014	4108	7905	1405	4605	4
57	5234	0786	6049	1021	5700	0084	4173	7966	1460	4656	3
58	5329	0877	6134	1101	5775	0155	4239	8026	1516	4707	2
59	5424	0967	6220	1181	5850	0225	4305	8087	1572	4757	1
	19°	18°	17°	16°	15°	14°	13°	12°	11°	10°	Min.
	Natural Co-sines.										
P. P. to 1″.	1.62	1.54	1.46	1.38	1.30	1.21	1.13	1.05	0.97	0.88	

Min.	70°	71°	72°	73°	74°	75°	76°	77°	78°	79°	
0	2.74748	2.90421	3.07768	3.27085	3.48741	3.73205	4.01078	4.33148	4.70463	5.14455	60
1	4997	0696	8073	7426	9125	3640	1576	3723	1137	5256	59
2	5246	0971	8379	7767	9509	4075	2074	4300	1813	6058	58
3	5496	1246	8685	8109	9894	4512	2574	4879	2490	6863	57
4	5746	1523	8991	8452	3.50279	4950	3076	5459	3170	7671	56
5	5996	1799	9298	8795	0666	5388	3578	6040	3851	8480	55
6	6247	2076	9606	9139	1053	5828	4081	6623	4534	9293	54
7	6498	2354	9914	9483	1441	6268	4586	7207	5219	5.20107	53
8	6750	2632	3.10223	9829	1829	6709	5092	7793	5906	0925	52
9	7002	2910	0532	3.30174	2219	7152	5599	8381	6595	1744	51
10	2.77254	2.93189	3.10842	3.30521	3 52609	3.77595	4.06107	4.38969	4.77286	5.22566	50
11	7507	3468	1153	0868	3001	8040	6616	9560	7978	3391	49
12	7761	3748	1464	1216	3393	8485	7127	4.40152	8673	4218	48
13	8014	4028	1775	1565	3785	8931	7639	0745	9370	5048	47
14	8269	4309	2087	1914	4179	9378	8152	1340	4.80068	5880	46
15	8523	4591	2400	2264	4573	9827	8666	1936	0769	6715	45
16	8778	4872	2713	2614	4968	3.80276	9182	2534	1471	7553	44
17	9033	5155	3027	2965	5364	0726	9699	3134	2175	8393	43
18	9289	5437	3341	3317	5761	1177	4.10216	3735	2882	9235	42
19	9545	5721	3656	3670	6159	1630	0736	4338	3590	5.30080	41
20	2.79802	2.96004	3.13972	3.34023	3.56557	3.82083	4.11256	4.44942	4.84300	5.30928	40
21	2.80059	6288	4288	4377	6957	2537	1778	5548	5013	1778	39
22	0316	6573	4605	4732	7357	2992	2301	6155	5727	2631	38
23	0574	6858	4922	5087	7758	3449	2825	6764	6444	3487	37
24	0833	7144	5240	5443	8160	3906	3350	7374	7162	4345	36
25	1091	7430	5558	5800	8562	4364	3877	7986	7882	5206	35
26	1350	7717	5877	6158	8966	4824	4405	8600	8605	60[illegible]0	34
27	1610	8004	6197	6516	9370	5284	4934	9215	9330	6936	33
28	1870	8292	6517	6875	9775	5745	5465	9832	4.90056	7805	32
29	2130	8580	6838	7234	3.60181	6208	5997	4.50451	0785	8677	31
30	2.82391	2.98868	3.17159	3.37594	3.60588	3.86671	4.16530	4.51071	4.91516	5.39552	30
31	2653	9158	7481	7955	0996	7136	7064	1693	2249	5.40429	29
32	2914	9447	7804	8317	1405	7601	7600	2316	2984	1309	28
33	3176	9738	8127	8679	1814	8068	8137	2941	3721	2192	27
34	3439	3.00028	8451	9042	2224	8536	8675	3568	4460	3077	26
35	3702	0319	8775	9406	2636	9004	9215	4196	5201	3966	25
36	3965	0611	9100	9771	3048	9474	9756	4826	5945	4857	24
37	4229	0903	9426	3.40136	3461	9945	4.20298	5458	6690	5751	23
38	4494	1196	9752	0502	3874	3.90417	0842	6091	7438	6648	22
39	4758	1489	3.20079	0869	4289	0890	1387	6726	8188	7548	21
40	2.85023	3.01783	3.20406	3.41236	3.64705	3.91364	4.21933	4.57363	4.98940	5.48451	20
41	5289	2077	0734	1604	5121	1839	2481	8001	9695	9356	19
42	5555	2372	1063	1973	5538	2316	3030	8641	5.00451	5.50264	18
43	5822	2667	1392	2343	5957	2793	3580	9283	1210	1176	17
44	6089	2963	1722	2713	6376	3271	4132	9927	1971	2090	16
45	6356	3260	2053	3084	6796	3751	4685	4.60572	2734	3007	15
46	6624	3556	2384	3456	7217	4232	5239	1219	3499	3927	14
47	6892	3854	2715	3829	7638	4713	5795	1868	4267	4851	13
48	7161	4152	3048	4202	8061	5196	6352	2518	5037	5777	12
49	7430	4450	3381	4576	8485	5680	6911	3171	5809	6706	11
50	2.87700	3.04749	3.23714	3.44951	3.68909	3.96165	4.27471	4.63825	5.06584	5.57638	10
51	7970	5049	4049	5327	9335	6651	8032	4480	7360	8573	9
52	8240	5349	4383	5703	9761	7139	8595	5138	8139	9511	8
53	8511	5649	4719	6080	3.70188	7627	9159	5797	8921	5.60452	7
54	8783	5950	5055	6458	0616	8117	9724	6458	9704	1397	6
55	9055	6252	5392	6837	1046	8607	4.30291	7121	5.10490	2344	5
56	9327	6554	5729	7216	1476	9099	0860	7786	1279	3295	4
57	9600	6857	6067	7596	1907	9592	1430	8452	2069	4248	3
58	9873	7160	6406	7977	2338	4.00086	2001	9121	2862	5205	2
59	2.90147	7464	6745	8359	2771	0582	2573	9791	3658	6165	1
	19°	18°	17°	16°	15°	14°	13°	12°	11°	10°	Min.
	Natural Co-tangents.										
P. P. to 1″.	4.35	4.82	5.36	6.01	6.79	7.73	8.90	10.35	12.20	14.60	

Min.	80°	81°	82°	83°	84°	85°	86°	87°	88°	89°	
0	984808	987688	990268	992546	994522	996195	997564	998630	999391	999848	60
1	4858	7734	0309	2582	4552	6220	7584	8645	9401	9853	59
2	4909	7779	0349	2617	4583	6245	7604	8660	9411	9858	58
3	4959	7824	0389	2652	4613	6270	7625	8675	9421	9863	57
4	5009	7870	0429	2687	4643	6295	7645	8690	9431	9867	56
5	5059	7915	0469	2722	4673	6320	7664	8705	9441	9872	55
6	5109	7960	0509	2757	4703	6345	7684	8719	9450	9877	54
7	5159	8005	0549	2792	4733	6370	7704	8734	9460	9881	53
8	5209	8050	0589	2827	4762	6395	7724	8749	9469	9886	52
9	5259	8094	0629	2862	4792	6419	7743	8763	9479	9890	51
10	985309	988139	990669	992896	994822	996444	997763	998778	999488	999894	50
11	5358	8184	0708	2931	4851	6468	7782	8792	9497	9898	49
12	5408	8228	0748	2966	4881	6493	7801	8806	9507	9903	48
13	5457	8273	0787	3000	4910	6517	7821	8820	9516	9907	47
14	5507	8317	0827	3034	4939	6541	7840	8834	9525	9910	46
15	5556	8362	0866	3068	4969	6566	7859	8848	9534	9914	45
16	5605	8406	0905	3103	4998	6590	7878	8862	9542	9918	44
17	5654	8450	0944	3137	5027	6614	7897	8876	9551	9922	43
18	5703	8494	0983	3171	5056	6637	7916	8890	9560	9925	42
19	5752	8538	1022	3205	5084	6661	7934	8904	9568	9929	41
20	985801	988582	991061	993238	995113	996685	997953	998917	999577	999932	40
21	5850	8626	1100	3272	5142	6709	7972	8931	9585	9936	39
22	5899	8669	1138	3306	5170	6732	7990	8944	9594	9939	38
23	5947	8713	1177	3339	5199	6756	8008	8957	9602	9942	37
24	5996	8756	1216	3373	5227	6779	8027	8971	9610	9945	36
25	6045	8800	1254	3406	5256	6802	8045	8984	9618	9948	35
26	6093	8843	1292	3439	5284	6825	8063	8997	9626	9951	34
27	6141	8886	1331	3473	5312	6848	8081	9010	9634	9954	33
28	6189	8930	1369	3506	5340	6872	8099	9023	9642	9957	32
29	6238	8973	1407	3539	5368	6894	8117	9035	9650	9959	31
30	986286	989016	991445	993572	995396	996917	998135	999048	999657	999962	30
31	6334	9059	1483	3605	5424	6940	8153	9061	9665	9964	29
32	6381	9102	1521	3638	5452	6963	8170	9073	9672	9967	28
33	6429	9145	1558	3670	5479	6985	8188	9086	9680	9969	27
34	6477	9187	1596	3703	5507	7008	8205	9098	9687	9971	26
35	6525	9230	1634	3735	5535	7030	8223	9111	9694	9974	25
36	6572	9272	1671	3768	5562	7053	8240	9123	9701	9976	24
37	6620	9315	1709	3800	5589	7075	8257	9135	9709	9978	23
38	6667	9357	1746	3833	5617	7097	8274	9147	9716	9980	22
39	6714	9399	1783	3865	5644	7119	8291	9159	9722	9981	21
40	986762	989442	991820	993897	995671	997141	998308	999171	999729	999983	20
41	6809	9484	1857	3929	5698	7163	8325	9183	9736	9985	19
42	6856	9526	1894	3961	5725	7185	8342	9194	9743	9986	18
43	6903	9568	1931	3993	5752	7207	8359	9206	9749	9988	17
44	6950	9610	1968	4025	5778	7229	8375	9218	9756	9989	16
45	6996	9651	2005	4056	5805	7250	8392	9229	9762	9990	15
46	7043	9693	2042	4088	5832	7272	8408	9240	9768	9992	14
47	7090	9735	2078	4120	5858	7293	8425	9252	9775	9993	13
48	7136	9776	2115	4151	5884	7314	8441	9263	9781	9994	12
49	7183	9818	2151	4182	5911	7336	8457	9274	9787	9995	11
50	987229	989859	992187	994214	995937	997357	998473	999285	999793	999996	10
51	7275	9900	2224	4245	5963	7378	8489	9296	9799	9997	9
52	7322	9942	2260	4276	5989	7399	8505	9307	9804	9997	8
53	7368	9983	2296	4307	6015	7420	8521	9318	9810	9998	7
54	7414	990024	2332	4338	6041	7441	8537	9328	9816	9998	6
55	7460	0065	2368	4369	6067	7462	8552	9339	9821	9999	5
56	7506	0105	2404	4400	6093	7482	8568	9350	9827	9999	4
57	7551	0146	2439	4430	6118	7503	8583	9360	9832	1.00000	3
58	7597	0187	2475	4461	6144	7523	8599	9370	9837	0000	2
59	7643	0228	2511	4491	6169	7544	8614	9381	9843	0000	1
	9°	8°	7°	6°	5°	4°	3°	2°	1°	0°	Min.
	Natural Co-sines.										
P. P to 1″.	0.80	0.72	0.63	0.55	0.46	0.38	0.30	0.21	0.13	0.04	

Min.	80°	81°	82°	83°	84°	85°	86°	87°	88°	89°	
0	5.67128	6.31375	7.11537	8.14435	9.51436	11.4301	14.3007	19.0811	28.6363	57.2900	60
1	8094	2566	3042	6398	4106	4685	3607	1879	8771	58.2612	59
2	9064	3761	4553	8370	6791	5072	4212	2959	29.1220	59.2659	58
3	5.70037	4961	6071	8.20352	9490	5461	4823	4051	3711	60.3058	57
4	1013	6165	7594	2344	9.62205	5853	5438	5156	6245	61.3829	56
5	1992	7374	9125	4345	4935	6248	6059	6273	8823	62.4992	55
6	2974	8587	7.20661	6355	7680	6645	6685	7403	30.1446	63.6567	54
7	3960	9804	2204	8376	9.70441	7045	7317	8546	4116	64.8580	53
8	4949	6.41026	3754	8.30406	3217	7448	7954	9702	6833	66.1055	52
9	5941	2253	5310	2446	6009	7853	8596	20.0872	9599	67.4019	51
10	5.76937	6.43484	7.26873	8.34496	9.78817	11.8262	14.9244	20.2056	31.2416	68.7501	50
11	7936	4720	8442	6555	9.81641	8673	9898	3253	5284	70.1533	49
12	8938	5961	7.30018	8625	4482	9087	15.0557	4465	8205	71.6151	48
13	9944	7206	1600	8.40705	7338	9504	1222	5691	32.1181	73.1390	47
14	5.80953	8456	3190	2795	9.90211	9923	1893	6932	4213	74.7292	46
15	1966	9710	4786	4896	3101	12.0346	2571	8188	7303	76.3900	45
16	2982	6.50970	6389	7007	6007	0772	3254	9460	33.0452	78.1263	44
17	4001	2234	7999	9128	8931	1201	3943	21.0747	3662	79.9434	43
18	5024	3503	9616	8.51259	10.0187	1632	4638	2049	6935	81.8470	42
19	6051	4777	7.41240	3402	0483	2067	5340	3369	34.0273	83.8435	41
20	5.87080	6.56055	7.42871	8.55555	10.0780	12.2505	15.6048	21.4704	34.3678	85.9398	40
21	8114	7339	4509	7718	1080	2946	6762	6056	7151	88.1436	39
22	9151	8627	6154	9893	1381	3390	7483	7426	35.0695	90.4633	38
23	5.90191	9921	7806	8.62078	1683	3838	8211	8813	4313	92.9085	37
24	1236	6.61219	9465	4275	1988	4288	8945	22.0217	8006	95.4895	36
25	2283	2523	7.51132	6482	2294	4742	9687	1640	36.1776	98.2179	35
26	3335	3831	2806	8701	2602	5199	16.0435	3081	5627	101.107	34
27	4390	5144	4487	8.70931	2913	5660	1190	4541	9560	104.171	33
28	5448	6463	6176	3172	3224	6124	1952	6020	37.3579	107.426	32
29	6510	7787	7872	5425	3538	6591	2722	7519	7686	110.892	31
30	5.97576	6.69116	7.59575	8.77689	10.3854	12.7062	16.3499	22.9038	38.1885	114.589	30
31	8646	6.70450	7.61287	9964	4172	7536	4283	23.0577	6177	118.540	29
32	9720	1789	3005	8.82252	4491	8014	5075	2137	39.0568	122.774	28
33	6.00797	3133	4732	4551	4813	8496	5874	3718	5059	127.321	27
34	1878	4483	6466	6862	5136	8981	6681	5321	9655	132.219	26
35	2962	5838	8208	9185	5462	9469	7496	6945	40.4358	137.507	25
36	4051	7199	9957	8.91520	5789	9962	8319	8593	9174	143.237	24
37	5143	8564	7.71715	3867	6118	13.0458	9150	24.0263	41.4106	149.465	23
38	6240	9936	3480	6227	6450	0958	9990	1957	9158	156.259	22
39	7340	6.81312	5254	8598	6783	1461	17.0837	3675	42.4335	163.700	21
40	6.08444	6.82694	7.77035	9.00983	10.7119	13.1969	17.1693	24.5418	42.9641	171.885	20
41	9552	4082	8825	3379	7457	2480	2558	7185	43.5081	180.932	19
42	6.10664	5475	7.80622	5789	7797	2996	3432	8978	44.0661	190.984	18
43	1779	6874	2428	8211	8139	3515	4314	25.0798	6386	202.219	17
44	2899	8278	4242	9.10646	8483	4039	5205	2644	45.2261	214.858	16
45	4023	9688	6064	3093	8829	4566	6106	4517	8294	229.182	15
46	5151	6.91104	7895	5554	9178	5098	7015	6418	46.4489	245.552	14
47	6283	2525	9734	8028	9529	5634	7934	8348	47.0853	264.441	13
48	7419	3952	7.91582	9.20516	9882	6174	8863	26.0307	7395	286.478	12
49	8559	5385	3438	3016	11.0237	6719	9802	2296	48.4121	312.521	11
50	6.19703	6.96823	7.95302	9.25530	11.0594	13.7267	18.0750	26.4316	49.1039	343.774	10
51	6.20851	8268	7176	8058	0954	7821	1708	6367	8157	381.971	9
52	2003	9718	9058	9.30599	1316	8378	2677	8450	50.5485	429.718	8
53	3160	7.01174	8.00948	3155	1681	8940	3655	27.0566	51.3032	491.106	7
54	4321	2637	2848	5724	2048	9507	4645	2715	52.0807	572.957	6
55	5486	4105	4756	8307	2417	14.0079	5645	4899	8821	687.549	5
56	6655	5579	6674	9.40904	2789	0655	6656	7117	53.7086	859.436	4
57	7829	7059	8600	3515	3163	1235	7678	9372	54.5613	1145.92	3
58	9007	8546	8.10536	6141	3540	1821	8711	28.1664	55.4415	1718.87	2
59	6.30189	7.10038	2481	8781	3919	2411	9755	3994	56.3506	3437.75	1
	9°	8°	7°	6°	5°	4°	3°	2°	1°	0°	Min.
	Natural Co-tangents.										
P. P. to 1″.	17.80	22.19	28.46	37.83	5.28	7.88	13.01	....	....	....	

Deg.	0′	10′	20′	30′	40′	50′		P. Part to 1′.
0	1.000000	1.000004	1.000017	1.000038	1.000068	1.000106	89	2.5
1	000152	000207	000271	000343	000423	000512	88	7.6
2	000609	000715	000830	000953	001084	001224	87	12.7
3	001372	001529	001695	001869	002051	002242	86	17.8
4	002442	002650	002867	003092	003326	003569	85	22.9
5	003820	004080	004348	004625	004911	005205	84	28.1
6	005508	ι 05820	006141	006470	006808	007154	83	33.3
7	007510	007874	008247	008629	009020	009419	82	38.6
8	009828	010245	0·0671	011106	011550	012003	81	43.9
9	012465	012936	0.3416	013905	014403	014910	80	49.3
10	1.015427	1.015952	1.016487	1.017030	1.017583	1.018145	79	54.8
11	018717	019297	019887	020487	021095	021713	78	60.4
12	022341	022977	023624	024280	024945	025620	77	66.0
13	026304	026998	027702	028415	029138	029871	76	71.8
14	030614	031366	032128	032900	033682	034474	75	77.7
15	035276	036088	036910	037742	038584	039437	74	83.7
16	040299	041172	042055	042949	043853	044767	73	89.8
17	045692	046627	047573	048529	049496	050474	72	96.1
18	051462	052461	053471	054492	055524	056567	71	102.6
19	057621	058686	059762	060849	061947	063057	70	109.2
20	1.064178	1.065310	1.066454	1.067609	1.068776	1.069955	69	116.1
21	071145	072347	073561	074786	076024	077273	68	123.2
22	078535	079808	081094	082392	083703	085025	67	130.4
23	086360	087708	089068	090441	091827	093225	66	137.9
24	094636	096060	097498	098948	100411	101888	65	145.6
25	103378	104881	106398	107929	109473	111030	64	153.7
26	112602	114187	115787	117400	119028	120670	63	162.0
27	122326	123997	125682	127382	129096	130826	62	170.7
28	132570	134329	136104	137893	139698	141518	61	179.7
29	143354	145205	147073	148956	150854	152769	60	189.1
30	1.154701	1.156648	1.158612	1.160592	1.162589	1.164603	59	198.9
31	166633	168681	170746	172828	174927	177044	58	209.1
32	179178	181331	183501	185689	187895	190120	57	219.7
33	192363	194625	196906	199205	201523	203861	56	230.9
34	206218	208594	210991	213406	215842	218298	55	242.6
35	220775	223271	225789	228327	230886	233466	54	254.8
36	236068	238691	241336	244003	246691	249402	53	267.7
37	252136	254892	257671	260472	263298	266146	52	281.3
38	269018	271914	274834	277779	280748	283741	51	295.6
39	286760	289803	292872	295967	299088	302234	50	310.7
40	1.305407	1.308607	1.311833	1.315087	1.318368	1.321677	49	326.7
41	325013	328378	331771	335192	338643	342123	48	343.6
42	345633	349172	352742	356342	359972	363634	47	361.5
43	367327	371052	374809	378598	382420	386275	46	380.5
44	390164	394086	398042	402032	406057	410118	45	400.7
45	414214	418345	422513	426718	430960	435239	44	422.3
46	439557	443912	448306	452740	457213	461726	43	445.3
47	466279	470874	475509	480187	484907	489670	42	469.8
48	494477	499327	504221	509160	514145	519176	41	496.2
49	524253	529377	534549	539769	545038	550356	40	524.4
50	1 555724	1.561142	1.566612	1.572134	1.577708	1.583335	39	554.7
51	589016	594751	600542	606388	612291	618251	38	587.4
52	624269	630346	636483	642680	648938	655258	37	622.7
53	661640	668086	674597	681173	687815	694524	36	660.9
54	701302	708148	715064	722051	729110	736241	35	702.2
55	743447	750727	758084	765517	773029	780620	34	747.2
56	788292	796045	803881	811801	819806	827899	33	796.2
57	836078	844348	852707	861159	869704	878344	32	849.8
58	887080	895914	904847	913881	923017	932258	31	908.5
59	941604	951058	960621	970294	980081	989982	30	973.0
	60′	50′	40′	30′	20′	10′	Deg.	

Natural Co-secants.

Deg.	0′	10′	20′	30′	40′	50′		P. Part to 1′.
60	2.000000	2.010136	2.020393	2.030772	2.041276	2.051906	29	1044
61	062665	073556	084579	095739	107036	118474	28	1123
62	130054	141781	153655	165681	177859	190195	27	1210
63	202689	215346	228168	241158	254320	267657	26	1308
64	281172	294869	308750	322820	337083	351542	25	1417
65	366202	381065	396137	411421	426922	442645	24	1539
66	458593	474773	491187	507843	524744	541896	23	1678
67	559305	576975	594914	613126	631618	650396	22	1835
68	669467	688387	708514	728504	748814	769453	21	2015
69	790428	811747	833419	855451	877853	900635	20	2222
70	2.923804	2.947372	2.971349	2.995744	3.020569	3.045835	19	2461
71	3.071553	3.097736	3.124396	3.151545	179198	207367	18	2740
72	236068	265315	295123	325510	356490	388082	17	3068
73	420304	453173	486711	520937	555871	591536	16	3458
74	627955	665152	703151	741978	781660	822225	15	3925
75	863703	906125	949522	993929	4.039380	4.085913	14	4492
76	4.133565	4.182378	4.232394	4.283658	336215	390116	13	5190
77	445411	502157	560408	620226	681675	744821	12	6062
78	809734	876491	945169	5.015852	5.088628	5.163592	11	7171
79	5.240843	5.320486	5.402633	487404	574926	665333	10	8612
80	5.758770	5.855392	5.955362	6.058858	6.166067	6.277193	9	
81	6.392453	6.512081	6.636329	6.765469	6.899794	7.039622	8	
82	7.185297	7.337191	7.495711	7.661298	7.834433	8.015645	7	
83	8.205509	8.404659	8.613790	8.833671	9.065151	9.309170	6	
84	9.566772	9.839123	10.12752	10.43343	10.75849	11.10455	5	
85	11.47371	11.86837	12.29125	12.74549	13.23472	13.76311	4	
86	14.33559	14.95788	15.63679	16.38041	17.19843	18.10262	3	
87	19.10732	20.23028	21.49368	22.92559	24.56212	26.45051	2	
88	28.65371	31.25758	34.38232	38.20155	42.97571	49.11406	1	
89	57.29869	68.75736	85.94561	114.5930	171.8883	343.7752	0	
	60′	50′	40′	30′	20′	10′	Deg.	

Natural Co-secants.

LENGTHS OF CIRCULAR ARCS.

Degrees.						Minutes.		Seconds.	
°		°		°		′		″	
1	.0174533	26	.4537856	51	.8901179	1	.0002909	1	.0000048
2	.0349066	27	.4712389	52	.9075712	2	.0005818	2	.0000097
3	.0523599	28	.4886922	53	.9250245	3	.0008727	3	.0000145
4	.0698132	29	.5061455	54	.9424778	4	.0011636	4	.0000194
5	.0872665	30	.5235988	55	.9599311	5	.0014544	5	.0000242
6	.1047198	31	.5410521	56	.9773844	6	.0017453	6	.0000291
7	.1221730	32	.5585054	57	.9948377	7	.0020362	7	.0000339
8	.1396263	33	.5759587	58	1.0122910	8	.0023271	8	.0000388
9	.1570796	34	.5934119	59	1.0297443	9	.0026180	9	.0000436
10	.1745329	35	.6108652	60	1.0471976	10	.0029089	10	.0000485
11	.1919862	36	.6283185	65	1.1344640	11	.0031998	11	.0000533
12	.2094395	37	.6457718	70	1.2217305	12	.0034907	12	.0000582
13	.2268928	38	.6632251	75	1.3089969	13	.0037815	13	.0000630
14	.2443461	39	.6806784	80	1.3962634	14	.0040724	14	.0000679
15	.2617994	40	.6981317	85	1.4835299	15	.0043633	15	.0000727
16	.2792527	41	.7155850	90	1.5707963	16	.0046542	16	.0000776
17	.2967060	42	.7330383	100	1.7453293	17	.0049451	17	.0000824
18	.3141593	43	.7504916	110	1.9198622	18	.0052360	18	.0000873
19	.3316126	44	.7679449	120	2.0943951	19	.0055269	19	.0000921
20	.3490659	45	.7853982	130	2.2689280	20	.0058178	20	.0000970
21	.3665191	46	.8028515	140	2.4434610	25	.0072722	25	.0001212
22	.3839724	47	.8203047	150	2.6179939	30	.0087266	30	.0001454
23	.4014257	48	.8377580	160	2.7925268	40	.0116355	40	.0001939
24	.4188790	49	.8552113	170	2.9670597	50	.0145444	50	.0002424
25	.4363323	50	.8726646	180	3.1415927	60	.0174533	60	.0002909

Course.		Dist. 1.		Dist. 2.		Dist. 3.		Dist. 4.		Dist. 5.			
		Lat.	Dep.	Lat.	Dep.	Lat.	Dep.	Lat.	Dep.	Lat.	Dep.		
°	′											°	′
0	15	1.0000	0.0044	2.0000	0.0087	3.0000	0.0131	4.0000	0.0175	5.0000	0.0218	89	45
	30	0000	0087	1.9999	0175	2.9999	0262	3.9998	0349	4.9998	0436		30
	45	0.9999	0131	9998	0262	9997	0393	9997	0524	9996	0654		15
1	0	9998	0175	9997	0349	9995	0524	9994	0698	9992	0873	89	0
	15	9998	0218	9995	0436	9993	0654	9990	0873	9988	1091		45
	30	9997	0262	9993	0524	9990	0785	9986	1047	9983	1309		30
	45	9995	0305	9991	0611	9986	0916	9981	1222	9977	1527		15
2	0	9994	0349	9988	0698	9982	1047	9976	1396	9970	1745	88	0
	15	9992	0393	9985	0785	9977	1178	9969	1570	9961	1963		45
	30	9990	0436	9981	0872	9971	1309	9962	1745	9952	2181		30
	45	0.9988	0.0480	1.9977	0.0960	2.9965	0.1439	3.9954	0.1919	4.9942	0.2399		15
3	0	9986	0523	9973	1047	9959	1570	9945	2093	9931	2617	87	0
	15	9984	0567	9968	1134	9952	1701	9936	2268	9920	2835		45
	30	9981	0610	9963	1221	9944	1831	9925	2442	9907	3052		30
	45	9979	0654	9957	1308	9936	1962	9914	2616	9893	3270		15
4	0	9976	0698	9951	1395	9927	2093	9903	2790	9878	3488	86	0
	15	9973	0741	9945	1482	9918	2223	9890	2964	9863	3705		45
	30	9969	0785	9938	1569	9908	2354	9877	3138	9846	3923		30
	45	9966	0828	9931	1656	9897	2484	9863	3312	9828	4140		15
5	0	9962	0872	9924	1743	9886	2615	9848	3486	9810	4358	85	0
	15	0.9958	0.0915	1.9916	0.1830	2.9874	0.2745	3.9832	0.3660	4.9790	0.4575		45
	30	9954	0958	9908	1917	9862	2875	9816	3834	9770	4792		30
	45	9950	1002	9899	2004	9849	3006	9799	4008	9748	5009		15
6	0	9945	1045	9890	2091	9836	3136	9781	4181	9726	5226	84	0
	15	9941	1089	9881	2177	9822	3266	9762	4355	9703	5443		45
	30	9936	1132	9871	2264	9807	3396	9743	4528	9679	5660		30
	45	9931	1175	9861	2351	9792	3526	9723	4701	9653	5877		15
7	0	9925	1219	9851	2437	9776	3656	9702	4875	9627	6093	83	0
	15	9920	1262	9840	2524	9760	3786	9680	5048	9600	6310		45
	30	9914	1305	9829	2611	9743	3916	9658	5221	9572	6526		30
	45	0.9909	0.1349	1.9817	0.2697	2.9726	0.4046	3.9635	0.5394	4.9543	0.6743		15
8	0	9903	1392	9805	2783	9708	4175	9611	5567	9513	6959	82	0
	15	9897	1435	9793	2870	9690	4305	9586	5740	9483	7175		45
	30	9890	1478	9780	2956	9670	4434	9561	5912	9451	7390		30
	45	9884	1521	9767	3042	9651	4564	9534	6085	9418	7606		15
9	0	9877	1564	9754	3129	9631	4693	9508	6257	9384	7822	81	0
	15	9870	1607	9740	3215	9610	4822	9480	6430	9350	8037		45
	30	9863	1650	9726	3301	9589	4951	9451	6602	9314	8252		30
	45	9856	1693	9711	3387	9567	5080	9422	6774	9278	8467		15
10	0	9848	1736	9696	3473	9544	5209	9392	6946	9240	8682	80	0
	15	0.9840	0.1779	1.9681	0.3559	2.9521	0.5338	3.9362	0.7118	4.9202	0.8897		45
	30	9833	1822	9665	3645	9498	5467	9330	7289	9163	9112		30
	45	9825	1865	9649	3730	9474	5596	9298	7461	9123	9326		15
11	0	9816	1908	9633	3816	9449	5724	9265	7632	9081	9540	79	0
	15	9808	1951	9616	3902	9424	5853	9231	7804	9039	9755		45
	30	9799	1994	9598	3987	9398	5981	9197	7975	8996	9968		30
	45	9790	2036	9581	4073	9371	6109	9162	8146	8952	1.0182		15
12	0	9781	2079	9563	4158	9344	6237	9126	8316	8907	0396	78	0
	15	9772	2122	9545	4244	9317	6365	9089	8487	8862	0609		45
	30	9763	2164	9526	4329	9289	6493	9052	8658	8815	0822		30
	45	0.9753	0.2207	1.9507	0.4414	2.9260	0.6621	3.9014	0.8828	4.8767	1.1035		15
13	0	9744	2250	9487	4499	9231	6749	8975	8998	8719	1248	77	0
	15	9734	2292	9468	4584	9201	6876	8935	9168	8669	1460		45
	30	9724	2334	9447	4669	9171	7003	8895	9338	8618	1672		30
	45	9713	2377	9427	4754	9140	7131	8854	9507	8567	1884		15
14	0	9703	2419	9406	4838	9109	7258	8812	9677	8515	2096	76	0
	15	9692	2462	9385	4923	9077	7385	8769	9846	8462	2308		45
	30	9681	2504	9363	5008	9044	7511	8726	1.0015	8407	2519		30
	45	9670	2546	9341	5092	9011	7638	8682	0184	8352	2730		15
15	0	9659	2588	9319	5176	8978	7765	8637	0353	8296	2941	75	0
		Dep.	Lat.	Dep.	Lat.	Dep.	Lat.	Dep.	Lat.	Dep.	Lat.	Course.	
		Dist. 1.		Dist. 2.		Dist. 3.		Dist. 4.		Dist. 5.			

Course.		Dist. 6.		Dist. 7.		Dist. 8.		Dist. 9.		Dist. 10.			
°	′	Lat.	Dep.	Lat.	Dep.	Lat.	Dep.	Lat.	Dep.	Lat.	Dep.	°	′
0	15	5.9999	0.0262	6.9999	0.0305	7.9999	0.0349	8.9999	0.0393	9.9999	0.0436	89	45
	30	9998	0524	9997	0611	9997	0698	9997	0785	9996	0873		30
	45	9995	0785	9994	0916	9993	1047	9992	1178	9991	1309		15
1	0	9991	1047	9989	1222	9988	1396	9986	1571	9985	1745	89	0
	15	9986	1309	9983	1527	9981	1745	9979	1963	9976	2181		45
	30	9979	1571	9976	1832	9973	2094	9969	2356	9966	2618		30
	45	9972	1832	9967	2138	9963	2443	9958	2748	9953	3054		15
2	0	9963	2094	9957	2443	9951	2792	9945	3141	9939	3490	88	0
	15	9954	2356	9946	2748	9938	3141	9931	3533	9923	3926		45
	30	9943	2617	9933	3053	9924	3490	9914	3926	9905	4362		30
	45	5.9931	0.2879	6.9919	0.3358	7.9908	0.3838	8.9896	0.4318	9.9885	0.4798		15
3	0	9918	3140	9904	3664	9890	4187	9877	4710	9863	5234	87	0
	15	9904	3402	9887	3968	9871	4535	9855	5102	9839	5669		45
	30	9888	3663	9869	4273	9851	4884	9832	5494	9813	6105		30
	45	9872	3924	9850	4578	9829	5232	9807	5886	9786	6540		15
4	0	9854	4185	9829	4883	9805	5581	9781	6278	9756	6976	86	0
	15	9835	4447	9808	5188	9780	5929	9753	6670	9725	7411		45
	30	9815	4708	9784	5492	9753	6277	9723	7061	9692	7846		30
	45	9794	4968	9760	5797	9725	6625	9691	7453	9657	8281		15
5	0	9772	5229	9734	6101	9696	6972	9658	7844	9619	8716	85	0
	15	5.9748	0.5490	6.9706	0.6405	7.9664	0.7320	8.9622	0.8235	9.9580	0.9150		45
	30	9724	5751	9678	6709	9632	7668	9586	8626	9540	9585		30
	45	9698	6011	9648	7013	9597	8015	9547	9017	9497	1.0019		15
6	0	9671	6272	9617	7317	9562	8362	9507	9408	9452	0453	84	0
	15	9643	6532	9584	7621	9525	8709	9465	9798	9406	0887		45
	30	9614	6792	9550	7924	9486	9056	9421	1.0188	9357	1320		30
	45	9584	7052	9515	8228	9445	9403	9376	0578	9307	1754		15
7	0	9553	7312	9478	8531	9404	9750	9329	0968	9255	2187	83	0
	15	9520	7572	9440	8834	9360	1.0096	9280	1358	9200	2620		45
	30	9487	7832	9401	9137	9316	0442	9230	1747	9144	3053		30
	45	5.9452	0.8091	6.9361	0.9440	7.9269	1.0788	8.9178	1.2137	9.9087	1.3485		15
8	0	9416	8350	9319	9742	9221	1134	9124	2526	9027	3917	82	0
	15	9379	8610	9276	1.0044	9172	1479	9069	2914	8965	4349		45
	30	9341	8869	9231	0347	9121	1825	9011	3303	8902	4781		30
	45	9302	9127	9185	0649	9069	2170	8953	3691	8836	5212		15
9	0	9261	9386	9138	0950	9015	2515	8892	4079	8769	5643	81	0
	15	9220	9645	9090	1252	8960	2859	8830	4467	8700	6074		45
	30	9177	9903	9040	1553	8903	3204	8766	4854	8629	6505		30
	45	9133	1.0161	8989	1854	8844	3548	8700	5241	8556	6935		15
10	0	9088	0419	8937	2155	8785	3892	8633	5628	8481	7365	80	0
	15	5.9042	1.0677	6.8883	1.2456	7.8723	1.4235	8.8564	1.6015	9.8404	1.7794		45
	30	8995	0934	8828	2756	8660	4579	8493	6401	8325	8224		30
	45	8947	1191	8772	3057	8596	4922	8421	6787	8245	8652		15
11	0	8898	1449	8714	3357	8530	5265	8346	7173	8163	9081	79	0
	15	8847	1705	8655	3656	8463	5607	8271	7558	8079	9509		45
	30	8795	1962	8595	3956	8394	5949	8193	7943	7992	9937		30
	45	8743	2219	8533	4255	8324	6291	8114	8328	7905	2.0364		15
12	0	8689	2475	8470	4554	8252	6633	8033	8712	7815	0791	78	0
	15	8634	2731	8406	4852	8178	6974	7951	9096	7723	1218		45
	30	8578	2986	8341	5151	8104	7315	7867	9480	7630	1644		30
	45	5.8521	1.3242	6.8274	1.5449	7.8027	1.7656	8.7781	1.9863	9.7534	2.2070		15
13	0	8462	3497	8206	5747	7950	7996	7693	2.0246	7437	2495	77	0
	15	8403	3752	8137	6044	7870	8336	7604	0628	7338	2920		45
	30	8342	4007	8066	6341	7790	8676	7513	1010	7237	3345		30
	45	8281	4261	7994	6638	7707	9015	7421	1392	7134	3769		15
14	0	8218	4515	7921	6935	7624	9354	7327	1773	7030	4192	76	0
	15	8154	4769	7846	7231	7538	9692	7231	2154	6923	4615		45
	30	8089	5023	7770	7527	7452	2.0030	7133	2534	6815	5038		30
	45	8023	5276	7693	7822	7364	0368	7034	2914	6705	5460		15
15	0	7956	5529	7615	8117	7274	0706	6933	3294	6593	5882	75	0
		Dep.	Lat.	Dep.	Lat.	Dep.	Lat.	Dep.	Lat.	Dep.	Lat.	Course.	
		Dist. 6.		Dist. 7.		Dist. 8.		Dist. 9.		Dist. 10.			

Course.		Dist. 1.		Dist. 2.		Dist. 3.		Dist. 4.		Dist. 5.			
		Lat.	Dep.	Lat.	Dep.	Lat.	Dep.	Lat.	Dep.	Lat.	Dep.		
°	′											°	′
15	15	0.9648	0.2630	1.9296	0.5261	2.8944	0.7891	3.8591	1.0521	4.8239	1.3152	74	45
	30	9636	2672	9273	5345	8909	8017	8545	0690	8182	3362		30
	45	9625	2714	9249	5429	8874	8143	8498	0858	8123	3572		15
16	0	9613	2756	9225	5513	8838	8269	8450	1025	8063	3782	74	0
	15	9600	2798	9201	5597	8801	8395	8402	1193	8002	3991		45
	30	9588	2840	9176	5680	8765	8520	8353	1361	7941	4201		30
	45	9576	2882	9151	5764	8727	8646	8303	1528	7879	4410		15
17	0	9563	2924	9126	5847	8689	8771	8252	1695	7815	4619	73	0
	15	9550	2965	9100	5931	8651	8896	8201	1862	7751	4827		45
	30	9537	3007	9074	6014	8612	9021	8149	2028	7686	5035		30
	45	0.9524	0.3049	1.9048	0.6097	2.8572	0.9146	3.8096	1.2195	4.7620	1.5243		15
18	0	9511	3090	9021	6180	8532	9271	8042	2361	7553	5451	72	0
	15	9497	3132	8994	6263	8491	9395	7988	2527	7485	5658		45
	30	9483	3173	8966	6346	8450	9519	7933	2692	7416	5865		30
	45	9469	3214	8939	6429	8408	9643	7877	2858	7347	6072		15
19	0	9455	3256	8910	6511	8366	9767	7821	3023	7276	6278	71	0
	15	9441	3297	8882	6594	8323	9891	7764	3188	7204	6485		45
	30	9426	3338	8853	6676	8279	1.0014	7706	3352	7132	6690		30
	45	9412	3379	8824	6758	8235	0138	7647	3517	7059	6896		15
20	0	9397	3420	8794	6840	8191	0261	7588	3681	6985	7101	70	0
	15	0.9382	0.3461	1.8764	0.6922	2.8146	1.0384	3.7528	1.3845	4.6910	1.7306		45
	30	9367	3502	8733	7004	8100	0506	7467	4008	6834	7510		30
	45	9351	3543	8703	7086	8054	0629	7405	4172	6757	7715		15
21	0	9336	3584	8672	7167	8007	0751	7343	4335	6679	7918	69	0
	15	9320	3624	8640	7249	7960	0873	7280	4498	6600	8122		45
	30	9304	3665	8608	7330	7913	0995	7217	4660	6521	8325		30
	45	9288	3706	8576	7411	7864	1117	7152	4822	6440	8528		15
22	0	9272	3746	8544	7492	7816	1238	7087	4984	6359	8730	68	0
	15	9255	3786	8511	7573	7766	1359	7022	5146	6277	8932		45
	30	9239	3827	8478	7654	7716	1481	6955	5307	6194	9134		30
	45	0.9222	0.3867	1.8444	0.7734	2.7666	1.1601	3.6888	1.5468	4.6110	1.9336		15
23	0	9205	3907	8410	7815	7615	1722	6820	5629	6025	9537	67	0
	15	9188	3947	8376	7895	7564	1842	6752	5790	5940	9737		45
	30	9171	3987	8341	7975	7512	1962	6682	5950	5853	9937		30
	45	9153	4027	8306	8055	7459	2082	6612	6110	5766	2.0137		15
24	0	9135	4067	8271	8135	7406	2202	6542	6269	5677	0337	66	0
	15	9118	4107	8235	8214	7353	2322	6470	6429	5588	0536		45
	30	9100	4147	8199	8294	7299	2441	6398	6588	5498	0735		30
	45	9081	4187	8163	8373	7244	2560	6326	6746	5407	0933		15
25	0	9063	4226	8126	8452	7189	2679	6252	6905	5315	1131	65	0
	15	0.9045	0.4266	1.8089	0.8531	2.7134	1.2797	3.6178	1.7063	4.5223	2.1328		45
	30	9026	4305	8052	8610	7078	2915	6103	7220	5129	1526		30
	45	9007	4344	8014	8689	7021	3033	6028	7378	5035	1722		15
26	0	8988	4384	7976	8767	6964	3151	5952	7535	4940	1919	64	0
	15	8969	4423	7937	8846	6906	3269	5875	7692	4844	2114		45
	30	8949	4462	7899	8924	6848	3386	5797	7848	4747	2310		30
	45	8930	4501	7860	9002	6789	3503	5719	8004	4649	2505		15
27	0	8910	4540	7820	9080	6730	3620	5640	8160	4550	2700	63	0
	15	8890	4579	7780	9157	6671	3736	5561	8315	4451	2894		45
	30	8870	4617	7740	9235	6610	3852	5480	8470	4351	3087		30
	45	0.8850	0.4656	1.7700	0.9312	2.6550	1.3968	3.5400	1.8625	4.4249	2.3281		15
28	0	8829	4695	7659	9389	6488	4084	5318	8779	4147	3474	62	0
	15	8809	4733	7618	9466	6427	4200	5236	8933	4045	3666		45
	30	8788	4772	7576	9543	6365	4315	5153	9086	3941	3858		30
	45	8767	4810	7535	9620	6302	4430	5069	9240	3836	4049		15
29	0	8746	4848	7492	9696	6239	4544	4985	9392	3731	4240	61	0
	15	8725	4886	7450	9772	6175	4659	4900	9545	3625	4431		45
	30	8704	4924	7407	9848	6111	4773	4814	9697	3518	4621		30
	45	8682	4962	7364	9924	6046	4886	4728	9849	3410	4811		15
30	0	8660	5000	7321	1.0000	5981	5000	4641	2.0000	3301	5000	60	0
		Dep.	Lat.	Dep.	Lat.	Dep.	Lat.	Dep.	Lat.	Dep.	Lat.	Course.	
		Dist. 1.		Dist. 2.		Dist. 3.		Dist. 4.		Dist. 5.			

Course.		Dist. 6.		Dist. 7.		Dist. 8.		Dist. 9.		Dist. 10.			
		Lat.	Dep.	Lat.	Dep.	Lat.	Dep.	Lat.	Dep.	Lat.	Dep.		
°	′											°	′
15	15	5.7887	1.5782	6.7535	1.8412	7.7183	2.1042	8.6831	2.3673	9.6479	2.6303	74	45
	30	7818	6034	7454	8707	7090	1379	6727	4051	6363	6724		30
	45	7747	6286	7372	9001	6996	1715	6621	4430	6246	7144		15
16	0	7676	6538	7288	9295	6901	2051	6514	4807	6126	7564	74	0
	15	7603	6790	7203	9588	6804	2386	6404	5185	6005	7983		45
	30	7529	7041	7117	9881	6706	2721	6294	5561	5882	8402		30
	45	7454	7292	7030	2.0174	6606	3056	6181	5938	5757	8820		15
17	0	7378	7542	6941	0466	6504	3390	6067	6313	5630	9237	73	0
	15	7301	7792	6851	0758	6402	3723	5952	6689	5502	9654		45
	30	7223	8042	6760	1049	6297	4056	5835	7064	5372	3.0071		30
	45	5.7144	1.8292	6.6668	2.1341	7.6192	2.4389	8.5716	2.7438	9.5240	3.0486		15
18	0	7063	8541	6574	1631	6085	4721	5595	7812	5106	0902	72	0
	15	6982	8790	6479	1921	5976	5053	5473	8185	4970	1316		45
	30	6899	9038	6383	2211	5866	5384	5349	8557	4832	1730		30
	45	6816	9286	6285	2501	5754	5715	5224	8930	4693	2144		15
19	0	6731	9534	6186	2790	5641	6045	5097	9301	4552	2557	71	0
	15	6645	9781	6086	3078	5527	6375	4968	9672	4409	2969		45
	30	6558	2.0028	5985	3366	5411	6705	4838	3.0043	4264	3381		30
	45	6471	0275	5882	3654	5294	7033	4706	0413	4118	3792		15
20	0	6382	0521	5778	3941	5175	7362	4572	0782	3969	4202	70	0
	15	5.6291	2.0767	6.5673	2.4228	7.5055	2.7689	8.4437	3.1151	9.3819	3.4612		45
	30	6200	1012	5567	4515	4934	8017	4300	1519	3667	5021		30
	45	6108	1257	5459	4800	4811	8343	4162	1886	3514	5429		15
21	0	6015	1502	5351	5086	4686	8669	4022	2253	3358	5837	69	0
	15	5920	1746	5241	5371	4561	8995	3881	2619	3201	6244		45
	30	5825	1990	5129	5655	4433	9320	3738	2985	3042	6650		30
	45	5729	2233	5017	5939	4305	9645	3593	3350	2881	7056		15
22	0	5631	2476	4903	6222	4175	9969	3447	3715	2718	7461	68	0
	15	5532	2719	4788	6505	4043	3.0292	3299	4078	2554	7865		45
	30	5433	2961	4672	6788	3910	0615	3149	4442	2388	8268		30
	45	5.5332	2.3203	6.4554	2.7070	7.3776	3.0937	8.2998	3.4804	9.2220	3.8671		15
23	0	5230	3444	4435	7351	3640	1258	2845	5166	2050	9073	67	0
	15	5127	3685	4315	7632	3503	1580	2691	5527	1879	9474		45
	30	5024	3925	4194	7912	3365	1900	2535	5887	1706	9875		30
	45	4919	4165	4072	8192	3225	2220	2378	6247	1531	4.0275		15
24	0	4813	4404	3948	8472	3084	2539	2219	6606	1355	0674	66	0
	15	4706	4643	3823	8750	2941	2858	2059	6965	1176	1072		45
	30	4598	4882	3697	9029	2797	3175	1897	7322	0996	1469		30
	45	4489	5120	3570	9306	2651	3493	1733	7679	0814	1866		15
25	0	4378	5357	3442	9583	2505	3809	1568	8036	0631	2262	65	0
	15	5.4267	2.5594	6.3312	2.9860	7.2356	3.4125	8.1401	3.8391	9.0446	4.2657		45
	30	4155	5831	3181	3.0136	2207	4441	1233	8746	0259	3051		30
	45	4042	6067	3049	0411	2056	4756	1063	9100	0070	3445		15
26	0	3928	6302	2916	0686	1904	5070	0891	9453	8.9879	3837	64	0
	15	3812	6537	2781	0960	1750	5383	0719	9806	9687	4229		45
	30	3696	6772	2645	1234	1595	5696	0544	4.0158	9493	4620		30
	45	3579	7006	2509	1507	1438	6008	0368	0509	9298	5010		15
27	0	3460	7239	2370	1779	1281	6319	0191	0859	9101	5399	63	0
	15	3341	7472	2231	2051	1121	6630	0012	1209	8902	5787		45
	30	3221	7705	2091	2322	0961	6940	7.9831	1557	8701	6175		30
	45	5.3099	2.7937	6.1949	3.2593	7.0799	3.7249	7.9649	4.1905	8.8499	4.6561		15
28	0	2977	8168	1806	2863	0636	7558	9465	2252	8295	6947	62	0
	15	2853	8399	1662	3132	0471	7866	9280	2599	8089	7332		45
	30	2729	8630	1517	3401	0305	8173	9094	2944	7882	7716		30
	45	2604	8859	1371	3669	0138	8479	8905	3289	7673	8099		15
29	0	2477	9089	1223	3937	6.9970	8785	8716	3633	7462	8481	61	0
	15	2350	9317	1075	4203	9800	9090	8525	3976	7250	8862		45
	30	2221	9545	0925	4470	9628	9394	8332	4318	7036	9242		30
	45	2092	9773	0774	4735	9456	9697	8138	4659	6820	9622		15
30	0	1962	3.0000	0622	5000	9282	4.0000	7942	5000	6603	5.0000	60	0
		Dep.	Lat.	Dep.	Lat.	Dep.	Lat.	Dep.	Lat.	Dep.	Lat.		
		Dist. 6.		Dist. 7.		Dist. 8.		Dist. 9.		Dist. 10.		Course.	

Course.		Dist. 1.		Dist. 2.		Dist. 3.		Dist. 4.		Dist. 5.			
		Lat.	Dep.	Lat.	Dep.	Lat.	Dep.	Lat.	Dep.	Lat.	Dep.		
°	′											°	′
30	15	0.8638	0.5038	1.7277	1.0075	2.5915	1.5113	3.4553	2.0151	4.3192	2.5189	59	45
	30	8616	5075	7233	0151	5849	5226	4465	0302	3081	5377		30
	45	8594	5113	7188	0226	5782	5339	4376	0452	2970	5565		15
31	0	8572	5150	7143	0301	5715	5451	4287	0602	2858	5752	59	0
	15	8549	5188	7098	0375	5647	5563	4196	0751	2746	5939		45
	30	8526	5225	7053	0450	5579	5675	4106	0900	2632	6125		30
	45	8504	5262	7007	0524	5511	5786	4014	1049	2518	6311		15
32	0	8480	5299	6961	0598	5441	5898	3922	1197	2402	6496	58	0
	15	8457	5336	6915	0672	5372	6008	3829	1345	2286	6681		45
	30	8434	5373	6868	0746	5302	6119	3736	1492	2170	6865		30
	45	0.8410	0.5410	1.6821	1.0819	2.5231	1.6229	3.3642	2.1639	4.2052	2.7049		15
33	0	8387	5446	6773	0893	5160	6339	3547	1786	1934	7232	57	0
	15	8363	5483	6726	0966	5089	6449	3451	1932	1814	7415		45
	30	8339	5519	6678	1039	5017	6558	3355	2077	1694	7597		30
	45	8315	5556	6629	1111	4944	6667	3259	2223	1573	7779		15
34	0	8290	5592	6581	1184	4871	6776	3162	2368	1452	7960	56	0
	15	8266	5628	6532	1256	4798	6884	3064	2512	1329	8140		45
	30	8241	5664	6483	1328	4724	6992	2965	2656	1206	8320		30
	45	8216	5700	6433	1400	4649	7100	2866	2800	1082	8500		15
35	0	8192	5736	6383	1472	4575	7207	2766	2943	0958	8679	55	0
	15	0.8166	0.5771	1.6333	1.1543	2.4499	1.7314	3.2666	2.3086	4.0832	2.8857		45
	30	8141	5807	6282	1614	4423	7421	2565	3228	0706	9035		30
	45	8116	5842	6231	1685	4347	7527	2463	3370	0579	9212		15
36	0	8090	5878	6180	1756	4271	7634	2361	3511	0451	9389	54	0
	15	8064	5913	6129	1826	4193	7739	2258	3652	0322	9565		45
	30	8039	5948	6077	1896	4116	7845	2154	3793	0193	9741		30
	45	8013	5983	6025	1966	4038	7950	2050	3933	0063	9916		15
37	0	7986	6018	5973	2036	3959	8054	1945	4073	3.9932	3.0091	53	0
	15	7960	6053	5920	2106	3880	8159	1840	4212	9800	0265		45
	30	7934	6088	5867	2175	3801	8263	1734	4350	9668	0438		30
	45	0.7907	0.6122	1.5814	1.2244	2.3721	1.8367	3.1628	2.4489	3.9534	3.0611		15
38	0	7880	6157	5760	2313	3640	8470	1520	4626	9401	0783	52	0
	15	7853	6191	5706	2382	3560	8573	1413	4764	9266	0955		45
	30	7826	6225	5652	2450	3478	8675	1304	4901	9130	1126		30
	45	7799	6259	5598	2518	3397	8778	1195	5037	8994	1296		15
39	0	7771	6293	5543	2586	3314	8880	1086	5173	8857	1466	51	0
	15	7744	6327	5488	2654	3232	8981	0976	5308	8720	1635		45
	30	7716	6361	5432	2722	3149	9082	0865	5443	8581	1804		30
	45	7688	6394	5377	2789	3065	9183	0754	5578	8442	1972		15
40	0	7660	6428	5321	2856	2981	9284	0642	5712	8302	2139	50	0
	15	0.7632	0.6461	1.5265	1.2922	2.2897	1.9384	3.0529	2 5845	3.8162	3.2306		45
	30	7604	6494	5208	2989	2812	9483	0416	5978	8020	2472		30
	45	7576	6528	5151	3055	2727	9583	0303	0110	7878	2638		15
41	0	7547	6561	5094	3121	2641	9682	0188	6242	7735	2803	49	0
	15	7518	6593	5037	3187	2555	9780	0074	6374	7592	2967		45
	30	7490	6626	4979	3252	2469	9879	2.9958	6505	7448	3131		30
	45	7461	6659	4921	3318	2382	9976	9842	6635	7303	3294		15
42	0	7431	6691	4863	3383	2294	2.0074	9726	6765	7157	3457	48	0
	15	7402	6724	4804	3447	2207	0171	9609	6895	7011	3618		45
	30	7373	6756	4746	3512	2118	0268	9491	7024	6864	3780		30
	45	0.7343	0.6788	1.4686	1.3576	2.2030	2.0364	2.9373	2.7152	3.6716	3.3940		15
43	0	7314	6820	4627	3640	1941	0460	9254	7280	6568	4100	47	0
	15	7284	6852	4567	3704	1851	0555	9135	7407	6419	4259		45
	30	7254	6884	4507	3767	1761	0651	9015	7534	6269	4418		30
	45	7224	6915	4447	3830	1671	0745	8895	7661	6118	4576		15
44	0	7193	6947	4387	3893	1580	0840	8774	7786	5967	4733	46	0
	15	7163	6978	4326	3956	1489	0934	8652	7912	5815	4890		45
	30	7133	7009	4265	4018	1398	1027	8530	8036	5663	5045		30
	45	7102	7040	4204	4080	1306	1120	8407	8161	5509	5201		15
45	0	7071	7071	4142	4142	1213	1213	8284	8284	5355	5355	45	0
		Dep.	Lat.	Dep.	Lat.	Dep.	Lat.	Dep.	Lat.	Dep.	Lat.	Course.	
		Dist. 1.		Dist. 2.		Dist. 3.		Dist. 4.		Dist. 5.			

Course.		Dist. 6.		Dist. 7.		Dist. 8.		Dist. 9.		Dist. 10.			
		Lat.	Dep.	Lat.	Dep.	Lat.	Dep.	Lat.	Dep.	Lat.	Dep.		
°	′											°	′
30	15	5.1830	3.0226	6.0468	3.5264	6.9107	4.0302	7.7745	4.5340	8.6384	5.0377	59	45
	30	1698	0452	0314	5528	8930	0603	7547	5678	6163	0754		30
	45	1564	0678	0158	5791	8753	0903	7347	6016	5941	1129		15
31	0	1430	0902	0002	6053	8573	1203	7145	6353	5717	1504	59	0
	15	1295	1126	5.9844	6314	8393	1502	6942	6690	5491	1877		45
	30	1158	1350	9685	6575	8211	1800	6738	7025	5264	2250		30
	45	1021	1573	9525	6835	8028	2097	6532	7359	5035	2621		15
32	0	0883	1795	9363	7094	7844	2394	6324	7693	4805	2992	58	0
	15	0744	2017	9201	7353	7658	2689	6116	8025	4573	3361		45
	30	0603	2238	9037	7611	7471	2984	5905	8357	4339	3730		30
	45	5.0462	3.2458	5.8873	3.7868	6.7283	4.3278	7.5694	4.8688	8.4104	5.4097		15
33	0	0320	2678	8707	8125	7094	3571	5480	9018	3867	4464	57	0
	15	0177	2898	8540	8381	6903	3863	5266	9346	3629	4829		45
	30	0033	3116	8372	8636	6711	4155	5050	9674	3389	5194		30
	45	4.9888	3334	8203	8890	6518	4446	4832	5.0001	3147	5557		15
34	0	9742	3552	8033	9144	6323	4735	4613	0327	2904	5919	56	0
	15	9595	3768	7861	9396	6127	5024	4393	0652	2659	6280		45
	30	9448	3984	7689	9648	5930	5312	4171	0977	2413	6641		30
	45	9299	4200	7515	9900	5732	5600	3948	1300	2165	7000		15
35	0	9149	4415	7341	4.0150	5532	5886	3724	1622	1915	7358	55	0
	15	4.8998	3.4629	5.7165	4.0400	6.5331	4.6172	7.3498	5.1943	8.1664	5.7715		45
	30	8847	4842	6988	0649	5129	6456	3270	2263	1412	8070		30
	45	8694	5055	6810	0897	4926	6740	3042	2582	1157	8425		15
36	0	8541	5267	6631	1145	4721	7023	2812	2901	0902	8779	54	0
	15	8387	5479	6451	1392	4516	7305	2580	3218	0644	9131		45
	30	8231	5689	6270	1638	4309	7586	2347	3534	0386	9482		30
	45	8075	5899	6088	1883	4100	7866	2113	3849	0125	9832		15
37	0	7918	6109	5904	2127	3891	8145	1877	4163	7.9864	6.0182	53	0
	15	7760	6318	5720	2371	3680	8424	1640	4476	9600	0529		45
	30	7601	6526	5535	2613	3468	8701	1402	4789	9335	0876		30
	45	4.7441	3.6733	5.5348	4.2855	6.3255	4.8977	7.1162	5.5100	7.9069	6.1222		15
38	0	7281	6940	5161	3096	3041	9253	0921	5410	8801	1566	52	0
	15	7119	7146	4972	3337	2825	9528	0679	5718	8532	1909		45
	30	6956	7351	4783	3576	2609	9801	0435	6026	8261	2251		30
	45	6793	7555	4592	3815	2391	5.0074	0190	6333	7988	2592		15
39	0	6629	7759	4400	4052	2172	0346	6.9943	6639	7715	2932	51	0
	15	6464	7962	4207	4289	1951	0616	9695	6943	7439	3271		45
	30	6297	8165	4014	4525	1730	0886	9446	7247	7162	3608		30
	45	6131	8366	3819	4761	1507	1155	9196	7550	6884	3944		15
40	0	5963	8567	3623	4995	1284	1423	8944	7851	6604	4279	50	0
	15	4.5794	3.8767	5.3426	4.5229	6.1059	5.1690	6.8691	5.8151	7.6323	6.4612		45
	30	5624	8967	3228	5461	0832	1956	8437	8450	6041	4945		30
	45	5454	9166	3030	5693	0605	2221	8181	8748	5756	5276		15
41	0	5283	9364	2830	5924	0377	2485	7924	9045	5471	5606	49	0
	15	5110	9561	2629	6154	0147	2748	7666	9341	5184	5935		45
	30	4937	9757	2427	6383	5.9916	3010	7406	9636	4896	6262		30
	45	4763	9953	2224	6612	9685	3271	7145	9929	4606	6588		15
42	0	4589	4.0148	2020	6839	9452	3530	6883	6.0222	4314	6913	48	0
	15	4413	0342	1815	7066	9217	3789	6620	0513	4022	7237		45
	30	4237	0535	1609	7291	8982	4047	6355	0803	3728	7559		30
	45	4.4059	4.0728	5.1403	4.7516	5.8746	5.4304	6.6089	6.1092	7.3432	6.7880		15
43	0	3881	0920	1195	7740	8508	4560	5822	1380	3135	8200	47	0
	15	3702	1111	0986	7963	8270	4815	5553	1666	2837	8518		45
	30	3522	1301	0776	8185	8030	5068	5284	1952	2537	8835		30
	45	3342	1491	0565	8406	7789	5321	5013	2236	2236	9151		15
44	0	3160	1680	0354	8626	7547	5573	4741	2519	1934	9466	46	0
	15	2978	1867	0141	8845	7304	5823	4467	2801	1630	9779		45
	30	2795	2055	4.9928	9064	7060	6073	4193	3082	1325	7.0091		30
	45	2611	2241	9713	9281	6815	6321	3917	3361	1019	0401		15
45	0	2426	2426	9497	9497	6569	6569	3640	3640	0711	0711	45	0
		Dep.	Lat.	Dep.	Lat.	Dep.	Lat.	Dep.	Lat.	Dep.	Lat.	Course.	
		Dist. 6.		Dist. 7.		Dist. 8.		Dist. 9.		Dist. 10.			

LATITUDE.														
Min.	0°	1°	2°	3°	4°	5°	6°	7°	8°	9°	10°	11°	12°	Min.
0	0.0	60.0	120.0	180.1	240.2	300.4	360.7	421.1	481.6	542.2	603.1	664.1	725.3	0
1	1.0	61.0	21.0	81.1	41.2	01.4	61.7	22.1	82.6	43.3	04.1	65.1	26.3	1
2	2.0	62.0	22.0	82.1	42.2	02.4	62.7	23.1	83.6	44.3	05.1	66.1	27.4	2
3	3.0	63.0	23.0	83.1	43.2	03.4	63.7	24.1	84.6	45.3	06.1	67.1	28.4	3
4	4.0	64.0	24.0	84.1	44.2	04.4	64.7	25.1	85.6	46.3	07.1	68.2	29.4	4
5	5.0	65.0	25.0	85.1	45.2	05.4	65.7	26.1	86.6	47.3	08.2	69.2	30.5	5
6	6.0	66.0	26.0	86.1	46.2	06.4	66.7	27.1	87.6	48.3	09.2	70.2	31.5	6
7	7.0	67.0	27.0	87.1	47.2	07.4	67.7	28.1	88.6	49.3	10.2	71.2	32.5	7
8	8.0	68.0	28.0	88.1	48.2	08.4	68.7	29.1	89.6	50.3	11.2	72.2	33.5	8
9	9.0	69.0	29.0	89.1	49.2	09.4	69.7	30.1	90.7	51.4	12.2	73.3	34.5	9
10	10.0	70.0	130.0	190.1	250.2	310.4	370.7	431.1	491.7	552.4	613.2	674.3	735.6	10
11	11.0	71.0	31.0	91.1	51.2	11.4	71.7	32.1	92.7	53.4	14.2	75.3	36.6	11
12	12.0	72.0	32.0	92.1	52.2	12.4	72.7	33.1	93.7	54.4	15.3	76.3	37.6	12
13	13.0	73.0	33.0	93.1	53.2	13.4	73.7	34.2	94.7	55.4	16.3	77.3	38.6	13
14	14.0	74.0	34.0	94.1	54.2	14.4	74.7	35.2	95.7	56.4	17.3	78.4	39.6	14
15	15.0	75.0	35.0	95.1	55.2	15.4	75.7	36.2	96.7	57.4	18.3	79.4	40.7	15
16	16.0	76.0	36.0	96.1	56.2	16.4	76.8	37.2	97.7	58.4	19.3	80.4	41.7	16
17	17.0	77.0	37.0	97.1	57.2	17.5	77.8	38.2	98.7	59.4	20.3	81.4	42.7	17
18	18.0	78.0	38.0	98.1	58.2	18.5	78.8	39.2	99.8	60.5	21.3	82.4	43.7	18
19	19.0	79.0	39.0	99.1	59.2	19.5	79.8	40.2	500.8	61.5	22.4	83.5	44.8	19
20	20.0	80.0	140.0	200.1	260.2	320.5	380.8	441.2	501.8	562.5	623.4	684.5	745.8	20
21	21.0	81.0	41.0	01.1	61.3	21.5	81.8	42.2	02.8	63.5	24.4	85.5	46.8	21
22	22.0	82.0	42.0	02.1	62.3	22.5	82.8	43.2	03.8	64.5	25.4	86.5	47.8	22
23	23.0	83.0	43.0	03.1	63.3	23.5	83.8	44.2	04.8	65.5	26.4	87.5	48.9	23
24	24.0	84.0	44.0	04.1	64.3	24.5	84.8	45.2	05.8	66.6	27.4	88.6	49.9	24
25	25.0	85.0	45.0	05.1	65.3	25.5	85.8	46.3	06.8	67.6	28.5	89.6	50.9	25
26	26.0	86.0	46.0	06.1	66.3	26.5	86.8	47.3	07.8	68.6	29.5	90.6	51.9	26
27	27.0	87.0	47.0	07.1	67.3	27.5	87.8	48.3	08.9	69.6	30.5	91.6	53.0	27
28	28.0	88.0	48.0	08.1	68.3	28.5	88.8	49.3	09.9	70.6	31.5	92.6	54.0	28
29	29.0	89.0	49.0	09.1	69.3	29.5	89.8	50.3	10.9	71.6	32.5	93.6	55.0	29
30	30.0	90.0	150.0	210.1	270.3	330.5	390.8	451.3	511.9	572.6	633.5	694.7	756.0	30
31	31.0	91.0	51.0	11.1	71.3	31.5	91.8	52.3	12.9	73.7	34.6	95.7	57.1	31
32	32.0	92.0	52.0	12.1	72.3	32.5	92.9	53.3	13.9	74.7	35.6	96.7	58.1	32
33	33.0	93.0	53.1	13.1	73.3	33.5	93.9	54.3	14.9	75.7	36.6	97.7	59.1	33
34	34.0	94.0	54.1	14.1	74.3	34.5	94.9	55.3	15.9	76.7	37.6	98.7	60.1	34
35	35.0	95.0	55.1	15.1	75.3	35.5	95.9	56.3	16.9	77.7	38.6	99.8	61.1	35
36	36.0	96.0	56.1	16.1	76.3	36.5	96.9	57.3	18.0	78.7	39.6	700.8	62.2	36
37	37.0	97.0	57.1	17.1	77.3	37.5	97.9	58.4	19.0	79.7	40.7	01.8	63.2	37
38	38.0	98.0	58.1	18.1	78.3	38.5	98.9	59.4	20.0	80.8	41.7	02.8	64.2	38
39	39.0	99.0	59.1	19.1	79.3	39.6	99.9	60.4	21.0	81.8	42.7	03.8	65.2	39
40	40.0	100.0	160.1	220.2	280.3	340.6	400.9	461.4	522.0	582.8	643.7	704.9	766.3	40
41	41.0	01.0	61.1	21.2	81.3	41.6	01.9	62.4	23.0	83.8	44.7	05.9	67.3	41
42	42.0	02.0	62.1	22.2	82.3	42.6	02.9	63.4	24.0	84.8	45.8	06.9	68.3	42
43	43.0	03.0	63.1	23.2	83.3	43.6	03.9	64.4	25.0	85.8	46.8	07.9	69.3	43
44	44.0	04.0	64.1	24.2	84.3	44.6	04.9	65.4	26.0	86.8	47.8	09.0	70.4	44
45	45.0	05.0	65.1	25.2	85.3	45.6	05.9	66.4	27.1	87.9	48.8	10.0	71.4	45
46	46.0	06.0	66.1	26.2	86.3	46.6	07.0	67.4	28.1	88.9	49.8	11.0	72.4	46
47	47.0	07.0	67.1	27.2	87.3	47.6	08.0	68.4	29.1	89.9	50.8	12.0	73.4	47
48	48.0	08.0	68.1	28.2	88.3	48.6	09.0	69.5	30.1	90.9	51.9	13.1	74.5	48
49	49.0	09.0	69.1	29.2	89.3	49.6	10.0	70.5	31.1	91.9	52.9	14.1	75.5	49
50	50.0	110.0	170.1	230.2	290.3	350.6	411.0	471.5	532.1	592.9	653.9	715.1	776.5	50
51	51.0	11.0	71.1	31.2	91.3	51.6	12.0	72.5	33.1	93.9	54.9	16.1	77.5	51
52	52.0	12.0	72.1	32.2	92.4	52.6	13.0	73.5	34.1	95.0	55.9	17.1	78.6	52
53	53.0	13.0	73.1	33.2	93.4	53.6	14.0	74.5	35.1	96.0	57.0	18.2	79.6	53
54	54.0	14.0	74.1	34.2	94.4	54.6	15.0	75.5	36.2	97.0	58.0	19.2	80.6	54
55	55.0	15.0	75.1	35.2	95.4	55.6	16.0	76.5	37.2	98.0	59.0	20.2	81.7	55
56	56.0	16.0	76.1	36.2	96.4	56.6	17.0	77.5	38.2	99.0	60.0	21.2	82.7	56
57	57.0	17.0	77.1	37.2	97.4	57.6	18.0	78.5	39.2	600.0	61.0	22.3	83.7	57
58	58.0	18.0	78.1	38.2	98.4	58.6	19.0	79.5	40.2	01.0	62.1	23.3	84.7	58
59	59.0	19.0	79.1	39.2	99.4	59.7	20.0	80.5	41.2	02.1	63.1	24.3	85.8	59

LATITUDE.

Min.	13°	14°	15°	16°	17°	18°	19°	20°	21°	22°	23°	24°	Min.
0	786.8	848.5	910.5	972.7	1035.3	1098.2	1161.5	1225.1	1289.2	1353.7	1418.6	1484.1	0
1	87.8	49.5	11.5	73.8	36.3	99.3	62.5	26.2	90.3	54.8	19.7	85.2	1
2	88.8	50.5	12.6	74.8	37.4	1100.3	63.6	27.3	91.3	55.8	20.8	86.3	2
3	89.9	51.6	13.6	75.9	38.4	01.4	64.7	28.3	92.4	56.9	21.9	87.3	3
4	90.9	52.6	14.6	76.9	39.5	02.4	65.7	29.4	93.5	58.0	23.0	88.4	4
5	91.9	53.6	15.7	78.0	40.5	03.5	66.8	30.4	94.5	59.0	24.1	89.5	5
6	92.9	54.7	16.7	79.0	41.6	04.5	67.8	31.5	95.6	60.1	25.1	90.6	6
7	94.0	55.7	17.7	80.0	42.6	05.6	68.9	32.6	96.7	61.2	26.2	91.7	7
8	95.0	56.7	18.8	81.1	43.7	06.6	70.0	33.6	97.8	62.3	27.3	92.8	8
9	96.0	57.8	19.8	82.1	44.7	07.7	71.0	34.7	98.8	63.4	28.4	93.9	9
10	797.0	858.8	920.8	983.2	1045.8	1108.7	1172.1	1235.8	1299.9	1364.5	1429.5	1495.0	10
11	98.1	59.8	21.9	84.2	46.8	09.8	73.1	36.8	1301.0	65.6	30.6	96.1	11
12	99.1	60.9	22.9	85.2	47.9	10.8	74.2	37.9	02.0	66.6	31.7	97.2	12
13	800.1	61.9	23.9	86.3	48.9	11.9	75.2	39.0	03.1	67.7	32.8	98.3	13
14	01.2	62.9	25.0	87.3	49.9	12.9	76.3	40.0	04.2	68.8	33.9	99.4	14
15	02.2	64.0	26.0	88.4	51.0	14.0	77.4	41.1	05.3	69.9	34.9	1500.5	15
16	03.2	65.0	27.0	89.4	52.0	15.0	78.4	42.2	06.3	70.9	36.0	01.6	16
17	04.2	66.0	28.1	90.4	53.1	16.1	79.5	43.2	07.4	72.0	37.1	02.7	17
18	05.3	67.1	29.1	91.5	54.1	17.1	80.5	44.3	08.5	73.1	38.2	03.8	18
19	06.3	68.1	30.1	92.5	55.2	18.2	81.6	45.4	09.6	74.2	39.3	04.9	19
20	807.3	869.1	931.2	993.6	1056.2	1119.2	1182.7	1246.4	1310.6	1375.3	1440.4	1506.0	20
21	08.4	70.1	32.2	94.6	57.3	20.3	83.7	47.5	11.7	76.4	41.5	07.1	21
22	09.4	71.2	33.3	95.6	58.3	21.3	84.8	48.6	12.8	77.4	42.6	08.2	22
23	10.4	72.2	34.3	96.7	59.4	22.4	85.8	49.6	13.8	78.5	43.7	09.3	23
24	11.4	73.2	35.3	97.7	60.4	23.4	86.9	50.7	14.9	79.6	44.8	10.4	24
25	12.5	74.3	36.3	98.8	61.4	24.5	88.0	51.8	16.0	80.7	45.8	11.5	25
26	13.5	75.3	37.4	99.8	62.5	25.5	89.0	52.8	17.1	81.8	46.9	12.6	26
27	14.5	76.3	38.4	1000.8	63.5	26.6	90.1	53.9	18.1	82.8	48.0	13.7	27
28	15.5	77.4	39.5	01.9	64.6	27.6	91.1	55.0	19.2	83.9	49.1	14.8	28
29	16.6	78.4	40.5	02.9	65.6	28.7	92.2	56.0	20.3	85.0	50.2	15.9	29
30	817.6	879.4	941.6	1004.0	1066.7	1129.7	1193.2	1257.1	1321.4	1386.1	1451.3	1517.0	30
31	18.6	80.5	42.6	05.0	67.7	30.8	94.3	58.2	22.5	87.2	52.4	18.1	31
32	19.6	81.5	43.6	06.1	68.8	31.8	95.4	59.2	23.5	88.3	53.5	19.2	32
33	20.7	82.5	44.7	07.1	69.8	32.9	96.4	60.3	24.6	89.4	54.6	20.3	33
34	21.7	83.6	45.7	08.1	70.9	34.0	97.5	61.4	25.7	90.4	55.6	21.4	34
35	22.7	84.6	46.7	09.2	72.0	35.1	98.5	62.4	26.7	91.5	56.7	22.5	35
36	23.8	85.6	47.8	10.2	73.0	36.1	99.6	63.5	27.8	92.6	57.8	23.6	36
37	24.8	86.7	48.8	11.3	74.1	37.2	1200.7	64.6	28.9	93.7	58.9	24.7	37
38	25.8	87.7	49.9	12.3	75.1	38.2	01.7	65.6	30.0	94.8	60.0	25.8	38
39	26.9	88.7	50.9	13.4	76.2	39.3	02.8	66.7	31.1	95.8	61.1	26.9	39
40	827.9	889.8	951.9	1014.4	1077.2	1140.3	1203.9	1267.8	1332.1	1396.9	1462.2	1528.0	40
41	28.9	90.8	53.0	15.4	78.3	41.4	04.9	68.8	33.2	98.0	63.3	29.1	41
42	29.9	91.8	54.0	16.5	79.3	42.4	06.0	69.9	34.3	99.1	64.4	30.2	42
43	31.0	92.9	55.1	17.5	80.4	43.5	07.1	71.0	35.3	1400.2	65.5	31.3	43
44	32.0	93.9	56.1	18.6	81.4	44.6	08.1	72.1	36.4	01.3	66.6	32.4	44
45	33.0	94.9	57.1	19.6	82.5	45.6	09.2	73.1	37.5	02.4	67.7	33.5	45
46	34.1	96.0	58.2	20.6	83.5	46.7	10.2	74.2	38.6	03.4	68.8	34.6	46
47	35.1	97.0	59.2	21.7	84.6	47.7	11.3	75.3	39.7	04.5	69.8	35.7	47
48	36.1	98.0	60.2	22.7	85.6	48.8	12.4	76.3	40.7	05.6	70.9	36.8	48
49	37.2	99.1	61.3	23.8	86.7	49.9	13.4	77.4	41.8	06.7	72.0	37.9	49
50	838.2	900.1	962.3	1024.8	1087.7	1150.9	1214.5	1278.5	1342.9	1407.8	1473.1	1539.0	50
51	39.2	01.1	63.4	25.9	88.8	52.0	15.5	79.5	44.0	08.8	74.2	40.1	51
52	40.2	02.2	64.4	26.9	89.8	53.0	16.6	80.6	45.1	09.9	75.3	41.2	52
53	41.3	03.2	65.5	28.0	90 9	54.1	17.7	81.7	46.1	11.0	76.4	42.3	53
54	42.3	04.3	66.5	29.0	91.9	55.1	18.7	82.8	47.2	12.1	77.5	43.4	54
55	43.3	05.3	67.5	30.1	93.0	56.2	19.8	83.8	48.3	13.2	78.6	44.5	55
56	44.4	06.3	68.6	31.1	94.0	57.2	20.9	84.9	49.4	14.3	79.7	45.6	56
57	45.4	07.4	69.6	32.2	95.1	58.3	21.9	86.0	50.4	15.4	80.8	46.7	57
58	46.4	08.4	70.7	33.2	96.1	59.4	23.0	87.0	51.5	16.5	81.9	47.8	58
59	47.5	09.4	71.7	34.3	97.2	60.4	24.1	88.1	52.6	17.5	83.0	48.9	59

LATITUDE.												
Min.	25°	26°	27°	28°	29°	30°	31°	32°	33°	34°	35°	Min.
0	1550.0	1616.5	1683.5	1751.2	1819.4	1888.4	1958.0	2028.4	2099.5	2171.5	2244.3	0
1	51.1	17.6	84.6	52.3	20.6	89.5	59.2	29.6	2100.7	72.7	45.5	1
2	52.2	18.7	85.8	53.4	21.7	90.7	60.4	30.7	01.9	73.9	46.8	2
3	53.3	19.8	86.9	54.6	22.9	91.9	61.6	31.9	03.1	75.1	48.0	3
4	54.4	20.9	88.0	55.7	24.0	93.0	62.7	33.1	04.3	76.3	49.2	4
5	55.5	22.0	89.1	56.8	25.2	94.1	63.9	34.3	05.5	77.5	50.4	5
6	56.6	23.2	90.3	58.0	26.3	95.3	65.0	35.5	06.7	78.7	51.6	6
7	57.7	24.3	91.4	59.1	27.5	96.5	66.2	36.7	07.9	80.0	52.9	7
8	58.8	25.4	92.5	60.2	28.6	97.6	67.4	37.8	09.1	81.2	54.1	8
9	59.9	26.5	93.6	61.4	29.7	98.8	68.5	39.0	10.3	82.4	55.3	9
10	1561.0	1627.6	1694.8	1762.5	1830.9	1899.9	1969.7	2040.2	2111.5	2183.6	2256.5	10
11	62.1	28.7	95.9	63.6	32.0	1901.1	70.9	41.4	12.7	84.8	57.8	11
12	63.2	29.8	97.0	64.8	33.2	02.3	72.0	42.6	13.9	86.0	59.0	12
13	64.4	31.0	98.1	65.9	34.3	03.4	73.2	43.8	15.1	87.2	60.2	13
14	65.5	32.1	99.3	67.0	35.5	04.6	74.4	44.9	16.3	88.4	61.4	14
15	66.6	33.2	1700.4	68.2	36.6	05.7	75.6	46.1	17.5	89.6	62.7	15
16	67.7	34.3	01.5	69.3	37.8	06.9	76.8	47.3	18.7	90.8	63.9	16
17	68.8	35.4	02.6	70.5	38.9	08.1	77.9	48.5	19.8	92.0	65.1	17
18	69.9	36.5	03.8	71.6	40.1	09.2	79.1	49.7	21.0	93.3	66.3	18
19	71.0	37.6	04.9	72.7	41.2	10.4	80.2	50.8	22.2	94.4	67.5	19
20	1572.1	1638.8	1706.0	1773.9	1842.4	1911.5	1981.4	2052.0	2123.4	2195.7	2268.8	20
21	73.2	39.9	07.1	75.0	43.5	12.7	82.6	53.2	24.6	96.9	70.0	21
22	74.3	41.0	08.3	76.1	44.6	13.8	83.7	54.4	25.8	98.1	71.2	22
23	75.4	42.1	09.4	77.2	45.8	15.0	84.9	55.6	27.0	99.3	72.5	23
24	76.5	43.2	10.5	78.4	46.9	16.2	86.1	56.8	28.2	2200.5	73.7	24
25	77.6	44.3	11.6	79.5	48.1	17.3	87.3	58.0	29.4	01.7	74.9	25
26	78.7	45.5	12.8	80.6	49.2	18.5	88.4	59.1	30.6	03.0	76.1	26
27	79.8	46.6	13.9	81.8	50.4	19.6	89.6	60.3	31.8	04.2	77.4	27
28	80.9	47.7	15.0	83.0	51.5	20.8	90.8	61.5	33.0	05.4	78.6	28
29	82.1	48.8	16.1	84.1	52.7	21.9	92.0	62.7	34.2	06.6	79.8	29
30	1583.2	1649.9	1717.3	1785.2	1853.8	1923.1	1993.1	2063.9	2135.4	2207.8	2281.0	30
31	84.3	51.0	18.4	86.4	55.0	24.3	94.3	65.1	36.6	09.0	82.3	31
32	85.4	52.2	19.5	87.5	56.1	25.4	95.5	66.2	37.8	10.2	83.5	32
33	86.5	53.3	20.7	88.6	57.2	26.6	96.6	67.4	39.0	11.4	84.7	33
34	87.6	54.4	21.8	89.8	58.4	27.8	97.8	68.6	40.2	12.7	86.0	34
35	88.7	55.5	22.9	90.9	59.6	28.9	99.0	69.8	41.4	13.9	87.2	35
36	89.8	56.6	24.0	92.1	60.7	30.1	2000.2	71.0	42.6	15.1	88.4	36
37	90.9	57.8	25.2	93.2	61.9	31.3	01.3	72.2	43.8	16.3	89.7	37
38	92.0	58.9	26.3	94.3	63.0	32.4	02.5	73.4	45.0	17.5	90.9	38
39	93.1	60.0	27.4	95.5	64.2	33.6	03.7	74.5	46.2	18.7	92.1	39
40	1594.3	1661.1	1728.6	1796.6	1865.3	1934.7	2004.9	2075.7	2147.4	2219.9	2293.3	40
41	95.4	62.2	29.7	97.8	66.5	35.9	06.0	76.9	48.6	21.2	94.6	41
42	96.5	63.4	30.8	98.9	67.6	37.1	07.2	78.1	49.8	22.4	95.8	42
43	97.6	64.5	31.9	1800.0	68.8	38.2	08.4	79.3	51.0	23.6	97.0	43
44	98.7	65.6	33.1	01.2	69.9	39.4	09.6	80.5	52.2	24.8	98.3	44
45	99.8	66.7	34.2	02.3	71.1	40.5	10.7	81.7	53.4	26.0	99.5	45
46	1600.9	67.8	35.3	03.5	72.2	41.7	11.9	82.9	54.6	27.2	2300.7	46
47	02.0	69.0	36.5	04.6	73.4	42.9	13.1	84.0	55.8	28.5	02.0	47
48	03.1	70.1	37.6	05.7	74.5	44.0	14.3	85.2	57.0	29.7	03.2	48
49	04.2	71.2	38.7	06.9	75.7	45.2	15.4	86.4	58.2	30.9	04.4	49
50	1605.4	1672.3	1739.9	1808.0	1876.8	1946.4	2016.6	2087.6	2159.4	2232.1	2305.7	50
51	06.5	73.4	41.0	09.2	78.0	47.5	17.8	88.8	60.7	33.3	06.9	51
52	07.6	74.5	42.1	10.3	79.2	48.7	19.0	90.0	61.9	34.6	08.1	52
53	08.7	75.7	43.2	11.4	80.3	49.9	20.2	91.2	63.1	35.8	09.4	53
54	09.8	76.8	44.4	12.6	81.5	51.0	21.3	92.4	64.3	37.0	10.6	54
55	10.9	77.9	45.5	13.7	82.6	52.2	22.5	93.6	65.5	38.2	11.8	55
56	12.0	79.0	46.6	14.9	83.8	53.4	23.7	94.8	66.7	39.4	13.1	56
57	13.1	80.2	47.8	16.0	84.9	54.5	24.9	96.0	67.9	40.7	14.3	57
58	14.2	81.3	48.9	17.2	86.1	55.7	26.0	97.1	69.1	41.9	15.5	58
59	15.4	82.4	50.0	18.3	87.2	56.9	27.2	98.3	70.3	43.1	16.8	59

LATITUDE.

Min.	36°	37°	38°	39°	40°	41°	42°	43°	44°	45°	46°	Min.
0	2318.0	2392.6	2468.3	2545.0	2622.7	2701.6	2781.7	2863.1	2945.8	3030.0	3115.6	0
1	19.2	93.9	69.5	46.2	24.0	02.9	83.1	64.5	47.2	31.4	17.0	1
2	20.5	95.1	70.8	47.5	25.3	04.3	84.4	65.8	48.6	32.8	18.5	2
3	21.7	96.4	72.1	48.8	26.6	05.6	85.8	67.2	50.0	34.2	19.9	3
4	23.0	97.7	73.4	50.1	27.9	06.9	87.1	68.5	51.4	35.6	21.4	4
5	24.2	98.9	74.6	51.4	29.2	08.3	88.5	70.0	52.8	37.0	22.8	5
6	25.4	2400.2	75.9	52.7	30.5	09.6	89.8	71.3	54.2	38.4	24.2	6
7	26.7	01.4	77.1	54.0	31.9	10.9	91.2	72.7	55.6	39.8	25.7	7
8	27.9	02.7	78.5	55.3	33.2	12.2	92.5	74.1	57.0	41.3	27.1	8
9	29.1	03.9	79.7	56.6	34.5	13.5	93.8	75.4	58.3	42.7	28.5	9
10	2330.4	2405.2	2481.0	2557.8	2635.8	2714.9	2795.1	2876.8	2959.8	3044.1	3130.0	10
11	31.6	06.4	82.2	59.1	37.1	16.2	96.5	78.2	61.1	45.5	31.5	11
12	32.9	07.7	83.5	60.4	38.4	17.5	97.9	79.5	62.5	47.0	32.9	12
13	34.1	09.0	84.8	61.7	39.7	18.9	99.3	80.9	63.9	48.4	34.3	13
14	35.3	10.2	86.1	63.0	41.0	20.2	2800.6	82.3	65.3	49.8	35.8	14
15	36.6	11.5	87.4	64.3	42.3	21.5	02.0	83.7	66.7	51.2	37.2	15
16	37.8	12.7	88.6	65.6	43.6	22.9	03.3	85.0	68.1	52.6	38.7	16
17	39.0	14.0	89.9	66.9	44.9	24.2	04.7	86.4	69.5	54.1	40.1	17
18	40.3	15.2	91.2	68.2	46.3	25.5	06.0	87.8	70.9	55.5	41.6	18
19	41.5	16.5	92.4	69.5	47.6	26.8	07.3	89.1	72.3	56.9	43.0	19
20	2342.8	2417.8	2493.7	2570.7	2648.9	2728.2	2808.8	2890.5	2973.7	3058.3	3144.5	20
21	44.0	19.0	95.0	72.0	50.2	29.5	10.1	91.9	75.1	59.7	45.9	21
22	45.3	20.3	96.3	73.3	51.5	30.8	11.4	93.3	76.5	61.2	47.4	22
23	46.5	21.5	97.6	74.6	52.8	32.2	12.8	94.7	77.9	62.6	48.8	23
24	47.7	22.8	98.8	75.9	54.1	33.5	14.1	96.0	79.3	64.0	50.3	24
25	49.0	24.0	2500.1	77.2	55.5	34.8	15.5	97.4	80.7	65.4	51.7	25
26	50.2	25.3	01.4	78.5	56.8	36.2	16.8	98.8	82.1	66.9	53.2	26
27	51.5	26.5	02.7	79.8	58.1	37.5	18.2	2900.2	83.5	68.3	54.6	27
28	52.7	27.8	03.9	81.1	59.4	38.8	19.5	01.5	84.9	69.7	56.1	28
29	54.0	29.1	05.2	82.4	60.7	40.2	20.9	02.9	86.3	71.1	57.5	29
30	2355.2	2430.3	2506.5	2583.7	2662.0	2741.5	2822.3	2904.3	2987.7	3072.6	3159.0	30
31	56.5	31.6	07.8	85.0	63.3	42.9	23.6	05.7	89.1	74.0	60.4	31
32	57.7	32.9	09.0	86.3	64.6	44.2	25.0	07.1	90.5	75.4	61.9	32
33	58.9	34.1	10.3	87.6	66.0	45.5	26.3	08.4	91.9	76.9	63.3	33
34	60.2	35.4	11.6	88.9	67.3	46.9	27.7	09.7	93.3	78.3	64.8	34
35	61.4	36.7	12.9	90.2	68.6	48.2	29.0	11.2	94.7	79.7	66.2	35
36	62.7	37.9	14.2	91.5	69.9	49.5	30.4	12.6	96.1	81.1	67.7	36
37	63.9	39.2	15.4	92.8	71.2	50.9	31.7	14.0	97.5	82.6	69.1	37
38	65.2	40.4	16.7	94.1	72.5	52.2	33.1	15.3	98.9	84.0	70.6	38
39	66.4	41.7	18.0	95.4	73.9	53.5	34.5	16.7	3000.3	85.4	72.0	39
40	2367.6	2443.0	2519.3	2596.7	2675.2	2754.9	2835.8	2918.1	3001.8	3086.9	3173.5	40
41	68.9	44.2	20.5	98.0	76.5	56.2	37.2	19.5	03.2	88.3	75.0	41
42	70.2	45.5	21.8	99.3	77.8	57.6	38.6	20.9	04.6	89.7	76.4	42
43	71.4	46.8	23.1	2600.5	79.1	58.9	39.9	22.3	06.0	91.2	77.9	43
44	72.6	48.0	24.4	01.9	80.5	60.2	41.3	23.6	07.4	92.6	79.3	44
45	73.9	49.3	25.7	03.2	81.8	61.5	42.6	25.0	08.8	94.0	80.8	45
46	75.1	50.6	27.0	04.5	83.1	62.9	44.0	26.4	10.2	95.5	82.3	46
47	76.4	51.8	28.3	05.8	84.4	64.3	45.4	27.8	11.6	96.9	83.7	47
48	77.6	53.1	29.5	07.1	85.7	65.6	46.7	29.2	13.0	98.3	85.2	48
49	78.9	54.3	30.8	08.4	87.1	66.9	48.1	30.6	14.4	99.7	86.6	49
50	2380.1	2455.6	2532.1	2609.7	2688.4	2768.3	2849.5	2932.0	3015.8	3101.2	3188.1	50
51	81.4	56.9	33.4	11.0	89.7	69.6	50.8	33.3	17.2	02.6	89.6	51
52	82.6	58.1	34.7	12.3	91.0	71.0	52.2	34.7	18.7	04.1	91.0	52
53	83.9	59.4	36.0	13.6	92.3	72.3	53.5	36.1	20.1	05.6	92.5	53
54	85.1	60.7	37.2	14.9	93.7	73.7	54.9	37.5	21.5	07.0	94.0	54
55	86.4	61.9	38.5	16.2	95.0	75.0	56.3	38.9	22.9	08.4	95.4	55
56	87.6	63.2	39.8	17.5	96.3	76.3	57.7	40.3	24.3	09.8	96.9	56
57	88.9	64.5	41.1	18.8	97.6	77.7	59.0	41.7	25.7	11.2	98.4	57
58	90.2	65.8	42.4	20.1	99.0	79.0	60.5	43.1	27.1	12.7	99.8	58
59	91.4	67.0	43.6	21.4	2700.3	80.4	61.7	44.4	28.5	14.1	3201.3	59

LATITUDE.												
Min.	47°	48°	49°	50°	51°	52°	53°	54°	55°	56°	57°	Min.
0	3202.7	3291.5	3382.1	3474.5	3568.8	3665.2	3763.8	3864.6	3968.0	4073.9	4182.6	0
1	04.2	93.0	83.6	76.0	70.4	66.8	65.4	66.3	69.7	75.7	84.5	1
2	05.7	94.5	85.1	77.6	72.0	68.4	67.1	68.0	71.5	77.5	86.3	2
3	07.1	96.0	86.7	79.1	73.6	70.1	68.8	69.7	73.2	79.3	88.1	3
4	08.6	97.5	88.2	80.7	75.2	71.7	70.4	71.5	75.0	81.1	90.0	4
5	10.1	99.0	89.7	82.3	76.8	73.3	72.1	73.2	76.7	82.9	91.8	5
6	11.5	3300.5	91.3	83.8	78.4	75.0	73.7	74.9	78.4	84.7	93.7	6
7	13.0	02.0	92.8	85.4	79.9	76.6	75.4	76.6	80.2	86.4	95.5	7
8	14.5	03.5	94.3	87.0	81.5	78.2	77.1	78.3	82.0	88.2	97.3	8
9	15.9	05.0	95.8	88.5	83.1	79.8	78.7	80.0	83.7	90.0	99.2	9
10	3217.4	3306.5	3397.4	3490.1	3584.7	3681.5	3780.4	3881.7	3985.4	4091.8	4201.0	10
11	18.9	08.0	98.9	91.6	86.3	83.1	82.1	83.4	87.2	93.6	02.9	11
12	20.3	09.5	3400.4	93.2	87.9	84.7	83.7	85.1	88.9	95.4	04.7	12
13	21.8	11.0	02.0	94.7	89.5	86.4	85.4	86.8	90.7	97.2	06.6	13
14	23.3	12.5	03.5	96.3	91.1	88.0	87.1	88.5	92.5	99.0	08.4	14
15	24.8	14.0	05.0	97.9	92.7	89.6	88.8	90.2	94.2	4100.8	10.3	15
16	26.2	15.5	06.6	99.4	94.3	91.3	90.4	92.0	96.0	02.6	12.1	16
17	27.7	17.0	08.1	3501.0	95.9	92.9	92.1	93.7	97.7	04.4	14.0	17
18	29.2	18.5	09.6	02.6	97.5	94.5	93.8	95.4	99.5	06.2	15.8	18
19	30.7	20.0	11.1	04.1	99.1	96.2	95.5	97.1	4001.2	08.0	17.7	19
20	3232.1	3321.5	3412.7	3505.7	3600.7	3697.8	3797.1	3898.8	4003.0	4109.8	4219.5	20
21	33.6	23.0	14.2	07.3	02.3	99.4	98.8	3900.5	04.7	11.6	21.4	21
22	35.1	24.5	15.7	08.8	03.9	3701.1	3800.5	02.2	06.5	13.4	23.2	22
23	36.6	26.0	17.3	10.4	05.5	02.7	02.2	04.0	08.3	15.2	25.1	23
24	38.0	27.5	18.8	12.0	07.1	04.4	03.8	05.7	10.0	17.1	27.0	24
25	39.5	29.0	20.4	13.5	08.7	06.0	05.5	07.4	11.8	18.9	28.8	25
26	41.0	30.6	21.9	15.1	10.3	07.6	07.2	09.1	13.5	20.7	30.6	26
27	42.5	32.1	23.5	16.7	11.9	09.3	08.9	10.8	15.3	22.5	32.5	27
28	44.0	33.6	25.0	18.3	13.6	10.9	10.5	12.5	17.1	24.3	34.4	28
29	45.4	35.1	26.5	19.8	15.1	12.6	12.2	14.3	18.8	26.1	36.2	29
30	3246.9	3336.6	3428.0	3521.4	3616.7	3714.2	3813.9	3916.0	4020.6	4127.9	4238.1	30
31	48.4	38.1	29.6	23.0	18.4	15.8	15.6	17.7	22.4	29.7	40.0	31
32	49.9	39.6	31.1	24.6	20.0	17.5	17.3	19.4	24.1	31.5	41.8	32
33	51.4	41.1	32.7	26.1	21.6	19.1	18.9	21.2	25.9	33.3	43.7	33
34	52.8	42.6	34.2	27.7	23.2	20.8	20.6	22.9	27.7	35.2	45.5	34
35	54.3	44.1	35.8	29.3	24.8	22.4	22.3	24.6	29.4	37.0	47.4	35
36	55.8	45.7	37.3	30.8	26.4	24.1	24.0	26.3	31.2	38.8	49.3	36
37	57.3	47.2	38.8	32.4	28.0	25.7	25.7	28.1	33.0	40.6	51.1	37
38	58.8	48.7	40.4	34.0	29.6	27.4	27.4	29.8	34.8	42.4	53.0	38
39	60.3	50.2	41.9	35.6	31.3	29.0	29.1	31.5	36.5	44.2	54.9	39
40	3261.7	3351.7	3443.5	3537.1	3632.8	3730.7	3830.8	3933.2	4038.3	4146.1	4256.7	40
41	63.2	53.2	45.0	38.7	34.4	32.3	32.4	35.0	40.1	47.9	58.6	41
42	64.7	54.7	46.6	40.3	36.1	34.0	34.1	36.7	41.8	49.7	60.5	42
43	66.2	56.2	48.1	41.9	37.7	35.6	35.8	38.4	43.6	51.5	62.3	43
44	67.7	57.8	49.7	43.5	39.3	37.3	37.5	40.2	45.4	53.4	64.2	44
45	69.2	59.3	51.2	45.0	40.9	38.9	39.2	41.9	47.2	55.2	66.1	45
46	70.7	60.8	52.8	46.6	42.5	40.6	40.9	43.6	49.0	57.0	68.0	46
47	72.1	62.3	54.3	48.2	44.1	42.2	42.6	45.4	50.7	58.8	69.8	47
48	73.6	63.8	55.8	49.8	45.8	43.9	44.3	47.1	52.5	60.7	71.7	48
49	75.1	65.4	57.4	51.4	47.4	45.5	46.0	48.8	54.3	62.5	73.6	49
50	3276.6	3366.9	3458.9	3553.0	3649.0	3747.2	3847.7	3950.6	4056.1	4164.3	4275.5	50
51	78.1	68.4	60.5	54.6	50.6	48.8	49.4	52.3	57.8	66.1	77.4	51
52	79.6	69.9	62.0	56.1	52.2	50.5	51.1	54.0	59.6	68.0	79.2	52
53	81.1	71.4	63.6	57.7	53.8	52.1	52.8	55.8	61.4	69.8	81.1	53
54	82.6	73.0	65.2	59.3	55.5	53.8	54.4	57.5	63.2	71.6	83.0	54
55	84.1	74.5	66.7	60.9	57.1	55.5	56.1	59.3	65.0	73.5	84.9	55
56	85.6	76.0	68.3	62.5	58.7	57.1	57.8	61.0	66.8	75.3	86.8	56
57	87.1	77.5	69.8	64.0	60.3	58.8	59.5	62.7	68.5	77.1	88.6	57
58	88.5	79.0	71.4	65.6	61.9	60.4	61.2	64.5	70.3	79.0	90.5	58
59	90.0	80.6	73.0	67.2	63.6	62.1	62.9	66.2	72.1	80.8	92.4	59

LATITUDE.

Min.	58°	59°	60°	61°	62°	63°	64°	65°	66°	67°	68°	Min.
0	4294.3	4409.1	4527.4	4649.2	4775.0	4904.9	5039.4	5178.8	5323.5	5474.0	5630.8	0
1	96.2	11.1	29.4	51.3	77.1	07.1	41.7	81.2	26.0	76.6	33.5	1
2	98.1	13.0	31.4	53.4	79.3	09.4	44.0	83.5	28.4	79.1	36.2	2
3	4300.0	15.0	33.4	55.4	81.4	11.6	46.3	85.9	30.9	81.7	38.8	3
4	01.9	16.9	35.4	57.5	83.5	13.8	48.6	88.3	33.4	84.3	41.5	4
5	03.7	18.9	37.4	59.6	85.6	16.0	50.9	90.7	35.8	86.9	44.2	5
6	05.6	20.8	39.4	61.6	87.8	18.2	53.1	93.1	38.3	89.4	46.9	6
7	07.5	22.8	41.4	63.7	89.9	20.4	55.4	95.4	40.8	92.0	49.6	7
8	09.4	24.7	43.4	65.8	92.1	22.6	57.7	97.8	43.2	94.5	52.3	8
9	11.3	26.7	45.4	67.8	94.2	24.8	60.0	5200.2	45.7	97.1	54.9	9
10	4313.2	4428.6	4547.4	4669.9	4796.3	4927.0	5062.3	5202.6	5348.2	5499.7	5657.6	10
11	15.1	30.6	49.4	72.0	98.5	29.2	64.6	04.9	50.7	5502.3	60.3	11
12	17.0	32.5	51.4	74.1	4800.6	31.5	66.9	07.3	53.1	04.9	63.0	12
13	18.9	34.5	53.5	76.1	02.8	33.7	69.2	09.7	55.6	07.4	65.7	13
14	20.8	36.4	55.5	78.2	04.9	35.9	71.5	12.1	58.1	10.0	68.4	14
15	22.7	38.4	57.5	80.3	07.1	38.1	73.8	14.5	60.6	12.6	71.1	15
16	24.6	40.3	59.5	82.4	09.2	40.3	76.1	16.9	63.1	15.2	73.8	16
17	26.5	42.3	61.5	84.5	11.4	42.6	78.4	19.3	65.6	17.8	76.5	17
18	28.4	44.2	63.5	86.5	13.5	44.8	80.7	21.6	68.0	20.4	79.2	18
19	30.3	46.2	65.6	88.6	15.7	47.0	83.0	24.0	70.5	23.0	81.9	19
20	4332.2	4448.2	4567.6	4690.7	4817.8	4949.2	5085.3	5226.4	5373.0	5525.6	5684.6	20
21	34.1	50.1	69.6	92.8	20.0	51.5	87.6	28.8	75.5	28.1	87.3	21
22	36.0	52.1	71.6	94.9	22.1	53.7	90.0	31.2	78.0	30.7	90.0	22
23	37.9	54.1	73.6	97.0	24.3	55.9	92.3	33.6	80.5	33.3	92.7	23
24	39.8	56.0	75.7	99.1	26.4	58.2	94.6	36.0	83.0	35.9	95.5	24
25	41.8	58.0	77.7	4701.1	28.6	60.4	96.9	38.4	85.5	38.6	98.2	25
26	43.7	60.0	79.7	03.2	30.8	62.6	99.2	40.8	88.0	41.2	5700.9	26
27	45.6	61.9	81.7	05.3	32.9	64.9	5101.5	43.2	90.5	43.8	03.6	27
28	47.5	63.9	83.8	07.4	35.1	67.1	03.8	45.7	93.0	46.4	06.3	28
29	49.4	65.9	85.8	09.5	37.3	69.4	06.2	48.1	95.5	49.0	09.1	29
30	4351.3	4467.8	4587.8	4711.6	4839.4	4971.6	5108.5	5250.5	5398.0	5551.6	5711.8	30
31	53.2	69.8	89.9	13.7	41.6	73.8	10.8	52.9	5400.5	54.2	14.5	31
32	55.1	71.8	91.9	15.8	43.8	76.1	13.1	55.3	03.0	56.8	17.3	32
33	57.1	73.7	93.9	17.9	45.9	78.3	15.5	57.7	05.5	59.4	20.0	33
34	59.0	75.7	96.0	20.0	48.1	80.6	17.8	60.1	08.1	62.1	22.7	34
35	60.9	77.7	98.0	22.1	50.3	82.8	20.1	62.6	10.6	64.7	25.5	35
36	62.8	79.7	4600.0	24.2	52.4	85.1	22.4	65.0	13.1	67.3	28.2	36
37	64.7	81.6	02.1	26.3	54.6	87.3	24.8	67.4	15.6	69.9	30.9	37
38	66.7	83.6	04.1	28.4	56.8	89.6	27.1	69.8	18.1	72.6	33.7	38
39	68.6	85.6	06.1	30.5	59.0	91.8	29.4	72.2	20.6	75.2	36.4	39
40	4370.5	4487.6	4608.2	4732.6	4861.1	4994.1	5131.8	5274.7	5423.2	5577.8	5739.2	40
41	72.4	89.6	10.2	34.7	63.3	96.3	34.1	77.1	25.7	80.4	41.9	41
42	74.3	91.5	12.3	36.8	65.5	98.6	36.5	79.5	28.2	83.1	44.7	42
43	76.3	93.5	14.3	39.0	67.7	5000.8	38.8	82.0	30.8	85.7	47.5	43
44	78.2	95.5	16.4	41.1	69.9	03.1	41.1	84.4	33.3	88.4	50.2	44
45	80.1	97.5	18.4	43.2	72.0	05.4	43.5	86.8	35.8	91.0	52.9	45
46	82.1	99.5	20.5	45.3	74.2	07.6	45.8	89.3	38.4	93.6	55.7	46
47	84.0	4501.5	22.5	47.4	76.4	09.9	48.2	91.7	40.9	96.3	58.5	47
48	85.9	03.4	24.6	49.5	78.6	12.2	50.5	94.1	43.4	98.9	61.2	48
49	87.8	05.4	26.6	51.6	80.8	14.4	52.9	96.6	46.0	5601.6	64.0	49
50	4389.8	4507.4	4628.7	4753.7	4883.0	5016.7	5155.2	5299.0	5448.5	5604.2	5766.8	50
51	91.7	09.4	30.7	55.9	85.2	18.9	57.6	5301.5	51.0	06.9	69.5	51
52	93.6	11.4	32.8	58.0	87.4	21.2	59.9	03.9	53.6	09.5	72.3	52
53	95.6	13.4	34.8	60.1	89.5	23.5	62.3	06.3	56.1	12.2	75.1	53
54	97.5	15.4	36.9	62.2	91.7	25.8	64.6	08.8	58.7	14.8	77.9	54
55	99.4	17.4	39.0	64.4	93.9	28.0	67.0	11.2	61.2	17.5	80.6	55
56	4401.4	19.4	41.0	66.5	96.1	30.3	69.4	13.7	63.8	20.2	83.4	56
57	03.3	21.4	43.0	68.6	98.3	32.6	71.7	16.1	66.3	22.9	86.2	57
58	05.3	23.4	45.1	70.7	4900.5	34.9	74.1	18.6	68.9	25.5	89.0	58
59	07.2	25.4	47.2	72.9	02.7	37.1	76.4	21.1	71.4	28.2	91.8	59

LATITUDE.

Min.	69°	70°	71°	72°	73°	74°	75°	76°	77°	78°	79°	Min.
0	5794.6	5965.9	6145.7	6334.8	6534.4	6745.7	6970.3	7210.1	7467.2	7744.6	8045.7	0
1	97.4	68.8	48.8	38.1	37.8	49.4	74.2	14.2	71.7	49.4	51.0	1
2	5800.1	71.8	51.9	41.3	41.3	53.0	78.1	18.3	76.1	54.2	56.2	2
3	02.9	74.7	54.9	44.6	44.7	56.6	81.9	22.5	80.6	59.0	61.5	3
4	05.7	77.6	58.0	47.8	48.1	60.3	85.8	26.6	85.0	63.9	66.7	4
5	08.5	80.6	61.1	51.1	51.6	63.9	89.7	30.8	89.5	68.7	72.0	5
6	11.3	83.5	64.2	54.3	55.0	67.6	93.6	35.0	94.0	73.5	77.3	6
7	14.2	86.4	67.3	57.6	58.5	71.2	97.5	39.1	98.5	78.4	82.6	7
8	17.0	89.4	70.4	60.8	61.9	74.9	7001.4	43.3	7503.0	83.3	87.9	8
9	19.8	92.3	73.5	64.1	65.3	78.5	05.3	47.5	07.4	88.1	93.2	9
10	5822.6	5995.3	6176.6	6367.4	6568.8	6782.2	7009.2	7251.7	7511.9	7793.0	8098.5	10
11	25.4	98.2	79.7	70.6	72.3	85.9	13.1	55.8	16.5	97.9	8103.8	11
12	28.2	6001.2	82.8	73.9	75.7	89.6	17.0	60.0	21.0	7802.8	09.2	12
13	31.0	04.1	85.9	77.2	79.2	93.2	20.9	64.2	25.5	07.7	14.5	13
14	33.8	07.1	89.0	80.4	82.6	96.9	24.8	68.4	30.0	12.6	19.9	14
15	36.7	10.0	92.1	83.7	86.1	6800.6	28.8	72.6	34.5	17.5	25.2	15
16	39.5	13.0	95.2	87.0	89.6	04.3	32.7	76.8	39.1	22.4	30.6	16
17	42.3	16.0	98.3	90.3	93.0	08.0	36.6	81.1	43.6	27.3	36.0	17
18	45.1	18.9	6201.4	93.6	96.5	11.6	40.6	85.3	48.1	32.2	41.3	18
19	48.0	21.9	04.5	96.9	6600.0	15.4	44.5	89.5	52.7	37.2	46.7	19
20	5850.8	6024.9	6207.7	6400.2	6603.5	6819.1	7048.5	7293.7	7557.3	7842.1	8152.1	20
21	53.6	27.8	10.8	03.4	07.0	22.8	52.4	98.0	61.8	47.1	57.5	21
22	56.5	30.8	13.9	06.7	10.5	26.5	56.4	7302.2	66.4	52.0	62.9	22
23	59.3	33.8	17.0	10.1	14.0	30.2	60.3	06.4	71.0	57.0	68.4	23
24	62.2	36.8	20.2	13.4	17.5	33.9	64.3	10.7	75.5	61.9	73.8	24
25	65.0	39.8	23.3	16.7	21.0	37.6	68.3	15.0	80.1	66.9	79.2	25
26	67.8	42.7	26.5	20.0	24.5	41.3	72.2	19.2	84.7	71.9	84.7	26
27	70.7	45.7	29.6	23.3	28.0	45.1	76.2	23.5	89.3	76.9	90.1	27
28	73.5	48.7	32.7	26.6	31.5	48.8	80.2	27.7	93.9	81.9	95.6	28
29	76.4	51.7	35.9	29.9	35.0	52.5	84.2	32.0	98.5	86.9	8201.1	29
30	5879.2	6054.7	6239.0	6433.3	6638.5	6856.3	7088.2	7336.3	7603.2	7891.9	8206.6	30
31	82.1	57.7	42.2	36.6	42.1	60.0	92.2	40.6	07.8	96.9	12.1	31
32	85.0	60.7	45.3	39.9	45.6	63.8	96.2	44.9	12.4	7902.0	17.6	32
33	87.8	63.7	48.5	43.2	49.1	67.5	7100.2	49.2	17.0	07.0	23.1	33
34	90.7	66.7	51.7	46.6	52.6	71.3	04.2	53.5	21.7	12.0	28.6	34
35	93.6	69.7	54.8	49.9	56.2	75.0	08.2	57.8	26.3	17.1	34.1	35
36	96.4	72.7	58.0	53.3	59.7	78.8	12.2	62.1	31.0	22.1	39.7	36
37	99.3	75.7	61.2	56.6	63.3	82.6	16.3	66.4	35.6	27.2	45.2	37
38	5902.2	78.8	64.3	60.0	66.8	86.3	20.3	70.7	40.3	32.3	50.8	38
39	05.0	81.8	67.5	63.3	70.4	90.1	24.3	75.1	45.0	37.3	56.3	39
40	5907.9	6084.8	6270.7	6466.7	6673.9	6893.9	7128.4	7379.4	7649.7	7942.4	8261.9	40
41	10.8	87.8	73.9	70.0	77.4	97.7	32.4	83.7	54.3	47.5	67.5	41
42	13.7	90.8	77.1	73.4	81.0	6901.5	36.4	88.1	59.0	52.6	73.1	42
43	16.6	93.9	80.2	76.7	84.6	05.3	40.5	92.4	63.7	57.7	78.6	43
44	19.4	96.9	83.4	80.1	88.2	09.1	44.5	96.8	68.4	62.8	84.3	44
45	22.3	99.9	86.6	83.5	91.7	12.9	48.6	7401.1	73.2	68.0	89.9	45
46	25.2	6103.0	89.8	86.9	95.3	16.7	52.7	05.5	77.9	73.1	95.5	46
47	28.1	06.0	93.0	90.2	98.9	20.5	56.7	09.9	82.6	78.2	8301.1	47
48	31.0	09.0	96.2	93.6	6702.5	24.3	60.8	14.3	87.3	83.4	06.7	48
49	33.9	12.1	99.4	97.0	06.1	28.1	64.9	18.6	92.1	88.5	12.4	49
50	5936.8	6115.1	6302.6	6500.4	6709.7	6931.9	7169.0	7423.0	7696.8	7993.7	8318.1	50
51	39.7	18.2	05.8	03.8	13.2	35.7	73.1	27.4	7701.5	98.9	23.8	51
52	42.6	21.2	09.1	07.2	16.8	39.6	77.2	31.8	06.3	8004.0	29.4	52
53	45.5	24.3	12.3	10.6	20.4	43.4	81.2	36.2	11.1	09.2	35.1	53
54	48.4	27.3	15.5	14.0	24.0	47.2	85.3	40.6	15.8	14.4	40.8	54
55	51.3	30.4	18.7	17.4	27.7	51.1	89.5	45.1	20.6	19.6	46.5	55
56	54.2	33.4	21.9	20.8	31.3	54.9	93.6	49.5	25.4	24.8	52.2	56
57	57.2	36.5	25.1	24.2	34.9	58.8	97.7	53.9	30.2	30.0	58.0	57
58	60.1	39.6	28.4	27.6	38.5	62.6	7201.8	58.3	35.0	35.2	63.7	58
59	63.0	42.6	31.6	31.0	42.1	66.5	05.9	62.8	39.8	40.5	69.4	59

Mid. Lat.	DIFFERENCE OF LATITUDE.																				Mid. Lat.
	1°	2°	3°	4°	5°	6°	7°	8°	9°	10°	11°	12°	13°	14°	15°	16°	17°	18°	19°	20°	
°	′	′	′	′	′	′	′	′	′	′	′	′	′	′	′	′	′	′	′	′	°
15	0	1	2	3	5	7	9	12	15	18	22	26	31	36	41	47	52	59	65	72	15
16	0	1	2	3	4	6	9	11	14	18	21	25	30	34	39	44	50	56	62	69	16
17	0	1	2	3	4	6	8	11	14	17	20	24	28	33	38	43	48	54	60	66	17
18	0	1	1	3	4	6	8	10	13	16	20	23	27	32	36	41	46	52	58	64	18
19	0	1	1	3	4	6	8	10	13	16	19	22	26	30	35	40	45	50	56	61	19
20	0	1	1	2	4	5	7	10	12	15	18	22	25	29	34	38	43	48	54	6[illegible]	20
21	0	1	1	2	4	5	7	9	12	15	18	21	25	29	33	37	42	47	52	58	21
22	0	1	1	2	4	5	7	9	12	14	17	21	24	28	32	36	41	46	51	56	22
23	0	1	1	2	3	5	7	9	11	14	17	20	23	27	31	35	40	45	50	55	23
24	0	1	1	2	3	5	7	9	11	14	16	20	23	27	31	35	39	44	49	54	24
25	0	1	1	2	3	5	7	9	11	13	16	19	23	26	30	34	39	43	48	53	25
26	0	1	1	2	3	5	6	8	11	13	16	19	22	26	30	34	38	42	47	52	26
27	0	1	1	2	3	5	6	8	11	13	16	19	22	25	29	33	37	42	47	52	27
28	0	1	1	2	3	5	6	8	10	13	16	18	22	25	29	33	37	41	46	51	28
29	0	1	1	2	3	5	6	8	10	13	15	18	21	25	28	32	37	41	46	51	29
30	0	1	1	2	3	5	6	8	10	13	15	18	21	25	28	32	36	41	45	50	30
31	0	1	1	2	3	5	6	8	10	12	15	18	21	24	28	32	36	40	45	50	31
32	0	0	1	2	3	4	6	8	10	12	15	18	21	24	28	32	36	40	45	50	32
33	0	0	1	2	3	4	6	8	10	12	15	18	21	24	28	32	36	40	45	49	33
34	0	0	1	2	3	4	6	8	10	12	15	18	21	24	28	32	36	40	45	49	34
35	0	0	1	2	3	4	6	8	10	12	15	18	21	24	28	32	36	40	45	49	35
36	0	1	1	2	3	4	6	8	10	12	15	18	21	24	28	32	36	40	45	49	36
37	0	1	1	2	3	4	6	8	10	12	15	18	21	24	28	32	36	40	45	49	37
38	0	1	1	2	3	4	6	8	10	12	15	18	21	24	28	32	36	40	45	50	38
39	0	1	1	2	3	4	6	8	10	12	15	18	21	24	28	32	36	40	45	50	39
40	0	1	1	2	3	5	6	8	10	13	15	18	21	25	28	32	36	41	45	50	40
41	0	1	1	2	3	5	6	8	10	13	15	18	21	25	28	32	37	41	46	51	41
42	0	1	1	2	3	5	6	8	10	13	15	18	22	25	29	33	37	41	46	51	42
43	0	1	1	2	3	5	6	8	10	13	16	18	22	25	29	33	37	42	46	52	43
44	0	1	1	2	3	5	6	8	10	13	16	19	22	25	29	33	38	42	47	52	44
45	0	1	1	2	3	5	6	8	11	13	16	19	22	26	30	34	38	43	48	53	45
46	0	1	1	2	3	5	6	8	11	13	16	19	22	26	30	34	38	43	48	53	46
47	0	1	1	2	3	5	7	9	11	13	16	19	23	26	30	35	39	44	49	54	47
48	0	1	1	2	3	5	7	9	11	14	17	20	23	27	31	35	40	44	50	55	48
49	0	1	1	2	3	5	7	9	11	14	17	20	23	27	31	36	40	45	50	56	49
50	0	1	1	2	4	5	7	9	11	14	17	20	24	28	32	36	41	46	51	57	50
51	0	1	1	2	4	5	7	9	12	14	17	21	24	28	32	37	42	47	52	58	51
52	0	1	1	2	4	5	7	9	12	15	18	21	25	29	33	38	43	48	53	59	52
53	0	1	1	2	4	5	7	10	12	15	18	21	25	29	34	38	43	49	54	60	53
54	0	1	1	2	4	5	7	10	12	15	18	22	26	30	34	39	44	50	56	62	54
55	0	1	1	2	4	6	8	10	13	16	19	22	26	31	35	40	45	51	57	63	55
56	0	1	1	3	4	6	8	10	13	16	19	23	27	31	36	41	46	52	58	65	56
57	0	1	1	3	4	6	8	10	13	16	20	24	28	32	37	42	48	54	60	66	57
58	0	1	2	3	4	6	8	11	14	17	20	24	28	33	38	43	49	55	61	68	58
59	0	1	2	3	4	6	8	11	14	17	21	25	29	34	39	45	50	57	63	70	59
60	0	1	2	3	4	6	9	11	14	18	22	26	30	35	40	46	52	58	65	72	60
61	0	1	2	3	5	7	9	12	15	18	22	26	31	36	42	47	53	60	67	75	61
62	0	1	2	3	5	7	9	12	15	19	23	27	32	37	43	49	55	62	70	77	62
63	0	1	2	3	5	7	10	12	16	20	24	28	33	39	44	51	57	64	72	80	63
64	0	1	2	3	5	7	10	13	16	20	24	29	34	40	46	52	59	67	75	83	64
65	0	1	2	3	5	7	10	13	17	21	25	30	36	41	48	54	62	69	78	86	65
66	0	1	2	3	5	8	11	14	18	22	26	32	37	43	50	57	64	72	81	90	66
67	0	1	2	4	6	8	11	14	18	23	28	33	39	45	52	59	67	76	85	94	67
68	0	1	2	4	6	8	12	15	19	24	29	34	40	47	54	62	70	79	89	99	68
69	0	1	2	4	6	9	12	16	20	25	30	36	42	49	57	65	74	83	93	104	69
70	0	1	2	4	6	9	13	16	21	26	32	38	44	52	60	68	78	88	98	110	70
71	0	1	2	4	7	10	13	17	22	27	33	40	47	55	63	72	82	93	104	116	71
72	0	1	3	5	7	10	14	18	23	29	35	42	49	58	67	76	87	98	111	124	72

In computing compound interest for long periods of time, it is necessary to have the following logarithms to more than six places.

Number.	Logarithm.	Number.	Logarithm.
1.0025	.00108 43813	1.0425	.01807 60636
1.0050	.00216 60618	1.0450	.01911 62904
1.0075	.00324 50548	1.0475	.02015 40316
1.0100	.00432 13738	1.0500	.02118 92991
1.0125	.00539 50319	1.0525	.02222 21045
1.0150	.00646 60422	1.0550	.02325 24596
1.0175	.00753 44179	1.0575	.02428 03760
1.0200	.00860 01718	1.0600	.02530 58653
1.0225	.00966 33167	1.0625	.02632 89387
1.0250	.01072 38654	1.0650	.02734 96078
1.0275	.01178 18305	1.0675	.02836 78837
1.0300	.01283 72247	1.0700	.02938 37777
1.0325	.01389 00603	1.0725	.03039 73009
1.0350	.01494 03498	1.0750	.03140 84643
1.0375	.01598 81054	1.0775	.03241 72788
1.0400	.01703 33393	1.0800	.03342 37555

NUMBERS OFTEN USED IN CALCULATIONS.

		Logarithms.
Circumference of a circle to diameter 1; Surface of a sphere to diameter 1; Area of a circle to radius 1 .... =	3.1415926	0.497150
Area of a circle to diameter 1 .... =	.7853982	9.895090
Capacity of a sphere to diameter 1 .... =	.5235988	9.718999
Capacity of a sphere to radius 1 .... =	4.1887902	0.622089
1 ÷ 3.1415926 .... =	0.3183099	9.502850
Arc equal to radius expressed in degrees .... =	57°.2957795	1.758123
Arc equal to radius expressed in seconds .... =	206264″.8	5.314425
Length of 1 degree in parts of radius .... =	.0174533	8.241877
Length of 1 minute in parts of radius .... =	.0002909	6.463726
Sine of 1 second .... =	.00000485	4.685575
Sine of 2 seconds .... =	.00000970	4.986605
Sine of 3 seconds .... =	.00001454	5.162696
Sine of 4 seconds .... =	.00001939	5.287635
Sine of 5 seconds .... =	.00002424	5.384545
Sine of 6 seconds .... =	.00002909	5.463726
Sine of 7 seconds .... =	.00003394	5.530673
Sine of 8 seconds .... =	.00003879	5.588665
Sine of 9 seconds .... =	.00004363	5.639817
Base of Napier's system of logarithms .... =	2.7182818	0.434294
Modulus of the common logarithms .... =	.4342945	9.637784
360 degrees expressed in seconds .... =	1296000	6.112605
24 hours expressed in seconds .... =	86400	4.936514
Number of feet in one mile .... =	5280	3.722634

THE END.

Trigonometry and Tables.

Ninth Edition. 8vo, pp. 344, Sheep extra, $1 50. The *Trigonometry* and *Tables*, bound separately. The Trigonometry, $1 00; Tables, 50 cents.

This work contains an exposition of the nature and properties of logarithms; the principles of plane trigonometry; the mensuration of surfaces and solids; the principles of land surveying, with a full description of the instruments employed; the elements of navigation, and of spherical trigonometry. The tables furnish the logarithms of numbers to 10,000, with the proportional parts for a fifth figure in the natural number; logarithmic sines and tangents for every ten seconds of the quadrant, with the proportional parts to single seconds; natural sines and tangents for every minute of the quadrant; a traverse table; a table of meridional parts, &c.

In this work the principles of Trigonometry and its applications are discussed with the same clearness that characterizes the previous volumes. The portion appropriated to Mensuration, Surveying, &c., will especially commend itself to teachers, by the judgment exhibited in the extent to which they are carried, and the practically useful character of the matter introduced. What I have particularly admired in this, as well as the previous volumes, is the constant recognition of the difficulties, present and prospective, which are likely to embarrass the learner, and the skill and tact with which they are removed. The Logarithmic Tables will be found unsurpassed in practical convenience by any others of the same extent.—AUGUSTUS W. SMITH, LL.D., *President of the Wesleyan University.*

Elements of Analytical Geometry

and of the Differential and Integral Calculus. Seventh Edition. 8vo, pp. 278, Sheep extra, $1 50.

The first part of this volume treats of the application of algebra to geometry, the construction of equations, the properties of a straight line, a circle, parabola, ellipse, and hyperbola; the classification of algebraic curves, and the more important transcendental curves. The second part treats of the differentiation of algebraic functions, of Maclaurin's and Taylor's theorems, of maxima and minima, transcendental functions, theory of curves, and evolutes. The third part exhibits the method of obtaining the integrals of a great variety of differentials, and their application to the rectification and quadrature of curves, and the cubature of solids. All the principles are illustrated by an extensive collection of examples. The work was prepared to meet the wants of the mass of college students of average abilities.

Analytical Geometry is treated, amply enough for elementary instruction, in the short compass of 112 pages, so that nothing need be omitted, and the studen can master his text-book as a whole. The Calculus is treated in like manner in 167 pages, and the opening chapter makes the nature of the art as clear as it can possibly be made. We recommend this work, without reserve or limitation, as the best text-book on the subject we have yet seen.—*Methodist Quarterly Review.*

Introduction to Practical Astronomy,

with a Collection of Astronomical Tables. 8vo, pp. 497, Sheep extra, $1 50.

This work furnishes a description of the instruments required in the outfit of an observatory, as also the methods of employing them, and the computations growing out of their use. It treats particularly of the Transit Instrument and of Graduated Circles; of the method of determining time, latitude, and longitude; with the computation of eclipses and occultations. The work is designed for the use of amateur observers, practical surveyors, and engineers, as well as students who are engaged in a course of training in our colleges. The tables which accompany this volume are such as have been found most useful in astronomical computations, and to them has been added a catalogue of 1500 stars, with the constants required for reducing the mean to the apparent places.

Letters commendatory of this work have been received from G. B. Airy, Astronomer Royal of England; from William Whewell, D.D., Master of Trinity College, Cambridge, Eng.; from Prof. J. Challis, Plumian Professor of Astronomy in the University of Cambridge, Eng.; from J. C. Adams, late President of the Royal Astronomical Society; from Augustus De Morgan, Professor of Mathematics in University College, London; from M. J. Johnson, Director of the Radcliffe Observatory, Oxford, Eng.; from William Lassell, Astronomer of Liverpool, Eng.; from C. Piazzi Smyth, Astronomer Royal for Scotland; from Edward J. Cooper, of Markree Castle Observatory, Ireland; and from numerous astronomers from every part of the United States.

It appears to me that Prof. Loomis' work on Practical Astronomy is likely to be extensively useful, as containing the most recent information on the subject, and giving the information in such a manner as to make it accessible to a large class of readers. I am of opinion that Practical Astronomy is a good *educational* subject even for those who may never take observations, and that a work like this of Prof. Loomis should be a text-book in every University. The want of such a work has long been felt here, and if my astronomical duties had permitted, I should have made an attempt to supply it. It is remarkable, that in England, where Practical Astronomy is so much attended to, no book has been written which is at all adapted to making a learner acquainted with the recent improvements and actual state of the science.—JAMES CHALLIS, *Plumian Professor of Astronomy in the University of Cambridge, Eng.*

The science of the age was most assuredly in want of a work on Practical Astronomy, and I am delighted to find that want now supplied from America, and from the pen of Prof. Loomis. I propose to make this volume a text-book for my class of Practical Astronomy in the University of Edinburgh.—C. PIAZZI SMYTH, *Astronomer Royal for Scotland.*

No work since that of Professor Woodhouse places the reader so directly in communication with the interior of the Observatory as the work on Practical Astronomy by Prof. Loomis; and he has supplied a want which young astronomers, actually wishing to observe, must have felt for a long time. It is more than possible that this work may establish itself as a text-book in England.—AUGUSTUS DE MORGAN, *Professor of Mathematics in University College, London.*

Recent Progress of Astronomy,

especially in the United States. A thoroughly revised Edition of this Work is now in course of Preparation.

This volume is designed to exhibit, in a popular form, the most important astronomical discoveries of the past ten years. It treats particularly of the discovery of the planet Neptune, of the new asteroids, of the new satellite, and the new ring of Saturn, of the great comet of 1843, Biela's comet, Miss Mitchell's comet, &c.; of the parallax of fixed stars, motion of the stars, resolution of the nebulæ, &c.; the history of American observatories, determination of longitude by the electric telegraph, manufacture of telescopes in the United States, &c.

Books for Schools and Colleges

PUBLISHED BY

HARPER & BROTHERS, FRANKLIN SQUARE, N. Y.

ALFORD'S GREEK TESTAMENT. 4 vols. 8vo. Vol. I., containing the Four Gospels. (*Just Ready.*)

ANDREWS'S LATIN-ENGLISH LEXICON, founded on the larger German-Latin Lexicon of Dr. WM. FREUND. With Additions and Corrections from the Lexicons of Gesner, Facciolati, Scheller, Georges, &c. Royal 8vo, Sheep, $5 00.

ANTHON'S CLASSICAL SERIES.
Latin Lessons. 75 cents.
Zumpt's Latin Grammar. 75 cents.
Zumpt's Abridgment. 50 cents.
Latin Prose Composition. 75 cents.
Latin Prosody and Metre. 75 cents.
Latin Versification. 75 cents.
Cæsar's Commentaries. $1 00.
Cicero's Select Orations. $1 00.
Sallust's Jugurthine War, &c. 75 cents.
The Æneid of Virgil. $1 25.
The Works of Horace. $1 25.
Eclogues and Georgics of Virgil. $1 25.
The Germania, &c., of Tacitus. $1 00.
Cicero de Senectute, &c. 75 cents.
Cornelius Nepos. $1 00.
Cicero's Tusculan Disputations. $1 00.
Juvenal and Persius. $1 00.
First Greek Lessons. 75 cents.
Greek Prose Composition. 75 cents.
Greek Grammar. 75 cents.
New Greek Grammar. 75 cents.
Greek Prosody and Metre. 75 cents.
Jacob's Greek Reader. $1 00.
Xenophon's Anabasis. $1 25.
Xenophon's Memorabilia of Socrates. $1 00.
Homer's Iliad. First Six Books. $1 25.
Manual of Greek Antiquities. 87½ cents.
Manual of Roman Antiquities. 87½ cents.
Manual of Greek Literature. $1 00.
A Latin-English and English-Latin Dictionary. Small 4to, Sheep, $2 00.
A Classical Dictionary. Royal 8vo, Sheep, $4 00.
Smith's Dictionary of Greek and Roman Antiquities. Royal 8vo, Sheep, $4 00.

BARTON'S GRAMMAR. 16mo, Muslin, 37½ cents.

MISS BEECHER'S PHYSIOLOGY AND CALISTHENICS. With Wood-cuts. 16mo, Paper, 37½ cents; Muslin, 50 cents.

BOYD'S ECLECTIC MORAL PHILOSOPHY: prepared for Literary Institutions and general use. 12mo, Muslin, 75 cents.

BOYD'S RHETORIC. Elements of Rhetoric and Literary Criticism, with copious Practical Exercises and Examples: including also a succinct History of the English Language, and of British and American Literature, from the earliest to the present Times. On the Basis of the Recent Works of ALEXANDER REID and R. CUNNELL; with large Additions from other Sources. 18mo, Half Bound, 50 cents.

BUTLER'S ANALOGY OF RELIGION, Natural and Revealed, to the Constitution and Course of Nature. With an Analysis, left unfinished, by the late ROBERT EMORY, D.D., President of Dickinson College. Completed and Edited, with a Life of Bishop Butler, Notes, and Index, by G. B. CROOKS. 12mo, Muslin, 75 cents.

BUTLER'S ANALOGY. By HOBART. Analysis of Butler's Analogy of Religion, Natural and Revealed, to the Constitution and Course of Nature, with Notes. Also CRAUFORD'S Questions for Examination, revised and adapted to the use of Schools. By CHARLES E. WEST. 18mo, Muslin, 40 cents.

BUTTMANN'S GREEK GRAMMAR, for the use of High Schools and Universities. Revised and enlarged by his Son, ALEXANDER BUTTMANN. Translated from the 18th German Edition, by EDWARD ROBINSON, D.D., LL.D. 8vo, Sheep, $2 00.

COMBE'S PHYSIOLOGY. Questions. Engravings. 18mo, Muslin, 45 cents; Half Sheep, 50 cents.

DICKENS AND BONNER'S CHILD'S HISTORIES. Adapted for Reading-Books in Schools.

A CHILD'S HISTORY OF ENGLAND. By CHARLES DICKENS. 2 vols. 16mo, Muslin, 60 cents.

A CHILD'S HISTORY OF THE UNITED STATES. By JOHN BONNER. With Illustrations. 2 vols. 16mo, Muslin, $1 00. (Uniform with "Dickens's Child's History of England.")

A CHILD'S HISTORY OF ROME. By JOHN BONNER. Illustrations. 2 vols. 16mo, Muslin, $1 00.

A CHILD'S HISTORY OF GREECE. By JOHN BONNER. Illustrations. 2 vols. 16mo, Muslin, $1 00.

DOCHARTY'S INSTITUTES OF ALGEBRA. Being the First Part of a Course of Mathematics, designed for the use of Schools, Academies, and Colleges. Sixth Edition. To which is added a Suggestive Key. 12mo, Sheep, 75 cents.

DOCHARTY'S ARITHMETIC. A Practical and Commercial Arithmetic: containing Definitions of Terms, and Rules of Operations, with numerous Examples. The whole forming a complete Treatise for the use of Schools and Academies. 12mo, Sheep extra, 75 cents.

DOCHARTY'S GEOMETRY. Elements of Plane and Solid Geometry, together with the Elements of Plane and Spherical Trigonometry, and an Article on Inverse Trigonometrical Functions. 12mo, Sheep, 75 cents.

DRAPER'S TEXT-BOOK ON CHEMISTRY, for the use of Schools and Colleges. Carefully Revised, with Additions. With 300 Illustrations. 12mo, Sheep extra, 75 cents.

DRAPER'S TEXT-BOOK ON NATURAL PHILOSOPHY, for the use of Schools and Colleges. Containing the most recent Discoveries and Facts, compiled from the best Authorities. With nearly 400 Illustrations. 12mo, Sheep extra, 75 cents.

DRAPER'S PHYSIOLOGY. Human Physiology, Statical and Dynamical; or, The Conditions and Course of the Life of Man: being the Text of the Lectures delivered in the Medical Department of the University. By JOHN W. DRAPER, M.D., LL.D., Professor of Chemistry and Physiology in the University of New York. Illustrated with nearly 300 fine Wood Engravings. 8vo, Muslin, $4 00; Sheep extra, $4 25.

DUFF'S BOOK-KEEPING. The North American Accountant: embracing Single and Double Entry Book-keeping, practically adapted to the Inland and Maritime Commerce of the United States. Exemplifying all Modern Improvements in the Science, with a new and certain Method of detecting Errors and proving the Ledger. Embracing an improved Plan of Instruction. Complete in two parts. 8vo, School Edition, Half Sheep, 75 cents; Mercantile Edition, Muslin, $1 50.

FINDLAY'S CLASSICAL ATLAS, to illustrate Ancient Geography. Comprised in 25 Maps, showing the various Divisions of the World as known to the Ancients. With an Index of the Ancient and Modern Names. 8vo, Half Bound, $3 35.

FOSTER'S CHEMISTRY. First Principles of Chemistry, illustrated by a Series of the most recently discovered and brilliant Experiments known to the Science. Adapted specially for Classes. 12mo, Sheep extra, 60 cents.

The Publishers are prepared to furnish a complete set of all the apparatus necessary to perform the experiments laid down in the work. The apparatus is manufactured expressly for this purpose by Dr. JAMES R. CHILTON. Price, neatly packed, $23 00.

FOSTER'S CHART of the Organic Elements. For the use of Schools and Academies. Beautifully colored, mounted on Rollers, with Cloth Back, $4 00.

FOWLER'S ENGLISH LANGUAGE, in its Elements and Forms. With a History of its Origin and Development, and a full Grammar. Designed for use in Colleges and Schools. New and Revised Edition. 8vo, Muslin, $1 50; Sheep extra, $1 75.

FOWLER'S SCHOOL GRAMMAR. Abridged from the Octavo Edition. Designed for general use in Schools and Families. 12mo, Sheep, $1 00.

GRAY AND ADAMS'S GEOLOGY. Engravings. 12mo, Sheep extra, 75 cents.

GRAY'S NATURAL PHILOSOPHY. Designed as a Text-book for Academies, High Schools, and Colleges. Illustrated by 360 Woodcuts. 12mo, Sheep extra, 75 c.

HARPER'S SCHOOL HISTORY. Narrative of the General Course of History, from the Earliest Periods to the Establishment of the American Constitution. Prepared with Questions for the use of Schools, and illustrated with 150 Maps and Engravings. Square 12mo, Muslin, $1 25; Sheep, $1 38.

HARRISON'S LATIN GRAMMAR. An Exposition of some of the Laws of the Latin Grammar. 12mo, Sheep extra, 75 cents.

HOOKER'S CHILD'S BOOK OF NATURE. For the Use of Families and Schools; intended to aid Mothers and Teachers in Training Children in the Observation of Nature. In Three Parts. PART I. Plants.—PART II. Animals.—PART III. Air, Water, Heat, Light, &c. By WORTHINGTON HOOKER, M.D., Author of "Physician and Patient," "Human Physiology," &c. Illustrated by Engravings. With Questions for the use of Teachers. The Three Parts complete in one vol. Small 4to, Muslin, $1 25; Separately, Muslin, 50 cents each.

LIDDELL'S HISTORY OF ROME. A School History of Rome, from the Earliest Times to the Establishment of the Empire, with Chapters on the History of Literature and Art. By HENRY G. LIDDELL, D.D., Dean of Christ Church, Oxford. Illustrated by Numerous Wood-cuts. Uniform with Smith's "History of Greece." 12mo, Muslin, $1 00.

LIDDELL AND SCOTT'S GREEK-ENGLISH LEXICON, based on the German work of FRANCIS PASSOW. With Corrections and Additions, and the Insertion, in Alphabetical Order, of the Proper Names occurring in the Principal Greek Authors, by HENRY DRISLER, M.A., Prof. of Latin Language and Literature in Columbia College. Royal 8vo, Sheep extra, $5 00.

LOOMIS'S SCHOOL AND COLLEGE SERIES.

- **A TREATISE ON ARITHMETIC.** 12mo, Sheep, 75 cents.
- **ELEMENTS OF ALGEBRA.** 12mo, Sheep, 62½ c.
- **A TREATISE ON ALGEBRA.** 8vo, Sheep, $1 00.
- **ELEMENTS OF GEOMETRY AND CONIC SECTIONS.** 8vo, Sheep, 75 cents.
- **TRIGONOMETRY AND TABLES.** 8vo, Sheep, $1 50. The *Trigonometry* and *Tables*, bound separately. The Trigonometry, $1 00; Tables, $1 00.
- **ELEMENTS OF ANALYTICAL GEOMETRY AND OF THE DIFFERENTIAL AND INTEGRAL CALCULUS.** 8vo, Sheep, $1 50.
- **PRACTICAL ASTRONOMY.** 8vo, Sheep, $1 50.
- **RECENT PROGRESS OF ASTRONOMY,** especially in the United States. 12mo, Muslin, $1 00.
- **ELEMENTS OF NATURAL PHILOSOPHY,** for the use of Academies and High Schools. 12mo, Sheep, $1 00.

M'CLINTOCK'S FIRST BOOK IN LATIN. Containing Grammar, Exercises, and Vocabularies, on the Method of Constant Imitation and Repetition. With Summaries of Etymology and Syntax. 12mo, Sheep extra, 75 cents.

M'CLINTOCK'S SECOND BOOK IN LATIN. Containing Syntax and Reading Lessons in Prose; forming a sufficient Latin Reader, with Imitation Exercises and a Vocabulary. 12mo, Sheep extra, 75 cents.

M'CLINTOCK'S FIRST BOOK IN GREEK. Containing a full View of the Forms of Words, with Vocabularies and copious Exercises, on the Method of constant Imitation and Repetition. Revised Edition. With brief Summaries of the Doctrine of the Verb, and of the Rules of Syntax. 12mo, Sheep extra, 75 cents.

M'CLINTOCK'S SECOND BOOK IN GREEK. Containing Syntax, with Reading Lessons in Prose; Prosody and the Dialects, with Reading Lessons in Verse. Forming a sufficient Greek Reader, with Notes and copious Vocabulary. 12mo, Sheep extra, 75 cents.

MORSE'S SCHOOL GEOGRAPHY. A new System of Geography, for the use of Schools. Illustrated by more than 50 Cerographic Maps, and numerous Engravings on Wood. 4to, Half Bound, 50 cents.

PARKER'S AIDS TO ENGLISH COMPOSITION. Prepared for Students of all Grades, embracing Specimens and Examples of School and College Exercises, and most of the higher Departments of English Composition, both in Prose and Verse. A new Edition, with Additions and Improvements. 12mo, Muslin, 80 cents; Sheep, 90 cents.

PARKER'S GEOGRAPHICAL QUESTIONS, adapted for the use of Morse's, Woodbridge's, Worcester's, Mitchell's, Field's, Malte Brun's, Smith's, Olney's Goodrich's, or any other respectable Collection of Maps: embracing, by way of Question and Answer, such Portions of the Elements of Geography as are necessary as an Introduction to the Study of the Maps. To which is added a concise Description of the Terrestrial Globe. 12mo, Muslin, 20 cents.

PARKER'S OUTLINES OF GENERAL HISTORY. Designed as the Foundation and Review of a Course of Historical Reading. 12mo, Sheep extra, $1 00.

PLAUTUS. "The Captives." A Comedy of Plautus. With English Notes for the use of Students. By JOHN PROUDFIT, D.D. 18mo, Paper, 37½ cents.

POTTER'S AND EMERSON'S THE SCHOOL AND SCHOOLMASTER. PART I. The School; its Objects, Relations, and Uses. With a Sketch of the Education most needed in the United States, the present state of Common Schools, the best Means of improving them, and the consequent Duties of Parents, Trustees, and Inspectors, &c.—PART II. The proper Character, Studies, and Duties of the Teacher, with the best Methods for the Government and Instruction of Common Schools, and the Principles on which School-houses should be Built, Arranged, Warmed, and Ventilated. By ALONZO POTTER, D.D., and GEORGE B. EMERSON, A.M. Engravings. 12mo, Muslin, $1 00.

POTTER'S POLITICAL ECONOMY: its Objects, Uses, and Principles; considered with Reference to the Condition of the American People. With a Summary for the use of Students. 18mo, Half Sheep, 50 cents.

RENWICK'S CHEMISTRY. Questions. Engravings. 18mo, Half Sheep, 75 cents.

RENWICK'S NATURAL PHILOSOPHY. Illustrations. 18mo, Half Sheep, 75 cents.

RENWICK'S MECHANICS. Applications of the Science of Mechanics to Practical Purposes. Engravings. 18mo, Half Sheep, 90 cents.

RIDDLE AND ARNOLD'S ENGLISH-LATIN LEXICON, founded on the German-Latin Dictionary of Dr. C. E. GEORGES. Carefully Revised, and containing a copious Dictionary of Proper Names. By CHARLES ANTHON, LL.D. Royal 8vo, Sheep extra, $3 00.

SALKELD'S FIRST BOOK IN SPANISH. Adapted to every Class of Learners; containing full Instructions in Pronunciation; a Grammar; Reading Lessons, &c. 12mo, Sheep extra, $1 00.

SMITH'S (PROF. A. W.) MECHANICS. Embracing the Theory of Statics and Dynamics, and its Application to Solids and Fluids. Illustrations. 12mo, Muslin, $1 50; Sheep extra, $1 75.

SMITH'S (DR. WM.) HISTORY OF GREECE, from the Earliest Times to the Roman Conquest, with Supplementary Chapters on the History of Literature and Art. For Schools and Students. Illustrated with 100 Wood-cuts. Edited by Professor GREENE. 12mo, Muslin, $1 00.

SMITH'S (DR. WM.) STUDENT'S GIBBON. The History of the Decline and Fall of the Roman Empire. By EDWARD GIBBON. Abridged. Incorporating the Researches of Recent Commentators. By WILLIAM SMITH, LL.D., Editor of the "Classical Dictionary" and "A Dictionary of Greek and Roman Antiquities." Illustrated by 100 Engravings on Wood. Uniform with "Liddell's Rome." 12mo, Muslin, $1 00.

SMITH'S (DR. WM.) NEW CLASSICAL DICTIONARY of Greek and Roman Biography, Mythology, and Geography. Edited by CHARLES ANTHON, LL.D. Royal 8vo, Sheep extra, $2 50.

SPENCER'S GREEK TESTAMENT, with English Notes, Critical, Philological, and Exegetical; Maps, Indexes, &c. 12mo, Muslin, $1 00; Sheep extra, $1 25.

STORY ON THE CONSTITUTION. 12mo, Muslin, 75 cents.

UPHAM ON THE WILL. Philosophical and Practical Treatise on the Will. By T. C. UPHAM. 12mo, Sheep extra, $1 25.

UPHAM'S MENTAL PHILOSOPHY, embracing the two Departments of the Intellect and Sensibilities. 2 vols. 12mo, Sheep extra, $2 50.

UPHAM'S MENTAL PHILOSOPHY, ABRIDGED. Designed as a Text-Book in Academies. 12mo, Sheep extra, $1 25.

WHATELY'S ELEMENTS OF LOGIC. 18mo, Muslin, 37½ cents.

WHATELY'S ELEMENTS OF RHETORIC. 18mo, Muslin, 37½ cents.

Harper's New Catalogue.

A NEW DESCRIPTIVE CATALOGUE OF HARPER & BROTHERS' PUBLICATIONS is now ready for diſtribution, and may be obtained gratuitouſly on application to the Publiſhers perſonaily, or by letter encloſing ſix cents in poſtage ſtamps.

The attention of gentlemen, in town or country, deſigning to form Libraries or enrich their literary collections, is reſpectfully invited to this Catalogue, which will be found to compriſe a large proportion of the ſtandard and moſt eſteemed works in Engliſh Literature —COMPREHENDING MORE THAN TWO THOUSAND VOLUMES—which are offered in moſt inſtances at leſs than one half the coſt of ſimilar productions in England.

To Librarians and others connected with Colleges, Schools, etc., who may not have acceſs to a reliable guide in forming the true eſtimate of literary productions, it is believed the preſent Catalogue will prove eſpecially valuable as a manual of reference.

To prevent diſappointment, it is ſuggeſted that, whenever books can not be obtained through any bookſeller or local agent, applications with remittance ſhould be addreſſed direct to the Publiſhers, which will be promptly attended to.

FRANKLIN SQUARE, NEW YORK.

2578128R00198

Printed in Great Britain
by Amazon.co.uk, Ltd.,
Marston Gate.